Self and Society

BLACKWELL READERS IN SOCIOLOGY

Each volume in this authoritative series aims to provide students and scholars with comprehensive collections of classic and contemporary readings for all the major sub-fields of sociology. They are designed to complement single-authored works, or to be used as stand-alone textbooks for courses. The selected readings sample the most important works that students should read and are framed by informed editorial introductions. The series aims to reflect the state of the discipline by providing collections not only on standard topics but also on cutting-edge subjects in sociology to provide future directions in teaching and research.

- *From Modernization to Globalization: Perspectives on Development and Social Change* edited by J. Timmons Roberts and Amy Hite
- *Aging and Everyday Life* edited by Jaber F. Gubrium and James A. Holstein
- *Popular Culture: Production and Consumption* edited by C. Lee Harrington and Denise D. Bielby
- *Self and Society* edited by Ann Branaman

Self and Society

Edited by

Ann Branaman

First published 2001

2 4 6 8 10 9 7 5 3 1

Blackwell Publishers Inc.
350 Main Street
Malden, Massachusetts 02148
USA

Blackwell Publishers Ltd
108 Cowley Road
Oxford OX4 1JF
UK

Library of Congress Cataloging-in-Publication Data

Self and society / edited by Ann Branaman.
    p. cm.—(Blackwell readers in sociology)
   Includes bibliographical references and index.
   ISBN 0–631–21539–5 (alk. paper)—ISBN 0–631–21540–9 (pb.: alk. paper)
   1. Social psychology.   2. Identity (Psychology)   3. Self.   4. Knowledge, Sociology of.
   I. Branaman, Ann.   II. Series.
  HM1111.   S45 2000
  302—dc21

                                                     00–028942

British Library Cataloguing in Publication Data
A CIP catalogue record for this book is available from the British Library.

Typeset in 10/12 Sabon
by Kolam Information Services Pvt. Ltd, Pondicherry, India
Printed in Great Britain by TJ International, Padstow, Cornwall

This book is printed on acid-free paper.

Contents

Contributors

Leon Anderson is Associate Professor of Sociology at Ohio University. He is co-author (with David Snow) of *Down on Their Luck: A Study of Homeless Street People* (1993).

Philip Blumstein, now deceased, was Professor of Sociology at the University of Washington. He co-authored (with Pepper Schwartz) *American Couples: Money, Work, Sex* (1983).

Gordon Clanton is Adjunct Professor of Sociology at San Diego State University. He is co-editor (with Lynn G. Smith) of *Jealousy* (1998).

L. Richard Della Fave is Professor of Sociology at North Carolina State University, teaching in areas of theory, racial and ethnic relations, and social stratification.

Charles Derber is Professor of Sociology at Boston College. He is the author of *The Pursuit of Attention: Power and Ego in Everyday Life* (2000), *Power in the Highest Degree* (1990), and *The Wilding of America: How Greed and Violence Are Eroding Our Nation's Character* (1996).

Joe R. Feagin is Professor of Sociology at the University of Florida. He is the author of *The New Urban Paradigm* (1998), and co-author of *Living with Racism: The Black Middle Class Experience* (with Melvin P. Sikes, 1994), *Double Burden: Black Women and Everyday Racism* (with Y. St Jean, 1998), and *Racial and Ethnic Relations* (with C. Feagin, 1999).

Kenneth J. Gergen is Professor of Sociology at Swarthmore College. He is the author of *The Social Construction of the Person* (1985), *The Saturated Self* (1991), and *Realities and Relationships: Soundings in Social Construction* (1994).

Erving Goffman, now deceased, was Professor of Anthropology and Psychology at the University of Pennsylvania.

Nancy M. Henley is Professor of Psychology at the University of California at Los Angeles. She is the author of *Body Politics: Power, Sex, and Nonverbal Communication* (1977).

John P. Hewitt is Professor of Sociology at the University of Massachusetts, Amherst. He is the author of *Dilemmas of the American Self* (1989) and *Self and Society: A Symbolic Interactionist Social Psychology* (1991).

Arlie Russell Hochschild is Professor of Sociology at the University of California at Berkeley. She is the author of *The Managed Heart: Commercialization of Human*

Feeling (1983), *The Second Shift: Working Parents and the Revolution at Home* (1989), and *The Time Bind: When Work Becomes Home and Home Becomes Work* (1997).

Judith A. Howard is Professor of Sociology at the University of Washington. She is the co-author (with Jocelyn A. Hollander) of *Gendered Situations, Gendered Selves: A Gender Lens in Social Psychology* (1997), and co-editor (with Peter L. Callero) of *The Self-Society Dynamic: Cognition, Emotion, Action* (1991).

Mary Jackman is Professor of Sociology at the University of California at Davis. She is the author of *The Velvet Glove: Paternalism and Conflict in Gender, Class, and Race* (1994).

Melvin Kohn is Professor of Sociology at Johns Hopkins University. He is the author of *Class and Conformity: A Study in Values* (1989), and co-author (with Kazimierz M. Slomczynski) of *Social Structure and Self-Direction: A Comparative Analysis of the United States and Poland* (1990).

Aafke Komter is the editor of *The Gift: An Interdisciplinary Perspective* (1996).

Yale Magrass is Professor of Sociology at Southeast Massachusetts University. His fields of interest include social theory, social problems, social psychology, historical and political sociology, and sociology of knowledge.

Leslie Margolin is Professor of Counselor Education at the University of Iowa. She is the author of *Goodness Personified: The Emergence of Gifted Children* (1994) and *Under the Cover of Kindness: The Invention of Social Work* (1997).

Horace Miner, now deceased, received his Ph. D. from the University of Chicago in 1937. He became Professor of Anthropology and Sociology at the University of Michigan in 1964, and retired in 1987.

Peggy Orenstein is a journalist and the author of *School Girls: Young Women, Self-Esteem, and the Confidence Gap* (1995).

Cecilia L. Ridgeway is Professor of Sociology at Stanford University. She is the author of *The Dynamics of Small Groups* (1983) and the editor of *Gender, Interaction, and Inequality* (1991).

Barbara J. Risman is Professor of Sociology at North Carolina State University. She is the author of *Gender Vertigo* (1998) and co-editor (with Kristen A. Myers and Cynthia D. Anderson) of *Feminist Foundations: Toward Transforming Sociology* (1998).

D. L. Rosenhan is Professor of Psychology and Law at Stanford University. He is co-author (with Martin E. P. Seligman) of *Abnormal Psychology* (1984) and *Abnormality* (1998).

Melvin P. Sikes is an educator and psychological consultant. He is co-author (with Joe R. Feagin) of *Living With Racism: The Black Middle Class Experience* (1994).

Kazimierz M. Slomczynski is Professor of Sociology at Ohio State University. He is co-author (with Melvin Kohn) of *Social Structure and Self-Direction: A Comparative Analysis of the United States and Poland* (1990), and editor of *Social Stratification in Poland: Eight Empirical Studies* (1986).

David Snow is Professor of Sociology at the University of Arizona. He is co-author (with Leon Anderson) of *Down on Their Luck: A Study of Homeless Street People* (1993).

Mark Snyder is Professor of Psychology at the University of Minnesota. He is the author of *Public Appearances, Private Realities: The Psychology of Self-Monitoring* (1987).

Ralph H. Turner is Professor Emeritus of Sociology at the University of California at Los Angeles. He is the author of *Collective Behavior* (1987).

Henry A. Walker is Professor of Sociology at the University of Arizona. He is co-editor (with Phyllis Moen and Donna Dempster-McClain) of *A Nation Divided: Diversity, Inequality, and Community in America* (1999).

Viviana Zelizer is Professor of Sociology at Princeton University. She is the author of *Morals and Markets: The Development of Life Insurance in the United States* (1979), *Pricing the Priceless Child: The Changing Social Value of Children* (1985), and *The Social Meaning of Money* (1994).

Acknowledgments

The editor and publishers gratefully acknowledge permission to reproduce the copyright material listed below. The publishers apologize for any errors or omissions in the list and would be pleased to be notified of any corrections that should be incorporated in the next edition or reprint of this book.

Blumstein, Philip, "The Production of Selves in Personal Relationships," from *The Self–Society Dynamic*, ed. J. Howard and P. Callero (Cambridge University Press, 1991).

Clanton, Gordon, "Jealousy in American Culture, 1945–1985: Reflections from Popular Literature," from *The Sociology of Emotions: Original Essays and Research Papers*, ed. David D. Franks and E. Doyle McCarthy (JAI Press, Greenwich, Conn. and London, 1989).

Della Fave, L. Richard, "The Meek Shall Not Inherit the Earth: Self-Evaluation and the Legitimacy of Stratification," *American Sociological Review* 45 (December 1980). Reprinted by permission American Sociological Association.

Derber, Charles, with Magrass, Yale, "Attention for Sale," in *The Pursuit of Attention: Power and Ego in Everyday Life*, by Charles Derber, 2nd edn (Oxford University Press, New York, 2000).

Feagin, Joe R. and Sikes, Melvin P., *Living with Racism: The Black Middle Class Experience*. Copyright © 1994 by Joe R. Feagin and Melvin P. Sikes. Reprinted by permission of Beacon Press, Boston.

Gergen, Kenneth J., *The Saturated Self*. Copyright © 1991 by Basic Books Inc. Reprinted by permission of Basic Books, a member of Perseus Books, L.L.C., New York.

Goffman, Erving, from *The Presentation of Self in Everyday Life* by Erving Goffman. Copyright © 1959 by Erving Goffman. Used by permission of Doubleday, a division of Random House, Inc., New York.

Henley, Nancy M., "Body Politics: Power, Sex and Nonverbal Communication." Reprinted with the permission of Simon & Schuster, Inc., from *Body Politics* by Nancy M. Henley. Copyright © 1977 by Prentice-Hall, Inc.

Hewitt, John P., *The Myth of Self-Esteem*. Copyright © 11/97 by St. Martin's Press, Inc. Reprinted with permission of Bedford/St. Martin's Press, Inc., New York.

Hochschild, Arlie Russell, "Emotion Work, Feeling Rules, and Social Structure," *American Journal of Sociology* 85 (1979). © 1979 by The University of Chicago. Reprinted by permission of The University of Chicago Press.

Howard, Judith A., "A Sociological Framework of Cognition," *Advances in Group Processes* 7, 1990. Copyright © 1990 by JAI Press Inc.

Jackman, Mary, *The Velvet Glove: Paternalism and Conflict in Gender, Class and Race Relations* (University of California Press, Berkeley, 1994. Copyright © 1994 The Regents of the University of California).

Kohn, Melvin and Slomczynski, Kazimierz M., *Social Structure and Self-direction: A Comparative Analysis of the United States and Poland* (Blackwell Inc., Cambridge, Mass., 1990, reprinted by permission of Professor Melvin L. Kohn).

Komter, Aafke, "Hidden Power in Marriage," *Gender and Society* 3(2), 1989, pp. 187–216. Copyright © 1989 by Sage Publications, Inc. Reprinted by permission of Sage Publications Inc., Thousand Oaks, Calif.

Margolin, Leslie, "Goodness Personified: The Emergence of Gifted Children," *Social Problems* 40(4) (November 1993), pp. 510–32. © 1993 by The Society for the Study of Social Problems.

Miner, Horace, "Body Ritual among the Nacirema," *American Anthropologist* 58(3), 1956, Reprinted with permission of the American Anthropological Association, Arlington, Va.

Orenstein, Peggy, from *School Girls: Young Women, Self-Esteem, and the Confidence Gap* by Peggy Orenstein, American Association of University Women. Copyright © 1994 by Peggy Orenstein. Reprinted by permission of the author and the Sandra Dijkstra Literary Agency.

Ridgeway, Cecilia L. and Walker, Henry A., "Status Structures," from *Sociological Perspectives on Social Psychology* (Allyn and Bacon, Boston and London, 1995).

Risman, Barbara J., "Intimate Relationships from a Microstructural Perspective: Men Who Mother," *Gender and Society* 1(1), pp. 6–32. Copyright © 1987, by Sage Publications, Inc. Reprinted by permission of Sage Publications Inc., Thousand Oaks, Calif.

Rosenhan, D. L., "On Being Sane in Insane Places," reprinted with permission from *Science* 179 (January), 1973. Copyright 1973 American Association for the Advancement of Science.

Snow, David and Anderson, Leon, *Down on Their Luck: A Study of Homeless Street People* (University of California Press, Berkeley, 1993, Copyright © 1993 The Regents of the University of California).

Snyder, Mark, "Self-Fulfilling Stereotypes," reprinted with permission of *Psychology Today* magazine. Copyright 1982 (Sussex Publishers, Inc.).

Turner, Ralph H., "The Real Self: From Institution to Impulse," *American Journal of Sociology* 81, 1976. Reprinted by permission of The University of Chicago Press.

Zelizer, Viviana, *Pricing the Priceless Child: The Changing Social Value of Children*. Copyright © 1985 by Basic Books Inc. Reprinted by permission of Basic Books, a member of Perseus Books, L.L.C., New York.

Editor's Introduction

The readings collected here illustrate four core topics of sociological social psychology and these topics constitute the four parts of the book: (1) the social construction of reality; (2) the sociology of thought and emotions; (3) the self in social context; and (4) interaction and inequality. The volume is divided into four parts representing each of these topics.

The selected topics and readings by no means comprehensively survey the diverse work that is done by sociologists who specialize in social psychology.[1] The purpose of this volume, however, is to bring together readings that focus on themes distinguishing sociological social psychology from the version of social psychology more typically practiced and taught in psychology departments.

Though not all sociologists and psychologists fall neatly on their respective sides of the disciplinary divide, there are basic differences between the sociological perspective and the psychological perspective in social psychology. These differences can be illustrated by comparing psychological and sociological approaches to two central topics of social psychology: social influence and social cognition.

Both versions of social psychology have a central emphasis on social influence. That human beings are powerfully influenced by their social environments is the most elementary insight of either version of social psychology. Psychological and sociological social psychologists differ, however, in their approach to social influence. Psychologists are more interested in the individual, in understanding how human beings typically respond to social influence. It could be argued that psychological social psychologists seek to discover an essential human social nature. In other words, they want to discover some basic truths about the ways that human beings (allowing for differences based on personality, temperament, or other factors) are socially influenced. How do groups influence individuals? Do the opinions and attitudes of individuals change when they are subjected to a new social milieu with its own climate of opinions and attitudes? How are the perceptions of individuals influenced by the perceptions of others? Do individuals conform to authority, regardless of the content of the authority's directive? These are the topics of classic studies in social psychology, including Ted Newcomb's study of political attitudes at Bennington College during the 1930s (Newcomb 1958), Muzafer Sherif's study of norm formation (Sherif 1935), and Stanley Milgram's study of obedience to authority (Milgram 1963). These and many other studies that have been conducted during the twentieth century illustrate the elementary insight of social psychology that human beings are powerfully influenced by their social environments.

Sociological social psychologists are similarly interested in social influence. But whereas psychological social psychologists are most interested in understanding how individuals respond to social influence, sociological social psychologists are more interested in understanding the social, cultural, and historical contexts of human experience. Taking for granted the basic social psychological insight that human beings are influenced by their social environment, sociological social psychologists are interested in the *societal context* and *content* of social influence. In other words, sociological social psychologists want to know what beliefs, values, norms, and categories of people are more influential than others in a particular society at a particular time in history, and they want to understand the social, cultural, and historical forces that make them so.

A second major focus of psychological social psychology is social cognition, or the study of how human beings process information about themselves, others, and their social world. Cognitive social psychologists emphasize that human beings do not respond directly to reality itself, but instead to their perceptions of reality. In the same way that psychological social psychologists have defined some general principles about the ways that individuals respond to social influence, they have attempted to identify some general principles about the ways that individuals process information about their social world. The "belief perseverance phenomenon" (the tendency for our current beliefs to control our perceptions and our memories of reality) (Myers 1987: 118–19) and the "fundamental attribution error" (the tendency to underestimate situational causes and overestimate internal causes of behavior) (Ross 1977) are two examples of such principles. Sociological social psychology, also interested in the topic of social cognition, gives more emphasis to the societal, cultural, and historical bases of human thought processes than to the cognitive biases of individual human beings (Howard 1990).

In addition to the differences between the sociological and psychological perspectives on social influence and social cognition, there are a number of themes more characteristic of the sociological approach to social psychology than to the psychological. First, sociologically-oriented social psychologists are more likely to study the cultural patterning of human experience. Sociologists study the interrelationship of culture, language, and thought, i.e., the ways the language we speak and the words we most heavily use reflect our society and culture *and* influence the way we think about ourselves and the world (Whorf 1956). Sociological social psychologists pay special attention to social norms, or the everyday social rules that guide human behavior. While all social psychologists accept that human behavior is guided by social norms, sociologists are particularly concerned to examine the content of the norms and to link them to their societal context. Psychological social psychologists ask, "Given that there is a social norm about X, how are individuals affected and how do individuals tend to respond?" They are not particularly concerned with the content of the social norm. Sociological social psychologists, on the other hand, examine the norm and try to understand its connection to the larger social context. Sociologists also distinguish themselves from psychological social psychologists in their focus on socialization in relation to the larger social context. They are interested not merely in establishing that the development of human beings depends on socialization, but in studying the content of that socialization within any particular society, culture, or social group.

Further, sociological social psychologists are concerned with the influence of social structure (the patterns of relationships in a society) on human experience. In particular, they study how a person's place in the social structure – i.e., social roles and relative position in various social hierarchies – affects thought, behavior, and personality. The work of Melvin Kohn and Carmi Schooler, for instance, focuses on how the different characteristics of jobs typically held by middle-class and working-class persons produces differences in personality (Kohn and Schooler 1973).

Study of the interrelationship of the self, social interaction, and social structure has been one of the distinctive contributions of sociological social psychology. Here, it is important to distinguish two distinct perspectives in sociological social psychology: the structural perspective and the interactionist perspective. In addition to research such as Kohn and Schooler's that examines how personality is affected by social structural factors such as social class, social psychologists who work from the structural perspective ask such questions as: How is experience in social interaction influenced by a person's position within society? How is interaction influenced by the culture and structure of the larger society? How do inequalities in the larger society affect patterns of everyday social interaction? How do these patterns of everyday social interaction, in turn, shape the self? Following the work of Herbert Blumer (1969) and Erving Goffman (1959), by contrast, interactionist social psychologists focus on the processes whereby definitions of social reality and definitions of self are constructed and negotiated in social interaction. They are interested both in how these definitions of social reality and definitions of self reflect the structure and culture of the larger society and in how these interaction processes contribute to making and remaking the structure and culture of the larger society.

Another distinctive theme of sociological social psychology is the social psychology of inequality. Sociological social psychologists study the role of social psychological processes in making and perpetuating social inequality and examine the effects of social inequality on the experiences of both dominant and subordinate social groups. For example, they ask such questions as how one's social class influences the kind of attention one receives in social situations (Derber 1979), how race bias affects performance in job interviews (Snyder 1994), or how gender inequality is perpetuated by the different standards of popularity for boys and girls in school (Eder et al. 1995).

Sociologically-oriented social psychologists also examine the influence of historical and cultural contexts of human experience, particularly how these contexts affect how we think, what we value, and even and especially what it means to be a "self." For example, in what ways are our goals different today than they were for our great-grandparents? What, if any, are the differences in psychological characteristics between persons living in modern cities and those living in rural areas or between persons living in the United States and persons living in India?

Sociological social psychology is concerned with the relationship between the individual and society and, unlike psychological social psychology, does not take society for granted. To summarize, the main difference between the two social psychologies is that psychological social psychology is concerned with the ways in which social influence typically affects human beings (i.e., that most people will conform to the behavior of others when in a group of three or more) and with the way that individuals process information about the social world. Sociological social psychology, on the other hand, is concerned with the ways in which human experience is patterned differently according to one's social position (e.g. race, class, gender, occupational role) and according to the specific social, historical, and cultural contexts in which one lives. Sociological social psychology does not take the world "out there" for granted, but instead examines the specific content of the various social influences on our lives and the ways in which we, as individuals, groups, and societies, construct reality.

Note

1 For a comprehensive view of sociological social psychology, the collection edited by Cook, Fine, and House, *Sociological Perspectives on Social Psychology* (1995), is an invaluable resource.

References

Blumer, Herbert. 1969. *Symbolic Interactionism: Perspective and Method*. Englewood Cliffs, NJ: Prentice-Hall.

Cook, Karen S., Fine, Gary Alan, and House, James S. (eds.). 1995. *Sociological Perspectives on Social Psychology*. Boston: Allyn and Bacon.

Derber, Charles. 1979. *The Pursuit of Attention: Power and Individualism in Everyday Life*. New York: Oxford University Press.

Eder, Donna, with Evans, Catherine and Parker, Stephen. 1995. *School Talk: Gender and Adolescent Culture*. New Brunswick, NJ: Rutgers University Press.

Goffman, Erving. 1959. *The Presentation of Self in Everyday Life*. New York: Anchor Books.

Howard, Judith A. 1990. "A sociological framework of cognition." *Advances in Group Processes* 7: 75–99.

Kohn, Melvin L. and Schooler, Carmi. 1973. "Occupational experience and psychological functioning: An assessment of reciprocal effects." *American Sociological Review* 38: 97–118.

Milgram, Stanley. 1963. "Behavioral study of obedience." *Journal of Abnormal and Social Psychology* 67: 371–8.

Myers, David G. 1987. *Social Psychology*, 2nd edn. New York: McGraw-Hill.

Newcomb, T. M. 1958. "Attitude development as a function of reference groups." In E. E. Maccoby, T. M. Newcomb, and E. L. Hartley (eds.) *Readings in Social Psychology*, 3rd edn. New York: Holt, Rinehart, and Winston, pp. 265–75.

Ross, L. D. 1977. "The intuitive psychologist and his shortcomings: Distortions in the attribution process." In L. Berkowitz (ed.) *Advances in Experimental Social Psychology*, vol. 10. New York: Academic Press, pp. 174–221.

Sherif, Muzafer. 1935. "A study of some social factors in perception." *Archives of Psychology* 27 (187): 1–60.

Snyder, Mark. 1994. "Self-fulfilling stereotypes." In Paula Rothenberg (ed.) *Race, Class, and Gender in the United States*, 3rd edn. New York: St. Martin's Press, pp. 325–31.

Whorf, Benjamin. 1956. *Language, Thought, and Reality: Selected Writings of Benjamin Lee Whorf*. Cambridge, Mass.: MIT Press.

Additional reading

Adamopoulos, John and Kashima, Yoshihisa (eds.). 1999. *Social Psychology and Cultural Context*. Thousand Oaks, Calif.: Sage Publications.

Gergen, Kenneth and Gergen, Mary (eds.). 1984. *Historical Social Psychology*. Hillsdale, NJ: Erlbaum.

House, James S. 1977. "The three faces of social psychology." *Sociometry* 40: 161–77.

Lindesmith, Alfred, Strauss, Anselm L. and Denzin, Norman K. 1991. *Social Psychology*, 8th edn. Thousand Oaks, Calif.: Sage Publications.

Parker, Ian and Shotter, John (eds.). 1990. *Deconstructing Social Psychology*. London: Routledge.

Rosenberg, Morris and Turner, Ralph H. (eds.). 1981. *Social Psychology: Sociological Perspectives*. New York: Basic Books.

Wexler, Philip. 1996. *Critical Social Psychology*. New York: P. Lang.

Part I

The Social Construction of Reality

Introduction

> The man in the street does not ordinarily trouble himself about what is "real" to him and about what he "knows" unless he is stopped short by some sort of problem. He takes his "reality" and his "knowledge" for granted. The sociologist cannot do this, if only because of his systematic awareness of the fact that men in the street take quite different "realities" for granted as between one society and another. The sociologist is forced by the very logic of his discipline to ask, if nothing else, whether the difference between the two "realities" may not be understood in relation to various differences between the two societies. (Berger and Luckmann 1966: 2)

"The social construction of reality," the title of Peter Berger and Thomas Luckmann's 1966 classic, is one of the central themes of sociological social psychology. The passage quoted above indicates something of the meaning of this phrase. To say that reality is socially constructed means that the reality experienced by human beings depends on the meanings they learn from others in their society and social groups. One of the major aims of sociological social psychology is to demonstrate that many of the assumptions, beliefs, values, norms, and patterns of everyday life that we take to be natural and inevitable are human constructs.

The phrase "the social construction of reality" is typically associated with symbolic interactionism and related interpretive traditions in sociology. The three main tenets of symbolic interactionism, as defined by Herbert Blumer (1969), explain part of the meaning of "the social construction of reality": (1) "human beings act toward things on the basis of the meanings that the things have for them"; (2) "the meaning of such things is derived from, or arises out of, the social interaction that one has with one's fellows"; and (3) "meanings are handled in, and modified through, an interpretative process used by the person in dealing with the things he encounters" (Blumer 1969: 2).

Although the social construction of reality is often associated with symbolic interactionism, the idea is, in fact, quite central to sociology as a whole. Many sociologists, however, believe that symbolic interactionism overemphasizes the individual's freedom to construct the realities of everyday life and does not give sufficient weight to the power of societal structures, culture, and social institutions. Erving Goffman, for example, emphasized that most social situations are defined prior to the individual's arrival at them (Goffman 1974). It is important, therefore, to recognize that the concept "the social construction of reality" does not itself specify who or what is responsible for the constructing and how fixed or mutable the constructed reality may be.

There are a number of dimensions to the idea that reality is socially constructed, each of which will be illustrated by the readings included in this section. The most basic meaning is represented by W. I. Thomas's famous statement: "If men define situations as real, they are real in their consequences" (Thomas 1928). If, for example, we define gender as a significant basis of differentiation, gender becomes a significant basis of differentiation. Thomas's theorem does not mean that individuals are at liberty to define an experience any way they want. Their definitional liberty is restricted in a number of ways. In the first place, definitions of reality are a collective, social process. For instance, an individual could not single-handedly define gender as an insignificant basis of differentiation and expect the significance of gender in society to disappear. Second, the definitions of reality of various persons, groups, and categories of people are not equally influential. One crucial component of social hierarchies based on categories such as age, gender, race, class, educational status, and occupational status is inequality in the power to define reality. Third, definitions of reality often predate the existence of any particular individual. Norms, beliefs, and patterns of social relationships preexist in the social group into which the individual is born or enters. The family and community and the society and culture, not the individual, are the primary defining agencies. These restrictions of the individual's definitional liberty, in fact, powerfully illustrate what it means to say that reality is socially constructed.

One reason that our definitions of reality have real consequences is that definitions influence perceptions of reality. A classic example is provided by a study by the famous social psychologist Solomon Asch (1946). On the first day of class, Asch informs the 9 a.m. introductory psychology class that they will be taught by Professor A. Asch not only describes Professor A's academic and teaching accomplishments, but adds that he is quite warm and friendly. Asch informs the 10 a.m. introductory class that they will be taught by Professor B. Asch describes Professor B's academic and teaching accomplishments in an identical manner to his description of Professor A, but adds that professor B is quite analytic in manner. In fact Professor A and Professor B were the same person. Yet, as a result of the preconceptions of the students, the professor was perceived quite differently by the two classes. The 9 a.m. class loved their professor, while the 10 a.m. class wished to drop the course.

The paper by David Rosenhan, "On being sane in insane places," similarly illustrates the power of a definition of reality to influence the perception of reality. Rosenhan sent eight psychologically normal individuals into a psychiatric hospital, who feigned psychiatric disturbance merely by reporting that they had been hearing voices saying "empty," "hollow," and "thud," as if telling them that their lives were empty. Having obtained admission to the hospital with a diagnosis of schizophrenia, the pseudopatients reported no more symptoms and behaved in their usual manner. The initial definition of the pseudopatients as "insane," however, had already done its work. Their behaviors were viewed through the lens of the label "insane" and were interpreted as manifestations of mental illness. The power of definitions of reality to create a perception of reality, and sometimes even to influence behavior in such a way as to confirm the preconception, is the core insight of "labeling theory" (Becker 1963).

Not only do our definitions of reality influence our perceptions of reality, but another way that our definitions of situations may become real in their consequences is through the self-fulfilling prophecy. A self-fulfilling prophecy is a process in which our expectations of reality lead us to behave in such a way as to produce that reality. If, for example, I believe that one of my colleagues dislikes me, I may behave coldly towards this person. Though I might have initially been wrong about her dislike of me, my coldness towards my colleague actually produces the dislike and thereby confirms my initial belief. The idea of the self-fulfilling prophecy is derived from basic principles of social cognition developed by psychological social psychology.

First, we perceive reality in accordance with our preconception of it. Second, our perceptions of another person affect our behavior towards that person. Finally, our behavior influences the person in such a way that they fulfill our expectation. The reading by Mark Snyder, "Self-fulfilling stereotypes," examines how stereotypes about race, gender, and physical attractiveness produce self-fulfilling prophecies.

If our beliefs and preconceptions influence our perception of reality, certainly the language we use also influences the way we see the world. A distinctive theme of sociological social psychology is the analysis of the interrelationship between language, thought, and society. According to the sociological view, language is an important agent of socialization. As the carrier of the shared meanings of a culture, our language leads us to perceive reality through a culturally-specific lens. The idea that the reality one experiences is determined by the language one speaks is known as the Whorf–Sapir hypothesis (Whorf 1956). In contrast to the commonsense view that we use language to *express* our thoughts, feelings, and experience, the Whorf–Sapir theory holds that our language shapes our thoughts, feelings, and experiences. For example, they noted that Standard Average European (SAE) languages have a grammatical structure which distinguishes nouns and verbs and subjects and predicates. The language of the Hopi, on the other hand, does not. English-speaking people say, "The lightning flashed." The Hopi say, "Lightning." Because SAE languages break up nature into nouns and verbs and subjects and predicates, those who speak such languages tend to look at the world in terms of time. The Hopi, conversely, tend to view reality in terms of events.

Though most do not go so far as to argue that language *determines* our thought, sociologists do believe that language is an essential carrier of culture and thus an important social influence on our thought and experience. Even within our own language, the concepts we use to describe reality powerfully influence our perception of reality. The reading by Rosenhan, for example, illustrates that the hospital staff responded more to the label "insane" than they did to the actual behavior of the pseudopatients. The reading by Peggy Orenstein, "Sluts and studs" from *School Girls* illustrates not only how concepts shape our response to reality but also how the words we use to speak about reality reflect the beliefs, norms, attitudes, and values of our culture.

A second meaning of the idea that reality is socially constructed is that what we think of as "normal" is socially constructed. In other words, we take for granted that the way we, or most people in our society, live our daily lives is the normal and natural way to do so. Horace Miner's "Body ritual among the Nacirema" illustrates one of the elementary sociological insights that what is "normal" or "bizarre" varies by culture. Miner's essay is a description of American culture from the perspective of an outsider, demonstrating that everyday practices that we take for granted as normal human behavior do not seem all that natural from the perspective of an outsider. Phenomenological sociology (Schutz 1970) and ethnomethodology (Garfinkel 1967) emphasize this point, calling for the sociologists to play the role of "stranger" in their own worlds and to expose the taken-for-granted assumptions of social life.

Finally, to say that reality is socially constructed means that definitions of reality are products of their social and cultural context. In contemporary American society, for example, many consider self-esteem to be a reality that affects many important outcomes in a person's life. In *The Myth of Self-Esteem* (1998), John Hewitt makes the case that "self-esteem" is only one of many possible ways of interpreting emotional responses to our own successes and failures. In the context of individualistic American culture, however, it is the favored interpretation. Hewitt's book analyzes the social and cultural factors that gave rise to the American focus on self-esteem. In addition to the extract from Hewitt's work, the readings by Zelizer (1985) and Margolin (1993) offer two more examples of socially constructed realities: the "priceless child" and the "gifted child." Like Hewitt, Zelizer and Margolin's analyses place these constructed realities in their social and cultural contexts.

References

Asch, Solomon. 1946. "Forming impressions of personality." *Journal of Abnormal and Social Psychology* 41: 258–90.

Becker, Howard. 1963. *Outsiders*. New York: Free Press.

Berger, Peter and Luckmann, Thomas. 1966. *The Social Construction of Reality*. New York: Doubleday.

Blumer, Herbert. 1969. *Symbolic Interactionism: Perspective and Method*. Englewood Cliffs, NJ: Prentice-Hall.

Garfinkel, Harold. 1967. *Studies in Ethnomethodology*. Englewood Cliffs, NJ: Prentice-Hall.

Goffman, Erving. 1974. *Frame Analysis: An Essay on the Organization of Experience*. New York: Harper and Row.

Hewitt, John P. 1998. *The Myth of Self-Esteem: Finding Happiness and Solving Problems in America*. New York: St. Martin's Press.

Margolin, Leslie. 1993. "Goodness personified: The emergence of gifted children." *Social Problems* 40(4): 510–32.

Miner, Horace. 1956. "Body ritual among the Nacirema." *American Anthropologist* 58(3): 503–7.

Orenstein, Peggy. 1994. *School Girls: Young Women, Self-Esteem, and the Confidence Gap*. New York: Doubleday.

Rosenhan, D. L. 1973. "On being sane in insane places." *Science* 179 (January): 250–8.

Schutz, Alfred. 1970. *On Phenomenology and Social Relations*, ed. and with introduction by Helmut Wagner. Chicago: University of Chicago Press.

Snyder, Mark. 1994. "Self-fulfilling stereotypes." In Paula Rothenberg (ed.) *Race, Class, and Gender in the United States*, 3rd edn. New York: St. Martin's Press.

Thomas, William I. with Thomas, Dorothy Swaine. 1928. *The Child in America*. New York: Alfred A. Knopf.

Whorf, Benjamin. 1956. *Language, Thought, and Reality: Selected Writings of Benjamin Lee Whorf*. Cambridge, Mass.: MIT Press.

Zelizer, Viviana. 1985. *Pricing the Priceless Child: The Changing Social Value of Children*. New York: Basic Books.

Additional reading

Becker, Howard S. 1953. "Becoming a marijuana user." *American Journal of Sociology* 59: 235–42.

Conrad, Peter. 1975. "The discovery of hyperkinesis: Notes on the medicalization of deviant behavior." *Social Problems* 23: 12–21.

Emerson, Joan P. 1970. "Behavior in private places: Sustaining definitions of reality in gynecological examinations." In P. Dreitsel (ed.) *Recent Sociology*. New York: Macmillan, pp. 74–97.

Sarbin, T. and Kitsuse, J. (eds.). 1994. *Constructing the Social*. London: Sage Publications.

Zerubavel, Eviatar. 1991. *The Fine Line: Making Distinctions in Everyday Life*. New York: Free Press.

1 On Being Sane in Insane Places

D. L. Rosenhan

If sanity and insanity exist, how shall we know them?

The question is neither capricious nor itself insane. However much we may be personally convinced that we can tell the normal from the abnormal, the evidence is simply not compelling. It is commonplace, for example, to read about murder trials wherein eminent psychiatrists for the defense are contradicted by equally eminent psychiatrists for the prosecution on the matter of the defendant's sanity. More generally, there are a great deal of conflicting data on the reliability, utility, and meaning of such terms as "sanity," "insanity," "mental illness," and "schizophrenia."[1] Finally, as early as 1934, Benedict suggested that normality and abnormality are not universal.[2] What is viewed as normal in one culture may be seen as quite aberrant in another. Thus, notions of normality and abnormality may not be quite as accurate as people believe they are.

To raise questions regarding normality and abnormality is in no way to question the fact that some behaviors are deviant or odd. Murder is deviant. So, too, are hallucinations. Nor does raising such questions deny the existence of the personal anguish that is often associated with "mental illness." Anxiety and depression exist. Psychological suffering exists. But normality and abnormality, sanity and insanity, and the diagnoses that flow from them may be less substantive than many believe them to be.

At its heart, the question of whether the sane can be distinguished from the insane (and whether degrees of insanity can be distinguished from each other) is a simple matter: do the salient characteristics that lead to diagnoses reside in the patients themselves or in the environments and contexts in which observers find them? From Bleuler, through Kretchmer, through the formulators of the recently revised *Diagnostic and Statistical Manual* of the American Psychiatric Association, the belief has been strong that patients present symptoms, that those symptoms can be categorized, and, implicitly, that the sane are distinguishable from the insane. More recently, however, this belief has been questioned. Based in part on theoretical and anthropological considerations, but also on philosophical, legal, and therapeutic ones, the view has grown that psychological categorization of mental illness is useless at best and downright harmful, misleading, and pejorative at worst. Psychiatric diagnoses, in this view, are in the minds of the observers and are not valid summaries of characteristics displayed by the observed.[3]

Gains can be made in deciding which of these is more nearly accurate by getting normal people (that is, people who do not have, and have never suffered, symptoms of serious psychiatric disorders) admitted to psychiatric hospitals and then determining whether they were discovered to be sane and, if so, how. If the sanity of such

Reprinted from *Science* 179 (January 1973): 250–8.

pseudopatients were always detected, there would be prima facie evidence that a sane individual can be distinguished from the insane context in which he is found. Normality (and presumably abnormality) is distinct enough that it can be recognized wherever it occurs, for it is carried within the person. If, on the other hand, the sanity of the pseudopatients were never discovered, serious difficulties would arise for those who support traditional modes of psychiatric diagnosis. Given that the hospital staff was not incompetent, that the pseudopatient had been behaving as sanely as he had been outside of the hospital, and that it had never been previously suggested that he belonged in a psychiatric hospital, such an unlikely outcome would support the view that psychiatric diagnosis reveals little about the patient but much about the environment in which an observer finds him.

This article describes such an experiment. Eight sane people gained secret admission to 12 different hospitals. Their diagnostic experiences constitute the data of the first part of this article; the remainder is devoted to a description of their experiences in psychiatric institutions. Too few psychiatrists and psychologists, even those who have worked in such hospitals, know what the experience is like. They rarely talk about it with former patients, perhaps because they distrust information coming from the previously insane. Those who have worked in psychiatric hospitals are likely to have adapted so thoroughly to the settings that they are insensitive to the impact of that experience. And while there have been occasional reports of researchers who submitted themselves to psychiatric hospitalization,[4] these researchers have commonly remained in the hospitals for short periods of time, often with the knowledge of the hospital staff. It is difficult to know the extent to which they were treated like patients or like research colleagues. Nevertheless, their reports about the inside of the psychiatric hospital have been valuable. This article extends those efforts.

Pseudopatients and their Settings

The eight pseudopatients were a varied group. One was a psychology graduate student in his twenties. The remaining seven were older and "established." Among them were three psychologists, a pediatrician, a psychiatrist, a painter, and a housewife. Three pseudopatients were women, five were men. All of them employed pseudonyms, lest their alleged diagnoses embarrass them later. Those who were in mental health professions alleged another occupation in order to avoid the special attentions that might be accorded by staff, as a matter of courtesy or caution, to ailing colleagues. With the exception of myself (I was the first pseudopatient and my presence was known to the hospital administrator and chief psychologist and, so far as I can tell, to them alone), the presence of pseudopatients and the nature of the research program was not known to the hospital staffs.

The settings were similarly varied. In order to generalize the findings, admission into a variety of hospitals was sought. The 12 hospitals in the sample were located in five different states on the East and West coasts. Some were old and shabby, some were quite new. Some were research-oriented, others not. Some had good staff–patient ratios, others were quite understaffed. Only one was a strictly private hospital. All of the others were supported by state or federal funds or, in one instance, by university funds.

After calling the hospital for an appointment, the pseudopatient arrived at the admissions office complaining that he had been hearing voices. Asked what the voices said, he replied that they were often unclear, but as far as he could tell they said "empty," "hollow," and "thud." The voices were unfamiliar and were of the same sex as the pseudopatient. The choice of these symptoms was occasioned by their apparent similarity to existential symptoms. Such symptoms are alleged to arise from painful concerns about the perceived meaninglessness of one's life. It is as if the hallucinating person were saying, "My life is empty and hollow." The choice of these symptoms was also determined by the *absence* of a single report of existential psychoses in the literature.

Beyond alleging the symptoms and falsifying name, vocation, and employment, no further alterations of person, history, or circumstances were made. The significant events of the pseudopatient's life history were presented as they had actually occurred. Relationships with parents and siblings, with spouse and children, with people at work and in school, consistent with the aforementioned exceptions, were described as they were or had been. Frustrations and upsets were described along with joys and satisfactions. These facts are important to remember. If anything, they strongly biased the subsequent results in favor of detecting sanity, since none of their histories or current behaviors were seriously pathological in any way.

Immediately upon admission to the psychiatric ward, the pseudopatient ceased simulating *any* symptoms of abnormality. In some cases, there was a brief period of mild nervousness and anxiety, since none of the pseudopatients really believed that they would be admitted so easily. Indeed, their shared fear was that they would be immediately exposed as frauds and greatly embarrassed. Moreover, many of them had never visited a psychiatric ward; even those who had, nevertheless had some genuine fears about what might happen to them. Their nervousness, then, was quite appropriate to the novelty of the hospital setting, and it abated rapidly.

Apart from that short-lived nervousness, the pseudopatient behaved on the ward as he "normally" behaved. The pseudopatient spoke to patients and staff as he might ordinarily. Because there is uncommonly little to do on a psychiatric ward, he attempted to engage others in conversation. When asked by staff how he was feeling, he indicated that he was fine, that he no longer experienced symptoms. He responded to instructions from attendants, to calls for medication (which was not swallowed), and to dining-hall instructions. Beyond such activities as were available to him on the admissions ward, he spent his time writing down his observations about the ward, its patients, and the staff. Initially these notes were written "secretly," but as it soon became clear that no one much cared, they were subsequently written on standard tablets of paper in such public places as the dayroom. No secret was made of these activities.

The pseudopatient, very much as a true psychiatric patient, entered a hospital with no foreknowledge of when he would be discharged. Each was told that he would have to get out by his own devices, essentially by convincing the staff that he was sane. The psychological stresses associated with hospitalization were considerable, and all but one of the pseudopatients desired to be discharged almost immediately after being admitted. They were, therefore, motivated not only to behave sanely, but to be paragons of cooperation. That their behavior was in no way disruptive is confirmed by nursing reports, which have been obtained on most of the patients.

These reports uniformly indicate that the patients were "friendly," "cooperative," and "exhibited no abnormal indications."

The Normal are not Detectably Sane

Despite their public "show" of sanity, the pseudopatients were never detected. Admitted, except in one case, with a diagnosis of schizophrenia,[5] each was discharged with a diagnosis of schizophrenia "in remission." The label "in remission" should in no way be dismissed as a formality, for at no time during any hospitalization had any question been raised about any pseudopatient's simulation. Nor are there any indications in the hospital records that the pseudopatient's status was suspect. Rather, the evidence is strong that, once labeled schizophrenic, the pseudopatient was stuck with that label. If the pseudopatient was to be discharged, he must naturally be "in remission"; but he was not sane, nor, in the institution's view, had he ever been sane.

The uniform failure to recognize sanity cannot be attributed to the quality of the hospitals, for, although there were considerable variations among them, several are considered excellent. Nor can it be alleged that there was simply not enough time to observe the pseudopatients. Length of hospitalization ranged from 7 to 52 days, with an average of 19 days. The pseudopatients were not, in fact, carefully observed, but this failure clearly speaks more to traditions within psychiatric hospitals than to lack of opportunity.

Finally, it cannot be said that the failure to recognize the pseudopatients' sanity was due to the fact that they were not behaving sanely. While there was clearly some tension present in all of them, their daily visitors could detect no serious behavioral consequences – nor, indeed, could other patients. It was quite common for the patients to "detect" the pseudopatients' sanity. During the first three hospitalizations, when accurate contents were kept, 35 of a total of 118 patients on the admissions ward voiced their suspicions, some vigorously. "You're not crazy. You're a journalist, or a professor [referring to the continual note-taking]. You're checking up on the hospital." While most of the patients were reassured by the pseudopatient's insistence that he had been sick before he came in but was fine now, some continued to believe that the pseudopatient was sane throughout his hospitalization. The fact that the patients often recognized normality when staff did not raises important questions.

Failure to detect sanity during the course of hospitalization may be due to the fact that physicians operate with a strong bias toward what statisticians call the type 2 error.[6] This is to say that physicians are more inclined to call a healthy person sick (a false positive, type 2) than a sick person healthy (a false negative, type 1). The reasons for this are not hard to find: it is clearly more dangerous to misdiagnose illness than health. Better to err on the side of caution, to suspect illness even among the healthy.

But what holds for medicine does not hold equally well for psychiatry. Medical illnesses, while unfortunate, are not commonly pejorative. Psychiatric diagnoses, on the contrary, carry with them personal, legal, and social stigma.[7] It was therefore important to see whether the tendency toward diagnosing the sane insane could be reversed. The following experiment was arranged at a research and teaching hospital whose staff had heard these findings but doubted that such an error could occur in their hospital. The staff was informed that at some time during the following 3 months, one or more pseudopatients would attempt to be admitted into the psychiatric hospital. Each staff member was asked to rate each patient who presented himself at admissions or on the ward according to the likelihood that the patient was a pseudopatient. A 10-point scale was used, with a 1 and 2 reflecting high confidence that the patient was a pseudopatient.

Judgments were obtained on 193 patients who were admitted for psychiatric treatment. All staff who had had sustained contact with or primary responsibility for the patient – attendants, nurses, psychiatrists, physicians, and psychologists – were asked to make judgments. Forty-one patients were alleged, with high confidence, to be pseudopatients by at least one member of the staff. Twenty-three were considered suspect by at least one psychiatrist. Nineteen were suspected by one psychiatrist *and* one other staff member. Actually, no genuine pseudopatient (at least from my group) presented himself during this period.

The experiment is instructive. It indicates that the tendency to designate sane people as insane can be reversed when the stakes (in this case, prestige and diagnostic acumen) are high. But what can be said of the 19 people who were suspected of being "sane" by one psychiatrist and another staff member? Were these people truly "sane," or was it rather the case that in the course of avoiding the type 2 error the staff tended to make more errors of the first sort – calling the crazy "sane"? There is no way of knowing. But one thing is certain: any diagnostic process that lends itself so readily to massive errors of this sort cannot be a very reliable one.

The Stickiness of Psychodiagnostic Labels

Beyond the tendency to call the healthy sick – a tendency that accounts better for diagnostic behavior on admission than it does for such behavior after a lengthy period of exposure – the data speak to the massive role of labeling in psychiatric assessment. Having once been labeled schizophrenic, there is nothing the pseudopatient can do to overcome the tag. The tag profoundly colors others' perceptions of him and his behavior.

From one viewpoint, these data are hardly surprising, for it has long been known that elements are given meaning by the context in which they occur. Gestalt psychology made this point vigorously, and Asch[8] demonstrated that there are "central" personality traits (such as "warm" versus "cold") which are so powerful that they markedly color the meaning of other information in forming an impression of a given personality.[9] "Insane," "schizophrenic," "manic-depressive," and "crazy" are probably among the most powerful of such central traits. Once a person is designated abnormal, all of his other behaviors and characteristics are colored by that label. Indeed, that label is so powerful that many of the pseudopatients' normal behaviors were overlooked entirely or profoundly misinterpreted. Some examples may clarify this issue.

Earlier I indicated that there were no changes in the pseudopatient's personal history and current status beyond those of name, employment, and, where necessary, vocation. Otherwise, a veridical description of personal history and circumstances was offered. Those circumstances were not psychotic. How were they made consonant with the diagnosis of psychosis? Or were those diagnoses modified in such a way as to bring them into accord with the circumstances of the pseudopatient's life, as described by him?

As far as I can determine, diagnoses were in no way affected by the relative health of the circumstances of a pseudopatient's life. Rather, the reverse occurred: the perception of his circumstances was shaped entirely by the diagnosis. A clear example of such translation is found in the case of a pseudopatient who had had a close relationship with his mother but was rather remote from his father during his early childhood. During adolescence and beyond, however, his father became a close friend, while his relationship with his mother cooled. His present relationship with his wife was characteristically close and warm. Apart from occasional angry exchanges, friction was minimal. The children had rarely been spanked. Surely there is nothing especially pathological about such a history. Indeed, many readers may see a similar pattern in their own experiences, with no markedly deleterious consequences. Observe, however, how such a history was translated in the psychopathological context, this from the case summary prepared after the patient was discharged.

> This white 39-year-old male . . . manifests a long history of considerable ambivalence in close relationships, which begins in early childhood. A warm relationship with his mother cools during his adolescence. A distant relationship to his father is described as becoming very intense. Affective stability is absent. His attempts to control emotionality with his wife and children are punctuated by angry outbursts and, in the case of the children, spankings. And while he says that he has several good friends, one senses considerable ambivalence embedded in those relationships also.

The facts of the case were unintentionally distorted by the staff to achieve consistency with a popular theory of the dynamics of a schizophrenic reaction. Nothing of an ambivalent nature had been described in relations with parents, spouse, or friends. To the extent that ambivalence could be inferred, it was probably not greater than is found in all human relationships. It is true the pseudopatient's relationships with his parents changed over time, but in the ordinary context that would hardly be remarkable – indeed, it might very well be expected. Clearly, the meaning ascribed to his verbalizations (that is, ambivalence, affective instability) was determined by the diagnosis: schizophrenia. An entirely different meaning would have been ascribed if it were known that the man was "normal."

All pseudopatients took extensive notes publicly. Under ordinary circumstances, such behavior would have raised questions in the minds of observers, as, in fact, it did among patients. Indeed, it seemed so certain that the notes would elicit suspicion that elaborate precautions were taken to remove them from the ward each day. But the precautions proved needless. The closest any staff member came to questioning these notes occurred when one pseudopatient asked his physician what kind of medication he was receiving and began to write down the response. "You needn't write it," he was told gently. "If you have trouble remembering, just ask me again."

If no questions were asked of the pseudopatients, how was their writing inter-preted? Nursing records for three patients indicate that the writing was seen as an aspect of their pathological behavior. "Patient engages in writing behavior" was the daily nursing comment on one of the pseudopatients who was never questioned about his writing. Given that the patient is in the hospital, he must be psychologically disturbed. And given that he is disturbed, continuous writing must be a behavioral manifestation of that disturbance, perhaps a subset of the compulsive behaviors that are sometimes correlated with schizophrenia.

One tacit characteristic of psychiatric diagnosis is that it locates the sources of aberration within the individual and only rarely within the complex of stimuli that surrounds him. Consequently, behaviors that are stimulated by the environment are commonly misattributed to the patient's disorder. For example, one kindly nurse found a pseudopatient pacing the long hospital corridors. "Nervous, Mr X?" she asked. "No, bored," he said.

The notes kept by pseudopatients are full of patient behaviors that were misinter-preted by well-intentioned staff. Often enough, a patient would go "berserk" because he had, wittingly or unwittingly, been mistreated by, say, an attendant. A nurse coming upon the scene would rarely inquire even cursorily into the environmental stimuli of the patient's behavior. Rather, she assumed that his upset derived from his pathology, not from his present interactions with other staff members. Occasionally, the staff might assume that the patient's family (especially when they had recently visited) or other patients had stimulated the outburst. But never were the staff found to assume that one of themselves or the structure of the hospital had anything to do with a patient's behavior. One psychiatrist pointed to a group of patients who were sitting outside the cafeteria entrance half an hour before lunchtime. To a group of young residents he indicated that such behavior was characteristic of the oral-acquisitive nature of the syndrome. It seemed not to occur to him that there were very few things to anticipate in a psychiatric hospital besides eating.

A psychiatric label has a life and an influence of its own. Once the impression has been formed that the patient is schizophrenic, the expectation is that he will continue to be schizophrenic. When a sufficient amount of time has passed, during which the patient has done nothing bizarre, he is considered to be in remission and available for discharge. But the label endures beyond discharge, with the unconfirmed expectation that he will behave as a schizophrenic again. Such labels, conferred by mental health professionals, are as influential on the patient as they are on his relatives and friends, and it should not surprise anyone that the diagnosis acts on all of them as a self-fulfilling prophecy. Eventually, the patient himself accepts the diagnosis, with all of its surplus meanings and expectations, and behaves accordingly.[10]

The inferences to be made from these matters are quite simple. Much as Zigler and Phillips have demonstrated that there is enormous overlap in the symptoms pres-ented by patients who have been variously diagnosed,[11] so there is enormous overlap in the behaviors of the sane and the insane. The sane are not "sane" all of the time. We lose our tempers "for no good reason." We are occasionally depressed or anxious, again for no good reason. And we may find it difficult to get along with one or another person – again for no reason that we can specify. Similarly, the insane are not always insane. Indeed, it was the impression of the pseudopatients while living with them that they were sane for long periods of time – that the bizarre behaviors upon which their diagnoses were allegedly predicated constituted only a small fraction of their total behavior. If it makes no sense to label ourselves permanently depressed on the basis of an occasional depression, then it takes better evidence than is presently available to label all patients insane or schizophrenic on the basis of bizarre behaviors or cognitions. It seems more useful, as Mischel has pointed out,[12] to limit our discussions to *behaviors*, the stimuli that provoke them, and their correlates.

It is not known why powerful impressions of personality traits, such as "crazy" or "insane," arise. Conceivably, when the origins of and stimuli that give rise to a behavior are remote or unknown, or when the behavior strikes us as immutable, trait labels regarding the *behaver* arise. When, on the other hand, the origins and stimuli are known and available, discourse is limited to the behavior itself. Thus, I may hallucinate because I am sleeping, or I may hallucinate because I have ingested a peculiar drug. These are termed sleep-induced hallucinations, or dreams, and drug-induced hallucinations, respectively. But when the stimuli to my hallucinations are unknown, that is called craziness, or schizophrenia – as if that inference were somehow as illuminating as the others.

The Experience of Psychiatric Hospitalization

The term "mental illness" is of recent origin. It was coined by people who were humane in their inclinations and who wanted very much to raise the station of (and the public's sympathies toward) the psychologically disturbed from that of witches and "crazies" to one that was akin to the physically ill. And they were at least partially successful, for the treatment of the mentally ill *has* improved considerably over the years. But while treatment has improved, it is doubtful that people really regard the mentally ill in the same way that they view the physically ill. A broken leg is something one recovers from, but mental illness allegedly endures forever. A broken leg does not threaten the observer, but a crazy schizophrenic? There is by now a host of evidence that attitudes toward the mentally ill are characterized by fear, hostility, aloofness, suspicion, and dread.[13] The mentally ill are society's lepers.

That such attitudes infect the general population is perhaps not surprising, only upsetting. But that they affect the professionals – attendants, nurses, physicians, psychologists, and social workers – who treat and deal with the mentally ill is more disconcerting, both because such attitudes are self-evidently pernicious and because they are unwitting. Most mental health professionals would insist that they are sympathetic toward the mentally ill, that they are neither avoidant nor hostile. But it is more likely that an exquisite ambivalence characterizes their relations with psychiatric patients, such that their avowed impulses are only part of their entire attitude. Negative attitudes are there too and can easily be detected. Such attitudes should not surprise us. They are the natural offspring of the labels patients wear and the places in which they are found.

Consider the structure of the typical psychiatric hospital. Staff and patients are strictly segregated. Staff have their own living space, including their dining facilities, bathrooms, and assembly places. The glassed quarters that contain the professional staff, which the pseudopatients came to call "the cage," sit out on every dayroom. The staff emerge primarily for caretaking purposes – to give medication, to conduct a therapy or group meeting, to instruct or reprimand a patient. Otherwise, staff keep to themselves, almost as if the disorder that afflicts their charges is somehow catching.

So much is patient–staff segregation the rule that, for four public hospitals in which an attempt was made to measure the degree to which staff and patients mingle, it was necessary to use "time out of the staff cage" as the operational measure. While it was not the case that all time spent out of the cage was spent mingling with patients (attendants, for example, would occasionally emerge to watch television in the dayroom), it was the only way in which one could gather reliable data on time for measuring.

The average amount of time spent by attendants outside of the cage was 11.3 percent (range, 3 to 52 percent). This figure does not represent only time spent mingling with patients, but also includes time spent on such chores as folding laundry, supervising patients while they shave, directing ward clean-up, and sending patients to off-ward activities. It was the relatively rare attendant who spent time talking with patients or playing games with them. It proved impossible to obtain a "percent mingling time" for nurses, since the amount of time they spent out of the cage was too brief. Rather, we counted instances of emergence from the cage. On the average, daytime nurses emerged from the cage 11.5 times per shift, including instances when they left the ward entirely (range, 4 to 39 times). Late afternoon and night nurses were even less available, emerging on the average 9.4 times per shift (range, 4 to 41 times). Data on early morning nurses, who arrived usually after midnight and departed at 8 a.m., are not available because patients were asleep during most of this period.

Physicians, especially psychiatrists, were even less available. They were rarely seen on the wards. Quite commonly, they would be seen only when they arrived and departed, with the remaining time being spent in their offices or in the cage. On the average, physicians emerged on the ward 6.7 times per day (range, 1 to 17 times). It proved difficult to make an accurate estimate in this regard, since physicians often maintained hours that allowed them to come and go at different times.

The hierarchical organization of the psychiatric hospital has been commented on before,[14] but the latent meaning of that kind of organization is worth noting again. Those with the most power have least to do with patients, and those with the least power are most involved with them. Recall, however, that the acquisition of role-appropriate behaviors occurs mainly through the observation of others, with the most powerful having the most influence. Consequently, it is understandable that attendants not only spend more time with patients than do any other members of the staff – that is required by their station in the hierarchy – but also, insofar as they learn from their superiors' behavior, spend as little time with patients as they can. Attendants are seen mainly in the cage, which is where the models, the action, and the power are.

I turn now to a different set of studies, these dealing with staff response to patient-initiated contact. It has long been known that the amount of time a person spends with you can be an index of your significance to him. If he initiates and maintains eye

Table 1.1 Self-initiated contact by pseudopatients with psychiatrists and nurses and attendants, compared to contact with other groups

Contact	Psychiatric hospitals		University campus (nonmedical)	University medical center Physicians		
	(1) Psychiatrists	(2) Nurses and attendants	(3) Faculty	(4) "Looking for a psychiatrist"	(5) "Looking for an internist"	(6) No additional comment
Responses						
Moves on, head averted (%)	71	88	0	0	0	0
Makes eye contact (%)	23	10	0	11	0	0
Pauses and chats (%)	2	2	0	11	0	10
Stops and talks (%)	4	0.5	100	78	100	90
Mean number of questions answered (out of 6)	*	*	6	3.8	4.8	4.5
Respondents (no.)	13	47	14	18	15	10
Attempts (no.)	185	1283	14	18	15	10

* Not applicable.

contact, there is reason to believe that he is considering your requests and needs. If he pauses to chat or actually stops and talks, there is added reason to infer that he is individuating you. In four hospitals, the pseudopatient approached the staff member with a request which took the following form: "Pardon me, Mr [or Dr or Mrs] X, could you tell me when I will be eligible for grounds privileges?" (or " . . . when I will be presented at the staff meeting?" or " . . . when I am likely to be discharged?"). While the content of the question varied according to the appropriateness of the target and the pseudopatient's (apparent) current needs the form was always a courteous and relevant request for information. Care was taken never to approach a particular member of the staff more than once a day, lest the staff member become suspicious or irritated. In examining these data, remember that the behavior of the pseudopatients was neither bizarre nor disruptive. One could indeed engage in good conversation with them.

The data for these experiments are shown in table 1.1, separately for physicians (column 1) and for nurses and attendants (column 2). Minor differences between these four institutions were overwhelmed by the degree to which staff avoided continuing contacts that patients had initiated. By far, their most common response consisted of either a brief response to the question, offered while they were "on the move" and with head averted, or no response at all.

The encounter frequently took the following bizarre form: (pseudopatient): "Pardon me, Dr X. Could you tell me when I am eligible for grounds privileges?" (physician): "Good morning, Dave. How are you today?" (moves off without waiting for a response).

It is instructive to compare these data with data recently obtained at Stanford University. It has been alleged that large and eminent universities are characterized by faculty who are so busy that they have no time for students. For this comparison, a young lady approached individual faculty members who seemed to be walking purposefully to some meeting or teaching engagement and asked them the following six questions.

1 "Pardon me, could you direct me to Encina Hall?" (at the medical school: "...to the Clinical Research Center?").
2 "Do you know where Fish Annex is?" (there is no Fish Annex at Stanford).
3 "Do you teach here?"
4 "How does one apply for admission to the college?" (at the medical school: "...to the medical school?").
5 "Is it difficult to get in?"
6 "Is there financial aid?"

Without exception, as can be seen in table 1.1 (column 3), all of the questions were answered. No matter how rushed they were, all respondents not only maintained eye contact, but stopped to talk. Indeed, many of the respondents went out of their way to direct or take the questioner to the office she was seeking, to try to locate "Fish Annex," or to discuss with her the possibilities of being admitted to the university.

Similar data, also shown in table 1.1 (columns 4, 5, and 6), were obtained in the hospital. Here too, the young lady came prepared with six questions. After the first question, however, she remarked to 18 of her respondents (column 4), "I'm looking for a psychiatrist," and to 15 others (column 5), "I'm looking for an internist." Ten other respondents received no inserted comment (column 6). The general degree of cooperative responses is considerably higher for these university groups than it was for pseudopatients in psychiatric hospitals. Even so, differences are apparent within the medical school setting. Once having indicated that she was looking for a psychiatrist, the degree of cooperation elicited was less than when she sought an internist.

Powerlessness and Depersonalization

Eye contact and verbal contact reflect concern and individuation; their absence, avoidance and depersonalization. The data I have presented do not do justice to the rich daily encounters that grew up around matters of depersonalization and avoidance. I have records of patients who were beaten by staff for the sin of having initiated verbal contact. During my own experience, for example, one patient was beaten in the presence of other patients for having approached an attendant and told him, "I like you." Occasionally, punishment meted out to patients for misdemeanors seemed so excessive that it could not be justified by the most radical interpretations of psychiatric canon. Nevertheless, they appeared to go unquestioned. Tempers were often short. A patient who had not heard a call for medication would be roundly excoriated, and the morning attendants would often wake patients with, "Come on, you m—f—s, out of bed!"

Neither anecdotal nor "hard" data can convey the overwhelming sense of powerlessness which invades the individual as he is continually exposed to the depersonalization of the psychiatric hospital. It hardly matters *which* psychiatric hospital – the excellent public ones and the very plush private hospital were better than the rural and shabby ones in this regard, but, again, the features that psychiatric hospitals had in common overwhelmed by far their apparent differences.

Powerlessness was evident everywhere. The patient is deprived of many of his legal rights by dint of his psychiatric commitment.[15] He is shorn of credibility by virtue of his psychiatric label. His freedom of movement is restricted. He cannot initiate contact with the staff, but may only respond to such overtures as they make. Personal privacy is minimal. Patient quarters and possessions can be entered and examined by any staff member, for whatever reason. His personal history and anguish is available to any staff member (often including the "grey lady" and "candy striper" volunteer) who chooses to read his folder, regardless of their therapeutic relationship to him. His personal hygiene and waste evacuation are often monitored. The water closets may have no doors.

At times, depersonalization reached such proportions that pseudopatients had the sense that they were invisible, or at least unworthy of account. Upon being admitted, I and other pseudopatients took the initial physical examinations in a semipublic room, where staff members went about their own business as if we were not there.

On the ward, attendants delivered verbal and occasionally serious physical abuse to patients in the presence of other observing patients, some of whom (the pseudo-patients) were writing it all down. Abusive behavior, on the other hand, terminated quite abruptly when other staff members were known to be coming. Staff are credible witnesses. Patients are not.

A nurse unbuttoned her uniform to adjust her brassiere in the presence of an entire ward of viewing men. One did not have the sense that she was being seductive. Rather, she didn't notice us. A group of staff persons might point to a patient in the dayroom and discuss him animatedly, as if he were not there.

One illuminating instance of depersonalization and invisibility occurred with regard to medications. All told, the pseudopatients were administered nearly 2,100 pills, including Elavil, Stelazine, Compazine, and Thorazine, to name but a few. (That such a variety of medications should have been administered to patients presenting identical symptoms is itself worthy of note.) Only two were swallowed. The rest were either pocketed or deposited in the toilet. The pseudopatients were not alone in this. Although I have no precise records on how many patients rejected their medications, the pseudopatients frequently found the medications of other patients in the toilet before they deposited their own. As long as they were cooperative, their behavior and the pseudopatients' own in this matter, as in other important matters, went unnoticed throughout.

Reactions to such depersonalization among pseudopatients were intense. Although they had come to the hospital as participant observers and were fully aware that they did not "belong," they nevertheless found themselves caught up in and fighting the process of depersonalization. Some examples: a graduate student in psychology asked his wife to bring his textbooks to the hospital so he could "catch up on his homework" – this despite the elaborate precautions taken to conceal his professional association. The same student, who had trained for quite some time to get into the hospital, and who had looked forward to the experience, "remembered" some drag races that he had wanted to see on the weekend and insisted that he be discharged by that time. Another pseudopatient attempted a romance with a nurse. Subsequently, he informed the staff that he was applying for admission to graduate school in psychology and was very likely to be admitted, since a graduate professor was one of his regular hospital visitors. The same person began to engage in psychotherapy with other patients – all of this as a way of becoming a person in an impersonal environment.

The Sources of Depersonalization

What are the origins of depersonalization? I have already mentioned two. First are attitudes held by all of us toward the mentally ill – including those who treat them – attitudes characterized by fear, distrust, and horrible expectations on the one hand, and benevolent intentions on the other. Our ambivalence leads, in this instance as in others, to avoidance.

Second, and not entirely separate, the hierarchical structure of the psychiatric hospital facilitates depersonalization. Those who are at the top have least to do with patients, and their behavior inspires the rest of the staff. Average daily contact with psychiatrists, psychologists, residents, and physicians combined ranged from 3.9 to 25.1 minutes, with an overall mean of 6.8 (six pseudopatients over a total of 129 days of hospitalization). Included in this average are time spent in the admissions interview, ward meetings in the presence of a senior staff member, group and individual psychotherapy contacts, case presentation conferences, and discharge meetings. Clearly, patients do not spend much time in interpersonal contact with doctoral staff. And doctoral staff serve as models for nurses and attendants.

There are probably other sources. Psychiatric installations are presently in serious financial straits. Staff shortages are pervasive, staff time at a premium. Something has to give, and that something is patient contact. Yet, while financial stresses are realities, too much can be made of them. I have the impression that the psychological forces that result in depersonalization are much stronger than the fiscal ones and that the addition of more staff would not correspondingly improve patient care in this regard. The incidence of staff meetings and the enormous amount of record-keeping on patients, for example, have not been as substantially reduced as has patient contact. Priorities exist, even during hard times. Patient contact is not a significant priority in the traditional psychiatric hospital, and fiscal pressures do not account for this. Avoidance and depersonalization may.

Heavy reliance upon psychotropic medication tacitly contributes to depersonalization by convincing staff that treatment is indeed being conducted and that further patient contact may not be necessary. Even here, however, caution needs to be exercised in understanding the role of psychotropic drugs. If patients were powerful rather than powerless, if they were viewed as interesting individuals rather than diagnostic entities, if they were socially significant rather than social lepers, if their anguish truly and wholly compelled our sympathies and concerns, would we not *seek* contact with them, despite the availability of medications? Perhaps for the pleasure of it all?

The Consequences of Labeling and Depersonalization

Whenever the ratio of what is known to what needs to be known approaches zero, we tend to invent "knowledge" and assume that we understand more than we actually do. We seem unable to acknowledge that we simply don't know. The needs for diagnosis and remediation of behavioral and emotional problems are enormous. But rather than acknowledge that we are just embarking on understanding, we continue to label patients "schizophrenic," "manic-depressive," and "insane," as if in those words we had captured the essence of understanding. The facts of the matter are that we have known for a long time that diagnoses are often not useful or reliable, but we have nevertheless continued to use them. We now know that we cannot distinguish insanity from sanity. It is depressing to consider how that information will be used.

Not merely depressing, but frightening. How many people, one wonders, are sane but not recognized as such in our psychiatric institutions? How many have been needlessly stripped of their privileges of citizenship, from the right to vote and drive to that of handling their own accounts? How many have feigned insanity in order to avoid the criminal consequences of their behavior, and, conversely, how many would rather stand trial than live interminably in a psychiatric hospital – but are wrongly thought to be mentally ill? How many have been stigmatized by well-intentioned, but nevertheless erroneous, diagnoses? On the last point, recall again that a "type 2 error" in psychiatric diagnosis does not have the same consequences it does in medical diagnosis. A diagnosis of cancer that has been found to be in error is cause for celebration. But psychiatric diagnoses are rarely found to be in error. The label sticks, a mark of inadequacy forever.

Finally, how many patients might be "sane" outside the psychiatric hospital but seem insane in it – not because craziness resides in them, as it were, but because they are responding to a bizarre setting, one that may be unique to institutions which harbor nether people? Goffman[16] calls the process of socialization to such institutions "mortification" – an apt metaphor that includes the processes of depersonalization that have been described here. And while it is impossible to know whether the pseudopatients' responses to these processes are characteristic of all inmates – they were, after all, not real patients – it is difficult to believe that these processes of socialization to a psychiatric hospital provide useful attitudes or habits of response for living in the "real world."

Summary and Conclusions

It is clear that we cannot distinguish the sane from the insane in psychiatric hospitals. The hospital itself imposes a special environment in which the meanings of behavior can easily be misunderstood. The consequences to patients hospitalized in such an environment – the powerlessness, depersonalization, segregation, mortification, and self-labeling – seem undoubtedly countertherapeutic.

I do not, even now, understand this problem well enough to perceive solutions. But two matters seem to have some promise. The first concerns the proliferation of community mental health facilities, of crisis intervention centers, of the human potential movement, and of behavior therapies that, for all of their own problems, tend to avoid psychiatric labels, to focus on specific problems and behaviors, and to retain the individual in a relatively non-pejorative environment. Clearly, to the extent that we refrain from sending the distressed to insane places, our impressions of them are less likely to be distorted. (The risk of distorted perceptions, it seems to me, is always present, since we are much more sensitive to an individual's behaviors and verbalizations than we are to the subtle contextual stimuli that often promote them. At issue here is a matter of magnitude. And, as I have shown, the magnitude of distortion is exceedingly high in the extreme context that is a psychiatric hospital.)

The second matter that might prove promising speaks to the need to increase the sensitivity of mental health workers and researchers to the *Catch 22* position of psychiatric patients. Simply reading materials in this area will be of help to some such workers and researchers. For others, directly experiencing the impact of psychiatric hospitalization will be of enormous use. Clearly, further research into the social psychology of such total institutions will both facilitate treatment and deepen understanding.

I and the other pseudopatients in the psychiatric setting had distinctly negative reactions. We do not pretend to describe the subjective experiences of true patients. Theirs may be different from ours, particularly with the passage of time and the necessary process of adaptation to one's environment. But we can and do speak to the relatively more objective indices of treatment within the hospital. It could be a mistake, and a very unfortunate one, to consider that what happened to us derived from malice or stupidity on the part of the staff. Quite the contrary, our overwhelming impression of them was of people who really cared, who were committed and who were uncommonly intelligent. Where they failed, as they sometimes did painfully, it would be more accurate to attribute those failures to the environment in which they, too, found themselves than to personal callousness. Their perceptions and behavior were controlled by the situation, rather than being motivated by a malicious disposition. In a more benign environment, one that was less attached to global diagnosis, their behaviors and judgments might have been more benign and effective.

Notes

1 P. Ash, *Journal of Abnormal Psychology* 44 (1949): 272; A. T. Beck, *American Journal of Psychiatry* 119 (1962): 210; A. T. Boisen, *Psychiatry* 2 (1938): 233; N. Kreitman, *Journal of Mental Science* 107 (1961): 876; N. Kreitman, P. Sainsbury, J. Morrisey, J. Towers, and J. Scrivener, *Journal of Mental Science* 107 (1961): 887; H. O. Schmitt and C. P. Fonda, *Journal of Abnormal Social Psychology* 52 (1956): 262; W. Seeman, *Journal of Nervous and Mental Disease* 118 (1953): 541.

   For an analysis of these artifacts and summaries of the disputes, see: J. Zubin, *Annual Review of Psychology* 18 (1967): 373; L. Phillips and G. Draguns, *Annual Review of Psychology* 22 (1971): 447.
2 R. Benedict, *Journal of General Psychology* 10 (1934): 59.

3 See in this regard: H. Becker, *Outsiders: Studies in the Sociology of Deviance*, New York: Free Press, 1963; B. M. Braginsky, D. D. Braginsky, and K. Ring, *Methods of Madness: The Mental Hospital as a Last Resort*, New York: Holt, Rinehart and Winston, 1969. G. M. Crocetti and P. V. Lemkau, *American Sociological Review* 30 (1965): 577; E. Goffman, *Behavior in Public Places*, New York: Free Press, 1963; R. D. Laing, *The Divided Self: A Study of Sanity and Madness*, Chicago: Quadrangle Books, 1960; D. L. Phillips, *American Sociological Review* 28 (1963): 963; T. R. Sarbin, *Psychology Today* 6 (1972): 18; E. Schur, *American Journal of Sociology* 75 (1969): 309; T. Szasz, *Law, Liberty and Psychiatry*, New York: Macmillan, 1963; T. Szasz, *The Myth of Mental Illness: Foundations of a Theory of Mental Illness*, New York: Hoeber-Harper, 1963.

For a critique of some of these views, see: W. R. Gove, *American Sociological Review* 35 (1970): 873.

See also: E. Goffman, *Asylums*, Garden City, NY: Doubleday, 1966; T. J. Scheff, *Being Mentally Ill: A Sociological Theory*, Chicago: Aldine, 1966.

4 A. Barry, *Bellevue is a State of Mind*, New York: Harcourt, Brace, Jovanovich, 1971; I. Belknap, *Human Problems of a State Mental Hospital*, New York: McGraw-Hill, 1956; W. Caudill, F. C. Redlich, H. R. Gilmore, and E. B. Brody, *American Journal of Orthopsychiatry* 22 (1952): 314; A. R. Goldman, R. H. Bohr, and T. A. Steinberg, *The Professional Psychologist* 1 (1970): 427; unauthored, *Roche Report* 1, no. 13 (1971): 8.

5 On the relations between social class and psychiatric diagnosis, see: A. deB. Hollingshead and F. C. Redlich, *Social Class and Mental Illness: A Community Study*, New York: Wiley, 1958.

6 Scheff, *Being Mentally Ill*.

7 J. Cumming and E. Cumming, *Community Mental Health* 1 (1965): 135; A. Farina and K. Ring, *Journal of Abnormal Psychology* 70 (1965): 47; H. E. Freeman and O. G. Simmons, *The Mental Patient Comes Home*, New York: Wiley, 1963; W. J. Johannsen, *Mental Hygiene* 53 (1969): 218; A. S. Linsky, *Social Psychiatry* 5 (1970): 166.

8 S. E. Asch, *Journal of Abnormal Social Psychology* 41 (1946): 258; S. E. Asch, *Social Psychology*, New York: Prentice-Hall, 1952.

9 See also: J. S. Bruner and R. Tagiuri, in G. Lindzey (ed.) *Handbook of Social Psychology*, vol. 2, Cambridge, Mass.: Addison-Wesley, 1954, pp. 634–54; J. S. Bruner, D. Shapiro, and R. Tagiuri, in R. Tagiuri and L. Petrullo (eds.) *Person Perception and Interpersonal Behavior*, Stanford, Calif.: Stanford University Press, 1958, pp. 277–88; I. N. Mensch and J. Wishner, *Journal of Personality* 16 (1947): 188; J. Wishner, *Psychological Review* 67 (1960): 96.

10 Scheff, *Being Mentally Ill*.

11 E. Zigler and L. Phillips, *Journal of Abnormal Social Psychology* 63 (1961): 69. See also R. K. Freudenberg and J. P. Robertson, *AMA Archives of Neurology and Psychiatry* 76 (1956): 14.

12 W. Mischel, *Personality and Assessment*, New York: Wiley, 1968.

13 J. C. Nunnally, Jr., *Popular Conceptions of Mental Health*, New York: Holt, Rinehart and Winston, 1961; T. R. Sarbin, *Journal of Clinical Consulting Psychiatry* 31 (1967): 31; T. R. Sarbin and J. C. Mancuso, *Journal of Clinical Consulting Psychiatry* 35 (1970): 159.

14 A. H. Stanton and M. S. Schwartz, *The Mental Hospital: A Study of Institutional Participation in Psychiatric Illness and Treatment*, New York: Basic Books, 1954.

15 D. B. Wexler and S. E. Scoville, *Arizona Law Review* 13 (1971): 1.

16 Goffman, *Asylums*.

2 Self-Fulfilling Stereotypes

Mark Snyder

Gordon Allport, the Harvard psychologist who wrote a classic work on the nature of prejudice, told a story about a child who had come to believe that people who lived in Minneapolis were called monopolists. From his father, moreover, he had learned that monopolists were evil folk. It wasn't until many years later, when he discovered his confusion, that his dislike of residents of Minneapolis vanished.

Allport knew, of course, that it was not so easy to wipe out prejudice and erroneous stereotypes. Real prejudice, psychologists like Allport argued, was buried deep in human character, and only a restructuring of education could begin to root it out. Yet many people whom I meet while lecturing seem to believe that stereotypes are simply beliefs or attitudes that change easily with experience. Why do some people express the view that Italians are passionate, blacks are lazy, Jews materialistic, and lesbians mannish in their demeanor? In the popular view, it is because they have not learned enough about the diversity among these groups and have not had enough contact with members of the groups for their stereotypes to be challenged by reality. With more experience, it is presumed, most people of good will are likely to revise their stereotypes.

My research over the past decade convinces me that there is little justification for such optimism – and not only for the reasons given by Allport. While it is true that deep prejudice is often based on the needs of pathological character structure, stereotypes are obviously quite common even among fairly normal individuals. When people first meet others, they cannot help noticing certain highly visible and distinctive characteristics: sex, race, physical appearance, and the like. Despite people's best intentions, their initial impressions of others are shaped by their assumptions about such characteristics.

What is critical, however, is that these assumptions are not merely beliefs or attitudes that exist in a vacuum; they are reinforced by the behavior of both prejudiced people and the targets of their prejudice. In recent years, psychologists have collected considerable laboratory evidence about the processes that strengthen stereotypes and put them beyond the reach of reason and good will.

My own studies initially focused on first encounters between strangers. It did not take long to discover, for example, that people have very different ways of treating those whom they regard as physically attractive and those whom they consider physically unattractive, and that these differences tend to bring out precisely those kinds of behavior that fit with stereotypes about attractiveness.

In an experiment that I conducted with my colleagues Elizabeth Decker Tanke and Ellen Berscheid, pairs of college-age men and women met and became acquainted in telephone conversations. Before the conversations began, each man received a Polaroid snapshot, presumably taken just moments before, of the woman he would soon meet. The photograph, which had actually been prepared before the experiment

Reprinted from *Race, Class, and Gender in the United States*, 3rd edn, edited by Paula Rothenberg, New York: St Martin's Press, 1994, pp. 325–31. Originally published in *Psychology Today* magazine, 1982.

began, showed either a physically attractive woman or a physically unattractive one. By randomly choosing which picture to use for each conversation, we insured that there was no consistent relationship between the attractiveness of the woman in the picture and the attractiveness of the woman in the conversation.

By questioning the men, we learned that even before the conversations began, stereotypes about physical attractiveness came into play. Men who looked forward to talking with physically attractive women said that they expected to meet decidedly sociable, poised, humorous, and socially adept people, while men who thought that they were about to get acquainted with unattractive women fashioned images of rather unsociable, awkward, serious, and socially inept creatures. Moreover, the men proved to have very different styles of getting acquainted with women whom they thought to be attractive and those whom they believed to be unattractive. Shown a photograph of an attractive woman, they behaved with warmth, friendliness, humor, and animation. However, when the woman in the picture was unattractive, the men were cold, uninteresting, and reserved.

These differences in the men's behavior elicited behavior in the women that was consistent with the men's stereotyped assumptions. Women who were believed (unbeknown to them) to be physically attractive behaved in a friendly, likeable, and sociable manner. In sharp contrast, women who were perceived as physically unattractive adopted a cool, aloof, and distant manner. So striking were the differences in the women's behavior that they could be discerned simply by listening to tape recordings of the woman's side of the conversations. Clearly, by acting upon their stereotyped beliefs about the women whom they would be meeting, the men had initiated a chain of events that produced *behavioral confirmation* for their beliefs.

Similarly, Susan Anderson and Sandra Bem have shown in an experiment at Stanford University that when the tables are turned – when it is women who have pictures of men they are to meet on the telephone – many women treat the men according to their presumed physical attractiveness, and by so doing encourage the men to confirm their stereotypes. Little wonder, then, that so many people remain convinced that good looks and appealing personalities go hand in hand.

Sex and Race

It is experiments such as these that point to a frequently unnoticed power of stereotypes: the power to influence social relationships in ways that create the illusion of reality. In one study, Berna Skrypnek and I arranged for pairs of previously unacquainted students to interact in a situation that permitted us to control the information that each one received about the apparent sex of the other. The two people were seated in separate rooms so that they could neither see nor hear each other. Using a system of signal lights that they operated with switches, they negotiated a division of labor, deciding which member of the pair would perform each of several tasks that differed in sex-role connotations. The tasks varied along the dimensions of masculinity and femininity: sharpen a hunting knife (masculine), polish a pair of shoes (neutral), iron a shirt (feminine).

One member of the team was led to believe that the other was, in one condition of the experiment, male; in the other, female. As we had predicted, the first member's belief about the sex of the partner influenced the outcome of the pair's negotiations. Women whose partners believed them to be men generally chose stereotypically masculine tasks; in contrast, women whose partners believed that they were women usually chose stereotypically feminine tasks. The experiment thus suggests that much sex-role behavior may be the product of other people's stereotyped and often erroneous beliefs.

In a related study at the University of Waterloo, Carl von Baeyer, Debbie Sherk, and Mark Zanna have shown how stereotypes about sex roles operate in job interviews. The researchers arranged to have men conduct simulated job interviews with women supposedly seeking positions as research assistants. The investigators informed half of the women that the men who would interview them held traditional views about the ideal woman, believing her to be very emotional, deferential to her husband, home-oriented, and passive. The rest of the women were told that their interviewer saw the ideal woman as independent, competitive, ambitious, and dominant. When the women arrived for their interviews, the researchers noticed that most of them had dressed to meet the stereotyped expectations of their prospective interviewers. Women who expected to see a traditional interviewer had chosen very feminine-looking makeup, clothes, and accessories. During the interviews (videotaped through a one-way mirror) these women behaved in traditionally feminine ways and gave traditionally feminine answers to questions such as "Do you have plans to include children and marriage with your career plans?"

Once more, then, we see the self-fulfilling nature of stereotypes. Many sex differences, it appears, may result from the images that people create in their attempts to act out accepted sex roles. The implication is that if stereotyped expectations about sex roles shift, behavior may change, too. In fact, statements by people who have undergone sex-change operations have highlighted the power of such expectations in easing adjustment to a new life. As the writer Jan Morris said in recounting the story of her transition from James to Jan: "The more I was treated as a woman, the more woman I became."

The power of stereotypes to cause people to confirm stereotyped expectations can also be seen in interracial relationships. In the first of two investigations done at Princeton University by Carl Word, Mark Zanna, and Joel Cooper, white undergraduates interviewed both white and black job applicants. The applicants were actually confederates of the experimenters, trained to behave consistently from interview to interview, no matter how the interviewers acted toward them.

To find out whether or not the white interviewers would behave differently toward white and black job applicants, the researchers secretly videotaped each interview and then studied the tapes. From these, it was apparent that there were substantial differences in the treatment accorded blacks and whites. For one thing, the interviewers' speech deteriorated when they talked to blacks, displaying more errors in grammar and pronunciation. For another, the interviewers spent less time with blacks than with whites and showed less "immediacy," as the researchers called it, in their manner. That is, they were less friendly, less outgoing, and more reserved with blacks.

In the second investigation, white confederates were trained to approximate the immediate or the nonimmediate interview styles that had been observed in the first investigation as they interviewed white job applicants. A panel of judges who evaluated the tapes agreed that applicants subjected to the nonimmediate styles performed less adequately and were more nervous than job applicants treated in the immediate style. Apparently, then, the blacks in the first study did not have a chance to display their qualifications to the best advantage. Considered together, the two investigations suggest that in interracial encounters, racial stereotypes may constrain behavior in ways to cause both blacks and whites to behave in accordance with those stereotypes.

Rewriting Biography

Having adopted stereotyped ways of thinking about another person, people tend to notice and remember the ways in which that person seems to fit the stereotype, while resisting evidence that contradicts the stereotype. In one investigation that I conducted with Seymour Uranowitz, student subjects read a biography of a fictitious woman named Betty K. We constructed the story of her life so that it would fit the stereotyped images of both lesbians and heterosexuals. Betty, we wrote, never had a steady boyfriend in high school, but did go out on dates. And although we gave her a steady boyfriend in college, we specified that he was more of a close friend than anything else. A week after we had distributed this biography, we gave our subjects some new information about Betty. We told some students that she was now living with another woman in a lesbian relationship; we told others that she was living with her husband.

To see what impact stereotypes about sexuality would have on how people remembered the facts of Betty's life, we asked each student to answer a series of questions about her life history. When we examined their answers, we found that the students had reconstructed the events of Betty's past in ways that supported their own stereotyped beliefs about her sexual orientation. Those who believed that Betty was a lesbian remembered that Betty had never had a steady boyfriend in high school, but tended to neglect the fact that she had gone out on many dates in college. Those who believed that Betty was now a heterosexual tended to remember that she had formed a steady relationship with a man in college, but tended to ignore the fact that this relationship was more of a friendship than a romance.

The students showed not only selective memories but also a striking facility for interpreting what they remembered in ways that added fresh support for their stereotypes. One student who accurately remembered that a supposedly lesbian Betty never had a steady boyfriend in high school confidently pointed to the fact as an early sign of her lack of romantic or sexual interest in men. A student who correctly remembered that a purportedly lesbian Betty often went out on dates in college was sure that these dates were signs of Betty's early attempts to mask her lesbian interests.

Clearly, the students had allowed their preconceptions about lesbians and heterosexuals to dictate the way in which they interpreted and reinterpreted the facts of Betty's life. As long as stereotypes make it easy to bring to mind evidence that supports them and difficult to bring to mind evidence that undermines them, people will cling to erroneous beliefs.

Stereotypes in the Classroom and Workplace

The power of one person's beliefs to make other people conform to them has been well demonstrated in real life. Back in the 1960s, as most people well remember, Harvard psychologist Robert Rosenthal and his colleague Lenore Jacobson entered elementary-school classrooms and identified one out of every five pupils in each room as a child who could be expected to show dramatic improvement in intellectual achievement during the school year. What the teachers did not know was that the children had been chosen on a random basis. Nevertheless, something happened in the relationships between teachers and their supposedly gifted pupils that led the children to make clear gains in test performance.

It can also do so on the job. Albert King, now a professor of management at Northern Illinois University, told a welding instructor in a vocational training center that five men in his training program had unusually high aptitude. Although these five had been chosen at random and knew nothing of their designation as high-aptitude workers, they showed substantial changes in performance. They were absent less often than were other workers, learned the basics of the welder's trade in about half the usual time, and scored a full 10 points higher than other trainees on a welding test. Their gains were noticed not only by the researcher and by the welding instructor, but also by other trainees, who singled out the five as their preferred co-workers.

Might not other expectations influence the relationships between supervisors and workers? For example, supervisors who believe that men are better suited to some jobs and women to others may treat their workers (wittingly or unwittingly) in ways that encourage them to perform their jobs in accordance with stereotypes about differences between men and women. These same stereotypes may determine who gets which job in the first place. Perhaps some personnel managers allow stereotypes to influence, subtly or not so subtly, the way in which they interview job candidates, making it likely that candidates who fit the stereotypes show up better than job-seekers who do not fit them.

Unfortunately, problems of this kind are compounded by the fact that members of stigmatized groups often subscribe to stereotypes about themselves. That is what Amerigo Farina and his colleagues at the University of Connecticut found when they measured the impact upon mental patients of believing that others knew their psychiatric history. In Farina's study, each mental patient cooperated with another person in a game requiring teamwork. Half of the patients believed that their partners knew they were patients, the other half believed that their partners thought they were nonpatients. In reality, the nonpatients never knew a thing about anyone's psychiatric history. Nevertheless, simply believing that others were aware of their history led the patients to feel less appreciated, to find the task more difficult, and to perform poorly. In addition, objective observers saw them as more tense, more anxious, and more poorly adjusted than patients who believed that their status was not known. Seemingly, the belief that others perceived them as stigmatized caused them to play the role of stigmatized patients.

Consequences for Society

Apparently, good will and education are not sufficient to subvert the power of stereotypes. If people treat others in such a way as to bring out behavior that supports stereotypes, they may never have an opportunity to discover which of their stereotypes are wrong.

I suspect that even if people were to develop doubts about the accuracy of their stereotypes, chances are they would proceed to test them by gathering precisely the evidence that would appear to confirm them.

The experiments I have described help to explain the persistence of stereotypes. But, as is so often the case, solving one puzzle only creates another. If by acting as if false stereotypes were true, people lead others, too, to act as if they were true, why do the stereotypes not come to *be* true? Why, for example, have researchers found so little evidence that attractive people are generally friendly, sociable, and outgoing, and that unattractive people are generally shy and aloof?

I think that the explanation goes something like this: Very few among us have the kind of looks that virtually everyone considers either very attractive or very unattractive. Our looks make us rather attractive to some people but somewhat less attractive to other people. When we spend time with those who find us attractive they will tend to bring out our more sociable sides, but when we are with those who find us less attractive, they will bring out our less sociable sides. Although our actual physical appearance does not change, we present ourselves quite differently to our admirers and to our detractors. For our admirers we become attractive people, and for our detractors we become unattractive. This mixed pattern of behavior will prevent the development of any consistent relationship between physical attractiveness and personality.

Now that I understand some of the powerful forces that work to perpetuate social stereotypes, I can see a new mission for my research. I hope, on the one hand, to find out how to help people see the flaws in their stereotypes. On the other hand, I would like to help the victims of false stereotypes find ways of liberating themselves from the constraints imposed on them by other members of society.

3 Sluts and Studs

Peggy Orenstein

Sex Education: Don't Ask, Don't Tell

Desire and the dynamics of power embedded in it are rarely broached in sex education curricula, especially as it pertains to girls. Educator Michelle Fine has written that boys' desire is included in classrooms, intrinsic to the biological lessons of erections, ejaculation, and wet dreams. Girls' pleasure, however, is evaded, and their sexuality is discussed primarily through the veil of reproduction: the onset of menstruation, the identification of ovaries and the uterus. Desire, as it relates to girls, is reduced in most classrooms to one element: whether to say "yes" or "no" – not even to themselves, but to boys. By emphasizing refusal and ignoring desire, Fine argues, schools contribute to the repression of girls' sexual selves. The "official" version of sexuality that is taught, she says, becomes a discourse "based on the male in search of desire and the female in search of protection."

At Weston Middle School, as in many schools, the community dictates what children may or may not learn in sex education classes. Principal Andrea Murray estimates that 25 percent of the students at Weston are already sexually active. And if "sexually active" is measured solely by engaging in intercourse, that's probably about right: the average age of sexual initiation dropped steadily in the 1980s, and some studies have found that up to 53 percent of middle and junior high school students have had sexual intercourse at least once. If national statistics hold, one out of five of those sexually active girls at Weston will become pregnant before she graduates high school. Yet the sex education curriculum endorsed by the community forbids a discussion of contraception until tenth grade, precisely because of the fear that contraceptive knowledge will promote desire.

Maureen Webster, a young, maternal woman with a throaty voice, teaches the middle school's sex education course, which students take as seventh graders. During the course, she may not mention birth control in class – she is even prohibited from informing her students that condoms are a source of protection against HIV, lest the information in some way sanction homosexuality (activity which, free from the possibility of procreation, is necessarily based on desire).

"It's got to change," she tells me when I visit her classroom one day. "But right now some parents think that if you talk about contraception you're giving the kids a license." Ms Webster says that if a student specifically asks about condoms, or some other taboo topic, she may answer the question, saying, for instance, "a condom is a sheath that fits over the penis," without revealing its purpose or in any way detailing its proper use. Essentially, though, if Weston's students want to know how to prevent unwanted pregnancy or sexually transmitted diseases, she says, "they have to find it out elsewhere." Ms Webster says that the Weston community even bridles at her

Reprinted from *School Girls: Young Women, Self-Esteem, and the Confidence Gap*, New York: Doubleday, 1994, pp. 58–61.

clinical explanation of masturbation, an activity that provides plenty of entertainment without the side effects of either pregnancy or disease. "I try to answer as correctly as I can," she says, "but I know that the parents are concerned. So when some boy asks, 'How do girls masturbate?' I'll say, 'Just as boys can fondle their private areas, likewise a girl can,' and leave it at that."

The curriculum Ms Webster uses includes a month's worth of lessons, but since the course falls within a larger, quarter-long health class, and time is limited, she usually condenses it into a week or two, which is still somewhat longer than most sex education classes. That leaves one class period each for male and female anatomy and one class period devoted to a lecture on how sexually transmitted diseases are spread (but not how they can be prevented). Given both communal and temporal constraints, a useful discussion of sexual desire – or any talk of sexual activity that isn't grounded in "consequences" – would be unthinkable. Yet although issues of sexual entitlement are never overtly addressed in Ms Webster's class, when the bell rings, the power dynamics of "slut" and "stud" are firmly in place.

Ms Webster had invited me to visit on the fourth day of the sex education unit. The students have already zipped through male and female anatomy, which included a lecture on the female reproductive system but – because there wasn't time for the more comprehensive film Ms Webster had planned to show – no identification of the clitoris or even the labia. Today, Ms Webster is trying to illustrate the effect of sleeping with multiple partners on disease transmission. She has passed out a photo-copied work sheet which summarizes the symptoms of eight STDs and now stands at the front of the room.

"We'll use a woman," she says, drawing the Greek symbol for woman on the blackboard. "Let's say she is infected, but she hasn't really noticed yet, so she has sex with three men."

Ms Webster draws four symbols for man on the board, and as she does, a heavyset boy in a Chicago Bulls cap stage-whispers, "What a slut," and the class titters.

"Okay," says Ms. Webster, who doesn't hear the comment. "Now the first guy has three sexual encounters in six months." She turns to draw three more women's signs, her back to the class, and several of the boys point at themselves proudly, striking exaggerated macho poses.

"The second guy was very active, he had intercourse with five women." As she turns to the diagram again, two boys stand and take bows.

"Now the third guy was smart – he didn't sleep with *anyone*." She draws a happy face and the boys point at each other derisively, mouthing, "You! You!"

During the entire diagramming process, the girls in the class remain silent.

This drama is played out without the teacher's noticing. She goes on to explain the remaining diseases, allotting several minutes to each and ten minutes to AIDS. When the bell rings, the students shove the handout into their backpacks. I doubt whether, in this short time, they've truly learned the risks of disease; but they certainly have been reminded of the rules of desire.

4 Body Ritual among the Nacirema

Horace Miner

The anthropologist has become so familiar with the diversity of ways in which different peoples behave in similar situations that he is not apt to be surprised by even the most exotic customs. In fact, if all of the logically possible combinations of behavior have not been found somewhere in the world, he is apt to suspect that they must be present in some yet undescribed tribe. This point has, in fact, been expressed with respect to clan organization by Murdock (1949: 71). In this light, the magical beliefs and practices of the Nacirema present such unusual aspects that it seems desirable to describe them as an example of the extremes to which human behavior can go.

Professor Linton first brought the ritual of the Nacirema to the attention of anthropologists twenty years ago (1936: 326), but the culture of this people is still very poorly understood. They are a North American group living in the territory between the Canadian Cree, the Yaqui and Tarahumare of Mexico, and the Carib and Arawak of the Antilles. Little is known of their origin, although tradition states that they came from the east. According to Nacirema mythology, their nation was originated by a culture hero, Notgnihsaw, who is otherwise known for two great feats of strength – the throwing of a piece of wampum across the river Pa-To-Mac and the chopping down of a cherry tree in which the Spirit of Truth resided.

Nacirema culture is characterized by a highly developed market economy which has evolved in a rich natural habitat. While much of the people's time is devoted to economic pursuits, a large part of the fruits of these labors and a considerable portion of the day are spent in ritual activity. The focus of this activity is the human body, the appearance and health of which loom as a dominant concern in the ethos of the people. While such a concern is certainly not unusual, its ceremonial aspects and associated philosophy are unique.

The fundamental belief underlying the whole system appears to be that the human body is ugly and that its natural tendency is to debility and disease. Incarcerated in such a body, man's only hope is to avert these characteristics through the use of the powerful influences of ritual and ceremony. Every household has one or more shrines devoted to this purpose. The more powerful individuals in the society have several shrines in their houses and, in fact, the opulence of a house is often referred to in terms of the number of such ritual centers it possesses. Most houses are of wattle and daub construction, but the shrine rooms of the more wealthy are walled with stone. Poorer families imitate the rich by applying pottery plaques to their shrine walls.

While each family has at least one such shrine, the rituals associated with it are not family ceremonies but are private and secret. The rites are normally only discussed with children, and then only during the period when they are being initiated into

Reprinted from *American Anthropologist* 58(3) (1956): 503–7.

these mysteries. I was able, however, to establish sufficient rapport with the natives to examine these shrines and to have the rituals described to me.

The focal point of the shrine is a box or chest which is built into the wall. In this chest are kept the many charms and magical potions without which no native believes he could live. These preparations are secured from a variety of specialized practitioners. The most powerful of these are the medicine men, whose assistance must be rewarded with substantial gifts. However, the medicine men do not provide the curative potions for their clients, but decide what the ingredients should be and then write them down in an ancient and secret language. This writing is understood only by the medicine men and by the herbalists who, for another gift, provide the required charm.

The charm is not disposed of after it has served its purpose, but is placed in the charm-box of the household shrine. As these magical materials are specific for certain ills, and the real or imagined maladies of the people are many, the charm-box is usually full to overflowing. The magical packets are so numerous that people forget what their purposes were and fear to use them again. While the natives are very vague on this point, we can only assume that the idea in retaining all the old magical materials is that their presence in the charm-box, before which the body rituals are conducted, will in some way protect the worshipper.

Beneath the charm-box is a small font. Each day every member of the family, in succession, enters the shrine room, bows his head before the charm-box, mingles different sorts of holy water in the font, and proceeds with a brief rite of ablution. The holy waters are secured from the Water Temple of the community, where the priests conduct elaborate ceremonies to make the liquid ritually pure.

In the hierarchy of magical practitioners, and below the medicine men in prestige, are specialists whose designation is best translated "holy-mouth-men." The Nacirema have an almost pathological horror of and fascination with the mouth, the condition of which is believed to have a supernatural influence on all social relationships. Were it not for the rituals of the mouth, they believe that their teeth would fall out, their gums bleed, their jaws shrink, their friends desert them, and their lovers reject them. They also believe that a strong relationship exists between oral and moral characteristics. For example, there is a ritual ablution of the mouth for children which is supposed to improve their moral fiber.

The daily body ritual performed by everyone includes a mouth-rite. Despite the fact that these people are so punctilious about care of the mouth, this rite involves a practice which strikes the uninitiated stranger as revolting. It was reported to me that the ritual consists of inserting a small bundle of hog hairs into the mouth, along with certain magical powders, and then moving the bundle in a highly formalized series of gestures.

In addition to the private mouth-rite, the people seek out a holy-mouth-man once or twice a year. These practitioners have an impressive set of paraphernalia, consisting of a variety of augers, awls, probes, and prods. The use of these objects in the exorcism of the evils of the mouth involves almost unbelievable ritual torture of the client. The holy-mouth-man opens the client's mouth and, using the above mentioned tools, enlarges any holes which decay may have created in the teeth. Magical materials are put into these holes. If there are no naturally occurring holes in the teeth, large sections of one or more teeth are gouged out so that the supernatural substance can be applied. In the client's view, the purpose of these ministrations is to arrest decay and to draw friends. The extremely sacred and traditional character of the rite is evident in the fact that the natives return to the holy-mouth-men year after year, despite the fact that their teeth continue to decay.

It is to be hoped that, when a thorough study of the Nacirema is made, there will be careful inquiry into the personality structure of these people. One has but to watch the gleam in the eye of a holy-mouth-man, as he jabs an awl into an exposed nerve, to suspect that a certain amount of sadism is involved. If this can be established, a very interesting pattern emerges, for most of the population shows definite masochistic tendencies. It was to these that Professor Linton referred in discussing a distinctive part of the daily body ritual which is performed only by men. This part of the rite involves scraping and lacerating the surface of the face with a sharp instrument. Special women's rites are performed only four times during each lunar month, but what they lack in frequency is made up in barbarity. As part of this ceremony, women bake their heads in small ovens for about an hour. The theoretically interesting point is that what seems to be a preponderantly masochistic people have developed sadistic specialists.

The medicine men have an imposing temple, or *lati pso*, in every community of any size. The more elaborate ceremonies required to treat very sick patients can only be performed at this temple. These ceremonies involve not only the thaumaturge but a permanent group of vestal maidens who move sedately about the temple chambers in distinctive costume and headdress.

The *lati pso* ceremonies are so harsh that it is phenomenal that a fair proportion of the really sick natives who enter the temple ever recover. Small children whose indoctrination is still incomplete have been known to resist attempts to take them to the temple because "that is where you go to die." Despite this fact, sick adults are not only willing but eager to undergo the protracted ritual purification, if they can afford to do so. No matter how ill the supplicant or how grave the emergency, the guardians of many temples will not admit a client if he cannot give a rich gift to the custodian. Even after one has gained admission and survived the ceremonies, the guardians will not permit the neophyte to leave until he makes still another gift.

The supplicant entering the temple is first stripped of all his or her clothes. In every-day life the Nacirema avoids exposure of his body and its natural functions. Bathing and excretory acts are performed only in the secrecy of the household shrine, where they are ritualized as part of the body-rites. Psychological shock results from the fact that body secrecy is suddenly lost upon entry into the *lati pso*. A man, whose own wife has never seen him in an excretory act, suddenly finds himself naked and assisted by a vestal maiden while he performs his natural functions into a sacred vessel. This sort of ceremonial treatment is necessitated by the fact that the excreta are used by a diviner to ascertain the course and nature of the client's sickness. Female clients, on the other hand, find their naked bodies are subjected to the scrutiny, manipulation and prodding of the medicine men.

Few supplicants in the temple are well enough to do anything but lie on their hard beds. The daily ceremonies, like the rites of the holy-mouth-men, involve discomfort and torture. With ritual precision, the vestals awaken their miserable charges each dawn and roll them about on their beds of pain while performing ablutions, in the formal movements of which the maidens are highly trained. At other times they insert magic wands in the supplicant's mouth or force him to eat substances which are supposed to be healing. From time to time the medicine men come to their clients and jab magically treated needles into their flesh. The fact that these temple cere-monies may not cure, and may even kill the neophyte, in no way decreases the people's faith in the medicine men.

There remains one other kind of practitioner, known as a "listener." This witch-doctor has the power to exorcise the devils that lodge in the heads of people who have been bewitched. The Nacirema believe that parents bewitch their own children. Mothers are particularly suspected of putting a curse on children while teaching them the secret body rituals. The counter-magic of the witch-doctor is unusual in its lack of ritual. The patient simply tells the "listener" all his troubles and fears, beginning with the earliest difficulties he can remember. The memory displayed by the Nacirema in these exorcism sessions is truly remarkable. It is not uncommon for the patient to bemoan the rejection he felt upon being weaned as a babe, and a few individuals even see their troubles going back to the traumatic effects of their own birth.

In conclusion, mention must be made of certain practices which have their base in native esthetics but which depend upon the pervasive aversion to the natural body and its functions. There are ritual fasts to make fat people thin and ceremonial feasts to make thin people fat. Still other rites are used to make women's breasts larger if they are small, and smaller if they are large. General dissatisfaction with breast shape is symbolized in the fact that the ideal form is virtually outside the range of human variation. A few women afflicted with almost inhuman hypermammary develop-ment are so idolized that they make a handsome living by simply going from village to village and permitting the natives to stare at them for a fee.

Reference has already been made to the fact that excretory functions are ritualized, routinized, and relegated to secrecy. Natural reproductive functions are similarly distorted. Intercourse is taboo as a topic and scheduled as an act. Efforts are made to avoid pregnancy by the use of magical materials or by limiting intercourse to certain phases of the moon. Conception is actually very infrequent. When pregnant, women dress so as to hide their condition. Parturition takes place in secret, without friends or relatives to assist, and the majority of women do not nurse their infants.

Our review of the ritual life of the Nacirema has certainly shown them to be a magic-ridden people. It is hard to understand how they have managed to exist so long under the burdens which they have imposed upon themselves. But even such exotic customs as these take on real meaning when they are viewed with the insight provided by Malinowski when he wrote (1948: 70):

> Looking from far and above, from our high places of safety in the developed civilization, it is easy to see all the crudity and irrelevance of magic. But without its power and guidance early man could not have mastered his practical difficulties as he has done, nor could man have advanced to the higher stages of civilization.

References

Linton, Ralph. 1936. *The Study of Man*. New York: D. Appleton-Century.
Malinowski, Bronislaw. 1948. *Magic, Science, and Religion*. Glencoe, Ill: Free Press.
Murdock, George P. 1949. *Social Structure*. New York: Macmillan.

5 The Reality of Self-Esteem

John P. Hewitt

Self-esteem is the center of a powerful mythology, but it is not merely an empty word that signifies nothing. The proponents of self-esteem are mistaken in their faith in its capacity to guarantee individual happiness and solve social problems, but indirectly and perhaps unwittingly they have grasped something of importance about the psychology of contemporary people. Opponents are correct in their skepticism about claims made on behalf of self-esteem, but they are mistaken in dismissing the phenomenon out of hand. Self-esteem has a social and psychological reality, and my task in this chapter is to explore it.

My purpose is not to adjudicate between the proponents and opponents of self-esteem or between alternative definitions of what self-esteem is or how to get it. The arguments and differences of meaning [I] have examined represent disagreements about what the social world should be like and how people should behave. They are not resolvable by scientific evidence or theory. My purpose is to develop an alternative perspective on self-esteem, a way of looking at the phenomenon that sheds a new and perhaps unexpected light on it.

Is Self-Esteem Universal?

I begin this task by addressing a key question, namely whether self-esteem is the universal phenomenon that its proponents claim it to be. My skepticism about self-esteem might lead you to expect my answer to be an unequivocal "no," but the question does not lend itself to a simple answer. Self-esteem, we will see, is both universal and culturally specific, hence it is both reality and myth. Its proponents think they have discovered something that they have in reality invented. But their invention of self-esteem and its incorporation as a key element of the American psyche is possible only because of universal features of human nature.

Self-esteem is universal in the same way that the self is universal; to understand the reality of the former we must grapple with the reality of the latter. What is universal about the self and what is culturally shaped? How is the experience of the self different from one culture to another and how is it the same? And how is self-esteem related to the more general concept of the self?

Is the self a universal human experience or phenomenon? The answer depends in part upon how we define our terms. If by "self" we mean something very much like the ideas and beliefs Americans have in mind when they use this term, then the answer is essentially "no." Human cultures have created a variety of ideas about the nature and importance of individuals, the relationship between the individual and

Reprinted from *The Myth of Self-Esteem: Finding Happiness and Solving Problems in America*, New York: St. Martin's Press, 1998, pp. 123–31, 137–43.

society, what motivates people, and where individuals acquire their capacities or traits. Most contemporary Americans tend to believe that the individual has a distinctive if not unique self that sets him or her apart from others. A traditional member of the Hopi people of Arizona, however, would find this a foreign and rather unpleasant way of thinking, taking the view that the person is a member of a people who have found their way to this earth and can find fulfillment only by pursuing traditional cultural practices.[1]

If by self, however, we mean *reflexivity* – the capacity of human beings to be the object of their own thoughts, feelings, and actions – then the answer is clearly "yes." The contemporary yuppie obsessed with acquiring and displaying wealth and status and the traditional Hopi immersed in a community that measures the individual by his or her participation in the "Hopi way" both possess the human propensity for reflexivity. They share the capacity to think about themselves, attach feelings to themselves, and become the object of their own actions. They also share the means of acquiring reflexivity. Both grasp themselves indirectly by seeing themselves from what they imagine to be the perspectives of others – not only the specific others with whom they interact but the community as a whole of which they are a part and the gods or spirits in which they believe.

Both the yuppie and the Hopi have the capacity to recognize themselves as individuals and to imagine how they measure up to the standards of the community and its culture. Both can formulate goals for themselves, be satisfied or dissatisfied with themselves, and reward or punish themselves for success or failure. Both have the capacity for self-consciously governing conduct in accordance with the standards of the group. Both have the capacity to disregard or disobey these standards. The cultural expectations that apply to yuppies and Hopis are very different, of course, for the former is expected to strive for individual success and distinction, whereas the latter is expected to immerse himself or herself in a communal way of life. But each is a reflexive creature.

The experience of reflexivity – however culture shapes the content or nature of the self – is both cognitive and affective. The social world provides the social groups, situations, roles, and social acts within which people experience reflexivity. People see themselves as holding up their end of a conversation, meeting the responsibilities of parenthood, having fun at a party, or being members of a committee or social class. Culture provides people with not only a vocabulary of terms with which to label themselves but also with a set of ideas about human nature, a ready-made discourse about human wants and needs that permits them to interpret their self-experiences.

Human beings also respond affectively – with feeling – to the surrounding world and to themselves. They are bored or elated by conversations, love or resent their children, feel proud or ashamed of their accomplishments. Moreover, they do not merely see themselves as they think others see them, but respond positively or negatively to the real or imagined evaluative responses of others. They are satisfied or disappointed in what they see in themselves, they love or despise themselves, they feel sad about or elated with themselves. They are capable of a variety of emotions directed toward themselves – such as pride, shame, honor, love, guilt – the experience of which is shaped both by the particulars of culture and the universal features of the human experience.[2]

The reality of self-esteem lies in the fact that it is one of these self-referential emotions. Like other such emotions, it depends crucially, but not entirely, on culture. Like all emotions, reflexive ones depend on the vocabulary of emotions the culture makes available. We experience most keenly and fully that which we can name and talk about. We can experience self-esteem, in other words, only if we have a name for it, just as we can experience pride or shame only because we have names for these emotions.

Like all emotions, self-esteem also involves neurological, muscular, visceral – in short, bodily – responses and sensations that are precipitated by human experiences. The grief that contemporary Americans feel over the death of a parent or spouse, for example, involves depressed energy, feelings of being lost or hopeless, intense sadness, crying, and other feeling states that are bodily and not merely "mental." Just as the fact of death is a universal human experience, some of the intense bodily feelings it precipitates probably also have a universal character. This is not to say that all human beings experience grief in this situation. Rather, they have some common bodily, affective reactions that our culture elaborates into what we call grief. Other cultures call the same or similar bodily states by other names, experiencing them as illness, for example, and elaborate a different set of meanings and activities.

The idea that self-esteem is likewise a culturally named emotion is novel and will meet vociferous objection from some quarters. Those convinced of the importance of self-esteem will especially resist categorizing it in this way, for they view it as a universal fact of human nature, not a cultural invention. Nonetheless, by viewing self-esteem as an emotion, we can gain a better grasp of its significance and contemporary meaning.

Self-Esteem as an Emotion

As a beginning point for viewing self-esteem as an emotion, I ask the reader to imagine an analogy with the emotion we commonly call "love." Like self-esteem, love is an elusive feeling, subject to a variety of definitions and to some disagreement about its importance or desirability. Those who are in love generally have no difficulty recognizing the fact, even if they cannot define what love is. Just as self-esteem is often associated with feelings of exuberance or energy, love is associated with feelings of breathless excitement, heart palpitations, and sexual arousal. People seek love, just as they do self-esteem, though they may believe they will never find it or that they do not deserve it. Experts on love offer pronouncements on how to find it, or how to "do" it, just as self-esteem experts offer advice. Love is, in short, a socially constructed emotion – a name for a state of being that involves powerful feelings, renders intense bodily experiences meaningful, and provides people with motives and explanations for their actions. So is self-esteem.

Both self-esteem and love resemble other human emotions, for each consists of a culturally significant and relatively standardized *interpretation* of a set of *feelings* that are aroused in various situations. The feelings associated with emotions take many different forms, depending on the circumstances in which the person finds himself or herself. Under conditions of threat or danger, for example, the individual feels highly mobilized to act, whether by fleeing or fighting. Bodily processes not immediately relevant to survival – such as digestion – slow down or shut down, and the body's resources are directed to the task of meeting the threat. Pulse and respiration speed up, and the body receives an extra supply of adrenalin.

The human experience of emotions associated with such arousal – fear and anger – is not dictated simply by physiological events. There is always a process of interpretation that occurs before, during, and after the arousal of such feelings, and the emotion consists of *both* the feelings *and* the interpretation of them. The belief that one *might* be in danger, as for example when one is alone at night in a place where people have been mugged, is sufficient to produce the physiological arousal we associate with fear. The arousal in turn shapes the way one interprets events – noises and shadows take on new significance, for example, when we believe they may signify that someone is about to attack us. And if one breaks into a run, determined to escape the perceived danger, the experience of fear – which is the named emotion associated with this situation – is as much a result of the activity of running as it is a cause of it. Although we say that we run because we are afraid, it is the act of running from danger that leads us to label our emotional state as fear.

Emotions, then, consist of interpreted physiological or bodily changes. A variety of situations provoke the individual not only to grasp cognitively what is happening so appropriate actions may be taken but also to be affected physiologically in various ways. Sometimes, as in situations that provoke fear, the physiological response is essentially one of arousal or mobilization for action. At other times, the response is nearly the opposite of arousal. The death of a loved one, for example, can provoke a profound depression – that is, an inability or unwillingness to act, a sense of lethargy that makes even physical movement difficult. Whatever the physiological response to a situation, individuals must ordinarily perform actions and interpret their own responses and feelings. We account for the quickened heartbeat in part by calling it "fear" and by associating this emotion with a course of action, perhaps running away. We account for the feeling of dullness and lethargy by calling it "sadness" or "grief" and by associating it with the actions we call mourning.

What are the situations associated with self-esteem, and what kinds of physiological arousal do they produce? There are a variety of ways one might go about answering this question, but the one I will develop here strikes me as a promising and useful way of thinking about self-esteem. It can be stated simply as follows: Self-esteem is interpreted mood. That is, self-esteem is a culturally specific emotion associated with a general human affective response that we can call *mood*.

Mood is a generalized human response to success and failure. All of the diverse situations in which human beings find themselves have an impact on mood. Those situations in which people successfully achieve their goals (or even exceed them) encourage a state of *euphoria*, which is the positive pole of mood. Euphoria entails feelings of energy, alertness, generalized well-being, and an eagerness to face whatever situation next occurs. Situations in which people fail to achieve their goals or fall short of them promote *dysphoria*, which involves a lack of energy, hesitancy to act, and feelings of anxiety, depression, and generalized gloom. Mood ordinarily falls somewhere between these poles. People are seldom either completely dysphoric or euphoric, but rather react to situations in proportion to their degree of success or failure.

Mood, like any other affective response, is experienced when it is named, interpreted, and associated with a line of conduct. It is, therefore, difficult to define mood without using words that themselves provide interpretations of it. Euphoria is not equivalent to "energy" or "well-being," for these are words we use to interpret the feeling. Rather, euphoria is an underlying feeling that is brought into conscious focus by words such as these. Likewise, dysphoria is not equivalent to "gloom" or "sadness," but rather is a state that people interpret and thus experience through these words.

From an evolutionary perspective, we can think of mood as a built-in reward and protection system. That is, successful action is rewarded not only by the results of that action – earning a good grade as a result of studying hard for an examination, for example – but by the positive mood that success promotes. The positive mood reinforces the actions that led to success, and in so doing it encourages the individual to do more of the same. By the same token, the negative mood that occurs as a result of failure operates as a protective mechanism, for it tends to inhibit actions that have led to failure and in so doing keeps the individual out of further difficulty.

Like any kind of human feeling, mood tends to be consciously associated with various lines of conduct and to draw meaning from the actions with which it is associated and the names we give to it. In other words, culture provides both names and courses of action that we can associate with mood, just as it provides names and courses of action we associate with other feelings. The question, then, is how do we name this dimension of human experience and what actions do we associate with it? Self-esteem is part of the answer, but as we will see, only a part.

It seems unlikely that such a general response as mood would have only one name. Every human situation in one way or another involves goals and expectations; sometimes they are met and sometimes they are not. The employee follows the rules and works hard, only to find that his or her job has been eliminated through corporate downsizing. An indifferent student does poorly on an examination but earns an "A" in the course because the professor made an arithmetical mistake in calculating the grade. An imaginary future Boston Red Sox team actually makes it to the World Series and wins, and the incredulous fans exult. A medical researcher spends years in the laboratory perfecting a vaccine and earns fame and fortune as a result. Each of these situations surely has an impact on what we have called mood, but people are apt to interpret these experiences in different ways, with self-esteem being only sometimes a part of the interpretation.

Moreover, cultures differ markedly from one another in the ways they explain or interpret success or failure. The Puritan immigrant to New England in the 1630s, for example, was determined to build a new and more godly community in the American wilderness and was keenly interested in the fate of his or her soul. Convinced that human beings were inherently sinful, Puritans also believed that some were predestined for salvation, and they scrutinized themselves and their experiences intently for signs that they might be among the elect. While Puritans certainly had the fundamental human response we have labeled as mood, they interpreted their feelings with reference to sin and salvation, not self-esteem. It is the contemporary corporate employee carrying the cultural burden of individual responsibility who, feeling depressed or demoralized because of the loss of a job, may interpret the feeling in terms of self-esteem.

Mood, in short, lends itself to a variety of interpretations, and these are shaped both by general cultural ideas and expectations and by the way the culture encourages people to interpret specific experiences. It is American culture generally, we will see, that frequently transforms mood into the self-referential emotion we call self-esteem. It is the actions of conceptual entrepreneurs operating within that cultural framework that give self-esteem its particular meanings. And it is a more particular set of cultural understandings that sometimes employ self-esteem as an interpretation of mood and sometimes employ other terms.

Self-Esteem and the Culture of Individualism

Viewing self-esteem as a named emotion that provides a culturally relevant and appropriate interpretation of mood gives us a novel way of understanding self-esteem. There is nothing new or unexpected, however, in the assertion that self-esteem rests upon a foundation of individualism. It is the tendency to place the individual on center stage and to believe that the individual possesses a distinctive self that makes an emphasis on self-esteem possible. However, self-esteem is not the only interpretation of mood that a culture of individualism could create; thus we must raise and answer a number of questions: What are the alternatives to self-esteem as an interpretation of personal experience? Are they the same alternatives that existed a century ago or two centuries ago? If they are not, why has the change occurred? Does the change in vocabulary indicate a major change in the experience of self? What shapes our choice of self-esteem versus other possible interpretations of feelings?

The English language makes available many words individuals can use to interpret the positive or negative feelings that result from success or failure. Having achieved fame, obtained a good grade, or won the lottery, a person might describe himself or herself as happy, joyful, glad, blessed, or fortunate, or some combination of these and similar adjectives. Likewise, the person who has encountered failure might speak of being dejected, unhappy, sad, unlucky, or cursed. Words such as these are self-referential, for they attempt to capture something of the personal meaning of a particular experience. They also frequently mix an interpretation of an emotional state with an explanation of the event that has caused it. To say one is happy to have succeeded describes the emotion one is experiencing; to say one is lucky or blessed is to explain why something has occurred to make one experience this emotion. And just as the individual might make such statements about himself or herself, so others might make such statements about the individual.

There is another array of terms that might be applied, both by individuals experiencing a feeling state and those who observe them doing so. One can imagine an individual saying "I am proud of myself," or "I feel that I have proven my worth." Assertions of pride, self-respect, dignity, value, or self-satisfaction are clearly self-referential. They also contain implicit explanations of success: to be "proud" is to claim credit for an accomplishment as much as to describe the feelings one is experiencing. One can imagine others using these terms as well, but also applying a related set of labels with more negative connotations. Egotism, vanity, narcissism, and conceit come to mind as words others sometimes use to give a negative cast to feelings people themselves describe in positive terms.

People likewise have an array of terms with which to characterize their own and others' dysphoric feelings. They use such general expressions as depression, gloom, dejection, sadness, and unhappiness to describe and explain feelings. And pride and similar terms have their counterparts in modesty, humility, diffidence, reticence, self-hatred, and self-restraint. Each of these words, like those mentioned previously, both describe the emotions the individual is experiencing and provide a way for others to make their own interpretations.

One pair of terms deserves special mention. "Pride" is one of the most common terms people use to express the euphoria that stems from success; "shame" is its dysphoric counterpart. To fall short of one's individual expectations is typically to fall short also of cultural expectations or the expectations of specific other people. To lose a job or fail a test is not merely to fall short of an individual goal, but to fail to live up to one's obligations to others. A common response to such failure is to be *ashamed* at having failed in one's responsibilities, just as to be *proud* is a common response to success.

But just how common are these responses? Are all Americans (or all human beings) always ashamed when they fall short of expectations and proud when they meet them? Or are they sometimes ashamed and sometimes sad, sometimes proud and sometimes happy? And what are the differences between sadness and shame, or pride and happiness? Do such different words merely provide alternative ways for individuals to describe and experience themselves? Or, in contrast, do such differing words and the emotional experiences they make possible have significant conse-quences for individuals and for the society in which they live?

All of the words mentioned describe self-referential emotions. Pride and shame, however, seem to have a reference outside the individual that appears lacking in such words as sadness and happiness. To say "I am happy to have succeeded" or "I am depressed that I failed" is to define one's emotional experience almost entirely with reference to oneself. *I* am the person experiencing this emotion, these statements seem to assert. To say "I am proud" or "I am ashamed," in contrast, is to associate the emotion one is experiencing with the expectations and responses of others. To be proud is not only to interpret one's emotional state but also to link it to the related emotional states of others, for one can hardly be proud without imagining an audience that is also proud of one. Likewise, one is not only ashamed, but conscious that others are ashamed of one.

Both happiness and pride (or sadness and shame) involve a real or imagined audience, but the individual's relationship with the audience seems to differ. To say, for example, "I'm happy that I got the promotion" is to ask others to approve of or applaud one's happiness and to invite their identification with one. It is the emotional state itself – the individual's happiness – that forms the main basis of the social bond between the happy person and his or her audience. To say, "I'm proud of my promotion" is also to ask for approval and invite identification, but there is more to the social bond than the individual's feeling of pride. The proud person and the approving audience are bound together not only by the emotion, but by a shared sense of the standards or expectations on which it is based.

Some emotional states, then, seem better able than others to foster connections with people. Pride and shame build stronger social ties than happiness and sadness.

. . .

Self-Esteem and the Medicalization of the Self

For the last century or so, the nature of the person has increasingly been subject to definition by scientists and experts. The invention of psychology and psychiatry established a beachhead for science in the territories of the mind, and their control over this territory has steadily increased. The development of humanistic psychology in the 1940s, exemplified by the client-centered approach of Carl Rogers, furthered this development. Even though Rogers departed from the scientific psychology of his day by making individual subjectivity central to his work, the nature of the person was still a matter held to lie within the province of the psychologist. Indeed, even religious positive thinkers such as Norman Vincent Peale turned to psychology for some of their ideas, signaling the decline of religion's ownership of this aspect of human experience.

In the last fifty years – roughly since the end of World War II – psychology in one form or another has become a major presence in our culture. It has spawned dozens of therapeutic systems and approaches, ranging from the scientifically and academically respectable to the bizarre. At one end of the spectrum, university psychology departments run training programs in clinical psychology, whose graduates must meet state licensing standards and who practice both in private offices and in various treatment facilities. At the other end of the spectrum, there is now a vast array of popular therapeutic methods, not taught within universities but rather in "institutes" and "schools" that are essentially entrepreneurial in nature.

All one need do to grasp the contemporary significance of this array of scientific and popular therapies is to consult the telephone book, which in my community contains about three pages of listings for psychologists, psychotherapists, and psychiatrists. These specialists practice in a small city with a small college and a nearby large town with a large university, with a total population of about 75,000. Academic places probably attract more than their share of people who think they need therapy and specialists who are eager to provide it. Even so, people in my vicinity can find a therapist almost more readily than they can find, say, a plumber or someone to repave the driveway. The area is likewise rich in alternative therapies.

During the same fifty years, medicine also made claims as a definer of human beings and their essential natures. Not only did medicine prove able to cure diseases and restore physical health, but increasingly it also claimed, through psychiatry, to hold the key to mental health. Orthodox Freudian psychoanalysis has given way to more diverse forms of therapy, and in recent years psychiatrists have turned increasingly to drugs in the treatment of mental illness. Although the basis of its claims has thus changed, organized medicine has nonetheless staked out the self, or what we call the self, as part of its territory.

The *Diagnostic and Statistical Manual*, on which mental health practitioners rely for the diagnosis and classification of mental illnesses, lists a bewildering array of forms of mental illness. More important, it brings under the rubric of illness many forms of behavior and problems of personal adjustment that once would have been viewed as problems of character or morality. The abuse of alcohol and other drugs, at one time thought to be forms of behavior that individuals could choose to abandon, now are regarded as treatable illnesses. Where once individuals were thought to be disagreeable or lacking in character, their behavior now is regarded as symptomatic of such illnesses as "narcissistic personality disorder" or "borderline personality disorder." Mental health practitioners have an arsenal of drugs and therapeutic techniques with which to treat these illnesses.

As the nature and problems of the person have fallen under the influence of this array of psychological and medical experts (or those who pretend to be experts) the self has become increasingly medicalized. The definition of a desirable or good self has not only gradually come to be shaped by these experts, but it has come to be seen in terms of health and illness. Behavior, once under the control of religion, law, and custom, has increasingly come under the control of one or another form of medicine. The person who was once thought to be capable of making rational choices, based upon adherence to social requirements, is now sometimes thought [of] as powerless to overcome various infirmities of the mind and psyche without medical assistance. And the self – the culturally created center of the person's essential being – is increasingly measured by criteria of health and illness. The good self, the desirable self, is coming to be the healthy self.

Where does self-esteem fit into this process of medicalization? Put most simply, I think both public and private uses of the word self-esteem are moving in a medical direction. Increasingly, I suspect, high self-esteem is becoming thought of as an indicator of psychological or mental health, and low self-esteem as a form of illness. Public discourse about self-esteem still touches a great many different cultural nerves, and by no means have its medical connotations come to dominate its use. In fact, given the current level of criticism of the self-esteem movement, I suspect we will see a diminution of public discourse using the word rather than a drastic transformation in that realm. But I also think that where public discourse about self-esteem persists, especially in private contexts, it will increasingly take a medical, health-related turn.

The best evidence that such a turn is underway comes from the apparently growing association between self-esteem and various forms of mental illness, particularly major depression. By a growing association, I do not mean that people diagnosed as depressed are also becoming more likely to have self-esteem problems. Self-esteem has long been associated with depression, and in fact the *DSM* defines low self-esteem as one of the key symptoms of major depression. Instead, I mean that professionals and the public alike are increasingly thinking of low self-esteem as a treatable illness, and thinking of it in much the same way they think of depression.

It is significant that self-esteem – which I have argued is interpreted mood – should be associated with depression, which is defined in broad terms as a "disorder of mood." High self-esteem is not becoming equivalent to mental health in general nor is low self-esteem to mental illness in general, for there are far too many ways in which mental functioning can become disordered for that to occur. But self-esteem is clearly becoming associated – in terms of conception, treatment, and public perception – with various mood disorders, including anxiety and major depression.

One form of evidence indicative of this growing conceptual association between self-esteem and depression is the use of similar forms of treatment for each condition. Significantly, both are being treated by psychiatrists and other physicians, not only with "talking therapies" but also with psychoactive drugs. The version of psychotherapy that is most successful in the treatment of depression – cognitive therapy – is also now used in the treatment of low self-esteem. Indeed, the most popular self-esteem book now on the market guides readers through the very same therapeutic strategies used to treat depression. The antidepressive drugs that have come to dominate the treatment of depression – including the well-known Prozac and similar drugs – also appear to have the effect of raising self-esteem. A brief examination of these treatments will make clear how far the medicalization of self-esteem has come – and also why I think it is useful to conceive of self-esteem as interpreted mood.

Ten Days to Self-Esteem, by psychiatrist David D. Burns, is a large, workbook-style publication with a picture of the smiling doctor on the cover, along with a bright gold sticker advising the potential buyer that the method has been "Pioneered and Tested at the Presbyterian Medical Center of Philadelphia" (Burns 1993). "In ten exciting steps," the cover advertises, "you will learn how to defeat depression, develop self-esteem, discover the secrets of joy in daily living." Burns also wrote *Feeling Good: The New Mood Therapy*, which is billed as a "breakthrough two and a half million best-seller" aimed at helping people with depression. Inside *Ten Days*, one learns that the book uses the method of cognitive therapy, which has proven to be as effective, if not more effective, the author says, than the use of antidepressant drugs in treating depression.

Ten Days to Self-Esteem is something of a marvel of medical technology – it is the latest in "bibliotherapy," as the author calls it. The book is chock-full of various tests that are to be taken by the reader as benchmarks in his or her progress in the treatment of low self-esteem. There is the Burns Anxiety Inventory, the Burns Depression Checklist, a Cost-Benefit Analysis on which the patient is to "list the advantages and disadvantages of a negative thought, feeling, or belief," a Daily Mood Log, and a Relationship Satisfaction Scale. There are multiple copies of these forms, since some of the scales are to be taken before and after each step. The steps themselves consist of exercises in which the reader becomes more aware of negative thoughts, analyzes them, finds new ways of describing the thoughts that makes him or her feel better, and thereby gradually reorients thinking from negative to positive. . . .

Throughout his book, Dr. Burns repeatedly associates [lack of] self-esteem and depression. In places, I found myself forgetting the book's focus on self-esteem, partly because the word depression so frequently appears, as do the methods used successfully to measure and treat depression. The confounding of depression and [lack of] self-esteem also reflects the fact that both are indeed grounded in mood. It seems to be, above all, the reader's mood that the author wishes to improve. "Feeling good feels wonderful," the back cover exclaims! "You owe it to yourself to feel good."

Depression is also treated by an arsenal of antidepressant drugs, most visibly in recent years by drugs such as Prozac. Such drugs work at the level of neurotransmission in the brain, and although the way in which they operate is not fully known, in general they increase the supply and prolong the action of such neurotransmitters as serotonin, norepinephrine, and dopamine. These neurotransmitters are responsible for the passing of messages along chains of neurons, and serotonin in particular is associated with the regulation of mood. By slowing the rate at which the neurotransmitters are reabsorbed by the transmitting neuron or destroyed by enzymes that work in the synapse, antidepressants have a reregulating effect on neural transmission.

Prozac, which works specifically on serotonin, has a range of positive effects on mental functioning. It brightens or lifts the person's mood, lessening or removing the negative and cloudy thinking, as well as the fog of despair that afflicts people suffering from major depression. It can make people more socially outgoing, more energetic, and more capable of functioning in everyday life. It also has the capacity to reduce anxiety, and it is approved for the treatment of obsessive-compulsive disorder, a form of mental illness in which the person repeatedly and uncontrollably engages in such behavior as washing hands or checking the locks on doors.

Prozac also raises self-esteem. As Peter Kramer, the author of the best-selling book *Listening to Prozac*, has pointed out, patients who seek treatment for depression frequently suffer from low self-esteem (1993: ch.7). As it brightens mood, Prozac also seems to raise self-esteem, not only for those with major depression but for those on the borderline of this illness whose symptoms do not quite meet the diagnostic criteria. Often this increased self-esteem has a rather swift onset – it does not occur gradually, but seemingly overnight. After the four weeks or so normally required for an antidepressant to take effect, some patients find their self-esteem rather markedly improved. They not only feel good, but they feel good about themselves.

It is not difficult to understand why Prozac has this effect, particularly if we think of self-esteem as an interpretation of mood. By helping individuals function better in relationships with others, antidepressants no doubt help them behave in ways that will earn them approval. But more fundamentally than that, Prozac directly brightens mood – it works precisely on the range of bodily feelings we have called mood, and in doing so it provides the individual with a new and desirable set of feelings to interpret. Given the availability of self-esteem as a label, and especially given the long-time clinical association of [low] self-esteem with depression, it is not surprising that both patients and their physicians interpret these changes in terms of self-esteem.

The significance of antidepressants for the medicalization of the self lies partly in the fact that physicians can now claim specific expertise in raising low self-esteem. Just as the success of cognitive therapy adds to the arsenal of the psychologist (or the psychiatrist inclined to try talk therapies before medication), Prozac adds to the arsenal of the psychiatrist and the family practitioner. Moreover, as people seek treatment for anxiety or low self-esteem, these conditions become defined as specific illnesses treatable by specific methods. Just as physicians treat diabetes with insulin injections, they treat low self-esteem with Prozac. And just as no one doubts the efficacy of insulin or the reality of diabetes, few will entertain doubts about antidepressants and low self-esteem.

Psychologists who use cognitive therapy and psychiatrists who use Prozac are often at odds with one another about treatment methods. The former dislike the rapidity with which the latter turn to drug therapy; and the latter are often dissatisfied with the reluctance of the former to accept the biochemical foundations of depression or self-esteem. Psychologists and psychiatrists alike are sometimes criticized and perhaps more often ignored by the legions of alternative health practitioners who have their own methods for improving self-esteem.

But what they all have in common is a tendency to think of high self-esteem as an indicator of health. We should not find this surprising. In a culture that makes happiness (however defined) a chief goal of life, we should not be surprised to find that individual mood gains in significance or that the words we use to describe and interpret this mood take a medical turn. If happiness is our cultural prime directive, being in a good mood is one of the chief ways we come to know we are happy. If we are ready to spend hundreds of millions of dollars on fitness equipment as well as hundreds of millions more on the care of the body, it is not surprising that we also spend our dollars on improving our moods. And if we can find a word like self-esteem, which has the virtue of avoiding at least some of the negative connotations of mental illness and depression, so much the better.

If there is something real about self-esteem, then, it is in the capacity of this word to label universal human somatic and psychological responses to success and failure in culturally appropriate ways. It is the latest word for happiness in a culture where happiness is important. Self-esteem is important, as its proponents recognize, but not because it is something whose pursuit will bring happiness. It is important because many of those who achieve happiness will increasingly call it self-esteem and think of it as a sign of health and vigor. The pursuit of self-esteem is something to worry about, as the critics have argued, but not because it undermines traditional cultural values. If anything, the babble of discourse about self-esteem reaffirms our cultural values and debates, and the varying meanings the term has acquired signify the vigor of the culture rather than its demise.

We should worry about the pursuit of self-esteem not because it will do harm, but because it will not do the good it promises. Psychic health, like physical health, is an unquestionable good, and it does not really matter what we call it. But neither form of health guarantees that people, individually or collectively, will do what they should do to remedy injustice, teach children skills that will help them lead productive and happy lives, or end the scourge of racism. Enhanced self-esteem is no more a shortcut to happiness or a better society than a low cholesterol count or well-defined abs. Healthy selves in healthy bodies can put their energies to good purposes or bad ones.

Notes

Words within square brackets have been inserted by the editor.

1 For helpful analyses of this question by anthropologists, see Schweder and Levine 1984.

2 The sociological view of emotions is explored in Hewitt 1997, chs 2 and 4.

References

Burns, David D., MD. 1993. *Ten Days to Self-Esteem*. New York: Quill.

Hewitt, John P. 1997. *Self and Society: A Symbolic Interactionist Social Psychology*, 7th edn. Boston: Allyn and Bacon.

Kramer, Peter. 1993. *Listening to Prozac*. New York: Viking.

Schweder, Richard A. and Levine, Robert A. (eds.). 1984. *Culture Theory: Essays on Mind, Self, and Emotion*. New York: Cambridge University Press.

6 Pricing the Priceless Child

Viviana Zelizer

My subject is the profound transformation in the economic and sentimental value of children –14 years of age or younger – between the 1870s and the 1930s. The emergence of this economically "worthless" but emotionally "priceless" child has created an essential condition of contemporary childhood.

For in strict economic terms, children today are worthless to their parents. They are also expensive. The total cost of raising a child – combining both direct maintenance costs and indirect opportunity costs – was estimated in 1980 to average between $100,000 and $140,000. In return for such expenses a child is expected to provide love, smiles, and emotional satisfaction, but no money or labor. One 1976 comprehensive time-budget study of 1,300 white, two-parent families in Syracuse, New York, found that children between the ages of 6 and 11 contributed on the average three and a half hours a week to household tasks, while their mothers spent some fifty hours doing housework (Walker and Woods 1976: 38).[1] Even the few chores that children perform are more often justified as an educational experience for their own benefit than an expected contribution to the household division of labor. Asked by researchers, "Why do you ask your children to work?," three-quarters of the parents in a study of 790 families from Nebraska explained children's domestic chores as character building. Only twenty-two parents responded, "I need the help" (White and Brinkerhoff 1981: 793; see also Straus 1962: 257–74). Money-making children, such as child actors or models, are considered an uncomfortable exception in our society; their parents are often suspected of callousness or greed.

Yet, children expect a regular income. While some "earn" their allowance by helping out around the house, many children, as *Parents Magazine* explains, receive it simply "in recognition of the fact that they are full members of the family" (Muenchow 1983: 55). After all, children must learn to spend their parents' money long before they begin to earn their own. Advertisers know it. As one prominent market-research firm points out, "there are 37 million children in the six to fourteen group [who] consume billions of dollars worth of goods and services every year" (cited by Goldsen 1977: 194). Parents cannot even expect significant public support to raise these expensive young consumers. While in all other major industrial countries a system of family allowances grants children at least partial monetary value, in America income-transfer programs remain notoriously inadequate and mostly restricted to female-headed, single-parent households below a certain income level. Tax exemptions for children, on the other hand, benefit primarily high-income families (see Kamerman and Kahn 1978).

In a recent book, *Costs of Children*, the economist Lawrence Olson concludes, "That so many young couples still decide to have children attests to the nonmonetary benefits they expect to derive from their progeny." After all, as he points out, "in

Reprinted from "Introduction," in *Pricing the Priceless Child: The Changing Social Value of Children*, New York: Basic Books, pp. 3–12.

purely monetary terms, couples would be better off putting their money in a bank as a way of saving for their old age" (Olson 1983: 58). A national survey of the psychological motivations for having children confirms their predominantly senti-mental value. Asked about "the advantages or good things about having children," the most common response was the desire for love and affection and the feeling of being a family (Hoffman and Manis 1979: 583–96).[2] A child is simply not expected to be useful. Significantly, in the many studies and articles written about the unequal distribution of household work, the roles of husbands and wives are examined, while the role of children is usually ignored.

In sharp contrast to contemporary views, the birth of a child in eighteenth-century rural America was welcomed as the arrival of a future laborer and as security for parents later in life. The economic value of children for agricultural families has been well documented by anthropologists. In many cultures, between the ages of 5 and 7, children assume a variety of work responsibilities–caring for younger children, help-ing with household work, or tending animals. In rural China today, for instance, researchers found children as young as 5 or 6 helping to feed the family fowl, clean the house, and prepare meals (Parish and Whyte 1978: 227; see also Whiting and Whiting 1977).

By the mid-nineteenth century, the construction of the economically worthless child had been in large part accomplished among the American urban middle class. Concern shifted to children's education as the determinant of future marketplace worth. Far from relying on his child as old-age "insurance," the middle-class father began insuring his own life and setting up other financial arrangements such as trusts and endowments, to protect the unproductive child. As one well-to-do father explained in *Harper's Weekly*, in 1904, "We work for our children, plan for them, spend money on them, buy life insurance for their protection, and some of us even *save* money for them. This last tribute is the most affecting of all...saving, for our children's start in life...is evidence of serious self-denial. Profound must be the depths of affection that will induce a man to save money for others to spend...." (Martin 1904: 1889).

However, the economic value of the working-class child increased, rather than decreased in the nineteenth century. Rapid industrialization after the 1860s intro-duced new occupations for poor children, and according to the 1870 census about one out of every eight children was employed. Working-class urban families in the late nineteenth century depended on the wages of older children and the household assistance of younger ones. Child labor laws and compulsory education, however, gradually destroyed the class lag. By the 1930s, lower-class children joined their middle-class counterparts in a new nonproductive world of childhood, a world in which the sanctity and emotional value of a child made child labor taboo. To make profit out of children, declared Felix Adler in 1905, was to "touch profanely a sacred thing" (cited in Bremner 1971: 653). To be sure, child labor did not magically and totally vanish. In the 1920s and 1930s, some children under 14 still worked in rural areas and in street trades. Moreover, the Great Depression temporarily restored the need for a useful child even in some middle-class households. But the overall trend was unmistakable. In the first three decades of the twentieth century, the economic-ally useful child become both numerically and culturally an exception. Although during this period the most dramatic changes took place among the working class, the sentimentalization of child life intensified even among the already "useless" middle-class children.

How did the social valuation of children change so dramatically within a relatively short period of time? Why did the sentimental value of children's lives increase just when their contributions to the household disappeared? And what accounts for the curious paradox that the market price of an economically useless child far surpassed the money value of a nineteenth-century useful child? By the 1930s, for example, childless couples were paying large sums of money to purchase a black market baby. In cases of accidental death, courts began to award increasingly large sums to compensate parents for the loss of their child.

The Price and Value of Children: A Sociological Approach

Although the shift in children's value from "object of utility" to object of sentiment is indisputable, historian Joseph F. Kett notes that a "precise characterization of this change has remained elusive" (Kett 1978: S196). The sociological impact has never been systematically explored. Indeed, since the 1930s, the study of children has been predominantly psychological in orientation. The sociology of childhood remains a surprisingly undeveloped specialty. Significantly, the latest edition of the *International Encyclopedia of the Social Sciences* has only two listings under child: child development and child psychiatry. Research on the value of children has been dominated by psychologists, economists, and demographers, all similarly concerned with parental motivation for childbearing and its relation to fertility patterns and population policy. For example, the recently completed cross-national Value of Children project interviewed national samples of married women under 40 and their husbands in seven countries in order to identify the perceived psychological satisfactions and costs of having children. According to one participating researcher, the investigation "is seen as important for predicting changes in fertility patterns and for affecting the motivation for fertility" (Hoffman and Manis 1979: 596; see also Arnold et al. 1975; Becker 1981; Sawhill 1977: 116–25; Schultz 1973: S2–S13). But, although these studies contribute to the understanding of children's value, they remain limited by a primarily individualistic and utilitarian framework and by an ahistorical perspective. They produce organized lists of children's costs and benefits, but largely ignore the cultural and social determinants of such international inventories.[3]

Microeconomic theories of fertility also focus on decision-making by rational, utility-maximizing parents. From this perspective, the demand for children is essentially dictated by their relative price and by income. Accordingly, as soon as children ceased to be profitable as economic investments, fertility declined and children became expensive consumption goods; their changing price determined their new value. The perceived utility of educated children outweighed the immediate benefits of their contribution to the family income. Thus, in the economic model, what matters are the choices made by individuals on the basis of their own assessment of the costs and benefits involved in the various alternatives. As with psychological theories, changes in the cultural and social context, which shape individual choice, are not examined.

American historians, for the most part, seem to be more intrigued with the social creation of adolescence than the changing status of younger pre-adolescent children. Existing historical interpretations of childhood are psychologically oriented or else focus mostly on the impact of structural change, in particular, changes in the economic system. From this perspective, the productive value of children disappeared with the success of industrial capitalism at the turn of the century, which required a skilled, educated labor force. (See, e.g., Huber 1976: 371–88 and Minge-Kalman 1978: 454–68.)[4]

Changes in the family are also linked with the shift in children's value. In his pioneer study, *Centuries of Childhood*, Philippe Ariès argues that the "discovery" of childhood as a separate stage of life in the sixteenth and seventeenth centuries in Europe was a measure of the growing importance of family life: "The concept of the family... is inseparable from the concept of childhood. The interest taken in childhood... is only one form, one particular expression of this more general concept – that of the family" (1962: 353). In nineteenth-century America, the increasing differentiation between economic production and the home transformed the basis of family cohesion. As instrumental ties weakened, the emotional value of all family members – including children – gained new saliency (see Hareven 1977: 57–70; Laslett 1978: 476–90; Zaretsky 1976). In particular, the sentimentalization of childhood was intimately tied to the changing world of their mothers. The increasing domestication of middle-class women in the nineteenth century, as Carl Degler points out in *At Odds*, "went hand in hand with the new conception of children as precious." The changing value of children, argues Degler, served women's interests: "Exalting the child went hand in hand with exalting the domestic role of woman; each reinforced the other while together they raised domesticity within the family to a new and higher level of respectability" (Degler 1980: 73–4).[5] The specialization of women into expert full-time motherhood intensified at the turn of the century, spreading (in ideal if not always in practice) to the working class. The creation of the family wage – a salary which would support a male wage earner and his dependent family – in the early twentieth century, was partly intended to implement the "cult of true womanhood" and "true" childhood among the working class. Feminist analysis suggests the collaboration of capitalism with patriarchy in this process:

> Capitalism needed a healthy, well-disciplined, and well-trained current and future labor force. Men in individual families needed to decrease competition with the large numbers of women and children working in the market (in the late nineteenth century); they also needed to have someone to take care of their household needs, especially children. The family wage helped ensure that it would be women who continued to perform these tasks. (Sokoloff 1981: 214)

The precise nature of the relationship between changes in the economic roles of women and children, however, remains unclear and largely undocumented. One historian, for instance, suggests that the decline in child labor pushed mothers into the labor force between 1920 and 1940: "It is possible that wives and mothers moved into the labor force in unconscious response to the withdrawal of children" (Wandersee 1981: 66). Thus, rather than a new shared domesticity, there was a substitution of secondary wage earners in many working-class and lower middle-class families. Mothers took over children's work responsibilities, without, however, relinquishing their former household duties.

Historian Christopher Lasch presents a very different, and more polemical interpretation of changes in family and child life. He sees the removal of children from the labor market as part of a general effort by Progressive reformers to remove children from family influence, especially the immigrant family. Public policy contributed not to the sentimentalization of domestic ties, but to their deterioration, specifically through the appropriation of parental functions by new "agencies of socialized reproduction" – educators, psychiatrists, social workers, penologists. Reformers, claims Lasch, "sought to remove children from the influence of their families, which they also blamed for exploiting child labor, and to place the young under the benign influence of state and school" (1979: 13). The sacralization of children was, in fact, their alienation from the home. It marked the beginning of the end of the family as a "haven in a heartless world."

Demographic theories, on the other hand, contend that the new emotional value of children is best explained by falling birth and mortality rates in the twentieth century. Philippe Ariès (1962) and Lawrence Stone, in a landmark study of the English family, suggest that in periods of high mortality parents protect themselves against the emotional pain of a child's death by remaining affectively aloof. From this perspective, it is "folly to invest too much emotional capital in such ephemeral beings" (Stone 1977: 105). The decline in early mortality, therefore, can be seen as an independent variable that encouraged "the deepening of emotional bonds" between parents and children (Uhlenberg 1983: 170). A similar cost–benefit accounting explains why falling birthrates and smaller family size augment the emotional value of each individual child. Between the mid-nineteenth century and 1915, for instance, the annual birthrate for native whites dropped nearly 40 percent, from 42.8 to 26.2 per thousand. Fewer children made each child more precious. But the economic equation of longevity or scarcity with value remains highly speculative. For instance, Demos submits that in seventeenth-century Plymouth a high death rate may have encouraged a special concern for and tenderness toward infants (1978: 157–65).

I will focus on one sociological dimension that has received little attention in the literature: the independent effect of cultural factors redefining the value of children in the United States.[6] I will argue that the expulsion of children from the "cash nexus" at the turn of the past century, although clearly shaped by profound changes in the economic, occupational, and family structures, was also part of a cultural process of "sacralization" of children's lives. The term sacralization is used in the sense of objects being invested with sentimental or religious meaning. While in the nineteenth century the market value of children was culturally acceptable, later the new normative ideal of the child as an exclusively emotional and affective asset precluded instrumental or fiscal considerations. In an increasingly commercialized world, children were reserved a separate noncommercial place, *extra-commercium*. The economic and sentimental value of children were thereby declared to be radically incompatible. Only mercenary or insensitive parents violated the boundary by accepting the wages or labor contributions of a useful child. Properly loved children, regardless of social class, belonged in a domesticated, nonproductive world of lessons, games, and token money. It was not a simple process. At every step, working-class and middle-class advocates of a useful childhood battled the social construction of the economically useless child.

Notes

1 On the costs of children, see Espenshade 1980: 1, 10–12.
2 On the emotional value of children for working-class mothers, see Rainwater 1960.
3 For a critique of current theories of fertility, see Blake 1968: 5–25; Katz and Stern 1981: 63–92; Turchi 1975: 107–25.
4 For a psychological approach to the history of childhood, see deMause 1975. On adolescence in a historical perspective, see Gillis 1981; Katz and Davey 1978: S81–S119; Kett 1977.
5 On the domestication of women, see Cott 1979; Welter 1983: 372–92.
6 There are some significant exceptions. For some studies that explore the cultural dimension, see Boli-Bennett and Meyer 1978: 797–812; Greven 1977; Smelser and Halpern 1978: S288–S315; Wells 1978: 516–32. In his explanation of changing family types in England, Stone (1977) relies primarily on a cultural explanation, contending that the rise of "affective individualism" was the determining factor.

References

Adler, Felix. 1905. "Child labor in the United States." Paper at the Annual Meeting of the National Child Labor Committee.
Ariès, Philippe. 1962. *Centuries of Childhood*. New York: Vintage.
Arnold, Fred, et al. 1975. *The Value of Children*. Honolulu: East-West Population Institute.
Becker, Gary S. 1981. *A Treatise on the Family*. Cambridge, Mass.: Harvard University Press.
Blake, Judith. 1968. "Are babies consumer durables? A critique of the economic theory of reproductive motivation." *Population Studies* 22 (March).
Boli-Bennett, John and Meyer, John. 1978. "Ideology of childhood and the state." *American Sociological Review* 43 (December).
Bremner, Robert H. 1971. *Children and Youth in America*, vol. II. Cambridge, Mass.: Harvard University Press.
Cott, Nancy F. 1979. *The Bonds of Womanhood: "Women's Sphere" in New England, 1780–1853*. New Haven, Conn.: Yale University Press.
Degler, Carl. 1980. *At Odds: Women and the Family in America from the Revolution to the Present*. New York: Oxford University Press.
deMause, Lloyd. 1975. "The evolution of childhood." In Lloyd deMause (ed.) *The History of Childhood*. New York: Harper and Row.
Demos, John. 1978. "Infancy and childhood in the Plymouth colony." In Michael Gordon (ed.) *The American Family in Social-Historical Perspective*, 1st edn. New York: St. Martin's Press.
Espenshade, Thomas J. 1980. "Raising a child can now cost $85,000." *Intercom* 8 (September).
Gillis, John R. 1981. *Youth and History*. New York: Academic Press.
Goldsen, Rose K. 1977. *The Show and Tell Machine*. New York: Dial Press
Greven, Philip. 1977. *The Protestant Temperament*. New York: Signet.
Hareven, Tamara. 1977. "Family time and historical time." *Daedalus* 106 (Spring).
Hoffman, Lois W. and Manis, Jean D. 1979. "The value of children in the United States: A new approach to the study of fertility." *Journal of Marriage and the Family* 41 (August).

Huber, Joan 1976. "Toward a sociotechnological theory of the women's movement." *Social Problems* 23 (April).

Kamerman, Sheila B. and Kahn, Alfred J. 1978. *Family Policy*. New York: Columbia University Press.

Katz, Michael B. and Davey, Ian E. 1978. "Youth and industrialization in a Canadian city." In John Demos and Sarane Spence Boocock (eds.) *Turning Points*. Chicago: University of Chicago Press.

Katz, Michael B. and Stern, Mark J. 1981. "Fertility, class, and industrial capitalism: Erie County, New York, 1855–1915." *American Quarterly* 33 (Spring).

Kett, Joseph F. 1977. *Rites of Passage*. New York: Basic Books.

—— 1978. "Curing the disease of precocity." In John Demos and Sarane Spence Boocock (eds.) *Turning Points*. Chicago: University of Chicago Press.

Lasch, Christopher. 1979. *Haven in a Heartless World*. New York: Basic Books.

Laslett, Barbara. 1978. "Family membership, past and present." *Social Problems* 25 (June).

Martin, E. S. 1904. "Children as an incentive." *Harper's Weekly* 48 (December 10).

Minge-Kalman, Wanda. 1978. "The Industrial Revolution and the European family: The institutionalization of 'childhood' as a market for family labor." *Comparative Studies in Society and History* 20 (September).

Muenchow, Susan. 1983. "Children and money: Teaching good habits." *Parents* 58 (December).

Olson, Lawrence. 1983. *Costs of Children*. Lexington, Mass.: Lexington Books.

Parish, William L. and Whyte, Martin K. 1978. *Village and Family in Contemporary China*. Chicago: University of Chicago Press.

Rainwater, Lee. 1960. *And the Poor Get Children*. Chicago: Quadrangle Books.

Sawhill, Isabel. 1977. "Economic perspectives on the family." *Daedalus* 106 (Spring).

Schultz, Theodore W. 1973. "The value of children: An economic perspective." *Journal of Political Economy* 81 (March–April).

Smelser, Neil J. and Halpern, Sydney. 1978. "The historical triangulation of family, economy, and education." In John Demos and Sarane Spence Boocock (eds.) *Turning Points*. Chicago: University of Chicago Press.

Sokoloff, Natalie J. 1981. *Between Money and Love*. New York: Praeger.

Stone, Lawrence. 1977. *The Family, Sex and Marriage in England 1500–1800*. New York: Harper and Row.

Straus, Murray A. 1962. "Work roles and financial responsibility in the socialization of farm, fringe, and town boys." *Rural Sociology* 27 (September).

Turchi, Boone A. 1975. "Microeconomic theories of fertility: A critique." *Social Forces* 54 (September).

Uhlenberg, Peter. 1983. "Death and the family." In Michael Gordon (ed.) *The American Family in Social-Historical Perspective*, 2nd edn. New York: St. Martin's Press.

Walker, Kathryn E. and Woods, Margaret. 1976. *Time Use: A Measure of Household Production of Family Goods and Services*. Washington, DC: Center for the Family of the American Home Economics Association.

Wandersee, Winifred D. 1981. *Women's Work and Family Values, 1920–1940*. Cambridge, Mass.: Harvard University Press.

Wells, Robert. 1978. "Family history and the demographic transition." In Michael Gordon (ed.) *The American Family in Social-Historical Perspective*, 1st edn. New York: St. Martin's Press.

Welter, Barbara. 1983. "The cult of true womanhood: 1820–1860." In Michael Gordon (ed.) *The American Family in Social-Historical Perspective*, 2nd edn. New York: St. Martin's Press.

White, Lynn K. and Brinkerhoff, David B. 1981. "Children's work in the family: Its significance and meaning." *Journal of Marriage and the Family* 43 (November).

Whiting, Beatrice B. and Whiting, John W. M. 1977. *Children of Six Cultures*. Cambridge, Mass.: Harvard University Press.

Zaretsky, Eli. 1976. *Capitalism, the Family, and Personal Life*. New York: Harper and Row.

7 Goodness Personified: The Emergence of Gifted Children

Leslie Margolin

> She is an attractive, merry, wholesome girl, who does all mental work with an ease, accuracy and expertness, which entitles her to be called a *"gifted child"*.
>
> **Genevieve Coy,*"The mentality of a gifted child"***

Seven academic journals specialize in gifted children.[1] Yet, there are no studies on the social construction of giftedness. Researchers who study gifted children attempt to determine their characteristics, but neglect the approach utilized in deviance and social problems research (Best 1987, 1989; Blumer 1971; Gusfield 1981; Spector and Kitsuse 1977) of studying the ways conceptions of such characteristics are developed. They ask how the gifted can be recognized, how many gifted there are, how giftedness is produced and supported, but do not inquire into the etiology of the meaning of giftedness.

This paper examines the emergence of giftedness as a recognized, enforceable social category and locates the gifted identity in the language used to describe and explain gifted children (Garfinkel 1967; Hilbert 1990; Zimmerman and Wieder 1970). The purpose of this methodological stance is to specify the language and imagery used to make the concept "gifted children" appear representative of something real, obdurate, and objective. Put somewhat differently, the analysis explores the methods used to display gifted children as objects of nature rather than of human imagination, as something discovered rather than created. This paper, then, is not about the "emergence" of a new class of people, nor is it strictly a description of claims made in conjunction with the gifted label. Instead, this paper examines the methods by which and through which scholars' claims about an intended object – the gifted – were (and are) taken as true (Zimmerman and Pollner 1970).

Given the intimate association of giftedness with scholarly activity, the focus is on a group of players who have received little attention in the social movement literature. While scholars are usually portrayed as the disinterested interpreters or mirrors of social change, here they are portrayed as a dynamic force in their own right. I examine how scholars' investigations defined and legitimated gifted children as a cultural entity, assembled gifted children in piece-by-piece fashion, provided detailed documentation of the gifteds' characteristics, and spread that vision to a community of believers.

Since Foucault (1977, 1980) argued that power in contemporary society is becoming increasingly "positive" – that is, less a matter of coercion than of inducing and

Reprinted from *Social Problems* 40(4) (November 1993): 510–32.

seducing – an examination of how a positive concept such as giftedness is established may offer a key to understanding modern social control (see Cohen 1985; Gross 1970; Rodger 1988). However, this examination is precarious because unlike repressive forms of control where power operates self-consciously, where there is a clear distinction between the deviant and the agent, positive power operates invisibly and effortlessly. Among gifted child educators, for example, there is little awareness of who the objects and agents of control are, or that social control is operating at all. The prevailing voices speak only in terms of liberation, self-actualization, and creative freedom. In the words of gifted child scholars: "Children who produce and create well beyond our expectations invigorate us and show us the possibilities of human potential. . . . In our own experience we have never met teachers more excited about teaching than when they work with gifted children" (Colangelo and Davis 1991: 4).

It may be difficult to associate the gifted and their activities with social control given the belief that positive labeling promotes self-esteem and achievement – the "Pygmalion effect" (Cooper and Good 1983; Rosenthal and Jacobson 1968). Nonetheless, the fact that positive labels are selectively assigned implies that some groups are given fewer advantages than others. In this regard, it is noteworthy that although African-American children make up 16 percent of the nation's school enrollment, only 8 percent of the students in programs for the gifted are of African-American descent (*New York Times* 1988). The selective distribution of positive labels in our schools parallels and supports the class differences and racial discrimination found in society as a whole (cf. Bowles and Gintis 1976; Lawler 1978; Mensh and Mensh 1991).

A second, and perhaps more subtle, aspect of social control in positive labeling is that its use implicitly constructs its negation. Good and evil are mutually defined; each is meaningful only in relation to the other. Thus, discourse on the gifted only occurs alongside an implied (or explicit) discourse on the nongifted. According to Douglas (1970: 5), any distinction between levels of worth is not only a matter of degree, that is, a comparison in terms of better or worse, it is absolute or categorical. However, unlike other "dividing practices" (Foucault 1965, 1973, 1977), whereby abnormals are defined and segregated from normals (e.g., the insane from the sane, the sick from the healthy, the criminal from the law-abiding citizen), here the social hierarchy is formed by attention to the positive idealization. This is consistent with Foucault's (1977: 304, 183) characterization of the modern "disciplines" as primarily engaged in "making" people, as procedures used to assign qualities and characteristics to human individuals. In Foucault's words, theirs "is the specific technique of power that regards individuals as both the objects and instruments of its exercise" (1977: 170).

Scholars' writings on the gifted may be a particularly good example of "people-making" since there was no public discourse on gifted children until social scientists first named and described them.[2] At the beginning of the twentieth century, stories of "child prodigies" appeared with increasing regularity in journals and newspapers, but these children were seen as curiosities, more as accidents of nature than as representatives of a stable class of people (see, for example, *Current Literature* 1910 and *North American Review* 1907). It was not until psychologists such as Lewis M. Terman, Henry H. Goddard, and Leta S. Hollingworth reported "findings" on gifted children that this social category received widespread acceptance. By making giftedness appear predictable, orderly, and explainable, psychologists assimilated the gifted into natural law, and made it possible to include them in everyday discourse.

Psychologists' interest in assessing differences in children's intellectual capacities can be traced to the sudden swelling of the school population at the turn of the century. Between 1890 and 1915, the US public elementary school enrollment increased by 47 percent (Chapman 1988: 42). The new students included children previously in the labor force before compulsory education and child labor laws were passed, and the vast number of children who had recently migrated from rural areas of the United States and eastern Europe (Oakes 1985: 19–21). Because a large proportion of these new students were beyond normal school entry age, the first grade in most urban elementary schools was enormously overpopulated, while the more advanced grades were proportionally underutilized. In 1904, the superintendent of New York City schools noted that 39 percent of the students were above the expected age for their grades (Ayres 1909). Given such numbers and the strain on the educational system, educators began to discuss methods for distinguishing overage children who could catch up from those who could not. They reasoned that if children's learning potential or intelligence could be estimated, teachers' attention could be channeled to those students more likely to advance. Thus, pressure to allocate limited educational resources created interest in methods for distinguishing and separating students with low, average, and above average native capacities (Chapman 1988).

These practical considerations ignited experts' interest in sorting children by their intellectual capacities. However, the eugenics movement provided this discourse's form and direction. By 1914, the year of the first National Conference on Race Betterment, the eugenics movement had gained significant influence over educators, medical professionals, and charitable organizations. From Galton's (1869, 1883, 1889) first inquiries into human heredity, there was a growing fascination in the United States with identifying, protecting, and preserving genetically superior cultural and racial groups (Hofstadter 1959: 161–7). As this paper will show, the eugenicist identification of superiority or "fitness" with membership in the upper classes and white race was shared by gifted child experts and was critical to their understanding of giftedness.

The paper begins with an analysis of the writings of the most influential gifted child scholars from the first decades of the century: Lewis Terman, Leta Hollingworth, and Henry Goddard.[3] The second half of the paper explores continuities and discontinuities with later scholars' writings.

Grounding Giftedness in the "Native Tongue"

If a conceptualization of a group's identity is to be adopted by a particular audience, it must be grounded in the "native tongue" of that audience's culture (Scott 1970). Thus, to successfully communicate the message that a social type exists, that message must be couched in language, and documented by examples, which express and support the culture's prevailing attitudes, beliefs, and values. The new social type must be defended in terms of people's "thinking as usual" (Schutz 1944: 501). Since experts on gifted children and the consumers of their reports are from the upper middle class, portrayals of gifted behavior and thinking – in order to appear valid and legitimate – must reflect upper-middle-class experience. To illustrate, the following dialogue was originally offered by Hollingworth as an example of the exactness of a gifted child's thinking.[4]

Q: What do you think is the most interesting vocation? What would you like to be when you grow up?
A: Well, the answer to those two questions is not the same.
Q: Then tell us first what you think is the most interesting vocation.
A: Science, especially astronomy.
Q: And what vocation would you like to follow when you grow up?
A: To be a medical doctor.
Q: But why not be what is most interesting?
A: Because a person cannot make much money being an astronomer. I never heard of anyone at the Lick Observatory earning fifty thousand dollars a year.
Q: But do medical doctors earn fifty thousand dollars a year?
A: It is possible for one to do it. Some of them do.
Q: Do you think being a medical doctor is the most lucrative occupation?
A: No. It would be more lucrative to get into Standard Oil.
Q: Then why not go into Standard Oil?
A: Because it isn't so interesting as being a medical doctor. (1926: 257)

The gifted children described by Hollingworth (1926) are portrayed as interested in upper-middle-class occupations and their career choices are explained, defended, and qualified in terms of upper-middle-class vocabularies of motive (cf. Mills 1940).

There also is a gender difference in presentation of the gifted child which is consistent with higher-class values and norms. Gifted girls "make sense" of their occupational choices in language grounded in upper-middle-class conceptions of feminine behavior.

Girl, IQ 133: Will be "a piano soloist." Expects "to graduate from university at 21 years, then marry and go on with piano work."
Girl, IQ 148: I want to be an authoress, actress, artist, and musician.
(Hollingworth 1926: 141–2, 253)

Gifted boys, on the other hand, explain their career choices with language that "makes sense" in terms of upper middle-class conceptions of masculinity.

Boy, IQ 162: Will take up the oil business, "because there is a lot of money in it, and because I like the work, and I have a lot of relatives in that business."
Boy, IQ 187: I want to work at whatever has the most mathematics in it, when I grow up.
(Hollingworth 1926: 141).

Not only is giftedness portrayed as mirroring upper-middle-class values, the gifted are portrayed as actual members of the upper middle class. For example, in the first volume of *Genetic Studies of Genius*, an examination of 1,528 gifted children, Terman (1925: 63) reported that among the 560 fathers of gifted children questioned, only one was a laborer, at a time when 15 percent of the population was in this job category. Similarly, only 2 fathers were farmers. By contrast, there were 33 lawyers; 38 engineers (with college degrees); 30 teachers; 32 physicians and dentists; and 103 executives, managers, and manufacturers. On average, parents of gifted children had covered twice as many school grades as other adults in the population. They lived in neighborhoods rated as "superior," and homes rated as "very superior." Each gifted child's home contained an average of 328 books.

For Schutz, a person's assessment of what is real within any sphere is guided primarily by self-interest. "He groups the world around himself (as the center) as a field of domination. . . . He singles out those of its elements which may serve as means or ends for his 'use and enjoyment,' for furthering his purposes, and for overcoming obstacles" (1944: 500). From this perspective, gifted child experts and consumers not only more readily comprehend gifted children's thinking as more intelligent, as truly "gifted," when that thinking is expressed in their cultural vernacular, they are also likely to support this designation because it conforms with their practical interests. After all, their children and values are labeled as gifted. The linkage of superior intellectual capacity to social class elevates their status and provides a rationale for superior privilege and wealth.

The Role of Heredity

A particularly soothing, self-serving and, hence, convincing dimension of gifted child discourse during the early part of this century was the effort to portray upper-middle-class status as a sequala or reward arising from giftedness. This is exhibited in Hollingworth's explanation of why most fathers of the gifted are highly educated, successful, and well-placed in professions or business. While Hollingworth acknowledges that "a few of the very gifted are born into homes where the father is an unskilled or semi-skilled manual laborer, and reared without 'advantages,'" she claims "these cases teach us that the gifted are not absolutely confined to any one set of environmental conditions" (1926: 57–8). They do not become gifted because they are given specific environmental stimuli or superior learning opportunities. Rather, gifted people earn and select superior environments. "If superior environment were the cause of high scores on [IQ] tests, no child living from birth in squalor could score high" (Hollingworth 1926: 58).

How, then, do gifted children come to live in "superior" environments? The answer was that their parents were gifted or, at least, came very close to this standard. Since giftedness results from heredity, not the social "advantages" accompanying giftedness, the significant correlation between giftedness and wealth is explained by the fact that "modern men, both voluntarily and involuntarily, allow more money to the more gifted. . . . Modern civilization bestows medals, appointments, professional, political, and military titles upon its best performers. It is clear that people always, even when their theories are aggressively democratic, create aristocracy within their group" (Hollingworth 1926: 2–3). In Terman's words: "The common opinion that the child from a cultured home does better in tests by reason of his superior home advantages is an entirely gratuitous assumption. . . . The children of successful and cultured parents test higher than children from wretched and ignorant homes for the simple reason that their heredity is better" (1922: 660).

So great was researchers' belief in the correspondence between social class and giftedness that Cox (1926), working under Terman's guidance, used "family standing" as a means of estimating the intelligence of children who did not take IQ tests. According to her methodology, a "family standing" at the "lower business and skilled labor level" was treated as equivalent to an IQ of 100, "semiprofessional and higher business" equalled an IQ of 110, and "professional" equalled an IQ of 120.

While social class is portrayed as correlated to giftedness, race has a cause and effect relation to giftedness: whites are portrayed as superior, and dark-skinned people as of inferior intellectual stock. Hollingworth notes several surveys testing the intelligence of black children, but contends "these surveys unexceptionally show a low average of intellect among children having Negro blood. Comparatively few of these children are found within the range which includes the best one per cent of white children" (1926: 69). Terman is even more direct:

> Their [dark-skinned people's] dullness seems to be racial, or at least inherent in the family stocks from which they come. The fact that one meets this type with such extraordinary frequency among Indians, Mexicans, and Negroes suggests quite forcibly that the whole question of racial differences in mental tests will have to be taken up anew and by experimental methods. The writer predicts that when this is done there will be discovered enormously significant racial differences in general intelligence, differences which cannot be wiped out by any scheme of mental culture. (1916: 91–2)

To reinforce the claim that giftedness is inborn (and, by implication, that upper-middle-class status results from hereditary advantage rather than socioeconomic opportunity), Hollingworth, Terman, and other psychologists from this period focused their analyses on individual level data and variables. For example, descriptions of early childhood development focus on the age when gifted children first stood, walked, spoke their first words, spoke complete sentences, learned the alphabet, began to read, and so forth. Thus, the first volume of Terman's *Genetic Studies of Genius: Mental and Physical Traits of a Thousand Gifted Children* (1925) contains chapters on "racial and social origin," "intellectually superior relatives," "vital statistics," "anthropometric measurements," "health and physical history," "medical examinations," "reading interests," "tests of character and personality traits." Other family members are discussed solely to demonstrate the heritability of giftedness (for example, see Hollingworth 1926: 181). The gifted are portrayed as scions of an aristocracy to which members are born, not raised (e.g., Terman 1925: 91–2; and Goddard 1928: 135–41).

Early gifted child texts contain lengthy descriptions of the educational and professional achievements of gifted children's ancestors but little or no information on their influence over gifted children's development. For example, although Hollingworth tells us nothing about J.M.'s family interactions, upbringing, or emotional and intellectual stimulation, we are told:

> [Her] father was educated as an electrical engineer, but subsequently went into investment banking. J.M.'s paternal grandfather was an architect who attended Edinburgh

University, and was trained in the Manchester School of Science. The paternal great-grandfather was an architect and ship builder, who engaged in laying out factories, and came from a line of builders. . . . J.M.'s maternal grandfather was first a teacher, then a merchant, very wealthy, and mayor of a southern town for eighteen years. The line of his descent was through southern planters. The maternal grandmother was the daughter of a college professor, who in turn was the son of a physician and surgeon. (1926: 234–5)

This attention to ancestors' social status appears to be modeled after Goddard's (1912) *The Kallikak Family*, which traces the genealogy of a "feebleminded" family by documenting members' long history of social and occupational failure. Efforts to connect intellectual capacity to income and social class are fully compatible with, and implicitly supported by, a culture which views financial success as a general indicator of worth. According to Douglas, a linkage between poverty and general moral devaluation underlies upper-middle-class language, "where the very means of saying that someone is both poor and virtuous – that is, 'poor but virtuous' – involves the presumption that one must normally . . . expect the poor to be wicked, since this 'but' implies a contradiction in normal expectation" (1970: 7).

Other Virtues

If upper-middle-class status represents general moral elevation, then the gifted, as the repository of these idealizations, can be expected to be superior in every area of human worth. Accordingly, they should be cognitively, as well as morally and spiritually superior. Goddard's exchange with a gifted education teacher confirms these beliefs. When asked how she disciplined her students, she responded incredulously, "Discipline, what do you mean by discipline?" Goddard attempted to clarify:

Q: Why punishment – what kind of punishment do you use?
A: Oh, we don't use any.
Q: Well, what do you do with the children who are bad?
A: Why, they are never bad.
Q: Oh, I mean when they are disobedient or don't do their work.
A: But there is no such thing in these classes. There is no such thing as not doing their work. (1928: 81)

The Protestant "valuation of restless, continuous, systematic work . . . as the highest means to asceticism, and at the same time the surest and most evident proof of rebirth and genuine faith" (Weber 1930: 172) is everywhere evident in scholars' descriptions of gifted children. From the earliest days of the movement, gifted children were characterized as tireless, obsessive, driven: at 7 years of age, D. was typing and editing his own newspaper (Hollingworth 1926: 244). "By her eighth birthday, Betty had read approximately seven hundred books, many of them twice" (Hollingworth 1926: 226). At the age of 5, R.W. was taking four violin lessons per week and practiced three to four hours daily (Stedman 1924: 25). At 3, K.D. made all her dolls' clothes (Stedman 1924: 52). At 6, H.H. kept his family's accounts and made out the bills (Terman 1919: 237). When L.M. was 10 he ran a lending library for the neighborhood children; his "interests take in the whole world; prohibition, Red Cross, Y.M.C.A., Boy Scouts, Athletics. Gives morality talks to anyone he thinks in need of them. Walks miles distributing literature for all the 'drives'" (1919: 213).

In Goddard's text, the gifted are paragons of classroom comportment. Each child appears cooperative yet self-reliant, independent but not self-centered:

> He doesn't ask, "May I get a pencil?" He goes and gets it, or a piece of paper or a book. If on his way to get the book he sees something that interests him and he stops to look at it, no one shouts at him to take his seat. If something strikes him as being funny, he laughs and no one reproves him unless he laughs unbecomingly loud, in which case very likely another child says, "William, I shouldn't laugh so loud as that; it isn't polite." And William accepts the reproof good-naturedly and has learned another lesson. (1928: 76)

Because our society regards "masculinity" as a primary virtue for boys, evidence that gifted boys are more masculine provides further support for the reality of giftedness. Terman (1925: 413) shows that gifted boys are not only more likely to be white, and upper middle class, their "Masculinity Index" is significantly higher. He provides statistics showing that gifted boys are less likely to play with dolls or "play dress up" (1925: 401), and are only one-fourth as likely to consider going into domestic and personal service occupations as nongifted boys.

Reflecting what Berger and Luckmann (1967: 64) call our "built-in need" to integrate meanings, to see the different dimensions of our experience as elements of a consistent whole, we expect virtue to be displayed in an orderly, coherent fashion. We expect people who excel in one way to excel in all ways. Thus, descriptions of the feebleminded as people born to every manner of vice, and the gifted as people born to every manner of goodness, "make sense" in terms of our expectation that phenomena hang together, that they "appear... in coherent arrangements of well-circumscribed objects having determinate properties" (Schutz and Luckmann 1973: 4). By demonstrating the congruence of the various details composing giftedness, it is transformed from a "mere congery of particulars" into a determinate ensemble (Pollner 1987: 34). For this reason, the most influential texts establishing giftedness are those showing the correlation of cognitive excellence with other human virtues.

Documenting Giftedness

To demonstrate the positive correlation among capacities, Hollingworth and Terman documented gifted children's superiority in a wide range of areas, including musical talent, artistic and mechanical ability, mental health, character, leadership, ambition, and discipline. In addition, Hollingworth (1926) devoted an entire chapter and Terman (1925) three chapters to displaying gifted children's superior physical and athletic endowments. Although both volumes provide an abundance of detail, Terman's is especially distinctive in this regard. To give one illustration, not only is the development of gifted children's pubic hair compared to that of the nongifted, subcategories are given for children with kinky and straight hair. In keeping with the anticipated pattern of gifted children's early maturation, they are shown to acquire pubic hair earlier than the nongifted regardless of their hair type (Terman 1925: 207). This heaping up of detail creates a sense of the inevitability of giftedness, its omniscience and prominence. Through these means, giftedness becomes a "master status" (Hughes 1945), a characteristic that can always be counted on to set the identified child apart from others.

Since truth is understood in opposition to myth, Goddard establishes the truth of giftedness by continually emphasizing the mythic foundations of beliefs opposing giftedness. For instance, he claims that many consider the gifted "conceited little prigs," but quickly points out that the gifted are more humble than ordinary children: "The narrowly conceited person who is snobbish and intolerant is not the person of ability" (1928: 26). According to Goddard, many say the gifted are flighty; "they cannot stick to anything that requires hard work" (1928: 24). However, Goddard warns that such a belief is not only unjust and untrue, it "is often expressive of jealousy" and "let anyone who thinks that gifted children have no perseverance watch one of them working on a program of his own" (1928: 25). Many are inclined to imagine the gifted are bookish, says Goddard, "that they are interested in little except reading" (1928: 92). But this too is false. "These children quickly become interested in mechanics, manual training, physical culture, music, foreign language, typewriting, nature study, art, anything which is within the reach of their mentality and which is presented to them in the right way" (1928: 92).

Hollingworth also rhetorically contrasts myth and fact. Recurrent differentiation between folk versions of reality and "scientifically proven assessments" creates the impression that experts' versions of gifted children are sophisticated, nonideological, and independent of any cultural stereotype. Above all, it creates the impression that any version of giftedness except that offered by Hollingworth and other scientists is capricious, arbitrary, and false (cf. Goode 1969). To illustrate, Hollingworth begins her chapter on "Physique and Movement" by noting:

> There is a current belief that very bright children are likely to be puny, weak, and undersized. It is supposed that the brain is active at the expense of the body, and that health is liable to deterioration in consequence. Thus the scholar has come down to us in poetry "sicklied o'er with the pale cast of thought." When the cartoonist wishes to portray the bright child, he draws a species of monstrosity, with large head, spindle legs, and a facial expression of deep melancholy. (1926: 78)

The remainder of Hollingworth's chapter is devoted to demolishing this imagery by showing that "objective" tests reveal gifted children as prodigiously large, strong, healthy, speedy, well proportioned, and well coordinated.

Photographs are used not only to demonstrate gifted children's size and physical capacities, but, more generally, to underscore their realness as a class of people, to embody their goodness, and to create the appearance of linkage between social class and intellectual endowment. Through the "retrospective illusion" whereby the impressions given by sense perceptions are felt to represent something with a reality all its own (Merleau-Ponty 1964: xiii), pictures permit observers to experience gifted children as part of a real world "out there" rather than an image existing only in the mind. For example, the photographs in Hollingworth's book display the gifted as extremely well-dressed, smiling, attractive children. This is also true of Goddard's (1928) book where photographs show smiling, comely children – the boys almost always dressed in white shirt and tie – standing next to their science projects or reading books, as if demonstrating their giftedness. One shows a group of children doing a variety of activities such as painting, typing, sewing, reading, and electronics work. The caption reads: "A high I.Q. class of children from first, second, and third grades. The children are not posing; this is a normal scene" (1928: 61). Perhaps the apotheosis of gifted child imagery is contained in the second volume of Terman's *Genetic Studies of Genius* (Cox 1926), a retrospective analysis of gifted children from earlier times. Across from the title page, a portrait appears of a prepubescent youth closely resembling Gainsborough's *Blue Boy* in silken attire with idealized facial beauty.

By contrast, the feebleminded displayed in textbooks during the first decades of the century are posed as if in mug shots, in side by side profile and full-faced photographs, their arms rigidly at their sides, wearing overalls and other cheap garments. On the whole, they appear unsmiling, unkempt, and uncomfortable (e.g., Goddard 1914; Holmes 1912; Huey 1912; Tredgold 1915). Goddard's *The Kallikak Family* serves as the archetype for this negative imagery. These photographs not only show the feebleminded dressed in working-class outfits, posed beside or within shacks, farms, and institutions for defectives, their faces were retouched with heavy dark lines around the eyes, eyebrows, mouth, nose, and hair to make them appear ugly and sinister (Gould 1981: 171).

In the mid-1930s, Hollingworth even attempted to establish the superior beauty of gifted children by proving it scientifically. She had a panel of judges rate the faces, heads, and shoulders of 40 gifted adolescents in comparison to a group of ordinary adolescents. The results are reported as clear-cut: "The photographed faces of highly intelligent adolescents are more attractive (more beautiful) to adult judges than are those of adolescents who represent the average population of adolescents" (1935: 279). Terman (1954) and Goddard (1928) also found gifted children physically superior. According to Goddard:

> These groups of children are physically the best in the system. Mentally they are more alert, they think quicker, they are more observing, they can see relationships more promptly. They have more good habits and fewer detrimental ones. They have a better use of language.... They have more curiosity and more energy. They see the end from the beginning more promptly. In short, they 'live' better, using that term with its fullest significance. (1928: 35)

For her part, Hollingworth does not find gifted children inferior in any area; while they are no better than others in music, drawing, mechanical aptitude, and some physical activities, they are also no worse. Moreover, Hollingworth shows that some of this apparent equality reveals other dimensions of gifted children's superiority. For example, the fact that gifted children are equal to ordinary children in the standing broad jump is taken as evidence of "their superior neuromuscular energy" (Monahan and Hollingworth 1927: 95) since they weigh seven pounds more. While Hollingworth found the gifted to be more conforming than other children, she interprets this as an unmitigated virtue, related to superior intelligence: "They quickly learn that 'it pays' in emotional tranquility, personal security, and sense of duty done, to regard the attitudes of others, and to meet the responsibility fully and promptly regardless of inclinations" (1926: 124). Similarly, behavior which might indicate questionable emotional stability is seen only as evidence of advanced development. This is apparent in her story of a gifted 6-year-old boy who was heard to weep one night after being put to bed, which he explained by saying: "I was crying to think how awfully the North taxed the South during the Civil War." Hollingworth argues such grief "is not a manifestation of nervous instability. It results from uncommon insight or intelligence. The very intelligent seldom weep at what moves the average person, but they weep when the average person perceives nothing to call forth tears" (1926: 129).

Attention to emotional health and other noncognitive dimensions of giftedness establishes giftedness as an orderly, consistent arrangement of positive qualities. People are thereby encouraged to believe that positive qualities suffuse the gifted child's entire being, from physical health, size, and beauty to character, temperament, and interests. Because these qualities represent upper-middle-class idealizations which conform to and occur within that culture's "native tongue," they are recognized and understood by gifted child consumers. Moreover, because the work that was done to make gifted children appear beautiful, brave, selfless, well off, strong, stable, and philosophical is masked or hidden from view, gifted child consumers do not trace these qualities back to the experts who produced them. Through "reification" (Berger and Luckmann 1967: 89–92), these constructed images are attributed to the gifted children themselves as facts of nature, as innate, objective differences.

The next sections examine how contemporary gifted child discourse shifted from an explicit hereditarian framework and incorporated the rhetoric of inclusion, pluralism, cultural relativity, and cultural diversity. I argue, however, that these vocabularies were adopted for precisely the same reasons the gifted child movement was originally framed in the "native tongue." By clothing gifted child education in acceptable terminologies, challenges to the project could be assimilated to it, allowing the gifted movement to continue and prosper.

New Rhetorics

As already noted, overcrowding in urban public schools at the turn of the century created pressure to separate pupils into ability tracks. Persell (1977: 85–6) argues that this pressure was less a function of the sheer number of students in the school system than of their racial and cultural mix: the greater the representation of minority group students, the greater the utilization of separate educational tracks. Thus, when the need to incorporate large numbers of foreign immigrants subsided in the 1930s and 1940s, ability tracking fell into disuse. However, when southern blacks moved into northern cities in increasing numbers in the 1950s, along with influxes of Mexican Americans and Puerto Ricans, the popularity of ability tracking surged (Persell 1977: 85–6). Accordingly, while gifted child scholars trace the sudden growth of gifted education during the 1950s to the launch of Sputnik and the mounting sense of competition with the Soviet Union (Davis and Rimm 1989;

Tannenbaum 1979), there is another, unacknowledged explanation for the cyclical interest in gifted education. Since ability tracking is most common in economically and racially diverse school systems (Oakes 1985: 65–7), it may provide the silent mechanism by which some social groups receive superior educations.

The language used to defend and rationalize ability tracking has gone through a cycle of its own since the era of Terman and Hollingworth. After Nazi racial policies and practices became known, eugenics talk "dropped below the horizon in social science" (Degler 1991: 204). In the 1950s and 1960s, the legal end to the "separate but equal" concept of educational equity (Oakes 1985), and the growing realization of de facto segregation's persistence (Cremin 1988: 265) produced mounting pressure on gifted child scholars and other educators to abandon explicit references to race and class superiority. In large measure as a result of this pressure, contemporary scholars now portray giftedness as more heterogeneous, flexible, and broad-based than did their forebears. As the *Gifted Child Quarterly* recently editorialized, "Educational services for highly able and talented students must be determined according to a philosophy of inclusion – 'who will benefit at this time from these services?' – and not a philosophy of exclusion" (Dettmer 1991: 165–6). Contemporary scholars refer to the multidimensionality and variety of intelligences:

> "Multiple talent" and "multiple criteria" are almost bywords of the present day gifted student movement, and most educators would have little difficulty in accepting a definition that includes almost every area of human activity that manifests itself in a socially useful form. (Renzulli 1978: 181)

A particularly graphic illustration of the effort to portray contemporary gifted child education according to a "philosophy of inclusion" is "Taylor's Talent Totem Poles" (Taylor 1978). This widely reproduced figure (see Davis and Rimm 1989; Eby and Smutny 1990; Sisk 1987) consists of the cartoon faces of seven children stacked on top of each other, forming six columns or "totem poles." Each totem pole is labeled for a different ability (e.g., "academic," "creative," "planning," "communicating," "forecasting," and "decision-making"). The faces at the top of the totem poles have the biggest smiles, indicating the most ability, while those at the bottom of the poles have the biggest frowns, indicating lower ability. Since the child grinning atop one pole can be found grimacing at the bottom of a neighboring pole, the central message is that no child can accurately be described as generically superior or inferior to others. Depending on the context, every child is both gifted and nongifted.

Also in keeping with the new rhetoric of inclusion, gifted child scholars are now conspicuously committed to cultural pluralism. Contemporary textbooks routinely include a chapter devoted to this theme (e.g., Colangelo and Davis 1991; Davis and Rimm 1989; Eby and Smutny 1990; Feldhusen et al. 1989; Pendarvis et al. 1990; Sisk 1987) and journal articles display passionate concern for minority issues (see, for example, Smith et al. (1991) "Underrepresentation of Minority Students in Gifted Programs: Yes! It Matters!"). In one of the most detailed of these statements, 35 gifted child scholars maintained that cultural minorities must be empowered to determine what giftedness means to themselves (Maker and Schiever 1989). As an American Indian scholar put it, "Gifted and talented American Indian students are who we say they are" (George 1989: 112).

Still, what initially appears as an effort to redefine giftedness as something local and culture-specific, falls far short of the anticipated outcome. There are pleas for "culture fair" and "culture free" tests, and calls to adjust scores on "biased" measures to compensate for the minority child's social "disadvantages," but underneath is the older presumption that once giftedness is located, the identified children share a common attribute whether they are American Indian, black, Cantonese, or white upper middle class. Accordingly, a contributor to a collection edited by Maker and Schiever writes:

> Gifted and talented students, regardless of ethnic background, need to associate with each other to share their ideas and experiences.... Their chief cause of anxiety is feeling alone and different from other children because of different interests, higher ethical standards, and different concerns. (Kirschenbaum 1989: 94–5)

In effect, giftedness is still treated as a child's most defining status, overriding considerations of ethnicity, age, and culture.

To further illustrate the similarity between contemporary and nascent gifted child discourse, consider the four tables contained within the collection edited by Maker and Schiever (1989: 4, 78, 152, 210) which describe the cultural variables affecting giftedness among Hispanics, American Indians, African Americans, and Asians. The columns of these tables list "absolute aspects of giftedness," the cultural values of the relevant minority group, and the behavioral characteristics of that minority group. Consistent with the rhetoric of Hollingworth and Terman, not only do these tables display giftedness as existing in a pure or "absolute" way, the characteristics of minority groups are displayed as often conflicting with these ideals. For example, "absolute" giftedness is described in unremittingly positive terms as: "high expectations of self," "ability to generate original ideas and solutions," "high level of language development," "extraordinary quantity of information," "idealism, a sense of justice, and advanced levels of moral judgment," and "emotional depth and intensity." By contrast, the language used to describe the values and behaviors of minority group members often reflects strikingly different, negative stereotypes. Black culture and children (1989: 210), for example, are characterized by terms such as "conformity," "manipulative behavior," "immediate or short-term gratification," "mastery of minimum academic skills," "physical punishment, blunt orders rather than discussion," "parental pressure conduct oriented, rather than task oriented," "acting out," "compliant behavior," and "leadership in street gangs."

Nothing's Changed

If giftedness in its "absolute" form is expected to be highly original and idealistic, and blacks are expected to be conforming and oriented to immediate or short-term gratification, the unstated implication is that blackness and giftedness exist in opposition to one another. This is not to imply that black people are inherently less gifted. In fact, contemporary gifted child scholars repeatedly reject this presumption. It is to say, rather, that black culture opposes giftedness, that it is an obstacle or disadvantage to the realization of giftedness in the black child. In the words of a gifted child scholar:

> Although gifted and talented students can be found in all walks of life and in all racial and ethnic groups, they are more likely to be found in some groups than others. The groups with high incidence of the gifted place a great emphasis on intellectual values and have more extensive opportunities to develop talents and skills already present in the child. (Gallagher, quoted in Greenlaw and McIntosh 1988: 50)

It is recognized that gifted children are born into families of cultural minorities, but it is assumed that these families cannot encourage or nurture their potentiality. Accordingly, Davis and Rimm reason that "gifted black children may perform only at an average level in school because of socioeconomic, language, motivational, personal, or cultural handicaps" (1985: 272). The implicit message is that black children can realize the full potentiality of their giftedness by distancing themselves from their culture of origin and assimilating to the dominant culture, a meaning encapsulated by the label "the disadvantaged gifted" (Van Tassel-Baska 1989; also see Clark 1983: 337).[5]

Contemporary gifted child scholars typify the need for "disadvantaged" gifted children to distance themselves from their cultures of origin through cautionary tales in which gifted children appear "held back" by the values and traditions of their ethnic groups. For example, Clark shares the story of Rosa, a Mexican-American girl whose father refused to let her accept a scholarship to Stanford because unmarried women should not go away from home. The story ends with Rosa, "who loved her family and loved the marvelous ability of her mind ... [being] forced to give up one to have the other" (1983: 337).

An interesting feature of the new emphasis on cultural inclusiveness is that it provides the appearance of radical change, of an effort to open gifted child education to those who have been traditionally excluded, without compromising the original core beliefs about giftedness. Because the potential for giftedness within the white upper classes is never questioned, while the potential for giftedness within minority groups is, the traditional biases of gifted education remain intact.

To illustrate further, Khatena provides a list of "descriptors for children affected by cultural diversity," that include such negatives as: "inability to trust or consider 'beauty in life,'" "outer locus of control rather than inner locus of control," "inability to attend to task without supervision," "lack of training and development," "anger and frustration increase animalistic desire to survive," and "a need to use subterfuge in environment to get message across" (1982: 247–9). Similarly, Clark describes "Japanese, Chinese, and other Asians" as strongly valuing "conformity, which inhibits creative activity or divergent thinking"; having a "quiet manner, which may foster unrealistic expectations and inappropriate assessments"; and exhibiting an "attitude of perfectionism, making using mistakes as learning experiences quite difficult." Jews are described as being "often overly competitive," manifesting a "perfectionistic attitude that causes tension and frustration in learning new material," with "pressure to achieve from family sometimes excessive, especially with males." Blacks are said to have "limited experience with varied or extended language patterns." And Mexican Americans are characterized by attitudes "depreciating education for family after high school," and "that differ on basic time, space reality" (1983: 339–40).

These negative descriptions stand in sharp contrast to the praise and wonder continually heaped on the gifted. While scholars emphasize various gifted child virtues, the specifics of each virtue seem insignificant against the totality and sheer number of virtues attributed to gifted children. Taken as a whole, these descriptors make gifted children appear divinely, quintessentially praiseworthy; they:

1 Are curious
2 Have a large vocabulary
3 Have long memories
4 Sometimes learn to read alone
5 Have a keen sense of time
6 Are persistent
7 Like to collect things
8 Are independent
9 Are healthy and well coordinated, but some may be delicate
10 May be bigger and stronger than average
11 Sustain interest in one or more fields over the years
12 Initiate their own activities
13 Develop earlier, sitting up, walking, talking
14 Learn easily
15 Have a keen sense of humor
16 Enjoy complicated games
17 Are creative and imaginative
18 Are interested and concerned about world problems
19 Analyze themselves, are often self-critical
20 Like older children when very young
21 Are original
22 Set high goals and ideals
23 Are leaders
24 Have talent(s) in art, music, writing, drama, dance
25 Use scientific methods of research
26 See relationships and draw sound generalizations
27 Produce work which is fresh, vital, and unique
28 Create new ideas, substances, and processes
29 Invent and build new mechanical devices
30 Often run counter to tradition
31 Continually question the status quo
32 Do the unexpected
33 Apply learning from one situation to different ones
34 Problem solve on a superior level, divergently, innovatively
35 May appear different
36 Enjoy reading, especially biography and autobiography.
    (Tuttle and Becker 1983: 34)

Gifted children are portrayed as specializing not only in cognitive and academic areas, but in everything. Thus, for Eby and Smutny, a "young gifted child" not only "learns rapidly," "is attentive, alert," and "highly imaginative," but also "is looked to by others for ideas and decisions," "is chosen first by peers," "easily repeats rhythm patterns," "makes up original tunes," "takes art activities seriously and derives satisfaction from them," and "shows mature sense of humor for age" (1990: 154–5).

Since, according to Pollner, "mundane inquiry constitutes itself and its world by remaining oblivious to its constitutive work, and part of that constitutive work includes that very obliviousness," the cultural presuppositions underlying these attributions are never examined (1987: 167). This obliviousness makes it possible for an educator to suggest that gifted children should visit brokerage firms, read the *Wall Street Journal*, and purchase stock, preferably a variety which pays a quarterly dividend so "the dividend can be added to the child's bank account four times a year" (Kanigher 1977: 50). Through this same obliviousness, another educator shows that the gifted might explore "the range and scope of a concept such as *heroes*" through exemplars in which the male "hero" is described as "blue-eyed and blond," and in which women appear only as "fair damsels" or as a wife who fixes the hero's breakfast and receives his grateful kiss (Gallagher 1985: 218–19). Similarly, after almost a decade of publishing pictures of neatly dressed white children demonstrating their giftedness by smiling into test tubes or making notations on "award winning compositions," the *Gifted Child Quarterly* finally published a picture of an African American in 1967. However, the African-American male appearing in this photograph was not portrayed as gifted, but as the subject of a photographic essay on hippies. The writing beside his photograph (in which he grasped a "Haight Ashbury" sign) referred to the "pity rather than contempt" that should be directed toward hippies (Ransohoff 1967: 181). The next photograph of an African American to appear in the *Gifted Child Quarterly* was titled "Disadvantaged gifted progress in new residential school" (vol. 12(1) 1968: 18).

Over 40 percent of the cartoon figures represented in Delisle's (1987) text on the gifted are dark skinned; yet there are no accompanying references to African-American, Hispanic, or American Indian cultures. Instead, giftedness is displayed as an ideal of homogeneity and assimilation. Take, for example, these statements of gifted children's "plans for the future":

> I will go to high school, and for college, I will go to the University of Florida. Then I'll become a real estator or get involved in computers. I will get married and then go into retirement and Medicare. (Boy, 10)

> To either teach children that are mentally handicapped or (most probably) go to hospitals and dance and sing for them. (Girl, 9)

> I would like to be a professor or a scientist. I think I would like to create things that would help the world. It would also be interesting to pass on the information I have learned to others. (Boy, 10)

> 1 Go to college and graduate school.
> 2 Get married and find a well-paying job.
> 3 Help my children to become good people. (Girl, 10) (Delisle 1987: 104)

As was true 60 years ago, gifted children's career aspirations are explained, defended, and qualified in terms of upper middle-class vocabularies of motive. Male children are still most often displayed as future scientists, lawyers, and surgeons, and females plan to "dance and sing" at hospitals, and to "help [their] children to become good people." Similarly, when contemporary scholars provide examples of gifted children's "exact" thinking, they do not use culturally neutral language. Like gifted child scholars from the 1920s, they call upon the vocabularies, values, and institutions of upper middle-class experience. Consider, for example, the dialogue offered by one scholar to demonstrate the thinking of highly gifted children:

The Boy: Do you always talk in such a strange manner?
Dr Levy: What do you mean?
The Boy: Well, your vocabulary is so limited. I thought you were on the faculty of the University of Pennsylvania.
Dr Levy: I thought you were a 4-year-old boy!
The Boy: I would prefer that you would talk to me as if I were a person. (Silverman 1989: 75)

Kaplan recommends that gifted children be enjoined to use phrases such as "Another point of view might be," "The accumulated evidence indicates that" "The issue germane or central to the point seems to value" and "The assumption proposed appears to be that" (1989: 173). The upper middle-class origins of these terms are not acknowledged; instead, this language is described as "the language of questioning, challenging, and verifying information," as if it existed apart from or transcended culture (1989: 173). Thus, expressed values and beliefs are not treated as human constructions representing one group's interests and visions. Giftedness and its features are treated as natural phenomena, as attributes existing independent of time, setting, and culture. Consider the following examples.

The *Gifted Child Quarterly* published 32 papers from 1988 through 1991 that used samples of children specifically described as "gifted," though the children came from different gifted child programs with different admission criteria (one used standardized achievement tests; eight were guided by IQ scores; the remaining sixteen programs used differing combinations of criteria such as IQ, achievement test scores, survey instruments, grades, class rank, references, and nominations). No concern was expressed over the fact that the children were enrolled in very different programs (including general "enrichment courses," "accelerated" classes, and specialized topical summer programs), that they came from different socioeconomic or cultural backgrounds, and were nominated to and accepted by these programs on the basis of highly discrepant information. Thus, despite researchers' stated beliefs about the heterogeneity and variety of intelligences and the cultural specificity of giftedness, empirical studies portray giftedness as a dichotomous variable that exists independently of the conditions of its discovery and occurrence. In other words, something with specific cultural origins is treated as the self-same thing over all past and prospective conditions.

Not only are gifted child samples treated as homogeneous, but findings are regarded as comparable regardless of the measures and procedures employed. In keeping with, and supporting, a model of continuous, linear development of knowledge, studies on the gifted are presented as increasingly refined portraits building on predecessors' works and observations which are treated as transcultural. To illustrate, a recent study (Wooding and Bingham 1988) examined 30 students enrolled in a Canadian junior high for the gifted to determine responses to a stressor. The gifted subjects were found to manage stress more efficiently and to recover sooner than a matched sample of nongifted children. The investigators portrayed these findings as comparable to, and supportive of, a host of other gifted child studies (e.g., Ludwig and Cullinan 1984; Reynolds and Bradley 1983; Terman 1925, 1954; Terman and Oden 1940, 1947, 1951) which utilized samples drawn from different countries, eras, and age groups, and based on different selection criteria. For example, the gifted children in Ludwig and Cullinan's study came from a Chicago suburb, were in grades 1–5, and were not in a school for the gifted, but in a pullout enrichment class. While the Canadian gifted were selected solely on the basis of IQ, the Chicago group was selected by six criteria, including "teacher referral," "general classroom functioning," and "ability to complete tasks." These groups were described as comparable though no effort was made to assess differences in race, social class, or culture. Through these means, gifted children's other characteristics fade into the background; giftedness operates as a child's central, or only, feature worth noting.

There are perhaps no better examples of scholars treating giftedness as a transcultural fact than the three books, *On Being Gifted* (American Association of Gifted Children 1978), *Gifted Children Speak Out* (Delisle 1984), and *Gifted Kids Speak Out* (Delisle 1987), devoted to children's comments about their giftedness. Although these books comprise hundreds of interviews of gifted children, the authors make no effort to place them in a cultural context, or to explain how these children came to be identified as gifted. Their giftedness is treated as nonconditional, as part of "that universal and publick Manuscript that lies expansed unto the eyes of all" (from Sir Thomas Browne, quoted in Woodbridge 1940: 3). Like Santayana's reference to "the stars, the seasons, the swarm of animals, the spectacle of birth and death," their giftedness is treated as something self-evidently seen and known, as "the facts before every man's eyes" (1924: x).

What gifted child scholars specifically exclude from inquiry is how children are found to serve as objects of gifted child research. They treat gifted children as an a priori facticity, as if they, gifted child scholars, had nothing to do with their existence. Through the "retrospective illusion" (Merleau-Ponty 1964), gifted child scholars and the consumers of their reports treat the object of perception as if it was the preexistent cause of perception; in so doing, they gloss the contingent character of what is perceived. The artifacts of giftedness (labeled children, gifted child programs, parent support groups, journals, books, institutes, etc.) help to obscure scholars' and others' essential contribution to giftedness. Having forgotten these contributions, scholars can carry on their activities as the authors of giftedness.

Positive Social Control

This paper's analysis has located the meaning of giftedness not in some special class of children, nor in experts' writings on giftedness, but, rather, in the intersection of experts' arguments and readers' understandings. Gifted child experts from the first decades of the century offered their readers a definition of giftedness which made sense within a particular cultural context. They took an unknown class of people (gifted children), and systematically related them to an associated but known class of people – members of the white upper middle class (cf. Strauss 1959). Since being gifted, upper middle class, and white imply "superior" status, the linking of these concepts appeared reasonable, particularly given that gifted child consumers were and are themselves upper middle class and white. The image of the gifted as the embodiment of goodness received widespread recognition at the same time that the feebleminded were increasingly perceived as the embodiment of social evil; together these images articulated the polar extremes of a moral order which assigns worth to all human characteristics, particularly social class and race.

Accepting these archetypes not only allowed gifted child scholars to recognize cognitively superior children, it changed the meaning of being upper middle class and white. Upper middle-class career choices, interests, and motivations, through their identification with giftedness, became sanctified. By portraying giftedness as a phenomenon of social class and race, experts provided legitimacy through scientific argument to a difference which had previously only been asserted. Gifted child discourse from the first decades of the century inadvertently supported people's general belief in the naturalness, sacredness, and correctness of white upper middle-class dominance.

For Foucault, the power of "positive" social control comes from its seamlessness, its invisibility, and ubiquitousness: "The judges of normality are everywhere. We are in the society of the teacher-judge, the doctor-judge, the educator-judge, the 'social-worker' judge; it is on them that the universal reign of the normative is based" (1977: 304). While harassment, defamation, and assault are easily named as repressive, efforts to identify people's strengths, to provide support and "advantages," appear irreproachable. It goes without saying that programs aimed at recognizing children's "gifts" are not comfortably classed with programs explicitly aimed at exerting hierarchical control and domination. The difficulty of making positive social control accountable explains its effectiveness: its capacity to quietly infiltrate democratic, egalitarian discourse and its ability to permeate modern social experience. It also explains why there is a well-developed literature on the social construction of retardation (e.g., Bogdan and Taylor 1982; Ferguson 1987; Mercer 1965, 1973; Smith 1985) without a comparable literature on the gifted.

To this day, criticisms of IQ testing almost always focus on the negative expectation created, and the identification of members of some cultural groups as slow, not on the identification of members of other groups as fast (e.g., Aguirre 1979; Beeghley and Butler 1974; Gould 1981; Mensh and Mensh 1991). Thus, when a federal district judge in California declared IQ tests invalid in 1979, it was because a disproportionately large percentage of black children had been assigned to classes for the "educable mentally retarded," not because a disproportionately small percentage of black children had been assigned to classes for the gifted.[6] Similarly, Gould's (1981) outrage in *The Mismeasure of Man* was aimed at psychologists and educators from the first decades of the century for coining negative terms such as: "feeble-minded," "high-grade defective," "moron," etc.; however, no mention was made of the selective use of positive terms such as "gifted." Despite widespread questioning in the academic literature of the various methods used to conceptualize, describe, and identify human intelligence, and despite the markedly unbalanced racial and ethnic composition of gifted child educational programming, use of the term "gifted" remains relatively immune to criticism.[7] For example, among the 408 reference sources listed by Aby (1990) on the "IQ Debate," only 3 are indexed under the topic heading "gifted children," 16 are indexed under "mental retardation and race," and no reference sources are listed (and, indeed, no topic heading is given) for "gifted children and race."

This selective attention cannot, of course, fully explain the continuing underrepresentation of blacks, Hispanics, American Indians, and other ethnic minorities in gifted education. However, it may partially explain why this underrepresentation is so resistant to change. Presumably any imagery which obscures and conceals the connection between giftedness and exclusionary ideology makes such a connection more difficult to address and discredit. Ironically, then, those elements of contemporary discourse which make gifted child programming *appear* democratic and integrated mystify efforts to identify the reasons such programs are *not* democratic and integrated. To exemplify, as in the days of Hollingworth and Goddard, contemporary textbooks on gifted children are illustrated with photographs of the gifted. However, unlike texts from the 1920s, a large number of the children represented in these photographs are of African-American descent (e.g., Davis and Rimm 1985; Eby and Smutny 1990; Kitano and Kirby 1986; Sisk 1987). While this display of "inclusiveness" may have a democratic intent – to create the expectation that groups long underrepresented in gifted child programs belong in and are welcomed by such programs – there is a second, unintended consequence. Since this positive imagery masks existing discrimination, that discrimination goes unchallenged.

By portraying gifted education as integrated or aspiring toward integration, responsibility for social control is concealed. Instead, the underrepresentation of minorities is attributed to factors located outside of, or peripheral to, gifted education itself. Most commonly, it is attributed to those who are excluded, to their "real learning deficits, not just hidden talents" (Tannenbaum 1990: 120). It is also attributed to the families of the excluded: "These children often come from families with low socioeconomic status and/or educational orientation. Typically these families provide little stimulation of higher level thinking skills through conversation, books, travel, shared problem solving, and educational activities" (Whitmore 1987: 147). Responsibility is attributed as well to "our schools, our attitudes, our values" (Zappia 1989: 26), to "minority children slipping through the cracks of a blind system" (Eby and Smutny 1990: 120), to the "social and cultural biases in standardized tests" (Richert 1987: 151), and to "insensitive" and "biased" teachers (Minner 1990: 37). What is conspicuously absent, however, is the suggestion that our very understanding of giftedness – the ways we study, validate, recognize, and describe this phenomenon – reflects and supports discrimination.

Many aspects of the relations between gifted child discourse and social control have changed over time. In the current climate it is impossible for a scholar to write, "The immemorial division of mankind into 'lower,' 'middle,' and 'upper' classes, economically speaking, rests on a biological foundation which guarantees the stubborn permanence with which it persists in spite of all efforts to abolish it by artifice" (Hollingworth 1926: 360). Yet the field of gifted child education which reiteratively displays its commitment to cultural pluralism continues to exclude minorities. This paper suggests that some discrimination may be traced to the cultural presuppositions underlying gifted child scholarship.

Notes

1 *Gifted Child Quarterly, Journal for the Education of the Gifted, Gifted Child Today, Gifted Education International, Roeper Review, Creativity Research Journal, Exceptional Children.*
2 The earliest use of the term "gifted child" I can find is in Van Sickle (1910: 357–66).
3 I concentrated on Leta Hollingworth and Lewis Terman because they are widely recognized as the "mother" and "father" of the gifted child movement (Davis and Rimm 1989: 6). While Henry Goddard is noted more for his writings on "feeblemindedness" than "gifted-ness," he was highlighted in this essay to emphasize the linkage between these discourses.

   There is an extraordinary volume and range of materials on gifted children. For example, as early as the 1920s (Henry 1924), the National Society for the Study of Education published a "Bibliography on Gifted Children" with 453 entries. To gain an overview of this literature's themes, origins, continuities and discontinuities, I examined all the citations under "gifted children" and "child prodigies" in the *New York Times Index* from the late nineteenth century to the present. I also went through all the issues of the *Journal of Educational Psychology* (from 1910 through the 1930s), and the leading gifted child journals, including the *Gifted Child Quarterly* and *Exceptional Children* (from the first volumes to 1993).
4 Hollingworth introduced the passage as follows: "The traits of character most frequently ascribed to C by those who know him well are honesty, reliability, bravery, loyalty, and precision. He is a stickler for the exact. No statement is right unless it is exactly right" (1926: 257).
5 Among American Indian students identified as gifted in Oklahoma, only 9 percent are listed as either full or three-fourths American Indian. By contrast, 68 percent of American Indian students identified as gifted have less than one-fourth American Indian blood (Maker and Schiever 1989: 81). This suggests that giftedness is recognized in relation to assimilation to the dominant culture.
6 *Larry P. v. Riles*, 495 F. Supp. 926 (1979).
7 Bettelheim (1958) may be the most prominent exception to this pattern.

References

Aby, Stephen H. 1990. *The IQ Debate: A Selective Guide to the Literature*. New York: Greenwood Press.

Aguirre, Adalberto. 1979. "Intelligence testing and Chicanos: A quality of life issue." *Social Problems* 27: 186–95.

American Association for Gifted Children. 1978. *On Being Gifted*. New York: Walker.

Ayres, Leonard P. 1909. *Laggards in Our Schools: A Study of Retardation and Elimination in City School Systems*. New York: Charities Publication Committee.

Beeghley, Leonard and Butler, Edgar W. 1974. "The consequences of intelligence testing in public schools before and after desegregation." *Social Problems* 21: 740–54.

Berger, Peter and Luckmann, Thomas. 1967. *The Social Construction of Reality*. Garden City, NY: Anchor Books.

Best, Joel. 1987. "Rhetoric in claims-making: Constructing the missing children problem." *Social Problems* 34: 101–21.

Best, Joel (ed.) 1989. *Images of Issues: Typifying Contemporary Social Problems*. New York: Aldine de Gruyter.

Bettelheim, Bruno. 1958. "Sputnik and segregation." *Commentary* 26 (October): 332–9.

Blumer, Herbert. 1971. "Social problems as collective behavior." *Social Problems* 18: 298–306.

Bogdan, Robert and Taylor, Steven. 1982. *Inside Out: The Social Meaning of Mental Retardation*. Toronto: University of Toronto.

Bowles, Samuel and Gintis, Herbert. 1976. *Schooling in Capitalist America: Educational Reform and the Contradictions of Economic Life*. New York: Basic Books.

Chapman, Paul Davis. 1988. *Schools as Sorters: Lewis M. Terman, Applied Psychology, and the Intelligence Testing Movement, 1890–1930*. New York: New York University Press.

Clark, Barbara. 1983. *Growing Up Gifted*. Columbus, Oh.: Charles E. Merrill.

Cohen, Stanley. 1985. *Visions of Social Control*. Cambridge: Polity Press.

Colangelo, Nicholas and Davis, Gary A. 1991. *Handbook of Gifted Children*. Boston: Allyn and Bacon.

Cooper, Harris M. and Good, Thomas L. 1983. *Pygmalion Grows Up*. New York: Longman.

Cox, Catherine Morris. 1926. *Genetic Studies of Genius: The Early Mental Traits of Three Hundred Geniuses*, vol. 2. Palo Alto, Calif.: Stanford University Press.

Coy, Genevieve L. 1918. "The mentality of a gifted child." *Journal of Applied Psychology* 2: 299–307.

Cremin, Lawrence A. 1988. *American Education. The Metropolitan Experience 1876–1980*. New York: Harper and Row.

Current Literature. 1910. "The boy prodigy of Harvard." 68 (March): 291–3.

Davis, Gary A. and Rimm, Sylvia B. 1985. *Education of the Gifted and Talented*. Englewood Cliffs, NJ: Prentice-Hall.

——,—— 1989. *Education of the Gifted and Talented*, 3rd edn. Englewood Cliffs, NJ: Prentice-Hall.

Degler, Carl N. 1991. *In Search of Human Nature: The Decline and Revival of Darwinism in American Social Thought*. New York: Oxford University Press.

Delisle, James R. 1984. *Gifted Children Speak Out*. New York: Walker.

—— 1987. *Gifted Kids Speak Out*. Minneapolis, Minn.: Free Spirit.

Dettmer, Peggy. 1991. "Gifted program advocacy: Overhauling bandwagons to build support." *Gifted Child Quarterly* 35: 165–71.

Douglas, Jack D. 1970. "Deviance and respectability: The social construction of moral meanings." In J. D. Douglas (ed.) *Deviance and Respectability*. New York: Basic Books, pp. 3–30.

Eby, Judy W. and Smutny, Joan F. 1990. *A Thoughtful Overview of Gifted Education*. New York: Longman.

Feldhusen, John, Van Tassel-Baska, Joyce, and Seeley, Ken. 1989. *Excellence in Educating the Gifted*. Denver: Love.

Ferguson, Phillip M. 1987. "The social construction of mental retardation." *Social Policy* 18: 51–6.

Foucault, Michel. 1965. *Madness and Civilization*. New York: Random House.

—— 1973. *The Birth of the Clinic*. New York: Pantheon.

—— 1977. *Discipline and Punish*. New York: Pantheon.

—— 1980. *Power/Knowledge*. New York: Pantheon.

Gallagher, James J. 1985. *Teaching the Gifted Child*. Boston: Allyn and Bacon.

Galton, Francis. 1869. *Hereditary Genius*. London: Macmillan.

—— 1883. *Inquiries into Human Faculty and its Development*. London: Macmillan.

—— 1889. *Natural Inheritance*. London: Macmillan.

Garfinkel, Harold. 1967. *Studies in Ethnomethodology*. Englewood Cliffs, NJ: Prentice-Hall.

George, R. Karlene. 1989. "Imagining and defining giftedness." In C. June Maker and Shirley W. Schiever (eds.) *Critical Issues in Gifted Education: Defensible Programs for Cultural and Ethnic Minorities*. Austin, Tex.: Pro-ed, pp. 107–12.

Goddard, Henry H. 1912. *The Kallikak Family: A Study in the Heredity of Feeble-mindedness*. New York: Macmillan.

—— 1914. *School Training of Defective Children*. Yonkers-on-Hudson, NY: World Book Co.

—— 1928. *School Training of Gifted Children*. Chicago: World Book Co.

Goode, Erich. 1969. "Marijuana and the politics of reality." *Journal of Health and Social Behavior* 10: 83–94.

Gould, Stephen Jay. 1981. *The Mismeasure of Man*. New York: Norton.

Greenlaw, Jean M. and McIntosh, Margaret E. 1988. *Educating the Gifted*. Chicago: American Library Association.

Gross, Bertram M. 1970. "Friendly fascism: A model for America." *Social Policy* 1 (November/December): 44–52.

Gusfield, Joseph R. 1981. *The Culture of Public Problems: Drinking-Driving and the Symbolic Order*. Chicago: University of Chicago Press.

Henry, Theodore S. 1924. "Annotated bibliography on gifted children and their education." In Guy M. Whipple (ed.) *Twenty-Third Yearbook of The National Society for the Study of Education*. Bloomington, Ill.: Public School Publishing Co, pp. 389–443.

Hilbert, Richard A. 1987. "Bureaucracy as belief, rationalization as repair: Max Weber in a post-functionalist age." *Sociological Theory* 5: 70–86.

—— 1990. "Ethnomethodology and the micro-macro order." *American Sociological Review* 55: 794–808.

Hofstadter, Richard. 1959. *Social Darwinism in American Thought*. New York: George Braziller.

Hollingworth, Leta S. 1926. *Gifted Children: Their Nature and Nurture*. New York: Macmillan.

—— 1935. "The comparative beauty of the faces of highly intelligent adolescents." *Journal of Genetic Psychology* 47: 268–81.

Holmes, Arthur. 1912. *The Conservation of the Child*. Philadelphia: Lippincott.

Huey, Edmund Burk. 1912. *Backward and Feeble-minded Children*. Baltimore: Warwick and York.

Hughes, Everett C. 1945. "Dilemmas and contradictions of status." *American Journal of Sociology* 50: 353–9.

Kanigher, Herbert. 1977. *Everyday Enrichment for Gifted Children at Home and School*. Los Angeles: National/State Leadership Training Institute on the Gifted and Talented.

Kaplan, Sandra N. 1989. "Language arts for gifted learners." In Roberta M. Milgram (ed.) *Teaching Gifted and Talented Learners in Regular Classrooms*. Springfield, Ill.: Charles C. Thomas, pp. 169–78.

Khatena, Joe. 1982. *Educational Psychology of the Gifted*. New York: Wiley.

Kirschenbaum, Robert J. 1989. "Identification of the gifted and talented American Indian student." In C. June Maker and Shirley W. Schiever (eds.) *Critical Issues in Gifted Education: Defensible Programs for Cultural and Ethnic Minorities*. Austin, Tex.: Pro-ed, pp. 91–101.

Kitano, Margie K. and Kirby, Darrell F. 1986. *Gifted Education: A Comprehensive View*. Boston: Little, Brown.

Lawler, James M. 1978. *IQ, Heritability, and Racism*. New York: International.

Ludwig, G. and Cullinan, D. 1984. "Behavior problems of gifted and nongifted elementary school girls and boys." *Gifted Child Quarterly* 28: 37–43.

Maker, C. June and Schiever, Shirley W. (eds.), 1989. *Critical Issues in Gifted Education: Defensible Programs for Cultural and Ethnic Minorities*. Austin, Tex.: Pro-ed.

Mensh, Elaine and Mensh, Harry. 1991. *The IQ Mythology: Class, Race, Gender, and Inequality*. Carbondale, Ill.: Southern Illinois University Press.

Mercer, Jane R. 1965. "Social system perspective and clinical perspective: Frames of reference for understanding career patterns of people labelled as mentally retarded." *Social Problems* 13: 18–34.

—— 1973. *Labeling the Retarded*. Berkeley, Calif.: University of California Press.

Merleau-Ponty, Maurice. 1964. *Signs*. Evanston, Ill.: Northwestern University Press.

Mills, C. Wright. 1940. "Situated actions and vocabularies of motive." *American Sociological Review* 5: 904–13.

Minner, Sam. 1990. "Teacher evaluations of case descriptions of LD gifted children." *Gifted Child Quarterly* 34: 37–9.

Monahan, Jane E. and Hollingworth, Leta S. 1927. "Neuromuscular capacity of children who test above 135 IQ (Stanford-Binet)." *Journal of Educational Psychology* 18: 88–96.

New York Times. 1988. "Study finds blacks twice as liable to school penalties as whites." 12 Dec.: A6.

North American Review. 1907. "An infant prodigy." 184: 887–8.

Oakes, Jeannie. 1985. *Keeping Track*. New Haven, Conn.: Yale University Press.

Pendarvis, Edwina D., Howley, Aimee A., and Howley, Craig B. 1990. *The Abilities of Gifted Children*. Englewood Cliffs, NJ: Prentice-Hall.

Persell, Caroline Hodges. 1977. *Education and Inequality*. New York: Free Press.

Pollner, Melvin. 1987. *Mundane Reason*. Cambridge: Cambridge University Press.

Ransohoff, Daniel J. 1967. "The hippies." *Gifted Child Quarterly* 11: 178–81.

Renzulli, Joseph S. 1978. "What makes giftedness? Reexamining a definition." *Phi Delta Kappa* 60: 180–4, 261.

Reynolds, C. R. and Bradley, M. 1983. "Emotional stability of intellectually superior children versus nongifted peers as estimated by chronic anxiety levels." *School Psychology Review* 12: 190–4.

Richert, E. Susanne. 1987. "Rampant problems and promising practices in the identification of disadvantaged gifted students." *Gifted Child Quarterly* 31: 149–54.

Rodger, J. John. 1988. "Social work as social control re-examined: Beyond the dispersal of discipline thesis." *Sociology* 22: 563–81.

Rosenthal, Robert and Jacobson, Lenore 1968. *Pygmalion in the Classroom*. New York: Holt.

Santayana, George. 1924. *Scepticism and Animal Faith*. New York: Scribner.

Schutz, Alfred. 1944. "The stranger: An essay in social psychology." *American Journal of Sociology* 49: 499–507.

Schutz, Alfred and Luckmann, Thomas. 1973. *The Structures of the Life-World*. Evanston, Ill.: Northwestern University Press.

Scott, Robert A. 1970. "The construction of conceptions of stigma by professional expert." In Jack D. Douglas (ed.) *Deviance and Respectability: The Social Construction of Moral Meanings*. New York: Basic Books, pp. 255–90.

Silverman, Linda Kreger. 1989. "The highly gifted." In John Feldhusen, Joyce Van Tassel-Baska, and Ken Seeley (eds.) *Excellence in Educating the Gifted*. Denver: Love, pp. 71–83.

Sisk, Dorothy. 1987. *Creative Teaching of the Gifted*. New York: McGraw-Hill.

Smith, Jacklyn, Le Rose, Barbara and Clasen, Robert E. 1991. "Underrepresentation of minority students in gifted programs: Yes! It matters!" *Gifted Child Quarterly* 35: 81–3.

Smith, John David. 1985. *Minds Made Feeble: The Myth and Legacy of the Kallikaks*. Rockville, Md.: Aspens Systems Corp.

Spector, Malcolm and Kitsuse, John I. 1977. *Constructing Social Problems*. Menlo Park, Calif.: Benjamin Cummings Publishing.

Stedman, Lulu. 1924. *Education of Gifted Children*. Yonkers-on-Hudson, NY: World Book Co.

Strauss, Anselm. 1959. *Mirrors and Masks*. New York: Free Press.

Tannenbaum, Abraham J. 1979. "Pre-Sputnik to post-Watergate concern about the gifted." In A. Harry Passow (ed.) *The Gifted and the Talented: Their Education and Development*. Chicago: National Society for the Study of Education.

—— 1990. "Defensible? Venerable? Vulnerable?" *Gifted Child Quarterly* 34: 84–6.

Taylor, Calvin W. 1978. "How many types of giftedness can your program tolerate?" *Journal of Creative Behavior* 12: 39–51.

Terman, Lewis M. 1916. *The Measurement of Intelligence*. Boston: Houghton Mifflin.

—— 1919. *The Intelligence of School Children: How Children Differ in Ability, the Use of Mental Tests in School Grading and the Proper Education of Exceptional Children*. Boston: Houghton Mifflin.

—— 1922. "Were we born that way?" *World's Work* 44 (October): 660.

—— 1925. *Genetic Studies of Genius: Mental and Physical Traits of a Thousand Gifted Children*, vol. 1. Stanford, Calif.: Stanford University Press.

—— 1954. "The discovery and encouragement of exceptional talent." *American Psychologist* 9: 221–30.

Terman, Lewis M. and Oden, Melita H. 1940. "Status of the California gifted group at the end of sixteen years." In National Society for the Study of Education, *Intelligence: Its Nature and Nurture*, 39th Yearbook, Bloomington, Ill.: Public School Publishing.

——, —— 1947. *Genetic Studies of Genius: The Gifted Child Grows Up*, vol. 4. Stanford, Calif.: Stanford University Press.

——, —— 1951. "The Stanford studies of the gifted." In Paul Witty (ed.) *The Gifted Child*. Boston: Heath, pp. 20–46.

Thorndike, E. L. 1924. "Measurement of intelligence." *Psychological Review* 31: 219–52.

Tredgold, A. F. 1915. *Mental Deficiency*. New York: William Wood.

Tuttle, Frederick B. Jr. and Becker, Laurence A. 1983. *Characteristics and Identification of Gifted and Talented Students*. Washington, DC: National Education Association.

Van Sickle, J. H. 1910. "Provision for gifted children in public schools." *Elementary School Teacher* 10: 357–66.

Van Tassel-Baska, Joyce. 1989. "The disadvantaged gifted." In John Feldhusen, Joyce Van Tassel-Baska, and Ken Seeley (eds.) *Excellence in Educating the Gifted*. Denver: Love, pp. 53–70.

Weber, Max. 1930. *The Protestant Ethic and the Spirit of Capitalism*. London: George Allen.

Whitmore, Joanne. 1987. "Conceptualizing the issue of underserved populations of gifted students." *Journal for the Education of the Gifted* 10: 141–54.

Woodbridge, Frederick J. E. 1940. *An Essay on Nature*. New York: Columbia University Press.

Wooding, G. Scott and Bingham, Ronald D. 1988. "Gifted children's responses to a cognitive stressor." *Gifted Child Quarterly* 32: 330–2.

Zappia, Irene Antonia. 1989. "Identification of gifted Hispanic students: A multidimensional view." In C. June Maker and Shirley W. Schiever (eds.) *Critical Issues in Gifted Education: Defensible Programs for Cultural and Ethnic Minorities*. Austin, Tex.: Pro-ed, pp. 19–26.

Zimmerman, Don H. and Pollner, Melvin. 1970. "The everyday world as phenomenon." In Jack D. Douglas (ed.) *Understanding Everyday Life*. Chicago: Aldine, pp. 80–103.

Zimmerman, Don H. and Wieder, Lawrence D. 1970. "Ethnomethodology and the problem of order: A comment on Denzin." In Jack D. Douglas (ed.) *Understanding Everyday Life*. Chicago: Aldine, pp. 221–38.

Part II

The Sociology of Thought and Emotions

Introduction

One of the basic insights of social psychology is that the thoughts, perceptions, attitudes, and emotions of human beings are subject to, and often determined by, social influence. This insight is the subject of many classic studies in social psychology. The "Asch conformity study" (Asch 1951) and Sherif's study of norm formation (1935), for instance, demonstrated that an individual's perception of reality (in these cases, the perception of the length of the line and of the movement of a light in a dark room) was influenced by the reported perceptions of others. A classic experimental study by Schacter and Singer (1962) involved giving "suproxin" injections to subjects and telling them what sensations they could expect the injections to produce. According to the findings of the study, what subjects were told they would potentially feel as a result of the injection largely determined what they did feel.

While also emphasizing that thought and emotion are subject to social influence, the sociological approach involves placing thought and emotion in social, cultural, and historical contexts. As with social influence generally, sociological social psychologists are particularly interested in the content of the thoughts and emotions that are common among specific groups or categories of people in specific societies at specific times in history.

Sociology of Cognition. The reading by Judith Howard, "A sociological framework of cognition," explains the distinctively sociological approach to cognition. The study of social cognition, she suggests, has largely been the domain of psychological social psychology. Like social psychology generally, the study of social cognition has been dominated by an individualistic bias. The psychological approach to the study of social cognition emphasizes that people act on the basis of their perceptions of the world. Using the behaviorist language of stimulus and response, the psychological approach to social cognition emphasizes that human thought intervenes between stimulus and response. The sociological approach, however, focuses on the *societal* context of human thought. Summarizing the sociological point of view, Howard states: "individual thought is influenced fundamentally by social categorizations and more generally by social context, by which I mean the real-world relationships among the groups upon which these categorizations are based" (1990: 77).

Howard illustrates the sociological approach to cognition by presenting a sociological framework for the study of attribution. Attribution, a central human thought-process by which we explain the behavior of ourselves, others, and social events, has been one of the central objects of study of cognitive social psychologists. Exemplifying the psychological focus on understanding the ways that individuals perceive their environment, classic attribution theory tries to identify some general principles that guide the individual's attribution of causality to behaviors and events. The choice to attribute behavior to internal causes (i.e., personal qualities or traits) or to external causes (i.e., the situation and the environment) is, according to the theory, the most basic decision that observers make when trying to understand behavior. When we are being rational, according to the attribution theory, we are likely to explain a person's behavior in terms of external causes when we notice that others behave similarly in similar situations, that the person behaves similarly in similar situations, or that the person behaves differently in dissimilar situations. Conversely, we are likely to explain a person's behavior in terms of traits or attributes of the person when we observe that others do not behave similarly in similar situations, that the person does not consistently behave similarly in similar situations, or that the person does behave similarly in dissimilar situations. Yet since we rarely have sufficient information to rationally determine internal or external causality, according to attribution theory, our attributions are often biased in a number of systematic ways. The actor–observer divergence (the tendency of actors to see situational causes of their own behavior but not that of others), the fundamental attribution error (the observer's tendency to underestimate situational factors and overemphasize internal factors as explanations of behavior), and the self-serving bias (the tendency for people to attribute success to internal factors and failure to external factors) have each been identified by attribution researchers as systematic and generalizable biases in attribution. The sociological approach to the study of the patterning of human thought, however, questions the generalizability of the biases identified by attribution theory and contends that principles of cognition cannot adequately account for how we explain reality.

Sociologists maintain that attribution is shaped by social, cultural, and political context (Howard 1990). Contradicting the view of the "fundamental attribution error" as universally generalizable, a number of studies have shown that adults in non-western culture place less emphasis on internal factors and more emphasis on external factors in explaining behavior. Miller (1984) explains this difference in terms of differences between western and non-western culture. Western culture is more individualistic, while non-western cultures place far more emphasis on the person's relation to the environment (1984: 962–3). In addition to the effect of cultural context, Howard's analysis identifies social categorization and social power relations as important determinants of attribution patterns. When we try to explain the behavior of another, studies show, we are more likely to blame the person rather than the situation for misconduct or failure when that person is a member of a different social group (Howard 1990: 91). Further, we are more likely to blame the person than the situation for misconduct or failure when that person is a member of a low-status social group, even if we are also a member of the same low-status group. In general, we are more likely to assign credit to the individual for success and blame situations for failures when the person is a member of a high-status social group (1990: 94). In other words, in attributing causality to a person's behavior, we consider not only the person's social category memberships relative to our own but also the relative social power of the social groups or social categories to which the person belongs.

In addition to focusing on the societal *context* of human thought, sociological social psychologists tend to analyze human thought-processes as they relate to one of the most central subjects of sociology: social inequality. Sociological social psychological studies of beliefs and attitudes tend to focus on beliefs and attitudes about various dimensions of social inequality, for example, racial attitudes, beliefs about inequality and about the justice of the society's system of social stratification, awareness of gender inequality. Some studies attempt to identify social factors (e.g., race, socioeconomic background, gender, marital status, education, political affiliation, region, age) that favor one set of beliefs or attitudes over another. For example, does one's socioeconomic class background influence attitudes towards affirmative action policies? Or, what is the relationship between years of education and one's beliefs about the justice of income distribution in American society? Examples of such studies include James Kluegel and Eliot Smith's work on beliefs about inequality (Kluegel and Smith 1986), Lawrence Bobo's studies of racial attitudes (Bobo 1988; Bobo and Kluegel 1993; Bobo and Zubrinsky 1996), and Nancy Davis and Robert Robinson's (1991) study of consciousness of gender inequality.

Other sociological work in this area draws on social psychological principles and processes to explain the emergence of beliefs that legitimate particular systems of social inequality. Status characteristics and expectations states (SCES) theory, initiated by Joseph Berger at Stanford University in the late 1960s and currently the leading approach in the social psychology of inequality, focuses on how societal inequalities based on such characteristics as race, class, and gender produce generalized beliefs about the competence of actors which in turn contribute to reproducing such inequalities. One of the most well-known researchers in this tradition, Cecilia Ridgeway (1991) argues that the unequal distribution of resources in society is often translated in goal-oriented interaction into unequal expectations of competence. In other words, a person who has less education, less occupational prestige, and less expensive clothing than another person will be thought to be less competent than the person with more education, more occupational prestige, and more expensive clothing. Because expectations affect perception and influence behavior in such a way as to produce self-fulfilling prophecies, the result of interactions between resource-rich and resource-poor individuals is that the resource-rich will typically seem to demonstrate higher competence. In societies where resources are unequally distributed according to nominal characteristics such as race and gender, competence expectations become attached to these characteristics as well. Then, in future situations, the characteristics of race and gender themselves come to generate competence expectations irrespective of the resources of any particular individual.

Typically, research on the relationship between societal inequality and the beliefs of individuals takes the reality of socially structured inequality in the larger society as a starting point and then attempts to explain how societal inequality affects the beliefs and behaviors of individual actors in such a way that these beliefs and behaviors contribute to the reproduction of the system of inequality. The reading by Richard Della Fave (1980), "The meek shall not inherit the earth: Self-evaluation and the legitimacy of stratification," is a classic example. Della Fave draws on equity theory, status attribution theory, and George Herbert Mead's theory of the development of the self to explain how individuals come to believe that the stratification system in their society is just.

Sociology of Emotions. A central premise in the sociology of emotions is that emotions are socially constructed.[1] According to Arlie Hochschild, "biological factors emerge as ingredients of emotions, but social factors determine the way we interpret and shape our emotions" (1990: 119). This basic premise is compatible with the social psychological view illustrated by Schacter's experimental studies. As with other social psychological topics, however, the sociological approach to emotions works with an expanded conception of the social. Sociologists of emotion are concerned not only with showing that emotions are experienced and defined in response to situational influences, but also seek to understand how emotions are shaped by the broader societal, cultural, and historical contexts. The readings by Hochschild and Clanton highlight the two core themes of the social constructionist approach to the sociology of emotions: (1) that emotions are socially constructed; (2) that emotion norms and emotional experiences vary according to social, cultural, and historical context.

Hochschild argues that management of emotions – i.e., the efforts we make to feel emotions we believe we should feel, to not feel emotions we believe we should not feel, to express emotions that we believe we should express, to avoid expressing emotions we believe we should not express – modifies emotional experience and sometimes even creates emotions (1990: 120). Emotion management is one way in which emotions are socially constructed. Simon, Eder, and Evans's study of emotion management among adolescent girls nicely illustrates Hochschild's point. One of the basic "feeling rules" of adolescent girl culture identified in their study was that girls "should always be in love." Striving to conform to this norm, girls would often have to manufacture romantic feelings for available boys to whom they were not initially attracted. The result of routinely performing such emotion work, according to the authors, is that it becomes difficult for girls to know the difference between "real" and manufactured feelings. Accordingly, manufacturing feelings for boys or men who are attracted to them comes to seem normal (Simon et al. 1992). So one crucial way in which emotions are socially constructed, according to the emotion management perspective, is through the norms or feeling rules about what emotions are suitable in various contexts (Kemper 1990: 16). The chapter by Arlie Hochschild, "Emotion work, feeling rules, and social structure," develops the emotion-management perspective.

In addition to feeling rules, another way that emotions are socially constructed is by the vocabulary of emotions and beliefs about emotions shared by members of societies or social groups (Gordon 1990: 146). The chapter in the previous section by John Hewitt, "The reality of self-esteem," illustrates this point. According to Hewitt, the wide circulation of the concept "self-esteem" in American culture is responsible for making self-esteem into a reality for most Americans. Experiencing dejection after failure to achieve a promotion, we say that a person "took a hit to his self-esteem." When another person is elated after obtaining the desired promotion, we say her self-esteem is high. We tend to attribute achievement to high self-esteem and failure to low self-esteem, and we also view high self-esteem as a response to success and low self-esteem as a response to failure. But why don't we instead think that the person who is dejected after failing to get promoted feels let down by his peers or feels that he has let down his peers? Or why do we attribute a person's achievement to their self-esteem and not instead to the favorable opportunities they have enjoyed? Hewitt argues that "self-esteem" is only one of many possible ways of interpreting the bodily responses and sensations that precede or follow successes and failures. The American cultural focus on self-esteem, a focus which indicates the individualistic view of success and failure as a reflection of the individual, makes "self-esteem" a widely accessible and common interpretation.

A second theme in the sociology of emotions is that norms about emotion vary according to social, historical, and cultural context. Franscesca Cancian and Steven Gordon's (1988) analysis of changing emotion norms in marriage exemplifies this theme. Analyzing US women's magazines since 1900, Cancian and Gordon identify changing norms about the feeling and expression of love and anger in marriage and offer an explanation of these changes in terms of broader societal changes that occurred during the twentieth century. Similarly, the reading by Gordon Clanton, "Jealousy in American culture" (1989), identifies a change in the typical experience and expression of jealousy in American culture and provides an analysis of the social causes of this change.

Hochschild's work similarly places emotion norms and feeling rules in societal context. Unlike Clanton and others who focus on historical changes in emotion norms, Hochschild's work focuses on the emotion norms associated with jobs and ideologies. In *The Managed Heart*, she examines the feeling rules associated with occupational roles (Hochschild 1983). As she points out in the reading included here, middle-class service jobs in particular require emotion management or "selling" of personality. *The Managed Heart* discusses the emotional management required of two jobs: the airline attendant and the bill collector. The airline attendant is charged with the task of appearing friendly, caring, and reassuring, while the bill collector must convey emotional coldness and avoid any expression of sympathy with the debtor. The link between jobs and emotion management, according to Hochschild, explains social class differences in emphasis on emotion management. Because middle-class persons are more likely to be employed in occupations that require emotion management, they are more likely than working-class persons to put an emphasis on the management of emotions. Hochschild argues that social class differences in parental socialization practices – i.e., the middle-class tendency to control the *feelings* of their children and to use emotional manipulation in doing so compared to the working-class tendency to emphasize behavioral conformity (Kohn 1977) – can be explained by the different demands for emotion management in middle-class and working-class jobs (Hochschild 1979: 570).

The Second Shift (1989), Hochschild's classic study of dual-career families, analyzes the feeling rules associated with gender ideology. Hochschild argues that ideologies include not only cognitive beliefs about what should be but also feeling rules defining appropriate emotional responses to various situations. Many couples described in Hochschild's study had conflicts over feeling rules. They struggled over how much gratitude they owe to their spouse and how much gratitude the spouse owes them, and they struggled over how much resentment they were entitled to feel towards their spouse and how much resentment the spouse was entitled to feel towards them. The feeling rules, according to Hochschild, were the "bottom side" of the gender ideologies held by husbands and wives. For example, a husband with a traditional gender-role ideology would feel entitled to appreciation for working long hours on the job and would feel justified in being irritated when his wife asks him to do more housework and childcare. Or a wife with an egalitarian gender-role ideology would feel entitled to equal regard for her work outside the home and would feel justified in feeling angry when her husband does not contribute equally to housework and childcare. In many cases, however, the feelings that the spouses actually experienced contradicted the surface gender-role ideology. Say, for example, that the same husband held an egalitarian gender-role ideology on the surface, but nonetheless felt angry that he did not receive more appreciation for his dedication to work and that his wife expected more from him at home. Or the wife held an egalitarian gender-role ideology on the surface, but nonetheless felt indebted to her husband for allowing her to work outside the home and felt guilty when she did not manage the majority of housework and childcare on her own. Some of the troubles experienced by couples that Hochschild studied were over conflicting feeling rules associated with conflicting gender-role ideologies. In other cases, however, the conflicts were between the feeling rules that corresponded to the surface gender-role ideology and the feelings that were actually experienced. Hochschild emphasizes that a full understanding of ideology must look beneath the surface gender ideology to the underlying feeling rules. As she puts it in the included selection, rules for managing feeling are the "bottom side" of ideology (1979: 566).

Note

1 Not all sociologists of emotion share this assumption. The readings in this volume represent the social constructionist approach to the sociology of emotions, currently the most popular perspective. Other important work in the sociology of emotions not represented here is listed in the additional reading section.

References

Asch, Solomon. 1951. "Effects of group pressure upon the modification and distortion of judgments." In H. Guetzkow (ed.) *Groups, Leadership, and Men.* Pittsburgh: Carnegie Press, pp. 177–90.

Bobo, Lawrence. 1988. "Group conflict, prejudice, and the paradox of contemporary racial attitudes." In Phyllis A. Katz and Dalmas A. Taylor (eds.) *Eliminating Racism: Profiles in Controversy.* New York: Plenum Press, pp. 85–116.

Bobo, Lawrence and Kluegel, James. 1993. "Opposition to race-targeting: Self-interest, stratification ideology, or racial attitudes?" *American Sociological Review* 58(4): 443–64.

Bobo, Lawrence and Zubrinsky, Camille. 1996. "Attitudes on residential integration: Perceived status differences, mere in-group preference, or racial prejudice?" *Social Forces* 74(3): 883–909.

Cancian, Francesca M. and Gordon, Steven L. 1988. "Changing emotion norms in marriage: Love and anger in U.S. women's magazines since 1900." *Gender and Society* 2: 308–42.

Clanton, Gordon. 1989. "Jealousy in American culture, 1945–1985: Reflections from popular literature." In David D. Franks and E. Doyle McCarthy (eds.) *The Sociology of Emotions: Original Essays and Research Papers.* Greenwich, Conn. and London: JAI Press, pp. 179–93.

Davis, Nancy J. and Robinson, Robert V. 1991. "Men's and women's consciousness of gender inequality: Austria, West Germany, Great Britain, and the United States." *American Sociological Review* 56: 72–84.

Della Fave, L. Richard. 1980. "The meek shall not inherit the earth: Self-evaluation and the legitimacy of stratification." *American Sociological Review* 45: 955–68.

Gordon, Steven L. 1990. "Social structural effects on emotions." In T. D. Kemper (ed.) *Research Agendas in the Sociology of Emotions.* Albany: State University of New York Press, pp. 145–79.

Hewitt, John. 1998. *The Myth of Self-Esteem*. New York: St. Martin's Press.

Hochschild, Arlie. 1979. "Emotion work, feeling rules, and social structure." *American Journal of Sociology* 85(3): 551–75.

—— 1983. *The Managed Heart: Commercialization of Human Feeling*. Berkeley: University of California Press.

—— 1990. "Ideology and emotion management: A perspective and path for future research." In T. D. Kemper (ed.) *Research Agendas in the Sociology of Emotions*. Albany: State University of New York Press, pp. 117–44.

Hochschild, Arlie, with Machung, Anne. 1989. *The Second Shift: Working Parents and the Revolution at Home*. New York: Viking.

Howard, Judith A. 1990. "A sociological framework of cognition." *Advances in Group Processes* 7: 75–99.

Kemper, Theodore. 1990. "Introduction," *Research Agendas in the Sociology of Emotions*. Albany: State University of New York Press.

Kluegel, James R. and Smith, Eliot R. 1981. "Beliefs about stratification," *Annual Review of Sociology* 7: 29–56.

—— and ——1986. *Beliefs About Inequality*. New York: Aldine De Gruyter.

Kohn, Melvin. 1977. *Class and Conformity: A Study in Values with a Reassessment, 1977*, 2nd edn. Chicago: University of Chicago Press.

Miller, Joan. 1984. "Culture and the development of everyday social explanation." *Journal of Personality and Social Psychology* 46: 961–78.

Ridgeway, Cecilia. 1991. "The social construction of status value: Gender and other nominal characteristics." *Social Forces* 70: 367–86.

Schacter, S. and Singer, J. 1962. "Cognitive, social, and physiological determinants of emotional state." *Psychological Review* 69: 379–99.

Sherif, Muzafer. 1935. "A study of some social factors in perception." *Archives of Psychology* 27(187): 1–60.

Simon, R., Eder, D., and Evans, C. 1992. "The development of feeling norms underlying romantic love among adolescent females." *Social Psychology Quarterly* 55(1): 29–46.

Additional Reading

Fineman, Stephen (ed.) 1993. *Emotions in Organizations*. London: Sage.

Franks, David D. and McCarthy, E. Doyle (eds.) 1989. *The Sociology of Emotions: Original Essays and Research Papers*. Stanford, Calif.: JAI Press.

Howard, Judith A. 1995. "Social cognition." In Karen S. Cook, Gary Alan Fine, and James S. House (eds.) *Sociological Perspectives on Social Psychology*. Needham Heights, Mass.: Mass.: Allyn and Bacon, pp. 90–117.

Howard, J. A. and Callero, P. L. (eds.). 1991. *The Self-Society Dynamic: Cognition, Emotion, and Action*. New York: Cambridge University Press.

Kemper, T. D. (ed.) 1990. *Research Agendas in the Sociology of Emotions*. Albany: State University of New York Press.

Morgan, David L. and Schwalbe, Michael L. 1990. "Mind and self in society: Linking social structure and social cognition." *Social Psychology Quarterly* 53: 148–64.

Moscovici, Serge. 1981. "On social representations." In J. P. Forgas (ed.) *Social Cognition: Perspectives on Everyday Understanding*. London: Academic, pp. 191–209.

Smith-Lovin, Lynn. 1995. "The sociology of affect and emotion." In Karen S. Cook, Gary Alan Fine, and James S. House (eds.) *Sociological Perspectives on Social Psychology*. Needham Heights, Mass:. Allyn and Bacon, pp. 118–48.

Scheff, Thomas. 1988. "Shame and conformity: The deference-emotion system." *American Sociological Review* 53: 395–406.

Scher, Steven J. and Heise, David R. 1993. "Affect and the perception of injustice." *Advances in Group Processes*, vol. 10, ed. Edward Lawler, Barry Markovsky, and Jodi O'Brien. Menlo Park, Calif.: JAI Press.

Stearns, Peter N. 1994. *American Cool: Constructing a Twentieth-Century Emotional Style.* New York: New York University Press.

Stearns, Carol Z. and Stearns, Peter N. 1986. *Anger: The Struggle for Emotional Control in America's History.* Chicago: University of Chicago Press.

8 A Sociological Framework of Cognition

Judith A. Howard

Introduction

Abbie Hoffman, a flamboyant 1960s anti-war activist, died on April 12, 1989, presumably by suicide. I and many of my colleagues experienced personal loss and regret, and were provoked by his death to sentimental reminiscing about "the old days." Why did we respond in this way to the death of Abbie Hoffman? Were these expressions of mourning manifestations of individual empathy? In contrast, we were notably less moved by the death that same week of Sugar Ray Robinson, arguably a person of equal historical significance. Although there are few feelings that might seem more personal than sorrow over a death, I suggest that these feelings were just as social as they were personal. For my colleagues and me, Abbie Hoffman symbolized the anti-war movement, an oppositional force to the US government that was active during an historical era in which these particular intergroup relationships were highly salient. His death holds symbolic meaning for those of us who identified with this movement, signaling both the death of the spirit of that movement and our own aging.

Several weeks before Hoffman's death, a catastrophic oil spill occurred in the Prince William Sound of Alaska. Initial projections were that this single spill would wreak more environmental damage than any other such event in history. The major focus of the media coverage of this event in the weeks that ensued was a self-conscious deliberation about who was responsible. Was it the mate in charge of the boat at the time, a man untrained for navigation? Was it the allegedly intoxicated captain who turned control of the boat over to the mate? Was it Exxon, the company that owned the boat? Was it the entire oil industry, which had aggressively pursued the development of oil reserves in Alaska? Was it the federal government, for failing to institute and monitor safeguards against such environmental disasters? Few US citizens failed to ponder these questions of accountability. But the answers people provided to these questions were shaped more by their sociopolitical investments than by objective processing of the available information. Representatives from business, for instance, were more likely to attribute responsibility to the captain than to the oil industry; Alaskans whose livelihood depended on fishing tended to blame Exxon.

Reactions to these events illustrate that sociopolitical and cultural contexts shape cognitive responses to objectively similar experiences. Despite the ubiquity of such examples, social cognition has been a highly individualistic field. The study of social cognition is guided by a basic assumption that behavior is a function of people's perceptions of their world, rather than of objective descriptions. That is, thought

Reprinted from *Advances in Group Processes* 7 (1990): 75–103.

intervenes between environmental stimuli and individuals' affective and behavioral responses to these stimuli (Fiske and Taylor 1984). Although this basic premise could incorporate attention to societal influences on thought, in practice social cognition has focused almost entirely on micro-level individual influences on cognition (Forgas 1981).

This view of social cognition stresses the individual at the expense of the societal, an emphasis that is in no way unique to social cognition. Although social psychology purports to be interdisciplinary, it has been and remains dominated by psychologists. Psychology as a discipline is marked by the study of the individual person, and this level of analysis is, in turn, marked by a North American account of the individual as highly self-contained and separate (Sampson 1977). Individual behavior is accounted for by personality traits. Even though the term "trait" has grown out of fashion (perhaps in response to growing sensitivity to the interaction between person and situation: Endler and Magnusson 1976), trait-like concepts continue to dominate social psychological explanations of social behavior (Feshbach 1984; McCrae and Costa 1984). My aim is to argue against this version of individualism and to demonstrate that individual thought is influenced fundamentally by social categorizations and more generally by social context, by which I mean the real-world relationships among the groups upon which these categorizations are based.

In order to develop this point, it is critical to distinguish between two different connotations of the term "social." Social can refer to small, interpersonal, typically face-to-face group interactions. One strand of research on groups does focus on small interpersonal groups and group dynamics, typically in experimental laboratory contexts (e.g., Back 1981; Ridgeway 1983). Social can also refer to groups at a more macro-level; a second strand of research on groups focuses on intergroup relations. From this perspective groups are conceived as nations or categories of stratification (Stephan 1985). Most research on social cognition assumes the former, and more limited, connotation of the term social (Senn 1989). In contrast, it is the latter, more sociological, connotation to which I refer in characterizing thought as fundamentally social. The basic premise is that individuals form social categorizations, cognitive representations of macro-level groups, or "discontinuous divisions of the social world into distinct classes or categories" (Tajfel 1972). Although social categorizations are formed on the basis of macro-level groups, they are not equivalent to groups. Social categories are cognitive structures; individuals carry their group memberships in their minds and thoughts. In this way memberships in social groups, and the historical, economic, political, and cultural relations among these groups, influence cognition, and ultimately behavior, without any necessary intervention of face-to-face interpersonal interaction.

In summary, I contend that: (1) individuals process information in terms of social categories, divisions that are defined on the basis of knowledge about and memberships in social groups; (2) social categorizations include the historical, political, and cultural content of both immediate and distal social context; (3) social categorizations not only produce but also are reproduced and changed by individual thought, both directly and through the effects of cognition on action. To support these contentions, I present a critical analysis of extant theory and research on cognitive structures and cognitive processes, emphasizing the process of attribution. I begin with a brief review of several related theories of social identity and social categorization, to provide the necessary theoretical framework. Through this discussion I intend to demonstrate the not fully acknowledged social, and even sociological, nature of individual thought.

Social Identity and Social Categorization

Social Identity Theory

Social identity theory, a cognitive-motivational theory of intergroup behavior developed by the late Henri Tajfel and his colleagues (Tajfel 1978; Turner and Giles 1981), is the most integrated and comprehensive of the several approaches to intergroup relations. Social identity theory developed from research on the process of social categorization, the seemingly ubiquitous tendency of individuals to classify others and to assign differential values to those categories, fostering intergroup discrimination (Tajfel 1982; Wilder 1986). Earlier research emphasized the psychodynamic functions of stereotyping, rather than the content or social functions of stereotypes (Allport 1954; Campbell 1956). Tajfel, in contrast, stresses the content of these intergroup conceptions, generated in particular sociohistorical contexts, and their social functions.

Social identity is that part of an individual's self-conception that derives from knowledge of her or his membership in a social group (or groups), together with the affective significance of that membership (Tajfel 1981; Tajfel and Turner 1979). In other words, social identity is the internalization of social categorizations, groupings of oneself and some class of stimuli as similar in contrast to other classes of stimuli. The construction of social identities is an intra-individual consequence of one function of stereotypes, positive differentiation of ingroups from outgroups. When interpersonal interactions occur in situations in which group memberships are salient, positive social identity must be achieved at least partially through intergroup social comparisons. Because situational variations may alter the salience of group memberships, social categorization may operate rapidly and transitorily. Thus the process of categorization may operate even in the relatively brief duration of most laboratory studies. Even a "minimal" social categorization (e.g., skill in dot estimation accuracy, Billig and Tajfel 1973) can exert discriminatory intergroup effects, because it provides a basis through social comparison for both positive ingroup distinctiveness and positive individual self-conceptions.

There is substantial empirical support for these components of social identity theory. Increases in the salience of group membership, for example, do lead to increases in individuals' ingroup favoritism (Doise et al. 1978; Turner et al. 1979). With respect to the introductory example of this paper, the salience of the environmentalist identity undoubtedly escalated dramatically subsequent to the Exxon oil spill, increasing in turn environmentalists' positive attitudes toward other environmentalists, and negative attitudes toward the oil industry. Allen and Wilder (1975) report that ingroup favoritism persists even when the beliefs of an ingroup member are known to be similar to those of members of an outgroup, and dissimilar to those of other ingroup members. Oakes and Turner (1980) make the link to individual social identity, demonstrating that increases in self-esteem are related to the opportunity to engage in intergroup discrimination. This suggests that environmentalists might have experienced increased self-esteem after the oil spill, a highly negative event that inspired outgroup discrimination.

Self-Categorization Theory

Social identity theory demonstrates the significance of social categorizations for intergroup relations and their motivational significance for the creation of positive social identity. John Turner's self-categorization theory (1987) focuses more directly on the components of social identity. Turner distinguishes among three levels of self-categorizations: highly abstract categorizations based on one's identity as a human being; an intermediate level of social categorizations based on ingroups and outgroups; and a third level of personal self-categorizations based on differentiating oneself from other ingroup members. He views each of these three levels of categorization as social in content, origin, and function. In asserting the social origins of all self-categorizations, Turner maintains that personal self-categorizations are not privileged as the true or authentic self. In contrast, virtually all other theories of the self assign greater authenticity to the personal than the social aspects of self, in accordance with the prevailing individualism of the field (Rosenberg 1979).

Although Turner assigns equal weight to the different types of self-categorizations, he parallels research on attention by asserting an inverse relationship between the salience of personal and social self-categorizations. Both cannot be salient at one and the same time. Factors which enhance the salience of ingroup–outgroup categorizations, and hence activate social categorizations, tend to increase the perceived identity between self and ingroup members and thus depersonalize individual self-perception on those dimensions that define ingroup membership. This constitutes a form of self-stereotyping whereby individuals view themselves as interchangeable members of a social category, more than as unique personalities. This is *not* a loss of individual identity in the sense of deindividuation. Rather, self-stereotyping refers simply to a cognitive shift from the salience of personal to social levels of identity.

The relative salience of social and personal identities depends in turn on: (1) the accessibility, or readiness of a category to become activated; and (2) the fit between the input in a given situation and stored category specifications (Oakes 1987). The dependence on accessibility reflects the fact that individuals can attend to only a limited set of stimuli at any one time. Accessibility is a function of cognitive variables such as recency of activation of the category or the relationship of the category to other accessible constructs, and affective variables such as the relative importance of group membership to the individual (Taylor and Fiske 1987). The affective meaning of the category reflects the content of social categorizations. Racial categories are likely to be of primary significance for South Africans, for example; socioeconomic categories are of special significance in Great Britain.

The concept of fit connects the perceptual activity of accessibility to reality; the degree of fit reflects the real-world characteristics of the relevant categories, and, importantly, the content of the social categorizations. Fit is both structural and normative. Structural fit reflects the degree to which observed behavioral differences and similarities between people are perceived as correlated with preexisting social categories. Different responses of faculty and younger students to the death of Abbie Hoffman make salient their generational differences, because these responses are consistent with preexisting social categories. Another example illustrates how the fit between input and stored category information affects the process of inference: a recent article in the *Seattle Times* reported the story of a woman who died trying to save her 2-year-old daughter from a house fire. Although little information was reported about the woman, the story did note her age, 19, the age of her own mother, 36, and of her grandmother, the child's great-grandmother, 54. Because of my prior knowledge that black women are likely to have children at substantially younger ages than are white women, this information suggested to me that the family was black. This example also illustrates the influence of affective significance on the accessibility of social categorizations. This story probably did not increase the salience of racial categories for all readers; racial stereotyping, the focus of some of my own work, is salient to me.

Normative fit reflects the ideologies prevalent in the social groups to whom the norms apply, and depends on the context in which these comparisons are made. What is normatively relevant to a given category, and hence socially meaningful, may vary widely across situations. For example, when a graduate student offers her faculty advisor a cup of coffee at the student's oral exam, this action may heighten the salience of their status differences; the same offer during the intermission of a symphony is unlikely to make salient their status relationship. Both structural and normative fit reflect the content of the relevant social categorizations. Their variability across social contexts indicates that these categorizations are social, rather than "natural."

A comparative context is a prerequisite for high category salience; therefore, the clarity and distinctiveness of a category are also determinants of salience. Category distinctiveness has been conceptualized by cognition researchers as the relative numerical infrequency of a stimulus within a given context. Membership in a numerical minority category should become more salient, the smaller the minority in relation to the majority. Research support for this prediction has been weak (Oakes 1987). Tajfel suggests that the definition of what constitutes a minority group may rest more on sociocultural factors than on sheer numbers. The clarity of the cultural boundaries separating majority and minority group members may be more crucial to the salience of the category memberships than their respective numbers (Tajfel 1981). Tajfel's emphasis on culture, together with the content-based criteria for assessing both structural and normative fit, add an important element to a purely cognitive perspective on self-categorization; the content of these categorizations is crucial for understanding the salience of social categories, and thus their effects.

Social Power and Social Identity

Social identity theory tends to take the terms self and identity for granted. Classic sociological definitions of self stress two components, I and Me, subject and object (Mead 1934). Although social psychologists treat subject and object as united and parallel aspects of self within a given individual, other philosophical traditions have theorized ways in which positions in social systems ascribe a subject position to some individuals, an object position to others. Post-structuralist (Derrida 1984) and feminist theories (de Beauvoir 1972; and see Jaggar 1983) maintain, for example, that the adult white middle-class male is the archetypal subject, whereas children, nonwhites, those who are economically disadvantaged, and women are objects, in most social systems. In other words, social power has immediate implications for social identity (Adam 1978; Deschamps 1983; Goode 1982). Those who dominate, subjects, even conceive of themselves as outside of any particular category, because they are members of the category that has the discursive power to define, locate and order others. Members of this group have the freedom to define themselves as specific, unique, individuals. Members of dominated groups, on the other hand, are viewed by those who dominate as undifferentiated representatives of their categories. Those who are dominated are thus caught in an ambiguity of identity between the subject position of the I that defines subjectivity for all individuals as individuals, and the object position to which they are assigned by the dominant group. Cast in terms of social identity theory, for those who dominate, personal identities are likely to be more salient than their social identities in most situations, whereas for those who are dominated, social identities are likely to be more salient than personal identities, not only in interactions with members of the dominant group, but also within their own consciousness. In this way social power is a major determinant of the salience of self-categorizations.

Content in Social Categorizations

Specific relations of social power are also part of the content of social categorizations. Incorporating social power into analyses of social identity is thus consistent with Tajfel's emphasis on sociocultural (as opposed to numerical) definitions of minority groups, and Oakes' emphasis on the normative, hence culturally constructed, criteria of fit between the input of a given situation and preexisting categories. A recent study of intergroup aggression provides further evidence of the significance of cultural content, and points to revisions in social identity theory (Struch and Schwartz 1989). This study evaluated the relative adequacy of belief congruence and social identity theories in predicting aggression directed by moderate Israelis against ultraorthodox Jews. Although there was some evidence of social identity processes, the results supported belief congruence theory. In accounting for these results, Struch and Schwartz suggest that members of existing groups in prolonged conflict share a history of cultural and social experiences that supports their distinctiveness from members of the other group. This allows them to maintain a sense of distinctiveness even in the face of contradictory information. Some of the propositions of social identity theory may need reevaluation that incorporates cultural content, in order to account for the behavior of members of existing groups as opposed to experimentally constructed groups that lack a real-world history.

Summary and Evaluation

There is a long social psychological tradition of regarding intergroup behavior as a regression to irrational or instinctual forms of behavior. In contrast, social identity and self-categorization theories cast ingroup identification as an adaptive social cognitive process that makes prosocial relations possible, while at the same time providing a social account for antisocial behavior. These theories maintain that individuals structure their perceptions of themselves and others by means of abstract social categories, that they internalize these categories as aspects of their self concepts, and that social cognitive processes relating to these self-conceptions produce group behavior. What they do not stress sufficiently is how these self-conceptions, through cognitive processes, also shape individual behavior, that is, how individual behavior reflects group memberships and identifications.

This omission may reflect the unnecessarily adversarial relationship between personal and social identities posed by social identity and self-categorization theories. The proposition that both cannot be salient at the same moment is consistent with research on the cognitive process of attention. However, the more general implication of an oppositional relationship between the two shows traces of the individualism characteristic of contemporary social psychology. In discussing the importance of roles in shaping attributions of responsibility, Lee Hamilton makes this same criticism: "what is missing from the view of role as an external force is precisely what makes us fully human: society acting in us, as well as on us" (1978: 321). In the same way, personal and social self-categorizations are intimately intertwined. Although personal self-categorizations emphasize how individuals differ from others within a relevant ingroup, these categorizations often fall on the same dimensions that comprise social self-categorizations. So, for example, reviews of Abbie Hoffman's life imply that the contemporary personal self-categorizations of former anti-war activists Hoffman, now businessman Jerry Rubin, and media star Tom Hayden might differ from each other, despite the fact that the social self-categorizations of each differentiate them as a group from those who were and are generally uncritical of the U S government. But in both cases the primary dimension of categorization is degree of sociopolitical radicalism, whether within an ingroup or between ingroup and outgroup. The relationship between personal and social self-categorizations thus may be best viewed as an indicator of the inseparability of person from society, rather than of their opposition.

This review of social identity and social categorization theories provides the necessary context for a critical analysis of social cognition and attribution research. In the next section I demonstrate the significance of memberships in social groups, through social categorization, for individual cognitive structures and cognitive processes, with particular attention to attribution theories and research.

Social Cognition

Social cognition is the study of how people gather, interpret, analyze, remember, and use information about the social world. Contemporary theories of social cognition share a basic metaphor of the human being as "cognitive miser." The environment presents individuals with much potential information; because we are limited in our cognitive capacities, we develop strategies for limiting and organizing information so that it becomes useable in goal-directed activity. From this perspective, the human being is a cognitive miser, seeking strategies to simplify complex situations.

This metaphor provides at least one plausible explanation for the content of stratification systems. The axes of the major systems of stratification are character-istics such as age, gender, race, and socioeconomic position. A cognitivist account of this content is that age, gender, race, and, less obviously, socioeconomic position are highly visible characteristics. Because human cognitive resources are limited, ca-tegorizations may have formed originally on the basis of the relative visibility of human characteristics. Each of these characteristics then developed its full cultural weight through prolonged and complex political histories.

Cognitive Structures

Cognitive structures are the basic elements of cognition. The major contemporary conception of cognitive structure is the social schema, a structure that incorporates organized knowledge about a given concept or domain. Three types of schemas have been emphasized: person schemas, knowledge about particular individuals, including one's self; role schemas, referring to social roles and categories; and event schemas, or scripts, knowledge about sequences of action in particular situations (Fiske and Taylor 1984). The striking lack of attention to the connections among these three types of schema attests to the implied separateness of person, role, and situation. Researchers have not asked, for example, how role schemas affect person schemas, a question directly relevant to social identity theory, how event schemas shift depending on one's role perspective, or which schemas are salient in different situations.

There is empirical evidence of the relevance of intergroup phenomena for schemas. Person schemas, directly analogous to social categorizations, are formed partly on the basis of group memberships. For instance, many individuals use sex as a category to organize information about themselves (Markus 1977). These gender-based person schemas, in turn, influence cognitive processes. Males who have strongly formed gender schemas take longer to ascribe masculine as opposed to feminine words to a male actor than do males who do not have a strong gender schema; the longer latencies of judgments among those with gender schemas reflect the longer time it takes them to search their larger array of information (Markus and Smith 1980). Role schemas also affect a variety of cognitive processes. Linville and Jones (1980), for example, demon-strate that racial schemas affect what third party evaluators expect from individuals in particular racial categories, resulting in different evaluations of job qualifications. There has been substantially less research that suggests how group memberships might affect event schemas. Event schemas provide behavioral expectations in specific situations, and thus should be equally susceptible to the influence of social group differentiation. It is important to specify whether members of particular social cate-gories differ in their expectations for particular situations, whether behavioral expec-tations in situations vary according to the social categories of the actors, and whether such differences affect the cognitive processing of the behaviors that actually occur.

Cognitive Processes

Cognitive processing of social information includes attention, encoding of informa-tion, the retrieval of information through memory, and the formation of a variety of inferences.

Attention

Research on attention generally has been highly individualistic. For example, one line of research addresses whether environmental stimuli direct attention inward or outward, creating states of objective and subjective self-awareness respectively (Carver and Scheier 1981). When objectively self-aware, one is thought to compare one's self to one's ideal standards. Objective self-awareness triggers an adjustment process; the individual adjusts his or her behavior, until the standard is met or the individual gives up. If external norms are more salient than individual standards, the individual will attempt to match her or his behavior with the external standards. But in either case, the individual is assumed to control his or her behavior. No account is made of how social categorizations might: create predispositions to focus either internally or externally; shape the content of one's ideal standards; or affect beliefs about the efficacy of adjustment actions.

Research has focused primarily on the effects of salience, the degree to which a stimulus stands out in the context (e.g., Langer et al. 1976). Salience can be created by the immediate context (e.g., through novelty); by tasks (e.g., attention may be goal-relevant); and by prior knowledge or expectations. It is this last route that most directly implicates social categories in directing the focus and intensity of attention; the salience of an individual's behavior depends on prior expectations for that individual (e.g., person schemas), for the social category of which he or she is a member (e.g., role schemas), or for people in general. Consistent with the premises of social identity theory, salience via group membership does affect attention, which affects cognitive processing (McArthur and Friedman 1980; Taylor et al. 1978). Moreover, the affective significance of particular social categories affects their salience, and hence attention. Allport and Kramer (1946) explain their finding that highly anti-Semitic students are more accurate in identifying Jewish faces than low anti-Semitic students, for example, by suggesting that anti-Semites are more willing to label a face Jewish on the basis of limited information.

Memory

Memory entails encoding, creating a mental representation of information to facilitate storage, and retrieval of that information, once stored. Representations are grouped into episodic and semantic or linguistic forms (Fiske and Taylor 1984). Consistent with the cognitive miser metaphor, semantic information is recalled more easily than episodic information, because semantic memory consists of a network of information, rather than isolated bits. For example, Hamilton et al. have demonstrated that the assigned task of impression formation, which requires that the perceiver form a coherent whole of many individual items of information, leads to more successful retrieval of information than memorization. These semantic networks of information are based largely on the prior expectancies perceivers bring to social situations (Hamilton et al. 1980). In this way, prior theories and expectations about social categories, as well as about particular individuals, influence encoding and subsequent retrieval of information.

Research on the normative criteria of memory, that is, the evaluation of memory against a standard of accuracy (not unlike the attributionists' concern with biases: Ross 1977) is especially indicative of the influence of social categorization. Concern for accuracy implies that correctness can be assessed, that there are objective stand-ards of fact. However, the hierarchical differences that accompany social categories allow particular groups to impose their definitions of fact and fiction on members of other groups. As one example, in October 1985, in Gainesville, Georgia, a Vietnamese man named Hen Van Nguyen stood trial for murder for several days, named by white eyewitnesses as the killer, despite his protestations that he was not the killer. A jail-booking officer finally realized that officials were taking the wrong man, another Vietnamese, to court. The County District Attorney observed by way of explanation that both of the men were missing front teeth, they had similar length hair, and the first name of one was the last name of the other. The memory of dominant group members, the eyewitnesses, the District Attorney, even the man's defense attorney, provided the definition of fact. This example also illustrates basic aspects of ingroup–outgroup categorization (Wilder 1986). These white judicial personnel had homogeneous per-ceptions of the Vietnamese defendants. Had the men been Caucasian, it it unlikely that similar length hair or similar first and last names would have lead to such a mistake.

Social inference

Social inferences combine new or retrieved information into social judgments. Infer-ence involves gathering information, sampling from the relevant information, and forming one of a variety of judgments. A host of "biases" in this process have been identified, most of which result from efficiency-maximizing strategies, or heuristics (Tversky and Kahneman 1974), such as tending to be guided by extreme data, or being unaware of the importance of sample size or of biases within samples (Nisbett and Ross 1980).

Many of these heuristics are vulnerable to the influence of social categorization. Representativeness, for example, involves identifying people as members of cate-gories, in order to form probability estimates. Representativeness relies on role schemas, often to the extent of minimizing other relevant information, such as population base rates (Tversky and Kahneman 1974). The anchoring and adjustment heuristic involves reducing ambiguity by starting from a reference point or anchor and then adjusting it to reach a judgment; social categories are an important source of these reference points (Markus and Smith 1981). The integration of information is also vulnerable to the limitations of the cognitive miser and to the effects of social categorization. People tend to underestimate covariation, for example, unless they have a strong prior expectation about the relationship between two variables (Jen-nings et al. 1982). Indeed, the existence of a strong prior expectation about the relationship between two variables is the most important influence on inaccuracy in covariation assessment (Nisbett and Ross 1980). When a relationship is expected, people greatly overestimate that relationship. This phenomenon of illusory correla-tion accounts for the persistence of role schemas; once expectations are formed about membership in a social category and particular behaviors and characteristics expected of members of that category, these expectations are resistant to change.

Social Categorization in Attribution

Attribution is the most prominent of the several inferential processes. Attribution refers to the formation of a causal inference, a judgment of what factors may have produced a particular outcome, or a trait inference, the assignment of a trait to an actor on the basis of her or his behavior. Heider views attribution as ubiquitous: "Whenever you cognize your environment you will find attribution occurring" (in Harvey et al. 1976: 18); Bruner (1957) maintains that all perception, including attribution, is necessarily the result of categorization. The pervasiveness of attribution and its reliance on categorization, taken together with the fact that attribution has been one of the most popular contemporary topics of social psychological research (Smith et al. 1980), make this an appropriate cognitive process with which to illustrate the fundamentally social character of cognition.

Classic theories of attribution

The initial groundwork for theories of attribution is presented in Heider's (1958) rather discursive discussion in *The Psychology of Interpersonal Relations*. Harold H. Kelley and Edward E. Jones each proposed more formal theories of attribution on the basis of Heider's work. The basic assumption of each of these three models of attribution is that the causes of behavior can be categorized into either internal factors, factors associated with an individual, or external factors, factors in the environment. For example, responsibility for the Alaskan oil spill could be attributed internally to the captain's negligence or externally to luck. Thus attribution theories also assume not only a division but also an oppositional relationship between internal and external, or individual and social factors.

Kelley (1967, 1973) asks under what circumstances people attribute a given behavior to the environment or to the actor. According to the full information model, attributions are based on profiles of covariation between behavior and three types of information: consensus, information about the behavior of other people; distinctiveness, information about how the actor behaves toward related stimuli; and consistency, information about the actor's past behavior. Applying Kelley's theory to the oil spill example, the incident might be classified as low consensus – not many boats sustain oil spills; high distinctiveness – other boats the crew had worked on had not had oil spills; and low consistency – this boat had never before had an oil spill. This information profile suggests an attribution to circumstance, due to the low consistency of the event.

However, this analysis reveals the difficulty of applying the model to complex real-world incidents. What is the relevant behavior? One could focus instead on the captain's decision to turn navigation of the boat over to an unqualified mate. This behavior is low consensus, because not many captains would do this, low distinctiveness, because the captain was alleged to have a history of being intoxicated on his boats (and of drunk driving violations), and high consistency, because he had been known to do this before. This profile supports an internal attribution to the captain. There are a number of other behaviors associated with this incident that might also be the focus of attributional analysis. This degree of complexity is not characteristic of most experimental research on attribution, but does characterize many real-world incidents.

Jones and Davis (1965) and Jones and McGillis (1976) propose the theory of correspondent inference, which addresses a different and more narrow question: under what circumstances does observation of an actor's behavior lead to attributions of particular dispositions to the actor? Prior expectancies for the behavior, taken together with an analysis of the effects that follow from this behavior and potential alternatives, influence whether a disposition is attributed. Two forms of expectancies are proposed; category-based expectancies are based on relevant social group memberships and social norms, and target-based expectancies are based on knowledge of the former behavior of the actor. Jones and Davis hypothesize that high prior expectancies militate *against* dispositional inference, an hypothesis that has come under substantial recent scrutiny (Howard 1985; Read 1987).

Beginning with Heider (1958), the study of attribution is defined as an investigation of the phenomenology of causality, how laypeople explain social behavior. Concern with the degree to which people deviate from objective standards of correctness would seem to have no place in such research. However, these theories of attribution have become accepted as normative criteria, and the degree to which laypeople conform to such theories has become a major preoccupation of attribution researchers. A number of "errors" have been identified, primary among them the "fundamental" attribution error – a preference for attributing causality to people rather than to the environment; the actor–observer difference – a preference for actors to attribute causality to the environment and for observers to make attributions to the actor; a tendency to underuse consensus information; the self-based consensus effect – a tendency to assume that others react as we ourselves would; and a variety of self-serving attributions, including both patterns that cast one's self in a positive light and self-denigrating attributions that serve positive ends for the actor (Ross 1977). Although these attributional biases were treated originally as generalizable, recent cross-cultural and cross-national research has begun to demonstrate the cultural specificity of these patterns (e.g., Miller 1984).

Despite the wealth of research on attribution, the covariational and correspondence inference theories are virtually the only major theoretical work. Although there is room for attention to social categorization phenomena in these theories, this has been implicit and undeveloped. The only reference to social phenomena in Kelley's model is consensus information, information about what others do. In hypothesizing that high consensus leads to an environmental attribution and low consensus to a person attribution, this model makes an assumption of fundamental importance to this review, that only individualized, idiosyncratic behavior is deliberate and internally motivated. Shared behavior is assumed to be externally constrained. The same assumption is made in the model of correspondent inference. Consensus is analogous to category-based expectancies, and the same prediction is made in both models. Normative behavior is assumed not to provide information about the actor. Intentional collective action thus has no conceptual place within these models. Kelley's (1967) model does not even specify who the others are upon whose behavior we form judgments of consensus. They might range from known friends of the actor, or the observer, to membership groups of the actor, or observer, or the "generalized other" of the observer. In other words, consensus judgments may reflect preconceptions of the observer, rather than a behavioral base. In conceptualizing behavioral expectancies as category-based, Jones and McGillis (1976) do specify more adequately the particular social groups upon whom consensus judgments are based.

To question this prevailing assumption that normative behavior does not provide information about the actor is also to question the distinction between category- and target-based expectancies, or between individual and society. To the extent that people internalize their group memberships, much of their individual behavior is guided by their conceptions of what behavior is normatively appropriate for the relevant reference group. Unfortunately, much of the relevant research has been conducted in asocial contexts. Research that makes social groups more salient might lead to revision of this aspect of these theories.

Oakes (1987) makes the important point that the validity of this assumption rests on the typical conceptualization of person attributions in terms of personality characteristics. No allowance is made for the possibility of any other type of person attribution: persons can be causal forces only by their individual personalities. If individuals have social as well as personal identities, however, it is important to consider what conditions produce attributions to people as social category members. Social category memberships can be treated as potentially causal factors in themselves, a type of dispositional property, representing social invariances in people's attitudes and behavior. That is, behavior can be explained in terms of people's shared, collective, social properties, in addition to their individual personalities. Oakes explores this possibility in an attitude attribution study, using membership in the Arts or Sciences faculty at a university as the basis of social categorization. This study strongly supports the distinctiveness of category membership as a third type of attribution, yet one that is perceived clearly as referring to an individual rather than to external factors.

Deschamps (1983) offers a very different, but equally social, critique of Jones and Davis's (1965) claim that the true person is revealed in idiosyncrasy. Deschamps argues that the adoption of a social role can be (indeed perhaps most often is) individualized without being deviant. In proposing that deviant behavior necessarily reflects personal dispositions, Jones and Davis oppose deviance to shared and culturally determined social norms. This approach is in striking contrast to a classic sociological view of deviance as a product of subcultures and subgroups, whose internal norms guide behavior defined as deviant by the culture at large (Scull 1988). These theories imply that group, rather than individual, characteristics should be attributed to the offenders. In other words, deviant behavior may reflect internalized group norms, rather than individual pathology.

A social theory of attribution

Hewstone and Jaspars (1984) note that most attribution research involves individuals explaining individual behavior in remarkably asocial situations. Few studies, according to Senn (1989), do the following: (1) treat individuals as group members; (2) focus on individuals interacting as social actors; (3) address the explanation of socially meaningful behavior; and/or (4) place that behavior in a broader societal context. Thus it has not been convincingly demonstrated that traditional theories of attribution can account for the explanations social actors provide for socially significant behavior. In discussing each of these points, I present relevant empirical research, where it is available. These points are intended to apply to cognitive structures and processes more generally; I use the process of attribution to illustrate the larger point that cognition is fundamentally social.

(1) *The process of attribution relies on the social categorization of actors and perceivers*. Categorization and attribution both rely on social representations, shared

systems of beliefs that individual members of social groups hold about their own and others' groups (Moscovici 1972, 1981). Social representations shape which characteristics are considered representative of a category, and hence are attributed to an individual who is classified as a member of that category. Trait attributions are one likely outcome of categorization. Categorization also underlies causal attribution. Social representations constitute causal schemas that influence information integration and processing. The content of social representations makes potential causes more accessible for retrieval (Hewstone and Jaspars 1984). The greater the accessibility, the less input needed for categorization to occur, the wider the range of input that will be accepted as fitting the category, and the more likely other categories that might provide a better fit will be ignored. Thus social categories and representations enhance the simplification and predictability of causal attributions.

There is substantial empirical evidence of the effects of social categorization on attribution. Duncan (1976), for example, has explored the influence of racial stereotypes on attributions about violence. White college students viewed a videotape of increasingly violent interactions between a black and a white. When the tape contained a black protagonist and a white victim, 75 percent of the subjects described the behavior as violent. When the roles were reversed, this label was chosen by 17 percent of the subjects. Equally important, subjects attributed the violent behavior primarily to the actor when the actor was black, and to the situation, when the actor was white. Similar patterns have been found in a non-western society in a study of Hindu–Muslim conflict (Taylor and Jaggi 1974). The authors hypothesized that Hindus would make internal attributions to other Hindus performing socially desirable acts and external attributions for undesirable acts. Opposite patterns were predicted for Hindu attributions about Muslims, outgroup members. The results were entirely consistent with the hypotheses.

These studies both demonstrate that social categorization produces asymmetric patterns of attribution that favor the ingroup and derogate the outgroup. Taylor and Doria (1979) evaluated the strength of ingroup favoritism, pitting it against the self-serving bias, the preference for self-promoting attributions. They used failure situations in which Canadian college athletes had to blame either themselves, contradicting the self-serving attributional bias, or their group, contradicting the principle of ingroup favoritism. Group-serving attributions predominated over self-serving explanations of game losses; players were more likely to attribute failure to themselves than to the team. This study attests to the strength of ingroup favoritism, and also addresses the relationship between social and personal identity. One plausible interpretation is that when group categorization is salient, basic self-serving attributional tendencies can be overturned, revealing how strongly attribution is a social phenomenon.

(2) *Behavior, the stimulus of the attributional process, is itself fundamentally social.*

(a) *The interactive context of behavior: social influence on attribution.* Social attributions may be created by and influenced through social interaction with other group members. The attributional constructs of consensus and category-based expectations imply social influence, but empirical research using these constructs has not developed the interactional details through which these variables influence attribution. Nonetheless, it might be useful to view the creation of social expectancies as a process of social influence. To do so is also to raise questions about the relative influence of preexisting expectations as opposed to expectations created or altered through immediate, contextualized, social influence. Investigation of such questions will require analysis of intergroup interactions such as group discussions among real-world, preexisting group members. In contrast to the three aspects of social attribution detailed above, this topic has received virtually no empirical or theoretical attention.

(b) *Socially meaningful situations in attributional research*. The behavioral and situational contexts of much attributional research have been remarkably asocial, to the theoretical decrement of the field. To take one example, one might draw a parallel between actor–observer attributional differences on the one hand, and ingroup–outgroup differences on the other. The bases for actor–observer differences have been viewed as perceptual and informational (Ross 1977), whereas ingroup–outgroup biases have been explained as a function of ethnocentrism. The perceptual bases of actor–observer differences could also be applied to attributional differences between ingroups and outgroups: ingroup members have more information on antecedents of observed behavior and have more detailed experiential information, and thus are more likely to analyze a situation in terms similar to those of the actor, than are outgroup members. An ingroup observer thus should make more dispositional attributions for the positive behavior of ingroup than outgroup members and more situational attributions for the negative behavior of ingroup than outgroup members. Ingroup ethnocentrism is a very different explanation for the same attributional pattern. Only by using a socially meaningful behavioral situation, one that involves not only actors and observers, but also a significant intergroup situation, would it be possible to ascertain the relative adequacy of these explanations.

I have addressed this aspect of social attribution in my own research on the effects of gender on attributions of blame for several types of assaults (Howard 1984a, 1984b). The selection of a victimization context in which to examine the effect of this social category was not coincidental. The range of victim characteristics investigated in related research is strikingly narrow. The victims have been exclusively female and almost always victims of sexual assault. They have been characterized in terms of sexually marked variables: respectability, physical attractiveness, previous acquaintance with the offender, and occupations such as nun, housewife, or, conversely, divorcée or dancer. More blame is attributed to female victims in the culturally proscribed than prescribed category of each of these variables. Because these cultural prescriptions are so pervasive as to be virtually invisible, however, no past research had explicitly compared the effects of gender in sexual and nonsexual contexts.

I assessed the extent to which the gender of an assault victim and the type of assault influence attributions of blame. I predicted that more blame would be attributed to female victims of sexual assault than to the three other types of victims, by both female and male subjects (thus assuming that social power would be more influential than ingroup bias). The results indicated a stronger effect of social categorization and power than had been predicted. Victim sex and type of assault did not interact significantly; instead, subjects attributed more general and characterological blame to female than to male victims, and more blame to the behavior of male than of female victims. Male (but not female) respondents attributed much more blame to the behavior of male than of female victims, exhibiting a defensive ingroup attribution bias.

In addition, the predicted effects of victim gender were found only among those with traditional gender role attitudes. Members of social categories vary in the degree to which their own ideological positions reflect their category memberships; the effects of category membership are not monolithic or seamless. The implications of category membership also vary over time and historical conditions. Gender is a particularly appropriate category with which to illustrate this variation, because the social representations of gender have been questioned deeply in the past two decades. The redefinition of gender may have produced greater variation in social representations of this particular category than of other more stable social categories.

Other analyses of these same data provide direct evidence of the fundamentally social nature of behavior (Howard 1984b). Subjects also provided trait evaluations of victims; social representations may exert more influence on cognitive evaluations than on attributions of blame, because attributions are likely to be more constrained by rules of logic. Because victimization is consistent with the female stereotype, being victimized should intensify prior expectations. Thus female victims were rated as higher than males on victimization-related feminine characteristics. I predicted that victim gender would not influence ratings on masculine characteristics, because being victimized contradicts male stereotypes, and this would erase sex differences that would obtain otherwise. Contradicting this prediction, but in a direction entirely consistent with this logic, male victims were perceived as less aggressive, strong, and active than females. Being raped also led to higher ratings of femininity than did being robbed, for *both* female and male victims. And, the more blame was attributed to a victim, whether male or female, the more feminine he or she was perceived to be. These patterns suggest that victimization is perceived to be not only a feminine, but also a feminizing, experience.

Although this study points to the importance of social context for understanding the effect of categorization on cognition, it does not explicitly vary situations. In a subsequent study with Kenneth Pike, I examined the effect of situational variations and the interaction between social category and situation, as well as the relative importance of ingroup bias and social power (Howard and Pike 1986). Using the categories of race and socioeconomic position, we hypothesized that more blame, more negative evaluations, and more severe sanctions would be attributed to black than to white actors, and to working-class than to middle-class actors, predictions that emphasize the importance of the ideological traces of social power.

White and primarily middle-class subjects read transcripts of one of two situations; in one a man was charged with disorderly conduct after creating a disturbance at a party, and in the other a social services caseworker was obtaining intake information on a man applying for unemployment benefits. The situation itself was influential: actors were blamed more and evaluated more negatively in the arrest than in the unemployment situation. Equally important, situation interacted with both race and class; blacks were blamed more than whites in the unemployment situation, for example, while whites were blamed more than blacks in the arrest situation. Moreover, class was somewhat more influential than race in the unemployment situation, and race was much more influential than class in the arrest situation. There was also substantial evidence of the influence of ideology on cognitive reactions; the direction of this influence differed by situation. Class ethnocentrism was found in the unemployment situation, but a pro-minority group racial bias was found in the arrest situation. These patterns suggest that these white college students are fairly conscious of racial discrimination, in contrast to class discrimination. These effects attest to the contextual embeddedness of social categorization, and hence cognitive processing. Future researchers would do well to place behaviors of interest within significant contexts, especially as these contexts are defined by existing systems of social categorization.

(3) *Attributions are shaped by the historical, economic and political context of intergroup relations.* Differential evaluation of specific categories appears always to accompany the process of categorization (Tajfel 1982). Thus social power relations are fundamental to the process of attribution, affecting both the direction and the content of causal and trait attributions. For example, the positive ingroup bias hypothesized to underlie attributions for all individuals is altered by the culturally prevalent negative image of dominated groups; thus attributions made by members of socially subordinate groups, in some circumstances, echo the attributions of those who are dominant, and thus are self-denigrating, rather than self-serving.

Assessment of the effects of social power relations on ingroup–outgroup biases requires that attributions be elicited from members of both majority and minority groups. In one such study, Sagar and Schofield (1980) replicated Duncan's (1976) study of the effect of racial stereotypes in a sample of both black and white sixth-grade students. They found similar results among both black and white students; prevailing social hierarchies were more influential to attribution than an ingroup bias. A study of the effects of gender hierarchy reports similar results (Deaux and Emswiller 1974). Independent of the type of task, a good performance by a male is attributed to skill, whereas a similar performance by a female is attributed to chance. When a task is typed as feminine, and thus associated with the lower status group, a male is perceived as just as competent as a female. These patterns were found in attributions made by both female and male subjects, another indication of the pervasive influence of social power on attribution.

Deschamps (1983) replicates Taylor and Doria's (1979) evaluation of the relative strength of the ingroup and self-serving attributional biases, but places this question in the context of social power. Categorizations were based on gender and on the construction of experimental groups. Males show a stronger ingroup bias than females. Within gender, girls do not differentiate between self and other, but boys favor self over other. Across gender, girls devalue self in relation to the ingroup, although they do not distinguish between ingroup and outgroup. Boys diminish their overvaluation of self, when ingroup–outgroup dynamics are introduced, as social identity theory suggests. Deschamps concludes that the egocentric tendency is less strong than ethnocentrism in the case of socially subordinate categories such as girls. When multiple categories are involved, the inferiority of the subordinate group category is manifested at the individual rather than the group level, hence attributions to self are less favorable than attributions either to ingroup or to outgroup.

A study by Mann and Taylor (1974) addresses a different intersection of categorization and culture, investigating the effect on attributions of what Deschamps

(1983) calls crossed versus simple categorizations. Cross-cutting social categorizations refer to overlapping categories (e.g., social class and ethnicity). In this study, French and English Canadians were asked to judge the degree to which positive or negative acts were caused by personality traits of the actor. Each subject received three forms, one identifying the ethnicity of the actor, a second identifying the social class, and a third identifying both variables (a highly reactive procedure). The attributions of French Canadians were more ethnocentric than the attributions of the English, which the authors attribute to the ethnic minority position of the French Canadians. This pattern reflects social power relationships; the content of the social representations was also influential. English Canadians placed more emphasis on class than on ethnicity, whereas the French emphasized ethnicity over class. The specificity of these patterns to particular categories reflects the influence of cultural content.

Guimond and Simard (1979) extend this line of research in exploring attributions for intergroup inequality. Drawing on Lerner's "just world theory" of attribution (Lerner and Miller 1978), they evaluate explanations of patterns of domination and subordination among French and English Canadians in Quebec. The dominant English Canadians tend to blame the French and attribute inequality to individuals, whereas the subordinate French Canadians blame the English and offer structural explanations. The attributions offered by the English are consistent with Lerner's just world theory, which posits a self-protective and individualistic attributional tendency to blame actors for their own misfortunes. The attributions offered by the French minority contradict just world theory. That the attributions of the dominant group support just world theory, and the attributions of the subordinate group contradict this theory suggests that attribution theory and research may represent more adequately the position of the politically dominant than a position of subordination. Evaluating the generalizability of attributional principles to subordinate groups is a critical task for the future.

General Conclusions

There is compelling theoretical and empirical evidence for the significance of social categorization, interactive social context, and sociopolitical hierarchy for a complete understanding of attribution, and, more generally, of social cognition. Despite this evidence, few attribution studies treat individuals as group members, focus on individuals interacting as social actors, address the explanation of socially meaningful behavior, or place that behavior in a broader societal context. This review of attribution theory and research demonstrates both the generally prevalent failure to recognize the social context of attribution, and the avenues within attribution likely to be receptive to research redressing these omissions.

This review questions the most basic assumption of all models of attribution, that the causes of behavior can be categorized into internal or external factors. This assumption implies that internal and external are clearly distinguishable. In contrast, according to a truly social theory of attribution, behavior must be explained in terms of people's shared, collective, social properties, in addition to their individual personalities. Attribution theories assume not only a division but also an oppositional relationship between internal and external, or individual and social factors. Theories of trait attribution go on to assume that only individualized, idiosyncratic behavior is deliberate and internally motivated. In contrast, a social theory of attribution must recognize the inseparability of individual and society; such a theory must be able to account for intentional collective action. Social category memberships must be treated as potentially causal factors in themselves. The cultural specificity or generality of attributional patterns must be demonstrated through not only cross-cultural, but also international intergroup research. Only this type of research can reveal the interactive influence of existing social categorizations and asymmetric power relations on cognitive reactions to social behavior.

What implications does this evidence suggest for traditional research on attribution and cognition? An adequate answer to this question requires an assessment of the pervasiveness of social categorization. In situations of apparent social homogeneity, social categorization may not seem relevant. However, substantial evidence indicates that in situations where there are no clear cues upon which to base differentiation, humans are prone to create groups, to categorize, on the basis of the flimsiest criteria (Billig and Tajfel 1973; Tajfel 1982). Moreover, even within socially homogenous situations, actors may well apply expectations based on culturally prevalent systems of categorization.

The prevailing view of social cognition emphasizes the cognitive capacities of the individual perceiver and the limits of those capacities. Differences in behavior are attributed typically to psychological differences among individuals. This review suggests that categorization, which develops in accord with culturally defined categories and category content, systematically explains presumably individual differences. Some behavior is idiosyncratic; there are circumstances in which behavioral differences are explained by individual characteristics. But when dimensions of categorization exist or have been constructed, and these categorizations are salient, behavioral differences are due to the mediation of environmental information by these systems of categorization and their location within existing sociopolitical hierarchies.

This analysis points to important qualifications on a substantial body of research on social cognition. Most of this research has focused on the responses of members of dominant groups to each other, and, less often, on the responses of members of dominant groups to the behaviors of members of subordinate outgroups. The limited nature of these intra- and intergroup profiles has been possible partly because the behavioral contexts considered in this research have been relatively asocial. These patterns cannot be generalized to account for the behavior of members of subordinate groups or for behaviors in more socially meaningful situations. Recently burgeoning cross-national research is beginning to demonstrate the cultural specificity of attributional and other cognitive patterns (Bond 1988). Ironically, there is much more resistance to recognizing that these patterns may not generalize to all categories within the US adult population.

In light of this evidence, it is intriguing that, on the whole, mainstream social psychologists in the United States continue to minimize the social aspects of attribution and cognition. Certainly some of the work cited here has appeared in US social psychology journals. However, the group of US researchers who have chosen to focus on the social aspects of cognition is small. This body of research has not had the general impact on the field as a whole that it merits. Moscovici's (1972) assertion that social circumstances create research questions is undoubtedly true, but it does not explain the prevailing minimization of the social aspects of cognition. The United States, like virtually all other nations, has a history of social conflict that should stimulate the kinds of questions explored in this article. I suggest that the void of research on such questions is due to the extreme individualism of North American social psychology. This individualism reflects the prevailing liberal humanist ideology, which asserts the distinctiveness of the individual from her or his environment, the control of the individual over the environment, and equality among individuals. Given the overwhelming evidence of the explanatory limits of this individualism, social psychologists must be skeptical about assertions of fundamental, primary, or general cognitive processes that do not take into account social categorization and intergroup differentiation and evaluation. Social categorization and hence intergroup relations are *central* to cognitive processes. I conclude with an articulate statement of a similar claim by Jeffrey Alexander (1987: 5):

> Focusing on individual consciousness...does not necessarily imply an individual*istic* position that sees this individual consciousness as unrelated to any distinctively social, or collective process. What it does mean, however, is that such collective force must be subjectively conceptualized.

References

Adam, B. D. 1978. *The Survival of Domination: Inferiorization and Everyday Life*. New York: Elsevier North-Holland.

Alexander, J. C. 1987. "From reduction to linkage: The long view of the micro–macro link." In J. C. Alexander, B. Giesen, R. Munch, and N. J. Smelser (eds.) *The Micro–Macro Link*. Berkeley, Calif.: University of California Press.

Allen, V. L. and Wilder, D. A. 1975. "Categorization, belief similarity, and group discrimination." *Journal of Personality and Social Psychology* 32: 971–7.

Allport, G. W. 1954. *The Nature of Prejudice*. Cambridge, Mass.: Addison-Wesley.

Allport, G. W. and Kramer, B. M. 1945. "Some roots of prejudice." *Journal of Psychology* 22: 9–39.

Back, K. 1981. "Small Groups." In M. Rosenberg and R. Turner (eds.) *Social Psychology: Sociological Perspectives*. New York: Basic Books.

Berger, J., Cohen, B. and Zelditch, M., Jr. 1972. "Status characteristics and social interaction." *American Sociological Review* 37: 241–55.

Billig, M. and Tajfel, H. 1973. "Social categorization and similarity in intergroup behavior." *European Journal of Social Psychology* 3: 27–52.

Bond, M. H. (ed.) 1988. *The Cross-Cultural Challenge to Social Psychology*. Newbury Park, Calif.: Sage Publications.

Bruner, J. S. 1957. "On perceptual readiness." *Psychological Review* 64: 123–51.

Campbell, D. T. 1956. "Enhancement of contrast as composite habit." *Journal of Abnormal Social Psychology* 3: 350–5.

Carver, C. S. and Scheier, M. F. 1981. *Attention and Self-Regulation: A Control-Theory Approach to Human Behavior*. New York: Springer-Verlag.

Deaux, K. 1976. "Sex: a perspective on the attribution process." In J. H. Harvey, W. Ickes, and R. F. Kidd (eds.) *New Directions in Attribution Research*, vol. 1. Hillsdale, NJ: Erlbaum.

Deaux, K. and Emswiller, T. 1974. "Explanations of successful performance on sex-linked tasks: What is skill for the male is luck for the female." *Journal of Personality and Social Psychology* 29: 80–5.

de Beauvoir, S. 1972. *The Second Sex*. Harmondsworth: Penguin Books.

Derrida, J. 1974. *Of Grammatology*. Baltimore: Johns Hopkins University Press.

——1984. *Signeponge/Signponge*, trans. Richard Rand. New York: Columbia University Press.

Deschamps, J.-C. 1983. "Social attribution." In J. Jaspars, F. D. Fincham, and M. Hewstone (eds.) *Attribution Theory and Research: Conceptual Developmental and Social Dimensions*. New York: Academic.

Doise, W., Deschamps, J.-C. and Meyer, G. 1978. "The accentuation of intracategory similarities." In H. Tajfel (ed.) *Differentiation Between Social Groups: Studies in the Social Psychology of Intergroup Relations*. London: Academic.

Duncan, B. L. 1976. "Differential social perception and attribution of intergroup violence: testing the lower limits of stereotyping of blacks." *Journal of Personality and Social Psychology* 34: 590–8.

Dweck, C. S. and T. E. Goetz. 1978. "Attributions and learned helplessness." In J. H. Harvey, W. Ickes, and R. F. Kidd (eds.) *New Directions in Attribution Research*, vol. 2. Hillsdale, NJ: Erlbaum.

Endler, N. S. and Magnusson, D. 1976. "Toward an interactional psychology of personality." *Psychological Bulletin* 83: 956–74.

Feshbach, S. 1984. "The 'personality' of personality theory and research." *Personality and Social Psychology Bulletin* 10: 446–56.

Fiske, S. T. and Taylor, S. E. 1984. *Social Cognition*. Reading, Mass.: Addison-Wesley.

Forgas, J. P. 1981. "What is social about social cognition?" In J. P. Forgas (ed.) *Social Cognition*. New York: Academic.

Gergen, K. J. 1985. "The social constructionist movement in modern psychology." *American Psychologist* 40: 266–73.

Goode, W. J. 1982. "Why men resist." In B. Thorne (ed.) *Rethinking the Family: Some Feminist Questions*. New York: Longman.

Guimond, S. and Simard, L. M. 1979. "Perception et interprétation des inégalités économiques entre Francophones et Anglophones au Quebec." Paper presented to the 40th Congress of the Canadian Psychological Society, Quebec.

Habermas, J. 1971. *Knowledge and Human Interests*. Boston: Beacon Press.

Hamilton, D. L. 1979. "A cognitive-attributional analysis of stereotyping." In L. Berkowitz (ed.) *Advances in Experimental Social Psychology*, vol. 12. New York: Academic.

Hamilton, D. L., Katz, L. B. and Leirer, V. O. 1980. "Organizational processes in impression formation." In R. Hastie, T. M. Ostrom, E. B. Ebbesen, R. S. Wyer, D. L. Hamilton, and D. E. Carlston (eds.) *Person Memory: The Cognitive Basis of Social Perception*. Hillsdale, NJ: Erlbaum.

Hamilton, V. L. 1978. "Who is responsible? Toward a *social* psychology of responsibility attribution." *Social Psychology Quarterly* 41: 316–28.

Harvey, J. H., Ickes, W. and Kidd. R. F. (eds.) 1976. *New Directions in Attribution Research*, vol. 1. Hillsdale, NJ: Erlbaum.

Harvey, J. H. and Weary, G. 1981. *Perspectives on Attributional Processes*. Dubuque, Ia: William C. Brown.

Heider, F. 1958. *The Psychology of Interpersonal Relations*. New York: Wiley.

Hewstone, M. and Jaspars, J. M. F. 1984. "Intergroup relations and attribution processes." In H. Tajfel (ed.) *The Social Dimension*, vol. 2. Cambridge: Cambridge University Press.

Hilton, D. J. and Slugoski, B. R. 1986. "Knowledge-based causal attribution: The abnormal conditions focus model." *Psychological Bulletin* 93: 75–88.

Horkheimer, M. and Adorno, T. W. 1972. *Dialectics of Enlightenment*. New York: Seabury Press.

Howard, J. A. 1984a. "Societal influences on attribution: Blaming some victims more than others." *Journal of Personality and Social Psychology* 47: 494–505.

——1984b. "The 'normal' victim: The effects of gender stereotypes on reactions to victims." *Social Psychology Quarterly* 47: 270–81.

——1985. "Further appraisal of correspondent inference theory." *Personality and Social Psychology Bulletin* 11: 467–77.

Howard, J. A. and Pike, K. C. 1986. "Ideological investment in cognitive processing: The influence of social statuses on attribution." *Social Psychology Quarterly* 49: 154–67.

Jaggar, A. 1983. *Feminist Politics and Human Nature*. Totowa, NJ: Rowman and Allanheld.

Jennings, D., Amabile, T. M. and Ross, L. 1982. "Informal covariation assessment: Data-based vs. theory-based judgments." In A. Tversky, P. Slovic, and D. Kahneman (eds.) *Judgment Under Uncertainty: Heuristics and Biases*. New York: Cambridge University Press.

Jones, E. E. and Davis, K. E. 1965. "From acts to dispositions." In L. Berkowitz (ed.) *Advances in Experimental Social Psychology*, vol. 2. New York: Academic.

Jones, E. E. and McGillis, D. 1976. "Correspondent inferences and the attribution cube: A comparative reappraisal." In J. H. Harvey, W. Ickes, and R. F. Kidd (eds.) *New Directions in Attribution Research*, vol. 1. Hillsdale, NJ: Erlbaum

Kassin, S. M. 1979. "Consensus information, prediction, and causal attribution: A review of the literature and issues." *Journal of Personality and Social Psychology* 37: 1966–81.

Kelley, H. H. 1967. "Attribution theory in social psychology." In D. Levine (ed.) *Nebraska Symposium on Motivation*, vol. 15. Lincoln: University of Nebraska Press.

Kelley, H. H. 1973. "The processes of causal attribution." *American Psychologist* 28: 107–28.

Langer, E. J., Fiske, S. T., Taylor, S. E. and Chanowitz, B. 1976. "Stigma, staring and discomfort: A novel stimulus hypothesis." *Journal of Experimental Social Psychology* 12: 451–63.

Lerner, M. J. and Miller, D. T. 1978. "'Just World' research and the attribution process: Looking back and ahead." *Psychological Bulletin* 85: 1030–51.

Linville, P. and Jones, E. E. 1980. "Polarized appraisals of out-group members." *Journal of Personality and Social Psychology* 38: 689–703.

McArthur, L. Z. 1972. "The how and what of why: Some determinants and consequences of causal attribution." *Journal of Personality and Social Psychology* 22: 171–93.

McArthur, L. Z. and Friedman, S. 1980. "Illusory correlation in impression formation: Variations in the shared distinctiveness effect as a function of the distinctive person's age, race, and sex." *Journal of Personality and Social Psychology* 39: 615–24.

McCrae, R. R. and Costa, P. T., Jr. 1984. "Personality is transcontextual: A reply to Veroff." *Personality and Social Psychology Bulletin* 10: 175–9.

Mann, J. F. and Taylor, D. M. 1974. "Attribution of causality: Role of ethnicity and social class." *Journal of Social Psychology* 94: 3–13.

Markus, H. 1977. "Self-schemata and processing information about the self." *Journal of Personality and Social Psychology* 35: 63–78.

Markus, H. and Smith, J. 1981. "The influence of self-schemas on the perception of others." In N. Cantor and J. Kihlstrom (eds.) *Personality, Cognition and Social Interaction*. Hillsdale, NJ: Erlbaum.

Mead, G. H. 1934. *Mind, Self and Society*. Chicago: University of Chicago Press.

Meeker, B. F. 1981. "Expectation states and interpersonal behavior." In M. Rosenberg and R. Turner (eds.) *Social Psychology: Sociological Perspectives*. New York: Basic Books.

Miller, J. G. 1984. "Culture and the development of everyday social explanation." *Journal of Personality and Social Psychology* 46: 961–78.

Moscovici, S. 1972. "Society and theory in social psychology." In J. Israel and H. Tajfel (eds.) *The Context of Social Psychology: A Critical Assessment*. New York: Academic.

Moscovici, S. 1981. "On social representations." In J. P. Forgas (ed.) *Social Cognition*. New York: Academic.

Moscovici, S. and Faucheux, C. 1972. "Social influence, conformity bias and the study of active minorities." In L. Berkowitz (ed.) *Advances in Experimental Social Psychology*, vol. 6. New York: Academic.

Nisbett, R. E. and Ross, L. 1980. *Human Inference: Strategies and Shortcomings of Social Judgment*. Englewood Cliffs, NJ: Prentice-Hall.

Oakes, P. 1987. "The salience of social categories." In J. C. Turner (ed.) *Rediscovering the Social Group: A Self-Categorization Theory*. Oxford: Blackwell Publishers.

Oakes, P. and Turner, J. C. 1980. "Social categorization and intergroup behavior: Does minimal intergroup discrimination make social identity more positive?" *European Journal of Social Psychology* 10: 295–301.

Read, S. J. 1987. "Constructing causal scenarios: A knowledge structure approach to causal reasoning." *Journal of Personality and Social Psychology* 52: 288–302.

Ridgeway, C. L. 1983. *The Dynamics of Small Groups*. New York: St. Martin's Press.

Rokeach, M. 1960. *The Open and Closed Mind*. New York: Basic Books.

Rosenberg, M. 1979. *Conceiving the Self*. Malabar, Fla.: Krieger.

Ross, L. 1977. "The intuitive psychologist and his shortcomings: Distortions in the attribution process." In L. Berkowitz (ed.) *Advances in Experimental Social Psychology*. New York: Academic.

Sagar, H. A. and Schofield, J. W. 1980. "Racial and behavioral cues in black and white children's perceptions of ambiguously aggressive acts." *Journal of Personality and Social Psychology* 39: 590–8.

Sampson, E. E. 1977. "Psychology and the American ideal." *Journal of Personality and Social Psychology* 35: 767–82.

Sampson, E. E. 1989. "The deconstruction of the self." In J. Shotter and K. J. Gergen (eds.) *Texts of Identity*. Newbury Park, Calif.: Sage.

Scull, A. T. 1988. "Deviance and social control." In N. J. Smelser (ed.) *Handbook of Sociology*. Newbury Park, Calif.: Sage.

Senn, D. J. 1989. "Myopic social psychology: An overemphasis on individualistic explanations of social behavior." In M. R. Leary (ed.) *The State of Social Psychology*, Calif.: Sage.

Smith, S. S., Richardson, D. and Hendrick, C. 1980. "Bibliography of journal articles in personality and social psychology: 1979." *Personality and Social Psychology Bulletin* 6: 606–36.

Stephan, W. H. 1985 "Intergroup relations." In G. Lindzey and E. Aronson (eds.) *Handbook of Social Psychology*, vol. II, 3rd edn. Hillsdale, NJ: Erlbaum.

Struch, N. and Schwartz, S. H. 1989. "Intergroup aggression: Its predictors and distinctness from in-group bias." *Journal of Personality and Social Psychology* 56: 364–73.

Tajfel, H. 1972. "Social categorization." In S. Moscovici (ed.) *Introduction a la Psychologie Sociale*, vol. 1. Paris: Larousse.

——1978. *Differentiation Between Social Groups: Studies in Intergroup Behavior* (European Monographs in Social Psychology, no. 14). London: Academic.

——1981. *Human Groups and Social Categories: Studies in Social Psychology*. Cambridge: Cambridge University Press.

——1982. "Social psychology of intergroup relations." *Annual Review of Psychology* 33: 1–39.

Tajfel, H. and Turner, J. C. 1979. "An integrative theory of intergroup conflict." In W. G. Austin and S. Worchel (eds.) *The Social Psychology of Intergroup Relations*. Monterey, Calif.: Brooks/Cole.

Taylor, S. E. and Fiske, S. T., 1978. "Salience, attention, and attribution: Top of the head phenomena." In L. Berkowitz (ed.) *Advances in Experimental Social Psychology*, vol. 11. New York: Academic.

Taylor, S. E., Fiske, S. T., Etcoff, N. L., and Ruderman, A. J. 1978. "Categorical and contextual bases of person memory and stereotyping." *Journal of Personality and Social Psychology* 36: 778–93.

Taylor, D. M. and Doria, J. R. 1979. "Self serving and group serving bias in attribution." Unpublished manuscript, McGill University, Montreal.

Taylor, D. M. and Jaggi, V. 1974. "Ethnocentrism and causal attribution in a south Indian context." *Journal of Cross-Cultural Psychology* 5: 162–71.

Turner, J. C. 1987. *Rediscovering the Social Group: A Self-Categorization Theory*. Oxford: Blackwell Publishers.

Turner, J. C., Brown, R. J. and Tajfel, H. 1979. "Social comparison and group interest in ingroup favoritism." *European Journal of Social Psychology* 9: 187–204.

Turner, J. C. and Giles, H. (eds.). 1981. *Intergroup Behavior*. Oxford: Blackwell Publishers.

Tversky, A. and Kahneman, D. 1974. "Judgment under uncertainty: Heuristics and biases." *Science* 185: 1124–31.

Weiner, B. 1974. *Achievement Motivation and Attribution Theory*. Morristown, NJ: General Learning Press.

Weiner, B., Russell, D. and Lerman, D. 1978. "Affective consequences of causal ascriptions." In J. H. Harvey, W. Ickes, and R. F. Kidd (eds.) *New Directions in Attribution Research*, vol. 2. Hillsdale, NJ: Erlbaum.

Wells, G. L. and Harvey, J. H. 1977. "Do people use consensus information in making causal attributions?" *Journal of Personality and Social Psychology* 35: 279–93.

Wilder, D. A. 1986. "Social categorization: Implications for creation and reduction of intergroup bias." In L. Berkowitz (ed.) *Advances in Experimental Social Psychology*, vol. 19. New York: Academic.

9 The Meek Shall Not Inherit the Earth

L. Richard Della Fave

One of the most persistent features of human societies has been the existence of some form of stratification. Theorists have tried to explain it: functionalists (Baltzell 1958; Davis 1948; Davis and Moore 1945; Keller 1963; Parsons 1949, 1953) have stressed the unequal functional importance of occupational roles; elitist conflict theorists (Dahrendorf 1959; Lenski 1966; Mosca 1939; Pareto 1935) have emphasized the inherently unequal ability of people to pursue the struggle over scarce resources; and radical conflict theorists (Anderson 1977, Habermas 1973; Harrington 1976; Marx and Engels 1959; Miliband 1969) have pointed to a succession of historically specific types of social systems whose very structures (principles of organization) insure continuing inequality.

Despite their considerable differences, each type of theorist regards legitimation as an important mechanism through which stratification is perpetuated (Coser 1956; Habermas 1973). Legitimation refers to a belief on the part of a large majority of the populace that institutionalized inequality in the distribution of primary resources – such as power, wealth, and prestige – is essentially right and reasonable (Alves and Rossi 1978; Feagin 1972; Jasso and Rossi 1977; Rainwater 1974). While the specific rationales used to justify inequality vary from one time and place to another (Bendix 1956; Dumont 1970; Wilson 1973), the essence of legitimation is based in the existence of some set of such justifications which is widely believed – indeed, justifications sometimes so taken for granted as not even to be questioned (Dumont 1970; Moore 1978; Shibutani and Kwan 1965).

Given the importance of legitimation in these writers' works, it is surprising that none, with the exception of Habermas (1973), has attempted to develop a systematic theory of legitimation, one that would specify its causes, explain its strength under various conditions, and describe the process through which it ultimately becomes part of the individual's thought. The propositions I will develop should be a component of this type of theory.

In developing a theory of legitimation it is important to understand that legitimation is only one of a number of means of maintaining stratification, namely through gaining at least the tacit consent of the populace, especially those who are relatively disadvantaged. In fact, legitimation is only one of several consent-generating mechanisms. Others include hopes for future upward mobility for self or children (Chinoy 1955; Form 1976; Lane 1962; Lopreato and Hazelrigg 1972); fear of jeopardizing one's absolute standard of living (Mankoff 1970); a feeling of powerlessness (Wright 1976); fear that the freedom and popular influence existing under representative democracy could be lost in a revolution aimed at bringing about greater equality (Anderson 1977); and the inability to imagine any egalitarian

Reprinted from *American Sociological Review* 45 (December 1980): 955–71.

alternative model of society (Dahl 1967; Mann 1970; Moore 1978; Sallach 1974; Sennett and Cobb 1972).

A comprehensive theory of stratification would need to consider all those mechanisms as well as all-important non-consensual factors such as coercion (Anderson 1977; Lenski 1966), the influence of moneyed interests over government (Domhoff 1967, 1971; Mills 1956; Prewitt and Stone 1973), and the structural imperatives of institutions in class-ridden societies (Harrington 1976; Miliband 1969; Parkin 1971). While the development of such a comprehensive theory is far beyond my intended scope here, this work can be seen as one aspect of some such larger project to which a growing number of social scientists are contributing.

Legitimation, we should be careful to note, can apply to any one of at least four system levels: (1) the particular status occupied by a given individual or group, (2) the particular regime in power, (3) a particular system of political economy, and (4) stratification itself (Della Fave 1974). The propositions to be developed here will focus primarily upon the fourth – the most general – level. However, the multileveled nature of legitimation must be kept in mind in order to understand how it is possible to make sense out of the seemingly paradoxical coexistence of interest group conflict, even to the point of revolution, and the continued legitimation of some form of stratification.

My objective is to develop propositions concerning legitimation through the use of the concept of self-evaluation. Throughout, legitimation is treated as a process in which the structure of the larger society becomes incorporated within the inner consciousness of the individual (Mead 1964: 141). I will show the compatibility of this approach with three widely differing orientations: in macrosociology, in the microsociology of social behaviorism, and with empirical evidence derived from both survey and observational research dealing with a wide range of specific topics.

Then, first, I review relevant aspects of the work of Marx, Mosca, and Parsons (representing three major approaches in macrosociology – namely, radical conflict theory, elite conflict theory and functionalism), respectively (Strasser 1976), pointing out, despite their differences, important similarities in their treatment of legitimation. Second, I turn to social psychology (namely, Mead's theory of the self, recent work on status attribution and equity theory, and Bem's critique of cognitive dissonance theory); I define the concept of self-evaluation, explicate its role in the legitimation process and, at that point, specify propositions. Third, I discuss the role of social institutions in the legitimation process and, fourth, conclude by exploring possible sources of delegitimation.

Macrosociology

The work of Marx, Mosca, and Parsons that I review is macrosociological in that its major focus is understanding why whole societies are organized as they are and why they change in particular ways. This does not mean that there is no concern with the social psychological processes that affect structure and change in societies – far from it. In fact, if these works lacked a social psychological side, it would have been far more difficult to identify relationships between them and the more explicitly social psychological work which I will also discuss.

Marx

Given Marx's view of capitalist society as rent by an irreconcilable conflict of interest between proletariat and bourgeoisie (Marx and Engels 1959), he was faced with the task of explaining why this objectively defined conflict was not translated directly into class warfare over the very existence of the capitalist system itself. The answer, of course, lay in the concept of class consciousness. Workers display class consciousness in its rudimentary form as a result of their concrete struggles with employers over wages and working conditions (Marx 1906: 396–7; Marx 1963: 170–5; Marx and Engels 1959: 19–20). Marx was confident that, after prolonged struggle and with the help of the radical party, workers would realize that only by overthrowing the capitalist system itself could they put an end to their own exploitation. He also believed they would come to see the pivotal role assigned to the working class by history – that of the liberator, rescuing mankind from the exploitation of class society (Marx and Engels 1959: 19) – by which action it would usher in a new era of equality and human freedom (Marx 1959).

Marx (1959) was convinced, however, that even a successful revolutionary proletariat would still be under the sway of a capitalist-oriented ideology that justified more than trivial inequalities in the distribution of primary resources. Only after a period during which the revolutionary proletariat had actually been running the society would the working class arrive at a level of consciousness that would support the idea of equality, with exceptions based solely on the basis of need. Therefore, it is understandable how, in the absence of fully developed class consciousness, bitter conflict could coexist with the legitimation of stratification (a point to which we will return, later). While Marx fails to explain how the ideology of the ruling class became incorporated in the consciousness of the workers in the first place, he gives us some potentially fruitful insights into the legitimation process, insights that can best be understood if we look at the way stratification is supposedly delegitimated.

In Marx's schema, three things precede the delegitimation of stratification. First, the workers embrace an ideology that casts them in the role of the deliverers of mankind from oppression. Second, they are actually victorious in revolution. And third, they have the experience of successfully running an entire society by themselves, without the aid of their "betters." All three things, especially when taken together, are powerful sources of confidence in one's ability to control one's world, to act competently. Conversely, the experiences faced by workers (in their subordinated positions within the normal workings of capitalism) work to undermine that confidence – to make them feel dependent, powerless, and of little value.

In our subsequent discussions of the work of Mosca and Parsons we shall see that similar implications can be drawn, despite the sharp disagreements between each of these writers and Marx and, indeed, despite their differences with each other.

Mosca

Unlike Marx, Mosca saw no Utopian vision of equality or freedom from the domination of some type of elite. In fact, central to his approach is the notion, often credited to Pareto (Meisel 1965), that the few, everywhere and always, shall rule the many (Mosca 1939).

While Mosca readily acknowledged that the dominance of elites rested heavily upon the use and threat of force, he was acutely aware of the importance of legitimation. Regardless of which elite happened to be in power, it promulgated a political formula that emphasized the allegedly superior qualities of its members (Mosca 1939: 82–92), by portraying them as being especially intelligent, moral, energetic, and/or strong. Most importantly, that political formula always portrays the ruling elite as embodying the society's most cherished values in greater measure than do other classes. Here, he introduces a theme that later recurs in the writing of Schumpeter (1951) as well as of functionalists such as Parsons (1949, 1953) and Davis and Moore (1945) – that is, the notion that members of the elite claim superior competence in precisely those activities (functions) that are most crucial to the particular society's survival and prosperity, those things such as military virtue, ritual purity, commercial acumen, or impartial justice.

Despite the variability in types of society and the qualities claimed by elites, his political formula is everywhere and always based upon the premise that superior people deserve to rule and enjoy the perquisites thereof. The successful promulgation of such a political formula cannot help but enhance, among members of the ruling elite, their feelings of competence and of being important and valued and yet undermine, among the masses, those same feelings.

Parsons

Turning now to the leading writer in the functionalist tradition, Talcott Parsons, we note a very different model of society than is characteristic of either Marx or Mosca. For Parsons (1949, 1951, 1953), a society is an organic whole in which the parts are differentiated, yet coordinated, to work toward the best interests of the whole. However, the functions (occupational roles) performed by the various parts are not of equal importance. In fact, there is a hierarchy of functional importance, with those roles most central to the survival and prosperity of society occupying the highest ranks (Parsons 1949: 83–4; 1953: 102–3).

For Parsons there is well-nigh total consensus among all segments of the population concerning the functional importance of the various occupational roles, a consensus embodied in the very moral order of society (Parsons 1949: 69–70). Successful performance of these highly ranked roles represents the highest level of conformity to society's norms. And since all societies must reward conformity and punish deviance, the incumbents of the most functionally important roles receive the greatest amount of rewards in the form of primary resources. For it to be otherwise would seem incongruous and wrong to any properly socialized member of a society.

Thus, the legitimacy accorded the unequal distribution of primary resources is based upon the deeply internalized norms of the society and is not subject to instrumental considerations of individual self-interest (Parsons 1951: 551). This implies that the belief in the superiority of those in the most functionally important positions is nearly universal and deeply internalized as well.

Parsons's notion of an internalized moral order, with its hierarchy of roles based upon the idea of differential functional importance for society, elevates the sense of worth of the functionally most important, while that of most others is humbled (Parsons 1949: 73).

We have seen a common thread running through the work of writers as diverse as Marx, Mosca, and Parsons. In each case there is an ideology that justifies a highly stratified system of resource allocation. But this ideology also allocates feelings of potency, competence, and, above all, importance and self-worth in a manner congruent with that of primary resources. In order to better understand the mechanisms through which distributions of primary resources are reflected in and reproduce congruent distributions of feelings of self-worth, we now examine works in social psychology.

Social Psychology

Any theory of legitimation must ultimately answer the question of how legitimations of stratification become part of the consciousness of the individuals who make up society. By focusing, primarily, on the concept of self, I will describe the various phases of a process through which this might occur, beginning with the work of Mead.

Mead

For Mead (1934) the self was a crucial concept in the study of human behavior because only by having a self does the human organism become a conscious, reflective person. The self is truly a creature of society as it can develop only from the reactions of others. We become conscious of ourselves when we realize that our gestures, including verbal ones, call out the same response in others as they do in ourselves. Once we have established this, we can then take the role of the "other" and anticipate others' reactions to us or to a third party. Thus, we become aware of ourselves through the reactions of others (Mead 1934: 141–9).

Because of the prolonged and acute dependency of the human infant we develop strong emotional bonds with those who satisfy our vital needs. They become our first significant others, and their reactions take on great importance. As we mature, our needs become more diversified and, as our circle of contacts broadens, we acquire a growing number of significant others.

As the development of the self continues, we become aware of certain similarities between what others expect of us and how they react to us. People, in general, see us as bright or dull, attractive or ugly, strong or weak, capable or incapable. This amalgam of perceived generalized expectations and reactions constitutes the generalized other. It is through the generalized other that we come to discover who we are and what is expected of us. Though our views (of who and what we are) vary not only over time but also from one situation to another, for most of us there remains a degree of consistency and stability commonly associated with maturity and mental health.

In an illustration of how the generalized other develops, Mead (1964) uses the example of the way in which we come to develop conceptions of the value of different goods in the marketplace: through observing how others react to the goods and, specifically, by noting for how much they offer them for sale and, in contrast, how much they are prepared to pay for them. Keeping in mind the ability of the self to view itself as object, we can see that selves are able to develop a conception of their own social value in very much the same way as they are able to understand the value of goods (Blau 1964). This important idea will be developed further when we review some of the work in equity theory.

Recent work in social psychology, relevant to the problem at hand, has stemmed from two related lines of theoretical development – namely, equity theory and status attribution theory. Both have benefited from extensive laboratory experimentation. Once they have been described, they will be linked to Mead's theory of the self through the work of Bem (1967).

Equity theory

Equity theory is based upon the notion of a balance; that is, individuals have a built-in tendency toward cognitive consistency (Festinger 1957; Heider 1958). Its main principle is that human beings carry around in their heads a notion that rewards should be proportional to investments, an idea Homans (1961, 1974) calls distributive justice. When the principle of distributive justice is violated, people become angry – morally outraged, one might even say. The individual who contributes more to the activities of a collectivity ought to receive a greater share of the rewards than one who contributes less. Contributions can be in the form of expenditure of energy, lending of expertise, donation of money, acceptance of responsibility, etc. Evidence supportive of this approach for small groups is abundant (Homans 1974; Leventhal 1975; Ofshe and Ofshe 1970).

The relevance of equity theory for a theory of legitimation of inequality in larger societies has been pointed out by Lerner (1975) and Walster and Walster (1975). Those in power are assumed to be contributing more and, therefore, are seen as deserving of greater rewards. If ego is not among the major contributors to the group, even he/she comes to feel deserving of lesser rewards. Thus, inequality is made to seem legitimate. However, the unanswered question is, *Why* do people tend to perceive those in power as contributing more? For an answer we must turn to status attribution theory. Before doing this, however, it is important to keep in mind several relevant differences between small groups and whole societies – especially large, highly differentiated ones. In societies, inequality of resources is enormous, as compared with small groups. In most small groups (certainly those studied in the laboratory), coercion is not available to enforce inequality, as it is in societies. Also, the life of small groups is very short; in fact, they lack a history. Thus, inequality cannot become institutionalized over generations. Finally, small groups are, by definition, collectivities in which the members interact face to face. There is none of the remoteness as exists between leaders and populace in large societies. Among other things, this means that it is much more difficult to manufacture an impressive image of oneself, thereby to inflate one's importance, in a small group than in a large society.

Status attribution theory

The development of status attribution theory, like that of equity theory, is based upon the assumption of a strain toward cognitive consistency within the individual.

The central problem lies in how an individual assesses the status of another when only one (or a few) status-relevant clues are known (Berger et al. 1972; Webster and Driskell 1978). Normally, the individual generalizes from what is known and assumes that a person's unknown status-relevant characteristics are consistent with the known ones.

Since status attribution theory describes the process through which the overall picture of an individual's status is pieced together from fragmentary clues, we can see, once this picture is completed, how it is used to assess, retrospectively, the individual's "contributions."

The need to assess an individual's "contributions" in this manner is strongest when direct, face-to-face contact is at a minimum, which is the case with leaders in large, highly differentiated societies. Equity theory then describes how this, in turn, becomes the basis for an estimate of the level of reward deserved (Cook 1975). Thus, equity theory and status attribution theory are complementary. What is crucial is that the entire process through which the appropriate level of reward is determined is *circular*, in that the very fact of being wealthy or powerful influences our assessment of "contributions" and, on the basis of such assessment, we judge that person worthy of such a high reward.

In large societies the degree of inequality of resources is most often very great (Lenski 1966), making it likely that the disadvantaged will be awed by the size of the gap and attribute very large differences to "contributions."

Bem

As impressive and promising as status attribution theory and equity theory appear to be in developing propositions about legitimation, their primary assumption – that there exists a strain toward cognitive consistency within the individual psyche – has been challenged by Bem (1967). He argues that a whole range of heretofore inexplicable findings in laboratory research dealing with balance theory can be readily explained, were that assumption altered.

Bem suggests that we do not postulate any hypothetical strain toward cognitive consistency but, rather, we assume that an individual derives judgements from what [he believes] an "objective outside observer" would view as reasonable. This shift in assumptions solves an important problem. Social psychologists have long been plagued by the accusation that their findings reflect culture-bound thought patterns rather than universal human tendencies (Sampson 1975). If the definition of what is reasonable (consistent) emanates not from the innate structure of mind but from an image of an external observer, it follows that the observer can vary in his/her judgements, depending upon the culture with which a researcher is dealing and upon the nature of the subject's individual experience.

But what external, objective observer is available and also, at the same time, likely to have his/her judgements internalized? Mead's generalized other has precisely these characteristics. As in his example of buying and selling goods, the way we develop an idea of what is a "reasonable" price or value of goods is what we see others regularly charging and/or paying for them. We have just seen that this is precisely the way in which Mead sees the generalized other developing.

This observation enables us to link equity and status attribution theory with Mead's theory of the self, for it is from the generalized other that individuals form an evaluation of self and, thus, of the worth of their "contributions." It is upon these evaluations, in turn, that judgements of equity are made in accordance with the principle of distributive justice.

So far we have achieved two major objectives. The first was to locate a common thread running through the macrosociology of writers as diverse as Marx, Mosca, and Parsons, with respect to their treatment of legitimation. This common thread is a relationship between legitimation and self-worth or, as we shall refer to it hereafter, self-evaluation. The second objective was to show that recent work in social psychology (specifically, equity theory and status attribution theory) is complementary, and that this work can be linked to Mead's theory of the self. Taken together, the social psychological works describe several aspects of the legitimation process. What remains now is to tie this in with macrosociology, in order to generate propositions about legitimation.

Before moving to the propositions themselves, the concept of self-evaluation must be explicated. The individual develops conceptions of self with respect to any number of possible characteristics. However, here we are concerned with those characteristics relevant to the individual's relationship with the institutions of the larger society, from which come rewards in the form of primary resources, specifically those characteristics enabling the individual to dominate or gain favor within these institutions.

The basic dependency of human beings makes impressive any ability to dominate the environment, either physically or socially. In the face-to-face context, leaders – those who are treated as most socially valuable and who are granted disproportionate rewards – are those who demonstrate their personal competence or, at least, those who do so before others can demonstrate theirs (Webster and Sobieszek 1974). However, in large societies, the "demonstration" of the ability to dominate is mediated through a number of factors mentioned earlier in discussing equity theory. Dominance of the external world is most effective when it permits the formation of a *publicly defensible* positive evaluation of self, that is, an evaluation that is defensible before the widest possible audience. The extent of the audience is important as the apparent objectivity of societal reactions contributes so heavily to their power to convince. As objectivity is defined as inter-subjective agreement, the wider the audience, the more certain one can be of the objectivity of the assessment. Thus, self-evaluation, as defined here, is the individual's perception of the social value that others attribute to him/her. Those who perceive that they are viewed as important by the widest audience, and particularly by others who are also viewed as important, have the highest self-evaluation. We are finally at the point where the diverse material presented so far can be pulled together and the propositions derived.

The Legitimation Process

The primary question to which this paper is addressed is, How do ideologies that justify structured inequality in the distribution of primary resources become part of the social consciousness of individuals? The main proposition of the theory states:

The level of primary resources that an individual sees as just for him/herself, relative to others, is directly proportional to his/her level of self-evaluation. The individual's level of self-evaluation is developed through a process of comparison (Rosenberg and Pearlin 1978). Thus, individuals with relatively high self-evaluations will see themselves as deserving of high levels of resources relative to others, whereas those with relatively low self-evaluations will see themselves as deserving of relatively little in comparison with others.

A corollary of this proposition allows us to deal with a related question, namely, Under what circumstances will the stratification system of any society enjoy relatively high or low levels of legitimacy? It states: *The strength of legitimacy of stratification in any society is directly proportional to the degree of congruence between the distribution of primary resources and the distribution of self-evaluations.* What follows is a discussion of the ways in which these propositions are derived.

Those possessing greater wealth and power in a society will tend to be perceived as having more of a whole range of other positive characteristics than those less fortunate or powerful. Through the status attribution process, those possessing greater amounts of primary resources come to be seen as actually being superior. At this point, the principle of equity takes over, and people believe that those who appear to be superior deserve to be more richly rewarded. This generalization, derived from previously reviewed laboratory studies, finds support in survey research as well (Fox et al. 1977; Lopreato and Hazelrigg 1972).

Of course, the attribution of superior characteristics to those with greater wealth and power implies that those lower in the stratification system will attribute to themselves relatively inferior characteristics, through comparison (Jacques and Chason 1977; Rosenberg and Pearlin 1978). Thus, if they are, in relevant ways, inferior, then they deserve to have lesser wealth and power. This is consistent with research on relative deprivation (Runciman 1966; Rushing 1972) in which members of different strata tend to compare themselves with others of their own stratum, rather than with those noticeably either richer or poorer than themselves. The latter type of comparison is meaningless precisely because those persons substantially higher or lower than oneself are obviously deserving of correspondingly greater or lesser rewards. The differences are simply taken for granted. It is the relatively small differences in rewards between oneself and those similar to self that excite feelings of deprivation.

Because of the circular nature of the process just described, a given distribution of primary resources tends to reproduce itself in a congruent distribution of self-evaluations which, in turn, reinforces the very status quo that generated it in the first place. While this describes the basic logic behind the main proposition, a closer study (of the mechanisms through which the process may be operating) is warranted.

Discussion of the status attribution process revealed that when ego meets alter and knows only one or two of alter's status-relevant characteristics, ego attributes other characteristics to alter – which, in the eyes of an imagined generalized other, are consistent with the ones ego knows. However, the work of Goffman (1959) strongly suggests that alter often behaves in ways that help the attribution process along. Highly placed individuals, by virtue of their greater wealth and power, are able to control or stage their encounters with subordinates in such ways as to impress them.

For example, they may display their wealth in their personal appearance and in the very settings in which encounters take place. Also, the subordinate goes to his/her superior, not the reverse. Another staging device is the appearance of being calm and in control (Hall and Hewitt 1970). The power to dictate explicitly, or better yet implicitly, where a meeting will be held is a convincing display of power. The subordinate's constant awareness of his/her asymmetrical dependence upon the superior serves this function (Emerson 1962), as well as the superior's ability to make the subordinate wait (Schwartz 1974).

Finally, the ability of superiors to stage their encounters allows them to shield their shortcomings from the view of subordinates. A good illustration of this is the fact that the deviance of the poor is more often performed in public places and is, thus, more visible than that of the rich (Chambliss 1973; Johnson et al. 1977).

The process that generates differential self-evaluation does not operate in a vacuum but, rather, within the framework of social institutions – especially institutions such as the school and the workplace which are instrumental in determining one's place in the distribution of primary resources (Bowles and Gintis 1976). Differential placement within these institutions, resulting from both competitive achievement and ascription, generates, within individuals, conceptions of where they stand in the larger society.

We have seen how the possession of greater primary resources allows dominants to control (through social institutions) the character of relationships between themselves and subordinates. One result of the establishment of these controlled relationships is the development of a generalized conception within the culture of the superiority of those who are highly rewarded and, by implication, the inferiority of others. This generalized conception develops out of communication among status-homogeneous groups. This is important because dominants maintain a certain degree of social distance between themselves and subordinates, which means that encounters with any one subordinate may not be frequent. Sharing of experience through communication creates a generalized set of expectations surrounding such relationships, expectations that become internalized through their embodiment in the generalized other. Through this process, the individual develops an evaluation of self with respect to the larger society. When the self-evaluations are congruent with actual command over primary resources, legitimacy emerges – as our corollary states. Through the resulting ideology, the circular logic of the legitimation process reinforces the stratified status quo.

If this description of the legitimation process is accurate, then the inverse of the corollary should also be true, namely: *The more incongruent the distribution of resources and self-evaluations, the more likely is the delegitimation of stratification.* This last point cannot be emphasized too strongly. Simply because I have referred to the legitimation process as self-reinforcing does not mean that "might becomes right," automatically. It is only when the distributions of resources and self-evaluations are congruent that it appears to do so. However, it is important to realize that, under most circumstances, the condition of congruence holds very well. This is precisely what accounts for the seemingly automatic character of the legitimation process, which may well have (mis)led functionalists into seeing it as universal. However, I maintain that incongruence between the two distributions can be produced by a number of forces, both internal and external to a society.

In order to round out the exposition of self-evaluation theory we must return to a question raised earlier, namely, How can the legitimation of stratification coexist with extensive intergroup conflict, and even revolution? The first step toward resolving this apparent paradox is to refer to our discussion of the four (system) levels at which legitimation can exist: (1) the position of the individual or group within a stratified order, (2) the particular regime in power, (3) the system of political economy, and (4) stratification itself. The specification of these levels shows how it is logically possible for legitimation to exist on some levels while conflict might prevail on others. This suggests that theories based upon conflict and those based upon consensus need not be incompatible but, rather, may simply be applicable to different system levels, but it fails to explain why this occurs or at which levels legitimation or conflict could be expected to be the dominant pattern.

Note also that these four levels fall along a continuum ranging from the more concrete to the more abstract. There appears to be a pattern in which conflict prevails at the more concrete levels while legitimation remains on the more abstract levels. For example, Marx and Engels (1959) note the tendency of workers to focus their discontent over poverty, harsh working conditions, and economic insecurity upon what appears to them to be its most immediate source: their employers or the machines being introduced into the factories. Similarly, Lenin (1963) observed that, left to their own devices, workers would not go beyond "trade union consciousness."

More contemporary writers have echoed that theme. Mills (1956) argued that people tend to be absorbed almost totally within their own limited milieux and are seldom able to connect private troubles with public issues. Both Mann (1970) and Parkin (1971) have pointed to the importance of a radical ideology which enables people to see the linkage between everyday discontents and their systemic causes. Giddens (1973) has gone furthest in specifying a rather exacting set of conditions that must be fulfilled if workers are to proceed beyond a mere struggle with employers over economic issues (conflict consciousness) to the point where the legitimacy of the capitalist system is called into question (revolutionary consciousness).

Additional support for the existence of this pattern can be cited. Liebow's (1967) observations of unemployed blacks, and Sennett and Cobb's (1972) interviews with blue-collar workers both revealed, on the one hand, considerable resentment over material conditions and the low regard in which society holds them and, on the other hand, a virtually total failure to bring the legitimacy of the system itself into question. Needless to say, in no instance was the legitimacy of stratification itself ever challenged. Similar observations are reported by students of the Hindu caste system (Dumont 1970; Mandelbaum 1968).

On the basis of this evidence I might frame a second proposition: *The probability that legitimation will prevail is directly related to the system level of abstraction.* That is, the higher the level of abstraction, the more likely a self-reinforcing legitimation process is to be found. At the very highest level – which is the focus of this paper – it has been nearly universal while, at the lowest level, conflict manifest in various forms has been the rule. Examples of those forces that might promote delegitimation and, therefore, signal the applicability of conflict theory at the highest level are now discussed.

Summary and Discussion

In recent years, conflict theory has gained an important place in American sociology and has shed much light upon the way in which stratification systems are initially established. However, conflict theories are much less effective in explaining exactly how stratification becomes legitimated; they offer concepts such as false consciousness and political formula but fail to describe the mechanisms through which the legitimation process operates (e.g. Marx and Engels 1947).

Functional theory, which assumes the existence and internalization of a common value system among all strata of the population, has always purported to explain how an ongoing stratification system is legitimated. However, it has done so in a manner that is incompatible with the considerable achievements of conflict theory, for it has all but ignored the role of power and conflict. Moreover, it has assumed the inevitability of stratification and its legitimation and, therefore, precludes a priori the search for the conditions under which it might not exist (Gouldner 1970).

The self-evaluation hypothesis is fully compatible with a conflict orientation in both its radical and elitist varieties. Like most conflict theories it, too, goes beyond the conception of stratified societies being held together exclusively by either force or the threat of force. However, it does more than simply allude to the role of ideology or ruling ideas in legitimating stratification. It describes legitimation as the outgrowth of social psychological processes operating within the confines of asymmetrical relationships embedded in major social institutions. A major strength of the self-evaluation hypothesis is that it can account for the coexistence of both legitimated inequality and a self-interested struggle over resources on the part of all strata in society.

Unlike functionalism, the self-evaluation hypothesis does not *assume* the existence of a common value system. It achieves compatibility with functionalism by describing a process through which an ideology which justifies stratification comes to be commonly accepted by all strata – even the poor, in apparent contradiction to their self-interest. It also proposes an explanation of why this process *appears* to be inevitable and universal. In this sense, it takes seriously functionalism's insistence upon the existence of a common, objective standard of evaluation that is widely internalized (Kraus et al. 1978), in a way that conflict theory never really has.

The self-evaluation hypothesis has also shown its ability to interpret a range of empirical data from both surveys and observational studies. While direct tests of the propositions stated here have not yet been made, their compatibility with so many theoretical orientations and existing findings suggests that they merit serious consideration.

One of their most promising features is their ability to explain why so many disadvantaged persons hold beliefs concerning stratification seemingly contrary to their "objective self-interest" while the views of the privileged seem to be more consistent with their interests (Cheal 1979; Feagin 1972). Among the privileged, in terms of the propositions, self-evaluations coincide with self-interest. They tend to have high self-evaluations based upon their advantaged circumstances and success in dealing with the world. Such evaluations lead to their feelings that they *deserve* what they have. Among the disadvantaged, however, their self-evaluations are inconsistent with their interests. Having relatively low self-evaluations, they don't see themselves as *deserving* equality with those "better" than themselves (at least in terms of power and wealth). If the propositions are correct, the exceptions who are egalitarians ought to be precisely those individuals, among the disadvantaged, who have especially high self-evaluations (Feagin 1972).

However, no claim is made that this is an exhaustive theory of mass support for inequality. As I pointed out from the start, factors other than self-evaluation are very likely to generate such support – even among people whose self-interest would seem to dictate support for equality. Only by taking all of these factors together can the maintenance of stratification in modern society be explained.

No discussion of legitimation would be complete without a consideration of the conditions under which stratification might be delegitimized.

Delegitimizing Stratification

It is important that we recognize the "dual nature" of the legitimation process. On the one hand, as I have argued repeatedly, it is self-reinforcing. Any given distribution of primary resources has a strong tendency to produce a congruent distribution of self-evaluations through a set of very basic social psychological mechanisms. On the other hand, the process is not totally automatic. In a thousand little ways it must be maintained and reconstructed, anew, on a daily basis (Berger and Luckmann 1966).

Maintenance of legitimation involves the staging process in which social distance must be maintained and people must be duly impressed. The generalized conception (within the culture of elite superiority) must be reinforced directly through the mass media; control of subordinates and manipulation of their sense of self-worth must be continued within major social institutions through the exercise of hierarchical authority; channels of upward mobility must be kept open to the most talented members of subordinate strata.

While isolated cases of failure to maintain any of these facets of the system are unlikely to be fatal, a large-scale pattern of failure could initiate a chain of events which, under appropriate conditions, might undermine the legitimation of stratification. Since, theoretically, the delegitimation of stratification is possible, under what conditions might it occur?

I have hypothesized that delegitimation comes about when incongruence develops between the distribution of primary resources and that of self-evaluations. Though there are many logically possible ways in which incongruence may develop, I will focus on only a few here. In the first instance, the evaluation of the elite is lowered in the eyes of the populace so that, for most, the gap between the evaluation of self and that of the highly rewarded is narrowed, without any concomitant narrowing of the gap in terms of resources. In this case it is also possible that highly rewarded persons, reacting to the incongruity, would lower their evaluations of themselves to a point at which they feel overrewarded and experience a "loss of nerve."

One way in which such an eventuality might come about is through a failure of the dominant stratum to continue to keep the economy running smoothly and/or to fail to maintain order (Gurr 1970; Mankoff 1970). In either case, an objective failure on the part of the regime would weaken the ability of leaders to present themselves as possessing superior competence.

In the second instance, the actual extent of inequality of resources is suddenly shown to be much greater than was previously suspected. This could occur either through changing ecological patterns that force rich and poor to observe at close hand the way each other lives, or through media exposure.

While both of these instances result in incongruity, it is of a negative sort, brought on by disenchantment with superiors. Elites, as leadership groups, are seen as those who are needed to perform society's most vital functions and make its most important decisions. Negative reactions to elites, with no concomitant rise in the self-evaluations of the masses, are very likely to simply initiate a search for more worthy elites to take the place of the fallen ones. Stratification still remains.

This leads to the third instance. Here, incongruity is generated through a rise in the self-evaluations of the disadvantaged. As a result, the privileged no longer seem especially worthy by comparison. In this instance, the disadvantaged come to feel more confident about their ability to shape their own destiny in the larger world.

While my main concern has been class stratification, one might argue that a hypothesis as general as the one advanced here should be applicable to other forms of stratification, as well, such as racial or sexual. But these forms of stratification involve only the first system level of abstraction, the placement of particular categories of individuals within a given stratification system. They can, theoretically, be eliminated while the society remains class-stratified – that is, members of previously subordinate racial groups, or women, can have an equal chance of high or low placement, with inequality itself being firmly entrenched. This would be the prototypical meritocracy. Thus we should expect a much higher probability of conflict and a much lower level of consensus over the legitimacy of these forms of stratification than over the very idea of stratification itself. Yet it might be fruitful to explore the possible relevance of the relationship between the distribution of resources among racial groups and their self-evaluations, particularly the effect of suddenly elevated levels of minority self-evaluations or the high self-evaluations of members of minority elites whose opportunities for advancement are blocked. But these issues are much too extensive to be treated here and must be relegated to another study.

The self-evaluation hypothesis overcomes the static bias that afflicts not only functionalism but also the elitist types of conflict theory that treat stratification and its legitimation as being inevitable. By taking a dialectical approach (Ball 1979) it opens up the very question of the conditions under which these two persistent characteristics of social life are likely to be present in varying degrees or, even, entirely absent.

References

Alves, W. M. and Rossi, P. H. 1978. "Who should get what? Fairness judgements of the distribution of earnings." *American Journal of Sociology* 84: 541–63.
Anderson, P. 1977. "The antinomies of Antonio Gramsci." *New Left Review* 100: 5–78.
Ball, R. A. 1979. "The dialectical method: Its application to social theory." *Social Forces* 57: 785–98.

Baltzell, E. D. 1958. *Philadelphia Gentlemen: The Making of a National Upper Class*. New York: Free Press.

Bem, D. J. 1967. "Self-perception: An alternative interpretation of cognitive dissonance phenomena." *Psychological Review* 74: 183–200.

Bendix, R. 1956. *Work and Authority in Industry: Ideologies of Management in the Course of Industrialization*. New York: Wiley.

Berger, P. L. and Luckmann, T. 1966. *The Social Construction of Reality: A Treatise in the Sociology of Knowledge*. Garden City, NY: Doubleday.

Berger. J., Zelditch, M., Anderson, B. and Cohen, B. P. 1972. "Structural aspects of distributive justice: A status value formulation." In J. Berger, M. Zelditch, and B. Anderson (eds.) *Sociological Theories in Progress*, vol. 2. Boston: Houghton Mifflin.

Blau, P. M. 1964. *Exchange and Power in Social Life*. New York: Wiley.

Bowles, S. and Gintis, H. 1976. *Schooling in Capitalist America*. New York: Basic Books.

Chambliss, W. 1973. "The saints and the roughnecks." *Society* 11: 24–31.

Cheal, D. J. 1979. "Hegemony, ideology, and contradictory consciousness." *Sociological Quarterly* 20: 109–17.

Chinoy, E. 1955. *Automobile Workers and the American Dream*. Boston: Beacon.

Clark, K. B. 1965. *Dark Ghetto*. New York: Harper and Row.

Cook, R. 1975. "Expectations, evaluations, and equity." *American Sociological Review* 40: 372–88.

Coser, L. 1956. *The Functions of Social Conflict*. New York: Free Press.

Dahrendorf, R. 1959. *Class and Class Conflict in Industrial Society*. Stanford, Calif.: Stanford University Press.

Dahl, R. A. 1967. *Pluralist Democracy in America*. Chicago: Rand-McNally.

Davis, K. 1948. *Human Society*. New York: Macmillan.

Davis, K. and Moore, W. E. 1945. "Some principles of stratification." *American Sociological Review* 10: 242–9.

Della Fave, L. R. 1974. "On the structure of egalitarianism." *Social Problems* 22: 199–213.

Domhoff, G. W. 1967. *Who Rules America?* Englewood Cliffs, NJ: Prentice-Hall.

—— 1971. *The Higher Circles*. New York: Vintage.

Dumont, L. 1970. *Homo Hierarchicus: An Essay on the Caste System*. Chicago: University of Chicago Press.

Emerson, R. 1962. "Power-dependence relations." *American Sociological Review* 27: 31–41.

Feagin, J. 1972. "When it comes to poverty, it's still, 'God helps those who help themselves.'" *Psychology Today* 6: 101–29.

Festinger, L. 1957. *A Theory of Cognitive Dissonance*. Evanston, Ill.: Row-Peterson.

Form, W. H. 1976. *Blue Collar Stratification*. Princeton: Princeton University Press.

Fox, W., Payne, D., Priest, T. and Philiber, W. 1977. "Authority position, legitimacy of authority structure, and acquiescence to authority." *Social Forces* 55: 966–73.

Giddens, A. 1973. *The Class Structure of the Advanced Societies*. London: Hutchinson.

Goffman, E. 1959. *The Presentation of Self in Everyday Life*. Garden City, NY: Doubleday.

Gouldner, A. W. 1970. *The Coming Crisis of Western Sociology*. New York: Avon.

Gurr, T. R. 1970. *Why Men Rebel*. Princeton: Princeton University Press.

Habermas, J. 1973. *Legitimation Crisis*. Boston: Beacon.

Hall, P. M. and Hewitt, J. P. 1970. "The quasi theory of communication and the management of dissent." *Social Problems* 18: 17–26.

Harrington, M. 1976. *The Twilight of Capitalism*. New York: Simon and Schuster.

Heider, F. 1958. *The Psychology of Interpersonal Relations*. New York: Wiley.

Homans, G. C. 1961. *Social Behavior: Its Elementary Forms*. New York: Harcourt, Brace, and World.

—— 1974. *Social Behavior: Its Elementary Forms* (rev. edn). New York: Harcourt, Brace, Jovanovich.

Jacques, J. and Chason, K. 1977. "Self-esteem and low status groups." *Sociological Quarterly* 18: 399–412.

Jasso, G. and Rossi, P. H. 1977. "Distributive justice and earned income." *American Sociological Review* 42: 639–51.

Johnson, W., Petersen, R., and Wells, E. 1977. "Arrest probabilities for marijuana users as indicators of selective law enforcement." *American Journal of Sociology* 83: 681–99.

Keller, S. 1963. *Beyond the Ruling Class: Strategic Elites in Modern Society*. New York: Random House.

Kraus, V., Schild, E. and Hodge, R. 1978. "Occupational prestige in the collective conscience." *Social Forces* 56: 900–18.

Lane, R. E. 1962. *Political Ideology: Why the American Common Man Believes As He Does*. New York: Free Press.

Lenin, V. I. 1963. *What Is to Be Done?* New York: Oxford University Press.

Lenski, G. 1966. *Power and Privilege*. New York: McGraw-Hill.

Lerner, M. J. 1975. "The justice motive in social behavior: Introduction." *Journal of Social Issues* 31: 1–20.

Leventhal, G. 1975. "The distribution of rewards and resources in groups and organizations." In L. Berkowitz and E. Walster (eds.) *Advances in Experimental Social Psychology*, vol. 9. New York: Academic Press.

Liebow, E. 1967. *Tally's Corner*. Boston: Little, Brown.

Lopreato, J. and Hazelrigg, L. 1972. *Class, Conflict, and Mobility*. San Francisco: Chandler.

Mandelbaum, D. G. 1968. "Status seeking in Indian villages." *Trans-Action* 15: 48–52.

Mankoff, M. 1970. "Power in advanced capitalist society: A review essay on recent elitist and Marxist criticism of pluralist theory." *Social Problems* 17: 418–29.

Mann, M. 1970. "The social cohesion of liberal democracy." *American Sociological Review* 35: 423–39.

Marx, K. 1906. *Capital*, vol. 1. New York: Modern Library.

—— 1959. "Critique of the Gotha program." In L. S. Feuer (ed.) *Marx and Engels: Basic Writings on Politics and Philosophy*. Garden City, NY: Doubleday.

—— 1963. *The Poverty of Philosophy*. New York: International Publishers.

Marx, K. and Engels, F. 1947. *The German Ideology*. New York: International Publishers.

——and—— 1959. "Manifesto of the Communist party." In L. S. Feuer (ed.) *Marx and Engels: Basic Writings on Politics and Philosophy*. Garden City, NY: Doubleday.

Mead, G. H. 1934. *Mind, Self, and Society*. Chicago: University of Chicago Press.

—— 1964. *G. H. Mead: Selected Writings*, ed. Andrew J. Reck. Indianapolis: Bobbs-Merrill.

Meisel, J. H. 1965. *Pareto and Mosca*. Englewood Cliffs, NJ: Prentice-Hall.

Miliband, R. 1969. *The State in Capitalist Society*. New York: Basic Books.

Mills, C. W. 1956. *The Power Elite*. New York: Oxford University Press.

Moore, B. 1978. *Injustice: The Social Bases of Obedience and Revolt*. White Plains, NY: Sharpe.

Mosca, G. 1939. *The Ruling Class*. New York: McGraw-Hill.

Ofshe, L. and Ofshe, R. 1970. *Utility and Choice in Social Interaction*. Englewood Cliffs, NJ: Prentice-Hall.

Pareto, V. 1935. *The Mind and Society: A Treatise on General Sociology*. New York: Harcourt, Brace.

Parkin, F. 1971. *Class Inequality and Political Order*. New York: Praeger.

Parsons, T. 1949. "An analytical approach to the theory of social stratification." In T. Parsons (ed.) *Essays in Sociological Theory*. New York: Free Press.

—— 1951. *The Social System*. New York: Free Press.

—— 1953. "A revised analytical approach to the theory of social stratification." In R. Bendix and S. M. Lipset (eds.) *Class, Status, and Power*. New York: Free Press.

Prewitt, K. and Stone, A. 1973. *The Ruling Elites*. New York: Harper and Row.

Rainwater, L. 1974. *What Money Buys: Inequality and the Social Meanings of Income*. New York: Basic Books.

Rosenberg, M. and Pearlin, L. I. 1978. "Social class and self-esteem among children and adults." *American Journal of Sociology* 84: 53–77.

Runciman, W. G. 1966. *Relative Deprivation and Social Justice*. Baltimore: Penguin Books.

Rushing, W. 1972. *Class, Culture, and Alienation*. Reading, Mass.: D. C. Heath.

Sallach, D. 1974. "Class domination and ideological hegemony." *Sociological Quarterly* 15: 39–50.

Sampson, E. E. 1975. "On justice as equality." *journal of Social Issues* 31: 45–64.

Schumpeter, J. 1951. *Imperialism and Social Classes*. New York: Meridian.

Schwartz, B. 1974. "Waiting, exchange, and power: The distribution of time in social system." *American Journal of Sociology* 79: 841–70.

Sennett, R. and Cobb, J. 1972. *The Hidden Injuries of Class*. New York: Vintage.

Shibutani, T. and Kwan, K. 1965. *Ethnic Stratification*. New York: Macmillan.

Strasser, H. 1976. *The Normative Structure of Sociology*. London: Routledge and Kegan Paul.

Walster, E. and Walster, G. W. 1975. "Equity and social justice." *Journal of Social Issues* 31: 21–44.

Webster, M. J. and Driskell, J. E. 1978. "Status generalization: A review of some new data." *American Sociological Review* 43: 220–36.

Webster, M. and Sobieszek, B. 1974. *Source of Self-Evaluation: A Formal Theory of Significant Others and Social Influence*. New York: Wiley.

Wilson, W. J. 1973. *Power, Racism, and Privilege*. New York: Macmillan.

Wright, J. 1976. *The Dissent of the Governed: Alienation and Democracy in America*. New York: Academic Press.

10 Emotion Work, Feeling Rules, and Social Structure

Arlie Russell Hochschild

Social psychology has suffered under the tacit assumption that emotion, because it seems unbidden and uncontrollable, is not governed by social rules. Social rules, for their part, are seen as applying to behavior and thought, but rarely to emotion or feeling. If we reconsider the nature of emotion and the nature of our capacity to try shaping it, we are struck by the imperial scope of social rules. Significant links emerge among social structure, feeling rules, emotion management, and emotive experience – links I try to trace in this essay. The purpose is to suggest an area for inquiry.

Why is the emotive experience of normal adults in daily life as orderly as it is? Why, generally speaking, do people feel gay at parties, sad at funerals, happy at weddings? This question leads us to examine, not conventions of appearance or outward comportment, but conventions of feeling. Conventions of feeling become surprising only when we imagine, by contrast, what totally unpatterned, unpredictable emotive life might actually be like at parties, funerals, weddings, and in the family or work life of normal adults.

Erving Goffman suggests both the surprise to be explained and part of the explanation: "We find that participants will hold in check certain psychological states and attitudes, for after all, the very general rule that one enter into the prevailing mood in the encounter carries the understanding that contradictory feelings will be in abeyance.... So generally, in fact, does one suppress unsuitable affect, that we need to look at offenses to this rule to be reminded of its usual operation" (1961: 23). If we take this passage seriously, as I urge we do, we may be led back to the classic question of social order from a particular vantage point – that of emotion management. From this vantage point, rules seem to govern how people try or try not to feel in ways "appropriate to the situation." Such a notion suggests how profoundly the individual is "social," and "socialized" to try to pay tribute to official definitions of situations, with no less than their feelings.

Let me pause to point out that there are two possible approaches to the social ordering of emotive experience. One is to study the social factors that induce or stimulate primary (i.e., nonreflective, though by definition conscious) emotions – emotions passively undergone. The other is to study *secondary acts* performed upon the ongoing nonreflective stream of primary emotive experience. The first approach focuses on how social factors affect what people feel, the second on how social factors affect what people think and do about what they feel (i.e., acts of assessment and management). Those who take the first approach might regard those who take the second as being "overly cognitive." But in fact the two approaches are compatible, and indeed the second, taken here, relies on some accumulation of knowledge garnered from the first.

Reprinted from *American Journal of Sociology* 85(3) (1979): 551–75.

If we take as our object of focus what it is people think or do about feelings, several questions emerge. First, with what assumptions about emotion and situation do we begin? In other words, (a) how responsive is emotion to deliberate attempts to suppress or evoke it? (b) What sociological approach is most fruitful? Second, what are the links among social structure, ideology, feeling rules, and emotion management? To begin with, (c) are there feeling rules? (d) How do we know about them? (e) How are these rules used as baselines in social exchanges? (f) What in the nature of work and child rearing might account for different ways adults of varying classes manage their feelings? I shall sketch outlines of possible answers with the aim, in some measure, of refining the questions.

Two Accounts of Emotion and Feeling

In order to address the first question, we might consider two basic accounts of emotion and feeling found in social psychology: the *organismic* account and the *interactive* account. The two approaches differ in what they imply about our capacity to manage emotion, and thus in what they imply about the importance of rules about managing it. I cannot do full justice here to the question of what emotion is and how it is generated, nor can I offer a full reaction to the ample literature on that question.

According to the organismic view, the paramount questions concern the relation of emotion to biologically given "instinct" or "impulse." In large part, biological factors account for the questions the organismic theorist poses. The early writings of Sigmund Freud (1911, 1915a, 1915b; see Lofgren 1968), Charles Darwin (1955), and in some though not all respects, William James (James and Lange 1922) fit this model. The concept "emotion" refers mainly to strips of experience in which there is no conflict between one and another aspect of self; the individual "floods out," is "overcome." The image that comes to mind is that of a sudden, automatic reflex syndrome: Darwin's instant snarl expression, Freud's tension discharge at a given breaking point of tension overload, James and Lange's notion of an instantaneous unmediated visceral reaction to a perceived stimulus, the perception of which is also unmediated by social influences.

In this first model, social factors can enter in only in regard to how emotions are stimulated and expressed (and even here Darwin took the universalist position) (see Ekman 1972, 1973). Social factors are not seen as an influence on how emotions are actively suppressed or evoked. Indeed, emotion is characterized by the fixity and universality of a knee-jerk reaction or a sneeze. In this view, one could as easily manage an emotion as one could manage a knee jerk or a sneeze. If the organismic theorist were to be presented with the concept of feeling rules, he or she would be hard put to elucidate what these rules impinge on, or what capacity of the self could be called on to try to obey a feeling rule (see Hochschild 1977). Recent attempts to link an organismic notion of emotion to social structure, such as Randall Collins's (1975) wonderfully bold attempt, suffer from the problems that were implicit in the organismic account to begin with. By Collins, as by Darwin on whom he draws, emotions are seen as capacities (or susceptibilities) within a person, to be automatically triggered, as Collins develops it, by one or another group in control of the ritual apparatus that does the "triggering" (1975: 59). A wholly different avenue of social control, that of feeling rules, is bypassed, because the individual's capacity to try to, or try not to feel – that to which the rule applies – is not suggested by the organismic model with which Collins begins.

In the interactive account, social influences permeate emotion more insistently, more effectively, and at more theoretically posited junctures. In large part, socio-psychological factors account for the questions the interactive theorist poses. The writings of Gerth and Mills (1964), Goffman (1956, 1959, 1961, 1967, 1974), Lazarus (1966), Lazarus and Averill (1972), Schachter and Singer (1962), Schachter (1964), Kemper (1978), Averill (1976), and aspects of late Freudian and neo-Freudian thought fit this model. To invoke the Freudian vocabulary, the image here is not that of a "runaway id," but of an ego and superego, acting upon, shaping, nagging, however ineffectively, temporarily, or consciously, the id. Emotion is sometimes posited as a psychobiological means of adaptation, an analogue to other adaptive mechanisms, such as shivering when cold or perspiring when hot. But emotion differs from these other adaptive mechanisms, in that thinking, perceiving, and imagining – themselves subject to the influence of norms and situations – are intrinsically involved.

As in the first model, social factors affect how emotions are elicited and expressed. However, in addition, social factors guide the microactions of labeling (Katz 1977; Schachter 1964; Schachter and Singer 1962), interpreting (Gerth and Mills 1964), and managing emotion (Lazarus 1966). These microactions, in turn, reflect back on that which is labeled, interpreted, and managed. They are, finally, intrinsic to what we call "emotion" (see Schafer 1976). Emotion, in this second school of thought, is seen as more deeply social. Lazarus's (1966) work in particular lends empirical weight to the interactive model. It suggests that normal adults, such as university students on whom he conducted experiments, have a considerable capacity to control emotion. It is more control than one might expect from a small child, an insane adult, or an animal, from all of which Freud, in his earlier writings, and Darwin drew inspiration. But since it is the emotive experience of normal adults we seek to understand, we would do well to begin with the interactive account.

The Interactive Account of Emotion and Social Psychology

If emotions and feelings can to some degree be managed, how might we get a conceptual grasp of the managing act from a social perspective? The interactive account of emotion leads us into a conceptual arena "between" the Goffmanian focus on consciously designed appearances on the one hand and the Freudian focus on unconscious intrapsychic events on the other. The focus of Mead (1934) and Blumer (1969) on conscious, active, and responsive gestures might have been most fruitful had not their focus on deeds and thought almost entirely obscured the importance of feeling. (See Shott (1979) for an attempt to consider emotion from a symbolic interactionist perspective.) The self as emotion manager is an idea that borrows from both sides – Goffman and Freud – but squares completely with neither. Here I can only sketch out a few basic borrowings and departures, focusing on the departures.

Erving Goffman

Goffman guides our attention to social patterns in emotive experience. He catches an irony: moment to moment, the individual is actively negotiating a course of action, but in the long run, all the action seems like passive acquiescence to social convention. The conserving of convention is not a passive business. Goffman's approach might simply be extended and deepened by showing that people not only try to conform outwardly, but do so inwardly as well. "When they issue uniforms, they issue skins" (Goffman 1974) could be extended: "and two inches of flesh."

Yet, ironically, to study why and under what conditions "participants . . . hold in check certain psychological states . . ." (Goffman 1961: 23), we are forced partly out of the perspective which gave birth to the insight. I shall try to show why this is so, what the remedies might be, and how the results could be conceptually related to aspects of the psychoanalytic tradition.

First, Goffman, for reasons necessary to his purpose, maintains for the most part a studied disregard for the links between immediate social situations and macrostructure on the one hand, and individual personality on the other. If one is interested in drawing links among social structure, feeling rules, and emotion management, this studied disregard becomes a problem.

Goffman's "situationism" is a brilliant achievement, one that must be understood as a development in the intellectual history of social psychology. Earlier in the century a number of classic works linked social structure to personality, or "dominant institutions" to "typical identities," and thus also related findings in sociology and anthropology to those in psychology or psychoanalytic theory. These studies appeared in a number of fields: in anthropology, Ruth Benedict (1946); in psychoanalysis, Erich Fromm (1942), Karen Horney (1937), and Erik Erikson (1950); in sociology, David Riesman (1952, 1960), Swanson and Miller (1966), and Gerth and Mills (1964).

Possibly in response to this paradigm Goffman proposed an intermediate level of conceptual elaboration, "between" social structure and personality. His focus is on situations, episodes, encounters. The situation, the episodically emergent encounter, is not only nearly divorced from social structure and from personality; he even seems to intend his situationism as an analytic substitute for these concepts (see Goffman 1976: 77). Structure, he seems to say, can be not only transposed but reduced "in and down," while personality can be reduced "up and out" to the study of here-now, gone-then interactional moments.

Each interactional episode takes on the character of a minigovernment. A card game, a party, a greeting on the street exacts from us certain "taxes" in the form of appearances which we "pay" for the sake of sustaining the encounter. We are repaid in the currency of safety from disrepute. (Thanks to Harvey Farberman for discussion on this point.)

This model of the situation *qua* minigovernment, while useful for Goffman's purposes, leads us away from social structure and personality – two concepts with which any study of feeling rules and emotion management would be wise to deal. To study why and under what conditions "participants . . . hold in check certain psychological states" (Goffman 1961: 23), we are forced out of the here-now, gone-then situationism and back, in part at least, to the social structure and personality model. We are led to appreciate the importance of Goffman's work, as it seems he does not, *as the critical set of conceptual connecting tissues by which structure and personality, real in their own right, are more precisely joined.*

Specifically, if we are to understand the origin and causes of change in "feeling rules" – this underside of ideology – we are forced back out of a study of the immediate situations in which they show up, to a study of such things as changing relations between classes or the sexes.

If we are to investigate the ways people try to manage feeling, we shall have to posit an actor capable of feeling, capable of assessing when a feeling is "inappropriate," and capable of trying to manage feeling. The problem is that the actor Goffman proposes does not seem to feel much, is not attuned to, does not monitor closely or assess, does not actively evoke, inhibit, shape – in a word, *work on* feelings in a way an actor would have to do to accomplish what Goffman says is, in fact, accomplished in one encounter after another. We are left knowing about "suppressive work" as a final result, but knowing nothing of the process or techniques by which it is achieved. If we are to argue that social factors influence how we try to manage feelings, if we are to carry the social that far, we shall have to carry our analytic focus beyond the "black box" to which Goffman ultimately refers us.

Goffman's actors actively manage outer impressions, but they do not actively manage inner feelings. For example, a typical Goffmanian actor, Preedy at the beach (Goffman 1959), is exquisitely attuned to outward appearance, but his glances inward at subjective feeling are fleeting and blurred. The very topic, sociology of emotion, presupposes a human capacity for, if not the actual habit of, reflecting on and shaping inner feelings, a habit itself distributed variously across time, age, class, and locale. This variation would drop from sight were we to adopt an exclusive focus on the actor's attentiveness to behavioral façade and assume a uniform passivity *vis-à-vis* feelings.

This skew in the theoretical actor is related to what from my viewpoint is another problem: Goffman's concept of acting. Goffman suggests that we spend a good deal of effort managing impressions – that is, acting. He posits only *one* sort of acting: the direct management of behavioral expression. His illustrations, though, actually point to *two* types of acting: the direct management of behavioral expression (e.g., the given-off sigh, the shoulder shrug), and the management of feeling from which expression can follow (e.g., the thought of some hopeless project). An actor playing the part of King Lear might go about his task in two ways. One actor, following the English school of acting, might focus on outward demeanor, the constellation of minute expressions that correspond to Lear's sense of fear and impotent outrage. This is the sort of acting Goffman theorizes about. Another actor, adhering to the American or Stanislavsky school of acting, might guide his memories and feelings in such a way as to elicit the corresponding expressions. The first technique we might call "surface acting," the second "deep acting." Goffman fails to distinguish the first from the second, and he obscures the importance of "deep acting." Obscuring this, we are left with the impression that social factors pervade only the "social skin," the tried-for outer appearances of the individual. We are left underestimating the power of the social.

In sum, if we are to accept the interactive account of emotion and to study the self as emotion manager, we can learn from Goffman about the link between social rule and feeling. But to elaborate this insight we might well selectively relax the theoretical strictures Goffman has stoically imposed against a focus on social structure and on personality.

Freud

The need to replace Goffman's "black-box psychology" with some theory of self, in the full sense of the term, might seem to lead to Freudian or neo-Freudian theory. Yet, here, as with Goffman, only some aspects of the Freudian model seem useful to my understanding of conscious, deliberate efforts to suppress or evoke feeling. I shall briefly discuss psychoanalytic theory to show some points of departure.

Freud, of course, dealt with emotions, but for him they were always secondary to drive. He proposed a general theory of sexual and aggressive drives. Anxiety, as a derivative of aggressive and sexual drives, was of paramount importance, while a wide range of other emotions, including joy, jealousy, depression, were given relatively little attention. He developed, and many others have since elaborated, the concept of ego defenses as generally unconscious, involuntary means of avoiding painful or unpleasant affect. Finally the notion of "inappropriate affect" is used to point to aspects of the individual's ego functioning and not used to point to the social rules according to which a feeling is or is not deemed appropriate to a situation.

The emotion-management perspective is indebted to Freud for the general notion of what resources individuals of different sorts possess for accomplishing the task of emotion work (as I have defined it) and for the notion of unconscious involuntary emotion management. The emotion-management perspective differs from the Freudian model in its focus on the full range of emotions and feelings and its focus on conscious and deliberate efforts to shape feeling. From this perspective, we note too that "inappropriate emotion" has a clearly important social as well as intrapsychic side.

Let me briefly illustrate the differences between the two perspectives. In Shapiro's well-known work on "neurotic style," he gives an example:

> An obsessive-compulsive patient – a sober, technically minded and active man – *was usually conspicuously lacking in enthusiasm or excitement in circumstances that might seem to warrant them.* On one occasion, as he talked about a certain prospect of his, namely, the good chance of an important success in his work, his sober expression was momentarily interrupted by a smile. After a few more minutes of talking, during which he maintained his soberness only with difficulty, he began quite hesitantly to speak of certain hopes that he had only alluded to earlier. Then he broke into a grin. *Almost immediately, however, he regained his usual somewhat worried expression.* As he did this, he said, "Of course, the outcome is by no means certain," and he said this in a tone that, if anything, would suggest the outcome was almost certain to be a failure. After ticking off several of the specific possibilities for a hitch, he finally seemed to be himself again, so to speak. (Shapiro 1965: 192, emphasis mine)

What seems interesting about this example differs according to whether one takes the psychiatric perspective or the emotion-management perspective. First, to the psychiatrist in the case above, what circumstances warrant what degree and type of feeling seems relatively unproblematic. A doctor "knows" what inappropriate affect is; the main problem is not so much to discern misfits of feeling to situation but to explain them and to cure the patient of them. From the emotion-management perspective, on the other hand, the warranting function of circumstances is problematic. Further, the means used to assess this warranting function may well be the same for a psychiatrist as for a salesclerk or school disciplinarian. For, in a sense we all act as lay psychiatrists using unexamined means of arriving at a determination about just "what" circumstances warrant "that much" feeling of "that sort."

What the psychiatrist, the salesclerk, and the school disciplinarian may share is a habit of comparing situation (e.g., high opportunity, associated with an accomplishment at work) with role (e.g., hopes, aspirations, expectations typical of, and expected from, those enacting the role). Social factors can enter in, to alter how we expect a role to be held, or played. If, for example, the patient were a "sober, technically minded and active" *woman* and if the observer (rightly or wrongly) assumed or expected her to value family and personal ties over worldly success, less enthusiasm at the prospect of advance might seem perfectly "appropriate." Lack of enthusiasm would have a warrant of that social sort. Again, if the patient was an antinuclear activist and his discovery had implications for nuclear energy, that would alter the hopes and aspirations he might be expected to have at work and might warrant dismay, not enthusiasm.

We assess the "appropriateness" of a feeling by making a comparison between feeling and situation, not by examining the feeling *in abstracto*. This comparison lends the assessor a "normal" yardstick – a *socially* normal one – from which to factor out the personal meaning systems which may lead a worker to distort his view of "the" situation and feel inappropriately with regard to it. The psychiatrist holds constant the socially normal benchmark and focuses on what we have just factored out. The student of emotion management holds constant what is factored out and studies the socially normal benchmark, especially variations in it.

There is a second difference in what, from the two perspectives, seems interesting in the above example. From the emotion-management perspective, what is interesting is the character and direction of volition and consciousness. From the psychiatric perspective, what is of more interest is pre-will and nonconsciousness. The man above is not doing emotion work, that is, making a conscious, intended try at altering feeling. Instead he is controlling his enthusiasm by "being himself," by holding, in Schutz's term, a "natural attitude." He "no longer needs to struggle not to grin; he is not in a grinning mood" (Shapiro 1965: 164). In order to avoid affective deviance, some individuals may face a harder task than do others, the task of consciously working on feelings in order to make up for "a natural attitude" – explainable in psychoanalytic terms – that gets them in social trouble. The hysteric working in a bureaucratic setting may face the necessity for more emotion work than the obsessive compulsive who fits in more naturally.

In sum, the emotion-management perspective fosters attention to how people try to feel, not, as for Goffman, how people try to appear to feel. It leads us to attend to how people consciously feel and not, as for Freud, how people feel unconsciously. The interactive account of emotion points to alternate theoretical junctures: between consciousness of feeling and consciousness of feeling rules, between feeling rules and emotion work, between feeling rules and social structure. In the remainder of this essay, it is these junctures we shall explore.

By "emotion work" I refer to the act of trying to change in degree or quality an emotion or feeling. To "work on" an emotion or feeling is, for our purposes, the same as "to manage" an emotion or to do "deep acting." Note that "emotion work" refers to the effort – the act of trying – and not to the outcome, which may or may not be successful. Failed acts of management still indicate what ideal formulations guide the effort, and on that account are no less interesting than emotion management that works.

The very notion of an attempt suggests an active stance *vis-à-vis* feeling. In my exploratory study respondents characterized their emotion work by a variety of active verb forms; "I *psyched myself up*.... I *squashed* my anger down.... I *tried hard* not to feel disappointed....I *made* myself have a good time....I *tried* to feel grateful....I *killed* the hope I had burning." There was also the actively passive form, as in, "I *let myself* finally feel sad."

Emotion work differs from emotion "control" or "suppression." The latter two terms suggest an effort merely to stifle or prevent feeling. "Emotion work" refers more broadly to the act of evoking or shaping, as well as suppressing, feeling in oneself. I avoid the term "manipulate" because it suggests a shallowness I do not mean to imply. We can speak, then, of two broad types of emotion work: *evocation*, in which the cognitive focus is on an undesired feeling which is initially absent, and *suppression*, in which the cognitive focus is on an undesired feeling which is initially present. One respondent, going out with a priest twenty years her senior, exemplifies the problems of evocative emotion work: "Anyway, I started to try and make myself like him. I made myself focus on the way he talked, certain things he'd done in the past.... When I was with him I did like him but I would go home and write in my journal how much I couldn't stand him. I kept changing my feeling and actually thought I really liked him while I was with him but a couple of hours after he was gone, I reverted back to different feelings." Another respondent exemplifies the work, not of working feeling up, but of working feeling down:

> Last summer I was going with a guy often, and I began to feel very strongly about him. I knew though, that he had just broken up with a girl a year ago because she had gotten too serious about him, so I was afraid to show any emotion. I also was afraid of being hurt, so I attempted to change my feelings. *I talked myself into not caring about Mike* ... but I must admit it didn't work for long. *To sustain this feeling I had to almost invent bad things about him and concentrate on them or continue to tell myself he didn't care. It was a hardening of emotions*, I'd say. It took a lot of work and was unpleasant, because I had to concentrate on anything I could find that was irritating about him.

Often emotion work is aided by setting up an emotion-work system, for example, telling friends of all the worst faults of the person one wanted to fall out of love with, and then going to those friends for reinforcement of this view of the ex-beloved. This suggests another point: emotion work can be done by the self upon the self, by the self upon others, and by others upon oneself.

In each case the individual is conscious of a moment of "pinch," or discrepancy, between what one does feel and what one wants to feel (which is, in turn, affected by what one thinks one ought to feel in such a situation). In response, the individual may try to eliminate the pinch by working on feeling. Both the sense of discrepancy and the response to it can vary in time. The managing act, for example, can be a five-minute stopgap measure, or it can be a more long-range gradual effort suggested by the term "working through."

There are various techniques of emotion work. One is *cognitive:* the attempt to change images, ideas, or thoughts in the service of changing the feelings associated with them. A second is *bodily:* the attempt to change somatic or other physical symptoms of emotion (e.g., trying to breathe slower, trying not to shake). Third, there is *expressive* emotion work: trying to change expressive gestures in the service of changing inner feeling (e.g., trying to smile, or to cry). This differs from simple display in that it is directed toward change in feeling. It differs from bodily emotion work in that the individual tries to alter or shape one or another of the classic public channels for the expression of feeling.

These three techniques are distinct theoretically, but they often, of course, go together in practice. For example:

> I was a star halfback in high school. Before games I didn't feel the upsurge of adrenalin – in a word I wasn't "psyched up." (This was due to emotional difficulties I was experiencing and still experience – I was also an A student whose grades were dropping.) Having been in the past a fanatical, emotional, intense player, a "hitter" recognized by coaches as a very hard worker and a player with "desire," this was very upsetting. *I did everything I could to get myself "up." I would try to be outwardly "rah rah" or get myself scared of my opponents – anything to get the adrenalin flowing.* I tried to look nervous and intense before games, so at least the coaches wouldn't catch on. . . . When actually I was mostly bored, or in any event, not "up." I recall before one game wishing I was in the stands watching my cousin play for his school, rather than "out here."

Emotion work becomes an object of awareness most often, perhaps, when the individual's feelings do not fit the situation, that is, when the latter does not account for or legitimate feelings in the situation. A situation (such as a funeral) often carries with it a proper definition of itself ("this is a time facing loss"). This official frame carries with it a sense of what it is fitting to feel (sadness). It is when this tripartite consistency among situation, conventional frame, and feeling is somehow ruptured, as when the bereaved feels an irrepressible desire to laugh delightedly at the thought of an inheritance, that rule and management come into focus. It is then that the more normal flow of deep convention – the more normal fusion of situation, frame, and feeling – seems like an accomplishment.

The smoothly warm airline hostess, the ever-cheerful secretary, the unirritated complaint clerk, the undisgusted proctologist, the teacher who likes every student equally, and Goffman's unflappable poker player may all have to engage in deep acting, an acting that goes well beyond the mere ordering of display. Work to make feeling and frame consistent with situation is work in which individuals continually and privately engage. But they do so in obeisance to rules not completely of their own making.

Feeling Rules

We feel. We try to feel. We want to try to feel. The social guidelines that direct how we want to try to feel may be describable as a set of socially shared, albeit often latent (not thought about unless probed at), rules. In what way, we may ask, are these rules themselves known and how are they developed?

To begin with, let us consider several common forms of evidence for feeling rules. In common parlance, we often talk about our feelings or those of others as if rights and duties applied directly to them. For example, we often speak of "having the right" to feel angry at someone. Or we say we "should feel more grateful" to a benefactor. We chide ourselves that a friend's misfortune, a relative's death, "should have hit us harder," or that another's good luck, or our own, should have inspired more joy. We know feeling rules, too, from how others react to what they infer from our emotive display. Another may say to us, "You *shouldn't feel* so guilty; it wasn't your fault," or "You *don't have a right* to feel jealous, given our agreement." Another may simply declare an opinion as to the fit of feeling to situation, or may cast a claim upon our managerial stance, presupposing this opinion. Others may question or call for an account of a particular feeling in a situation, whereas they do not ask for an accounting of some other situated feeling (Lyman and Scott 1970). Claims and callings for an account can be seen as *rule reminders*. At other times, a person may, in addition, chide, tease, cajole, scold, shun – in a word, sanction us for "mis-feeling." Such sanctions are a clue to the rules they are meant to enforce.

Rights and duties set out the proprieties as to the *extent* (one can feel "too" angry or "not angry enough"), the *direction* (one can feel sad when one should feel happy), and the *duration* of a feeling, given the situation against which it is set. These rights and duties of feeling are a clue to the depth of social convention, to one final reach of social control.

There is a distinction, in theory at least, between a feeling rule as it is known by our sense of what we can *expect* to feel in a given situation, and a rule as it is known by our sense of what we *should* feel in that situation. For example, one may realistically expect (knowing oneself and one's neighbor's parties) to feel bored at a large New Year's Eve party and at the same time acknowledge that it would be more fitting to feel exuberant. However, "expect to feel" and "should ideally feel" often coincide, as below:

> Marriage, chaos, unreal, completely different in many ways than I imagined. Unfortunately we rehearsed the morning of our wedding at eight o'clock. The wedding was to be at eleven o'clock. It wasn't like I thought (everyone would know what to do). They didn't. That made me nervous. My sister didn't help me get dressed or flatter me (nor did anyone in the dressing room until I asked them). I was depressed. I wanted to be so happy on our wedding day. I never dreamed how anyone would cry at their wedding. A wedding is "the happy day" of one's life. I couldn't believe that some of my best friends couldn't make it to my wedding and that added to a lot of little things. So I started out to the church and all these things that I always thought would not happen at my wedding went through my mind. I broke down – I cried going down. "Be happy" I told myself. Think of the friends, and relatives that are present. (But I finally said to myself, "Hey people aren't getting married, you are. It's for Rich (my husband) and

you.") From down the pretty long aisle we looked at each other's eyes. His love for me changed my whole being. From that point on we joined arms. I was relieved and the tension was gone. In one sense it meant misery – but in the true sense of two people in love and wanting to share life – it meant the world to me. It was beautiful. It was indescribable.

In any given situation, we often invest what we expect to feel with idealization. To a remarkable extent these idealizations vary socially. If the "old-fashioned bride" above anticipates a "right" to feel jealous at any possible future infidelity, the young "flower child" below rejects just this right.

> when I was living down south, I was involved with a group of people, friends. We used to spend most evenings after work or school together. We used to do a lot of drugs, acid, coke or just smoke dope and we had this philosophy that we were very communal and did our best to share everything – clothes, money, food, and so on. I was involved with this one man – and thought I was "in love" with him. He in turn had told me that I was very important to him. Anyway, this one woman who was a very good friend of mine at one time and this man started having a sexual relationship, supposedly without my knowledge. I knew though and had a lot of mixed feelings about it. I thought, intellectually, that I had no claim to the man, and believed in fact that no one should ever try to *own* another person. I believed also that it was none of my business and I had no reason to worry about their relationship together, for it had nothing really to do with my friendship with either of them. I also believed in sharing. But I was horribly hurt, alone and lonely, depressed and I couldn't shake the depression and on top of those feelings I felt guilty for having those possessively jealous feelings. And so I would continue going out with these people every night, and try to suppress my feelings. My ego was shattered. I got to the point where I couldn't even laugh around them. So finally I confronted my friends and left for the summer and traveled with a new friend. I realized later what a heavy situation it was, and it took me a long time to get myself together and feel whole again.

Whether the convention calls for trying joyfully to possess, or trying casually not to, the individual compares and measures experience against an expectation often idealized. It is left for motivation ("what I want to feel") to mediate between feeling rule ("what I should feel") and emotion work ("what I try to feel"). Some of the time many of us can live with a certain dissonance between "ought" and "want," or between "want" and "try to." But the attempts to reduce emotive dissonance are our periodic clues to rules of feeling.

A feeling rule shares some formal properties with other sorts of rules, such as rules of etiquette, rules of bodily comportment, and those of social interaction in general (Goffman 1961). A feeling rule is like these other kinds of rules in the following ways: It delineates a zone within which one has permission to be free of worry, guilt, or shame with regard to the situated feeling. Such zoning ordinances describe a metaphoric floor and ceiling, there being room for motion and play between the two. Like other rules, feeling rules can be obeyed halfheartedly or boldly broken, the latter at varying costs. A feeling rule can be in varying proportions external or internal. Feeling rules differ curiously from other types of rules in that they do not apply to action but to what is often taken as a precursor to action. Therefore they tend to be latent and resistant to formal codification.

Feeling rules reflect patterns of social membership. Some rules may be nearly universal, such as the rule that one should not enjoy killing or witnessing the killing of a human being, including oneself. Other rules are unique to particular social groups and can be used to distinguish among them as alternate governments or colonizers of individual internal events.

Framing Rules and Feeling Rules: Issues in Ideology

Rules for managing feeling are implicit in any ideological stance; they are the "bottom side" of ideology. Ideology has often been construed as a flatly cognitive framework, lacking systematic implications for how we manage feelings, or, indeed, for how we feel. Yet, drawing on Durkheim (1961), Geertz (1964), and in part on Goffman (1974), we can think of ideology as an interpretive framework that can be described in terms of framing rules and feeling rules. By "framing rules" I refer to the rules according to which we ascribe definitions or meanings to situations. For example, an individual can define the situation of getting fired as yet another instance of capitalists' abuse of workers or as yet another result of personal failure. In each case, the frame may reflect a more general rule about assigning blame. By "feeling rules" I refer to guidelines for the assessment of fits and misfits between feeling and situation. For example, according to one feeling rule, one can be legitimately angry at the boss or company; according to another, one cannot. Framing and feeling rules are back to back and mutually imply each other.

It follows that when an individual changes an ideological stance, he or she drops old rules and assumes new ones for reacting to situations, cognitively and emotively. A sense of rights and duties applied to feelings in situations is also changed. One uses emotion sanctions differently and accepts different sanctioning from others. For example, feeling rules in American society have differed for men and women because of the assumption that their natures differ basically. The feminist movement brings with it a new set of rules for framing the work and family life of men and women: the same balance of priorities in work and family now ideally applies to men as to women. This carries with it implications for feeling. A woman can now as legitimately (as a man) become angry (rather than simply upset or disappointed) over abuses at work, since her heart is supposed to be in that work and she has the right to hope, as much as a man would, for advancement. Or, a man has the right to feel angry at the loss of custody if he has shown himself the fitter parent. "Old-fashioned" feelings are now as subject to new chidings and cajolings as are "old-fashioned" perspectives on the same array of situations.

One can defy an ideological stance not simply by maintaining an alternative frame on a situation but by maintaining an alternative set of feeling rights and obligations. One can defy an ideological stance by inappropriate affect and by refusing to perform the emotion management necessary to feel what, according to the official frame, it would seem fitting to feel. Deep acting or emotion work, then, can be a form of obeisance to a given ideological stance, lax emotion management a clue to an ideology lapsed or rejected.

As some ideologies gain acceptance and others dwindle, contending sets of feeling rules rise and fall. Sets of feeling rules contend for a place in people's minds as a governing standard with which to compare the actual lived experience of, say, the senior prom, the abortion, the wedding, the birth, the first job, the first layoff, the divorce. What we call "the changing climate of opinion" partly involves a changed framing of the "same" sorts of events. For example, each of two mothers may feel guilty about leaving her small child at day care while working all day. One mother, a feminist, may feel that she should not feel as guilty as she does. The second, a traditionalist, may feel that she should feel more guilty than, in fact, she does feel.

Part of what we refer to as the psychological effects of "rapid social change," or "unrest," is a change in the relation of feeling rule to feeling and a lack of clarity about what the rule actually is, owing to conflicts and contradictions between contending sets of rules. Feelings and frames are deconventionalized, but not yet reconventionalized. We may, like the marginal man, say, "I don't know how I should feel."

It remains to note that ideologies can function, as Randall Collins rightly notes (1975), as weapons in the conflict between contending elites and social strata. Collins suggests that elites try to gain access to the emotive life of adherents by gaining legitimate access to ritual, which for him is a form of emotive technology. Developing his view, we can add that elites, and indeed social groups in general, struggle to assert the legitimacy of their framing rules and their feeling rules. Not simply the evocation of emotion but laws governing it can become, in varying degrees, the arena of political struggle.

Feeling Rules and Social Exchange

The seemingly static links among ideology, feeling rules, and emotion management come alive in the process of social exchange. Students of social interaction have meant two things by the term "social exchange." Some have referred to the exchange of goods and services between people (Blau 1964; Simpson 1972; Singelmann 1972). Others (Mead 1934) have referred to an exchange of gestures, without the cost–benefit accounting referred to in the first usage. Yet acts of display, too, may be considered "exchanged" in the limited sense that the individual very often feels that a gesture is owed to oneself or another. I refer, then, to exchange of acts of display based on a prior, shared understanding of patterned entitlement. Any gesture – a cool greeting, an appreciative laugh, the apology for an outburst – is measured against a prior sense of what is reasonably owed another, given the sort of bond involved. Against this background measure, some gestures will seem more than ample, others less.

The exchange of gestures has, in turn, two aspects; it is an exchange of display acts (Goffman 1969, 1967) – that is, of surface acting – and also an exchange of emotion work – that is, of deep acting. In either case, rules (display rules or feeling rules), once agreed upon, establish the worth of a gesture and are thus *used* in social exchange as a medium of exchange. Feeling rules establish the basis of worth to be ascribed to a range of gestures, including emotion work. Emotion work is a gesture in a social exchange; it has a function there and is not to be understood merely as a facet of personality.

There seem to be two ways in which feeling rules come into play in social exchange. In the first, the individual takes the "owed" feeling to heart, takes it seriously. For example, a young woman on the eve of her college graduation felt anxious and depressed but thought that she "ought to feel happy," and that she "owed this happiness" to her parents for making her graduation possible. The parents felt entitled to a series of gestures indicating her pleasure. The young graduate could "pay" her parents in emotive display, a surface acting dissociated from her "real" definition of the situation. Going one step further, she could pay them with a gesture of deep acting – of trying to feel. The most generous gesture of all is the act of successful self-persuasion, of genuine feeling and frame change, a deep acting that jells, that works, that in the end is not phony (since it is what the emotion *is)* though it is none the less not a "natural" gift.

The second way feeling rules come into play in exchange is shown when the individual does not take the affective convention seriously; he or she plays with it. For example, an airport observation: There are two airline ticket agents, one experienced, one new on the job. The new agent is faced with the task of rewriting a complex ticket (involving change of date, lower fare, and credit of the difference between the previous and present fare to be made toward an air travel card, etc.). The new ticket agent looks for the "old hand," who is gone, while the customers in line shift postures and stare intently at the new agent. The "old hand" finally reappears after ten minutes, and the following conversation takes place: "I was looking for you. You're supposed to be my instructor." Old hand: "Gee," with an ironic smile, "I am *really* sorry. I feel *so* bad I wasn't here to help out" (they both laugh). The inappropriate feeling (lack of guilt, or sympathy) can be played upon in a way that says, "Don't take my nonpayment in emotion work or display work personally. I don't want to work here. You can understand that." The laughter at an ironic distance from the affective convention suggests also an intimacy; we do not need these conventions to hold us together. What we share is the defiance of them.

Commoditization of Feeling

In the beginning we asked how feeling rules might vary in salience across social classes. One possible approach to this question is via the connections among social exchange, commoditization of feeling, and the premium, in many middle-class jobs, on the capacity to manage meanings.

Conventionalized feeling may come to assume the properties of a commodity. When deep gestures of exchange enter the market sector and are bought and sold as an aspect of labor power, feelings are commoditized. When the manager gives the company his enthusiastic faith, when the airline stewardess gives her passengers her psyched-up but quasi-genuine reassuring warmth, what is sold as an aspect of labor power is deep acting.

But commoditization of feeling may not have equal salience for all social classes. It may have more salience for the middle class than for the working class. The way each class socializes its children may, furthermore, prepare them for future demands for the skill of emotion management.

When I speak of social class, it is not strictly speaking to income, education, or occupational status that I refer, but to something roughly correlated to these – the on-the-job task of creating and sustaining appropriate meanings. The bank manager, the IBM executive, for example, may be required, in part, to sustain a definition of self, office, and organization as "up and coming," or "on the go," "caring," or "reliable," meanings most effectively sustained through acts upon feeling. Feeling rules are of utmost salience in jobs such as these; rule reminders and sanctions are more in play. It is not, as Erich Fromm suggests, that the modern middle-class man "sells his personality," but that, more precisely, many jobs call for an appreciation of display rules, feeling rules, and a capacity for deep acting.

Working-class jobs more often call for the individual's external behavior and the products of it – a car part assembled, a truck delivered 500 miles away, a road repaired. The creation and sustaining of meanings goes on, but it is not such an important aspect of work. Physical labor is more commoditized, meaning-making and feeling, less. Surely, too, there are working- or lower-class jobs that do require the capacity to sustain meanings and to do so, when necessary, by emotion work; the jobs of prostitute (Elmer Pascua, work in progress) and personal servant require feeling management. But to the extent that meaning-making work tends to be middle-class work, feeling rules are more salient in the middle class.

There are jobs, like that of secretary or airline stewardess, with relatively low financial rewards and little authority, which nonetheless require a high degree of emotion and display management. Such jobs are often filled by women, many of whom come from the middle class. Such workers are especially important as a source of insight about emotion management. Being less rewarded for their work than their superiors, they are more likely to feel detached from, and be perceptive about, the rules governing deep acting. Deep acting is less likely to be experienced as part of the self and more likely to be experienced as part of the job. Just as we can learn more about "appropriate situation-feeling fits" by studying misfits, so too we can probably understand commoditized feeling better from those for whom it is a salient form of alienation (see Kanter's (1977) excellent chapters on secretaries).

Class, Child Rearing, and Emotion Work

Middle- and working-class parents tend to control their children in different ways (Bernstein 1971; Kohn 1963, 1969). Given the general pattern of class inheritance, each class tends to prepare its children with the skills necessary to "its" type of work environment and to pass on class-appropriate ways.

Middle-class parents tend to control via appeals to feeling, and the control is more *of* feeling. The working-class parent, by contrast, tends to control via appeals to behavior, and the control is more *of* behavior and its consequences (Bernstein 1971; Kohn 1963). That is, the middle-class child is more likely to be punished for "feeling the wrong way, or seeing things in the wrong light," or having the "wrong intention," whereas the working-class child is more likely to be punished for wrong behavior and its consequences. The class difference in socialization amounts to different degrees of training for the commoditization of feeling. This is yet another way the class structure reproduces itself. (Thanks to Caroline Persell for this point.)

It may well be that, especially among the middle class, a corresponding value is now placed on "authenticity," on things as they "truly are" or "once were." Authenticity, which Lionel Trilling has described as the "new moral virtue," when it refers to unworked-over feeling, may be rendered scarce for those in the meaning-making sector. For this sector, the pattern may be that of conventionalizing feeling, putting it on the market, and looking for "authenticity" (see Trilling 1972).

Summary and Conclusion

Why, we asked at the beginning, do we feel in ways appropriate to the situation as much of the time as we do? One suggested answer is: because we actively try to manage what we feel in accordance with latent rules. In order to elaborate this suggestion we considered first the responsiveness of emotion to acts of management as it is treated in the organismic and interactive account of emotion. According to the interactive account, we are not always passive *vis-à-vis* an uncontrollable flood of feeling, and those occasional efforts to actively shape our feeling can sometimes be effective. Taking this account I began to articulate the emotion-management perspective first by distinguishing it from the dramaturgical perspective on the one hand and the psychoanalytic perspective on the other. I then suggested some links among emotive experience, deep acting, and feeling rules. In turn, feeling rules were seen as the bottom side of ideology and therefore subject to the same pressures for change as are ideologies.

Conventions of feeling (i.e., what one is supposed to feel) are used in social exchange between individuals. Individuals operate their exchanges according to a prior sense of what is owed and owing. Individuals see themselves as being owed and as owing gestures of emotion work, and they exchange such gestures. People bond, in the emotive sense, either by fulfilling the emotive requirements situations call forth (e.g., the graduate trying to feel happy) or by holding just these requirements to one side (the ironic ticket agent acknowledging the sincere feeling "due" the other even while playing with that notion of debt).

Just as gestures of emotion work can be exchanged in private, so they can be exchanged in the marketplace, as an aspect of what is sold and bought as labor power. In such a case we can speak of the "commoditization" of emotion work. This prevails more for workers whose job it is to make and sustain meanings (e.g., "this is an up-and-coming company"; "this is a pleasant, safe airplane") – jobs found more in the middle class. Commoditization is less salient for those in physical labor or nonsocial mental labor, more common in the working class. A reexamination of class differences in child rearing suggests that middle-class families prepare their children for emotion management more, working-class families less. Each, in this way, prepares its children to psychologically reproduce the class structure.

The emotion-management perspective can be applied to any number of areas. We know little about how feeling rules vary in content from one occupation to another. The funeral parlor director, the doctor, the complaints clerk, the day-care worker all apply a sense of "should" to the situated feelings that emerge in the course of a week. How do these "shoulds" differ? Crosscutting occupational and class differences, they are likely to exhibit cultural differences associated with gender and ethnicity. Indeed, a good place to study change in feeling rules would be the strata of persons for whom the *right* of men to cry, or feel fearful, is extended over a greater range of situations, and for whom the *right* of women to open anger is extended over a larger, sanction-free, zone. How has this set of feeling rules, as the underside of feminist ideology, altered the understanding between men and women as to what feelings are latently "owed" and "owing"? We need to ask how different sexes, classes, and ethnic and religious groups differ in the sense of what one "ought to" or "has the right to" feel in a situation. How different is the burden of hidden work trying to obey latent laws? Finally, in whose interest are these feeling rules? Some managing of feeling promotes the social good. Some does not. Surely the flight attendant's sense that she "should feel cheery" does more to promote profit for United than to enhance her own inner well-being.

References

Averill, James R. 1976. "Emotion and anxiety: Sociocultural, biological, and psychological determinants." In M. Zuckerman and C. D. Spielberger (eds.) *Emotion and Anxiety: New Concepts, Methods and Applications*. New York: Wiley, pp. 87–130.

Benedict, Ruth. 1946. *Patterns of Culture*. New York: Penguin.

Bernstein, Basil. 1971. *Class, Codes and Control*. New York: Schocken.

Blau, Peter. 1964. *Exchange and Power in Social Life*. New York: Wiley.

Blumer, Herbert. 1969. *Symbolic Interactionism: Perspective and Method*. Englewood Cliffs, NJ: Prentice-Hall.

Collins, Randall. 1975. *Conflict Sociology*. New York: Academic Press.

Darwin, C. [1872] 1955. *The Expression of the Emotions in Man and Animals*. New York: Philosophical Library.

Durkheim, Émile. 1961. *The Elementary Forms of the Religious Life*. New York: Collier.

Ekman, P. 1972. "Universals and cultural differences in facial expressions of emotion." In J. K. Cole (ed.) *Nebraska Symposium on Motivation 1971*. Lincoln: University of Nebraska Press, pp. 207–83.

—— (ed.) 1973. *Darwin and Facial Expression*. New York: Academic Press.

Erikson, Eric. 1950. *Childhood and Society*. New York: Norton.

Foster, George M. 1972. "The anatomy of envy: A study in symbolic behavior." *Current Anthropology* 13: 165–202.

Freud, Sigmund. 1911. "Formulations regarding the two principles in mental function." In *Collected Papers*, vol. 4. New York: Basic Books, pp. 13–21.

—— 1915a. "Repression." In *Standard Edition*, vol. 14. London: Hogarth Press, pp. 146–58.

—— 1915b. "The unconscious." In *Standard Edition*, vol. 14. London: Hogarth Press, pp. 177–9.

Fromm, Erich. 1942. *Escape from Freedom*. New York: Farrar and Rinehart.

Geertz, Clifford. 1964. "Ideology as a cultural system." In *The Interpretation of Cultures*. London: Hutchinson, pp. 49–76.

Gerth, Hans and Mills, C. Wright. 1964. *Character and Social Structure: The Psychology of Social Institutions*. New York: Harcourt, Brace and World.

Goffman, Erving. 1956. "Embarrassment and social organization." *American Journal of Sociology* 62 (November): 264–71.

—— 1959. *The Presentation of Self in Everyday Life*. Garden City, NY: Doubleday.

—— 1961. "Fun in games." In *Encounters*. Indianapolis: Bobbs-Merrill, pp. 17–84.

—— 1967. *Interaction Ritual*. Garden City, NY: Doubleday.

—— 1969. *Strategic Interaction*. Philadelphia: University of Pennsylvania Press.

—— 1974. *Frame Analysis*. New York: Harper and Row.

—— 1976. "Gender advertisements." *Studies in the Anthropology of Visual Communication* 3, 2 (Fall).

Hochschild, Arlie Russell. 1977. "Reply to Scheff." *Current Anthropology* 18, 3 (September): 494–5.

Horney, Karen. 1937. *The Neurotic Personality of Our Time*. New York: Norton.

James, William, and Lange, Carl B. 1922. *The Emotions*. Baltimore: Williams and Wilkins.

Kanter, Rosabeth. 1977. *Men and Women of the Corporation*. New York: Basic Books.

Katz, Judith. 1977. "Discrepancy, arousal and labelling: Towards a psycho-social theory of emotion." Mimeographed. Toronto: York University.

Kemper, Thomas D. 1978. "Toward a sociological theory of emotion: Some problems and some solutions." *American Sociologist* 13 (February): 30–41.

Kohn, Melvin. 1963. "Social class and the exercise of parental authority." In Neil Smelser and William Smelser, (eds.) *Personality and Social System*, New York: Wiley, pp. 297–313.

—— 1969. *Class and Conformity*. Homewood, Ill.: Dorsey.

Lazarus, Richard S. 1966. *Psychological Stress and the Coping Process*. New York: McGraw-Hill.

Lazarus, Richard S. and Averill, James R. 1972. "Emotion and cognition: With special reference to anxiety." In D. C. Spielberger (ed.) *Anxiety: Current Trends in Theory and Research*, vol 2. New York: Academic Press.

Lofgren, L. Borge. 1968. "Psychoanalytic theory of affects." *Journal of the American Psychoanalytic Association* 16 (July): 638–50.

Lyman, S. and Scott, Marvin. 1970. *Sociology of the Absurd*. New York: Appleton-Century-Crofts.

Mead, G. H. 1934. *Mind, Self and Society*, ed. Charles Morris. Chicago: University of Chicago Press.

Riesman, David. 1952. *Faces in the Crowd: Individual Studies in Character and Politics*. New Haven, Conn.: Yale University Press.

—— 1960. *The Lonely Crowd: A Study of the Changing American Character*. New Haven, Conn.: Yale University Press.

Schachter, Stanley. 1964. "The interaction of cognitive and physiological determinants of emotion states." In P. H. Leiderman and D. Shapiro (eds.) *Psychobiological Approaches to Social Behavior*. Stanford, Calif.: Stanford University Press.

Schachter, S. and Singer, J. 1962. "Cognitive, social and physiological determinants of emotional state." *Psychological Review* 69: 379–99.

Schafer, Roy. 1976. *A New Language for Psychoanalysis*. New Haven, Conn.: Yale University Press.

Shapiro, David. 1965. *Neurotic Styles*. New York: Basic Books.

Shott, Susan. 1979. "Emotion and social life: A symbolic interactionist analysis." *American Journal of Sociology* 84 (May): 1317–34.

Simpson, Richard. 1972. *Theories of Social Exchange*. Morristown, NJ: General Learning Press.

Singelmann, Peter. 1972. "Exchange as symbolic interaction: Convergences between two theoretical perspectives." *American Sociological Review* 37(4): 414–24.

Swanson, Guy E. and Miller, Daniel. 1966. *Inner Conflict and Defense*. New York: Schocken.

Trilling, Lionel. 1972. *Sincerity and Authenticity*. Cambridge, Mass.: Harvard University Press.

11 Jealousy in American Culture, 1945–1985

Gordon Clanton

Emotions in Sociological Perspective

Emotions are social as well as psychological phenomena. Emotions are responses to situations interpreted on the basis of previous social learning. They reflect the norms, attitudes, and values of groups as well as individuals. They are useful and dangerous for groups as well as individuals. These and other *social* aspects of emotions are the subject matter of the sociology of emotions. Until recently, sociology has had little to say about emotions despite their obvious importance in human affairs. Emotions have social dimensions. It is the business of sociology to explore them.

Emotions are shaped by society. Private experiences of emotion are embedded in history, in culture, in social structure. Not only our feelings but also our feelings about our feelings are shaped by psychological, philosophical, and theological frameworks which are institutionalized in social life. Thus, patterns of emotional experience change in response to changes in society and culture. A powerful illustration of this principle is found in the evolution over the last four decades of the experience of jealousy.

For present purposes jealousy may be defined as a protective reaction to a perceived threat to a valued relationship or to its quality (Clanton and Smith 1986: vi, 239). The protective reaction can involve thoughts, feelings, or actions. Although jealous behavior sometimes damages relationships, jealousy always *intends* the protection of the relationship and/or the protection of the ego of the threatened partner. Adult jealousy typically results when one believes that a romantic relationship is threatened by a real or imaginary rival. As Goffman (1967) notes about embarrassment, jealousy is not an irrational impulse breaking through socially prescribed behavior but part of this orderly behavior itself.

An analysis of articles in popular magazines reveals that the experience, expression, interpretation, and treatment of jealousy have changed substantially in the United States since World War II. Before about 1970, much jealousy was seen by many people as proof of love. Since 1970, jealousy has been seen by many people as a personal defect rooted in low self-esteem. Applying the sociology of knowledge to this patterning of human emotion, this paper summarizes these changes, explores their social causes and effects, and suggests some implications for clinical practice and for self-understanding. In addition, some educated guesses about the future of jealousy are offered.

Reprinted from *The Sociology of the Emotions: Original Essays and Research Papers*, ed. David D. Franks and E. Doyle McCarthy, Greenwich, Conn. and London: JAI Press, 1989, pp. 179–93.

Jealousy in Popular Magazines

The popular media of a society can serve as an imprecise but useful barometer of the interests and concerns of the populations served by the media in question. Seeking to understand how jealousy has been viewed in the United States since World War II, I used the *Readers' Guide to Periodical Literature* to identify every article on jealousy published from 1945 to 1985 in the magazines indexed. The *Readers' Guide* is a cumulative index to general interest periodicals published in the United States. Thus it provides a wide cross-section of publications sufficient for identification of trends. The *Readers' Guide*, which currently lists almost 200 periodicals, is arranged so that one can look up the subject of jealousy and find out which magazines included articles on this topic for a given time period. The *Readers' Guide* does not index fiction by subject so this survey included only non-fiction treatments of jealousy.

In addition to articles on adult jealousy in romantic relationships and in marriage, the entries for "Jealousy" typically include articles on sibling rivalry and other family jealousies as well as miscellaneous advice columns and other short items in which jealousy is one of several issues discussed. It is not always possible to tell from the title just what the article is about. Similarly, it is not always possible to classify articles as representing the "old" or "new" view of jealousy summarized later in this article.

If one considers only major articles on adult jealousy, one finds about one article per year from 1945 through the late 1950s and about two per year in the early 1960s. Almost nothing was published about adult jealousy from 1966 to 1972. From 1973 through 1978 there were, once again, about two articles per year. Since 1978, the average number of articles has increased to about five per year. To summarize: except for the period from 1966 to 1972 when almost nothing was published about jealousy, the number of articles on jealousy in the magazines indexed in the *Readers' Guide* increased about five-fold over the four decades surveyed – with most of the increase occurring since 1978.

It should be noted that the survey was not intended to generate a precise or systematic survey of the contents of the approximately eighty articles published and reviewed. Rather, the intention was to read the articles in order to identify axial shifts taking place over four decades in people's views of jealousy, their evaluation of jealousy, and its social significance. For this reason, this report will highlight those specific articles that best communicate the "old" and "new" views of jealousy during the post-World War II period.

Over the forty-year span surveyed an interesting shift has occurred in the relative numbers of articles on adult jealousy as opposed to sibling rivalry and other jealousies among family members. Prior to 1966, articles on sibling rivalry and other family jealousies were more numerous than articles on adult jealousy in romantic relationships and in marriage. Since 1970, however, among the articles indexed under "Jealousy" in the *Readers' Guide*, those on adult jealousy have outnumbered articles on family jealousies by roughly *six to one*. Over this period, articles on sibling rivalry continued to appear and to be filed under "Siblings" or "Sibling rivalry." Apparently, however, fewer and fewer of these articles used the word "jealousy" in their titles. As a result, they are not indexed under "Jealousy." Thus, it appears that prior to 1966, the word "jealousy" was commonly used with reference to both adult jealousy and sibling rivalry. Since about 1970, the word "jealousy" has been used primarily with reference to adult jealousy in romantic relationships and marriage.

Another subtle shift in the connotations of the word "jealousy" is revealed by these data. Prior to 1966, most articles about adult jealousy focused on relatively innocent *flirtations*, for example, what to do if, at a party, your mate spends most of the evening in animated conversation with an attractive member of the other gender. Since about 1970, many articles on adult jealousy are about the threat of *real sexual adventures and affairs*, for example, what to do if your mate betrays you sexually or proposes an "open marriage."

Canvassing all the listed articles on jealousy over the forty-year period, one notes that the great bulk of them appeared in magazines oriented toward women readers. A supplemental analysis finds little mention of jealousy in *Playboy or Penthouse*. This pattern suggests that women, undoubtedly due to both their social positions and the social meanings attributed to these positions, express both a greater interest in jealousy and other emotions and a greater willingness to talk about them than men.

Jealousy as Proof of Love: 1945–1965

From the end of World War II until the late 1960s, virtually all of the articles in popular magazines said that a certain amount of jealousy was natural, proof of love, and good for marriage. The reader (typically a woman) was advised to keep her jealous feelings "under control" and to avoid the "unreasonable" jealousy which is marked by suspicion, hostility, accusations, and threats. The woman was told to avoid situations which might make her husband jealous *but* to interpret *his* expressions of jealousy as evidence of love. If jealousy threatened the stability of the marriage, professional help was advised.

Representative of this approach was a short piece in *McCall's* magazine (May 1962) by David R. Mace, a well-known marriage counselor and author. The article, titled "Two faces of jealousy," hinged on the distinction between normal and abnormal (or pathological) jealousy and moved from the assumption that the differences between the two were self-evident and nonproblematic. Normal jealousy, according to Mace, "is the instinct that flashes a warning when the exclusiveness of marriage is threatened.... Normal jealousy is a protective instinct that has saved many a marriage. Abnormal jealousy is a destructive obsession and often requires professional treatment." In this article, no attention was given to the possibility that definitions of "normal" and "abnormal" jealousy might vary from time to time, from place to place, and from couple to couple.

Judith Viorst's March 1970 *Redbook* article, "Confessions of a jealous wife," summed up the view of jealousy that had prevailed in the middle sectors of American society until about that time. Jealousy was approved and defended as a normal accompaniment of love. Some conventional strategies for coping with jealousy were discussed, including sarcasm, violence, and trying to make the spouse jealous. What Viorst refers to as the "civilized" response and the open marriage approach were ruled out. The author concluded that nothing really works. Jealousy is inevitable: "A man who wasn't attractive to other women, a man who wasn't alive enough to enjoy other women, a man who was incapable of making me jealous, would never be the kind of man I'd love."

Although it appeared in 1970, Viorst's "Confessions" represented the "old view" of jealousy which was taken-for-granted in the 1950s and early 1960s. Nearly all articles on adult jealousy in popular magazines prior to 1970 reflected this point of view: jealousy is natural; it is proof of love; it is good for marriage. Although the possibility of pathological jealousy was acknowledged and warned against, the focus was on little episodes of "normal" jealousy which show that love is alive and which need not threaten the quality to the relationship. After 1970, this "old view" of jealousy largely disappeared from the popular media for more than a decade.

Jealousy as a Personal Defect: 1970–1980

The magazines listed in the *Readers' Guide* and the popular media in general were largely silent about jealousy from 1966 to 1972. This is surprising in light of the fact that the same period produced an explosion of popular writing on sex, love, relationships, and personal growth. Perhaps the prevailing view of jealousy was changing so fast that writers and editors were unsure how to characterize it.

By about 1970, a new view of jealousy was taking root in a substantial and influential minority of Americans. Magazine articles began to question the appropriateness of jealous feelings in love relationships. Many people no longer assumed that jealousy is evidence of love. For the first time *guilt* about jealousy became an issue for large numbers of people. According to the emerging view, jealousy was not natural; it was learned. Jealousy was no longer seen as proof of love; it was, rather, evidence of a defect such as low self-esteem or the inability to trust. Thus, jealousy was not seen as good for relationships; it was bad for them. From this it followed that one could and should seek to eradicate every trace of jealousy from one's personality. Various prescriptions for achieving this were offered by therapists, gurus, and advice-givers.

Typical of magazine articles espousing the "new view" of jealousy was "Taming the green-eyed monster" by veteran writer Norman Lobsenz. Like the article by Judith Viorst previously discussed, the Lobsenz article also appeared in *Redbook* – exactly five years later (March 1975). Its thrust and tone, however, were quite different. Lobsenz cited psychologists and sociologists who suggested that jealousy was becoming outdated as society moved into an era of "liberated" relationships between men and women. He recounted the experiences of several young couples who tried to minimize jealousy in their marriages. He described how he overcame his own moment of jealousy when, at a party, his wife spent most of the evening in animated conversation with a good-looking man: "Once I realized that my wife's conversation with someone else took nothing away from me, ... I also realized that there was no reason for jealousy." As with most articles reflecting the "new view," little attention was given to situations in which there *is* a threat to the relationship and, therefore, a reason for jealousy. The semantics of the "new view" lead us to lose sight of appropriate jealousies rooted in real threats to valued relationships.

Lobsenz acknowledged that the would-be "liberated" are sometimes troubled by *unexpected* jealous feelings which are all the more painful because these people are convinced that they *ought not* feel jealous. But even here, he is suggesting that it is *desirable* to be completely without jealousy. Reading such an article, one could easily believe that only defective people with poor reality-testing ever feel jealousy.

Lobsenz found the roots of jealousy in self-doubt and lack of self-esteem. He was confident that we can learn from our experiences of jealousy and that we can constructively redirect our jealous energy. This article offered an optimistic, rational, and one might say, a masculine counterpart to the treatments of jealousy published before 1970.

Not all articles advocating the new "liberated" view of jealousy were so optimistic. In the *Village Voice* (October 18, 1973), Karen Durbin observed that jealousy is "well on the way to becoming the New Sin of the liberated generation." In her own counter-cultural milieu with its emphasis on radical politics and women's liberation, possessiveness in love relationships was criticized as "emotional imperialism." Thus, Durbin *tried* to be liberated and felt guilty when she became jealous. For her and for others she knew, "The energy required for all that coping was too much, and I fled." All jealousy, Durbin concluded, is a cry of pain. It "will probably be with us as long as sex remains an expression of love and as long as love remains the most effective means (apart from religion) of assuaging our essential isolation." Durbin's article and her TV talk show appearances were much discussed in New York City and elsewhere. No doubt, many of the would-be liberated were relieved to hear a voice from the left suggesting it might sometimes be all right to feel jealous.

As different as they are in outcome and mood, the underlying assumptions about jealousy which characterize the articles by Lobsenz and Durbin are very similar. Both reflect the "new view" of jealousy as (1) a learned behavior which can and should be unlearned, (2) rooted in the personal defects of the jealous person, and (3) bad for relationships and for one's soul.

The change in the understanding of jealousy was accompanied by semantical shifts – changes in language which reflected new beliefs. Whereas in the 1950s the word "jealousy" was often used to describe normal and possibly beneficial feelings and behaviors, by the early 1970s the word was increasingly used primarily with reference to inappropriate, unconstructive, and even pathological reactions such as suspiciousness, paranoia, and violence. In the common speech of the 1970s, the jealous person was usually characterized as unduly possessive, insecure, and suffering from low self-esteem.

Of course, many people continued to hold onto the idea that some jealousy is appropriate and constructive even as the popular media increasingly focused on its inappropriate manifestations. *McCall's*, for example, bucked the trend with a May 1974 article titled "In Defense of Jealousy." The United States is a pluralistic society. Amid rapid social change, old styles are *joined*, not replaced, by new styles. As a result, the number of styles is always increasing. Among more conventional people, "jealousy" continued to refer primarily to little misunderstandings and flirtations. For these people, a little jealousy continued to be seen as proof of love. Among those with more liberal views of sexual rules and gender roles, "jealousy" had to do with the possibility of greater personal freedom including, for some, levels of sexual freedom previously seen as incompatible with marriage. For these people, jealousy came to be associated with low self-esteem, poor reality-testing, inappropriate possessiveness, and unconstructive behavior. Given the demographics of the magazines in which the "new view" articles were published, it appears that the new view of jealousy was found more among the affluent than the poor, more among the better-educated than the less-well-educated, and more among the urban and the suburban than the rural.

Sociology of Knowledge and Sociology of Emotions

Although some social scientists and helping professionals are among the advocates of the "new view" of jealousy, it is not the business of sociology to approve one of these interpretations as truer or better than the other. The rather more modest goal of sociology is to describe the change and to *explain* it by locating its social causes and social effects.

The search for the social roots and social functions of information, ideas, and opinions is the work of the sociology of knowledge. Early work in this field looked for the social sources of "big ideas" such as political philosophies and religions – often with the goal of discrediting the ideas and beliefs of others by pointing to their social causes. In a major theoretical advance, Peter L. Berger and Thomas Luckmann (1966) proposed that the sociology of knowledge could and should be employed to analyze everything that people "know," everything they believe to be true. In other words, the many "small ideas" – the attitudes, beliefs, and values which make up one's picture of reality (one's *Weltanschauung)* – are socially constructed and can be analyzed in terms of the social processes which gave rise to them.

To call attention to the social causes and social functions of ideas and attitudes need not necessarily involve the attempt to discredit or impugn them (Berger 1981). *All* knowledge is socially grounded. My beliefs, no less than my opponent's beliefs, are shaped by social forces. Thus, regarding this or that belief pertaining to an emotion such as jealousy, the sociology of knowledge asks *not* "Is this true?" but rather "Where did this idea come from?" and "How and why has it changed over time?"

This paper is an exercise in the sociology of knowledge. We are searching for the social roots of the knowledge – the attitudes, beliefs, and values – on which the experience and interpretation of jealousy depend. In other words, we are looking for the social sources of the changing fashions in jealousy summarized above, namely, the shift from seeing jealousy as proof of love to seeing jealousy as a defect rooted in low self-esteem.

The experience and expression of emotions depend on what one "knows," what one believes to be true. Jealousy, as previously noted, is a protective reaction to a perceived threat to a valued relationship or to its quality (Clanton and Smith 1986: vi, 239). Thus, the experience and expression of jealousy depend on what one knows about (1) what constitutes a valued relationship (i.e., its boundaries and rules), (2) what constitutes a threat to the relationship or to its quality, and (3) what one ought to do to protect a threatened relationship. Jealousy and other emotions can be analyzed in terms of the social causes that give rise to the substantive beliefs and norms on which they depend.

Jealousy, in other words, is a consequence of social organization and will vary as forms of social organization vary. For example, swingers do not view sexual exclusiveness as a necessary condition for a happy marriage and so appear to be without jealousy in situations which would make most people jealous (Gilmartin 1986). Similarly, people in other cultures get jealous in situations in which we do not (and vice versa) because of cultural variations in definitions of relationship boundaries, threats, and protective strategies (Hupka 1981; Mead 1986).

Social Sources of the New View of Jealousy

The new view of jealousy which arose in the late 1960s and peaked in the early 1970s was a by-product of a larger shift in the shape of love relationships in the United States. The 1950s and early 1960s were characterized by an emphasis on *relationship commitment* or "togetherness." There was almost no talk about personal freedom in marriage. The "sexual revolution" and the women's movement were not yet topics of conversation. In such a time, jealousy is seen as a natural proof of love and as good for marriage. In contrast, in the late 1960s and early 1970s, many individuals sought to enhance *personal freedom* in relationships, often at the cost of the forms of commitment characteristic of earlier times. Cohabitation became much more common. Women demanded fairness. The divorce rate rose. The media reported on nude beaches, communes, and gay pride. A book titled *Open Marriage* topped the best sellers list for over a year in 1972. (For more on these trends, see Clanton 1984, Gagnon 1977, and Swidler 1980.) As a result of these and other manifestations of concern for personal freedom in love relationships, jealousy came to be viewed by many as a personal defect. If one emphasizes freedom in relationships, one will see much jealousy as inappropriate and undesirable.

The quest for more personal freedom in love relationships and in marriage was part of a larger trend in favor of more freedom, more experimentation, and a more positive view of pleasure. These qualities often are associated with the youth counterculture of the late 1960s but, in fact, various manifestations of these themes diffused through the whole culture in the 1970s and 1980s. Although flowers and beads are less fashionable now than they were in the late 1960s, the countercultural view of jealousy as a defect remains quite strong today – even though the rhetoric of the 1980s includes a certain amount of backlash against 1960s themes and values.

A longer view of history, amplified by cross-cultural comparisons, reveals that jealousy functions to protect love and other forms of valued relationships (Davis 1986). In every culture people form valued relationships in accordance with prevailing norms. Jealousy protects whatever kinds of relationships cultures teach people to value. Specific jealous behaviors vary enormously across cultures because of the great diversity of human beliefs about relationship boundaries, threats, and protection. The experience and the interpretation of jealousy change as beliefs about these matters change.

To summarize: The sexual conservatism of the period before about 1965 produced a relatively positive view of jealousy while the liberalization of the late 1960s and early 1970s produced a negative appraisal of jealousy. Today many people still hold some version of the late 1960s view that jealousy is a personal defect. At the same time, "commitment" seems to be making something of a comeback. One hears less talk than before about freedom, adventure, and open marriage. Insofar as fear of AIDS and other developments make North American culture somewhat more conservative about sex, jealousy will, to some degree, be "rehabilitated" and more generally approved.

Implications for Therapy and Self-Understanding

A sociological view of jealousy can facilitate better self-understanding and more effective therapy. Although full discussion of these matters is not possible in the space available, I shall attempt briefly to illustrate that awareness of social forces can (1) enhance understanding of the contemporary experience of jealousy and (2) provide a basis for a critique of the fashionable but misleading view of jealousy as caused by low self-esteem.

Jealousy Today

The emphasis on personal freedom in relationship and the related view of jealousy as a personal defect peaked in the early 1970s. For more than a decade now, Americans have been integrating the new input of the late 1960s and recovering some of the concern for commitment which characterized the "togetherness" of earlier times. In the United States today one finds adherents of both views of jealousy. As noted above, the "new view" that jealousy is evidence of personal defects remains very strong. But many contemporary people are skeptical of a too simple emphasis on either commitment or freedom. For more and more individuals and couples, the stated goal is to strike a balance between commitment and freedom in love relationships (Swidler 1980).

Such a balance is not easy to achieve. American society is increasingly pluralistic. This means that husband and wife are more likely than in the past to have different values in connection with issues that bear on relationship quality. As a result, the management of jealousy will increasingly depend on good communication between partners of their personal needs and values *and* on honest negotiations where their respective needs and values are incongruent (Margolin 1981). Such negotiations are not easy to achieve because most individuals in most relationships are reluctant to give up any power or benefit they hold.

C. Wright Mills (1959) reminded us that biography is embedded in history. Self-understanding often is enhanced by considering one's life against the backdrop of the events of one's time. The recent historical shift from an emphasis on commitment to an emphasis on freedom to an emphasis on balancing the two is analogous to the sequence of personal experience for most individuals. In the life-cycle of the developing person, attention first is given to the establishment of a committed relationship. Later there may emerge a concern for personal freedom in the context of commitment. Still later, perhaps following a break-up or divorce, many individuals rediscover the importance of commitment and seek to achieve a workable balance of commitment and freedom. Striking such a balance is the challenge of our time, especially for middle-aged individuals whose young adulthood coincided with the culture's emphasis on the personal freedom which, in the words of songwriter Kris Kristofferson, was sometimes "just another word for nothing left to lose."

Individuals who are aware of the cultural shifts described in this article will better understand important changes in their own lives. They will be less likely to adopt uncritically the still-fashionable view that jealousy is a personal defect. They will be more likely to look for the roots of jealousy in *relationship dysfunctions* rather than in intrapsychic disturbances. They will seek a *balance* of commitment and freedom rather than focus exclusively on one or the other. They will attempt to *negotiate* that balance rather than adopt some standard external to the couple or imposed by one partner. Awareness of the social forces does not guarantee that we shall find easy answers to complex personal questions, but, without such awareness, we are at the mercy of fads and fashions which may be harmful to our love relationships and to our mental health.

Jealousy and Self-Esteem

Today it is fashionable to assume that low self-esteem is a major cause of jealousy and that raising one's self-esteem is a good way to reduce or "cure" jealousy. The sociology of knowledge encourages a search for the social roots of this assumption.

Explanations of jealousy as evidence of low self-esteem are part of the larger tendency in the 1970s and 1980s to view a wide range of personal failures and problems as caused by low self-esteem. This view is widely taken for granted by both helping professionals and lay people. It is, nevertheless, erroneous and dangerous. In fact, one may have high self-esteem in general but still be uncertain and vulnerable in some areas. One may have high self-esteem but still experience jealousy if a valued relationship appears to be threatened.

Although it enjoys the status of a "scientific" principle of great therapeutic usefulness, the notion that emotional upsets are *caused* by low self-esteem is, in fact, an erroneous extension of the commonsense principle that success is associated with self-confidence and with liking oneself and that failure is associated with lack of self-confidence and not liking oneself (i.e., low self-esteem). Explanations of human behavior often assert that low self-esteem *causes* failure but it is at least as true that *failure causes low self-esteem* (or, that the relationship is reciprocal). Thus, most statements in the popular psychological literature about the relationship between low self-esteem and various personal failures or inadequacies are, at best, circular and, at worst, backward. That is, such statements either say nothing beyond the truism that successful people feel better about themselves than do failures, or, worse: they actually *invert* the causal relationship and view low self-esteem as the cause of failure when, in fact, failure is more often the cause of lowered self-esteem.

Leaving aside the methodological problems which characterize many of the studies of jealousy and self-esteem (Clanton and Smith 1986: 242ff.), several kinds of evidence suggest that, despite wide-spread opinion to the contrary, low self-esteem is *not* the principal cause of jealousy.

1 Cross-cultural surveys reveal that low self-esteem plays little or no role in explanations of jealousy in various cultures (Hupka 1981). In all cultures, jealousy is provoked by perceived violations of marriage rules, by real events in the social world, not by personal defects in isolated individuals (Davis 1936).

2 The "low self-esteem" explanation for jealousy is not found in the popular media in the United States before about 1970. If it were a timeless truth, you would expect *some*body to write about it earlier.

3 Empirical research has not found a consistent correlation between low self-esteem and jealousy. David J. Kosins (1983: 75f.) reviews the literature and finds five studies which report modest correlations and five more which find no significant correlation. Gray L. Hansen (1985: 263) cites one study which finds a negative relationship between self-esteem and jealousy for both men and women, one which finds this relationship only for men, and three which find no relationship between the two variables. In his own research, Hansen (p. 267) finds low self-esteem to be associated with jealousy for females but not for males. To summarize: Empirical research has not demonstrated a consistent *correlation* between jealousy and low self-esteem. Furthermore, most studies do not address at all the question of *causation*.

4 The Kosins study finds no statistically significant relationship between jealousy and several developmental variables including childhood conflicts with siblings, separations and losses during childhood, harshness of parental discipline, quality of early parent–child relations, and emotional support from peers in childhood. Furthermore, there was no significant difference in the intensity of jealousy reported by college students (representing the "normal" or nonclinical population), psychotherapy outpatients, and a small sample of psychiatric inpatients. These surprising findings suggest that most jealousy is not best viewed as an emotional disorder rooted in the psychological deficiencies of the jealous person.

5 Those who assume that low self-esteem causes jealousy (rather than the other way around) are also likely to assume that low self-esteem causes delinquent behavior in young people. Contrary to this expectation, John D. McCarthy and Dean R. Hoge (1984) found that the effect of self-esteem on subsequent delinquent behavior is negligible. Instead, they found consistent but weak negative effects of delinquent behavior on subsequent self-esteem. In other words, low self-esteem does not cause delinquency but delinquency has some tendency to lower self-esteem. The "commonsense" assumption of causal direction is backward. Furthermore, it is reasonable to assume that delinquent behavior sometimes *raises* self-esteem for persons who can find no other route to "success." At the very minimum, this study challenges the automatic assumption that low self-esteem is responsible for problematic behavior including jealousy.

With these bits of evidence before us, we can re-evaluate the widespread assumption that low self-esteem is the principal cause of jealousy. Reflecting this viewpoint, a psychotherapist recently told me, "I have never had a jealous patient who was not also suffering from low self-esteem." She was puzzled when I asked her which caused which. Like many others, she *assumed* that the low self-esteem caused the jealousy. *It is at least as plausible that the jealousy caused the low self-esteem.* That is, individuals' experiences of jealousy resulted in their feeling less good about themselves, a tendency encouraged by the "new view" which sees jealousy as a personal defect.

If, as I have suggested, low self-esteem is more often an *effect* than a cause of jealousy, then one cannot reasonably hope to reduce jealousy by artificially pumping up one's self-esteem. To the contrary, one would need to find ways of reducing jealousy in order to raise self-esteem. The focus on raising self-esteem might actually divert attention away from the kind of work on one's jealousy that would be necessary if self-esteem is to be raised. As Gayla Margolin (1981) has noted, jealousy is an interactional problem more often than it is an individual problem. Jealousy is often a reflection of larger issues of relationship satisfaction and dissatisfaction.

Conclusion

This paper, an exercise in the sociology of emotions, has argued that the experience, the expression, the interpretation, and the treatment of jealousy change as society and culture change. Since about 1970, jealousy has been seen by many as a personal defect rooted in low self-esteem. Awareness of the social roots of this shift illuminates the contemporary experience of jealousy and calls into question the still-fashionable view of jealousy as a useless emotion which grows out of low self-esteem.

References

Berger, Bennett M. 1981. *The Survival of a Counterculture.* Berkeley: University of California Press.

Berger, Peter L. and Luckmann, Thomas. 1966. *The Social Construction of Reality.* Garden City, NY: Doubleday.

Clanton, Gordon. 1984. "Social forces and the changing family." In Lester A. Kirkendall and Arthur E. Gravatt (eds.) *Marriage and the Family in the Year 2020.* Buffalo, NY: Prometheus Press.

Clanton, Gordon, and Smith, Lynn G. (eds.) [1977] 1986. *Jealousy.* Lanham, Md.: University Press of America.

Davis, Kingsley. [1936] 1986. "Jealousy and sexual property." In Gordon Clanton and Lynn G. Smith (eds.) *Jealousy.* Lanham, Md.: University Press of America, pp. 129–34.

Gagnon, John H. 1977. *Human Sexualities.* Glenview, Ill.: Scott-Foresman.

Gilmartin, Brian G. [1977] 1986. "Jealousy among the Swingers." In Gordon Clanton and Lynn G. Smith (eds.) *Jealousy.* Lanham, Md.: University Press of America, pp. 152–8.

Goffman, Erving. 1967. "Embarrassment and social organization." In his *Interaction Ritual.* Garden City, NY: Doubleday.

Hansen, Gary L. 1985. "Perceived threats and marital jealousy." *Social Psychology Quarterly* 48(3): 262–8.

Hupka, Ralph B. 1981. "Cultural determinants of jealousy." *Alternative Lifestyles* 4(3): 310–56.

Kosins, David J. 1983. "Developmental correlates of sexual jealousy." Doctoral dissertation, California School for Professional Psychology, San Diego.

Margolin, Gayla. 1981. "A behavioral-systems approach to the treatment of jealousy." *Clinical Psychology Review* 1: 469–87.

McCarthy, John D. and Hoge, Dean R. 1984. "The dynamics of self-esteem and delinquency." *American Journal of Sociology* 90(2): 396–410.

Mead, Margaret. [1931] 1986. "Jealousy: Primitive and civilized." In Gordon Clanton and Lynn G. Smith (eds.) *Jealousy.* Lanham, Md.: University Press of America, pp. 115–26.

Mills, C. Wright. 1959. *The Sociological Imagination.* New York: Grove Press.

Swidler, Ann. 1980. "Love and adulthood in American culture." In Neil J. Smelser and Erik H. Erikson (eds.) *Themes of Work and Love in Adulthood.* Cambridge, Mass.: Harvard University Press.

Part III

The Self in Social Context

Introduction

The idea that the self is fundamentally a social phenomenon has been central in sociological social psychology since George Herbert Mead and Charles Horton Cooley developed the idea of the social self in the early twentieth century. Mead argued that human communication and role-taking (viewing oneself from the perspective of another person and, ultimately, from the perspective of society as a whole) were essential to the development of the self. According to Mead, we first see ourselves and come to experience a "self" when we see ourselves from the perspective of others. As Mead puts it,

> The individual experiences himself as such, not directly, but only indirectly, from the particular standpoints of other individual members of the same social group, or from the generalized standpoint of the social group as a whole to which he belongs. For he enters his own experience as a self or individual, not directly or immediately, not by becoming a subject to himself, but only insofar as he first becomes an object to himself just as other individuals are objects to him or in his experience; and he becomes an object to himself only by taking the attitudes of other individuals toward himself within a social environment or context of experience and behavior in which both he and they are involved. (Mead 1934: 138)

More simply, Mead says, "We are more or less seeing ourselves as others see us" (pp. 68–9).

The newborn infant, Mead would say, initially is not a self. The baby begins to experience itself as an object only when it recognizes that it is an object to the parents. Only through the responses of the parents or other significant others does the child come to experience itself as a self. What kind of self depends on how the parents and other significant others respond to it. In adult life, Mead would argue, we continue to experience ourselves indirectly by taking the attitudes of other people and of the "generalized other" towards ourselves. Many of us view ourselves according to standards prevalent in our culture. We decide if we are attractive or not, if we are talented or not, if we are successful or not, if we are a good person or not, by looking at ourselves from the perspective of others and from the generalized standpoint of our culture. We decide who we are on the basis of how other people respond to us. Whether or not I define myself as a musician, for example, depends largely on how other people respond to my attempts at making music.

Similar to Mead's idea was Cooley's use of the concept the "looking-glass self" to describe how the self develops in the context of social environment. According to Cooley, we develop a concept of self from the reflection we get from other people. First, we look in the faces of others as we would in a mirror, imagining from what we see how we appear to them. Second, we try to discern how others judge our appearance. On the basis of how we imagine we appear to others and on how we imagine they judge that appearance, finally, we feel pride or mortification. Cooley came up with the idea of the "looking-glass self" through observing his own children.

Accordingly, he focused on the role of our initial looking-glasses – i.e., our parents or other primary caretakers – in forming our selves. Moving out of the initial parent–child context, however, sociological social psychologists have focused on the impact of extra-familial social contexts in shaping the self. Representing the distinctively sociological approach to the analysis of the self, the readings included in this section examine the role of social interaction, personal relationships, social roles, jobs, social identities, social hierarchies, and social-historical context in shaping the self.

Going beyond Mead's claim that the self *arises* in the context of social experience, Erving Goffman makes the more radical claim that the self is a product of performance in social interaction. Goffman argues that self-presentation is a crucial determinant of one's very sense of self. In contrast to the common-sense view that self-presentation either expresses the self or a false image of the self, Goffman emphasizes that the self is shaped in the process of self-presentation. "The general notion that we make a presentation of ourselves to others is hardly novel; what ought to be stressed in conclusion is that the very structure of the self can be seen in terms of how we arrange for such performances in our Anglo-American society" (Goffman 1959: 252). The extract from his *The Presentation of Self in Everyday Life* (1959) explains that self-presentation is an essential aspect of social interaction and that the self is a dramatic effect rather than the cause of these performances.

Also illustrating Goffman's idea that the self is produced and not merely expressed in social interaction, the chapter by Philip Blumstein, "The production of selves in personal relationships," examines how "selves are created, maintained, and changed by virtue of the structure of intimate relationships and the nature of interaction that occurs in them" (Blumstein 1991: 305). Defining the self as a personal intrapsychic structure and identity as the self presented in social interaction, Blumstein notes that the commonsensical way of understanding the relationship between self and identity is to think of the self as the basis of identity. Blumstein challenges this causal ordering, arguing that identity actually affects the self (p. 306). If we project certain identities frequently enough, as we tend to do in intimate relationships, we tend to become the person that we have enacted. The chapter by Blumstein examines a number of processes by which selves are created in intimate relationships.

The central premise of the microstructural perspective is that human behavior cannot be adequately explained by stable internalized personality traits of individuals but must instead be understood in the context of social forces and situational experiences in everyday life. This perspective is explained and illustrated in the chapter by Barbara Risman, "Intimate relationships from a microstructural perspective: Men who mother." Here, Risman argues that most differences between men and women cannot be attributed to internalized personality traits but can better be explained by "differential experiences, opportunities, and access to social networks" (1987: 9). Studying men who had involuntarily adopted the primary caretaker role after the death of, or desertion by, their wives, Risman's study demonstrated that the mothering role was much more important than the sex or personality attributes of the parent in producing mothering behavior. Further, her study found that holding the primary caretaker role was more important than a respondent's sex in predicting self-reported femininity. In applying her findings to the analysis of the self in general, Risman points out that the microstructural perspective "suggests that selves are constantly constructed and sustained by the situational experiences in everyday life" (1987: 23).

Moving from a microstructural to a macrostructural level of analysis, the chapter by Melvin Kohn and Kazimierz Slomczynski examines the relationship between social class, jobs, and personality. Exemplifying an approach that distinguishes sociological from psychological social psychology, they argue that social psychologists must move beyond studying the effects of the interpersonal environment on human life and begin paying attention to the impact of the concrete conditions under which people live and work. Particularly, this work focuses on how the different levels of occupational self-direction characteristic of middle-class and working-class jobs produce differences in values, orientations, and cognitive functioning. The central thesis of Kohn's research is that "members of more 'advantaged' social classes would be more intellectually flexible, would value self-direction more highly for their children, and would have more self-directed orientations to self and society than would members of less advantaged social classes" (Kohn and Slomczynski 1990: 233). This chapter summarizes the main elements of Kohn's thesis and research findings concerning the relationship between social class, jobs, and personality.

Other work that examines macrostructural effects on the self focuses on how social categories such as social class, race, and gender affect one's evaluation of self. The most central in this tradition is Morris Rosenberg's research on social determinants of the self-concept. Noting the unequal evaluation of many social identity elements in society, Rosenberg was particularly interested in how the unequal prestige accorded to social identities would affect a person's self-esteem. In studying the relationship between social class and self-esteem, for example, Rosenberg found no relationship for children 8–11 years old, a modest association for adolescents, and a considerably larger relationship among adults (1979: 129). He explained these findings using three principles of self-esteem formation: (1) the principle of reflected appraisals; (2) social comparison, the evaluation of ourselves on the basis of comparisons to others; and (3) self attribution, the evaluation of ourselves on the basis of the outcomes of our behavior. Young children, he explained, are often in socioeconomically homogenous backgrounds and, accordingly, evaluate themselves on the basis of appraisals of and comparison with others from similar socioeconomic backgrounds. In assessing their worth on the basis of their achievements, furthermore, children rely on their own scholastic achievements rather than the socioeconomic success of their parents. Adults, conversely, are more likely to work in socioeconomically heterogeneous environments, to be more aware of socioeconomic inequality than children, and to evaluate themselves on the basis of their socioeconomic achievements. Accordingly, among adults, self-esteem is positively related to social class.

Generally, the idea that a person's definition of self is powerfully influenced and constrained by social roles, social power, and social status is central to the sociological view of the self. A theme emphasized in Erving Goffman's work is that the image that an individual is able to present and have accepted by others in social interaction is in large part determined by the person's social categories, social status, and resources. The individual is socially constrained to express a "workable definition of himself" – in other words, a definition that others will be prepared to accept (Goffman 1971: 366). As the chapter by Goffman points out, presentation of self in social interaction is a powerful determinant of the self. But, as the work from which it was abstracted emphasizes, individuals are very dependent on others to support the images they present. Generally, others are willing to accept only definitions of self that are more or less compatible with what they have come to expect of persons of similar category, rank, and resources. For members of devalued social categories and of limited resources, sustaining a favorable image of self in social interaction is quite difficult. Goffman's *Asylums* (1961), a study of the self in the context of institutions that strip the individual of autonomy, demonstrates how dependent we are on certain props (control of material resources, space, privacy, autonomy, respect from others) to sustain an image of ourselves as competent and worthy persons. Under such conditions of deprivation, however, individuals may employ a variety of techniques to resist complete degradation. The chapter by Snow and Anderson, "Salvaging the self," identifies a number of ways that homeless people attempt to salvage self-worth in spite of their lack of resources and the demeaning treatment they received from the domiciled.

Finally, in addition to studying the impact of social interaction, social relationships, social roles, social categories, and social hierarchies on the self, sociological social psychologists have also emphasized that self-experience varies according to social, cultural, and historical context. David Riesman's classic *The Lonely Crowd* (1961), for instance, identified three distinct types of selves – the tradition-directed individual, the inner-directed individual, and the other-directed individual – which he believed to be predominant at particular points in history, and provided a theory of how changing social and cultural conditions produced these different types of selves. The chapter by Ralph Turner, "The real self: From institution to impulse," similarly provides a social-historical analysis of changing ways of defining the "real self." Turner argues that there has been a cultural shift from defining the real self in terms of institutional roles to defining the self in terms of impulses. To the institutionally-oriented, according to Turner, the real self is something that is achieved in the process of living up to high standards in the performance of institutional roles. The institutional self believes in individualism, defining individualism as the resistance of social influences that divert a person from achievement, adherence to ethical standards, and other institutional goals (Turner 1976: 994–5). To those who define the self more in terms of impulses, however, the "real self" is revealed when the individual is released from the demands of institutional roles. The real self is something to be discovered, something that is revealed in spontaneous actions and in uninhibited moments. The impulsive self also believes in individualism, but defines it very differently. For the impulsive self, individualism entails rejecting institutional standards that compete with the expression of impulses (p. 995). Turner considers a number of possible social and cultural explanations for this shift. One is that a person's tendency to define the "real self" in terms of impulses rather than institutional roles can be explained by changes in the ways that people are integrated into society (p. 1001). In an earlier time in history, when production and disciplined work habits were vital to the development of industrialization, it was more fitting for individuals to define themselves in terms of their institutional roles. In a postindustrial society organized more around consumption than production, however, it makes more sense for people to define themselves in terms of their tastes, leisure pursuits, and inner thoughts and feelings.

The analysis of the self in the context of the conditions of late modern, postindustrial or postmodern society is a theme that has been pursued by a number of sociologists in recent decades (Berger 1973; Gergen 1991; Giddens 1991; Zurcher 1977). A key problem commonly identified is the precariousness of identities in social worlds characterized by continuous change. In *Modernity and Self-Identity* (1991), Anthony Giddens writes that late modern individuals are utterly forced to make numerous lifestyle choices and to "find" themselves in the absence of traditional guidelines. In the extract from *The Saturated Self* (1991), Kenneth Gergen argues that the multiplication of mass media, information, and communication technologies in postmodern society has multiplied the relationships, involvements, demands, choices, and standards of evaluation of the individual. The self, he argues, is "populated" by "multiple and disparate potentials for being" (1991: 69), casting the individual into doubt about the viability of any particular investment of self the individual makes (pp. 73–4).

References

Berger, Peter. 1973. *The Homeless Mind*. New York: Random House.
Blumstein, Philip. 1991. "The production of selves in personal relationships." In J. Howard and P. Callero (eds.) *The Self-Society Dynamic*. New York: Cambridge University Press.
Gergen, Kenneth. 1991. *The Saturated Self*. New York: Basic Books.
Giddens, Anthony. 1991. *Modernity and Self-Identity*. Stanford: University of Stanford Press.
Goffman, Erving. 1959. *The Presentation of Self in Everyday Life*. New York: Anchor Books.
—— 1961. *Asylums*. Garden City, NY: Doubleday, Anchor Books.
—— 1971. *Relations in Public*. New York: Basic Books.
Kohn, Melvin and Slomczynski, Kazimierz. 1990. *Social Structure and Self-Direction: A Comparative Analysis of the United States and Poland*. Cambridge, Mass.: Blackwell Publishers.
Mead, George Herbert. 1934. *Mind, Self, and Society*. Chicago: University of Chicago Press.
Riesman, David. 1961. *The Lonely Crowd*. New Haven, Conn.: Yale University Press.
Risman, Barbara J. 1987. "Intimate relationships from a microstructural perspective: Men who mother." *Gender and Society* 1(1): 6–32.
Rosenberg, Morris. 1979. *Conceiving the Self*. New York: Basic Books.
Snow, David and Anderson, Leon. 1993. *Down on Their Luck: A Study of Homeless Street People*. Berkeley: University of California Press.
Turner, Ralph. 1976. "The real self: From institution to impulse." *American Journal of Sociology* 81: 980–1016.
Zurcher, Louis A., Jr. 1977. *The Mutable Self*. Beverly Hills, Calif.: Sage.

Additional Readings

Casey, Catherine. 1995. *Work, Self, and Society after Industrialism*. London and New York: Routledge.
Calhoun, Craig (ed.) 1994. *Social Theory and the Politics of Identity*. Cambridge, Mass.: Blackwell Publishers.
Gecas, Viktor and Burke, Peter J. 1995. "Self and identity." In Karen Cook, Gary Fine, and James S. House (eds.) *Sociological Perspectives on Social Psychology*. Boston, Mass.: Allyn and Bacon.
Hewitt, John P. 1988. *Dilemmas of the American Self*. Philadelphia: Temple University Press.

Kohn, Melvin L. and Schooler, Carmi. 1983. *Work and Personality: An Inquiry into the Impact of Social Stratification.* Norwood, NJ: Ablex Publishing.

Rosenberg, Morris. 1989. "Self-concept research: A historical overview." *Social Forces* 68: 34–44.

Schwalbe, Michael L. 1986. *The Psychological Consequences of Natural and Alienated Labor.* Albany: State University of New York Press.

Shotter, John and Gergen, Kenneth J. 1989. *Texts of Identity.* Newbury Park, Calif.: Sage.

Taylor, Charles. 1989. *Sources of the Self.* New Haven, Conn.: Yale University Press.

12 The Presentation of Self in Everyday Life

Erving Goffman

Introduction

When an individual enters the presence of others, they commonly seek to acquire information about him or to bring into play information about him already possessed. They will be interested in his general socioeconomic status, his conception of self, his attitude toward them, his competence, his trustworthiness, etc. Although some of this information seems to be sought almost as an end in itself, there are usually quite practical reasons for acquiring it. Information about the individual helps to define the situation, enabling others to know in advance what he will expect of them and what they may expect of him. Informed in these ways, the others will know how best to act in order to call forth a desired response from him.

For those present, many sources of information become accessible and many carriers (or "sign-vehicles") become available for conveying this information. If unacquainted with the individual, observers can glean clues from his conduct and appearance which allow them to apply their previous experience with individuals roughly similar to the one before them or, more important, to apply untested stereotypes to him. They can also assume from past experience that only individuals of a particular kind are likely to be found in a given social setting. They can rely on what the individual says about himself or on documentary evidence he provides as to who and what he is. If they know, or know of, the individual by virtue of experience prior to the interaction, they can rely on assumptions as to the persistence and generality of psychological traits as a means of predicting his present and future behavior.

However, during the period in which the individual is in the immediate presence of the others, few events may occur which directly provide the others with the conclusive information they will need if they are to direct wisely their own activity. Many crucial facts lie beyond the time and place of interaction or lie concealed within it. For example, the "true" or "real" attitudes, beliefs, and emotions of the individual can be ascertained only indirectly, through his avowals or through what appears to be involuntary expressive behavior. Similarly, if the individual offers the others a product or service, they will often find that during the interaction there will be no time and place immediately available for eating the pudding that the proof can be found in. They will be forced to accept some events as conventional or natural signs of something not directly available to the senses. In Ichheiser's terms, the individual will have to act so that he intentionally or unintentionally *expresses* himself, and the others will in turn have to be *impressed* in some way by him (Ichheiser 1949: 6–7).

Reprinted from "Introduction," "Performances," and "Conclusion," in *The Presentation of Self in Everyday Life*, New York: Anchor Books, 1959, pp. 1–5, 17–21, 252–5.

The expressiveness of the individual (and therefore his capacity to give impressions) appears to involve two radically different kinds of sign activity: the expression that he *gives*, and the expression that he *gives off*. The first involves verbal symbols or their substitutes which he uses admittedly and solely to convey the information that he and the others are known to attach to these symbols. This is communication in the traditional and narrow sense. The second involves a wide range of action that others can treat as symptomatic of the actor, the expectation being that the action was performed for reasons other than the information conveyed in this way. As we shall have to see, this distinction has an only initial validity. The individual does of course intentionally convey misinformation by means of both of these types of communication, the first involving deceit, the second feigning.

Taking communication in both its narrow and broad sense, one finds that when the individual is in the immediate presence of others, his activity will have a promissory character. The others are likely to find that they must accept the individual on faith, offering him a just return while he is present before them in exchange for something whose true value will not be established until after he has left their presence. (Of course, the others also live by inference in their dealings with the physical world, but it is only in the world of social interaction that the objects about which they make inferences will purposely facilitate and hinder this inferential process.) The security that they justifiably feel in making inferences about the individual will vary, of course, depending on such factors as the amount of information they already possess about him, but no amount of such past evidence can entirely obviate the necessity of acting on the basis of inferences. As William I. Thomas suggested:

> It is also highly important for us to realize that we do not as a matter of fact lead our lives, make our decisions, and reach our goals in everyday life either statistically or scientifically. We live by inference. I am, let us say, your guest. You do not know, you cannot determine scientifically, that I will not steal your money or your spoons. But inferentially I will not, and inferentially you have me as a guest. (quoted in Volkart 1951: 5)

Let us now turn from the others to the point of view of the individual who presents himself before them. He may wish them to think highly of him, or to think that he thinks highly of them, or to perceive how in fact he feels toward them, or to obtain no clear-cut impression; he may wish to ensure sufficient harmony so that the interaction can be sustained, or to defraud, get rid of, confuse, mislead, antagonize, or insult them. Regardless of the particular objective which the individual has in mind and of his motive for having this objective, it will be in his interests to control the conduct of the others, especially their responsive treatment of him. This control is achieved largely by influencing the definition of the situation which the others come to formulate, and he can influence this definition by expressing himself in such a way as to give them the kind of impression that will lead them to act voluntarily in accordance with his own plan. Thus, when an individual appears in the presence of others, there will usually be some reason for him to mobilize his activity so that it will convey an impression to others which it is in his interests to convey. Since a girl's dormitory mates will glean evidence of her popularity from the calls she receives on the phone, we can suspect that some girls will arrange for calls to be made, and Willard Waller's finding can be anticipated:

> It has been reported by many observers that a girl who is called to the telephone in the dormitories will often allow herself to be called several times, in order to give all the other girls ample opportunity to hear her paged. (Waller 1937: 730).

Of the two kinds of communication – expressions given and expressions given off – this report will be primarily concerned with the latter, with the more theatrical and contextual kind, the non-verbal, presumably unintentional kind, whether this communication be purposely engineered or not. As an example of what we must try to examine, I would like to cite at length a novelistic incident in which Preedy, a vacationing Englishman, makes his first appearance on the beach of his summer hotel in Spain:

> But in any case he took care to avoid catching anyone's eye. First of all, he had to make it clear to those potential companions of his holiday that they were of no concern to him whatsoever. He stared through them, round them, over them – eyes lost in space. The beach might have been empty. If by chance a ball was thrown his way, he looked surprised; then let a smile of amusement lighten his face (Kindly Preedy), looked round dazed to see that there *were* people on the beach, tossed it back with a smile to himself and not a smile *at* the people, and then resumed carelessly his nonchalant survey of space.
>
> But it was time to institute a little parade, the parade of the Ideal Preedy. By devious handlings he gave any who wanted to look a chance to see the title of his book – a Spanish translation of Homer, classic thus, but not daring, cosmopolitan too – and then gathered together his beach-wrap and bag into a neat sand-resistant pile (Methodical and Sensible Preedy), rose slowly to stretch at ease his huge frame (Big-Cat Preedy), and tossed aside his sandals (Carefree Preedy, after all).
>
> The marriage of Preedy and the sea! There were alternative rituals. The first involved the stroll that turns into a run and a dive straight into the water, thereafter smoothing into a strong splashless crawl towards the horizon. But of course not really to the horizon. Quite suddenly he would turn on to his back and thrash great white splashes with his legs, somehow thus showing that he could have swum further had he wanted to, and then would stand up a quarter out of water for all to see who it was.
>
> The alternative course was simpler, it avoided the cold-water shock and it avoided the risk of appearing too high-spirited. The point was to appear to be so used to the sea, the Mediterranean, and this particular beach, that one might as well be in the sea as out of it. It involved a slow stroll down and into the edge of the water – not even noticing his toes were wet, land and water all the same to *him!* – with his eyes up at the sky gravely surveying portents, invisible to others, of the weather (Local Fisherman Preedy). (Sansom 1956: 230–2)

. . .

Performances

Belief in the Part One is Playing

When an individual plays a part he implicitly requests his observers to take seriously the impression that is fostered before them. They are asked to believe that the character they see actually possesses the attributes he appears to possess, that the task he performs will have the consequences that are implicitly claimed for it, and that, in general, matters are what they appear to be. In line with this, there is the popular view that the individual offers his performance and puts on his show "for the benefit of other people." It will be convenient to begin a consideration of performances by turning the question around and looking at the individual's own belief in the impression of reality that he attempts to engender in those among whom he finds himself.

At one extreme, one finds that the performer can be fully taken in by his own act; he can be sincerely convinced that the impression of reality which he stages is the real reality. When his audience is also convinced in this way about the show he puts on – and this seems to be the typical case – then for the moment at least, only the sociologist or the socially disgruntled will have any doubts about the "realness" of what is presented.

At the other extreme, we find that the performer may not be taken in at all by his own routine. This possibility is understandable, since no one is in quite as good an observational position to see through the act as the person who puts it on. Coupled with this, the performer may be moved to guide the conviction of his audience only as a means to other ends, having no ultimate concern in the conception that they have of him or of the situation. When the individual has no belief in his own act and no ultimate concern with the beliefs of his audience, we may call him cynical, reserving the term "sincere" for individuals who believe in the impression fostered by their own performance. It should be understood that the cynic, with all his professional disinvolvement, may obtain unprofessional pleasures from his masquerade, experiencing a kind of gleeful spiritual aggression from the fact that he can toy at will with something his audience must take seriously.

It is not assumed, of course, that all cynical performers are interested in deluding their audiences for purposes of what is called "self-interest" or private gain. A cynical individual may delude his audience for what he considers to be their own good, or for the good of the community, etc. For illustrations of this we need not appeal to sadly enlightened showmen such as Marcus Aurelius or Hsun Tzŭ. We know that in service occupations practitioners who may otherwise be sincere are sometimes forced to delude their customers because their customers show such a heartfelt demand for it. Doctors who are led into giving placebos, filling station attendants who resignedly check and recheck tire pressures for anxious women motorists, shoe clerks who sell a shoe that fits but tell the customer it is the size she wants to hear – these are cynical performers whose audiences will not allow them to be sincere. Similarly, it seems that sympathetic patients in mental wards will sometimes feign bizarre symptoms so that student nurses will not be subjected to a disappointingly sane performance (see Taxel 1953: 4).[1] So also, when inferiors extend their most lavish reception for visiting superiors, the selfish desire to win favor may not be the chief motive; the inferior may be tactfully attempting to put the superior at ease by simulating the kind of world the superior is thought to take for granted.

I have suggested two extremes: an individual may be taken in by his own act or be cynical about it. These extremes are something a little more than just the ends of a continuum. Each provides the individual with a position which has its own particular securities and defenses, so there will be a tendency for those who have traveled close to one of these poles to complete the voyage. Starting with lack of inward belief in one's role, the individual may follow the natural movement described by Park:

> It is probably no mere historical accident that the word person, in its first meaning, is a mask. It is rather a recognition of the fact that everyone is always and everywhere, more or less consciously, playing a role . . . It is in these roles that we know each other; it is in these roles that we know ourselves. (Park 1950: 249)

> In a sense, and in so far as this mask represents the conception we have formed of ourselves – the role we are striving to live up to – this mask is our truer self, the self we would like to be. In the end, our conception of our role becomes second nature and an integral part of our personality. We come into the world as individuals, achieve character, and become persons. (ibid.: 250)

This may be illustrated from the community life of Shetland. For the last four or five years the island's tourist hotel has been owned and operated by a married couple of crofter origins. From the beginning, the owners were forced to set aside their own conceptions as to how life ought to be led, displaying in the hotel a full round of middle-class services and amenities. Lately, however, it appears that the managers have become less cynical about the performance that they stage; they themselves are becoming middle class and more and more enamored of the selves their clients impute to them.

Another illustration may be found in the raw recruit who initially follows army etiquette in order to avoid physical punishment and eventually comes to follow the rules so that his organization will not be shamed and his officers and fellow soldiers will respect him.

As suggested, the cycle of disbelief-to-belief can be followed in the other direction, starting with conviction or insecure aspiration and ending in cynicism. Professions which the public holds in religious awe often allow their recruits to follow the cycle in this direction, and often recruits follow it in this direction not because of a slow realization that they are deluding their audience – for by ordinary social standards the claims they make may be quite valid – but because they can use this cynicism as a means of insulating their inner selves from contact with the audience. And we may even expect to find typical careers of faith, with the individual starting out with one kind of involvement in the performance he is required to give, then moving back and forth several times between sincerity and cynicism before completing all the phases and turning-points of self-belief for a person of his station. Thus, students of medical schools suggest that idealistically oriented beginners in medical school typically lay aside their holy aspirations for a period of time. During the first two years the students find that their interest in medicine must be dropped that they may give all their time to the task of learning how to get through examinations. During the next two years they are too busy learning about diseases to show much concern for the persons who are diseased. It is only after their medical schooling has ended that their original ideals about medical service may be reasserted (Becker and Greer 1958: 50–6)

While we can expect to find natural movement back and forth between cynicism and sincerity, still we must not rule out the kind of transitional point that can be sustained on the strength of a little self-illusion. We find that the individual may attempt to induce the audience to judge him and the situation in a particular way, and he may seek this judgment as an ultimate end in itself, and yet he may not completely believe that he deserves the valuation of self which he asks for or that the impression of reality which he fosters is valid. Another mixture of cynicism and belief is suggested in Kroeber's discussion of shamanism:

> Next, there is the old question of deception. Probably most shamans or medicine men, the world over, help along with sleight-of-hand in curing and especially in exhibitions of power. This sleight-of-hand is sometimes deliberate; in many cases awareness is perhaps not deeper than the foreconscious. The attitude, whether there has been repression or not, seems to be as toward a pious fraud. Field ethnographers seem quite generally convinced that even shamans who know that they add fraud nevertheless also believe in their powers, and especially in those of other shamans: they consult them when they themselves or their children are ill. (Kroeber 1952: 311)

. . .

Staging and the Self

The general notion that we make a presentation of ourselves to others is hardly novel; what ought to be stressed in conclusion is that the very structure of the self can be seen in terms of how we arrange for such performances in our Anglo-American society.

In this report, the individual was divided by implication into two basic parts: he was viewed as a *performer*, a harried fabricator of impressions involved in the all-too-human task of staging a performance; he was viewed as a *character*, a figure, typically a fine one, whose spirit, strength, and other sterling qualities the perform-ance was designed to evoke. The attributes of a performer and the attributes of a character are of a different order, quite basically so, yet both sets have their meaning in terms of the show that must go on.

First, character. In our society the character one performs and one's self are somewhat equated, and this self-as-character is usually seen as something housed within the body of its possessor, especially the upper parts thereof, being a nodule, somehow, in the psychobiology of personality. I suggest that this view is an implied part of what we are all trying to present, but provides, just because of this, a bad analysis of the presentation. In this report the performed self was seen as some kind of image, usually creditable, which the individual on stage and in character effect-ively attempts to induce others to hold in regard to him. While this image is entertained *concerning* the individual, so that a self is imputed to him, this self itself does not derive from its possessor, but from the whole scene of his action, being generated by that attribute of local events which renders them interpretable by witnesses. A correctly staged and performed scene leads the audience to impute a self to a performed character, but this imputation – this self – is a *product* of a scene that comes off, and is not a *cause* of it. The self, then, as a performed character, is not an organic thing that has a specific location, whose fundamental fate is to be born, to mature, and to die; it is a dramatic effect arising diffusely from a scene that is presented, and the characteristic issue, the crucial concern, is whether it will be credited or discredited.

In analyzing the self, then, we are drawn from its possessor, from the person who will profit or lose most by it, for he and his body merely provide the peg on which something of collaborative manufacture will be hung for a time. And the means for producing and maintaining selves do not reside inside the peg; in fact these means are often bolted down in social establishments. There will be a back region with its tools for shaping the body, and a front region with its fixed props. There will be a team of persons whose activity on stage in conjunction with available props will constitute the scene from which the performed character's self will emerge, and another team, the audience, whose interpretive activity will be necessary for this emergence. The self is a product of all of these arrangements, and in all of its parts bears the marks of this genesis.

The whole machinery of self-production is cumbersome, of course, and sometimes breaks down, exposing its separate components: back region control; team collusion; audience tact; and so forth. But, well oiled, impressions will flow from it fast enough to put us in the grips of one of our types of reality – the performance will come off and the firm self accorded each performed character will appear to emanate intrinsically from its performer.

Let us turn now from the individual as character performed to the individual as performer. He has a capacity to learn, this being exercised in the task of training for a part. He is given to having fantasies and dreams, some that pleasurably unfold a triumphant performance, others full of anxiety and dread that nervously deal with vital discreditings in a public front region. He often manifests a gregarious desire for teammates and audiences, a tactful considerateness for their concerns; and he has a capacity for deeply felt shame, leading him to minimize the chances he takes of exposure.

These attributes of the individual *qua* performer are not merely a depicted effect of particular performances; they are psychobiological in nature, and yet they seem to arise out of intimate interaction with the contingencies of staging performances.

And now a final comment. In developing the conceptual framework employed in this report, some language of the stage was used. I spoke of performers and audiences; of routines and parts; of performances coming off or falling flat; of cues, stage settings and backstage; of dramaturgical needs, dramaturgical skills, and dramaturgical strategies. Now it should be admitted that this attempt to press a mere analogy so far was in part a rhetoric and a maneuver.

The claim that all the world's a stage is sufficiently commonplace for readers to be familiar with its limitations and tolerant of its presentation, knowing that at any time they will easily be able to demonstrate to themselves that it is not to be taken too seriously. An action staged in a theater is a relatively contrived illusion and an admitted one; unlike ordinary life, nothing real or actual can happen to the performed characters – although at another level of course something real and actual can happen to the reputation of performers *qua* professionals whose everyday job is to put on theatrical performances.

And so here the language and mask of the stage will be dropped. Scaffolds, after all, are to build other things with, and should be erected with an eye to taking them down. This report is not concerned with aspects of theater that creep into everyday life. It is concerned with the structure of social encounters – the structure of those entities in social life that come into being whenever persons enter one another's immediate physical presence. The key factor in this structure is the maintenance of a single definition of the situation, this definition having to be expressed, and this expression sustained in the face of a multitude of potential disruptions.

A character staged in a theater is not in some ways real, nor does it have the same kind of real consequences as does the thoroughly contrived character performed by a confidence man; but the *successful* staging of either of these types of false figures involves use of *real* techniques – the same techniques by which everyday persons sustain their real social situations. Those who conduct face to face interaction on a theater's stage must meet the key requirement of real situations; they must expressively sustain a definition of the situation: but this they do in circumstances that have facilitated their developing an apt terminology for the interactional tasks that all of us share.

Note

1 Harry Stack Sullivan has suggested that the tact of institutionalized performers can operate in the other direction, resulting in a kind of *noblesse oblige* sanity. See his "Socio-psychiatric research," pp. 987–8.

References

Becker, H. S. and Greer, Blanche. 1958. "The fate of idealism in medical school." *American Sociological Review* 23.

Ichheiser, Gustav. 1949. "Misunderstandings in human relations," supplement to *American Journal of Sociology* 55 (September).

Kroeber, A. L. 1952. *The Nature of Culture*. Chicago: University of Chicago Press.

Park, Robert Ezra. 1950. *Race and Culture*. Glencoe, Ill.: Free Press.

Sansom, William. 1956. *A Contest of Ladies*. London: Hogarth Press.

Sullivan, Harry Stack. "Socio-psychiatric research." *American Journal of Psychiatry* 10.

Taxel, Harold. 1953. "Authority structure in a mental hospital." Unpublished master's thesis, Department of Sociology, University of Chicago.

Volkart, E. H. (ed.) 1951. *Social Behavior and Personality: Contributions of W. I. Thomas to Theory and Social Research*. New York: Social Science Research Council.

Waller, Willard. 1937. "The rating and dating complex." *American Sociological Review* 2.

13 The Production of Selves in Personal Relationships

Philip Blumstein

Introduction

Innumerable words have been written and uttered on the fundamental relationship between the person and society, many of them inspiring discussion of the *social* nature of the self. As Rosenberg (1981: 593) summarizes,

> social factors play a major role in...formation [of the self]....[It] arises out of social experience and interaction; it both incorporates and is influenced by the individual's location in the social structure; it is formed within institutional systems...; it is constructed from the materials of the culture; and it is affected by immediate social and environmental contexts.

The significance of this simple point cannot be overstated: It has been one of sociology's guiding principles for many years, it has been offered as an epiphany to generations of undergraduates, and it has inspired countless research studies. Nevertheless, the concrete social processes captured in the simple but elegant notion of the social creation of the self remain, after all these years, only vaguely understood. The picture is incomplete. Surely social interaction generates selves, but the question that continues to deserve our attention is *how*.

From the early work of Cooley (1902), it has been a commonplace to locate much of the development of self in *primary groups*, by which is generally meant families and similar intimate relationships. This classical theme is the point of departure for this chapter, in which I address the question of how selves are created, maintained, and changed by virtue of the structure of intimate relationships and the nature of interaction that occurs in them.

Self and Identity

The terms *self* and *identity* have been used in a dizzying diversity of ways, and no definitional synthesis will be attempted here. My approach here is largely dramaturgical, relying on the numerous discussions of self and identity that followed the 1959 publication of Goffman's *Presentation of Self in Everyday Life* (e.g., Blumstein 1975; Gergen 1968; McCall and Simmons 1966; Messinger et al. 1962; Weinstein and Deutschberger 1963). In my usage, *self* is a personal intrapsychic structure and is only knowable by the person to whom it belongs. In this view the self can be part of the mechanics that motivate the actor's behavior (Blumstein 1975; McCall and

Reprinted from *The Self-Society Dynamic*, ed. J. Howard and P. Callero, New York: Cambridge University Press, 1991, pp. 305–22.

Simmons 1966; Rosenberg 1981; Swann 1987). In contrast, I will use the term *identity* as a shorthand for *situational* or *situated identity* (Alexander and Wiley 1981; Weinstein and Deutschberger 1963), referring to the *face* that is publicly displayed, perhaps quite fleetingly, in interaction. In this usage, identity is Goffman's *presented self* and, as such, it requires no private commitment on the part of actor or audience to its being a valid reflection of the "true" self.

Numerous attempts have been made to characterize the relationship between identity and self (Blumstein 1975; Gergen 1968; McCall and Simmons 1966; Swann and Read 1981; Wiley and Alexander 1987). First, it is necessary to consider the relationship between self and behavior. Although the various approaches to this question differ in detail, a common theme can be identified: The self finds expression in behavior, even if that expression may be mediated in complex ways. The actor's behavior, according to the most general model, invokes a response in alter. Out of that response ego receives information with implications for his or her self, information that ultimately may modify that self. The self, it is posited, has enormous motivation consequences for interactive behavior, and all interactive behavior, it is further posited, can be analyzed in terms of the situated identities being presented. Perhaps the best articulated version of the view that self produces identity is found in McCall and Simmons's (1966: 73) discussion of individuals' ubiquitous motive to seek *role-support*, which they define as "a set of reactions and performances by others the expressive implications of which tend to confirm one's detailed and imaginative view of himself.... Role-support is centrally the implied confirmation of the specific *content* of one's idealized and idiosyncratic imaginations of self." Since people are universally motivated to seek role-support for cherished aspects of the self, they tend to present (enact) identities consistent with that self in order to maximize the likelihood of receiving that role-support.

I have no quarrel with this view of the relationship between self and identity. However, in this chapter I wish to explore a different causal ordering, one less commonly considered, that is, that identity affects self. Going back to the work of Bem (1972), numerous social psychologists have argued that actors perceive their own behavior (whatever its sources), and in the process they make attributions to the self. If one translates this into a dramaturgical framework, instead of *behavior*, one may speak of the *identities* people project. Individuals observe the identities they project, and in some circumstances they may attribute this enactment to a true expression of the self. In spite of any constraints the self may place on the identities presented (Blumstein 1975), these enacted behaviors may frequently have nothing to do with any sincere underlying dimensions of self.

A central assertion of this chapter is that if identities are projected frequently enough, they eventually produce modifications in the self. In searching for a term to capture this process whereby repeated enactment of identities produce selves, I have chosen the concept of *ossification*. Whereas the work of people on self-attribution has dealt with the intrapsychic process whereby one's own behavior is observed and inferences are made about it, I focus more on the interpersonal aspects of how and why identities ossify into selves.

The process of ossification is very slow and gradual, and consequently is not easy to study with our conventional research methods. It is the process that we infer has occurred when we awaken one morning to discover we are not the same person we were twenty years earlier. Or more commonly when we encounter a person from our past and are reminded by the interaction of how much our self has drifted over the years. Surely the meanderings of our social environment are responsible for the drift, but I would argue that it is particularly in our intimate relationships that the ossification process takes place. To say that the self is subject to drift does not contradict the idea of ossification. Indeed the two concepts may be seen as constituting two ends of a continuum. Drift occurs as a function of changes in the individual's interpersonal environment. Ossification has as a necessary condition continuity in the interpersonal environment, and accelerates during those periods of continuity. Ossification means that we enact identities with great frequency and we *become* the person whom we have enacted.

Why, in so much writing about the self, has the idea of ossification (or some equivalent) not been prominent? The answer lies in a shortcoming of dramaturgical analysis, that is, its inattention to the development of durable social structures. Microsociology seems recently to have undergone a shift away from an exclusive focus on interaction to a greater recognition of ongoing relationships. When the model, especially in Goffman's work, was built on unanchored, situationally bounded, evanescent exchanges between near strangers, the implications for self of the identity presented seemed trivial. But so much of social life occurs in relationships that, even if not always intense, have histories and futures, and for that reason the identities that are enacted in intimate relationships should have important implications for the self.

Couple Identity Work

There is a form of seemingly insignificant talk heard frequently from husbands, wives, and from partners in other kinds of intimate marriagelike relationships. Possibly it is occasionally heard in the speech of close friends. Here are three simulated examples:

> My husband can't be allowed into the kitchen. He wouldn't know how to boil water. He would ruin it and make a mess in the process.

> We are different about dirt. I hate it and clean it up the minute it appears. She waits until it begins to accumulate and then goes after it with a vengeance. We are both very clean, just different about it.

> We are not like other couples. They are all interested in showing what they earn and what they can buy, but we prefer to content ourselves with a more spiritual approach to life.

This form of verbal behavior, *couple identity work*, is often heard when one interviews couples, as well as in the spontaneous speech of ordinary people. It is frequently directed to persons outside the relationship, but I believe it also arises when intimates are alone talking together about themselves and about their relationship. As is clear from the examples, these are not ponderous discussions of "the relationship," but instead rather mundane characterizations of who the two partners are, frequently with a tone of who they are *vis-à-vis* one another.

I have called this process couple *identity* work; what does it have to do with the *self*? Although there is certainly identity work going on in the examples, it has already been acknowledged that situated identities and selves are not the same. However, one of the important ways in which personal relationships differ from simple Goffmanesque interaction is that in the former situated identities are potentially much more apt to have long-lasting implications for the self. Again, this is the process I have called ossification.

One might argue that these people are only announcing the truth about themselves and their partners. Indeed this is a compelling observation because who will be more keenly aware of the dispositions of another than his or her spouse or partner? The very nature of intimacy implies that two people have developed a profound awareness of who the other is. It is, however, the publicness of the display, the apparent felt necessity of locating oneself, one's partner, and the relatedness of the two in some kind of conceptual space that suggests that the relationship engenders or demands reality creation work that is separate and apart from the simple reporting on a preexisting reality (cf. Goffman 1971, on tie-signs). In these interactions couples are displaying a reality they have created, while at the same time they are allowing us to witness a sample of the processes through which this reality was created over the months and years.

Motivation

A husband may learn for the first time that he cannot cook as his wife describes his culinary failures to a group of assembled friends. If he hears such commentary with sufficient frequency, both in front of guests and in solitary conversation with his wife, one may expect that he will come to incorporate culinary incompetence into his self. Moreover, if no circumstances arise to propel him into the kitchen, he will have no opportunity to challenge that aspect of self. This example is particularly useful because it leads to speculations about motivation: What goals or purposes would a wife be likely to achieve by fostering the reality that her husband is incompetent in the kitchen? What goals or purposes does a husband achieve in passively acceding to that definition of the situation? One can ask a further set of questions, more on the level of social structure, such as, What is it about the institution of marriage that led to this bit of reality creation in which, ultimately, both spouses have colluded? Moreover, in what ways did this minute exercise in reality creation contribute to the reproduction of the marital institution?

A fundamental concept in dramaturgical analysis is *interpersonal control* (Weinstein 1969). It links the motivational states of purposive actors to the self-presentational strategies they employ. It draws attention to the connection between hedonistic actors and processes of reality presentation and reality negotiation. A focus on interpersonal control lends motivational enrichment to the dramaturgical model, with the simple principle that actors' purposes (desires, goals) can best be served by the identities they choose to enact and the identities into which they are able to cast their interaction partner(s) (Weinstein 1969; Weinstein and Deutschberger 1963, 1964). If one accepts that frequently enacted identities eventually may ossify into selves, then the implication of interpersonal control as a motivational concept is that selves grow out of motivational states (both ego's and alter's – the opposite of the usual position on causality).

In close relationships, just as in Goffman's disconnected focused gatherings, it must be acknowledged that ego takes active, though perhaps not conscious, involvement in shaping alter's identity, and his or her motivation may frequently be purely selfish. Ego may best pursue his or her desired outcomes in interaction and/or relationship by shaping the distribution of identities (both ego's and alter's) that are incorporated into the working consensus. But intimate relationships are significantly different from the interactions that Goffman analyzed. Among intimates, who have durable relationships with anticipatable futures, it is generally much more efficient to shape the underlying self of alter, such that by simply *being* that self, alter will assume a situated identity congruent with ego's goals. The less efficient alternative would be for ego to try to manipulate alter's situational identity afresh in each encounter. For example, once a husband has incorporated as a part of his self a sense of ineptitude in the kitchen, then his wife need never again altercast him in that light because his sense of self keeps him from entering her mysterious domain.

So far, little has been said about the content of actors' motivational systems. Aside from the everyday motivations – scratch my neck, take the children off my hands, do not drink too much in front of my parents – I would posit one central motivation in close relationships: the desire to keep alter committed to the relationship, and equally or more committed than oneself. The first part of this motivation involves the creation of solidarity through interdependence; the second involves the potential creation of hierarchy, that is, a partner who is either equal or inferior in terms of power and status. Both can be achieved if one finds ways to encourage alter's dependency (Emerson 1962). But alter's dependency is encouraged at the same time that he or she is encouraged to perform services that increase his or her worth and consequently ego's own dependency (Emerson 1972).

Definitions of Reality

The process of identity negotiations should be viewed as ubiquitous because there are identity implications (hence potential self-implications) in even the most insignificant nuances of communication. For example, in a study of the division of labor in conversation, Kollock et al. (1985) showed that interruptions (violations of turn-taking norms) appear to be the right of the powerful. It is reasonable to argue a related phenomenon, that is, that actors infer from how much they successfully achieve interruption, or how often they are successfully interrupted, what their power or status is in an encounter. Some evidence indirectly supports this assertion: In an experimental study Robinson and Reis (1988) found that people who interrupt are more likely than those who do not to be perceived as more masculine and less feminine. On the basis of the research of Kollock et al., it could be argued that the dimensions being measured by Robinson and Reis as perceived masculinity and perceived femininity are really perceived hierarchy in the relationship between the speakers. If research subjects make such judgments about third parties who interrupt, it seems very reasonable that ordinary people make similar judgments about the interruptions that occur in their own ongoing relationships. To be interrupted at alter's will is to learn the worth of one's contribution, and if this pattern is experienced repeatedly, it should affect the self in significant ways, even if alter is not intentionally trying to altercast ego into a subordinate position by his or her interruptions.

Another example of this logic comes from a study of influence tactics used by couples (Howard et al. 1986) that found the weaker partner tends to use indirection to get his or her way. By extension, one might expect that by using indirection, one *becomes* a certain kind of person in the shared definition of reality, and that eventually this is incorporated into the self. Additionally, Goody (1978) has argued very convincingly that the simple act of asking a question is, for the lowly, one of the few legitimate avenues for inducing a high-status other into conversation. How one is required to enter a conversation, with head raised or bowed, sets a situational identity, and if this scenario occurs repeatedly, it eventually shapes the self.

Situations of open conflict have particular capacity for creating realities that may force modifications in the self. Frequently in the opening rounds of conflict in intimate relationships one partner offers a definition of the situation, usually a narrative containing complaints easily translatable into assertions both about situational identities and about dispositions, that is, selves, of the actors (see Turner (1970) for an analysis of conflict between intimates). Information expressed in conflict situations has the patina of deep veracity because the extreme emotions are believed to undermine the expressive control necessary for strategic interaction. The other partner may find the asserted characterizations of self that emerge during intense conflict enormously discontinuous with respect to the self held dear, and must come to grips with what may be a persuasive but unsettling definition offered by a person who has been granted unparalleled permission to define situations. Alter may also have a counterdefinition to offer, one that may neutralize the self-implications of ego's statements. Nevertheless, alter has learned a possibly new way of framing the self, and even if ego recants his or her asserted truth, that truth, once uttered, continues to exist as a potential resource in the production of self for alter.

An intimate dyad has two fundamental properties when it comes to defining reality: (1) By being intimate, each partner grants the other enormous authority to shape the collective reality of the pair, and (2) by being a dyad, there may often be little in the way of third-party adjudication as to whose definition of reality – definition of selves – bears resemblance to some reality above or beyond the couple (a reality that actors take to be objective). This is why members of couples in conflict feel a need to discuss their problems with third parties, in order to bring the weight of validation to bear on one or the other of the potentially competing realities. And, of course, central to the realities being crafted are the selves of both parties.

This brings us back to dependency. Even in a structure as simple as a dyad, the process of reality construction can be very complex. Two of the many factors that enter into the process are *power* and *competence*. For the relationship to be close, both partners are highly dependent on one another and therefore both are very powerful. Nevertheless, in most cases one is likely to be even more powerful than the other, reflecting differences in resources and alternatives (Emerson 1962). The generally more powerful partner, one might expect, will not only have greater capacity to get his or her way, but also in more subtle ways to control the definition of the situation, and by extension, the selves expressed within that definition (Scheff 1968).

Not all forms of power are the same, and indeed one should expect that power that reflects one partner's particular expertise will be especially useful in defining relevant realities. For example, modern women have been granted the right of expertise over the subject of love (Cancian 1985), and as a consequence, one would expect women in heterosexual relationships to have legitimacy in defining their partner's competence at such qualities as expressiveness, tenderness, and the like. This does not mean that these women are either generally more powerful or generally more capable of shaping the collective definition of the situation.

Interpersonal competence is an aggregation of skills that allow one actor to prevail over another in defining the situation, that is, in assuring that the working consensus captures a reality that supports his or her goals and desires. It includes such qualities as role-taking ability and the possession of a large and unfettered repertoire of lines of actions (Weinstein 1969). Competent actors will generally be more successful at shaping their partner's identity *and* their partner's self, even without being relatively more powerful. Indeed the less powerful partner is more likely to resort to interpersonal tactics of indirection (Howard et al. 1986), and one form of indirection may be the subtle yet constant efforts to change alter's self so that he or she will behave more cooperatively. Following this line of argument, one encounters an interesting paradox: The more powerful partner is in a better position to change alter's definition of himself or herself, yet the less powerful partner has a greater desire to change alter's self because he or she does not have as many alternative means to change alter's behavior.

Another aspect of reality work in relationships is worth noting: In the everyday negotiation of reality, there is a norm of passive acceptance such that if the costs are small to endorsing alter's definition of the situation, then people will permit that definition to prevail. Given this premise, dramaturgically astute actors can gradually create a definition of the relationship and the selves of its members that will take enormous effort, and possibly engender hostility and conflict, if alter wishes to amend it. Collective meanings may accrue that one partner feels unable to modify, even though he or she neither believes in them nor feels strategically safe by accepting their implications. This is why such culturally significant relationships as marriage have developed rich elaboration around defining the relationship in an inescapable way. For example, ego's proposal of marriage is a last chance, however fraught with risk of momentary unpleasantness and discomfort, for alter to say that the inadvertent accretion of meaning that may have occurred cannot be sustained.

Roles and Relationships

The motivational states of the actors are not the only place to look for sources of the reality-creating processes in intimate relationships whereby selves are likely to be produced. Other places include the social structure and the structure of intimacy.

There is evidence in the work of social psychologists that roles shape selves (e.g., Huntington 1957; Kadushin 1969; Turner 1978). The role structure of heterosexual marriage, in particular, has clear self-producing properties. Marital roles set important markers that are widely used to define traits or dispositions of role incumbents. The *provider* role, the *homemaker* roles, the *parent* role, the *lover* role, and so on, all have highly elaborated cultural standards that can be used to measure one's own and one's partner's adequacy as a person, as a man, as a woman, and so on. I will not attempt it here, but I think it would be a fruitful enterprise to analyze some of the subtleties in the content of marital roles with respect to the potential for self-implications. For example, what are the implications for the self to live under the conception that one's house can never be too clean, that one can never earn too much money, or that the delinquency of one's children reflects the quality of their home life?

Intimate relationships are at the same time *role relationships* and *personal relationships* (Blumstein and Kollock 1988). As role relationships they provide common cultural scripts for their enactment, and these scripts, I have argued, shape selves. As personal relationships they have a set of internal processes, growing from the structure of intimacy, that also shape selves. Unlike roles, which are scripted particularly for each type of relationships, these internal processes have more to do with the structure of intimacy *per se*.

I would posit two dynamics in intimate relationships, particularly those that involve the complex coordination problems of living together: the *centripetal* and *centrifugal*. They are akin to the dual and contradictory needs for security/inclusion and autonomy/freedom. The former leads to projections of similarity or sameness; the latter to projections of difference or uniqueness (Maslach 1974; Snyder and Fromkin 1980). Projections of difference are very risky because they easily and inadvertently (perhaps inevitably) shade off into hierarchy.

In order to predict when these two dynamics will occur, one must consider both the motivational states of the actors and the constraints of social structure. What can ego accomplish by being different? Or better? How does the relationship function when there is a shared reality of sameness? If there is a shared reality of difference?

Differentiation

Differentiation is one of the internal processes inherent to close relationships. Some differentiation comes with the role structure, as in the case of traditional heterosexual marriage, although the institution of marriage seems to be losing some of its role rigidity. However, this does not mean that as the cultural and structural sources of difference wither, spouses will not create differences, perhaps smaller, more subtle, more idiosyncratic, and personally less repugnant, but differences nevertheless.

There are several connections between forces of differentiation and self-production processes: the contrast effect, the division of labor, and the avoidance of competition. The first, and most evident, is the *contrast effect*. Inevitably, as two people become intimately acquainted with one another, they simply will note that they react differently to a situation. The question is how such a simple set of personal observations may enter the interpersonal realm, and from there be elaborated upon to the point where they have potency in the production of selves.

The situation occurs frequently when there are serious potential coordination problems that are being exacerbated by the perceived difference. A good example is in the realm of sexuality, where small differences in sexual appetite or preferred sexual scripts can become highly elaborated under some circumstances. The coordination problems help to heighten each partner's awareness of his or her own dispositions, and this awareness in itself can transform a disposition into a feature of self. But at another level, the couple may need to achieve a shared conceptualization to account for enduring imperfection or compromises in their solutions to the problems of sexual coordination. The consequence is that the dispositional differences are magnified, abstracted, reified, and typified. Through this process, the small differences become a more real feature of the individuals' selves.

Much of our thinking about intimacy derives from a heterosexual marital or dating context. Here a wealth of cultural resources is available for the creation of differences, and it is interesting to wonder whether this availability increases or decreases the potential impact on selves. Returning to the example of sexual coordination, one might wonder what occurs when a wife has a ready cultural basis for understanding the difference between her sexual appetite and that of her husband (i.e., Men are more sexual than women). What are the consequences for her self? In structuring an answer to this question, it might prove fruitful to contrast the wife's situation to that of a partner in a lesbian couple where a similar asymmetry of initiating and declining sex is present. In this case, it is much more difficult to find relevant cultural materials for contextualizing the observed differences between the two partners. Without an obvious categorical basis of observed differences, then any differences are likely to be treated as idiosyncratic (cf. Jones et al. 1961). The questions, then, become: In which kind of couple – two sexes or one – are the problematics of sexual coordination more likely to become part of the shared consciousness and rhetoric? In which kind of couple is that shared definition going to lead to a creation of a reality of dispositional difference? In which kind of couple will the creation of a reality of difference become ossified in the selves of the actors? Given the cultural belief that women have less sexual appetite than men, it would seem that the wife in our example would have as a central feature of her self her female sex, but that the *typical* aspects associated with her sex would in general not feature centrally in her self. The lesbian in our example does not have any category membership to account for her comparatively low sexual appetite and so her uniqueness (relative to her partner) would make sexual appetite a more salient dimension of self-organization. Indeed she may carry her typification of self as a person low in sexual appetite into a subsequent relationship where the facts might cast her self-perception in doubt.

The second force of differentiation is the tendency for all forms of social organization to create a *division of labor* even when there is none pre-assigned. In my research I have observed that, struggle as some couples might to avoid differentiation in household tasks and other instrumental activities, they face a monumental uphill battle. The antagonism to a division of labor seems to have two sources: (1) a fear that it will resemble the traditional patriarchal divisions of heterosexual marriage with their attendant inequality, and (2) a desire to perform tasks together in order to maximize the amount of shared couple time. Couples report, however, that the pressures of efficiency, differences in aptitude, and different tastes all conspire to push them into a division of labor even when they fervently wish to avoid one.

The third process has some parallels to the creation of a division of labor. It involves the *avoidance of competition*. Inspiration for focusing the discussion of competition avoidance comes from the work on self-evaluation maintenance processes described by Tesser (1988). Couples face the problem of competitiveness whenever their selves are constructed such that the realms in which competence is salient are the same for both of them. This means that rather than identifying with the other's success, each may feel diminished by it. The powerful bonds of identification (Turner 1970) are inhibited by the evils of social comparison processes (Festinger 1954; Suls and Miller 1977). According to Tesser's model, there are two dynamic processes: *reflection processes*, which involve what has been called identification by others, such that the successful performance of a person with whom we are close reflects favorably on us (see Cialdini and Richardson 1980), and *comparison processes*, which involve the sense of diminished worth of our own performance in comparison to the superior performance of the other. Turner (1970) has argued persuasively that bonds based on identification are salutary for intimate relationships, and by implication, the competitiveness that can grow out of comparison processes is detrimental.

The traditional differentiation of gender and its institutionalization in marital roles provided a significant buffer against competitiveness between spouses. However, as these institutions have changed, as men's and women's lives have become more similar and the distinction between their realms (private versus public) has withered, couples have clearly developed an increased potential for competition. Although many couples are probably crippled or brought to dissolution by that competition, I believe I have observed among couples I have interviewed that many others find ways of moving away from the conditions that lead to competitiveness.

On the basis of my impressionistic observation, I would suggest that couples whose similarity in skills, talents, and performances makes them vulnerable to competition rather than identification work collectively to create rich elaborations on tiny differences. Initially this is an act of reality construction, and eventually an act of self-production. By focusing and elaborating on small and apparent differences, they eventually *become* different. The couple who early in their relationship develop a shared hobby of cooking discovers that one is slightly better at desserts and the other slightly better at salads. Years later they may be discovered to have one salad-maker and one pastry chef, with each taking pride in the other's "unique" talent. Of course, the system is self-perpetuating, that is, the more each partner comes to define herself or himself as different from the other, the more that partner will come to behave differently and thereby be validated in the reflection from others in that self-definition. There is not a lot of strong evidence on the consequences of such differentiation for couples, but one study suggests that when couples can agree on which partner has greater knowledge in various domains, they also express greater satisfaction with their relationship (Wegner 1986).

Sameness

The creation of differentness, both symbolic and real, must have limits in order for close relationships to survive. Indeed, it might be hypothesized that relationships can only create differentness to the extent that their solidarity or bondedness (Turner

1970) is secure. Indeed, similarity abounds. Homogamy among married couples is one of the most durable empirical facts in the social sciences (Buss 1984, 1985; Buss and Barnes 1986), and there is also recent evidence for homogamy in same-sex couples (Howard et al. 1989; Kurdek and Schmitt 1987) as well as in friendship choice (Duck and Craig 1978; Feld 1982; Kandel 1978; Verbrugge 1977). The usual discussion of homogamy is based on assumptions of similarity of stable values, opinions, social statuses, and personality traits, all qualities the partners bring to the relationship. Without denying the validity of the literature on homogamy, I would suggest that homogamy in the "softer" areas, that is, values, opinions, *perceived* dispositions, may be something that couples *achieve* together once in the relationship. They accomplish the achievement through interpersonal processes of reality construction layered with supporting self-modifications.

Some examples of the social construction of sameness come from my study in collaboration with Pepper Schwartz on four types of couples: married couples, heterosexual cohabitors, lesbian couples, and gay male couples (Blumstein and Schwartz 1983). One of the lesbian couples was striking in this regard. When they arrived for their interview they wore the same hairstyle and virtually identical clothes. During the interview one partner exemplified couple identity work directed at sameness (Blumstein and Schwartz 1983: 454):

> I could honestly believe in reincarnation. We think so much alike and we have so much in common and we do these dumb things like get the same clothes on. We buy the same things. We bought each other the same valentine at different stores at different times.... We go out and buy the same groceries, not having discussed what we wanted ahead of time.... We'll shop at the same place and drift into each other. We drive up nose to nose in the same parking lots at the same moments.

There is little to be gained in treating these coincidences as either valid facts or as hallucinations. Rather one can look at these *stories* (which in the interview did not seem to be told for the first time), and the narrative they formed. One can understand how this narrative allows the couple to key into deep cultural themes of *love as merger*, and thereby multiply the symbolic solidarity and perfect taken-for-grantedness of the *happily ever after scenario* for their relationship. One can also understand how by the telling of these stories by both women (or when one woman tells them in the other's presence and the latter does not balk or object), each is saying something, either actively or passively, about her self and about the self of her partner. And if one is cynical about it, one can imagine each woman awaking in the morning and subconsciously choosing what clothing to wear in order to enhance the likelihood of confirming that they have "discovered" the uniquely perfect match in partners. I would suggest that she would choose that dress, not because she is consciously taking the role of her partner, but rather because she has come to see herself as "the kind of person who looks good in and likes wearing pastel colors." The motive is to construct togetherness through coincidence; the product is a pair of selves that will allow that motive to succeed.

Another example (Blumstein and Schwartz 1983) comes from a partner in a gay male relationship, who said:

We go to the opera and I know that at the first intermission he will have a strong opinion one way or the other. Sometimes I have a gut level reaction to the opera, but generally I fall somewhere in the middle. The opera is somewhere between pretty good and quite bad, and I'm really not sure how I feel. But I do know that I feel a need to have an opinion to express at the intermission. And I realized the other night as I sit there, I'm getting anxious about what my opinion will be. So I asked myself why I was anxious about having an opinion, and I realized that when we both spontaneously love something, or we both spontaneously hate something, I feel this great, euphoric sense of rapport, of we-ness, that we are well matched and are therefore a "natural," "meant-to-be" couple. And when we disagree, or see the same thing very differently, I feel distant and alienated from him. It's like the spell has been broken. So as I sit in the opera wondering what my opinion is, I am really hoping that I will wind up with the opinion that will allow us to blend into one sweep of unanimity and be overwhelmed with that warm glow of coupleness.

This couple may not be typical; many couples feel free to disagree over heartfelt issues without any constraint to create a mystical couple reality, and do not experience their relationship as diminished by the agreement to disagree. They have learned that they agree on enough basic matters that a few displays of uniqueness is not distressing. Indeed such displays may be salutary in precisely the ways described in our discussion of differentiation processes. Examples such as this are probably most common in the early phases of relationships, where the participants may be eager to give assistance to whatever emerging similarities they may be discovering in one another. They feel genuine in the exaggerated sameness they project, but as I have argued, the projection of a self has the grave potential for the becoming of a self.

Anchors against Drift

A fundamental fact about close relationships is that their attractiveness emerges from their predictability (Bateson 1972; Kelley and Thibaut 1978; Kelly 1955). Costs associated with learning new scripts with each new person one meets are reduced, role taking is simplified, coordination problems are minimized. How do couples accomplish this predictability? It is more than simply learning the other; rather it is by imposing a set of constraints on selves such that partners actually *become* more predictable. I would posit a fundamental overarching obligation in close relationships: to live up to the dispositional qualities that have become part of the working consensus (Athay and Darley 1981; Swann 1984). That is why personal relationships are inherently conservative, because an actor is constrained today to be the same person he or she was yesterday. Because of the constraints on actors to exhibit stable dispositional traits, close relationships can depart rather markedly from cultural scripts as the two participants create and maintain their own private culture.

Many people might object to this view of the conservative effects of intimate relationships. They would see close relationships as vehicles of personal growth and change (Aron and Aron 1989; Cancian 1987). They would argue that the extreme interdependence found in close relationships would provide a safe haven for the partners to explore alternative definitions of self. Although this logic is very persuasive, it ignores the fact that the selves of the partners are finely interwoven.

One partner cannot express a self if there is no complementary self with which to resonate. One cannot enact incompetent dependency unless one's partner plays effective authority. To the extent that each partner has cathected the elements of his or her self, then that person is deeply invested in the complementary aspects of the self of the other. Certainly relationships can sometimes survive significant and abrupt changes in one of the selves. But it is indeed a matter of survival, because newly adopted selves create new demands on the other to give role-support, demands that cannot always be met, even with the best of intentions.

References

Alexander, C. Norman, Jr. and Wiley, Mary. 1981. "Situated activity and identity formation." In M. Rosenberg and R. H. Turner (eds.) *Social Psychology: Sociological Perspectives*. New York: Basic Books, pp. 269–89.

Aron, Arthur and Aron, Elaine. 1989. "New research on the self-expansion model." Paper presented at the Nags Head Conference on Interaction Process and Analysis, Nags Head, NC.

Athay, M. and Darley, John M. 1981. "Toward an interaction centered theory of personality." In N. Cantor and J. F. Kihlstrom (eds.) *Personality, Cognition, and Social Interaction*. Hillsdale, NJ: Erlbaum, pp. 281–308.

Bateson, Gregory. 1972. *Steps to an Ecology of Mind*. New York: Ballantine.

Bem, Daryl J. 1972. "Self-perception theory." In Leonard Berkowitz (ed.) *Advances in Experimental Social Psychology*, vol. 6. New York: Academic Press, pp. 1–62.

Blumstein, Philip W. 1975. "Identity bargaining and self-conception." *Social Forces* 53: 476–85.

Blumstein, Philip and Kollock, Peter. 1988. "Personal relationships." *Annual Review of Sociology* 14: 467–90.

Blumstein, Philip, and Schwartz, Pepper. 1983. *American Couples: Money, Work, and Sex*. New York: Morrow.

Buss, David M. 1984. "Toward a psychology of person–environment (PE) correlations: The role of spouse selection." *Journal of Personality and Social Psychology* 47: 361–77.

—— 1985. "Human mate selection." *American Scientist* 73: 47–51.

Buss, David M. and Barnes, Michael. 1986. "Preferences in human mate selection." *Journal of Personality and Social Psychology* 50: 559–70.

Cancian, Francesca. 1985. "Gender politics: Love and power in the private and public spheres." In Alice S. Rossi (ed.) *Gender and the Life Course*. New York: Aldine, pp. 253–64.

—— 1987. *Love in America: Gender and Self-development*. New York: Cambridge University Press.

Cialdini, Robert B. and Richardson, K. D. 1980. "Two indirect tactics of image management: Basking and blasting." *Journal of Personality and Social Psychology* 39: 406–15.

Cooley, Charles Horton. 1902. *Human Nature and the Social Order*. New York: Scribner's.

Duck, Steve W. and Craig, R. G. 1978. "Personality similarity and the development of friendship." *British Journal of Social and Clinical Psychology* 17: 237–42.

Emerson, Richard M. 1962. "Power-dependence relations." *American Sociological Review* 27: 31–41.

—— 1972. "Exchange theory, part II: Exchange relations and networks." In J. Berger, M. Zelditch, and B. Anderson (eds.) *Sociological Theories in Progress*, vol. 2. Boston: Houghton Mifflin, pp. 58–87.

Feld, Scott L. 1982. "Social structural determinants of similarity among associates." *American Sociological Review* 47: 797–801.

Festinger, Leon. 1954. "A theory of social comparison processes." *Human Relations* 7: 117–40.

Gergen, Kenneth J. 1968. "Personal consistency and the presentation of self." In C. Gordon and K. J. Gergen (eds.) *The Self in Social Interaction*. New York: Wiley, pp. 299–308.

Goffman, Erving. 1959. *The Presentation of Self in Everyday Life*. New York: Doubleday.

Goffman, Erving. 1971. *Relations in Public: Microstudies of the Public Order*. New York: Basic Books.

Goody, Esther N. 1978. "Toward a theory of questions." In E. N. Goody (ed.) *Questions and Politeness: Strategies in Social Interaction*. London: Cambridge University Press, pp. 17–43.

Howard, Judith A., Blumstein, Philip, and Schwartz, Pepper. 1986. "Sex, power, and influence tactics in intimate relationships." *Journal of Personality and Social Psychology* 51: 102–9.

——, ——, and —— 1989. "Homogamy in intimate relationships: Why birds of a feather flock together." Paper presented at the annual meeting of the American Sociological Association, San Francisco.

Huntington, Mary Jean. 1957. "The development of a professional self image." In R. K. Merton, G. G. Reeder, and P. Kendall (eds.) *The Student Physician*. Cambridge, Mass.: Harvard University Press, pp. 179–87.

Jones, Edward E., Davis, Keith E. and Gergen, Kenneth J. 1961. "Role playing variations and their informational value for person perception." *Journal of Abnormal and Social Psychology* 63: 302–10.

Kadushin, Charles. 1969. "The professional self-concept of music students." *American Journal of Sociology* 75: 389–404.

Kandel, Denise B. 1978. "Homophily, selection and socialization in adolescent friendships." *American Journal of Sociology* 84: 427–36.

Kelley, Harold H. and Thibaut, John W. 1978. *Interpersonal Relations: A Theory of Interdependence*. New York: Wiley.

Kelly, George A. 1955. *The Psychology of Personal Constructs*. New York: Norton.

Kollock, Peter, Blumstein, Philip and Schwartz, Pepper. 1985. "Sex and power in interaction: Conversational privileges and duties." *American Sociological Review* 50: 34–46.

Kurdek, Lawrence and Schmitt, J. Patrick. 1987. "Partner homogamy in married, heterosexual cohabiting, gay, and lesbian couples." *Journal of Sex Research* 23: 212–32.

Maslach, Christina. 1974. "Social and personal bases of individuation." *Journal of Personality and Social Psychology* 29: 411–25.

McCall, George J. and Simmons, J. L. 1966. *Identities and Interactions*. New York: Free Press.

Messinger, Sheldon L., with Sampson, Harold and Towne, Robert D. 1962. "Life as theatre: Some notes on the dramaturgical approach to social reality." *Sociometry* 25: 98–110.

Robinson, Laura F. and Reis, Harry T. 1988. "The effects of interruption, gender, and leadership position on interpersonal perceptions." Paper presented at the International Conference on Personal Relationships, Vancouver, Canada.

Rosenberg, Morris. 1981. "The self-concept: Social product and social force." In M. Rosenberg and R. H. Turner (eds.) *Social Psychology: Sociological Perspectives*. New York: Basic Books, pp. 593–624.

Scheff, Thomas J. 1968. "Negotiating reality: Notes on power in the assessment of responsibility." *Social Problems* 16: 3–17.

Snyder, C. R. and Fromkin, Howard L. 1980. *Uniqueness: The Human Pursuit of Difference*. New York: Plenum Press.

Suls, Jerry M. and Miller, Richard L. (eds.) 1977. *Social Comparison Processes: Theoretical and Empirical Perspectives*. Washington, DC: Hemisphere.

Swann, William B., Jr. 1984. "Quest for accuracy in person perception: A matter of pragmatics." *Psychological Review* 91: 457–77.

—— 1987. "Identity negotiation: Where two roads meet." *Journal of Personality and Social Psychology* 53: 1038–51.

Swann, William B., Jr. and Read, S. J. 1981. "Self-verification processes: How we sustain our self-conceptions." *Journal of Experimental Social Psychology* 17: 351–72.

Tesser, Abraham. 1988. "Toward a self-evaluation maintenance model of social behavior." In Leonard Berkowitz (ed.) *Advances in Experimental Social Psychology*, vol. 21. San Diego: Academic Press, pp. 181–227.

Turner, Ralph. 1970. *Family Interaction*. New York: Wiley.

—— 1978. "The role and the person." *American Journal of Sociology* 84: 1–23.

Verbrugge, Lois M. 1977. "The structure of adult friendship choices." *Social Forces* 56: 576–97.

Wegner, Daniel M. 1986. "Transactive memory: A contemporary analysis of the group mind." In B. Mullen and G. R. Geothals (eds.) *Theories of Group Behavior*. New York: Springer-Verlag, pp. 185–208.

Weinstein, Eugene A. 1969. "The development of interpersonal competence." In D. A. Goslin (ed.) *Handbook of Socialization Theory and Research*. Chicago: Rand McNally, pp. 753–75.

Weinstein, Eugene A. and Deutschberger, Paul. 1963. "Some dimensions of altercasting." *Sociometry* 26: 454–66.

—— and —— 1964. "Tasks, bargains, and identities in social interaction." *Social Forces* 42: 451–6.

Wiley, Mary Glenn and Alexander, Norman C. 1987. "From situated activity to self-attribution: The impact of social structural schemata." In K. Yardley and T. Honess (eds.) *Self and Identity: Psychosocial Perspectives*. Chichester: Wiley, pp. 105–17.

14 Intimate Relationships from a Microstructural Perspective: Men Who Mother

Barbara J. Risman

While much feminist theory has focused on how macroinstitutional forces create gender inequality (e.g., Blumberg 1978; Chafetz 1984; Margolis 1984), little attention has been paid to how immediate contextual variables create gender in everyday life. Structural explanations for gendered behavior in interpersonal relationships have thus far received short shrift from sociologists. After a critique of the predominant individualist model for gendered interpersonal relations, I analyze the ways social forces at the microstructural level create gendered behavior. The presentation of a microstructural theory for gendered behavior is followed by an empirical test of the hypothesis that microstructural conditions are more important to the creation of male "mothers" than individual attitudes and socialized personality traits. I then discuss why the individualist paradigm for gender in intimate relationships has been so readily accepted not only by lay audiences but also by feminist social scientists. Finally, I end with the suggestion that a microstructural perspective is necessary for effective feminist social policy.

The Individualist Perspective on Interpersonal Relations

Although the study of gender in interpersonal relationships has flourished in the last two decades, the research has concentrated on individualist variables. The presumption that gender roles are internalized as stable personality traits is the hallmark of any individualist paradigm. Researchers using this perspective are biased toward psychological explanations for behavioral differences between men and women and do not consider seriously enough how these classes of actors are shaped by their immediate social settings. An individualist model suggests that by adulthood, men and women have developed very different personalities. Women have become nurturant, person-oriented, and child-centered, and men have become competitive and work-oriented. In an often cited statement of the individualist perspective, Bem and Bem (1976) argue that gender-role socialization is so powerful that adults actually have little choice in their roles. They argue, for example, that a 21-year-old woman is not free to choose a nonstereotypical life-style because "society has controlled not only her alternatives, but her motivation to choose any but one of those alternatives" (p. 184). Particular personality types are developed through child-rearing techniques

Reprinted from *Gender and Society* 1(1) (March 1987): 6–32.

and gender-appropriate role models. According to individualist theorists, there are limits to individual flexibility. Intensely held emotions, values, and predispositions develop during childhood and coalesce into a person's core identity.

The literature on gender in interpersonal settings implicitly attributes primary causal status to internalized psychic predispositions. Exclusive mothering and childhood socialization together are assumed to affect – if not predetermine – adult preferences and choices. Tavris and Offir (1977) suggest that social psychologists often explain "women's second class status by pointing to different personality traits men and women acquire as they grow up" (p. 197). Internalized socialization shapes individual motivation to follow socially proscribed roles.

The variety of individualist explanations for gendered behavior is impressive. Nancy Chodorow's (1978) analysis in *The Reproduction of Mothering* of how gendered personalities develop as a result of exclusive female mothering is an influential feminist psychoanalytic-oriented theory. Two of the most commonly accepted individualist explanations for gender-differentiated behavior are reinforcement socialization theory (e.g., Bandura and Walters 1963; Lever 1976; Lewis and Weinraub 1979; Mischel 1966; Weitzman 1979) and cognitive development theory (e.g., Gilligan 1982; Kohlberg 1966). Although sociobiological theories (e.g., Symons 1979; Van den Berghe 1979; Wilson 1978) and biosocial theories (Rossi 1977, 1984) merge evolutionary, genetic, hormonal, and social variables, they also ultimately locate the source of gendered behavior in individual motivation.

The defining characteristics of these different individualist paradigms is the presumption that gendered behavior is the result of *internalized* traits. While individualist theorists do not negate the role of social structural influences on family patterns (see especially, Chodorow 1978), they focus on how culturally determined family patterns create gendered personalities, which then provide the motivations for individuals to fill their socially appropriate roles. For example, individualist theorists debate whether women desire to stay home with their children because they have been mothered by same-sex parents and have therefore developed the desire for intense intimacy, or whether the social reinforcement girls receive for doll play and other nurturant behavior is a better explanation for the female motivation to mother. Although individualist theory does not necessarily deny the usefulness of studying ongoing interpersonal interaction, the implicit presumption within this tradition is that internalized psychological motivation is a more salient explanation for gendered behavior than immediate social relations.

A Microstructural Perspective on Gendered Behavior in Interpersonal Relations

Microstructural theory in its most extreme manifestation would suggest that identical behavioral expectations and identical socially structured opportunities would produce identical behavior in men and women. That is, if D is the difference between women's and men's behavior after gender-linked structural opportunities and social expectations have been controlled (or in "real life," hypothetically eliminated), then a pure microstructural hypothesis predicts D would equal zero. More realistically, the actual magnitude of D would be the variation in human behavior left for analysis by individualist theorists after the effect of structural conditions has been explained. For example, the physical experience of childbirth and breast-feeding may differentiate the parental behavior of some women from men, but the parenting behavior of adopting, non-breast-feeding mothers should be potentially identical to that of fathers. Social class, birth order, responsibility for child care, or time spent with the child are some of the microstructural forces that may produce differences in parental behavior that might or might not be gender-linked (cf. Gekas 1979; Kohn 1969, 1979).

Individualist and microstructural theory can be differentiated by their predictions about the source of gender differences. Microstructural theory suggests that most differences between women and men arise from differential experiences, opportunities, and access to social networks. The empirical question for microstructural theory is the relative magnitude and variability of the social processes that produce gender. In a microstructural approach, behavior is not viewed as fixed by early socialization and biological conditions but rather as adaptive to ongoing interaction.

An analysis of how structural factors influence gender has been hindered by the inconsistent definition of the term "structure." The relationships between economic or historical forces and social institutions are usually considered structural (e.g. Goode 1960; Merton 1975). Indeed, Mayhew (1980) argues vehemently that only these macro-level relationships actually merit the term structural. Other theorists more interested in interpersonal interaction (e.g., Hewitt 1979; Stryker 1980, 1981) use the term "structural" to refer to one mechanism through which institutional social forces may affect human behavior.

I presume that situational interaction is necessarily a component of structural theory because it is the only way that structural exigencies are experienced by human actors. Macrostructural approaches often presume direct causal relationships between societal conditions and human action (see Gerson 1985, for a critique of these theories), while the approach developed here presumes that behavior emerges from social interaction. The behaviors (and identities) that can conceivably be enacted are circumscribed by the social organization of experiences available to particular types of actors. I propose a specifically microstructural perspective to link institutionally organized social forces with the experiences, expectations, and opportunities individual actors encounter in their everyday interaction. My work goes beyond the notion of socially created personality toward a theory of the way concrete social relations create gender.

Two traditions inform a microstructural theory of gender: symbolic interaction and status expectations theory. The importance of interactional and situational factors in shaping behavior has been well documented empirically (Fine and Kleinman 1979; Hewitt 1979; McHugh 1968; Rosenthal and Jacobsen 1968). Status expectations theory suggests that ascribed social statuses, including gender, affect social interaction even when such statuses are irrelevant to the task at hand (Berger et al. 1972; Eagly and Steffen 1984; Meeker and Weitzell-O'Neill 1977; Ridgeway 1982; Wagner et al. 1986).

The concept of embeddedness recently elaborated by Granovetter (1985) to explain nonutilitarian economic behavior is useful for integrating interactional and status expectations theories into a more general microstructural explanation for gendered behavior. My premise is that gender status affects behavior not only, or even primarily, through role internalization but because of placement and experiences within social networks. Concrete social relations create gendered behavior because in nearly all social interaction, men and women are embedded in different social networks. Further, they face different experiences even when in similar positions within networks of relationships.

The small body of research that even implicitly uses this notion of embeddedness to explain apparent differences between men and women focuses almost exclusively on labor force participation. In 1977, Kanter critiqued the studies on female labor force participation for their individualist presumptions. The findings she reports in *Men and Women of the Corporation* provide strong support for the microstructuralist theory that an actor's place in social networks – variables such as his or her access to powerful mentors, the numbers of like others, and the possibility for upward mobility – better explain behavior at work than internalized femininity or masculinity. Other researchers (Geis et al. 1984; Lorber 1984; Meeker and Weitzell-O'Neill 1977; Thompson 1981) have provided empirical support for a microstructural framework using both labor force and laboratory research.

A microstructural approach to gendered behavior within domestic settings was used by Kollock et al. (1985) in their study of the allocation of conversational privileges and duties among same-sex and opposite-sex couples. They find that dyadic power dynamics often create the conversational division of labor usually attributed to internalized gender roles. Researchers who focus on the influence of interpersonal power on body language (see review by Henley 1977) also report that apparent sex differences are often really differences in power. In *Hard Choices*, Gerson (1985) argues that situational opportunities often determine women's decisions about childbearing. Gerson finds no identifiable internalized feminine personality type or biological instinct that propelled the women in her sample toward motherhood. Over half of the baby-boom women in Gerson's sample shifted their orientations between domesticity and work (in both directions) because of the microstructural forces in their lives, such as the existence, or lack thereof, of stable heterosexual relationships, the opportunities and rewards available or lacking in the labor force, and the relative interest of male partners in fatherhood.

An Empirical Test of Microstructural Theory: Men Who Mother

The research reported here is a study specifically designed to test the relative strength of individualist versus microstructural explanations for one set of behaviors that is usually gender-typed, mothering. Mothering is defined here as the task of providing physical maintenance and psychological nurturance to young children. Mothering is one of the few behaviors that appears almost universally gender-specific. According to the individualist paradigm (e.g., Chodorow 1978; Dinnerstein 1976; Rossi 1984), mothering is primarily a woman's activity not because of the social organization of work or kinship, but because women psychologically desire to "mother" and men do not. In a critique of this individualist position, Lorber (1981: 482–6) argues that we need to focus more attention on the situational factors that encourage full-time mothering by women. Gerson's (1985) research suggests that microstructural forces do explain women's choices about childbearing.

Research Design

Social forces in a sex or gender system influence behavior through two distinct paths: (1) the socialization of individual personalities and belief systems (individualist factors) and (2) the organization of experiences available to persons based on the ascribed characteristic of gender (microstructural factors). The first path, the process of personality development and gendered socialization, has long been considered a mechanism by which society creates both gender and patriarchy (Chodorow 1978; Hartmann 1981; Rubin 1975). The second path, the interplay of microstructural factors, has less often been examined as a distinct route by which society creates gender, particularly in the realm of interpersonal relations. My hypothesis is that microstructural factors, such as situational demands and embeddedness in social networks, will be better predictors of mothering behaviors than individualist factors, such as gendered socialization and gender-typed internalized personality traits.

The research is designed to disentangle the individual and microstructural determinants of mothering behaviors. Any attempt to disentangle these factors is hindered by the self-selection of most actors into whatever counternormative positions they fill. Those who select positions inconsistent with traditional gender roles may have experienced atypical socialization. This study bypasses the self-selection problem by using as subjects people playing social roles they did not voluntarily choose: widowed or deserted single fathers. These men provide primary care and nurturance to young children without having chosen to do so. The death or desertion of a wife severs the usual relationship between personal motivation and social role. The single fathers in this sample faced situations for which they had not been socialized.

The parental behaviors and household strategies of these single fathers are compared with those of single mothers and of parents in two-paycheck and in traditional mother-at-home families. If individualist factors are the key to parental behavior, these single fathers will have neither the motivation nor the skills to provide primary care for children, to mother with all its subtlety; their care will not be equivalent to the care provided by women who mother. If microstructural factors are more influential, reclassification of the father into the primary caretaker role and the continuing expectations of children to be nurtured will produce mothering by men that is nearly indistinguishable from the behavior of women in the same situation.

. . .

Discussion of Findings

The central hypothesis is that much of the variation in gender-typed behavior usually attributed to individual variables, such as biology or gendered socialization, can be better accounted for by the differential situational exigencies and opportunities faced by women and men. The results of this research generally, although not exclusively, support this hypothesis.

Table 14.1 presents the equations that represent the empirical path model used to explain variation in reported parental strategies for housework, parent-child intimacy, and parental displays of affection. The rows in table 14.1 present the

Table 14.1   Reduced and structural equations for housework, intimacy and affection

Dependent variables	Predictor variables						
	Sex	Primary	Share	Role priority	Femininity	Masculinity	R^2
(1A) Housework	—	—	—				0.56‡
	(0.55)‡	(1.23)‡	(0.80)‡				
(1B) Housework	—	—	—	-0.04	0.06	-0.07	0.56‡
	(0.50)‡	(1.23)‡	(0.81)‡	(-0.02)	(0.07)	(-0.06)	
(2A) Affection	—	—	—				0.11‡
	(0.47)‡	(0.20)	(0.38)*				
(2B) Affection	—	—	—	0.04	0.12	0.04	0.12‡
	(0.43)‡	(0.13)	(0.37)*	(0.02)	(0.16)	(0.04)	
(3A) Intimacy	—	—	—				0.03†
	(0.28)*	(0.35)	(0.25)				
(3B) Intimacy	—	—	—	0.12*	0.38	-0.07	0.13‡
	(0.04)	(0.16)	(0.23)	(0.08)	(0.55)‡	(-0.08)	

Note: Both standardized and metric regression coefficients are reported for continuous variables with metric coefficients in parentheses. Metric coefficients only are reported for dichotomous dummy variables.
*$p \leq 0.05$;   †$p \leq 0.01$;   ‡$p \leq 0.001$.

Table 14.2 Reduced and structural equations for housework by sex

	Predictor variables			
	Men		Women	
	Share	Primary	Share	Primary
Housework	—	—	—	
	(0.55)‡	(1.28)‡	(-0.17)‡	a
	$R^2 = 0.46$‡		$R^2 = 0.10$†	

Note: Metric coefficients only are reported for dichotomous dummy variables.
a. All women – single mothers and housewives – who do not share roles are primary caretakers; therefore, primary drops out of the equation because there is no variation in this cell.
† $p \leq 0.01$; ‡ $p \leq 0.001$.

dependent variables and the coefficients resulting from their regression on the independent variables.

The relative strengths of microstructural factors (i.e., primary caretaker role, sharing breadwinner role) and individualist factors (i.e., respondent's sex) are presented separately for each dependent variable.

Housework

Both sex and parental role appear to affect reported personal responsibility for housework directly (see table 14.1, equation 1A). Measures for the definitions of self were not significant intervening variables between either respondent's sex or parental role variables and housework (table 14.1, Equation 1B). Tests for interactions between parenting roles and respondent's sex were significant, however, indicating that parental roles have differential effects on men and women. (See table 14.2, which presents the coefficients for the effects of parental roles on housekeeping estimated separately for men and women.)

The equation presented in table 14.2 indicates that sharing parental roles affects men's and women's reported housekeeping behaviors quite differently. Sharing economic and homemaker roles with a wife increases men's reported responsibility for household chores significantly ($b = 0.555$, $p = 0.001$). Inversely, wives who share economic roles reported doing significantly less housework than other women report ($b = -0.17$, $p = 0.001$). Therefore, these results indicate that husbands' responsibility increased in proportion to the decrease in their wives' responsibility.

The influence of primary parental responsibility for young children on men, that is, being a single father, seems to increase personal household responsibility dramatically. Such men did not report hiring outsiders to take responsibility for household chores. The effect of primary parental responsibility on women cannot be assessed because all the women respondents except employed wives (the role-sharers) were primary caretakers of children. This lack of variation precluded estimating the effects of the primary caretaker role on women. Although table 14.2 indicates that parental role explained considerably more of the variation in men's reported responsibility for housework than in women's responsibility, this may be attributed to the smaller variation in parental role responsibility among women respondents.

Unlike previous research, these data suggest that reported responsibility for housework is much better explained by parental role than by sex. Primary parents, whether men or women (housewives or single parents) reported doing much more housework than other parents reported. More surprising, given previous research results (e.g., Blumstein and Schwartz 1983), is the finding that traditional gender roles seem to be challenged in role-sharing couples: Women reported doing significantly less and men reported doing significantly more housework than their traditionally married counterparts reported. Indeed, almost half of all the variation in men's reported responsibility for housework can be attributed to parental role ($R^2 = 0.46$). Therefore, the microstructural hypothesis that much of the variation in housework often attributed to sex can be better explained by situational exigencies is strongly supported.

Overt Affection

Both parental role and respondent's sex influenced parental reports of affectionate displays almost equally (see table 14.1, equation 2A). Being female and sharing parental roles were positively related to reports of displays of affection. When the measures for definition of self were added to the analysis (equation 2B), sex and parental role still directly affected the frequency of reported parental displays of affection. While the increased variation explained by introducing measures for the definition of self was statistically significant, it was so small as to be substantively trivial. The possible interactions between respondent's sex and parental role variables were tested and found nonsignificant.

The microstructural variable of parental role was an important predictor of reported parent–child affection. Men and women who shared responsibility for child care reported being more physically affectionate with their children than men and women who were either primary caretakers or traditional fathers. However, sex also remained a powerful predictor of parents' reports of physical expressions of affection toward children, with women reporting more affectionate behavior than men. Perhaps, as Pleck and Sawyer (1974) suggest, gendered socialization is particularly effective in instilling inexpressiveness in men, or respondents may have reported what they perceived to be socially desirable behavior. Overall, these analyses suggest the importance, but not exclusivity, of the microstructural hypothesis concerning parental displays of affection.

Parent–Child Intimacy

Respondent's sex and parenting role appeared to be equally strong predictors of reported parent–child intimacy (see table 14.1, equation 3A). However, when measures for definition of self were added to the analysis, the effect of respondent's sex almost disappeared while the effect of sharing roles was only slightly weakened. table 14.1, equation 3B indicates that when parental role, respondent's sex, and measures of definition of self were considered simultaneously, femininity was by far the strongest predictor of reported parent–child intimacy. The possible interactions among sex, primary caretaker, and sharing roles for predicting reported intimacy were estimated and found nonsignificant.

Definition of self was particularly salient for understanding reports of parent–child intimacy. Those respondents who described themselves with more feminine personality traits reported more intimate relationships with their children. The explained variance for intimacy increased from 3 to 13 percent when measures for definition of self were included as intervening variables. Therefore, although not predicted, the respondent's definitions of self as measured by the femininity score had an *independent* effect on reported parent–child intimacy. Perhaps the more feminine the parent, the more likely he or she is to elicit intimacy in children. Or perhaps, once again, respondents reported what they perceived to be socially desirable responses, with feminine persons particularly likely to report parent–child intimacy. Overall, these analyses partially support the microstructural theory. Individualist factors affect intimacy indirectly via definitions of self, and microstructural variables directly affect the level of parent–child intimacy.

Definition of Self

Definition of self had an independent effect on reported parent–child intimacy. (Table 14.3 presents the coefficients for the measures of definitions of self with parental-role variables and respondent's sex as predictor variables). This unpredicted result suggests that it would be informative to explore the relative importance of microstructural versus individualist factors for explaining respondents' definitions of self. Individualist theorists merely presume that socialization creates stable feminine and masculine personality traits, while a microstructuralist approach suggests that

Table 14.3 Structural equations for role priority, femininity and masculinity

| | Predictor variables | | | |
Dependent variables	Sex	Primary	Share	R^2
(1) Role priority	—	—	—	0.02^*
	$(0.44)^*$	(0.32)	(0.27)	
(2) Femininity	—	—	—	0.11†
	(0.31)‡	(0.33)†	(0.01)	
(3) Masculinity	—	—	—	0.06‡
	(-0.50)‡	(0.26)	(0.08)	

Note: Metric coefficients only are reported for dichotomous dummy variables.
$*p \leq 0.05$; †$p \leq 0.01$; ‡$p \leq 0.001$.

selves are constantly constructed and sustained by the situational experiences in everyday life.

However, neither microstructural nor individual variables together predicted much of the variation of respondents' definitions of self. Jointly they explained only 2 percent of the variance in role priorities as measured by the TST; femaleness alone was positively, although weakly, related to giving parental roles high priority. Parental-role variables and respondents' sex together predicted 11 and 6 percent of the variance in femininity and masculinity scores, respectively.

Parental-role responsibility was as good a predictor of self-reported femininity as was respondent's sex. The effect of the primary caretaker role was slightly larger than the effect of respondent's sex in predicting femininity scores. The mean scores on femininity and masculinity show that single fathers and dual-paycheck mothers reported almost identical levels of femininity (see table 14.4). This is an important finding for the theoretical understanding of gender, because the individualist theorists who dominate the field usually assume that women are more feminine than are men because they have internalized feminine personality traits during the process of socialization. These results suggest that it is just as plausible that at least some women and men display feminine traits because the roles they play demand such characteristics. Social roles – even if not chosen, as is the case for the single men in this study – influence self-perceived femininity. These results suggest that definition

Table 14.4 Mean femininity and masculinity scores

	Femininity	Masculinity
Traditional father	6.31	6.79
Dual-paycheck father	6.34	6.96
Single father	6.54	6.86
Single mother	6.95	6.47
Dual-paycheck mother	6.61	6.23
Traditional mother	6.98	6.43

Note: Range = 1 to 9;   1 = low.

of self, at least as it relates to femininity, ought to be conceptualized as not only socially created but also socially sustained, reflective of ongoing role demands. While the scores on femininity reflected parental roles, the scores on masculinity did not. Overall, the findings about femininity support a microstructural hypothesis, but the findings on masculinity do not.

Summary of Findings

There was clear empirical support for the importance of microstructural factors in determining parenting behavior. These data indicated that parental role is an important predictor of reported responsibility for housework and reported parent–child affection. Those parents who share responsibility for child care, whatever their sex, reported more intimate relationships with their children than did other respondents. Parental role was the only variable directly related to reports of parent–child intimacy. Parental-role responsibility was as good a predictor of self-reported feminine personality characteristics as biological sex.

These analyses also indicate, however, the concurrent importance of individualist factors for parenting behavior. Sex remained a significant predictor of reported parental physical expressions of affection and had an important, although indirect, effect on reported parent–child intimacy. In addition, respondent's sex was a powerful predictor of self-reported masculinity.

The central hypothesis proposed was that much of the variation in gender-typed behavior usually attributed to individual variables, such as biology or socialization, can be accounted for by the differential situational exigencies and opportunities faced by women and men. The results of this research support the hypothesis. Microstructural factors are important, although not exclusive, explanations for gendered behavior.

References

Bandura, Albert and Walters, Richard H. 1963. *Social Learning and Personality Development*. New York: Holt, Rinehart and Winston.

Bem, Sandra L. and Bem, Darby J. 1976. "Case study of a nonconscious ideology: Training the woman to know her place." In S. Cox (ed.) *Female Psychology: The Emerging Self*. Chicago: Science Research Associates, pp. 180–90.

Berger, Joseph, Cohen, Bernard P., and Zelditch, Morris, Jr. 1972. "Status characteristics and social interaction." *American Sociological Review* 37: 241–55.

Blumberg, Rae Lesser. 1978. *Stratification: Socioeconomic and Sexual Inequality*. Dubuque, Ia.: W. C. Brown.

Blumstein, Philip and Schwartz, Pepper. 1983. *American Couples: Money, Work, and Sex*. New York: William Morrow.

Chafetz, Janet Saltzman. 1984. *Sex and Advantage: A Comparative Macro-Structural Theory of Sex Stratification*. Totowa, NJ: Rowman and Allanheld.

Chodorow, Nancy. 1978. *The Reproduction of Mothering*. Berkeley: University of California Press.

Dinnerstein, Dorothy. 1976. *The Mermaid and the Minotaur: Sexual Arrangements and the Human Malaise*. New York: Harper and Row.

Eagly, Alice H. and Steffen, Valerie J. 1984. "Gender stereotypes stem from the distribution of women and men into social roles." *Journal of Personality and Social Psychology* 46: 735–54.

Fine, Gary Alan and Kleinman, Sherryl. 1979. "Rethinking subculture: An interactionist analysis." *American Journal of Sociology* 85: 1–20.

Geis, Florence L., Brown, Virginia, Jennings, Joyce, and Corrado-Taylor, Denise. 1984. "Sex vs. status in sex-associated stereotypes." *Sex Roles* 11: 771–85.

Gekas, Victor. 1979. "The influence of social class on socialization." In W. R. Burr, R. Hill, F. I. Nye, and I. R. Reiss (eds.) *Contemporary Theories About the Family*, vol. 1. New York: Free Press, pp. 365–403.

Gerson, Kathleen. 1985. *Hard Choices*. Berkeley: University of California Press.

Gilligan, Carol. 1982. *In a Different Voice*. Cambridge, Mass.: Harvard University Press.

Goode, William J. 1960. "A theory of role strain." *American Sociological Review* 24: 38–47.

Granovetter, Mark. 1985. "Economic action, social structure and embeddedness." *American Journal of Sociology* 91: 481–510.

Hartmann, Heidi I. 1981. "The family as the locus of gender, class and political struggle: The example of housework." *Signs: Journal of Women in Culture and Society* 6: 366–94.

Henley, Nancy M. 1977. *Body Politics: Power, Sex, and Nonverbal Communication*. Englewood Cliffs, NJ: Prentice-Hall.

Hewitt, John P. 1979. *Self and Society: A Symbolic Interactionist Social Psychology*. Boston: Allyn and Bacon.

Kohn, Melvin. 1969. *Class and Conformity*. Homewood, Ill.: Dorsey Press.

—— 1979. "The effects of social class on parental values and practices." In D. Reiss and H. A. Hoffman (eds.) *The American Family*. New York: Plenum Press.

Kohlberg, Lawrence. 1996. "A cognitive-developmental analysis of children's sex-role concepts and attitudes." In E. Maccoby (ed.) *The Development of Sex Differences* Stanford, Calif.: Stanford University Press, pp. 82–172.

Kollock, Peter, Blumstein, Philip and Schwartz, Pepper. 1985. "Sex and power in interaction: Conversational privileges and duties." *American Sociological Review* 50: 34–46.

Lever, Janet. 1976. "Sex differences in the games children play." *Social Problems* 23: 479–89.

Lewis, Michael and Weinraub, Marsha. 1979. "Origins of early sex role development." *Sex Roles* 5: 135–55.

Lorber, Judith. 1981. "On the reproduction of mothering: A methodological debate." *Signs: Journal of Women in Culture and Society* 6: 482–86.

Margolis, Maxine L. 1984. *Mothers and Such: Views of American Women and Why They Changed*. Berkeley: University of California Press.

Mayhew, Bruce H. 1980. "Structuralism versus individuals: Part I, Shadow boxing in the dark." *Social Forces* 59: 335–75.

McHugh, Peter. 1968. *Defining the Situation*. Indianapolis: Bobbs-Merrill.

Meeker, B. J. and Weitzell-O'Neill, P. A. 1977. "Sex roles and interpersonal behavior in task-oriented groups." *American Sociological Review* 42: 91–105.

Merton, Robert K. 1975. "Structural analysis in sociology." In P. M. Blau (ed.) *Approaches to the Study of Social Structure*. New York: Free Press, pp. 21–52.

Mischel, Walter. 1966. "A social learning view of sex differences in behavior." In E. Maccoby (ed.) *The Development of Sex Differences*. Stanford, Calif.: Stanford University Press.

Pleck, Joseph and Sawyer, Jack (eds.) 1974. *Men and Masculinity*. Englewood Cliffs, NJ: Prentice-Hall.

Ridgeway, Cecilia L. 1982. "Status in groups: The importance of motivation." *American Sociological Review* 47: 76–88.

Rosenthal, Robert and Jacobson, Lenore. 1968. *Pygmalion in the Classroom*. New York: Holt, Rinehart and Winston.

Rossi, Alice. 1977. " A biosocial perspective on parenting." *Daedalus* 106(2): 1–32.

—— 1984. "Gender and parenthood." *American Sociological Review* 49: 1–19.

Rubin, Gayle. 1975. "The traffic in women: Notes on the political economy of sex." In R. R. Reiter (ed.) *Toward an Anthropology of Women*. New York: Monthly Review Press, pp. 157–210.

Stryker, Sheldon. 1980. *Symbolic Interactionism: A Social Structural View*. Menlo Park, Calif.: Benjamin-Cummings.

—— 1981. "Symbolic interactionism: Themes and variations." In M. Rosenberg and R. H. Turner (eds.) *Social Psychology: Sociological Perspectives*. New York: Basic Books.

Symons, Donald. 1979. *The Evolution of Human Sexuality*. New York: Oxford University Press.

Tavris, Carol and Offir, Carole. 1977. *The Longest War: Sex Differences in Perspective*. New York: Harcourt Brace Jovanovich.

Thompson, Martha E. 1981. "Sex differences: Differential access to power or sex-role socialization?" *Sex Roles* 7: 413–24.

Van den Berghe, Pierre L. 1979. *Human Family Systems: An Evolutionary View*. New York: Elsevier.

Wagner, David G., Ford, Rebecca S., and Ford, Thomas W. 1986. "Can gender inequalities be reduced?" *American Sociological Review* 51: 47–60.

Weitzman, Lenore J. 1979. *Sex Role Socialization*. Palo Alto, Calif.: Mayfield.

15 Social Structure and Self-Direction: A Comparative Analysis of the United States and Poland

Melvin Kohn and Kazimierz M. Slomczynski

Class, Stratification, and Psychological Functioning

We hypothesized [earlier in our book] that members of more "advantaged" social classes would be more intellectually flexible, would value self-direction more highly for their children, and would have more self-directed orientations to self and society than would members of less advantaged social classes. By "advantaged," we do *not* mean higher in social-stratification position, but rather advantaged in terms of the very definition of social class: having greater control over the means of production and greater control over the labor power of others.

Hence, we expected managers and (in the United States) employers, who have greatest control over the means of production and the labor power of others, to value self-direction most highly, to be the most intellectually flexible, and to have the most self-directed orientations of all the social classes. We expected manual workers, who have least control over the means of production and the labor power of others, to be at the other extreme. These expectations were strikingly confirmed.

We similarly expected men of higher social-stratification position to value self-direction more highly for their children, to be more intellectually flexible, and to have more self-directed orientations to self and society than do men of lower social-stratification position. These expectations, too, were strikingly confirmed. Moreover, we found that class and stratification each have at least some significant effect on psychological functioning, independent of one another.

Occupational Self-Direction as a Key Intervening Link

Why do men's positions in the social structure affect their psychological functioning? Our basic premise is that what is psychologically crucial to social-structural position is control over the conditions of one's life. We therefore advanced the same hypothesis for both class and stratification: that position in the social structure – whether

Reprinted from "A re-evaluation of the thesis and its implications for understanding the relationship between social structure and personality," in *Social Structure and Self-Direction: A Comparative Analysis of the United States and Poland*, Cambridge, Mass: Blackwell Publishers, 1990, pp. 232–6, 256–62.

the class structure or the stratification order – affects psychological functioning in large part because such position greatly affects one's opportunities to be self-directed in one's work. Thus, men who are more advantageously located in the class structure or have a higher position in the stratification order have greater opportunity to be self-directed in their work; the experience of occupational self-direction, in turn, profoundly affects their values, orientations, and cognitive functioning.

As we have noted, this is a very strong hypothesis. We defined social class in terms of control over the means of production and the labor power of others; but we hypothesize that the reason why social class affects values, intellectual flexibility, and self-directedness of orientation is that class position greatly affects how much control one has over the conditions of one's own work. We defined social stratification in terms of a hierarchy of power, privilege, and prestige, and we measured social-stratification position in terms of occupational status, educational attainment, and job income; but we hypothesize that stratification position affects psychological functioning not because of the status the job confers, or the income that it affords, but because higher stratification position affords greater opportunities for occupational self-direction. Even the education component of social stratification matters only in part because the educational process itself affects psychological functioning; education matters, too, because educational attainment greatly affects the substantive complexity of one's job.

We have found, in fact, that the relationships of both social class and social stratification with occupational self-direction are very strong in both countries. More advantageous positions in the class structure and higher positions in the stratification order markedly increase men's opportunities to be self-directed in their work. Moreover, and crucially, the exercise of occupational self-direction plays a major part in explaining the psychological effects of class and stratification. For both the United States and Poland, the effects of class and stratification position on parental valuation of self-direction, intellectual flexibility, and self-directedness of orientation are attributable in very substantial degree to occupational self-direction.

Directions of Effects in the Relationships of Social Structure and Personality

Our entire thesis rests on the premises that social-structural position not only is correlated with, but actually affects, men's opportunities to exercise self-direction in their work; and that doing self-directed work is not only correlated with, but actually affects, off-the-job psychological functioning.

Our analyses demonstrate that men's class and stratification positions do affect their exercise of occupational self-direction. These analyses further demonstrate that occupational self-direction decidedly affects men's values, intellectual flexibility, and self-directedness of orientation. There is solid evidence that self-direction in work leads one to value self-direction more highly, to be more intellectually flexible, and to have a more open, flexible orientation to society. Lack of opportunity for self-direction in work leads one to value conformity to external authority, to be less intellectually flexible, and to have a generally conformist orientation to self and society.

The analyses further indicate that, over time, personality also affects class placement and status attainment. The relationships are quintessentially reciprocal.

Occupational self-direction plays a pivotal role in explaining both the effects of social structure on personality and the effects of personality on position in the social structure. Men's positions in the class structure and in the stratification order affect their values, intellectual flexibility, and self-directedness of orientation primarily because class and stratification affect occupational self-direction, which in turn affects these facets of personality. These facets of personality affect men's attained positions in the class structure and the stratification order mainly because personality affects occupational self-direction.

Intergenerational Processes

We next hypothesized that the effects of social structure on job conditions, and of job conditions on *parental* values, would extend intergenerationally to *offspring's* values.

We found that, for both the United States and Poland, the class and stratification positions of the parental family have a considerable effect on the values of adolescent and young-adult offspring. The process is primarily one of family social-structural position affecting parents' opportunities for occupational self-direction, parents' experience of occupational self-direction affecting their values, and parents' values affecting their children's values.

Just as occupational self-direction affects their parents' values, so too does *educational* self-direction affect the values of adolescents and young adults. We see in this finding a confirmation of the larger thesis that the experience of self-direction in one's work, whether in paid employment or in schoolwork, has a major impact on values at every stage of life.

· · ·

The Exercise of Self-direction in Other Realms of Life

In principle, the exercise of self-direction in other realms of life should have precisely the same psychological consequences as in the occupational realm, albeit not necessarily to the same degree. This belief is based on our fundamental premise – that what is psychologically crucial about position in the social structure is control over the conditions of one's life. Two of our US analyses – one of housework, the other of schooling – are directly in point and thus worth summarizing.

The exercise of self-direction in housework

We see housework as work, in many respects similar to the work that is done in paid employment, even though unpaid, carried out in a decidedly different organizational context, and subject to greater discretionary control. Some of the pivotal conditions of work experienced in paid employment are experienced as well in housework; there are exact analogues between such job conditions as the substantive complexity of work experienced in paid employment and the substantive complexity of house-work.

In the follow-up interviews of 1974, Kohn and Schooler asked both husbands and wives about their household activities, attempting to map the "job conditions" of housework. From this information, Schooler et al. (1983) developed indices of the substantive complexity of housework, its routinization, and several other conditions of work as experienced in housework. They then assessed the reciprocal relation-ships between housework and psychological functioning, using models similar to those that we have employed in this book.

In the main, they found that the conditions of work that *wives* experience in housework affect their psychological functioning much as do similar conditions of work as experienced in paid employment. For example, doing substantively complex work in the household, just as in paid employment, is conducive to intellectual flexibility, to having a self-directed orientation, and to a sense of well-being. More-over, this is true both for women who are employed outside the home and for those who are not. Further (unpublished) analyses of employed women show that sub-stantively complex housework and substantively complex work in paid employment independently (and additively) facilitate intellectual flexibility and self-directedness of orientation.

For *husbands*, the substantive complexity of housework seems to have little psychological impact; instead, heaviness of housework seems to be more important – physically heavy work facilitating intellectual flexibility, self-directedness of orientation, and a sense of well-being. This is somewhat puzzling. One possible explanation is that men's housework is likely to be solely in the realm of working with "things" (maintenance of household equipment and repairs, rather than reading recipes or books on child-rearing) and focused on delineated "projects" rather than on the everyday activities of running a household. In such circumstances, to do physically heavy work may be tantamount to having a substantial involvement in housework. Moreover, housework does not have the same demand characteristics for husbands that it has for wives. As Schooler et al. conclude:

> For many women, household work has much the same demand characteristics as does the work required in paid employment; thus, housework is a structural imperative whose psychological effects are similar to those of the structural imperatives of paid employment. For most men, in contrast, housework exerts no such imperative and thus does not have psychological effects similar to those of paid employment.... It may only be when it is imperative that work demands be met that the conditions of work have their usual psychological effects. (1983: 260)

These findings tell us that doing self-directed work may have much the same psychological effects whether or not that work is performed in paid employment. The findings also caution, though, that we should not necessarily expect the exercise of self-direction to have much psychological import where the work or activity is not an imperative.

Educational self-direction

In another extrapolation from occupational self-direction to the exercise of self-direction in other institutional realms, Kohn and Schooler hypothesized that students' exercise of self-direction in schoolwork would have psychological consequences quite similar to those of adults' exercise of self-direction in paid employment. To test this hypothesis, they built a battery of questions about "educational self-direction" into the interview schedule used for the children of the men in the follow-up study, most of these offspring still being students at the time they were interviewed. Miller et al. (1985, 1986) used these data to develop a measurement model of educational self-direction, which we have borrowed for our analysis of the transmission of values.

Using indices based on this measurement model and measurement models of personality similar to those that we have developed for adult men, they assessed the reciprocal effects of educational self-direction and personality. The data being cross-sectional, and there being no sensible way to approximate longitudinal models, these assessments could not take account of either "earlier" educational self-direction or "earlier" psychological functioning. The models could and did, however, statistically control the *parents'* psychological functioning, thus taking into account, to some substantial degree, family-experiential and genetic determinants of personality.

From their analysis of the reciprocal effects of educational self-direction and intellectual flexibility, Miller et al. concluded:

> that the exercise of self-direction by students in their schoolwork has a decided impact on their cognitive functioning and that their cognitive functioning, in turn, has a decided impact on their exercise of self-direction in schoolwork. These conclusions apply both to secondary-school and to college students. More specifically, the impact of educational self-direction on intellectual functioning results mainly from the substantive complexity of students' schoolwork – its scope, difficulty, and challenge. (1985: 941)

After extending their analyses to include self-directedness of orientation and distress, they further concluded that:

> educational self-direction affects *non-cognitive* aspects of personality as well. In models that examine separately each of the two major non-cognitive dimensions of personality – self-directedness versus conformity of orientation, and sense of distress versus well-being – we find that educational self-direction affects both. Greater self-direction in schoolwork – in particular, substantively more complex schoolwork – increases the self-directedness of the student's orientation. Greater self-direction in schoolwork also *decreases* the student's sense of distress, with both substantively complex schoolwork and freedom from close supervision contributing to a greater sense of well-being. (1986: 388)

These findings, too, apply to both high-school and college students.
As Miller et al. conclude,

> the causal relationship between the exercise of self-direction in work and personality is remarkably similar for students and adult workers. The similarity of findings suggests some fundamental linkages between work, regardless of setting, and the personality of the worker. For schooling, as for paid employment, the opportunity to exercise self-direction in one's own work appears to have impressive psychological effects. This

constitutes a striking affirmation of the applicability of an interpretive model designed to explain the social psychology of work in paid employment to the social psychology of work in school. (1986: 388–9)

We would now add: these findings lend further credibility to the belief that the exercise of self-direction may have similar psychological consequences in *any* realm where the work or activity is "an imperative."

These findings also help explain the importance of educational attainment for values, cognitive functioning, and self-directedness of orientation. We have repeatedly found that educational attainment decidedly affects these facets of psychological functioning, independently of occupational position, both for the United States and for Poland. We have also found that a substantial part of education's psychological impact is indirect, through educational attainment affecting job conditions (particularly the substantive complexity of the work), which, in turn, affect personality. But not all of the effect of educational attainment on personality is indirect; some is direct, a long-lasting residue of the educational experience itself. We see in the "educational self-direction" findings an explanation of this long-lasting direct effect: the core of the educational experience is educational self-direction – learning to think for oneself. Education is (or can be) doubly powerful, by itself providing experience conducive to the experience of self-direction and by providing both the credentials and the learned capacities for occupational careers that continue to afford opportunity for self-directed activity.

Self-direction and Other Structural Imperatives of Work and of Life

Our thesis is not that occupational self-direction explains everything, nor even that the experience of self-direction in paid employment and in other institutional settings has profound psychological consequences, but that the explanation of the psychological effects of social structure must always lie in the proximate conditions of life attendant on social-structural position.

In our research on class and stratification, this assumption has led us to emphasize job conditions, particularly those job conditions that are conducive to or restrictive of the opportunity to exercise self-direction in one's work: the substantive complexity of that work, how closely it is supervised, and how routinized it is. We have demonstrated that occupational self-direction plays a key role in explaining the effects of social class and social stratification on values, intellectual flexibility, and self-directedness of orientation. Certainly, there are other linkages between social structure and personality as well. Occupational self-direction does not completely explain the impact of class and stratification even on these dimensions of psychological functioning. And, as we have seen, other conditions of work – job protections, for example – play an important role in the processes whereby class and stratification affect distress. Still, our analyses do demonstrate that job conditions, particularly even if not solely those job conditions facilitative of occupational self-direction, play a crucial role in the psychological impact of class and stratification.

It is entirely understandable that a principal intervening link from class and stratification to personality is to be found in the conditions of life experienced in paid employment. After all, class and stratification are closely tied to occupational roles; one might even think of occupational self-direction as the job-structure analogue of class and stratification. Even housework and schoolwork are analogous to work in paid employment: we conceptualize them as work; we hypothesize that exercising self-direction in such work will affect psychological functioning in much the same way as does exercising self-direction in paid employment; and we find this indeed to be the case.

Nevertheless, the findings for housework and for schooling suggest that what is important for valuing self-direction, for effective cognitive functioning, and for holding a self-directed orientation is not necessarily *occupational* self-direction, but the *experience* of self-direction, whether in paid employment or in other institutional realms.

But what happens when we move even further from "work," in whatever realm? Many other facets of social structure are not so closely tied to work and work-like activities as are class, stratification, and even housework and schooling. It may well be that proximate conditions of life other than those directly involved in the exercise of self-direction may better explain the psychological impact of race, gender, and other dimensions of social structure. And – we are again reminded of our findings for distress – the experience of self-direction is not necessarily central for all facets of psychological functioning. Clearly, the experience of self-direction has direct carry-over to valuing self-direction, to having a self-directed orientation, and to thinking for oneself, all of which are direct psychological analogues to being self-directed. It may well be that other proximate conditions of life are more important for facets of psychological functioning that are more remote from the experience of self-direction.

We therefore would not *necessarily* expect conditions determinative of the opportunity for self-direction to play so large a role in explaining the psychological effects of other facets of social structure as they do in explaining those of class and stratification. Nor would we necessarily expect conditions determinative of the opportunity for self-direction to play so large a role in explaining the effects of social structure on other facets of psychological functioning as they do for values, cognitive functioning, and self-directedness of orientation. We would certainly want to search for *other* proximate conditions that might play a role for other facets of social structure analogous to that played by occupational self-direction for class and stratification, and to search for other proximate conditions that help explain the relationships of social structure to facets of psychological functioning other than values, cognitive functioning, and self-directedness of orientation. The challenge is to discover these proximate conditions and to demonstrate how they link social-structural position to personality.

Our findings for class, for stratification, for housework, and for schooling, though, do suggest that, in examining the psychological impact of *any* social institution or any component of social structure, one should always ask whether and how people's positions might affect their opportunities for self-direction. The place to look would not necessarily be *occupational* self-direction, but self-direction in the particular institutional realm, whether or not the activities be thought of as "work." The possibility that self-direction might provide the interpretive key should certainly be explored, no matter which institution or which facet of social structure one considers.

It is as well to remember in this connection that the central component of occupational (and of educational) self-direction is neither freedom from close supervision, which is merely the absence of a condition that would limit the possibilities for exercising self-direction, nor non-routinized conditions, but the substantive complexity of the activity. It is by engaging in substantively complex activity that one learns to value self-direction, enhances one's intellectual flexibility, and develops a self-directed orientation to self and to society. Our hypothesis would be that substantively complex *activity*, whether in paid employment, in housework, in schoolwork, or in any other realm of life where such activity is sufficiently important to take on the quality of a "structural imperative" would have similar psychological consequences. Paid employment is not the only realm of life that affords (or restricts) opportunities for engaging in substantively complex activities. The experience of thinking for oneself is too important to personality ever to be overlooked.

References

Miller, Karen A., Kohn, Melvin L., and Schooler, Carmi. 1985. "Educational self-direction and the cognitive functioning of students." *Social Forces* 63: 923–44.

——, ——, and —— 1986. "Educational self-direction and personality." *American Sociological Review* 51: 372–90.

Schooler, Carmi, Kohn, Melvin L., Miller, Karen A., and Miller, Joanne. 1983. "Housework as work." In Melvin L. Kohn and Carmi Schooler, *Work and Personality: An Inquiry into the Impact of Social Stratification*. Norwood, NJ: Ablex, pp. 242–60.

16 Salvaging the Self

David Snow and Leon Anderson

To be homeless in America is not only to have fallen to the bottom of the status system; it is also to be confronted with gnawing doubts about self-worth and the meaning of existence. Such vexing concerns are not just the psychic fallout of having descended onto the streets, but are also stoked by encounters with the domiciled that constantly remind the homeless of where they stand in relation to others.

One such encounter occurred early in the course of our fieldwork. It was late afternoon, and the homeless were congregating in front of the Sally for dinner. A school bus approached that was packed with Anglo junior high school students being bused from an eastside barrio school to their upper-middle- and upper-class homes in the city's northwest neighborhoods. As the bus rolled by, a fusillade of coins came flying out the windows, as the students made obscene gestures and shouted, "Get a job." Some of the homeless gestured back, some scrambled for the scattered coins – mostly pennies, others angrily threw the coins at the bus, and a few seemed oblivious to the encounter. For the passing junior high schoolers, the exchange was harmless fun, a way to work off the restless energy built up in school; but for the homeless it was a stark reminder of their stigmatized status and of the extent to which they are the objects of negative attention.

Initially, we did not give much thought to this encounter. We were more interested in other issues and were neither fully aware of the frequency of such occurrences nor appreciative of their psychological consequences. We quickly came to learn, however, that this was hardly an isolated incident. The buses passed by the Sally every weekday afternoon during the school year; other domiciled citizens occasionally found pleasure in driving by and similarly hurling insults at the homeless and pennies at their feet; and . . . the hippie tramps and other homeless in the university area were derisively called "Drag worms," the police often harassed the homeless, and a number of neighborhoods took turns vilifying and derogating them.

Not all encounters with the domiciled are so stridently and intentionally demeaning, of course, but they are no less piercingly stigmatizing. One Saturday morning, for instance, as we walked with Willie Hastings and Ron Whitaker along a downtown street, a woman with a station wagon full of children drove by. As they passed, several of the children pointed at us and shouted, "Hey, Mama, look at the street people!" Ron responded angrily:

> "Mama, look at the street people!" You know, it pisses me off the way fucking thieves steal shit and they can still hold their heads high 'cause they got money. Sure, they have to go to prison sometimes, but when they're out, nobody looks down on them. But I wouldn't steal from nobody, and look how those kids stare at us!

Reprinted from *Down on Their Luck: A Study of Homeless Street People*, Berkeley: University of California Press, 1993, pp. 198–230.

The pain of being objects of curiosity and negative attention are experienced fairly regularly by the homeless, but they suffer just as frequently from what has been called "attention deprivation." In *The Pursuit of Attention*, Charles Derber commented that "members of the subordinate classes are regarded as less worthy of attention in relations with members of dominant classes and so are subjected to subtle yet systematic face-to-face deprivation" (1979: 42). For no one is Derber's observation more true than for the homeless, who are routinely ignored or avoided by the domiciled. As previously noted, pedestrians frequently avert their eyes when passing the homeless on the sidewalk, and they often hasten their pace and increase the distance between themselves and the homeless when they sense they may be targeted by a panhandler. Pedestrians sometimes go so far as to cross the street in order to avoid anticipated interaction with the homeless. Because of the fear and anxiety presumably engendered in the domiciled by actual or threatened contact with the homeless, efforts are often made at the community level, as we saw earlier, to regulate and segregate the homeless both spatially and institutionally. Although these avoidance rituals and segregative measures are not as overtly demeaning as the more active and immediate kinds of negative attention the homeless receive, they can be equally stigmatizing, for they also cast the homeless as objects of contamination. This, too, constitutes an assault upon the self, albeit a more subtle and perhaps more insidious one.

Occurring alongside the negative attention and attention deprivation the homeless experience are an array of gestures and acts that are frequently altruistic and clearly indicative of goodwill. People do on occasion give to panhandlers and beggars out of sincere concern rather than merely to get them off their backs. Domiciled citizens sometimes even provide assistance without being asked. One evening, for instance, we found Pat Manchester sitting on a bench near the university eating pizza. "Man, I was just sitting here," he told us, "and this dude walked up and gave me half a pizza and two dollar bills." Several of the students who worked at restaurants in the university area occasionally brought leftovers to Rhyming Mike and other hippie tramps. Other community members occasionally took street people to their home for a shower, dinner, and a good night's sleep. Even Jorge Herrera, who was nearly incoherent, appeared never to wash or bathe, and was covered with rashes and open sores, was the recipient of such assistance. Twice during our field research he appeared on the streets after a brief absence in clean clothes, shaved, and with a new haircut. When we asked about the changes in his appearance, he told us that someone had taken him home, cleaned him up, and let him spend the night. These kinds of unorganized, sporadic gestures of goodwill clearly facilitate the survival of some of the homeless, but the numbers they touch in comparison to those in need are minuscule. Nor do they occur in sufficient quantity or consistently enough to neutralize the stigmatizing and demeaning consequences of not only being on the streets but being objects of negative attention or little attention at all.

In addition to those who make sporadic gestures of goodwill, thousands of domiciled citizens devote occasional time and energy to serving the homeless in an organized fashion in churches, soup kitchens, and shelters. Angels House kitchen was staffed in part by such volunteers, and their support was essential to the operation of the kitchen. Yet the relationship between these well-meaning volunteers and the homeless is highly structured and sanitized. The volunteers typically prepare sandwiches and other foods in a separate area from the homeless or encounter them only across the divide of a serving counter that underscores the distance between the servers and the served. Thus, however sincere and helpful the efforts of domiciled volunteers, the structure of their encounters with the homeless often underscores the immense status differences and thereby reminds the homeless again of where they stand in relation to others.

Gestures of goodwill toward the homeless and the kinds of attention they receive are not constant over time. Instead, they tend to follow an annual cycle, with sympathetic interest increasing with the first cold snap in the fall and reaching its zenith during the Christmas holiday season . . . . Moreover, once Christmas passes, coverage declines precipitously. This same pattern was seen in Austin in the activities both of the media and of many community residents. At times this expression of holiday concern reached almost comical dimensions. One Thanksgiving Day, for instance, the homeless were inundated with food. In the morning several domiciled citizens came to the Labor Corner to hand out sandwiches, and a few gave away whole turkeys, assuming they would be devoured on the spot. The Assembly of God Church served a large meal around noon, and the Salvation Army served its traditional Thanksgiving meal in midafternoon. At one point in the early afternoon the Sally officials appeared to be worried that only a few people would show up for the meal. Newspaper and television reporters lingered around the Sally much of the afternoon, taking pictures and interviewing both officials and street people for stories that would be aired that evening or would appear in the morning newspaper.

After Christmas, charitable interest in the homeless declined dramatically. The public span of sympathy seemed to have run its course. Thus, except for a two- to three-month period, the homeless tend to be recipients only of negative attention, ignored altogether, or dealt with in a segregated and sanitized fashion that underscores their stigmatized status.

The task the homeless face of salvaging the self is not easy, especially since wherever they turn they are reminded that they are at the very bottom of the status system. As Sonny McCallister lamented shortly after he became homeless, "The hardest thing's been getting used to the way people look down on street people. It's real hard to feel good about yourself when almost everyone you see is looking down on you." Tom Fisk, who had been on the streets longer, agreed. But he said that he had become more calloused over time:

> I used to let it bother me when people stared at me while I was trying to sleep on the roof of my car or change clothes out of my trunk, but I don't let it get to me anymore. I mean, they don't know who I am, so what gives them the right to judge me? I know I'm okay.

But there was equivocation and uncertainty in his voice. Moreover, even if he no longer felt the stares and comments of others, he still had to make sense of the distance between himself and them.

How, then, do the homeless deal with the negative attention they receive or the indifference they encounter as they struggle to survive materially? How do they salvage their selves? And to what extent do the webs of meaning they spin and the personal identities they construct vary with patterns of adaptation? We address these questions in the remainder of the chapter by considering two kinds of meaning:

existential and identity-oriented. The former term refers to the kinds of accounts the homeless invoke in order to make sense of their plight; the latter refers to the kinds of meaning they attach to self in interactions with others.

Making Sense of the Plight of Homelessness

The plight of human beings brought face-to-face with the meaning of their existence by suffocating social structures, unanticipated turns of events, dehumanizing living conditions, or the specter of death has been a long and persistent theme in both literature and philosophy. Underlying this strand of writing, generally discussed under the rubric of existentialism, are two consistent themes: that the quest for meaning, while an ongoing challenge in everyday life, is particularly pressing for those individuals whose routines and expectations have been disrupted; and that the burden of finding meaning in such disruptive moments rests on the shoulders of the individual. From this perspective, meaning is not an essence that inheres in a particular object or situation, but a construction or imputation; and the primary architects of such constructions are human actors. The burden of infusing problematic situations with meaning is heavier for some actors than for others, however. Certainly this is true of the homeless, with their pariah-like status, limited resources, and the often demeaning treatment they receive.

How do the homeless carve out a sense of meaning in the seemingly insane and meaningless situation in which they find themselves? Are they able to make sense of their plight in a fashion that helps to salvage the self?

Some are able to do so and others are not. Many of the homeless invoke causal accounts of their situation that infuse it with meaning and rescue the self; others abandon both concerns by drifting into the world of alcoholism or into an alternative reality that is in this world but not of it and that is often treated as symptomatic of insanity by those not privy to it. Of the two lines of response, the first is clearly the most pronounced.

Invoking Causal Accounts

By causal accounts we refer to the reasons people give to render understandable their behavior or the situations in which they find themselves. Such accounts are essentially common-sense attributions that are invoked in order to explain some problematic action or situation. Whether such accounts seem reasonable to an observer is irrelevant; what is at issue is their meaningfulness to the actor.

These explanatory accounts are seldom new constructions. Rather, they are likely to be variants of folk understandings or aphorisms that are invoked from time to time by many citizens and thus constitute part of a larger cultural vocabulary. This view of causal accounts accords with the contention that culture can best be thought of as a repertoire or "'tool kit' of symbols, stories, rituals, and world views which people use in varying configurations to solve different kinds of problems" (Swidler 1986: 273). These stories, symbols, or accounts are not pulled out of that cultural took kit at random, however. Instead, the appropriation and articulation process is driven by some pressing problem or imperative. In the case of the homeless, that predicament is the existential need to infuse their situation with a sense of meaning that helps to salvage the self. In the service of that imperative, three folk adages or accounts surfaced rather widely and frequently among the homeless in Austin in their conversations with us and each other. One says, "I'm down on my luck." Another reminds us, "What goes around, comes around." And the third says, "I've paid my dues."

"I'm down on my luck"

The term *luck*, which most citizens invoke from time to time to account for unanticipated happenings in their lives, is generally reserved for events that influence the individual's life but are thought to be beyond his or her control. To assert that "I'm down on my luck," then, is to attribute my plight to misfortune, to chance. For the homeless, such an attribution not only helps to make sense of their situation, but it does so in a manner that is psychologically functional in two ways: it exempts the homeless from responsibility for their plight, and it leaves open the possibility of a better future.

Exemption from personal responsibility was a consistent theme in the causal accounts we overheard. As Willie Hastings asserted aggressively in discussing with Ron Whitaker and us the negative attention heaped on all of us just a few minutes earlier by the children in the passing car:

> Shit, it ain't my fault I'm on the streets. I didn't choose to become homeless. I just had a lot of bad luck. And that ain't my fault. Hell, who knows? Those kids and their old lady might get unlucky and wake up on the streets someday. It can happen to anyone, you know!

Ron chipped in:

> Yeah, a lot of people think we're lazy, that we don't give a shit, that this is what we want. But that sure in hell ain't so – at least not for me. It wasn't my fault I lost my job in Denver. If I'd been working down the street, maybe I'd still be there. I was just at the wrong place at the wrong time. Like Willie said, some people just ain't got no luck!

Sonny McCallister, Tom Fisk, Tony Jones, Tanner Sutton, and Hoyt Page would all have agreed, in large part because their recently dislocated or straddler status makes them take street life less for granted than the outsiders do and therefore prompts them to try to explain their situation. But why invoke luck? Why not fix the blame for their plight on more direct, tangible factors, such as family discord, low wages, or being laid off? Not only are such biographic and structural factors clearly operative in their lives, but reference to them can also exempt people from personal responsibility for their plight. After all, it was not Tony Jones's fault that he lost his job as a security guard at a Chicago steel mill when the plant cut back. Yet, although he referred to this event as the one that triggered his descent onto the streets, he still maintained that he was primarily the victim of "bad luck" rather than less mysterious structural forces that clearly intruded into his life. Apparently, he felt that had he chanced to work at a different job or in a different factory, his fate would have been different.

The same logic is evident in Hoyt's efforts to make sense of his situation. His biography is strewn with a host of factors not of his own doing, such as having been orphaned and not having received proper attention for a learning disorder, which could have been woven into a responsibility-free account for being homeless. Yet, he too often said that he was simply "down on my luck."

This tendency to cling to the luck factor in lieu of structural or biographic accounts of homelessness does not stem from ignorance about these other factors or from false consciousness regarding their causal influence.... The homeless often name structural and biographic factors when discussing the reasons for their home-lessness. But the bad-luck account more readily allows for the possibility of a better day down the road. The victim of bad luck can become the recipient of good luck. "Luck changes," as we were frequently reminded. So, too, do structural trends and biographic experiences, but perhaps not so readily or positively from the standpoint of the homeless. Luck is also more fickle and mysterious, and its effects are sup-posedly distributed more randomly across the social order than are the effects of most structural trends. For good reason, then, some of the homeless cling to the luck factor.

Yet, the lives of most homeless are devoid of much good fortune, as is clear from the biographies of virtually all of our key informants. Why, then, do some of the homeless talk as if good luck is about to come their way? The answer resides in two other frequently invoked causal accounts that are intertwined with the luck factor: "What goes around, comes around," and "I've paid my dues."

"What goes around, comes around"

... Insofar as there is a moral code affecting interpersonal relations on the streets, it is manifested in the phrase, "What goes around, comes around." But the relevance of this phrase is not confined solely to the interpersonal domain. It is also brought into service with respect to the issue of meaning in general and the luck factor in particular.

Regarding the former, the contention that "what goes around, comes around" suggests a cyclical rather than linear conception of the process by which events unfold. This circularity implies, among other things, a transposition of opposites at some point in the life course. Biblical examples of such transpositions abound, as in the New Testament declarations that "The last shall be first and the first last" and "The meek shall inherit the earth." Although few homeless harbor realistic thoughts of such dramatic transpositions, many do assume that things will get better because "what goes around, comes around."

This logic also holds for luck. Thus, if a person has been down on his or her luck, it follows that the person's luck is subject to change. Hoyt, among others, talked as though he believed this proposition. "Look," he told us one evening over dinner and a few beers at a local steak house:

> I've been down on my luck for so damn long, it's got to change.... Like I said before, I believe what goes around, comes around, so I'm due a run of good luck, don't you think?

We nodded in agreement, but not without wondering how strongly Hoyt and others actually believed in the presumed link between luck and the cyclical principle of "what goes around, comes around." Whatever the answer, there is certainly good reason for harboring such a belief, for it introduces a ray of hope into a dismal situation and thereby infuses it with meaning of the kind that helps keep the self afloat.

"I've paid my dues"

This linkage is buttressed further by the third frequently articulated causal account: "I've paid my dues." To invoke this saying is to assert, as Marilyn Fisch often did in her more sober moments, that "I deserve better" after "what I've been through" or "what I've done." The phrase implies that if there are preconditions for a run of good luck, then those conditions have been met. Thus, Gypsy Bill told us one afternoon that he felt his luck was about to change as he was fantasizing about coming into some money. "You may think I'm crazy," he said, "but it's this feeling I've got. Besides, I deserve it 'cause I've paid my dues." A street acquaintance of Gypsy's, a man who fancied himself as "a great blues harmonica player," broke in:

> Yeah, man, I know what you mean. I was playing the blues on Bleeker Street once when Jeff Beck comes by and tells me I'm the best blues harmonica player he's ever heard. "Where do you live?" he asks me. And I tell him, "Here on this sidewalk, and I sleep in the subways." And he asks me, "What do you want from me?" And I tell him, "Nothing, man. A handshake." And he reaches into his pocket and pulls out a hundred-dollar bill and gives it to me 'cause I had it coming! I know the blues, man. I live them. I sleep on the fucking street, paying my dues. That's why no one plays the blues like me!

He then pointed to the knapsack on his back and asked if we knew what was in it. We shook our heads, and he said, "My jeans, man. I fucking pissed in 'em last night, I was so drunk. That's what I'm saying: I know the blues, man! I've paid my dues."

So a streak of good luck, however fleeting, or anticipation of such a streak, albeit a more sustained one, is rationalized in terms of the hardships endured. The more a person has suffered, the greater the dues that have been paid and the more, therefore, a run of good luck is deserved. Perhaps this is why some of those with the longest stretches of time on the streets, namely, outsiders, were heard to assert more often than others that "I've paid my dues." As Shotgun explained in one of his moments of sobriety, "I been on the streets for about fifteen years.... I've rode the boxcars and slept out in the wintertime. That's how you pay your dues." Yet, many outsiders do not often invoke this phrase. The reason, we suspect, is that they have been down on their luck for so long that their current fate seems impervious to change and they have therefore resigned themselves to life on the streets. Those who assert that they've paid their dues, however, invoke the phrase in service of the luck factor and the corollary principle of what goes around, comes around. And for good reason. Together, these accounts both exempt the homeless from responsibility for their plight and hold the door ajar for a change in luck.

Avenues of Escape: Alcohol and Alternative Realities

Not all homeless attend to the existential business of making sense of their situation by invoking conventional folk understandings. Some individuals may have been on the streets too long or have endured too many hardships, experienced too many frustrations, and suffered too many insults to the self to bother any longer with the accounting process. Instead, they gradually drift down alternative avenues for dealing with the oppressive realities of street life and the resultant brutalization of the self. These avenues, while stigmatized by the larger culture, are often consonant with the subculture of street life itself. One such avenue is alcoholism; the other involves the creation or adoption of alternative realities frequently associated with mental illness.

The suggestion that some of the homeless drift into alcoholism and mental illness as a consequence of the hopeless and demeaning situation in which they find themselves runs counter to the tendency to treat these conditions as precipitants of homelessness or at least as disabilities that increase vulnerability to becoming homeless. That this presumed causal connection holds for some of the homeless is no doubt true, but it is also true that alcoholism and mental illness sometimes function as means of coping psychologically with the traumas of street life. Clearly, they do not guarantee literal escape from the streets, but they can serve as insulation from further psychic assaults and thereby create illusions of personal autonomy and well-being. How often this process occurs is unclear, but that it is not an infrequent occurrence we are certain.

Evidence of this process is most pronounced with respect to the use of alcohol and drugs. This is clearly seen when we consider the mean scores for alcohol use among the different types of homeless in the field sample. Recalling that a mean score of 0 indicates infrequent use or engagement, whereas a score approaching 2 indicates frequent use, a mean score of 0.23 for the recently dislocated suggests that relatively few of the homeless are chronic alcoholics when they first hit the streets. Furthermore, the hippie tramps and traditional and redneck bums have the highest mean scores for alcohol use (1.33, 1.67, and 2.00, respectively), making it appear that the general tendency is for alcohol use to increase during the drift toward outsiderhood. Since outsiders have been on the streets much longer than the recently dislocated, it also follows that alcohol use is in part a function of time on the streets. Thus, the longer the time on the streets, the greater the probability of chronic alcohol use. The same general tendency also holds for drug use, although not quite as strongly.

Evidence of this tendency for substance use to escalate with increasing time on the streets also comes from our key informants. Hoyt is an avowed alcoholic, but he reminded us a number of times that he did not come to the streets as a chronic alcoholic. Instead, his "drinking problem," as he referred to it, developed over the course of eleven years on and off the streets. He began with drugs, primarily marijuana and speed, but gradually came to use alcohol more heavily because it was cheaper and "didn't get you into as much trouble with the law." During the past several years, he has used alcohol almost exclusively and has recently come to the realization that he has "a serious drinking problem" that must be attended to if he is to get off the streets permanently. Marilyn's experience with alcohol is similar. As she explained one morning over coffee:

> I didn't have much of a drinking problem before I landed on the streets. But I found it all so depressing. And everybody else was drinking and asking me to drink. So I said, "Why not?" I mean, what did I have to lose? Everything was so depressing. Drinking sure couldn't make it any worse!

Her claim of gradually increasing levels of drinking was substantiated by our frequent contacts with her for over two years. When we first met her, Marilyn, like many of the homeless, was a spree or binge drinker, but as time passed the period between the sprees became shorter and her drinking became more chronic, all of which was manifested in her increasingly emaciated, weathered, and scarred physical appearance. The experiences of Shotgun, Gypsy, Nona George, and JJ and Indio, as well as other outsiders we met, are all quite similar: increasing use of alcohol with the passage of time, resulting eventually in apparent physiological and psychological dependence.

Why this drift toward alcohol? Reasonable explanations are not hard to come by. One is subcultural. Drinking is, after all, one of the more salient features of street life, and, as Marilyn found, there is often normative pressure to join in either by sharing what one has or by drinking a portion of what has been offered. Boredom is another explanatory factor. Idleness is also a salient characteristic of street life, as the one thing many homeless have to fritter away is unscheduled time. But the explanatory factor that was most often cited by the homeless we came to know is psychological. In a word, it is escape – not so much from boredom as from the travails and miseries of street life, or from the past, or perhaps from both. Hoyt often noted how his reach for the bottle was driven by the need to escape the moment, to get away from the wretchedness and humiliation of his current experience. Shelters, he told us, activated this urge more than anything else:

> You're in there, with lotsa people you don't know. They look like shit and smell like it, too. And they remind you of where you are and who you are. It ain't pleasant. So you begin to crave a drink.

Hoyt was also aware that the drive to drink was sometimes prompted by the need to escape thoughts of the past. He told us once of a former street friend in Dallas who initially drank to obliterate the pain he experienced whenever he thought about the daughter he had lost through divorce:

> He did what a lot of us do when you think about something like that or about where you are now. You think about it and you get pissed off about it and you get drunk and forget about it. At least for a while, and then you start all over. It's just a cycle, a vicious cycle.

Hoyt, JJ, Indio, Nona, Marilyn, Gypsy, and others were all caught in this vicious cycle. Most were not ignorant about what they were doing, but they knew that they were ensnarled in a "catch-22" of sorts. On the one hand, there was awareness of both the physiological and the psychological hazards of chronic drinking; on the other hand, alcohol was often seen as the only avenue for escaping the traumas of the past or present and the meaningless of it all. "At times," as Hoyt once put it, "it seems like the only way out."

Viewed in this light, drinking clearly functions for some of the homeless as adaptive behavior that provides a psychological antidote to the pains of existence. For the chronic drinkers, to be sure, it is an adaptive behavior that has gotten out of control. But it did not begin that way for all of them. Much of the drinking behavior on the streets, including that which has gone awry, thus constitutes a variant of behaviors Erving Goffman has called "secondary adjustments," ways in which individuals who find themselves trapped in demeaning social contexts attempt to stand "apart from the role and the self" implied. They are "undertakings that provide something for the individual to lose himself in, temporarily blotting out all sense of the environment which, and in which, he must abide" (Goffman 1961: 309).

Like much of the drinking that occurs on the streets, some of the behaviors and verbalizations customarily read as symptomatic of mental illness can be construed as forms of adaptive behavior. Undoubtedly, some of the homeless who might be diagnosed as mentally ill were that way prior to their descent onto the streets, but others evince symptoms of such illness as a result of the trauma of living on the streets. The symptoms we refer to are not those of depression and demoralization, which are understandably widespread on the streets, but more "bizarre" patterns of thought and behavior that are less prevalent but more conspicuous. These include auditory and visual hallucinations, that is, hearing or seeing things to which others are not privy; conspiratorial delusions, such as the belief that others are talking about you or are out to get you; grandiose delusions, like the belief that you have extraordinary powers, insights, or contacts; and the public verbalization of these hallucinations and delusions as well as audible conversations with others not present. Such beliefs and behaviors suggest an alternative inner reality that is neither publicly shared nor fully accessible to others and is therefore "out of this world." Although such alternative realities frequently invite both folk labels of "nuts" and "crazy" and clinical labels of schizophrenia and paranoia, they may often be quite functional for some individuals who find themselves in a demeaning and inhumane context in which they are the frequent objects of negative attention or attention deprivation. After all, if you are rarely the recipient of any positive attention or are ignored altogether, creating and retreating into a private reality that grants you privileged insights and special status may be more adaptive than it appears at first glance.

Certainly this appeared to be the case with Tanner Sutton, the badly burned and disfigured Sally street employee who was preoccupied with the occult and higher forms of consciousness and who claimed to be a "spiritually gifted person" with "special mystical powers" that enabled him "to read people," live in "many different dimensions of space," and "look into the future when humans will be transformed into another life form." Taken at face value, such claims appear to be outlandish and perhaps even symptomatic of psychosis. Even some of Tanner's street associates regarded him as "far out." Yet Tanner was able to function quite resourcefully on the streets, as was evidenced by his ability to discharge his duties at the Sally. Moreover, however weird or bizarre Tanner's claims, to evaluate him in terms of their veracity misses the point. Tanner's biography and the context in which he found himself make the issue one not of verisimilitude but of psychological functionality. For Tanner, as for others who appear to have lodged their self in some alternative reality, that reality provides a psychological alternative to the material world in which they find themselves, thus insulating them from further psychic assaults emanating from that world and providing an alternative source of self-regard.

Such secondary adjustments, albeit psychological ones, are not fashioned in a highly conscious and intentional manner. Instead, they are drifted into unwittingly over a period of time in much the same way some of the homeless drift into chronic alcohol use. Evidence of this drifting process was clear in the life histories of both Tanner and Lance McCay. Lance's case is particularly revealing: he was admittedly and visibly mentally ill at the time we met him, but his behavior became increasingly bizarre over the two-year period we maintained contact with him. More often than not, such changes seemed to be triggered by an abbreviated visit home, after which he could be seen ranting and raving about his parents, incessantly talking to himself and engaging in more delusional thinking. It seemed clear to us that such outbursts were in large part defensive reactions to feelings of abandonment and exclusion that were magnified by the attention deprivation he experienced on the streets. Not only did we rarely see him conversing with others who were physically present, but other people made a point of avoiding him. In response, Lance retreated into his inner world. That world consisted of conspiratorial thoughts and behaviors, as when he wrote to his mother that he was considering moving to Billings, Montana, where "people won't be prejudiced against me because they won't even know me," as well as grandiose delusions, such as his claim to be "a writer like Hemingway."

Such statements and claims may appear to be strikingly outlandish at first glance, but their strangeness dissipates when they are put in context. For example, it seems less odd that Lance's talk and behavior were peppered with examples of paranoia and delusional thinking when it is remembered that he was frequently rejected and excluded. Moreover, these two sets of observations were linked together in a kind of interactive, self-fulfilling dynamic: the longer Lance was on the streets and the more he experienced rejection and exclusion, the more pronounced his conspiratorial and delusional thinking became and the more bizarre he appeared.

The point is that the bizarre patterns of thought and behavior exhibited by Tanner and Lance, among others, and commonly taken as symptomatic of mental illness can be understood, in part, in terms of their psychological survival value. This is not to suggest that individuals like Lance are not mentally ill in a clinical sense. But to frame their mental functioning and the realities they identify with solely in that fashion is to gloss the extent to which these alternative realities can function as adaptive shields against the painful realities of street life and thereby render superfluous the need to account for that existence in terms of conventional folk understandings. Like alcohol, then, bizarre, alternative realities can provide psychological escape from a brutalizing world out of which physical escape seems unlikely.

Constructing Identity-Oriented Meaning

However the homeless deal with the issue of existential meaning, whether by stringing together causal accounts borrowed from conventional cultural vocabularies or by seeking refuge in alcohol, drugs, or alternative realities, they are still confronted with establishing who they are in the course of interaction with others, for interaction between two or more individuals minimally requires that they be situated or placed as social objects. In other words, situationally specific identities must be established. Such identities can be established in two ways: they can be attributed or imputed by others, or they can be claimed or asserted by the actor. The former can be thought of as social or role identities in that they are imputations based primarily on information gleaned from the appearance or behavior of others and from the time and location of their action, as when children in a passing car look out the window and yell, "Hey, Mama, look at the street people!" or when junior high school students yell out the windows of their school bus to the homeless lining up for dinner in front of the Sally, "Get a job, you bums!" In each case, the homeless in question have been situated as social objects and thus assigned social identities.

When individuals claim or assert an identity, by contrast, they attribute meaning to themselves. Such self-attributions can be thought of as personal identities rather than social identities, in that they are self-designations brought into play or avowed during the course of actual or anticipated interaction with others. Personal identities may be consistent with imputed social identities, as when Shotgun claims to be "a tramp," or inconsistent, as when Tony Jones yells back to the passing junior high schoolers, "Fuck you, I ain't no lazy bum!" The presented personal identities of individuals who are frequent objects of negative attention or attention deprivation, as are the homeless, can be especially revealing, because they offer a glimpse of how those people deal interactionally with their pariah-like status and the demeaning social identities into which they are frequently cast. Personal identities thus provide further insight into the ways the homeless attempt to salvage the self.

What, then, are the personal identities that the homeless construct and negotiate when in interaction with others? Are they merely a reflection of the highly stereotypic and stigmatized identities attributed to them, or do they reflect a more positive sense of self or at least an attempt to carve out and sustain a less demeaning self-conception?

The construction of personal identity typically involves a number of complementary activities: (a) procurement and arrangement of physical settings and props; (b) cosmetic face work or the arrangement of personal appearance; (c) selective association with other individuals and groups; and (d) verbal construction and assertion of personal identity. Although some of the homeless engage in conscious manipulation of props and appearance – for example, Pushcart, with his fully loaded shopping cart, and Shotgun, who fancies himself a con artist – most do not resort to such measures. Instead, the primary means by which the homeless announce their personal identities is verbal. They engage, in other words, in a good bit of identity talk. This is understandable, since the homeless seldom have the financial or social resources to pursue the other identity construction activities. Additionally, since the structure of their daily routines ensures that they spend a great deal of time waiting here and there, they have ample opportunity to converse with each other.

Sprinkled throughout these conversations with each other, as well as those with agency personnel and, occasionally, with the domiciled, are numerous examples of identity talk. Inspection of the instances of the identity talk to which we were privy yielded three generic patterns: (1) distancing; (2) embracement; and (3) fictive storytelling. Each pattern was found to contain several subtypes that tend to vary in use according to whether the speaker is recently dislocated, a straddler, or an outsider. We elaborate in turn each of the generic patterns, their varieties, and how they vary in use among the different types of homeless.

Distancing

When individuals have to enact roles, associate with others, or utilize institutions that imply social identities inconsistent with their actual or desired self-conceptions, they often attempt to distance themselves from those roles, associations, or institutions. A substantial proportion of the identity talk we recorded was consciously focused on distancing from other homeless individuals, from street and occupational roles, and from the caretaker agencies servicing the homeless. Nearly a third of the identity statements were of this variety.

Associational distancing

Since a claim to a particular self is partly contingent on the imputed social identities of the person's associates, one way people can substantiate that claim when their associates are negatively evaluated is to distance themselves from those associates. This distancing technique manifested itself in two ways among the homeless: disassociation from the homeless as a general social category, and disassociation from specific groupings of homeless individuals.

Categoric associational distancing was particularly evident among the recently dislocated. Illustrative is Tony Jones's comment in response to our initial query about life on the streets:

> I'm not like the other guys who hang out down at the Sally. If you want to know about street people, I can tell you about them; but you can't really learn about street people from studying me, because I'm different.

Such categorical distancing also occurred among those individuals who saw themselves as on the verge of getting off the street. After securing two jobs in the hope of raising enough money to rent an apartment, Ron Whitaker indicated, for example, that he was different from other street people. "They've gotten used to living on the streets and they're satisfied with it, but not me!" he told us. "Next to my salvation, getting off the streets is the most important thing in my life." This variety of categorical distancing was particularly pronounced among homeless individuals who had taken jobs at the Sally and thus had one foot off the streets. These individuals were frequently criticized by other homeless for their condescending attitude. As Marilyn put it, "As soon as these guys get inside, they're better than the rest of us. They've been out on the streets for years, and as soon as they're inside, they forget it."

Among the outsiders, who had been on the streets for some time and who appeared firmly rooted in that life-style, there were few examples of categorical distancing. Instead, these individuals frequently distinguished themselves from other groups of homeless. This form of associational distancing was most conspicuous among those, such as the hippie tramps and redneck bums, who were not regular social-service or shelter users and who saw themselves as especially independent and resourceful. These individuals not only wasted little time in pointing out that they were "not like those Sally users," but were also given to derogating the more institutionally dependent. Indeed, although they are among the furthest removed from a middle-class life-style, they sound at times much like middle-class citizens berating welfare recipients. As Marilyn explained, "A lot of these people staying at the Sally, they're reruns. Every day they're wanting something. People get tired of giving. All you hear is gimme, gimme. And we transients are getting sick of it."

Role Distancing

Role distancing, the second form of distancing employed by the homeless, involves a self-conscious attempt to foster the impression of a lack of commitment or attachment to a particular role in order to deny the self implied. Thus, when individuals find themselves cast into roles in which the social identities implied are inconsistent with desired or actual self-conceptions, role distancing is likely to occur. Since the homeless routinely find themselves being cast into or enacting low-status, negatively evaluated roles, it should not be surprising that many of them attempt to disassociate themselves from those roles.

As did associational distancing, role distancing manifested itself in two ways: distancing from the general role of street person, and distancing from specific occupational roles. The former, which is also a type of categorical distancing, was particularly evident among the recently dislocated. It was not uncommon for these individuals to state explicitly that they should "not be mistaken as a typical street person." Role distancing of the less categoric and more situationally specific type was most evident among those who performed day labor, such as painters' helpers, hod carriers, warehouse and van unloaders, and those in unskilled service occupations such as dishwashing and janitorial work. As we saw earlier, the majority of the homeless we encountered would avail themselves of such job opportunities, but they seldom did so enthusiastically, since the jobs offered low status and low wages. This was especially true of the straddlers and some of the outsiders, who frequently reminded others of their disdain for such jobs and of the belief that they deserved better, as exemplified by the remarks of a drunk young man who had worked the previous day as a painter's helper: "I made $36.00 off the Labor Corner, but it was just nigger work. I'm 24 years old, man. I deserve better than that."

Similar distancing laments were frequently voiced over the disparity between job demands and wages. We were conversing with a small gathering of homeless men on a Sunday afternoon, for example, when one of them revealed that earlier in the day he had turned down a job to carry shingles up a ladder for $4.00 an hour because he found it demeaning to "do that hard a work for that low a pay." Since day-labor jobs seldom last for more than six hours, perhaps not much is lost monetarily in foregoing such jobs in comparison to what can be gained in pride. But even when the ratio of dollars to pride appears to make rejection costly, as in the case of permanent jobs, dissatisfaction with the low status of menial jobs may prod some homeless individuals to engage in the ultimate form of role distancing by quitting currently held jobs. As Ron Whitaker recounted the day after he quit in the middle of his shift as a dishwasher at a local restaurant:

> My boss told me, "You can't walk out on me." And I told her, "Fuck you, just watch me. I'm gonna walk out of here right now." And I did. "You can't walk out on me," she said. I said, "Fuck you, I'm gone."

The foregoing illustrations suggest that the social identities lodged in available work roles are frequently inconsistent with the desired or idealized self-conceptions of some of the homeless. Consequently, "bitching about," "turning down," and even "blowing off" such work may function as a means of social-identity disavowal, on the one hand, and personal-identity assertion on the other. Such techniques provide a way of saying, "Hey, I have some pride. I'm in control. I'm my own person." This is especially the case among those individuals for whom such work is no longer just a stopgap measure but an apparently permanent feature of their lives.

Institutional distancing

An equally prevalent distancing technique involved the derogation of the caretaker agencies that attended to the needs of the homeless. The agency that was the most frequent object of these harangues was the Sally. Many of the homeless who used it described it as a greedy corporation run by inhumane personnel more interested in lining their own pockets than in serving the needy. Willie Hastings claimed, for example, that "the major is money-hungry and feeds people the cheapest way he can. He never talks to people except to gripe at them." He then added that the "Sally is supposed to be a Christian organization, but it doesn't have a Christian spirit. It looks down on people.... The Salvation Army is a national business that is more worried about making money than helping people." Ron Whitaker concurred, noting on another occasion that the "Sally here doesn't nearly do as much as it could for people. The people who work there take bags of groceries and put them in their cars. People donate to the Sally, and then the workers there cream off the best." Another straddler told us after he had spent several nights at the winter shelter, "If you spend a week here, you'll see how come people lose hope. You're treated just like an animal."

Because the Salvation Army is the only local facility that provides free shelter, breakfast, and dinner, attention is understandably focused on it. But that the Sally would be frequently derogated by the people whose survival it facilitates may appear puzzling at first glance, especially given its highly accommodative orientation. The answer lies in part in the organization and dissemination of its services. Clients are processed in an impersonal, highly structured assembly line-like fashion. The result is a leveling of individual differences and a decline in personal autonomy. Bitching and complaining about such settings create psychic distance from the self implied and secure a modicum of personal autonomy. This variety of distancing, though observable among all of the homeless, was most prevalent among the straddlers and outsiders. Since these individuals have used street agencies over a longer period of time, their self-concepts are more deeply implicated in them, thus necessitating distancing from those institutions and the self implied. Criticizing the Sally, then, provides some users with a means of dealing with the implications of their dependency on it. It is, in short, a way of presenting and sustaining a somewhat contrary personal identity.

Thus far we have elaborated how some of the homeless distance themselves from other homeless individuals, from general and specific roles, and from the institutions that deal with them. Such distancing behavior and talk represent attempts to salvage a measure of self-worth. In the process, of course, the homeless are asserting more favorable personal identities. Not all homeless individuals engage in similar distancing behavior and talk, however. As is indicated in table 16.1, which summarizes the foregoing observations, categorical distancing tends to be concentrated among the recently dislocated. Among those who are more firmly entrenched in street life, distancing tends to be confined to distinguishing themselves from specific groups of

Table 16.1   Types of distancing, by type of homeless*

Types of homeless	Categoric distancing[a] (N: 16) %	Specific distancing[b] (N: 23) %	Institutional distancing[c] (N: 23) %
Recently dislocated	68.8	—	8.7
Straddlers	12.4	60.9	43.5
Outsiders	—	34.8	47.8
Mentally ill	18.7	4.3	—

* $\chi^2 = 41.88$, df = 6, P<0.001.

[a] Comments or statements coded as categoric distancing include those indicating dissociation or distancing from such general street-role identities as transient, bum, tramp, or drifter, or from other street people in general.

[b] Comments or statements coded as specific distancing include those indicating dissociation from specific groupings of homeless individuals or from specific survival or occupational roles.

[c] Comments or statements coded as institutional distancing include those indicating dissociation from or disdain for street institutions, such as the Salvation Army or soup kitchens.

homeless, such as novices and the institutionally dependent, from specific occupational roles, or from the institutions with which they have occasional contact.

Embracement

Embracement connotes a person's verbal and expressive confirmation of acceptance of and attachment to the social identity associated with a general or specific role, a set of social relationships, or a particular ideology. So defined, embracement implies that social identity is congruent with personal identity. Thus, embracement involves the avowal of implied social identities rather than their disavowal, as in the case of distancing. Thirty-four percent of the identity statements were of this variety.

Role embracement

The most conspicuous kind of embracement encountered was categoric role embracement, which typically manifested itself by the avowal and acceptance of street-role identities such as tramp and bum. Occasionally we would encounter an individual who would immediately announce that he or she was a tramp or a bum. A case in point is provided by our initial encounter with Shotgun, when he proudly told us that he was "the tramp who was on the front page of yesterday's newspaper." In that and subsequent conversations his talk was peppered with references to himself as a tramp. He said, for example, that he had appeared on a television show in St Louis as a tramp and that he "tramped" his way across the country, and he revealed several "cons" that "tramps use to survive on the road."

Shotgun and others like him identified themselves as traditional "brethren of the road" tramps. A number of other individuals identified themselves as "hippie tramps." When confronted by a passing group of young punk-rockers, for instance, Gimpy Dan and several other hippie tramps voiced agreement with the remark one made that "these kids will change but we'll stay the same." As if to buttress this claim, they went on to talk about "Rainbow," the previously mentioned annual gathering of old hippies which functions in part as a kind of identity-reaffirmation ritual. For these street people, there was little doubt about who they were; they not only saw themselves as hippie tramps, but they embraced that identity both verbally and expressively.

This sort of embracement also surfaced on occasion with skid row-like bums, as was evidenced by Gypsy Bill's repeated references to himself as a bum. As a corollary of such categoric role embracement, most individuals who identified themselves as tramps or bums adopted nicknames congruent with these roles, such as Shotgun, Boxcar Billie, Gypsy Bill, and Pushcart. Such street names thus symbolize a break with their domiciled past and suggest, as well, a fairly thoroughgoing embracement of life on the streets.

Role-specific embracement was also encountered occasionally, as when Gypsy would refer to himself as an "expert dumpster diver." Many street people occasionally engage in this survival activity, but relatively few pridefully identify with it. Other role-specific survival activities embraced included panhandling, small-time drug-dealing, and performing, such as playing a musical instrument or singing on a street corner for money. "Rhyming Mike," as we have seen, made his money by composing short poems for spare change from passersby, and routinely referred to himself as a street poet. For some homeless individuals, then, the street roles and routines they enact function as sources of positive identity and self-worth.

Associational embracement

A second variety of embracement entails reference to oneself as a friend or as an individual who takes his or her social relationships seriously. Gypsy provides a case in point. On one occasion he told us that he had several friends who either refused or quit jobs at the Sally because they "weren't allowed to associate with other guys on the streets who were their friends." Such a policy struck him as immoral. "They expect you to forget who your friends are and where you came from when you go to work there," he told us angrily. "They asked me to work there once and I told them, 'No way.' I'm a bum and I know who my friends are." Self-identification as a person who willingly shares limited resources, such as cigarettes and alcohol, also occurred frequently, particularly among self-avowed tramps and bums.

Associational embracement was also sometimes expressed in claims of protecting buddies. JJ and Indio repeatedly said they "looked out for each other." When Indio was telling about having been assaulted and robbed while walking through an alley, JJ said, almost apologetically, "It wouldn't have happened if I was with you. I wouldn't have let them get away with that." Similar claims were made to one of us, as when two straddlers said one evening after an ambiguous encounter with a clique of half a dozen other street people, "If it wasn't for us, they'd have had your ass."

Although protective behaviors that entailed risk were seldom observed, protective claims, and particularly promises, were heard frequently. Whatever the relationship between such claims and action, they not only illustrate adherence to the moral code of "what goes around, comes around," but they also express the claimant's desire to be identified as a trustworthy friend.

Ideological embracement

The third variety of embracement entails adherence to an ideology or an alternative reality and the avowal of a personal identity that is cognitively congruent with that ideology. Banjo, for example, routinely identifies himself as a Christian. He painted on his banjo case "Wealth Means Nothing Without God," and his talk is sprinkled with references to his Christian beliefs. He can often be found giving testimony about "the power and grace of Jesus" to other homeless around the Sally, and he witnesses regularly at the Central Assembly of God Church. Moreover, he frequently points out that his religious beliefs transcend his situation on the streets. As he told us once, "It would have to be a bigger purpose than just money to get me off the streets, like a religious mission."

A source of identity as powerful as religion, but less common, is the occult and related alternative realities. Since traditional occupational roles are not readily available to the homeless as a basis for identity, and since few street people have the material resources that can be used for construction of positive personal identities, it is little wonder that some of them find in alternative realities a locus for a positive identity. As we noted earlier, Tanner Sutton identifies himself as a "spirit guide" who can see into the future, prophesying, for instance, that "humans will be transformed into another life form."

Like mainstream religious traditions and occult realities, conversionist, restorative ideologies such as that associated with Alcoholics Anonymous provide an identity for some homeless people who are willing to accept AA's doctrines and adhere to its program. Interestingly, AA's successes seldom remain on the streets. Consequently, those street people who have previously associated with AA seldom use it as a basis for identity assertion. Nonetheless, it does constitute a potentially salient identity peg.

We have seen how the personal identities of the homeless may be derived from embracement of the social identities associated with certain stereotypic street roles, such as the tramp and the bum; with role-specific survival activities, such as dumpster-diving; with certain social relationships, such as friend and protector; or with certain religious and occult ideologies or alternative realities. We have also noted that the use of embracement tends to vary across the different types of homeless. This can be seen more clearly in table 16.2, which shows that categoric embracement in particular and embracement talk in general occur most frequently among outsiders and rarely among the recently dislocated.

Fictive Storytelling

A third form of identity talk engaged in by the homeless is fictive storytelling about past, present, or future experiences and accomplishments. We characterize as fictive stories that range from minor exaggerations of experience to full-fledged fabrications. We observed two types of fictive storytelling: embellishment of the past and present, and fantasizing about the future. Slightly more than a third of the identity statements we recorded fell into one of these two categories.

Table 16.2   Types of embracement, by type of homeless*

Types of homeless	Categoric embracement[a] (N: 16) %	Specific embracement[b] (N: 23) %	Ideological embracement[c] (N: 23) %
Recently dislocated	—	10.0	7.7
Straddlers	5.1	35.0	46.1
Outsiders	87.2	45.0	30.8
Mentally ill	7.7	10.0	15.4

*$\chi^2 = 21.11$, df = 6, P<0.05.

[a] Comments or statements coded as categoric embracement include those indicating acceptance of or attachment to street people as a social category or to such general street-role identities as bum, tramp, drifter, or transient.

[b] Comments or statements coded as specific embracement include those indicating identification with a situationally specific survival role, such as dumpster diver or street performer, or with a specific social-relational role, such as friend, lover, or protector, or with an occupational role.

[c] Comments or statements coded as ideological embracement include those indicating acceptance of a set of beliefs or ideas, such as those associated with a particular religion.

Embellishment

By *embellishment* we refer to the exaggeration of past or present experiences with fanciful and fictitious particulars so as to assert a positive personal identity. Embellishment involves enlargement of the truth, an overstatement of what transpired or is unfolding. Embellished stories, then, are only partly fictional.

Examples of embellishment for identity construction abound among the homeless. Although a wide array of events and experiences, ranging from the accomplishments of offspring to sexual and drinking exploits and predatory activities, were embellished, such storytelling was most commonly associated with past and current occupational and financial themes. The typical story of financial embellishment entailed an exaggerated claim regarding past or current wages. A case in point is provided by a 40-year-old homeless man who spent much of his time hanging around a bar boasting about having been offered a job as a Harley-Davidson mechanic for $18.50 per hour, although at the same time he constantly begged for cigarettes and spare change for beer.

Equally illustrative of such embellishment was an encounter we overheard between Marilyn, who was passing out discarded burritos, and a homeless man in his early twenties. After this fellow had taken several burritos, he chided Marilyn for being "drunk." She yelled back angrily, "I'm a sheetrock taper and I make 14 bucks an hour. What the fuck do you make?" In addition to putting the young man in his place, Marilyn thus announced to him and to others overhearing the encounter her desired identity as a person who earns a good wage and must therefore be treated respectfully. Subsequent interaction with her revealed that she worked only sporadically, and then most often for not much more than minimum wage. There was, then, a considerable gap between claims and reality.

Disjunctures between identity assertions and reality appear to be quite common and were readily discernible on occasion, as in the case of a 45-year-old straddler from Pittsburgh who had been on the streets for a year and who was given to substantial embellishment of his former military experiences. On several occasions he was overhead telling about "patrolling the Alaskan/Russian border in Alaskan Siberia" and his encounters with Russian guards who traded him vodka for coffee. Since there is no border between Alaska and Siberia, it is obvious that this tale is outlandish. Nonetheless, such tales, however embellished, can be construed as attempts to communicate specifics about the person and the person's sense of self. Additionally, they focus a ray of positive attention on the storyteller and thereby enable him or her to garner momentarily a valued resource that is typically in short supply on the streets.

Fantasizing

The second type of fictive storytelling among the homeless is verbal fantasizing, which involves the articulation of fabrications about the speaker's future. Such fabrications place the narrator in positively framed situations that seem far removed from, if at all connected to, his or her past and present. These fabrications are almost always benign, usually have a Walter Mitty/pipe dream quality to them, and vary from fanciful reveries involving little self-deception to fantastic stories in which the narrator appears to be taken in by his or her constructions.

Regardless of the degree of self-deception, the verbal fantasies we heard were generally organized around one or more of four themes: self-employment, money, material possessions, and women. Fanciful constructions concerning self-employment usually involved business schemes. On several occasions, for example, Tony Jones told us and others about his plans to set up a little shop near the university to sell leather hats and silver work imported from New York. In an even more expansive vein, two straddlers who had befriended each other seemed to be scheming constantly about how they were going to start one lucrative business after another. Once we overheard them talking about "going into business" for themselves, "either roofing houses or rebuilding classic cars and selling them." A few days later, they were observed trying to find a third party to bankroll one of these business ventures, and they even asked us if we "could come up with some cash."

An equally prominent source of fanciful identity construction is the fantasy of becoming rich. Some of the homeless just daydreamed about what they would do if they had a million dollars. Pat Manchester, for instance, assured us that if he "won a million dollars in a lottery," he was mature enough that he "wouldn't blow it." Others made bold claims about future riches without offering any details. And still others confidently spun fairly detailed stories about being extravagant familial providers in the future, as Tom Fisk did when he returned to town after a futile effort to establish himself in a city closer to his girlfriend. Despite his continuing financial setbacks, he assured us, "I'm going to get my fiancée a new pet monkey, even if it costs a thousand dollars. And I'm going to get her two parrots too, just to show her how much I love her."

Fanciful identity assertions were also constructed around material possessions and sexual encounters with women. These two identity pegs were clearly illustrated one evening among several homeless men along the city's major nightlife strip. During the course of making numerous overtures to passing women, two of the fellows jointly fantasized about how they would attract these women in the future. "Man, these chicks are going to be all over us when we come back into town with our new suits and Corvettes," one exclaimed. The other added, "We'll have to get some cocaine too. Cocaine will get you women every time." This episode and fantasy occurred early in the second month of our fieldwork, and we quickly came to learn that such fantasizing was fairly commonplace and that it was typically occasioned by "woman-watching," which exemplifies one of the ways in which homeless men are both deprived of attention and respond to that deprivation.

One place homeless men would often watch women was along a jogging trail in one of the city's parks adjacent to the river. Here on warm afternoons they would drink beer and call out to women who jogged or walked along the trail or came to the park to sun themselves. Most of the women moved nervously by, ignoring the overtures of the men. But some responded with a smile, a wave, or even a quick "Hi!" Starved for female attention, the homeless men are quick to fantasize, attributing great significance to the slightest response. One Saturday afternoon, for example, as we were sitting by the jogging trail drinking beer with Pat Manchester and Ron Whitaker, we noticed several groups of young women who had laid out blankets on the grassy strip that borders the trail. Pat and Ron were especially interested in the women who were wearing shorts and halter tops. Pat called out for them to take their tops off. It was not clear that they heard him, but he insisted, "They really want it. I can tell they do." He suggested we go over with him to "see what we can get," but he was unwilling to go by himself. Instead, he constructed a fantasy in which the young women were very interested in him. Occasionally the women glanced toward us with apprehension, and Pat always acted as though it was a sign of interest. "If I go over there and they want to wrap me up in that blanket and fuck me," he said, "man, I'm going for it." Nonetheless, he continued to sit and fantasize, unwilling to acknowledge openly the obdurate reality staring him in the face.

Although respectable work, financial wealth, material possessions, and women are intimately interconnected in actuality, only one or two of the themes were typically highlighted in the stories we heard. Occasionally, however, we encountered a particularly accomplished storyteller who wove together all four themes in a grand scenario. Such was the case with the straddler from Pittsburgh who told the following tale over a meal of bean stew and stale bread at the Sally, and repeated it after lights-out as he lay on the concrete floor of the winter warehouse: "Tomorrow morning I'm going to get my money and say, 'Fuck this shit.' I'm going to catch a plane to Pittsburgh and tomorrow night I'll take a hot bath, have a dinner of linguine and red wine in my own restaurant, and have a woman hanging on my arm." When encountered on the street the next evening, he attempted to explain his continued presence on the streets by saying, "I've been informed that all my money is tied up in a legal battle back in Pittsburgh," an apparently fanciful amplification of the original fabrication.

Although both embellished and fanciful fictive storytelling surfaced rather frequently in the conversations we overheard, they were not uniformly widespread or randomly distributed among the homeless. As is indicated in table 16.3, embellishment occurred among all the homeless but was most pronounced among the straddlers and outsiders. Fantasizing, on the other hand, occurred most frequently among those who still had one foot anchored in the world they came from and who could

Table 16.3 Types of fictive storytelling, by type of homeless*

Types of homeless	Embellishment[a] (N: 39) %	Fantasizing[b] (N: 31) %
Recently dislocated	2.6	45.2
Straddlers	42.1	32.2
Outsiders	50.0	9.7
Mentally ill	5.3	12.9

* $\chi^2 = 24.35$, df $=3$, P<0.001.

a Comments or statements were coded as embellishment if they entailed the elaboration and exaggeration of past and present experiences with fictitious particulars.

b Comments or statements were coded as fantasizing if they entailed future-oriented fabrications that placed the narrator in positively or strangely framed situations.

still envision a future, and it occurred least often among those individuals who appeared acclimated to street life and who tended to embrace one or more street identities. For these individuals, especially those who have been on the streets for some time, the future is apparently too remote to provide a solid anchor for identity-oriented fictions that are of this world. It is not surprising, then, that it is also these individuals who exhibit the greatest tendency to drift into alternative realities, as did a 33-year-old black female who claimed to be "the Interracial Princess," a status allegedly bestowed on her by "a famous astrologer from New York."

We have elaborated three generic patterns of talk through which the homeless construct and avow personal identities. We have seen that each pattern of this identity talk – distancing, embracement, and fictive storytelling – contains several varieties, and that their frequency of use varies among the types of homeless. Categoric role and associational distancing and the construction of fanciful identities occur most frequently among the recently dislocated, for example; whereas categoric embracement and embellishment tend to manifest themselves most frequently among the outsiders. Overall, then, many of the homeless are active agents in the construction and negotiation of identities as they interact with others. They do not, in other words, passively accept the social identities their appearance sometimes exudes or into which they are cast. This is not to suggest that the homeless do not sometimes view themselves in terms of the more negative, stereotypical identities frequently imputed to them. One afternoon, for example, we encountered Gypsy stretched out on a mattress in the back of his old car. Drunk and downhearted, he muttered glumly:

> I've just about given up on life. I can't get any work and all my friends do is keep me drunk. Crazy, just crazy – that's all I am. Don't have any desire to do anything for myself. This car is all I've got, and even it won't work. It's not even worth trying. I'm nothing but an asshole and a bum anymore.

But on other occasions, as we have seen, Gypsy was not only more cheerful but even managed to cull shreds of self-respect and dignity from his pariah-like existence. Moreover, we found that self-deprecating lamentations like Gypsy's were relatively rare compared to the avowal of positive personal identities. This should not be particularly surprising, since every human needs to be an object of value and since the homeless have little to supply that sense of value other than their own identity-construction efforts.

Summary

All animals are confronted with the challenge of material subsistence, but only humans are saddled with the vexing question of its meaning. We must not only sustain ourselves physically to survive, but we are also impelled to make sense of our mode of subsistence, to place it in some meaningful context, to develop an account of our situation that does not destroy our sense of self-worth. Otherwise, the will to persist falters and interest in tomorrow wanes. The biblical prophets understood this well when they told us that "man does not live by bread alone." The homeless appear to understand this existential dilemma, too, at least experientially; for while they struggle to subsist materially, they confront the meaning of their predicament and its implications for the self. These concerns weigh particularly heavily on the recently dislocated, but they gnaw at the other homeless as well – sometimes when they drift off at night, sometimes when they are jarred from sleep by their own dreams or the cries of others, and often throughout the day when their encounters with other homeless and with the domiciled remind them in myriad subtle and not-so-subtle ways of their descent into the lowest reaches of the social system and of their resultant stigmatized status.

In this chapter we have explored the ways the homeless deal with their plight, both existentially and interactionally, by attempting to construct and maintain a sense of meaning and self-worth that helps them stay afloat. Not all of the homeless succeed, of course. The selves of some have been so brutalized that they are abandoned in favor of alcohol, drugs, or out-of-this-world fantasies. And many would probably not score high on a questionnaire evaluating self-esteem. But the issue for us has not been how well the homeless fare in comparison to others on measures of self-esteem, but that they do, in fact, attempt to salvage the self, and that this struggle is an ongoing feature of the experience of living on the streets.

The homeless we studied are not the only individuals who have fallen or been pushed through the cracks of society who nevertheless try to carve a modicum of meaning and personal significance out of what must seem to those perched higher in the social order as an anomic void. Other examples of such salvaging work have been found in mental hospitals, concentration camps, and among black street-corner men. In these and presumably in other such cases of marginality, the attempt to carve out and maintain a sense of meaning and self-worth seems especially critical for survival because it is the one thread that enables those situated at the bottom to salvage their humanity. It follows, then, that it is not from lack of interest that some people find it difficult to salvage their respective selves, but that their difficulty results instead from the scarcity of material and social resources at their disposal.

That many of the homeless are indeed able to make some culturally meaningful sense of their situation and secure a measure of self-worth testifies to their psychological resourcefulness and resolve, and to the resilience of the human spirit.

Considering these observations, it is puzzling why most research on the homeless has focused almost solely on their demographics and disabilities, to the exclusion of their inner lives. Perhaps it is because many social scientists have long assumed that the issues of meaning and self-worth are irrelevant, or at least of secondary importance, in the face of pressing physiological survival needs. This assumption is firmly rooted in Abraham Maslow's well-known hierarchy of needs, which holds that the satisfaction of physiological and safety needs is a necessary condition for the emergence and gratification of higher-level needs such as the need for self-esteem or for a positive personal identity. This thesis has become almost a cliché in spite of the fact that relevant research is scanty and ambiguous at best. Our finding that concern with both existential and identity-oriented meaning can be readily gleaned from the talk of homeless street people, clearly some of the most destitute in terms of physiological and safety needs, provides an empirical counterpoint to this popular assumption. Moreover, our observations suggest that the salience of such cognitive concerns is not necessarily contingent on the prior satisfaction of physiological survival requisites. Instead, such needs appear to coexist, even at the most rudimentary levels of human existence. The homeless we came to know clearly evidence such concerns.

References

Derber, Charles. 1979. *The Pursuit of Attention: Power and Individualism in Everyday Life.* New York: Oxford University Press.

Goffman, Erving. 1961. *Asylums.* Garden City, NY: Anchor Books.

Swidler, Ann. 1986. "Culture in action: Symbols and strategies." *American Sociological Review* 51: 273–86.

17 The Real Self: From Institution to Impulse

Ralph H. Turner

Except at the most macroscopic and demographic levels, there is no way to study dynamics and change in social systems without attending to the attitudes and conceptions held by their members. Subjective data are essential, because people are not just miniature reproductions of their societies (Bendix 1952; Etzioni 1968; Wrong 1961).

One important sociological tradition for bringing personal dynamics into the analysis of social structure began with Thomas and Znaniecki's (1918) concept of *life organization*, which Park (1931) translated into *conceptions of self* and Kuhn and McPartland (1954) converted into an easily applied set of empirical operations. The *self-conception* as an object arises in connection with self-process (Mead 1934). From early experience with the distinction between *mine* and *yours*, I learn to distinguish between *myself* and others (Cooley 1902).

The present discussion emphasizes a related point, that the idea of a self-as-object permits me to distinguish among the various feelings and actions that emanate from my person. Some emanations I recognize as expressions of my real self; others seem foreign to the real me. I take little credit and assume little blame for the sensations and actions that are peripheral to my real self (Turner 1968). Others are of great significance, because they embody my true self, good or bad. The articulation of *real selves* with social structure should be a major link in the functioning and change of societies. This approach to linking person and social structure is especially compatible with symbolic interactionist and phenomenological perspectives which stress the ongoing creation of reality by each member of society.

The aim of this paper is to elaborate a dimension of self-conception that may have important implications for sociological theories of social control and other aspects of societal functioning. To varying degrees, people accept as evidence of their real selves either feelings and actions with an *institutional* focus or ones they identify as strictly *impulse*. There are suggestive signs that recent decades have witnessed a shift in the locus of self away from the institutional pole and toward that of impulse. This shift may have altered substantially the world of experience in which people orient themselves, setting it apart from the one that much established sociological theory describes. I describe these types, examine the hypothesized shift, suggest some theories that might explain it, and explore the implications for sociological thought.

In another publication I describe a modification of the "Who am I?" technique that I have developed specifically to gather data for analysis in these terms.

Before presenting the thesis, I must briefly outline my assumptions concerning self-conception. Out of the distinctively human reflexive process emerges a sense or

Reprinted from *American Journal of Sociology* 81(5) (1976): 989–1016.

conception of self as an object, which, however, has no existence apart from the conceptions and attitudes by which one constitutes it (Blumer 1966: 539–40). Identifying the self is not the same as identifying one's values, and self-conception is not to be confused with ideal self or ego ideal (Kuhn and McPartland 1954: 69). The self-conception identifies a person in qualitative and locational terms, not merely in evaluative ones such as self-esteem. The self is an object in relation to other objects, all of which are constantly modified in dynamic interrelationship (Berger 1966). Self-conception refers to the continuity – however imperfect – of an individual's experience of himself in a variety of situations. It is most usefully viewed as an intervening variable between some aspect of social structure and the working of the same or another aspect.

How the self can be so constituted as not to be coterminous with all the feelings and actions that emanate from a person has been a constant source of puzzlement. I suggest tentatively that the demarcation has three components. First, it relies on a more generalized discrimination between the real and the unreal in experience. We identify some experiences as fantasies, hallucinations, dreams, or other forms of the unreal. Under crisis conditions we sometimes go so far as to deceive ourselves concerning the reality of behavior and feelings that are not in accord with self (Spiegel 1969). More often we merely borrow the language of reality and unreality and employ its connotations. Second, bounding the self incorporates the general distinction between *attributions* to person and those to situation (Jones et al. 1971). Behaviors thought to reveal the true self are also ones whose causes are perceived as residing in the person rather than the situation. This distinction relies on a common-sense psychology held by the persons making attributions. The bases for bounding the self necessarily change whenever folk understandings of psychology change. The distinction also inextricably mixes normative conceptions of responsibility with naturalistic ones of cause. The emergence of self cannot be separated from the essentially moral process of establishing human accountability (Kilpatrick 1941). Third, the idea of self incorporates a further sense of a realm that is distinctly personal or *propriative* (Allport 1955). This realm has not been effectively defined; yet awareness of it is a crucial and almost irreducible intuition. Attribution theorists' evidence that self-attribution does not follow entirely the same rules as person attribution gives some clues to the proprium. But beyond the attribution of causation for behavior, the realm of self is characterized by possessiveness, privacy, and sacredness.

Institution and Impulse as Loci of Self

The self-conception is most frequently described sociologically by naming the roles that are preeminent in it. In a good example of this approach, Wellman (1971) finds that the self-conceptions of both black and white adolescents can be characterized on the basis of the same set of identities – namely, their age, gender, family, religion, race, and ethnic heritage, and their roles as students, athletes, and friends. Studies comparing the place of occupation and work in the life organizations of various groups of workers (Dubin 1956; Wilensky 1964) likewise relate the self-conception to particular roles in society.

Self-conceptions can also be compared on the basis of distinctions at a more abstract level. The relationship between self and social order is put in more comprehensive terms when we distinguish between self as anchored in *institutions* and self as anchored in *impulse*.

To one person, an angry outburst or the excitement of extramarital desire comes as an alien impetus that superficially beclouds or even dangerously threatens the true self. The experience is real enough and may even be persistent and gratifying, but it is still not felt as signifying the real self. The true self is recognized in acts of volition, in the pursuit of institutionalized goals, and not in the satisfaction of impulses outside institutional frameworks. To another person, the outburst or desire is recognized – fearfully or enthusiastically – as an indication that the real self is breaking through a deceptive crust of institutional behavior. Institutional motivations are external, artificial constraints and superimpositions that bridle manifestations of the real self. One plays the institutional game when one must, but only at the expense of the true self. The true self consists of deep, unsocialized, inner impulses. Mad desire and errant fancy are exquisite expressions of the self.

Again, conscientious acceptance of group obligations and unswerving loyalty can mean that the real self has assumed firm control and overcome the alien forces. But for those who find out who they really are by listening to the voice of impulse, the same behavior is a meaningless submission to institutional regimens and authoritarianism. A mother's self-sacrifice for her child is the measure of her real self when seen through institutional eyes, and it is a senseless betrayal of the parent's true being to those who find personal reality in the world of impulse.

It is no accident that this polarity parallels Freud's classic distinction between id and superego. To Freud, the id was more truly the person and the superego merely an external imposition. As he turned to examinations of society, he expressed the same conviction when he wrote, "Our civilization is entirely based upon the suppression of instincts" (1931: 13), and when he proposed a relaxation of social norms and standards as a solution to the discontents of modern civilization (1930). This position sharply contrasts with a view shared by many writers and exemplified in Park's assertion that "the role we are striving to live up to – this mask is our truer self" (1927: 739). Although in other writings Park sometimes expressed a different conviction, his statement epitomized the institutional locus of self, while Freud located the self chiefly in the world of impulse – until his belated concessions to ego.

The Key Differences

Several crucial differences between the two contrasting loci of self can be briefly stated.

1. Under the institution locus, the real self is revealed when an individual adheres to a high standard, especially in the face of serious temptation to fall away. A person shows his true mettle under fire. Under the impulse locus, the real self is revealed when a person does something solely because he wants to – not because it is good or bad or noble or courageous or self-sacrificing, but because he spontaneously wishes to do so.

2. To *impulsives*, the true self is something to be discovered. A young person drops out of school or out of the labor force in order to reflect upon and discover who he really is. To the *institutional*, waiting around for self-discovery to occur is ridiculous. The self is something attained, created, achieved, not something discovered. If vocational counseling to help the individual find his peculiar niche has elements of the impulse conception of self, the idea that a person can make of himself what he will, that one chooses a task and then works at it, is the view of institutionals. The contrast is well stated in a contemporary prescription for effective living, written from the institutional perspective:

> So if we reach a point of insight at which we become disgustedly aware of how we stage ourselves, play games, and ingratiate others, to say nothing of using defense mechanisms and strategies, and if at this point we want to enrich life by finding honest, deeply felt, loving interactions with others, it is tempting to believe that we can change simply by opening a door and letting out our "true" unsullied impulses. Change is never so simple. What is really involved is not the releasing of a true self but the making of a new self, one that gradually transcends the limitations and pettiness of the old. (White 1972: 387)

3. Under the institution locus, the real self is revealed only when the individual is in full control of his faculties and behaviors. Allport (1955) locates the self in planning and volition, in contrast to impulse. "When the individual is dominated by segmental drives, by compulsions, or by the winds of circumstances, he has lost the integrity that comes only from maintaining major directions of striving" (pp. 50–1). When control is impaired by fatigue, stress, alcohol, or drugs, an alien self displaces the true self. The danger of any of these conditions is that after repeated experiences the individual may lose the capacity to distinguish between the true self and the counterfeit and become progressively less able to resume control and reinstate the true self. If use of alcohol is viewed with favor, it is only on condition that the user is able to practice moderation or "hold his liquor," maintaining control in spite of alcohol.

But under the impulse locus, the true self is revealed only when inhibitions are lowered or abandoned. In a magnificent statement of an institutional perspective, Wordsworth (1807) called upon Duty, "stern daughter of the voice of God," for relief from the "weight of chance-desires" and for "a repose that ever is the same." But let the barest suspicion arise that a good deed has been motivated by a sense of duty, and it loses all value as a clue to self in the eyes of the impulsive. For some impulsives drugs and alcohol are aids – often indispensable – to the discovery of self, for without them socially instilled inhibitions irresistibly overpower the true self. A participant in a Los Angeles "love-in" in 1971 said: "It's a place where people can get out, get smashed, get stoned, or whatever. A love-in is a place to get away from the apartment. It's like being out and touching people for a change, rather than working with paper and working with inanimate objects. It's like being out in the real world for a change."

4. Hypocrisy is a concern of both types, but the word means different things to each. For the institutionals, hypocrisy consists of failing to live up to one's standards. The remedy is not to lower standards but to make amends and adhere to the standards the next time. If one's failings persist, one ceases to represent oneself as

what one cannot be, so that one at least escapes the charge of hypocrisy by presenting oneself only as what one is. For the impulsives, hypocrisy consists of asserting standards and adhering to them even if the behavior in question is not what the individual wants to do and enjoys doing. One who sets exacting standards for himself and by dint of dedicated effort succeeds in living up to them is still a hypocrite if he must suppress a desire to escape from these strict demands. Altruism, in the traditional sense of responding to duty and setting one's own interests aside, is a penultimate hypocrisy, compounded by the probability that it is a dissimulated self-seeking and manipulation. The institutional goal is correspondence between *prescription and behavior*; the goal of impulsives is correspondence between *impulse and behavior*: hypocrisy in either instance is a lack of the appropriate correspondence.

5. In the light of the foregoing differences, the qualities that make a performance admirable differ. The polished, error-free performance, in which the audience forgets the actor and sees only the role being played, is the most admired by institutionals. Whatever the task, perfection is both the goal and the means by which the real self finds expression. But impulsives find technical perfection repelling and admire instead a performance that reveals the actor's human frailties. They are in harmony with the motion picture star system, in which Gregory Peck, John Wayne, and Gina Lollobrigida, rather than the characters they play in a given picture, are the centers of attention. Ed Sullivan's popular appeal, generally attributed to his very awkwardness and ineptitude, is incomprehensible to the institutionals. Of course, the specific cues for spontaneity have changed, so a younger generation of impulsives no longer responds to these stars as did an older generation.

6. The difference between discovery and achievement also suggests a difference in time perspective. The self as impulse means a present time perspective, while the self as institution means a future time perspective. Institutionals, who build themselves a real world by making commitments, have difficulty retaining a vital sense of self when the future perspective is no longer tenable. The *malaise* of retirement is a common indication of this pattern. In contrast, freedom from past commitments is heralded poetically in the popular song "Gentle on my mind," by John Hartford.

7. Just as hypocrisy takes on different meanings within the two patterns, individualism is found in both settings with different implications. The individualist is one who rejects some kind of social pressure that threatens his true identity. But there are different kinds of pressure. In one view, social pressures can divert a person from achievement, from adherence to ethical standards, and from other institutional goals. The rugged individualists of nineteenth-century America thought in these terms. Children were imbued with an individualistic ethic in order to protect them from peer group pressures toward mediocrity or compromise of principle, either of which meant failure to realize the potential that was the true self. But individualism can also be a repudiation of the institutional and interindividual claims that compete with impulse. The individualist may be protecting himself against a conspiracy to force him into institutional molds, to make him do his duty, or to aspire. Both types would agree that one must resist the blandishments of friends and the threats of enemies in order to be true to oneself. But the institutional individualist is most attentive to pernicious pressures on the side of mediocrity and abandonment of principle; the impulsive individualist sees clearly the social pressures in league with a system of arbitrary rules and false goals.

Both institution and impulse loci allow for individualistic and non-individualistic orientations. We have found it useful to employ a cross-cutting distinction between *individual* and *social* anchorages for the self. Institutionals stress either achievement, a relatively individual goal, or altruism, a social aim, as the road to self-discovery. Somewhere between the two lies adherence to an ethical code which will vary according to whether ethics is viewed as applied altruism or a forum for individual achievement. Impulsives may stress the simple disregard of duties and inhibitions in order to gratify spontaneous impulses; this is essentially an individual route to self-discovery. Or they may seek self-discovery through expressing potentially tabooed feelings to other persons and thereby attain a state of interpersonal intimacy that transcends the normal barriers between people.

Related and Unrelated Distinctions

It is essential not to confuse these alternative anchorages with the question of whether people are preoccupied with maintaining appearances or conforming instead of "being themselves." Describing a mass gathering of youths, a student wrote, "People tend to forget how they would hope to come across, and instead act as their true selves." This is a terse statement of how participants felt in the situation and expresses the point of view of an impulse self-anchorage. But from an institutional perspective, the same youths appear to be tumbling over one another in their anxiety to comply with the latest youthful fad and to avoid any appearance of being square. The institutional hopes that after passing through this stage the youths will "find themselves," discovering their special niches in the institutional system. The self-anchorage determines which kinds of behavior seem genuine and which are concessions to appearances.

The polarity bears resemblances to several distinctions already advanced by others. McPartland's "Category B" responses and Kuhn and McPartland's consensual responses (Spitzer et al. 1973) to the Twenty Statements Test (TST) would all be institutional responses, but so would many responses in other categories. Institutionals have much in common with Riesman et al.'s (1950) inner-directed persons, but other-directed persons cannot be equated with impulsives. Sorokin's (1937–41) sensate types resemble the impulsives in their assignment of ultimate reality to the world of the senses. But Sorokin identifies striving for success with the sensate mind and altruism with the ideational, whereas I see these as alternative expressions of an institutional anchorage. Benedict's (1934) interpretation of Nietzsche's Dionysians suggests impulsives, who are unrestrained in acting on impulse and dream, while the Apollonians are more comfortable in an institutionally articulated system. But the dominating Apollonian theme of moderation certainly does not apply to heroic altruism or unrestrained striving for success.

Compared with the well-known dichotomies employed by Benedict, Sorokin, and Riesman et al., the institution–impulse distinction introduces a somewhat different dimension. It allows for the discovery of reality in either excess or moderation within both self-anchorages, and it allows in each orientation for both mystical and naturalistic realities and both individualizing and unifying realities. Goals of achievement, self-control, morality, and altruism lodge the self-conception more and more firmly in some institutional structure. The impulse release attained in encounter groups, expressive movements, and dropping out may in some forms promote a bond of intimacy with other individuals but always distinguishes the true self specifically from institutional values, norms, and goals.

This polarity has much in common with the widely discussed dimension of alienation. However, three important differences of approach make the concepts complementary rather than redundant. First, alienation is an intrinsically evaluative concept, incorporating a negative view of social trends and requiring that the search for explanation be directed toward disorganization in the social structure. Granted that each investigator's own self-locus will lead him to prefer one pole to the other, there are no a priori judgments that one locus is healthier than the other and no reasons to seek explanations for the shift in the pathologies of society. Second, while alienation implies a single continuum, self-locus implies two continua that may be loosely correlated but not identical. One is the continuum I have described. The other ranges from high to low *self-resolution*, according to whether the individual has a clear and stable self-conception or a vague and uncertain identity. Some scholars think of alienation as loss of self-resolution. But alienation from one's work can signify either an impulse locus or low self-resolution. And for some scholars in the Freudian tradition, self-estrangement *means* institutional anchorage.

A third distinction is that such concepts as alienation and anomie tell only where the self is *not*. The result is an effort to infer and explain self-estrangement without first exploring the possibility that the self may be securely lodged somewhere other than where the investigator has looked. Why *should* the self be lodged in work? Why should not work be carried out as a necessary but tolerable evil, its encroachment on the rest of life appropriately curtailed, as Seeman (1967) has suggested? Perhaps a decline of institutional self-anchorage is less a result of institutional failure than a consequence of the discovery of a new vitality in the world of impulse. Shils (1962) calls our attention to the new kinds of experience made possible for us by the mass society. The merit of examining these shifts in terms of self-loci rather than merely alienation is that we are sensitized to the possibility that the self has found new anchorages as well as losing the old.

Concerning this initial statement of the two loci of self, the reader should bear in mind that specifying polar types such as these is merely a way to start thinking about variation in the sense of self. Except on the fringes of society, we are unlikely to find the extremes. Elements of both anchorages probably coexist comfortably in the average person. Yet differences among groups of people in key facets of self may be of sufficient importance that their experience of each other is noncongruent, and little true communication can occur.

A Contemporary Trend

It is my speculative hypothesis that over the past several decades substantial shifts have occurred away from an institution and toward an impulse emphasis. Accounts of the "new sensibility" in American culture (Bell 1970: 59) or of "consciousness III" (Reich 1970) already associate many of the same features with the youthful protest of the 1960s. But it would be shortsighted not to see the shift in a more extended historical context or to overlook the possibility of rural–urban differences, class differences, and differences among national cultures, as well as generational differences. A revolutionary consciousness often unwittingly adopts perspectives that have been growing in established society, frees them from accommodation to other aspects of that society, and applies them to a contemporary crisis.

There is nothing novel in attending to changing values over the last few generations. But I suggest that the changes be viewed as a shift in what are conceived as valid indications of what is real about ourselves and our associates, telling us whether we really know a person or not. Distinguishing the real from the unreal is a matter of intuition, not of logic. Faultless logic that concerns unreal objects falls on deaf ears. A shifting locus of self means that successive generations are talking about different worlds of reality. At the heart of each are the shared and socially produced intuitions through which people identify their true selves.

Literary themes often presage shifts in popular consciousness. Examining the writings of James Frazer, Friedrich Nietzsche, Joseph Conrad, Thomas Mann, and Sigmund Freud, Lionel Trilling (1961) traces the theme that we must accept the reality of those human impulses that were judged unacceptable by an artificial and unreal civilization. He identifies "a certain theme which appears frequently in modern literature – so frequently, indeed, and in so striking a manner, that it may be said to constitute one of the shaping and controlling ideas of our epoch. I can identify it by calling it the disenchantment of our culture with culture itself – it seems to me that the characteristic element of modern literature, or at least of the most highly developed modern literature, is the bitter line of hostility to civilization which runs through it" (p. 26).

I have already noted Freud's penchant for the impulse perspective. Perhaps the greatest impact Freud had on the modern world was to discredit normative behavior and conscience as manifestations of our true selves and to elevate impulses to that position. Under his aegis, guilt has ceased to be the redemptive experience through which the real self reasserts itself and has become an external impediment to personal autonomy. Lynd (1958) exemplifies this newer intuition of reality when she writes,

> Living in terms of guilt and righteousness is living in terms of the sanctions and taboos of one immediate culture. To some extent such living is necessary for everyone. Living in terms of the confronting of shame – and allowing shame to become a revelation of oneself and one's society – makes way for living beyond the conventions of a particular culture. It makes possible the discovery of an integrity that is peculiarly one's own and of those characteristically human qualities that are at the same time most individualizing and most universal. (1958: 257)

Concern with discovery of the true self, vaguely identified as a set of impulses that have been repressed or dissipated under institutional constraint, turns up as a novel element in the political process of recent years. It became a prominent theme in youth movements, minority movements, and women's movements during the 1960s (Turner 1969). Miller (1973) traces the "politics of the true self" back to the poet William Blake and shows that violence is conceived of as the ultimate form of self-expression and self-discovery in the writings of Fanon and Sartre.

The term "soul" has often been used in much the same sense as our term "true self." It can be found in the work of poets as different as Richard Lovelace and William Wordsworth. But its meaning has changed to suit prevailing conceptions of personal reality. A century ago the soul was essentially a moral force. As secular psychology brought the term into disrepute, it disappeared, sank into obscurity, reemerging to describe a special quality attributed to blacks. It retains its character as a dynamic force, but a supposed lack of inhibition is a crucial criterion of "soul."

Miller and Swanson (1958) documented changing conceptions of child rearing as new middle-class parents evinced less concern about internalized controls and more about social adjustment than did parents from the old middle class. In studies of another stage in life, students, as they progressed through college or university, were found to look more favorably on the expression of impulses (Feldman and Newcomb 1969: 34). If the inner-directed person of Riesman et al. (1950) has much in common with our institutionals, the other-directed person may have been a transitional type, clinging to the institutional framework for his identity but finding a way to accept constant change. Perhaps the total repudiation of institutional identities is the product of a growing sense of unreality in *all* roles that comes from the other-directed person's efforts to *be* all his roles. In the world of business, the shift is from the view that human relations take care of themselves when tasks are effectively managed to the position that human-relations engineering is essential to effective production. In education the progressive movement promoted a conception of the child in terms of his impulses, and not merely his learning and conduct. Rieff's (1966) depiction of cultural change as "the shifting balance of controls and releases" (p. 233) and his account of the "triumph of the therapeutic" describe a historical change toward greater impulsiveness.

Recently Lifton (1970) has described a type of personality he believes is becoming much more common throughout the developed world. His "protean man" has no true shape of his own but assumes varied shapes according to circumstance. Except for the fact that Riesman et al. describe other-direction as a mode of conformity, "protean man" may be a new name for the same kind of person. But the idea that rapid social change makes fixed identities unworkable has also inspired Zurcher (1972, 1973) to identify the "mutable self" as a phenomenon unique to the present generation. Zurcher cites as evidence for the "mutable self" his discovery that students no longer answer Kuhn's TST as they used to. Early use of the procedure produced mostly "B mode" responses, meaning that the subject identified himself with various institutionalized roles and statuses. Now students give principally "C mode" responses which specify characteristic modes of acting, feeling, and responding.

"C mode" responses clearly attenuate the linkage between self and institutional anchorage. The real self is marked by characteristic orientations – attitudes, feelings, desires – rather than characteristic placement in social organization. Young people find self-realization in patterns that are viewed apart from their institutional settings. Consistent with this evidence is the contemporary view that, on meeting a stranger, it is inappropriate to ask where he comes from, what he does, and whether he is married, or to categorize him in other ways. Instead, one seeks to know him through his tastes and his feelings.

Theories and Explanations

If we are to explain and predict the self-loci of different populations, we must combine insights about individual dynamics with understanding of social structure and culture. The problem of individual dynamics is to identify circumstances under which experiences seem real or unreal in relation to self. Large-scale differences and shifts must then be linked with the exposure of individuals to such experiences.

An acceptable explanation must also address the question of whether impulse and institutional self-anchorages are the poles of a unitary variable, two separate variables related in a loose but imperfect inverse correlation, or even unrelated variable. If the conditions that weaken one locus intensify the other, a single continuum is indicated. But if, as seems more likely, the conditions that weaken one locus do not necessarily intensify the other, a more complex conception will be required.

My procedure has been inductive rather than deductive, starting with the observation of a difference and an apparent shift and then searching for explanations. Hence I now offer a set of alternative explanations rather than advance a single theory of self-locus.

Cultural Definitions of Reality

The most parsimonious principle is that people experience as real what they are taught is real. Definitions of reality are crucial components in all cultures, and a cultural shift may have occurred in recent times. Conceptions of reality are buttressed by systems of belief, and the decline of religious belief and its replacement by materialistic or naturalistic belief assigns more reality to physiological and allied psychological impulses. Cultural shift can explain the increasing personal reality attached to impulse as well as the declining personal relevance of institutions.

In tracing the historical evolution of public establishments designed to segregate deviants from the community, Rosen suggests that a new view of human nature came to the fore in the late seventeenth century, bringing with it the new idea of a personal self:

> Today the idea of a personal self appears as an indispensable assumption of existence. Actually, like other views of human nature, it is in large measure a cultural idea, a fact within history, the product of a given era. At any given period certain criteria are employed to establish normal human nature, as well as any deviation from it. (1969: 164).

If Rosen's evocative suggestion is correct, the locus of self was probably institutional at first. As Soellner (1972) interprets the recurring theme of self-discovery in Shakespeare's plays, the true self is formed in self-mastery. Cultural changes that occurred principally in the nineteenth and twentieth centuries turned attention increasingly toward impulse as the expression of self.

While economical, this explanation is somewhat question-begging, since we can do little with it except ask the revised question, Why has a cultural shift occurred? But as a starting point, the cultural explanation is useful. A related and well-established line of sociological explanation emphasizes uniformity and diversity of culture rather than its specific content. According to this view, certitudes come from unanimity – the vitality and reality of an experience come from the fact that it fits unmistakably into a consensual world-view. But the intimate experience of cultural diversity undermines certitudes. Institutional forms are seen in relativistic, rather than absolute, terms. No longer the locus of *real* behavior because they cannot be taken for granted, institutional frameworks begin to seem arbitrary and artificial.

While the latter construction escapes the danger of tautology in explanations that rely on the content of culture, it accounts for a decline in the institutional locus of self without indicating the basis for increasing impulse locus. By itself, this explanation suggests a generally weakened sense of identity instead of a shift from one locus to another.

The Terms of Social Integration

A second approach redirects our attention from culture to the fundamental terms of interpersonal relations. Early sociologists (Cooley 1902; Davis 1940; Young 1940) believed that human nature depends upon social interaction. The human meanings of experience come out of the sharing and exchange of experiences. We tend to believe in experiences we share with others and doubt those we cannot share (Blondel 1928; Halbwachs 1952). Events become real and vital when they become elements in the bonding of interpersonal and group relations. The integration of an individual into solidary groups is the ultimate source of any sense of reality concerning experience.

Festinger (1953) proposes that we often comply with group norms without accepting them as our own, but that, when we wish to be part of the group, our compliance is converted into private acceptance. Much earlier, Park's (1928) and Stonequist's (1937) depiction of the marginal man stressed the interplay between adherence to a particular culture and the desire for social incorporation. Social rejection led the marginal man to doubt his commitment to the group's values and images of reality. Warner and Lunt (1941) found confirmation of the conclusion that the stratification people experienced as real was the hierarchy of social identities and affiliations their economic assets helped them attain, not economic standing *per se*. Davie (1947) found that immigrants of relatively high status who came to the United States as refugees from Nazism felt they had lost in the move, even while acknowledging that their economic conditions were as good as or better than before. The loss of social recognition was salient in their estimate of overall position.

From this perspective, the self-conception should incorporate those actions and feelings that are involved in exchange with others and, through exchange, contribute materially to the individual's integration into groups. We are led to search for shifts in kinds of social relations that have relatively lasting and significant effects. One key may be the shift from the organization of group life around production and mutual protection groups to organization around consumption groups. From Veblen (1899), to Riesman et al. (1950), to Miller and Swanson (1958), observers have remarked a trend in the western world away from production orientation and toward consumption orientation. At an earlier period, the central problems of society revolved about how to produce efficiently and on a massive scale the goods that people wanted. The individual's round of life was concentrated in extended families, neighborhoods, small communities, and other social units, all of them organized about the aims of production. Disciplined work habits, aspirations that motivated work, and adherence to rules that facilitated collaboration for production were valued qualities that enhanced individual integration into stable and comprehensive social units. Since the same units were also vested with responsibility for mutual protection, altruism was the companion to productive contribution in making the individual an essential group member.

As production problems were increasingly resolved and production routinized and transferred to the domain of organizations with strictly segmental functions, the connections between production-related personal qualities and integration into primary groups became more tenuous and indirect. Likewise, protection became the routinized responsibility of experts who were external to the groups in which people lived. An altruistic act by an amateur could do more harm than good – witness warnings against amateurs moving automobile accident victims or trying to save drowning swimmers instead of waiting for paramedics or life guards! But of even greater significance, altruism toward a stranger has usually no significance for lasting social ties and identities in a highly segmented society. As their significance for interpersonal bonding declined, altruism, achievement, and righteousness became less credible clues to the real person.

As the consumption of goods, expressive activities, and pleasure became the aims about which the anchoring social groups were organized, a different set of qualities provided the interpersonal cement. The cultivation of personal tastes, expressive styles, and distinctive psychological "needs" was at a premium in groups whose vitality and continuation depended on collaboration for consumption. The family was increasingly viewed as a contrast, rather than an adjunct, to the world of production. When the links to production could not be totally severed, some relegated the family to the same sphere of unreality. Ogburn (1933) and Burgess and Locke (1950) noted that interpersonal response was becoming more prominent as a source of family cohesion.

This approach is consistent with the hypothesis that the institutional self is less prevalent and the impulsive self more so among segments of the population for whom production activities are aimed at maintenance rather than expansion. Rural and small-town folk are often characterized as bumpkins because they do not seek to play such rituals as initiations and funerals to dramatic perfection and fail to play their vocational and community roles to the hilt. I suggest that these are groups in which production is routinized and hence constitutes a less salient social bond. Where a genuine spirit of entrepreneurship prevails, the expansive aim makes routinization impossible, and the institutional self seems more real.

Deprivation and Desire

From psychodynamics comes a third principle that might explain varying loci of self. Sustained denial of any goal or impulse causes a preoccupation with the blocked tendency which makes the latter seem more real and important. While this is a cardinal Freudian assumption, it has a venerable history and is entirely consistent with George Mead's conception of impulse and social act. Lee gives the same process a different slant when she attempts to explain why Americans conceive of psycho-dynamics in terms of basic human needs instead of values:

> In maintaining our individual integrity and in passing on our value of individualism to the infant, we create needs for food, for security, for emotional response, phrasing these as distinct and separate.... We create needs in the infant by withholding affection and then presenting it as a series of approvals for an inventory of achievements or attributes. (1959: 74–5)

By contrast, in Hopi, Tikopia, Kwoma, Arapesh, Ontong-Javanese, and many other societies, value is undivided and positive. There is no separate motive or need for food, security, or social response.

Whether we start from Freud's or Lee's contrasting assumptions about the ultimate character of human motivation, we find agreement that modern urban, industrial civilization requires a great deal of control and suppression of impulse. If these requirements have increased, the result should be enhancement of the sense of reality associated with impulse. If modern civilization has also frustrated mankind's need for interpersonal response (Horney 1937), it is easy to understand that people may experience their longings for intimacy as manifestations of their real selves. We encounter more difficulty in developing a plausible account of lessened frustration in institutional spheres. Perhaps routinized social services and prepackaged solutions to all problems of production have eliminated the anxieties and potential frustrations in these areas and deprived such activities and concerns of their personal vitality.

Experience has shown how difficult it is for scholars to agree on such broad characterizations of societies as impulse repressive. A more plausible view may be that modern society is not so much repressive as it is contradictory, stimulating to an unparalleled degree the impulses whose expression is then inhibited. But if this is true of impulses Freud would have lodged in the id, it is equally true of achievement and service motivations that he would have placed in the superego. To some extent this entire approach may rest on a mythical conception of uninhibited life in preindustrial societies, based on selective reporting and disproportionate attention to premarital sexual play.

Opportunities and Consequences

A final principle is pragmatic and in some ways antithetical to the deprivation-enhancement approach. The postulate is that lines of action with plainly perceived and significant consequences are experienced as real, while ones with undependable or unidentifiable consequences seem less real. Consequences cannot be experienced without opportunity, so the reality of particular goals and impulses is enhanced by either augmented consequences or increased opportunities.

The waning vitality of institutional dispositions can be traced to the emasculation of rites of passage and the permeability of role boundaries. Disappointment over rites of passage, leading to a generalized sense of unreality, is poignantly conveyed in the popular song "Is that all there is?" Each of life's milestones turns out to be of little moment. A vital rite of passage initiates the individual into closely guarded secrets and skills and opens up new privileges, conditional upon his successful performance or endurance of the rite. When secrets, skills, and privileges are readily accessible to those who have not been through the rite, and when passage becomes pro forma, the entire sequence of institutional steps loses its reality. Likewise the potential of any institutional role for self-anchorage depends upon the degree to which it incorporates distinctive privileges, responsibilities, and skills. Such monopolies may have been progressively undermined in recent years.

There may be a key to the changing sense of what is real in the fate of the once-popular belief in self-discovery through self-sacrifice. One side of institutional identity is incorporation into the self of a whole range of socially generated objects that augment the interest, richness, and possibilities of gratification in life. The obverse, however, is the relinquishment of those random sensations and impulses which – like Blondel's (1928) *cénesthésie* – offer a constant threat to the ordered world of the institutional self. From the poet Francis Thompson (1893), writing in religious terms, to the psychoanalyst Fromm (1941), students of human nature have understood the appeal of self-surrender. For Thompson, the errant soul flees the Hound of Heaven in desperation until in abject surrender he discovers the fulfillment of his deepest desires. For Fromm, identification with an omnipotent, charismatic leader and his movement resolves the problems of the troubled self.

But implicit in self-discovery through surrender is the assumption that one has been absorbed into a caring, gratifying entity, both powerful and dependable. When Ruth of the Old Testament found a true self in surrendering her life to Naomi, she did so in the firm knowledge that Naomi would care for her, protect her, and give her a meaningful and rewarding place in her household. Thompson assures us that to those who surrender, God will grant many times more than they have given up. It is this rich return for surrender that vests the institutional self-conception with a vital sense of reality. The discovery of self in love for another is made real by the reciprocated love, the dependability of the relationship, and the new opportunities for gratification that come from the relationship. The discovery of self through immersion in an institutional framework is real when the dependability of that framework makes the world predictable and the rich body of objects opens up a new world of gratifications.

But if reciprocation does not occur, neither does the vital sense of a real self. When the institutional framework is characterized by disorder and undependability, when it fails as an avenue to expanded opportunity for gratification, the true self cannot be found in institutional participation. Because *perceived* consequences are crucial, objective order and dependability may be less important than whether consequences are early or delayed and whether effects are intrinsic or extrinsic. Here the analysis converges with many treatments of alienation in the Marxian tradition. The institutional order may still be relatively efficient and predictable, but the increasing time span between action and consequence and the increasing dependence on extrinsic rewards may contribute to a sense of unreality in institutional activities.

On the other hand, as Shils has eloquently indicated, mass society opened up opportunities for an augmented range of gratifications. As existence became less precarious, people could afford to act on their impulses. More of society's resources could be applied to creating avenues for the gratification of impulse:

> The individual organism has become a seeker after experience, a repository of experience, an imaginative elaborator of experience. To a greater extent than in the past, the

experience of the ordinary person, at least in youth, is admitted to consciousness and comes to form part of the core of the individual's outlook. There has come about a greater openness to experience, an efflorescence and intensification of sensibility.... In a crude, often grotesque way, the mass society has seen the growth, over wide areas of society, of an appreciation of the value of the experience of personal relationships, of the intrinsic value of a personal attachment.... (1962: 58–9)

In accordance with this more positive view of mass society, the sense of unreality attending institutional activity may be a crisis phenomenon, related to a stage in life or restricted to a small but vocal segment of the population. On the other hand, a relative decline in institutional self-anchorage may have occurred just because of the newly discovered vitality in the world of impulse. Instead of alienation from our institutions, we may be witnessing a reestablishment of balance between institutional and impulsive loci of the self.

Alternative Theories

I have by no means covered all plausible approaches to explaining the hypothesized shift in self-anchorage. For example, the massive amount of literature on patterns of deferred gratification should offer clues. Nor am I prepared to recommend a choice among theories. The major conflict is between deprivation theory, on the one hand, and opportunity theory and social integration theory, on the other. But even here the opposition may not be complete.

Evidence and experience suggest a curvilinear relationship between deprivation and the sense of reality. Severe and continued deprivation probably leads to a lessened sense of reality and sometimes even a complete divorcement between self and desire. "Narcotization" (Koos 1946: 48) and "analgesic" (Ball 1968) are terms sociologists have used to designate a pervading sense of unreality that stems from exceptional deprivation.

Furthermore, relative rather than absolute deprivation is probably the key. Hence, stimulation of desire without equivalent increase in gratification should also increase the sense of reality. With this modification, the deprivation approach need not be inconsistent with the others. Changing definitions of reality may be the source of, or bring an end to, relative deprivation. Modest relative deprivation may be the normal consequence when new opportunities for gratification become available. Just as competition may increase the interest in work of both winners and losers (Julian et al. 1966; Myers 1962) and a healthy anxiety enhance the excitement of love, the combination of accessible gratification and some degree of risk may create the most vital sense of reality. Individuals today may experience their impulses as more vital expressions of self than heretofore, because opportunities to gratify impulse have increased and norms against doing so have weakened, at the same time that lingering inhibitions from the past and contradictory cultural definitions add an increment of risk to the expression and pursuit of impulse.

Application of this approach to institutional activities suggests two phases. An early period of institutional innovation greatly elaborated the scope of potential human gratification, through family, work, community activity, and other institutional spheres; yet the growing and changing nature of the institutions maintained a universal element of risk. This combination of promise and risk led to a more profound personal investment in institutional pursuits than formerly, with the result that more people experienced their true selves as distinctively lodged in these spheres. As institutions came to perform more smoothly and routinely, the risk was reduced and the sense of reality declined. Thereafter ensued the second phase, already amply described.

Implications for Social Structure

Any massive shift in the locus of identity should have substantial consequences for social structure and may negate the implicit assumptions on which some sociological theories are founded. Theories deeply rooted in the past often take for granted an actor who locates his real self in an institutional setting. Conflict theories are no different from order theories in this respect, since they merely shift the locus of self to a class-bounded institutional framework. It is difficult to find sociological theories that locate bases for order rather than pathology when institutional participation is strictly instrumental and when only those impulses that seem unrelated to institutions are experienced as genuine and personal. I shall suggest how alternate loci of self bear on a few major concepts in sociology.

Role Distance

Few would deny that society exists only when members are enacting roles. Sartre (1956: 59) argues that society requires every person to play his roles to the hilt. Role theory assumes that role behavior is monitored and evaluated on scales of role adequacy. Evaluations by the actor and significant others influence subsequent role performance. When role theory is refined in accordance with self theory, evaluations of role adequacy are understood to have the greatest impact for roles that are paramount in the self-conception. Whatever society may expect, the actor usually plays to the hilt only those roles in which his ego is strongly involved (Sherif and Cantril 1947). So long as the roles attached to institutionally *key statuses* (Hiller 1947) are also most salient in personal identities, institutional and personal dynamics are mutually supporting.

But Goffman (1961) has identified a pervasive phenomenon of *role distance*. The role-distancing antics of parents on the merry-go-round with their children plainly ward off identification with a role that does violence to their self-conceptions. But when the surgeon engages in role distancing with nurses and assistants during a difficult operation, he can hardly be guarding against inappropriate institutional placement and identification. The distance is between the real person and *any* formalized role. If role distancing in such situations is as prevalent and important as Goffman suggests, it is difficult to accept Sartre's assertion.

The apparent contradiction between these two sensitive observers may come from their having viewed different cultures at different moments in time. When the self is securely lodged in institutions, the individual will play at least the most crucial roles to the hilt. When he does so, he will appear genuine to his institutional auditors. When he does not, he will seem insincere, because role distancing behavior is inappropriate flippancy, a denial of respect to significant others in the encounter. Indeed, the behavior of Goffman's surgeon would be so regarded in many medical circles. But when the true self is lodged in impulse, role distancing shows that one is not really the uptight, false, or plastic person one's conformity with institutional routine might suggest. Role distancing reminds significant others of a real self that is temporarily obscured by compliance with an institutional role.

On the one hand, organizational theorists should take account of role distancing as a crucial aspect of the meshing of person and institution. On the other hand, role distancing is probably not a universal feature of social behavior but a distinctive feature of societies like our own, in which the locus of self is widely found in non-institutional impulses.

Values and Norms

Sociologists distinguish between norms and values as part of the directing and regulating apparatus of society. Because of their preoccupation with distinguishing between these two components of social structure, sociologists often fail to notice that the difference is principally in the eye of the beholder: values and norms are largely the same phenomenon viewed in different ways. Honesty is a value; "thou shalt not lie" is a norm. But the two are inseparable, and, as Blake and Davis (1964) argue persuasively, neither can be derived from the other. But the object (value) and the rule (norm) are two constructions the individual can place on the same phenomenon. Which construction is foremost in his experience makes important differences in his relationship to social structure.

Honesty is a positively valued object, a goal to be achieved as a matter of self-respect and pride. One who values it does not feel that society is depriving him of the privilege of telling lies when he wishes, nor does he feel frustrated or constrained when he passes up the temptation to lie. Instead he has a positive sense of accomplishment and well-being from having lived up his values. But one who thinks in terms of the norm experiences deprivation and frustration. Like a driver adhering to the speed limit on an open highway, he gains no warm sense of worth and satisfaction from adhering to the rule; even when complying he often feels resentful of the restraint imposed upon him. The practice of premarital and marital chastity has been variously experienced as an opportunity for self-development and as an external restraint on a fundamental human need. *Self-as-impulse tends to transform the institutional order into a set of norms, all cramping expression of the true self. Self-as-institution subordinates the normative sense to a set of values, such as integrity, piety, patriotism, considerateness, and many others.*

Sociologists frequently prejudge the constructions people place on the social order and reify them into features of an objective social structure. They emphasize the constraints of society by seeing principally norms, or they emphasize the creation of new opportunities for self-fulfillment by underlining social values. A more adequate sociological understanding can be reached if we stop reifying the value–norm distinction and seek instead to understand what it is in the social structure that fosters anchorage of the self in either institution or impulse, with the resultant predisposition to see either values or norms in the institutional order.

Sentiments

Much of the spontaneous joy that lubricates the functioning of social orders resides in the social sentiments. Love is of paramount importance among the sentiments. Because sentiment seems to express the inner person, in contrast to external behavior that may be contrived, people seek agreement on signs by which to tell genuine from false sentiment. The choice of cues reflects the anchorage of self. Self-as-impulse can feel love as genuine, as a true reflection of self, only when it arises and persists as a spontaneous attachment, untrammeled by promises, covenants, and codes of behavior. Sentiment is not helped along by a facilitative social order: it erupts in spite of the order and threatens it. The less organization and preparation, the more easily can the individual discover his true sentiments. Institutionals, on the other hand, understand love as something that requires effort to attain and preserve. The infatuation that explodes impulsively is undependable and unreal. The institutional seeks to learn how to achieve true love and turns for guidance to such documents as Paul's chapter on love in the New Testament (1 Cor.: 13). The contrasting perspectives are represented in the analysis of popular sex manuals by Lewis and Brissett (1967). Manuals popular with married middle-class people in the past two or three decades [the 1940s to 1970s] are institutional in orientation. They offer readers an opportunity to enhance the vitality and mutuality of sexual experience, leading to a deeper union of the two selves. But Lewis and Brissett read the manuals from the impulsive perspective. Stripped of the institutional perspective, the quest for mutual self-attainment becomes sheer, meaningless "work." Thus, they write of "sex as work." To the extent to which the self-locus has moved away from institutions, the correlations found by Burgess and Cottrell (1939), Burgess and Wallin (1953), and Locke (1951) with persistence and love in marriage may become increasingly invalid, and new and different indicators may become relevant.

The Meaning of Ritual

In 1930, an article entitled "Ritual the conserver" (Cressman) appeared in the *American Journal of Sociology*. It elaborated the crucial part played by ritual in sustaining the Catholic church and its doctrines. To a contemporary reader, the paper seems peculiarly unconvincing. To those who find not only religious ritual but also marriage ceremonies, funerals and memorial services, initiation ceremonies, and graduation exercises devoid of meaning, it is unclear how ritual could add vitality and reality to anything. Yet plainly many people have been, and continue to be, moved deeply by participation in collective ritual, and for many people dedication to institutional goals and forms is strengthened in this way. The locus of self must be closely intertwined with the ability to gain vital experience from engaging in collective rituals. It would be premature to label one cause and the other effect, but the impulsive's self-fulfilling prophecy that he will not experience his real self through participation in institutional ritual contrasts with the equally self-fulfilling prophecy from the institutional.

But the matter cannot be reduced to a differential receptivity to ritual. Writing on the "collective search for identity," Klapp describes the contemporary poverty of ritual, then insists that "ritual is the prime symbolic vehicle for experiencing emotions and mystiques together with others – including a sense of oneself as sharing such emotions" (1969: 118). In the place of traditional forms, there have arisen new rituals that participants experience as spontaneous outpourings instead of institutional routines. Sitting on the floor in a circle and singing to the accompaniment of guitars takes the place of sitting in rows on pews and listening to an organ. Rock festivals and love-ins are only the more dramatic rituals, for even the conventional partying rituals of middle-class establishmentarians are experienced as a welcome contrast to institutional routine. Here, then, is another set of rituals that have meaning and vitality as opportunities for experiencing a self that contains more impulse than institution.

Ritual is commonly viewed as a support of the institutional order, and Klapp's "poverty of ritual" does indeed characterize many of the forms that have been employed to strengthen a collective sense of institutional commitment. But it is doubtful that there is any poverty of ritual today in those forms that increase the vitality of an impulsive view of self.

General Implications

Each of the foregoing points bears on the theory of social control. Concern with the prestige of one's role and the esteem that goes with high role adequacy buttresses the institutional structure. A sense of value eases the pathos of conformity with social norms. Social sentiments domesticate potentially disruptive emotions yet preserve their sensed vitality and spontaneity. And through collective ritual, group solidarity and dedication to the institutional structure are continually renewed. But all of this depends upon the individual's feeling that his real self is engaged in these experiences. If he finds that self elsewhere, control can only be instrumental.

One side of what I have described sounds much like a condition of anomie. But if people recognize their real selves in impulse, they become susceptible to social control from that quarter. And if impulses are generated in unrecognized ways by the social order and follow unsensed but consistent patterns, the impulsive self is as much a vehicle for social control as the institutional self. However, the relationship to recognized institutional structures will be complex and indirect. We need a theory of social control that relies more extensively on the creation and manipulation of situations and on symbiosis than on the internalization and enforcement of norms and values.

Afterthoughts

My chain of speculation has consisted of five links. First, I have assumed that each person develops at least a vague conception by which he recognizes some of his feelings and actions as more truly indicative of his real self than other feelings and actions. He does so in part on the basis of unique experience and in part in accordance with the guidelines shared by members of his society, subsocieties, and groups. Second, I have identified a distinction between locating the real self in sentiments and activities of an institutional and volitional nature, such as ambition, morality, and altruism, and recognizing the real self in the experience of impulse – for example, in apparently undisciplined desires and fancies and the wish to make intimate revelations in the presence of others. This appears to be a significant polarity in the contemporary relationship between individual and society. Third, I have assembled a number of suggestive indications to support the intuition that there has been a long-term shift in the direction of impulse, intensified in the [1960s and 1970s]. Fourth, I have drawn from analyses of contemporary society to suggest four theoretical approaches that might explain the shift in self-loci and differences in self-anchorage among diverse population segments. And fifth, I have assumed that many sociological theories, especially those having to do with social control, take for granted a population with institutional self-anchorages and need revision to allow for the more hidden ways in which societies control members who find their true selves in impulse.

I stress that there is no objectively, but only a subjectively, true self. Likewise institutional versus impulsive self is a subjective distinction and not a statement of psychogenesis. Institutional motivations are effective vehicles for a multitude of private impulses. And few of the instigations and sensations that people experience as impulse are not institutionally conditioned and generated. We are like the Plains Indians who sought purely personal visions to establish the basis of each individual's authority but faithfully replicated their culture in the form and content of their visions (Benedict 1934: p. 84).

One might suppose on the basis of attribution research that the self should necessarily be anchored overwhelmingly in impulse rather than institution. When an external cause is present, "the behavior is discounted, so to speak, as an indicator of personal disposition" (Kelley, in Jones et al. 1971: 155). But there are two important differences. First, although we understand achievement, ethical conformity, and altruism as rooted in institutions, the pattern is internalized, so there need be no sense of an external cause. Second, when we ask people to describe circumstances that reveal their true selves, the institutional replies usually involve going beyond requirements of a role or adhering to goals or norms in the face of obstacles that constitute acceptable excuses for failing to do so. Thus the behavior in question is unlikely to be ascribed to external causes.

As we explore the polarity of institution and impulse, we must ask whether choice between the two is of universal significance or peculiar to certain cultures and social structures. Thomas and Znaniecki (1918) discovered philistines and bohemians, but the fact that the society they studied tended to dichotomize people thus and force each person to choose between those polar types was probably more important than the objective typing of individuals. Mannheim (1952) described the distinctive socializing experience that sets one historical generation apart from others in terms of the *issues* over which people divide into rival camps rather than the association of a point of view with a generation. We must not, then, assume that a distinction between institutional and impulse self-anchorages found to be significant in contemporary American society should necessarily be significant in other societies.

We may indeed assume that because the polarity is important, most individuals will seek both kinds of anchorages. For much of life, these alternate anchorages will coexist in fairly easy accommodation. But at crucial transitions in the life cycle the coexistence will be interrupted. The latent opposition between institutional and impulsive selves then becomes manifest, figuring strongly in the turmoil of choice. The point of choice may be passed and the conflict recede into dormancy without the individual's self-conception being firmly anchored at one pole to the exclusion of the other.

Perhaps the feature of the distinction that warrants greatest stress and is most heavily freighted with implications for examining social structure is the hypothesized correlation between self-locus and a disposition to perceive either values or norms. Sociologists writing from a structural perspective often reify the distinction and speak as if values and norms existed as separate entities in society. To a large degree, however, it is the nature of the self-conception, in the way it identifies the individual's relationship to social structure, that leads one to perceive principally values or norms. Perceiving values and discovering the true self in the achievement of high institutional-role adequacy facilitates the operation of social control systems as they are commonly described in sociological theory. Perceiving norms and recognizing the true self specifically in the experience of impulses that are thought not to have an institutional basis subjects one to quite a different system of social control, one that is much less well described in sociological theory.

References

Allport, Gordon W. 1955. *Becoming: Basic Considerations for a Psychology of Personality.* New Haven, Conn: Yale University Press.

Ball, Richard A. 1968. "A poverty case: The analgesic subculture of the Southern Appalachians." *American Sociological Review* 33 (December): 885–95.

Bell, Daniel. 1970. "Quo warranto." *Public Interest* 19 (Spring) : 53–68.

Bendix, Reinhard. 1952. "Compliant behavior and individual personality." *American Journal of Sociology* 58 (November): 292–303.

Benedict, Ruth. 1934. *Patterns of Culture.* Boston: Houghton Mifflin.

Berger, Peter L. 1966. "Identity as a problem in the sociology of knowledge." *European Journal of Sociology* 7: 105–15.

Blake, Judith and Davis, Kingsley. 1964. "Norms, values, and sanctions." In Robert E. L. Faris (ed.) *Handbook of Modern Sociology.* Chicago: Rand-McNally, pp. 456–84.

Blondel, Charles. 1928. *The Troubled Conscience and the Insane Mind.* London: Kegan Paul, Trench, Trubner.

Blumer, Herbert. 1966. "Sociological implications of the thought of George Herbert Mead." *American Journal of Sociology* 17 (March): 535-48.

Burgess, Ernest W. and Cottrell, Leonard S. Jr. 1939. *Predicting Success or Failure in Marriage.* Englewood Cliffs, NJ: Prentice-Hall.

Burness, Ernest W. and Locke, Harvey J. 1950. *The Family: From Institution to Companionship.* New York: American Book.

Burgess, Ernest W. and Wallin, Paul. 1953. *Engagement and Marriage.* Chicago: Lippincott.

Cooley, Charles H. 1902. *Human Nature and the Social Order.* New York: Scribner.

Cressman, Luther H. 1930. "Ritual the conserver." *American Journal of Sociology* 35 (January): 564–72.

Davie, Maurice R. 1947. *Refugees in America.* New York: Harper.

Davis, Kingsley. 1940. "Final note on a case of extreme isolation of a child." *American Journal of Sociology* 45 (May); 554–65.

Dubin, Robert. 1956. "Industrial workers' world." *Social Problems* 3 (January): 131–42.

Etzioni, Amitai. 1968. "Basic human needs, alienation and inauthenticity." *American Sociological Review* 33 (December): 870–85.

Feldman, Kenneth A. and Newcomb, Theodore M. 1969. *The Impact of College on Students*, vol. 1. San Francisco: Jossey-Bass.

Festinger, Leon. 1953. "An analysis of compliant behavior." In Muzafer Sherif and M. O. Wilson (eds.) *Group Relations at the Crossroads*. New York: Harper, pp. 232–56.

Freud, Sigmund. 1930. *Civilization and Its Discontents*. London: Hogarth.

—— 1931. *Modern Sexual Morality and Modern Nervousness*. New York: Eugenics.

Fromm, Erich. 1941. *Escape from Freedom*. New York: Farrar and Rinehart.

Goffman, Erving. 1961. *Encounters*. Indianapolis: Bobbs-Merrill.

Halbwachs, Maurice. 1952. *Les Cadres sociaux de la mémoire*. Paris: Presses Universitaires de France.

Hiller, E. T. 1947. *Social Relations and Structures*. New York: Harper.

Horney, Karen. 1947. *The Neurotic Personality of Our Time*. New York: Norton.

Jones, Edward E., Kanouse, David E., Kelley, Harold H., Nisbett, Richard E., Valins, Stuart and Weiner, Bernard. 1971. *Attribution: Perceiving the Causes of Behavior*. Morristown, NJ: General Learning.

Julian, James W., Bishop, Doyle W. and Fiedler, Fred E. 1966. "Quasi therapeutic effects of intergroup competition." *Journal of Personality and Social Psychology* 3 (March): 321–7.

Kilpatrick, William H. 1941. *Selfhood and Civilization: A Study of the Self–Other Process*. New York: Macmillan.

Klapp, Orrin E. 1969. *Collective Search for Identity*. New York: Holt, Rinehart and Winston.

Koos, Earl L. 1946. *Families in Trouble*. New York: Kings Crown.

Kuhn, Manford H. and McPartland, Thomas S. 1954. "An empirical investigation of self-attitudes." *American Sociological Review* 19 (February): 68–76.

Lee, Dorothy D. 1948. "Are basic needs ultimate?" *Journal of Abnormal and Social Psychology* 43 (July): 391–5.

—— 1959. *Freedom and Culture*. Englewood Cliffs, NJ: Prentice-Hall.

Lewis, Lionel S. and Brissett, Dennis. 1967. "Sex as work: A study of avocational counselling." *Social Problems* 15 (Summer): 8–17.

Lifton, Robert J. 1970. *Boundaries: Psychological Man in Revolution*. New York: Random House.

Locke, Harvey J. 1951. *Predicting Adjustment in Marriage*. New York: Holt.

Lynd, Helen Merrell. 1958. *On Shame and the Search for Identity*. New York: Harcourt, Brace.

Mannheim, Karl. [1928] 1952. "The problem of generations." In Paul Kecskemeti (ed.) *Essays on the Sociology of Knowledge*. New York: Oxford University Press, pp. 276–322.

Mead, George H. 1934. *Mind, Self, and Society*. Chicago: University of Chicago Press.

Miller, Daniel R. and Swanson, Guy E. 1958. *The Changing American Parent*. New York: Wiley.

Miller, Stephen. 1973. "The politics of the 'true self.'" *Dissent* 20 (Winter): 93–8.

Myers, Albert. 1962. "Team competition, success, and the adjustment of group members." *Journal of Abnormal and Social Psychology* 65 (November): 325–32.

Ogburn, William F. 1933. "The family and its functions." In President's Research Committee on Social Trends (ed.) *Recent Social Trends in the United States*. New York: McGraw-Hill.

Park, Robert E. 1927. "Human nature and collective behavior." *American Journal of Sociology* 32 (March): 733–41.

—— 1928. "Human migration and the marginal man." *American Journal of Sociology* 33 (May): 881–93.

—— 1931. "Human nature, attitudes, and the mores." In Kimball Young (ed.) *Social Attitudes*. New York: Holt, pp. 17–45.

Reich, Charles A. 1970. *The Greening of America*. New York: Random House.

Rieff, Philip. 1966. *The Triumph of the Therapeutic*. New York: Harper and Row.

Riesman, David, Glazer, Nathan, and Denney, Reuel. 1950. *The Lonely Crowd*. New Haven, Conn.: Yale University Press.

Rosen, George. 1969. *Madness in Society*. New York: Harper and Row.

Sartre, Jean-Paul. 1956. *Being and Nothingness: An Essay on Phenomenological Ontology*. Translated by Hazel E. Barnes. New York: Philosophical Library.

Seeman, Melvin. 1967. "On the personal consequences of alienation in work." *American Sociological Review* 32 (April): 273–85.

Sherif, Muzafer and Cantril, Hadley. 1947. *The Psychology of Ego-Involvements*. New York: Wiley.

Shils, Edward. 1962. "The theory of mass society." *Diogenes* 39 (Fall): 45–66.

Soellner, Rolf. 1972. *Shakespeare's Patterns of Self-Knowledge*. Columbus: Ohio University Press.

Sorokin, Pitirim A. 1937–41. *Social and Cultural Dynamics*. Englewood cliffs, NJ: Bedminster.

Spiegel, John P. 1969. "Campus conflict and professorial egos." *Trans-action* 6 (October): 41–50.

Spitzer, Stephan, Couch, Carl and Stratton, John. 1973. *The Assessment of the Self*. Iowa City, Ia.: Sernoll.

Stonequist, Everett V. 1937. *The Marginal Man*. New York: Scribner.

Thomas, William I. and Znaniecki, Florian. 1918. *The Polish Peasant in Europe and America*. New York: Dover.

Thompson, Francis. 1893. "The Hound of Heaven."

Trilling, Lionel. 1961. "The modern element in modern literature." *Partisan Review* 28 (January): 9–25.

Turner, Ralph H. 1968. "The self in social interaction." In Chad Gordon and Kenneth Gergen (eds.) *The Self in Social Interaction*, vol.1. New York: Wiley.

—— 1969. "The theme of contemporary social movements." *British Journal of Sociology* 20 (December): 390–405.

—— 1975. "Is there a quest for identity?" *Sociological Quarterly* 16 (Spring): 148–61.

Veblen, Thorstein. 1899. *The Theory of the Leisure Class*. New York: New American Library.

Warner, W. Lloyd, and Paul S. Lunt. 1941. *The Status System of a Modern Community*. New Haven, Conn.: Yale University Press.

Wellman, Barry. 1971. "Social identities in black and white." *Sociological Inquiry* 41 (Winter): 57–66.

White, Robert W. 1972. *The Enterprise of Living: Growth and Organization in Personality*. New York: Holt, Rinehart and Winston.

Wilensky, Harold L. 1964. "Varieties of work experiences." In Henry Borow (ed.) *Man in a World at Work*. Boston: Houghton Mifflin.

Wordsworth, William. 1807. "Ode to Duty."

Wrong, Dennis H. 1961."The oversocialized conception of man in modern sociology." *American Sociological Review* 26 (April): 183–93.

Young, Kimball. 1940. *Personality and Problems of Adjustment*. New York: Crofts.

Zurcher, Lewis A. 1972. "The mutable self: An adaptation to accelerated sociocultural change." *Et al* 3(1): 3–15.

—— ,1973. "Alternative institutions and the mutable self: An overview." *Journal of Applied Behavioral Science* 9(2–3): 369–80.

18 The Saturated Self

Kenneth J. Gergen

These developments – computers, electronic mail, satellites, faxes – are only the beginning. Innovations now emerging will further accelerate the growth in social connectedness. At the outset is the digitization of all the major media – phonograph, photography, printing, telephone, radio, television. This means that the information conveyed by each source – pictures, music, voice – is becoming translatable to computer form. As a result, each medium becomes subject to the vast storage and rapid processing and transmission capabilities of the computer. Each becomes subject to home production and worldwide dissemination. We now face an age in which pressing a button will enable us to transmit self-images – in full color and sound – around the globe.

Fiberoptic cables increase the amount of information that can be received a thousandfold. This opens the possibility for a virtual infinity of new television and radio bands. Further, fiberoptic cable will allow the transmission of a television picture of twice the fidelity of what is now available (approximating 35mm motion picture film). Digital phone services can be carried on the cable, not only reproducing the voice with fidelity, but also enabling subscribers to see the other person. So much information can be carried on the cable that all these various services could be taking place while subscribers were simultaneously having their utility meters read and their electronic mail collected. With a home fax receiver, one could also have an instant *Los Angeles Times* or *National Geographic* at one's fingertips. Plans are now under way for people to designate the kinds of news they wish to see, and for computers to scan information services and compose individualized newspapers – to be printed on reusable paper.

Over a hundred nations (including the USSR) are now involved in linking all the world's phone systems. Simultaneously, the development of the cellular phone is mobilizing possibilities for communication. With the development of point-to-point contact around the world, the 12 million cellular phones now in use will represent but a bare beginning. One could be anywhere – from a woodside walk in Maine to a hut in the Malaysian jungle – and speak with a loved one or colleague on the other side of the globe. Plans are now afoot for the world system to carry *all* electronic signals, including phone, television, recorded music, written text. This would enable a user to plug into the system anywhere from Alabama to Zaire and immediately transmit and receive manuscripts, sound recordings, or videotapes. The process of social saturation is far from complete.

Reprinted from "Social saturation and the populated self," in *The Saturated Self*, New York: Basic Books, 1991, pp. 60–80.

The Process of Social Saturation

> Monocultural communication is the simplest, most natural, and – in the contemporary world – most fragile form of communication. At its best, it is a rich, satisfying, and effortless way of communicating; at its worst, it can be narrow-minded and coercive.
>
> W. Barnett Pearce, *Communication and the Human Condition*

A century ago, social relationships were largely confined to the distance of an easy walk. Most were conducted in person, within small communities: family, neighbors, townspeople. Yes, the horse and carriage made longer trips possible, but even a trip of thirty miles could take all day. The railroad could speed one away, but cost and availability limited such travel. If one moved from the community, relationships were likely to end. From birth to death one could depend on relatively even-textured social surroundings. Words, faces, gestures, and possibilities were relatively consistent, coherent, and slow to change.

For much of the world's population, especially the industrialized West, the small, face-to-face community is vanishing into the pages of history. We go to country inns for weekend outings, we decorate condominium interiors with clapboards and brass beds, and we dream of old age in a rural cottage. But as a result of the technological developments just described, contemporary life is a swirling sea of social relations. Words thunder in by radio, television, newspaper, mail, radio, telephone, fax, wire service, electronic mail, billboards, Federal Express, and more. Waves of new faces are everywhere – in town for a day, visiting for the weekend, at the Rotary lunch, at the church social – and incessantly and incandescently on television. Long weeks in a single community are unusual; a full day within a single neighborhood is becoming rare. We travel casually across town, into the countryside, to neighboring towns, cities, states; one might go thirty miles for coffee and conversation.

Through the technologies of the century, the number and variety of relationships in which we are engaged, potential frequency of contact, expressed intensity of relationship, and endurance through time all are steadily increasing. As this increase becomes extreme we reach a state of social saturation. Let us consider this state in greater detail.

Multiplying Relationships

In the face-to-face community the cast of others remained relatively stable. There were changes by virtue of births and deaths, but moving from one town – much less state or country – to another was difficult. The number of relationships commonly maintained in today's world stands in stark contrast. Counting one's family, the morning television news, the car radio, colleagues on the train, and the local news-paper, the typical commuter may confront as many different persons (in terms of views or images) in the first two hours of a day as the community-based predecessor did in a month. The morning calls in a business office may connect one to a dozen different locales in a given city, often across the continent, and very possibly across national boundaries. A single hour of prime-time melodrama immerses one in the lives of a score of individuals. In an evening of television, hundreds of engaging faces insinuate themselves into our lives. It is not only the immediate community that occupies our thoughts and feelings, but a constantly changing cast of characters spread across the globe.

Two aspects of this expansion are particularly noteworthy. First there is what may be termed the *perseverance of the past*. Formerly, increases in time and distance between persons typically meant loss. When someone moved away, the relationship would languish. Long-distance visits were arduous, and the mails slow. Thus, as one grew older, many active participants would fade from one's life. Today, time and distance are no longer such serious threats to a relationship. One may sustain an intimacy over thousands of miles by frequent telephone raptures punctuated by occasional visits. One may similarly retain relationships with high-school chums, college roommates, old military cronies, or friends from a Caribbean vacation five years earlier. Birthday books have become a standard household item; one's memory is inadequate to record the festivities for which one is responsible. In effect, as we move through life, the cast of relevant characters is ever expanding. For some this means an ever-increasing sense of stress: "How can we make friends with them? We don't even have time for the friends we already have!" For others there is a sense of comfort, for the social caravan in which we travel through life remains always full.

Yet at the same time that the past is preserved, continuously poised to insert itself into the present, there is an *acceleration of the future*. The pace of relationships is hurried, and processes of unfolding that once required months or years may be accomplished in days or weeks. A century ago, for example, courtships were often carried out on foot or horseback, or through occasional letters. Hours of interchange might be punctuated by long periods of silence, making the path from acquaintance-ship to intimacy lengthy. With today's technologies, however, it is possible for a couple to maintain almost continuous connection. Not only do transportation technologies chip away at the barrier of geographic distance, but through telephone (both stable and cordless), overnight mail, cassette recordings, home videos, photo-graphs, and electronic mail, the other may be "present" at almost any moment. Courtships may thus move from excitement to exhaustion within a short time. The single person may experience not a handful of courtship relationships in a lifetime but dozens. In the same way, the process of friendship is often accelerated. Through the existing technologies, a sense of affinity may blossom into a lively sense of interdependence within a brief space of time. As the future opens, the number of friendships expands as never before.

Bending the Life-Forms

> Our private sphere has ceased to be the stage where the drama of the subject at odds with his objects... is played out; we no longer exist as playwrights or actors, but as terminals of multiple networks.
>
> Jean Baudrillard, *The Ecstasy of Communication*

New patterns of relationship also take shape. In the face-to-face community one participated in a limited set of relationships: with family, friends, storekeepers, clerics, and the like. Now the next telephone call can thrust us suddenly into a new relationship – with a Wall Street broker, a charity solicitor, an alumni campaigner from the old school, a childhood friend at a nearby convention, a relative from across the country, a child of a friend, or even a sex pervert. One may live in a suburb with well-clipped neighbors, but commute to a city for frequent confrontation with street people, scam merchants, panhandlers, prostitutes, and threatening bands of juveniles. One may reside in Houston, but establish bonds – through business or leisure travel – with a Norwegian banker, a wine merchant from the Rhine Pfalz, or an architect from Rome.

Of course, it is television that most dramatically increases the variety of relationships in which one participates, even if vicariously. One can identify with heroes from a thousand tales, carry on imaginary conversations with talk-show guests from all walks of life, or empathize with athletes from around the globe. One of the most interesting results of this electronic expansion of relationships occurs in the domain of parent–child relationships. As Joshua Meyrowitz proposes in *No Sense of Place* (1985), children of the preceding century were largely insulated from information about the private lives of adults. Parents, teachers, and police could shield children from their adult proceedings by simply conducting them in private places. Further, books dealing with the misgivings, failings, deceits, and conflicts of the adult world were generally unavailable to children. Children remained children. Television has changed all that. Programming systematically reveals the full panoply of "backstage" trials and tribulations to the child. As a result the child no longer interacts with one-dimensional, idealized adults, but with persons possessing complex private lives, doubt-filled and vulnerable. In turn, parents no longer confront the comfortably naive child of yesteryear, but one whose awe is diminished and whose insights may be acute.

The technology of the age both expands the variety of human relationships and modifies the form of older ones. When relationships move from the face-to-face to the electronic mode, they are often altered. Relationships that were confined to specific situations – to offices, living rooms, bedrooms – become "unglued." They are no longer geographically confined, but can take place anywhere. Unlike face-to-face relationships, electronic relationships also conceal visual information (eye movement, expressive movements of the mouth), so a telephone speaker cannot read the facial cues of the listener for signs of approval or disapproval. As a result, there is a greater tendency to create an imaginary other with whom to relate. One can fantasize that the other is feeling warm and enthusiastic or cold and angry, and act accordingly. An acquaintance told me that he believed his first marriage to be a product of the heavy phoning necessary for a long-distance courtship. By phone she seemed the most desirable woman in the world; it was only months after the wedding that he realized he had married a mirage.

Many organizations are now installing electronic-mail systems, which enable employees to carry out their business with each other by computer terminals rather than by traditional, face-to-face means. Researchers find that employee relations have subtly changed as a result. Status differences begin to crumble as lower-ranking employees feel freer to express their feelings and question their superiors electronically than in person. Harvard Business School's Shoshana Zuboff suggests that the introduction of "smart machines" into businesses is blurring the distinctions between managers and workers. Managers are no longer the "thinkers" while the workers are consigned to the "doing" (Zuboff 1988). Rather, out of necessity the workers now become managers of information, and as a result, they considerably augment their power.

Relating in New Keys

Of the new forms of relationship that the saturation process has helped create, two are of special interest. First is the *friendly lover* relationship. For the essential romanticist, the object of love was all-consuming. He or she possessed value of such immense proportion that a lifetime of steadfast commitment could be viewed merely as preparation for an eternity of spiritual communion. The belief in marriage for "true love" is still pervasive, but as the social world is increasingly saturated, such relationships become unrealistic. Rather, men and women (especially professionals) are often in motion, traveling to business meetings, conferences, sales campaigns, consultations, vacations, and so on. Murmurings of "I can't live without you" lose their authenticity when one must add, "except until next Tuesday, and possibly again until the following Wednesday." And because many attractive members of the opposite sex are encountered along the way, providing professional benefits and companionships as well, a multiplicity of low level, or "friendly," romances is invited. To illustrate, a single professional woman from Maryland disclosed that she was "seeing" a local lawyer (unhappily married) because it was fun and convenient. At the same time, he took a back seat when a favorite "old friend" in her profession came in from Oklahoma. However, especially during the summer, she was keen to spend her weekends with a Boston consultant (relevant to her line of work) whose boat was moored at Martha's Vineyard. Each of these individuals, in turn, had other friendly lovers.

A second interesting pattern, the *microwave relationship*, is found increasingly on the domestic front. The ideal family unit has traditionally included a close, interdependent "nucleus," composed of a father-provider, a caretaking mother, and children whose lives are centered in the home until early adulthood. Social saturation has cut deeply into this traditional view. Husband and wife are now both likely to have work and recreational relations outside the family; day-care and babysitting facilities are increasingly required; children's social activities may be scattered across city and countryside; evening obligations or indulgences are frequent both for parents and for children over the age of 6; and family members are typically drawn into outside activities – sports, religious community, hobbies, visits – on the weekends. Differing television needs often thrust various family members into different trajectories even when they are at home together. In many families the crucial ritual of interdependence – dinner together – has become a special event. (In some households the dining-room table, once a family center, is strewn with books, papers, letters, and other objects dropped there by family members "passing through.") The home is less a nesting place than a pit stop.

At the same time, however, many parents are loath to give up the traditional image of the close-knit family. As a result, a new from of relationship emerges in which family members attempt to compensate for the vast expanses of nonrelatedness with intense expressions of bondedness. As many understand it, quantity is replaced by quality. The microwave oven is more than a technological support for those living a socially saturated life. It is also a good symbol of the newly emerging form of relationship: in both cases the users command intense heat for the immediate provision of nourishment. The adequacy of the result is subject to debate in both cases.

Intensifying Interchange

> Modern society is to be distinguished from older social formations by the fact that it affords more opportunities both for impersonal and for more intensive personal relationships.
>
> Niklas Luhmann, *Love as Passion*

Interestingly, technology also intensifies the emotional level of many relationships. People come to feel more deeply and express themselves more fully in an increasing number of relationships. This proposal may seem suspect. If persons pass through our lives in increasing numbers and speeds, wouldn't the outcome be a sense of superficiality and a disinclination to get involved? The attractive stranger you meet in Seattle is regrettably from Omaha; the fascinating new neighbors are returning in the spring to London; the absorbing seatmate on the plane is flying on to Bombay. What is there to do but keep it light and cool? To be sure, the vast share of the passing parade remains simply that. However, consider two aspects of the traditional, face-to-face community.

First, as relationships continue over a period of years they tend toward normalization. People choose to do things that reliably give them satisfaction. Changes in pattern mean risking these satisfactions. Thus, relationships over time tend toward a leveling of emotional intensity. As many married couples put it, "Exciting romance is replaced by a comfortable depth."

Second, the face-to-face community lends itself to a high degree of informal surveillance. People tend to know what the others are doing most of the time. They see each other across a room, through their windows, passing in the street, and so on. And where the social world remains stable, and new information is scant, the smallest details of one's life become everyone's topics of conversation. Petty gossip and strong community norms walk hand in hand. The intensity generated by the new, the novel, and the deviant is in scarce supply.

In the present context of saturation, neither of these conditions prevails. Because all relationships are constantly being disrupted, it is more difficult for any given relationship to normalize. The evening at home, once quiet, relaxed, and settling, is now – by dint of telephone, automobile, television, and the like – a parade of faces, information, and intrusions. One can scarcely settle into a calming rut, because who one is and the cast of "significant others" are in continuous motion. Further, because relationships range far and wide, largely through various electronic means, they cannot easily be supervised by others who care. One can find the intimacy of "telling all" to a close friend in Chicago, because those who would be horrified in Dallas or Topeka will never know. One can let the internal fires rage in Paris, because the folk in Peoria will never see the glow. One academic colleague spoke of his conversation with a woman while waiting in a check-in line for a return journey to the United States. The plane was to stop over in Iceland, and passengers had the choice of continuing the journey directly or remaining in Iceland and catching the next plane two days later. The professor found himself attracted to the lady and emboldened by the anonymity of the situation. Suddenly he found himself stammering a proposal to the woman to remain with him in Iceland for two days. Her complex smile gave him no answer. They silently approached the baggage carts on which travelers had to place their bags for either the direct flight or the layover. To his speechless amazement, she maneuvered her bag into the latter cart. After two days of bliss they parted company, never to communicate with each other again.

The press toward intensity is not limited to normalization and the breakdown of surveillance. There are also factors of fantasy and fleetingness at play. As the romanticists were well aware, little inspired the pen so much as the absence of the adored one. In the other's absence, one's fantasies were free to roan; one could project onto the favored person all virtues and desires. In this respect, nineteenth-century romanticism can be partially attributed to the combination of a cultural morality that discouraged a free play of relationships and the number of individuals educated in writing. Although standards of morality have liberalized since then, the increased possibility for relationships at a distance has had much the same effect as it did on the romantics. Relations at a distance can thus glow more brightly, and interchanges remain more highly charged.

The occasional meeting is intensified, finally, by its shortness. If it is agreed that the other is a "good friend," "very close," or a "special person," then the short periods of meeting must be similarly expressive. One must somehow demonstrate the significance of one's feelings and the high esteem in which the relationship is held. And, because there is little time, the demonstrations must be loud and clear. The result may be an elegantly prepared dinner, reservations at an unusual restaurant, entertainments or excursions planned, selected guests invited for sharing, and the like. Friends living in a central European city recently complained of what amounted to a delirium *ad* exhaustion. So frequently did visiting friends require a "display of significance" that both spirits and pocketbooks were depleted. Couples in frequently visited cities such as New York and Paris speak of the measures they take to ensure they have no spare bedrooms. With frequent visitors, no time remains for their nurturing capacities; spare rooms risk the evisceration of their private relationship.

Populating the Self

> The very din of imaginal voices in adulthood – as they sound in thought and memory, in poetry, drama, novels, and movies, in speech, dreams, fantasy, and prayer…can be valued not just as subordinate to social reality, but as a reality as intrinsic to human existence as the literally social.
>
> Mary Watkins, *Invisible Guests*

Consider the moments:

- Over lunch with friends you discuss Northern Ireland. Although you have never spoken a word on the subject, you find yourself heatedly defending British policies.
- You work as an executive in the investments department of a bank. In the evenings you smoke marijuana and listen to the Grateful Dead.

- You sit in a café and wonder what it would be like to have an intimate relationship with various strangers walking past.
- You are a lawyer in a prestigious midtown firm. On the weekends you work on a novel about romance with a terrorist.
- You go to a Moroccan restaurant and afterward take in the latest show at a country-and-western bar.

In each case individuals harbor a sense of coherent identity or self-sameness, only to find themselves suddenly propelled by alternative impulses. They seem securely to be one sort of person, but yet another comes bursting to the surface – in a suddenly voiced opinion, a fantasy, a turn of interests, or a private activity. Such experiences with variation and self-contradiction may be viewed as preliminary effects of social saturation. They may signal a *populating of the self*, the acquisition of multiple and disparate potentials for being. It is this process of self-population that begins to undermine the traditional commitments to both romanticist and modernist forms of being. It is pivotal importance in setting the stage for the postmodern turn. Let us explore.

The technologies of social saturation expose us to an enormous range of persons, new forms of relationships, unique circumstances and opportunities, and special intensities of feeling. One can scarcely remain unaffected by such exposure. As child-development specialists now agree, the process of socialization is lifelong. We continue to incorporate information from the environment throughout our lives. When exposed to other persons, we change in two major ways. We increase our capacities for *knowing that* and for *knowing how*. In the first case, through exposure to others we learn myriad details about their words, actions, dress, mannerisms, and so on. We ingest enormous amounts of information about patterns of interchange. Thus, for example, from an hour on a city street, we are informed of the clothing styles of blacks, whites, upper class, lower class, and more. We may learn the ways of Japanese businessmen, bag ladies, Sikhs, Hare Krishnas, or flute players from Chile. We see how relationships are carried out between mothers and daughters, business executives, teenage friends, and construction workers. An hour in a business office may expose us to the political views of a Texas oilman, a Chicago lawyer, and a gay activist from San Francisco. Radio commentators espouse views on boxing, pollution, and child abuse; pop music may advocate machoism, racial bigotry, and suicide. Paperback books cause hearts to race over the unjustly treated, those who strive against impossible odds, those who are brave or brilliant. And this is to say nothing of television input. Via television, myriad figures are allowed into the home who would never otherwise trespass. Millions watch as talk-show guests – murderers, rapists, women prisoners, child abusers, members of the KKK, mental patients, and others often discredited – attempt to make their lives intelligible. There are few 6-year-olds who cannot furnish at least a rudimentary account of life in an African village, the concerns of divorcing parents, or drug-pushing in the ghetto. Hourly our storehouse of social knowledge expands in range and sophistication.

This massive increase in knowledge of the social world lays the groundwork for a second kind of learning, a *knowing how*. We learn how to place such knowledge into action, to shape it for social consumption, to act so that social life can proceed effectively. And the possibilities for placing this supply of information into effective action are constantly expanding. The Japanese businessman glimpsed on the street today, and on the television tomorrow, may well be confronted in one's office the following week. On these occasions the rudiments of appropriate behavior are already in place. If a mate announces that he or she is thinking about divorce, the other's reaction is not likely to be dumb dismay. The drama has so often been played out on television and movie screens that one is already prepared with multiple options. If one wins a wonderful prize, suffers a humiliating loss, faces temptation to cheat, or learns of a sudden death in the family, the reactions are hardly random. One more or less knows how it goes, is more or less ready for action. Having seen it all before, one approaches a state of ennui.

In an important sense, as social saturation proceeds we become pastiches, imitative assemblages of each other. In memory we carry others' patterns of being with us. If the conditions are favorable, we can place these patterns into action. Each of us becomes the other, a representative, or a replacement. To put it more broadly, as the century has progressed selves have become increasingly populated with the character of others. We are not one, or a few, but like Walt Whitman, we "contain multitudes." We appear to each other as single identities, unified, of whole cloth. However, with social saturation, each of us comes to harbor a vast population of hidden potentials – to be a blues singer, a gypsy, an aristocrat, a criminal. All the selves lie latent, and under the right conditions may spring to life.

The populating of the self not only opens relationships to new ranges of possibility, but one's subjective life also becomes more fully laminated. Each of the selves we acquire from others can contribute to inner dialogues, private discussions we have with ourselves about all manner of persons, events, and issues. These internal voices, these vestiges of relationships both real and imagined, have been given different names; *invisible guests* by Mary Watkins, *social imagery* by Eric Klinger, and *social ghosts* by Mary Gergen, who found in her research that virtually all the young people she sampled could discuss many such experiences with ease (Gergen 1987; Klinger 1981; Watkins 1986; see also Baldwin and Holmes 1987). Most of these ghosts were close friends, often from earlier periods of their lives. Family members were also frequent, with the father's voice predominating, but grandparents, uncles, aunts, and other relatives figured prominently. Relevant to the earlier discussion of relations with media figures, almost a quarter of the ghosts mentioned were individuals with whom the young people had never had any direct interchange. Most were entertainers: rock stars, actors and actresses, singers, and the like. Others were religious figures such as Jesus and Mary, fictitious characters such as James Bond and Sherlock Holmes, and celebrities such as Chris Evert, Joe Montana, Barbara Walters, and the president.

The respondents also spoke of the many ways the social ghosts functioned in their lives. It was not simply that they were there for conversation or contemplation; they also served as models for action. They set standards for behavior; they were admired and were emulated. As one wrote, "Connie Chung was constantly being used as a role model for me and I found myself responding to a question about what I planned to do after graduation by saying that I wanted to go into journalism just because I had been thinking of her." Or, as another wrote of her grandmother, "She showed me how to be tolerant of all people and to show respect to everyone regardless of their state in life." Ghosts also voiced opinions on various matters. Most frequently they were used to bolster one's beliefs. At times such opinions were extremely important. As one wrote of the memory of an early friend, "She is the last link I have to

Christianity at this point in my life when I am trying to determine my religious inclinations." Still other respondents spoke of the way their ghosts supported their self-esteem: "I of think my father and I know that he would be proud of what I have accomplished." Many mentioned the sense of emotional support furnished by their ghosts: "My grandmother seems to be watching me and showing that she loves me even if I am not doing so well."

In closely related work, the psychologists Hazel Markus and Paula Nurius (1986) speak of *possible selves*, the multiple conceptions people harbor of what they might become, would like to become, or are afraid to become. In each case, these possible selves function as private surrogates for others to whom one has been exposed, either directly or via the media. The family relations specialists Paul Rosenblatt and Sara Wright (1984) speak similarly of the *shadow realities* that exist in close relationships. In addition to the reality that a couple shares together, each will harbor alternative interpretations of their lives together, interpretations that might appear unacceptable and threatening if revealed to the partner. These shadow realities are typically generated and supported by persons outside the relationship – possibly members of the extended family, but also figures from the media. Finally, the British psychologist Michael Billig and his colleagues (1988) have studied the values, goals, and ideals to which people are committed in their everyday lives. They found the typical condition of the individual to be internal conflict: for each belief there exists a strong counter-tendency. People feel their prejudices are justified, yet it is wrong to be intolerant; that there should be equality but hierarchies are also good; and that we are all basically the same, but we must hold on to our individuality. For every value, goal, or ideal, one holds to the converse as well. Billig proposes that the capacity for contradiction is essential to the practical demands of life in contemporary society.

This virtual cacophony of potentials is of no small consequence for either romanticist or modernist visions of the self. For as new and disparate voices are added to one's being, committed identity becomes an increasingly arduous achievement. How difficult for the romantic to keep firm grasp on the helm of an idealistic undertaking when a chorus of internal voices sing the praises of realism, skepticism, hedonism, and nihilism. And can the committed realist, who believes in the powers of rationality and observation, remain arrogant in the face of inner urges toward emotional indulgence, moral sentiment, spiritual sensitivity, or aesthetic fulfillment? Thus, as social saturation adds incrementally to the population of self, each impulse toward well-formed identity is cast into increasing doubt; each is found absurd, shallow, limited, or flawed by the onlooking audience of the interior.

Multiphrenia

> Modern man is afflicted with a permanent identity crisis, a condition conducive to considerable nervousness.
> Peter Berger, Brigitte Berger, and Hansfried Kellner, *The Homeless Mind*

It is sunny Saturday morning and he finishes breakfast in high spirits. It is a rare day in which he is free to do as he pleases. With relish he contemplates his options. The back door needs fixing, which calls for a trip to the hardware store. This would allow a much-needed haircut; and while in town he could get a birthday card for his brother, leave off his shoes for repair, and pick up shirts at the cleaners. But, he ponders, he really should get some exercise; is there time for jogging in the afternoon? That reminds him of a championship game he wanted to see at the same time. To be taken more seriously was his ex-wife's repeated request for a luncheon talk. And shouldn't he also settle his vacation plans before all the best locations are taken? Slowly his optimism gives way to a sense of defeat. The free day has become a chaos of competing opportunities and necessities.

If such a scene is vaguely familiar, it attests only further to the pervasive effects of social saturation and the populating of the self. More important, one detects amid the hurly-burly of contemporary life a new constellation of feelings or sensibilities, a new pattern of self-consciousness. This syndrome may be termed *multiphrenia*, generally referring to the splitting of the individual into a multiplicity of self-investments. This condition is partly an outcome of self-population, but partly a result of the populated self's efforts to exploit the potentials of the technologies of relationship. In this sense, there is a cyclical spiraling toward a state of multiphrenia. As one's potentials are expanded by the technologies, so one increasingly employs the technologies for self-expression; yet, as the technologies are further utilized, so do they add to the repertoire of potentials. It would be a mistake to view this multiphrenic condition as a form of illness, for it is often suffused with a sense of expansiveness and adventure. Someday there may indeed be nothing to distinguish multiphrenia from simply "normal living."

However, before we pass into this oceanic state, let us pause to consider some prominent features of the condition (see Berger et al. 1973 for a precursor to the present discussion). Three of these are especially noteworthy.

Vertigo of the Valued

> Because of the constant change and feeling "off balance," it is essential for men and women to develop . . . coping skills. First, understand that you will never "catch up" and be on top of things and accept this as all right. . . . Put a high priority on spending time relaxing and enjoying life, in spite of all that needs to be done.
>
> Bruce A. Baldwin, *Stress and Technology*

With the technology of social saturation, two of the major factors traditionally impeding relationships – namely time and space – are both removed. The past can be continuously renewed – via voice, video, and visits, for example – and distance poses no substantial barriers to ongoing interchange. Yet this same freedom ironically leads to a form of enslavement. For each person, passion, or potential incorporated into oneself exacts a penalty, a penalty both of *being* and of *being with*. In the former case, as others are incorporated into the self, their tastes, goals, and values also insinuate themselves into one's being. Through continued interchange, one acquires, for example, a yen for Thai cooking, the desire for retirement security, or an investment in wildlife preservation. Through others one comes to value whole-grain breads, novels from Chile, or community politics. Yet as Buddhists have long been aware, to desire is simultaneously to become a slave of the desirable. To "want" reduces one's choice to "want not." Thus, as others are incorporated into the self, and their desires become one's own, there is an expansion of goals, of "musts," wants, and needs. Attention is necessitated, effort is exerted, frustrations are encountered. Each new desire places its demands and reduces one's liberties.

There is also the penalty of being with. As relationships develop, their participants acquire local definitions: friend, lover, teacher, supporter, and so on. To sustain the relationship requires an honoring of the definitions, both of self and other. If two persons become close friends, for example, each acquires certain rights, duties, and privileges. Most relationships of any significance carry with them a range of obligations, for communication, joint activities, preparing for the other's pleasure, rendering appropriate congratulations, and so on. Thus, as relations accumulate and expand over time, there is a steadily increasing range of phone calls to make and answer, greeting cards to address, visits or activities to arrange, meals to prepare, preparations to be made, clothes to buy, makeup to apply... And with each new opportunity – for skiing together in the Alps, touring Australia, camping in the Adirondacks, or snorkeling in the Bahamas – there are "opportunity costs." One must unearth information, buy equipment, reserve hotels, arrange travel, work long hours to clear one's desk, locate babysitters, dogsitters, homesitters... Liberation becomes a swirling vertigo of demands.

In the professional world this expansion of "musts" is strikingly evident. In the university of the 1950s, for example, one's departmental colleagues were often vital to one's work. One could walk but a short distance for advice, information, support, and so on. Departments were often close-knit and highly interdependent; travels to other departments or professional meetings were notable events. Today, however, the energetic academic will be linked by post, long-distance phone, fax, and electronic mail to like-minded scholars around the globe. The number of interactions possible in a day is limited only by the constraints of time. The technologies have also stimulated the development of hundreds of new organizations, international conferences, and professional meetings. A colleague recently informed me that if funds were available he could spend his entire sabbatical traveling from one professional gathering to another. A similar condition pervades the business world. One's scope of business opportunities is no longer so limited by geography; the technologies of the age enable projects to be pursued around the world. (Colgate Tartar Control toothpaste is now sold in over forty countries.) In effect, the potential for new connection and new opportunities is practically unlimited. Daily life has become a sea of drowning demands, and there is no shore in sight.

The Expansion of Inadequacy

> Now You Can Read the Best Business Books of 1989 in Just 15 Minutes Each!
> Advertisement, *US Air Magazine*

> Information anxiety is produced by the ever-widening gap between what we understand and what we think we should understand.
> Richard Saul Wurman, *Information Anxiety*

It is not simply the expansion of self through relationships that hounds one with the continued sense of "ought." There is also the seeping of self-doubt into everyday consciousness, a subtle feeling of inadequacy that smothers one's activities with an uneasy sense of impending emptiness. In important respects this sense of inadequacy is a by-product of the populating of self and the presence of social ghosts. For as we incorporate others into ourselves, so does the range of proprieties expand, that is, the range of what we feel a "good," "proper," or "exemplary" person should be. Many of us carry with us the "ghost of a father," reminding us of the values of honesty and hard work, or a mother challenging us to be nurturing and understanding. We may also absorb from a friend the values of maintaining a healthy body, from a lover the goal of self-sacrifice, from a teacher the ideal of worldly knowledge, and so on. Normal development leaves most people with a rich range of "goals for a good life," and with sufficient resources to achieve a sense of personal well-being by fulfilling these goals.

But now consider the effects of social saturation. The range of one's friends and associates expands exponentially; one's past life continues to be vivid; and the mass media expose one to an enormous array of new criteria for self-evaluation. A friend from California reminds one to relax and enjoy life; in Ohio an associate is getting ahead by working eleven hours a day. A relative from Boston stresses the importance of cultural sophistication, while a Washington colleague belittles one's lack of political savvy. A relative's return from Paris reminds one to pay more attention to personal appearance, while a ruddy companion from Colorado suggests that one grows soft.

Meanwhile newspapers, magazines, and television provide a barrage of new criteria of self-evaluation. Is one sufficiently adventurous, clean, well traveled, well read, low in cholesterol, slim, skilled in cooking, friendly, odor-free, coiffed, frugal, burglarproof, family-oriented? The list is unending. More than once I have heard the lament of a subscriber to the Sunday *New York Times*. Each page of this weighty tome will be read by millions. Thus each page remaining undevoured by day's end will leave one precariously disadvantaged, a potential idiot in a thousand unpredictable circumstances.

Yet the threat of inadequacy is hardly limited to the immediate confrontation with mates and media. Because many of these criteria for self-evaluation are incorporated into the self – existing within the cadre of social ghosts – they are free to speak at any moment. The problem with values is that they are sufficient unto themselves. To value justice, for example, is to say nothing of the value of love; investing in duty will blind one to the value of spontaneity. No one value in itself recognizes the importance of any alternative value. And so it is with the chorus of social ghosts. Each voice of value stands to discredit all that does not meet its standard. All the voices at odds with one's current conduct thus stand as internal critics, scolding, ridiculing, and robbing action of its potential for fulfillment. One settles in front of the television for enjoyment, and the chorus begins: "12-year-old," "couch potato," "lazy," "irresponsible"... One sits down with a good book, and again, "sedentary," "antisocial," "inefficient," "fantasist"... Join friends for a game of tennis and "skin cancer," "shirker of household duties," "underexercised," "overly competitive" come up. Work late and it is "workaholic," "heart attack-prone," "overly ambitious," "irresponsible family member." Each moment is enveloped in the guilt born of all that was possible but now foreclosed.

Rationality in Recession

> A group of agents acting rationally in the light of their expectations could arrive at so many outcomes that none has adequate reasons for action.
>
> Martin Hollis, *The Cunning of Reason*

> LATIN DEBTS: LACK OF CONSENSUS
> Washington Awash in Arguments
> Dry on Agreements
>
> Headlines, *International Herald Tribune*

A third dimension of multiphrenia is closely related to the others. The focus here is on the rationality of everyday decision-making – instances in which one tries to be a "reasonable person." Why, one asks, is it important for one's children to attend college? The rational reply is that a college education increases one's job opportunities, earnings, and likely sense of personal fulfillment. Why should I stop smoking? one asks, and the answer is clear that smoking causes cancer, so to smoke is simply to invite a short life. Yet these "obvious" lines of reasoning are obvious only so long as one's identity remains fixed within a particular group.

The rationality of these replies depends altogether on the sharing of opinions – of each incorporating the views of others. To achieve identity in other cultural enclaves turns these "good reasons" into "rationalizations," "false consciousness," or "ignorance." Within some subcultures a college education is a one-way ticket to bourgeois conventionality: a white-collar job, picket fence in the suburbs, and chronic boredom. For many, smoking is an integral part of a risky life-style; it furnishes a sense of intensity, offbeatness, rugged individualism. In the same way, saving money for old age is "sensible" in one family, and "oblivious to the erosions of inflation" in another. For most westerners, marrying for love is the only reasonable (if not conceivable) thing to do. But many Japanese will point to statistics demonstrating greater longevity and happiness in arranged marriages. Rationality is a vital by-product of social participation.

Yet as the range of our relationships is expanded, the validity of each localized rationality is threatened. What is rational in one relationship is questionable or absurd from the standpoint of another. The "obvious choice" while talking with a colleague lapses into absurdity when speaking with a spouse, and into irrelevance when an old friend calls that evening. Further, because each relationship increases one's capacities for discernment, one carries with oneself a multiplicity of competing expectations, values, and beliefs about "the obvious solution." Thus, if the options are carefully evaluated, every decision becomes a leap into gray vapors. Hamlet's bifurcated decision becomes all too simple, for it is no longer being or nonbeing that is in question, but to which of multifarious beings one can be committed. T. S. Eliot began to sense the problem when Prufrock found "time yet for a hundred indecisions/And for a hundred visions and revisions,/Before taking of a toast and tea" (1930).

The otherwise simple task of casting a presidential vote provides a useful illustration. As one relates (either directly or vicariously) to various men and women, in various walks of life, and various sectors of the nation or abroad, one's capacities for discernment are multiplied. Where one might have once employed a handful of rational standards, or seen the issues in only limited ways, one can now employ a variety of criteria and see many sides of many issues. One may thus favor candidate A because he strives for cuts in the defense budget, but also worry about the loss of military capability in an unsteady world climate. Candidate B's plans for stimulating the growth of private enterprise may be rational from one standpoint, but the resulting tax changes seem unduly to penalize the middle-class family. At the same time, there is good reason to believe that A's cuts in defense spending will favor B's aims for a stimulated economy, and that B's shifts in the tax structure will make A's reductions in the military budget unnecessary. To use one criterion, candidate A is desirable because of his seeming intelligence, but from another, his complex ideas seem both cumbersome and remote from reality. Candidate B has a pleasing personality, useful for him to garner popular support for his programs, but in another sense his pleasant ways suggest he cannot take a firm stand. And so on.

Increasing the criteria of rationality does not, then, move one to a clear and univocal judgment of the candidates. Rather, the degree of complexity is increased until a rationally coherent stand is impossible. In effect, as social saturation steadily expands the population of the self, a choice of candidates approaches the arbitrary. A toss of a coin becomes equivalent to the diligently sought solution. We approach a condition in which the very idea of "rational choice" becomes meaningless.

So we find a profound sea change taking place in the character of social life during the twentieth century. Through an array of newly emerging technologies the world of relationships becomes increasingly saturated. We engage in greater numbers of relationships, in a greater variety of forms, and with greater intensities than ever before. With the multiplication of relationships also comes a transformation in the social capacities of the individual, both in knowing how and knowing that. The relatively coherent and unified sense of self inherent in a traditional culture gives way to manifold and competing potentials. A multiphrenic condition emerges in which one swims in ever-shifting, concatenating, and contentious currents of being. One bears the burden of an increasing array of oughts, of self-doubts and irrationalities. The possibility for committed romanticism or strong and single-minded modernism recedes, and the way is opened for the postmodern being.

References

Baldwin, Mark and Holmes, John G. 1987. "Private audiences and awareness of the self." *Journal of Personality and Social Psychology* 52: 1087–198.

Berger, Peter, Berger, Brigitte, and Kellner, Hansfried. 1973. *The Homeless Mind*. New York: Random House.

Billig, Michael et al. 1988. *Ideological Dilemmas*. London: Sage Publications.

Eliot, T. S. 1930. "The love song of J. Alfred Prufrock." In *The Waste Land and Other Poems*. New York: Harvest.

Gergen, Mary. 1987. "Social ghosts, our imaginal dialogues with others." Paper presented at the American Psychological Association meeting, New York, August.

Klinger, Eric. 1981. "The central place of imagery in human functioning." In Eric Klinger (ed.) *Imagery*, vol. 2: *Concepts, Results, and Applications*. New York: Plenum.

Markus, Hazel and Nurius, Paula. 1986. "Possible selves." *American Psychologist* 41: 954–69.

Meyrowitz, Joshua. 1985. *No Sense of Place: The Impact of Electronic Media on Social Behavior.* New York: Oxford University Press.

Rosenblatt, Paul C. and Wright, Sara E. 1984. "Shadow realities in close relationships." *American Journal of Family Therapy* 12: 45–54.

Watkins, Mary. 1986. *Invisible Guests: The Development of Imaginal Dialogues.* Hillsdale, NJ: Analytic Press.

Zuboff, Shoshana. 1988. *In the Age of the Smart Machine,* New York: Basic Books.

Part IV

Interaction and Inequality

Introduction

A fourth distinctive topic of sociological social psychology is the social psychology of inequality, i.e., the analysis of the ways in which social psychological processes reflect and contribute to patterns of inequality in the larger society. The readings included in this section focus on the relationship between interaction and inequality, the effects of social categories such as race, class, and gender on everyday social interaction, and the role of ideological beliefs in stabilizing and legitimating inequality.

Since about the 1960s, theories and research in the area of interaction and inequality have identified countless ways in which social inequality is expressed and maintained in social interaction. As Nancy Henley states in the extract from her classic *Body Politics:* "In front of, and defending, the political-economic structure that determines our lives and defines the context of human relationships, there is the micropolitical structure that helps maintain it" (1977: 3). Observed race, gender, or class differences in nonverbal patterns of communication, she argues, not only reflect the racial, gender, and class inequalities of power in the larger society but also contribute to maintaining it (p. 2).

In *Body Politics*, Henley draws connections between social inequality and several patterns of nonverbal communication. First, she argues that social power is expressed through the command of personal space (space surrounding a person's body) and control over the physical distance between self and others (1977: 33). Second, lower-status people more often wait for the time of higher-status people, while higher-status people may command immediate access to the time of lower-status people when they choose to do so (p. 45). Third, people with more power and status are accorded the conversational privileges of interrupting, contradicting, manipulating silence, and demanding speech (p. 69). Fourth, subordinates are expected to display a bodily formality in interactions with superiors, while superiors demonstrate their superiority with bodily relaxation (p. 85). Fifth, higher-status persons may legitimately initiate touch of subordinates, while the symmetrical privilege is denied to subordinates (p. 95). Sixth, higher-status people exhibit greater visual dominance behavior (i.e., a higher rate of looking while speaking than of looking while listening) than people with lower status (p. 156).

According to SCES theory, discussed in Part II and featured in Cecilia Ridgeway and Henry Walker's review article "Status structures" (1995), the level of competence expected of a person by other members of a task group depends on the person's external statuses, i.e., race, age, gender, occupational status, or educational background. Particularly in situations in which information about the ability of group members is unavailable, such characteristics are used to predict the contributions a person will likely make to the group's task. Because these predictions affect patterns of group interaction, the expectations attached to external status characteristics tend to become self-fulfilling.

According to research in this area, such expectations affect interaction in each of the following ways. First, higher-status group members are looked to and given more opportunities to contribute to the group's task. Not encouraged or supported in contributing, a lower-status member will have greater difficulty in demonstrating competence. Second, others tend to be more influenced by the suggestions of higher-status group members. The inability of the low-status member to influence others not only denies him or her the opportunity to demonstrate the potential usefulness of the suggestions but the lack of influence itself serves as a marker of incompetence. Third, independently of their objective merits, the contributions of high-status members tend to be evaluated more favorably than the contributions of lower-status members. Fourth, the use of double standards in evaluation contributes to the perpetuation of initial expectations. Research on double standards shows that higher-status group members are evaluated according to more lenient standards for success and failure, while lower-status group members are evaluated according to stringent standards for success and failure. Fifth, research shows that the burden of proof of non-relevance of external status characteristics rests on the low-status person (Ridgeway and Walker 1995: 289). The burden to demonstrate that her race, gender, and age has no bearing on her ability to succeed in a job, for example, falls on the young, black, female. She is considered incompetent until proven competent. Finally, low-status group members are hindered in overcoming negative expectations because their attempts to contribute to a group goal may be viewed as inappropriate. Research shows that the contributions and resulting status gains of high-status members are viewed as appropriate and beneficial to the achievement of the group's goals. The contributions of low-status members, on the other hand, are perceived as self-interested and inappropriate attempts to gain status in the group (p. 296). In each of these ways, inequalities in the larger society generate inequalities in social interaction which in turn contribute to maintaining societal inequality.

The readings by Derber, Feagin and Sikes, and Komter identify specific ways in which class, race, and gender inequality are manifested and experienced in everyday social interaction. The chapter by Charles Derber, "Attention for sale: The hidden privileges of class," examines how social class affects the amount and kind of attention one gives and receives in social interaction. *The Pursuit of Attention*, the book from which it was drawn, examines the relationship between the stratification system of the society and the dynamics of attention-giving and attention-getting in everyday social interaction. In all interactions, Derber suggests, the amount and kind of attention one receives is shaped by gender, social class, and other factors which are believed to determine one's worth. The distribution of attention in everyday interaction, Derber argues, mirrors the distribution of resources in the larger society. Whether one has an attention-getting or an attention-giving job, for instance, affects the amount of attention one gives and receives on a regular basis. Access to higher-status jobs, jobs that are more likely to involve attention-getting and less likely to require giving attention, varies according to social class and gender. Persons in middle-class occupations, e.g., executives, physicians, lawyers, and professors, are more likely to command the attention of secretaries, subordinates, and the public than are persons in working-class jobs. Both because of their lower status and because of the compatibility of such jobs with valued female traits, women are more likely than men to be employed in attention-providing occupations such as nursing, secretarial work, social work, day care, and elementary school teaching. Focusing exclusively on the impact of social class, the extract from Derber's book looks at how the amount of attention one receives in both formal and informal social interaction is affected by wealth, occupation, and education.

The extract from Feagin and Sikes's *Living With Racism: The Black Middle Class Experience* focuses on the psychological and interpersonal challenges faced by African Americans as they confront racial discrimination and the potential for racial discrimination in everyday interaction. Drawing on interviews with middle-class African Americans, they identify a number of ways in which discrimination or the possibility of discrimination affects everyday experience. Battling racial barriers to achievement, one respondent points out, takes energy away from pursuit of the original goal and is as much a barrier to achievement as the racist act itself (Feagin and Sikes 1994: 274). Facing apparent acts of discrimination, furthermore, many struggle with the question of whether they were being paranoid or overly sensitive (p. 294). When they conclude discrimination did indeed occur, they further face the difficulty of establishing the legitimacy of their view of the situation to potentially suspicious authorities. Many feel pressured to make no mistakes on their jobs, fearful of providing any shred of evidence to confirm negative racial stereotypes (pp. 277, 278). The stress caused by having to "prove oneself," Feagin and Sikes emphasize, is a major drain on the energy of African Americans (p. 296).

The chapter by Aafke Komter, "Hidden power in marriage," based on a study of married couples in the Netherlands, identifies informal ways in which power inequality between men and women is sustained in marital interaction. Particularly important for understanding how inequality in such relationships comes to be accepted and legitimated is the analysis of "invisible power." Komter's analysis shows how the inequalities of esteem between women and men and the unequal standards by which men and women are evaluated operate to disguise inequalities of power between husbands and wives. Komter found that wives were far more likely than husbands to report negative qualities about themselves, and that husbands and wives tended to attribute more overall competence to the husband. The higher regard in which both husband and wife held the husband resulted in the husband's greater influence being attributed to his superior competence and not experienced as an inequality of power. Furthermore, Komter found that many inequalities were concealed from view by perceptual biases. In particular, the study found that husbands tended to overestimate their own contributions and underestimate their wives' contributions to the household division of labor. At least in part, this bias can be explained by viewing women's and men's respective contributions through the lens of gender-specific cultural standards.

The final reading, the prologue to Mary Jackman's *The Velvet Glove: Paternalism and Conflict in Gender, Class, and Race Relations*, similarly focuses on the legitimation of inequality. Jackman argues that research on the ideology of inequality is dominated by a forced and misguided choice between "conflict and consensus" (1994: 1). This choice, she thinks, neglects the reality that consensus is often attached to exploitation in long-term relations of inequality. In such relationships, dominant groups are less likely to express blatant hostility and more likely to attempt to cover up conflict through befriending and emotionally disarming subordinates (p. 2). Dominant groups, she argues, always prefer a paternalistic relationship to subordinates when possible (p. 10). Paternalism obviates the costly necessity of conflict by emotionally and cognitively binding subordinates to the affection and rewards offered by dominants (p. 15). Despite the fact that dominant groups strive to pass off their paternalism as benevolence, Jackman emphasizes that the two must be distinguished. Unlike benevolence, paternalism entails exploitation. Counter to the view that love provides protection against abuse in human relationships, Jackman holds that love may serve as the cement of exploitation. The dominant has easier access to the resources of the subordinate when the relationship is infused with affection (p. 16). The remainder of Jackman's book explores the role of paternalism in class, race, and gender relations.

References

Derber, Charles. 1979. *The Pursuit of Attention: Power and Individualism in Everyday Life.* New York: Oxford University Press.

Feagin, Joe R. and Sikes, Melvin P. 1994. *Living With Racism: The Black Middle Class Experience.* Boston: Beacon Press.

Henley, Nancy M. 1977. *Body Politics: Power, Sex, and Nonverbal Communication.* Englewood Cliffs, NJ: Prentice-Hall.

Komter, Aafke. 1989. "Hidden power in marriage." *Gender & Society* 3(2): 187–216.

Jackman, Mary. 1994. *The Velvet Glove: Paternalism and Conflict in Gender, Class and Race Relations.* Berkeley: University of California Press.

Ridgeway, Cecilia and Walker, Henry. 1995. "Status structures." In Karen S. Cook, Gary Alan Fine, and James S. House (eds.) *Sociological Perspectives on Social Psychology.* Boston and London: Allyn and Bacon, pp. 281–96.

Additional reading

Archibald, W. Peter. 1976. "Face-to-face: The alienating effects of class, status, and power divisions." *American Sociological Review* 41: 819–37.

Berger, Joseph and Zelditch, Morris (eds.) 1985. *Status, Rewards, and Influence.* San Francisco: Jossey-Bass.

Foschi, Martha. 1997. "Double standards in the evaluation of men and women." Social *Psychology Quarterly* 59(3): 237–54.

Howard, Judith A., Blumstein, Philip, and Schwartz, Pepper. 1986. "Sex, power, and influence tactics in intimate relationships." *Journal of Personality and Social Psychology* 51(1): 102–9.

Kalbfleisch, Pamela J. and Cody, Michael J. (eds.) 1995. *Gender, Power, and Communication in Human Relationships.* Hillsdale, NJ: Erlbaum.

Kollock, Peter, Blumstein, Philip, and Schwartz, Pepper. 1985. "Sex and power in interaction." *American Sociological Review* 50: 34–47.

LaFrance, Marianne. 1992. "Gender and interruptions: Individual infraction or violation of the social order?" *Psychology of Women Quarterly* 16: 497–512.

Miller, Jean Baker. 1986. *Toward a New Psychology of Women.* Boston: Beacon Press.

Ridgeway, Cecilia L. (ed.) 1992. *Gender, Interaction, and Inequality.* New York: Springer-Verlag.

—— 1993. "Gender, status, and the social psychology of expectations." In Paula England (ed.) *Theory on Gender/Feminism on Theory.* New York: Aldine de Gruyter.

—— 1997. "Interaction and the conservation of gender inequality: Considering employment." *American Sociological Review* 62(2): 218–35.

Sagrestano, Lynda M. 1992. "Power strategies in interpersonal relationships: The effects of expertise and gender." *Psychology of Women Quarterly* 16: 481–95.

Stets, Jan E. 1997. "Status and identity in marital interaction." *Social Psychology Quarterly* 60(3): 185–217.

Tannen, Deborah (ed.) 1993. *Gender and Conversational Interaction*. New York and Oxford: Oxford University Press.

Thorne, Barrie and Henley, Nancy (eds.) 1975. *Language and Sex: Difference and Dominance*. Rowley, Mass.: Newbury House.

Thorne, Barrie, Kramarae, Cheris, and Henley, Nancy (eds.) 1983. *Language, Gender and Society*. Rowley, Mass.: Newbury House.

Webster, Murray Jr. and Foschi, Martha (eds.) 1988. *Status Generalization: New Theory and Research*. Stanford, Calif.: Stanford University Press.

West, Candace and Fenstermaker, Sarah. 1993. "Power, inequality, and the accomplishment of gender: An ethnomethodological view." In Paula England (ed.) *Theory on Gender/Feminism on Theory*. New York: Aldine de Gruyter.

19 Body Politics

Nancy M. Henley

Power and Nonverbal Communication

If you're looking at this you must be interested in nonverbal communication: how we say things with our body postures and movements, facial expression, gestures, touching, eye contact, use of space, and so on. You may have read other books, or articles, on the subject. If so, you may have noticed – or, with many authors, taken for granted – that most of the concerns of this field are ones such as closeness, like and dislike, intimacy, sexuality, expressions of emotion, or attempts to send or cover signals conveying positive or negative attitudes.

But there is another side to interpersonal relationship, one that affects us greatly but which we're encouraged to pay little attention to. This is the element of status, power, dominance, superiority: the vertical dimension of human relations, signalled by our spatial metaphor of "higher-ups," "underlings," "being over," and "looking up to" others. Friendship relations make up the horizontal dimension, and the corresponding spatial metaphor refers to closeness, "being near" and "being distant." The power relation is the "other" dimension in the study of nonverbal communication: important as it is in ordering human interaction, it has received little study from investigators of nonverbal behavior.

The "trivia" of everyday life – touching others, moving closer or farther away, dropping the eyes, smiling, interrupting – are commonly interpreted as facilitating social intercourse, but not recognized in their position as micropolitical gestures, defenders of the status quo – of the state, of the wealthy, of authority, of all those whose power may be challenged. Nevertheless these minutiae find their place on a continuum of social control which extends from internalized socialization at one end to sheer physical force at the other.

In front of, and defending, the political-economic structure that determines our lives and defines the context of human relationships, there is the micropolitical structure that helps maintain it. This micropolitical structure is the substance of our everyday experience. The humiliation of being a subordinate is often felt most sharply and painfully when one is ignored or interrupted while speaking, towered over or forced to move by another's bodily presence, or cowed unknowingly into dropping the eyes, the head, the shoulders. Conversely, the power to manipulate others' lives, to take graft, price gouge, or plan the bombing of far-off peasants is conferred in part by others' snapping to attention in one's presence, their smiling, fearing to touch or approach, their following one around for information and favors. These are the trivia that make up the batter for that great stratified waffle that we call our society.

There are some good anecdotal accounts that illustrate the working of nonverbal controls and point to truths about our unspoken power relationships that we can

Reprinted from "The other dimension" and "Advertisements for the self: Demeanor," in *Body Politics: Power, Sex, and Nonverbal Communication*, Englewood Cliff, NJ: Prentice-Hall, 1977, pp. 2–5, 82–91.

immediately recognize. One example is Jay Haley's tongue-in-cheek description of "The Art of Psychoanalysis," in which he analyzes the interaction between therapist and patient from the point of view of "gamesmanship" (Haley 1962). Besides calling attention to behaviors of the analyst and patient which emphasize their superior–inferior relationship, Haley shows features of the setting which also reinforce a pattern of dominance:

> By placing the patient on a couch, the analyst gives the patient the feeling of having his feet up in the air and the knowledge that the analyst has both feet on the ground. Not only is the patient disconcerted by having to lie down while talking, but he finds himself literally below the analyst and so his one-down position is geographically emphasized. In addition, the analyst seats himself behind the couch where he can watch the patient but the patient cannot watch him. This gives the patient the sort of disconcerted feeling a person has when sparring with an opponent while blindfolded. Unable to see what response his ploys provoke, he is unsure when he is one-up and when one-down.... It is essential that the rare patient who gets an opportunity to observe the analyst see only an impassive demeanor.
> Another purpose is served by the position behind the couch. Inevitably what the analyst says becomes exaggerated in importance since the patient lacks any other means of determining his effect on the analyst. The patient finds himself hanging on the analyst's every word, and by definition he who hangs on another's words is one-down. (1962: 208–10)

Superior or inferior spatial position . . . sitting or lying body posture . . . visibility or invisibility . . . impassive or expressive demeanor . . . these unnoticed details of an encounter are strong determiners of one person's power over another.

Another anecdotal description that tells us much about nonverbal power cues is Erving Goffman's insightful essay, "The nature of deference and demeanor" (1967: 47–95). Goffman draws a general principle from his many observations on a hospital ward: the principle of *symmetric relations between status equals and asymmetric ones between unequals*. That is, equals, such as co-workers on a job, can call each other by first name (e.g., Mike and Phil) and have equal rights to borrow each other's pen, sit in each other's chair, to touch one another or to invite each other out for a drink. Between unequals, though, one may be called by a title and the other by first name (e.g., Mrs Updegraff and Debbie), and one may have privileges in the relationship that the other does not. This is a principle we'll return to often in our examination of nonverbal behavior. Goffman also cites subtle aspects of verbal behavior – voice quality, pitch, interruption, self-disclosure – that signal superiority and subordination.

> Deferential pledges are frequently conveyed through spoken terms of address involving status-identifiers, as when a nurse responds to a rebuke in the operating room with the phrase, "yes, Doctor," signifying by term of address and tone of voice that the criticism has been understood and that, however unpalatable, it has not caused her to rebel. (1967: 60–1)

Between status equals we may expect to find interaction guided by symmetrical familiarity. Between superordinate and subordinate we may expect to find asymmetrical relations, the superordinate having the right to exercise certain familiarities which the subordinate is not allowed to reciprocate. Thus, in the research hospital, doctors tended to call nurses by their first name, while nurses responded with "polite" or "formal" address. Similarly, in American business organizations the boss may thoughtfully ask the elevator man how his children are but this entrance into another's life may be blocked to the elevator man, who can appreciate the concern but not return it. Perhaps the clearest form of this is found in the psychiatrist–patient relation, where the psychiatrist has a right to touch on aspects of the patient's life that the patient might not even allow himself to touch upon, while of course this privilege is not reciprocated. (1967: 64)

Here we see that the psychoanalyst's one-up game described by Jay Haley extends even into the nature of the analyst's listening role: who tells all, and who listens, makes a power game too. What is sympathy when extended symmetrically becomes privilege when it is one-sided. In the same way, the homely gesture of touching may involve privilege:

On Ward A, as in other wards in the hospital, there was a "touch system."... In addition to...symmetrical touch relations on the ward, there were also asymmetrical ones. The doctors touched other ranks as a means of conveying friendly support and comfort, but other ranks tended to feel that it would be presumptuous for them to reciprocate a doctor's touch, let alone initiate such a contact with a doctor. (1967: 73–4)

First names versus formal address...asking or answering personal questions ...touching or being touched...status references...tone of voice...Goffman calls attention to other unobtrusive aspects of an encounter that go with status differences. And more, he shows them as aspects of a group structure, not just a one-to-one relationship. Nonverbal cues, as Haley and Goffman have illustrated, play an extremely important and complex role in the maintenance of the social order: as signs and symbols of dominance, as subtle messages of threat, as gestures of submission.

Nonverbal cues also play an important role among people at the same social level; gestures of recognition, of friendship, loving, disdain, rejection, all regulate and maintain behavior. However, our focus here will be on the power aspect of nonverbal communication, both on the interpersonal and intergroup level, with particular reference to male dominance as one dimension of power. Overall in the social sciences, race dominance is a better known and better studied power manifestation, but there is little in the nonverbal literature written on patterns of interaction among people of different races. To say anything about the use of nonverbal cues maintaining race dominance, we usually must extrapolate from other studies. There is, on the other hand, plenty on sex differences, though it's seldom interpreted in a political (i.e., power-oriented) context.

. . .

Power and Demeanor

Certain behaviors oriented to one's own body are considered so gross that they regularly elicit expressions of disgust, even though we all engage in most or all of them at times. Yawning, scratching, spitting, picking one's nose or scabs, belching, hiccuping, and pasing gas are not countenanced in "polite" company, but do have a certain degree of acceptance among intimates and in extremely informal settings. (Coughing and blowing one's nose are at a lesser level of ceremonial breach.) "Polite" company, that is, the social elite and those who would imitate them, are so removed from their bodies (undoubtedly a sign of spirituality and near-divinity) that they are expected not to feel the need to itch, belch, or fart. Generally, pictures of respected public figures caught in this type of activities are suppressed. In fact, people of some power (often political figures) may demand that no pictures be taken showing them even with tobacco or alcohol, which would convey a certain physical indulgence they don't want to be associated with.

These outcast behaviors have an interesting position in social interaction, since many of them are seen as unavoidable physical impulses – e.g., yawning, belching, itching, hiccuping, farting – and, though disfavored, may be excused on petition of the offender. They are under a certain amount of willful control, however (probably the reason for their less-than-full excusability), especially by some expert practitioners. Goffman has noted a class of offenses called acts of malice or spite: "These often imply arrogance, disdain, and deep hostility, as when a middle-class person yawns directly before others in a slow and elaborate manner. ... When an individual wishes to show hostility to someone before whom he would ordinarily conduct himself tightly, extreme expressions of looseness become an available means" (1963: 218, 228). Anyone who has seen young boys deliver soulful belches one after another at a family gathering's elaborate meal, or seen the angry looks directed at them for uncontrolled flatulence, has seen this phenomenon in action. Goffman cites an illustration from T. E. Lawrence, on life in an RAF training depot in which the surest source of humor was an occasional "loud spirtle of wind," which caused wild laughter with impunity since "farts are not punishable like any other retort" (pp. 228–9).

This power of disruption is the ultimate power of the powerless. It can be a potent one; at the other extreme from unstuffing shirts, but on the same continuum, is the strength of a strike – when workers interrupt the steady flow of goods and services. Even deflating the pompous and disrupting authoritative situations have their place in the onslaught against unjust privilege. In the face-to-face situations described above, the object is to ruffle the composed demeanor of authority. (It is often played as a game to push the offense to the limit, with the least punishment.) Authority is supposed to "keep its cool," to show little emotion and to be unaffected by events in the world around. The same uninvolvement is used as a status cue in interaction between status unequals: to ignore another, to disdain the other's concern, is to show you are much more important to the other than vice versa. (This is again the Principle of Least Interest, acting on the general demeanor of two participants in a situation.) To ruffle that cool, then, is to bring down, if only momentarily, that authority.

It is tempting to romanticize disruptions by belch, yawn, and fart, as some authors have, as jolly shows of power against authority. However, this form of "power" is as much a sign of powerlessness as bowing and scraping; only the powerless must exercise their power in covert ways. And the powerless, lest we forget, are those who have little food or money, dress or shelter, comfort and mental peace. Justice speaks better to smiting one's oppressor with a weapon than with a fart.

Hang Loose

We tend to think of demeanor, the way one presents and conducts oneself, as a product of something termed "breeding" (which in usage has tended to include both genetic endowment *and* upbringing) and/or some mysterious quality of "class." Whatever we think its sources to be, we generally attribute demeanor to an individual, not to a situation or group identification. And yet, those things demeanor encompasses – deportment, dress, bearing – have distinctive class-determined characteristics. There are upper- and lower-class rules of deportment and modes of dress and carriage. Closely related, there are rules and modes that go with power and with powerlessness. For example, the forms of bodily laxness described above are extreme examples of "loose" demeanor. Less dramatic versions of tightness and looseness, however, are part of our everyday interaction and, like other forms of nonverbal communication, have much to indicate about our status and authority.

Demeanor, like deference, can be exhibited to others under either symmetrical or asymmetrical rules. As Goffman has written, symmetry in demeanor seems generally the case between social equals, but not between unequals. Here, those in higher positions are allowed more latitude in behavior, while underlings must be more circumspect:

> at staff meetings on the psychiatric units of the hospital, medical doctors had the privilege of swearing, changing the topic of conversation, and sitting in undignified position; attendants, on the other hand, had the right to attend staff meetings and to ask questions during them...but were implicitly expected to conduct themselves with greater circumspection than was required of doctors... Similarly, doctors had the right to saunter into the nurses' station, lounge on the station's dispensing counter, and engage in joking with the nurses; other ranks participated in this informal interaction with doctors, but only after doctors had initiated it. (1967: 78–9)

These behaviors fall into the complex that Goffman has organized into the idea of "tightness and looseness," that is, "how disciplined the individual is obliged to be in connection with the several ways in which respect for the gathering and its social occasion can be expressed" (1963: ch. 13). How disciplined a person must be relates closely to the degree of involvement the occasion requires. The discipline (or lack of it) is shown in such factors as the ceremonial rank and neatness of one's dress; engagement in side activities such as reading, studying the environment, daydreaming; and engaging in such personal physical caretaking as spitting, picking one's nose, belching, yawning.

Circumspection and tightness are the signals we offer up to superiors, or exhibit in public, to indicate our subordinate position. Mehrabian has presented experimental evidence for actual body tension as a correlate of status. Asymmetrical placement of the limbs, a sidways lean and/or reclining position when seated, and specific relaxations of the hands or neck are all indicators of postural relaxation, associated with a high status communicator. Communicators relax more when paired with an addressee of lower status than with one of higher status (Mehrabian 1972: 25–30).

The Watergate conspiracy trial gives an example of the relaxed demeanor of self-importance and unconcern, contrasted with the tension and thrust of intense involvement. Here former Attorney General John Mitchell relaxes on the witness stand, being questioned by government prosecutor James O. Neal; the reporter gives us a graphic picture of the contrast in their styles: "Neal leaned forward on the podium, pushed his glasses onto his forehead and unleashed a staccato of questions. Mitchell leaned back in his chair and offered terse, laconic replies" (Denison 1974: 32).

Of course, relaxation is also the form of demeanor used among intimates. The invitation to "Relax!" or "Loosen up," offered by the high status person, can be seen as another instance in which the higher status has the privilege of initiating greater intimacy. (Under the circumstances, however, it is easier said than done.) Such a suggestion can be compared, in fact, with the military command "At ease." "At ease" is not, in reality, an invitation to relax but a command to shift to a slightly more stable posture, while remaining as restrained and alert as before.

It may be observed that we have here another example of the norm in which that behavior exhibited by superiors to subordinates (looseness) is exhibited symmetrically among members of the lower social strata (when apart from those in power).

Goffman suggests that a pervasive difference exists between middle- and lower-class American males in their degree of public looseness (1963: ch. 13) He claims that lower-class males, not having to worry about keeping their clothes unrumpled or unsoiled, and having a social role that requires less orientation to public gatherings as such, are afforded much more looseness than their middle-class counterparts. These latter must keep relatively neat and clean, erect and stiff, alert to and involved in the gathering.

This picture, though, doesn't jibe with the earlier evidence of subordinates being required to conduct themselves with greater circumspection than superiors. One explanation for greater middle-class circumspection has been its hope for upward mobility, and therefore greater attention (than in either upper or lower classes) to the rules of conduct by which it must prove itself. Moreover, the situations described are different. The lower-class looseness is for public places, and isn't detailed for the presence of superiors, as in the staff meeting. We may well imagine that that looseness would evaporate in the presence of a recognized authority or superior, such as one's father, a police officer, or the boss. A distinction that might be made, then, is that subordinates' circumspection is exhibited only (or mainly) in the presence of dominants, not as a general marker of class. Working-class men perhaps spend more time in the presence of their peers than middle-class men (and than women of both classes), who work more often in proximity to superiors.

Clothes Make the Man not Responsible

We all know that the rich and powerful dress more expensively and exclusively, both because they can afford to and because dress is a primary indicator of their class status. And that the super-rich have more freedom to dress in ratty old clothes if they wish, being under no compulsion to indicate wealth that is everywhere self-evident. The ill fit of mass-produced clothes, the shabbiness of clothes one can't afford to replace, and the inappropriateness of clothes for some occasions because of limited wardrobe all proclaim low social status. What else is to be said about clothing? Are there clothes that dominate, that influence, that diminish?

A clothing consultant who "has spent more than a decade dressing men to succeed" would say so. His comments on clothing for the principals in the Watergate trials illustrate some aspects of influencing people through clothing, as well as aspects of class and race (Kunz 1974). When Haldeman, Ehrlichman, and Mitchell appeared before the Senate hearings, their need, according to the expert, John Molloy, was to appear credible to the public. Pinstripe suits were the prescription. "The pinstriped suit has been traditionally the most credible apparel for a man to wear when selling something important," he comments.

However, Molloy didn't think this was the proper tack when they went on trial. For one thing, "during the Watergate hearings the credibility of the pinstriped suit shrank." The purpose in a trial is different. Proper dress for defendants is that which, first, does not offend, and second, tries to relate to the jury and judge. The earlier traditional garb that appealed to primarily white middle-class TV hearing-watchers could not be expected to garner much identification from a predominantly black Washington jury.

Molloy suggested they should "borrow Jerry Ford's neckties": "A lot of the President's neckties are non-authoritarian and sporty. His light-colored suits are too. If you're trying to visually communicate to a jury that you weren't the man in charge, wearing non-authoritarian clothes could be a plus." He thought they should wear non-flashy shirts, suits in medium tones, and neckties that were neither flamboyant nor ultra-upper-class. He added, though, that these men's appearances were so well known that it would be hard to change their image.

However, even without his advice (for the trial) two of the defendants did make some change in image. Haldeman exchanged his famed crew-cut for longer, average-length hair. Molloy comments that the crew-cut, a 1950s hair style, had connoted 1950s thinking styles to blacks; longer hair made Haldeman look less prejudiced. Ehrlichman showed up at the trial suntanned, in lighter blue suits, eyeglass frames of fine gold wire (less foreboding than his old dark-rimmed half-glasses), and copious smiles. Perhaps these image changes had something to do with the relatively light sentences they received for their crimes; at the least, the new images must have helped to separate these men from their former boss and their former selves. These illustrations remind us that when they *did* wish to appear powerful and responsible, these men dressed in ways that proclaimed them as such. This is how intimidation may get the jump on any of us, and how the typical superior–subordinate relations are strengthened.

Walking Tall

The bearing with which one presents oneself also proclaims one's position in life. We are all familiar with the contrast between what is called "the bearing of a gentleman" and the shuffle of the servant, or the slump of a "nobody." Disease, fatigue, and occupational hazards of the poor and working classes have played a great part in stoop-shoulders, shuffles, limps, and other unpleasant "personal" characteristics, including ugliness. The "beautiful people" retain beauty and exhibit their class through not having to risk life or limb in work, and having the wealth to purchase many of the concomitants of beauty.

But there are postures of deference and dominance beyond those determined by class and occupation, of course. Scheflen describes, for example, habitual submissive behavior exhibited by hunched-down posture and avoiding the gaze of others (1973: 194). Military bearing is, on the other hand, an obvious example of the appearance of command. Drawing oneself up to one's full height, ramrod-straight and impassive of face, the aspect of the withdrawn and wooden, personality-absent commander, is certainly dominating. There is an apparent paradox, however: restriction of expression and movement (hands at the side) are characteristics usually imposed on subordinates, not superiors; one is puzzled to find them prescribed for officers. However, the military is a hierarchy in which every officer must be prepared to be a soldier too: obedience is much more emphasized and obvious in this than in other hierarchical structures, hence the mixture of nonverbal command and obedience in one body.

Standing tall is in itself a good way of achieving dominance; being tall is even better. It is well known now that tall men are more likely to be hired, to receive higher salaries, to be elected president, and to gain many other advantages than are short ones, as demonstrated by research and experience. And it works the other way around: important people seem bigger to us. When nursing students were asked to estimate heights of known faculty and student members (female) of their school, the heights of the two faculty members were overestimated, and of the two students, underestimated (Chelser and Goodman 1976: 72). Similarly, when other undergraduates (presumably both male and female) were asked to estimate the height of a man introduced to them as any one of five different academic ranks, the estimated height increased as the ascribed status increased (Dannenmaier and Thumin 1964: 63, 361–5; Wilson 1968: 74, 97–102). We are so used to according privileges and rank to all people (usually men) that when we see persons of rank, we automatically assume that they're tall.

Coming on Feminine

Demeanor has played a major part in the definition of femininity, and in the prescriptions for women's behavior. Clothing, one factor in demeanor, has been long a focus of attention on women, and in our culture has been particularly designed to emphasize their bodily contours. It has also been a showcase for the display of the frail materials (like lace and chiffon) associated with the female world, so it has been a major point of emphasis for women's weakness. The frailty of the material, its fineness and therefore difficulty of cleaning (compelling one to avoid getting it dirty), and the design of the clothing have combined to restrict women's movements in many ways. Skirts, for example, have kept many girls and women from engaging in certain physical activities and sitting in certain positions. In particular, straight skirts make it impossible to run; but some fashionable shoes make it almost impossible to walk, let alone run. Restrictive underwear – tight corsets, girdles, and the like – has also curtailed women's physical activities.

The design of women's clothing to stick to body contours has precluded the incorporation of pockets into women's clothing, a convenience that men's looser clothing has. Women are forced to carry pocketbooks, which further restricts their physical possibilities – it is awkward to carry other parcels, to deal with doors and children, or to run, with a purse. The function of the purse as women's albatross makes it a symbol of ridicule; many caricatures of women (by both females and males) utilize a purse as a comic focus, and impersonations of male homosexuals likewise use a purse as a sort of badge of shame. (Obviously, its psychoanalytic implications as a "vessel," a treasure chest that may be opened or closed, are not lost in these interpretations.)

Women's restrictive clothing is only part of the armament that keeps women in "dignified, ladylike" demeanor. Their schooling in proper posture for "ladies" is another. Young girls' training in posture is less likely to emphasize upright healthy ("military") bearing than is boys'. In fact, much of the example they see in magazine fashion models clearly glorifies the stylish slump of inactivity. Girls' postural training instead emphasizes propriety – keeping the legs properly closed when sitting, not leaning over so as to reveal breasts, keeping the skirt down to whatever is its current accepted leg coverage.... Women of all classes and status levels may not sit in undignified positions, swear, lounge on counters, or otherwise show the freedom in demeanor that Goffman describes as the privilege of those of higher status. Circumspection is required of them over and above their inferior work situations in life. As we saw earlier, there appears to be more class variation in demeanor among men.

This circumspection, the tightness of demeanor of the status inferior, is in the tension of their bodies too. Mehrabian's studies of body tension and relaxation found that females are generally less relaxed than are males, and he suggests that females convey more submissive attitudes by these tenser postures (1972: 27–30). In addition, in his communication studies, other communicators (of both sexes) assumed more relaxed positions when addressing females than males, as they are more relaxed with lower-status addressees than with higher-status ones.

A "loose woman" is one of bad reputation, and her attributed looseness comes from a lack of accepted control over her sexuality. But her portrayal in fiction and drama often carries other displays of looseness, e.g., in clothing, posture, and language as well. (The Italian actress Anna Magnani has often created such a character, for example, in *Open City or The Rose Tattoo*.) It is furthermore interesting to note that a "tight" woman, one who doesn't relax enough, is also often condemned, from the opposite end of the spectrum. These opposing demands are not as contradictory as they seem, however. They fit into the traditional view that a woman must restrict her sexuality (and its symbols) to all but the one (man) with whom she has a sanctified relationship: and to him she must be an endless fountain of sexuality.

Because of these restrictions on women's demeanor, the extreme looseness of body-focused functions (belching, nose-picking, and so on) is generally not open to women of our culture as an avenue of revolt. In fact, this controlled expression of "uncontrollable" functions may be a peculiarly male type of aggressiveness and hostility toward authority. If it should ever come into women's repertoire, however, it will carry great power, since it directly undermines the sacredness of women's bodies, a cornerstone of their suppression; and it will consequently command greater retaliation.

References

Chelser, Phyllis and Goodman, Emily Jane. 1976. *Women, Money and Power*. New York: Morrow.

Dannenmaier, W. D. and Thumin, F. J. 1964. "Authority status as a factor in perceptual distortion of size." *Journal of Social Psychology* 63: 361–5.

Denison, Jane. 1974. "Mitchell testifies he kept silent to ensure Nixon win." *Boston Globe*, November 28.

Feldman, Saul. 1971. "The presentation of shortness in everyday life – height and heightism in American society: Toward a sociology of stature." Paper presented at meetings of the American Sociological Association.

Goffman, Erving. 1963. *Behavior in Public Places: Notes on the Social Organization of Gatherings*. New York: Free Press.

——1967. *Interaction Ritual*. Garden City, NY: Doubleday.

Haley, Jay. 1962. "The art of psychoanalysis." In S. I. Hayakawa (ed.) *The Use and Misuse of Language*. Greenwich, Conn.: Fawcett, pp. 207–18.

Kunz, Marji. 1974. "Clothes make the defendant." *Boston Globe*, October 12.

Mehrabian, Albert. 1972. *Nonverbal Communication*. Chicago: Aldine-Atherton.

Scheflen, Albert. 1973. *Communicational Structure: Analysis of a Psychotherapy Transaction*. Bloomington, Ind.: Indiana University Press.

Wilson, Paul R. 1968. "Perceptual distortion of height as a function of ascribed academic status." *Journal of Social Psychology* 74: 97–102.

20 Status Structures

Cecilia L. Ridgeway and Henry A. Walker

Status structures are patterned inequalities of respect, deference, and influence among a group of people. Some in the group are "looked-up to," treated as more important, and have more privileges and power than others. In all known societies people exhibit regular patterns of differentiation on the basis of status. Observation of American society suggests that everyone from teenagers to corporate executives jockeys for a position of respect among those they deal with. Indeed, the development of status hierarchies is an enduring feature of human interaction and a fundamental aspect of the organization of social behavior. Explaining why or how they emerge and what their consequences are is essential to the sociological problems of inequality and social order.

To understand status relations, it is important to distinguish between status structures and status value. The word *status* has two traditional meanings in sociology. Linton (1936) used the term to mean a position in a social system, much like a role. For Veblen (1953), status was a position of value or worth in the community that was communicated through the cultural symbolism of one's possessions and consumption. Contemporary usage draws on both meanings but casts them differently into status structures and status value. In both contemporary concepts status refers to a position in a set of things that are rank-ordered by a standard of value. *Status structures* are rank-ordered relationships among *actors*. They describe the interactional inequalities formed from actors' implicit valuations of themselves and one another according to some shared standard of value. Status structures are inherently relational in that one actor is only high or low status in comparison to another. The actors can be individuals or corporate actors, such as nations or business; in this chapter we focus on individuals.

Anything that a society's or group's cultural beliefs associate with standing in status structures can take on *status value* in that collectivity. With status value, things become cultural symbols of worthiness in the collectivity. As sociologists since Veblen (1953) and Weber (1946) have observed, occupations, ethnic groups, genders, dress, automobiles, accents, and neighborhoods can all carry differential status value according to shared cultural beliefs. Some beliefs that rank-order the status value of certain things are widely held in entire societies (e.g., occupational prestige in the United States). Others are particular to smaller groups (e.g., dress styles among teenagers) and differ from one group to another.

Whatever their social basis, the principal effect of status value beliefs is on the behavior of actors who hold them. As we shall see, actors employ shared beliefs about the status value of their attributes, possessions, and behavior, and the social groups they belong to establish and maintain their own and others' positions in a

Reprinted from Karen S. Cook, Gary Alan Fine, and James S. House (eds.) *Sociological Perspectives on Social Psychology*, Boston and London: Allyn and Bacon, 1995, pp. 281–96, 305–10.

given status structure. Thus it is status structures themselves – the interactional hierarchies of esteem, deference, and influence that actors form – that are at the heart of sociological questions about status.

Since high-status members of these hierarchies are those more highly respected by a group standard, status creates the capacity to influence others in the structure. As a result, status structures are hierarchies of informal power as well as prestige. High-status members "call the shots" for the group in a way that low-status members do not. In fact, status structures, as influence hierarchies, are the central means by which groups of interactants organize their behavior and make collective decisions. This is what makes status structures important for understanding social order.

Although status structures are based in the person-to-person relationships of interaction, they are an important element in the larger, less personal process of social stratification in society. We have noted that the status significance society attaches to the social groups (e.g., economic, ethnic, sexual) to which a person belongs has an important impact on the status and influence a person achieves among a group of interactants. In turn, the influence and status a person achieves in interactional contexts has a powerful effect on his or her access to valued positions in organizations and to economic resources. Access to jobs, promotions, and economic opportunities are frequently mediated by interpersonal networks, encounters, and interviews where status processes operate and affect the outcome. Similarly, the actions of decision-making groups such as committees, panels, boards, councils, and ruling cliques reflect their status structures and, consequently, are likely better to represent the interests of their high- rather than low-status members or constituents. In fact, interactional status structures are the context in which many of the advantages and slights indicated by society's stratification system are actually delivered to the individual.

For a stratification system to persist, it must be enacted and supported in a variety of interactional contexts. There is an interdependence between society-level systems of stratification, formal hierarchies of power in a variety of organizations, and interactional status structures. The interdependence of these systems of status, power, and stratification is an important component of their legitimation, the process by which patterns of social action acquire a normative character. Within a legitimated status structure the deference and demeanors by which high- and low-status actors enact their positions take on a normative, ritual quality (E. Goffman 1956).

Legitimation can occur in systems of almost any size, from interactional status structures to formal organizations to systems of government. Legitimation transforms differences in status, influence, or power into systems of rights and obligations. As an example, actors whose exercise of power acquires legitimacy have the right to demand compliance from low-status actors, and low-status actors have the obligation to comply as long as the exercise of power is in accord with the accepted norms. Furthermore, those for whom high status has been legitimated can call on collective support to back up their directives, thereby increasing the level of compliance to their demands. Ironically, legitimate authorities are less likely to exercise power, since most actors voluntarily comply with normatively appropriate directives.

When status structures in interactional contexts reproduce patterns that exist in larger systems of stratification, they help maintain the legitimacy of those systems.

Actors' deference and demeanor in the status structure affirms the apparent moral order of the larger system. Similarly, the stratification of groups on the basis of qualities such as race, gender, or occupational status is an important source of legitimacy for interactional status structures that include members of such groups.

As our discussion suggests, both status-organizing processes and legitimation processes are inherently multilevel processes in complex societies. The study of status structures – how they emerge, the factors that account for their stability, how they change, and the manner in which they influence the behavior of individuals and groups – is an exciting convergence of work at the social structural and individual levels of investigation.

. . .

Status Structures

Early Research

Contemporary theories of status structures developed in response to a series of studies conducted from 1930 through the 1950s (e.g., Bales 1950; Roethlisberger and Dickson 1939; Whyte 1943). These studies provided a systematic empirical record of the emergence and operation of status hierarchies. They describe the behaviors by which status structures are enacted and some of the factors and circumstances out of which they emerge. Both for their descriptive value and because they provide the data that subsequent theories sought to explain, they offer a useful starting point.

Most influential were the observational studies of decision-making groups conduced by Bales (1950) and associates. Bales developed (1950, 1970) interaction process analysis, a scheme for coding behavior in task- or goal-oriented groups, that classifies each speech act in terms of who said it, to whom it was directed, and its instrumental (e.g., task suggestions, questions, and answers) or social-emotional content (i.e., positive and negative comments and reactions). Using this scheme. Bales developed empirical profiles of interaction in groups of three to seven previously unacquainted male undergraduates who met for several one-hour sessions to discuss and decide on human relations problems.

These groups are notable for two reasons. They began interaction with no structure imposed from the outside, since the members had no prior relationships with one another and no leader was appointed. Second, the members of the groups were homogeneous with respect to age, background, and social status. One of Bales's most striking findings was that despite this initial equality and lack of structure, these groups developed stable inequalities in participation by the end of the first one-hour session (Bales 1950, 1953). This finding has been replicated in several subsequent studies (e.g., Fisek and Ofshe 1970).

The inequalities that emerged were reflected in a series of correlated behaviors. First, the most talkative group member usually talks considerably more than the others, often accounting for upwards of 40 percent of the total speech acts (Bales 1970: 467–70). Second, the other group members are most likely to direct their own speech to the most talkative person. Finally, the higher a member's participation rank in the group, the more likely that member is to be rated by the others as having the best ideas and doing the most to guide and influence the group. Once these inequalities develop, they tend to persist over future group sessions.

While clear behavioral hierarchies emerged in his studies, Bales noted two complications. First, in an occasional group, an apparent power struggle resulted in a lack of consensus on who had the best ideas, slowing the development of a stable hierarchy. Second, Bales (1953: Bales and Slater 1955) and Slater (1955) argued that the most talkative, "best ideas" member was not always the best liked. Consequently, another member, usually the second most talkative, became the best-liked "social leader," while the most talkative was the "task leader." Although these studies are often cited, the extent to which Bales's and Slater's data support this interpretation has been challenged (Bonacich and Lewis 1973; Lewis 1972: Riedesel 1974). Subsequent research shows that the separation of task and social leadership occurs primarily when the task leader lacks legitimacy (Burke 1967, 1968, 1971). We return to this research later.

If stable inequalities emerge rather quickly in unstructured groups of initial equals, they are likely to develop in almost any group. In most actual groups, interactors differ somewhat in their social characteristics or background. Other early research focused on groups of this sort (Strodtbeck et al. 1957; Strodtbeck and Mann 1956; Torrance 1954). Typical is Strodtbeck et al.'s (1957) study of simulated juries composed of men and women selected from actual jury pools. In these groups, too, clear participation hierarchies developed, with the top two or three members doing half the talking. The most active members were also the most influential in the jury decisions. The most interesting finding, however, was that jurors' status in the larger society, as indicated by their occupations and sex, predicted how active and influential they became. It also predicted their likelihood of being chosen foreperson and how competent and helpful their fellow jurors perceived them to be. Clearly, standing in the outside society was translated into standing in the behavioral status order that emerged in the face-to-face group.

Studies of the emergence of status structures were supplemented by other early research documenting the consequences of established structures. As we have seen, members perceived to have higher standing in a group participate more and are more influential. Additional research demonstrated that standing in the group also determines how a member's contributions are evaluated by other members. Riecken (1958) found that the same idea expressed by a talkative member of a group was perceived to be more valuable than when it came from a less talkative member. Sherif et al. (1955) and Harvey (1953) both showed that group members overestimated the quality of performances by high-status members and underestimated those of low-status members, so that high-status members were seen as the better performers independent of their actual performances. Finally, and most dramatically, Whyte (1943) found that group members pressured one another to perform better or worse, to keep the quality of their contributions in line with their standing in the group. The status hierarchy, then, is an important regulator of the number, quality, and evaluation of members' contributions to group activities.

Whyte's (1943) classic study of the Nortons, a street-corner gang in Depression-era Boston, provides an excellent illustration of the way a status hierarchy regulates members' performances at group activities. Bowling was an important activity for the Nortons. Whyte observed that when they bowled together, the members' scores lined up almost perfectly with their positions in the gang's status hierarchy. The leader, "Doc," almost always scored the highest: "Alec," at the bottom of the hierarchy, always scored poorly. The interesting thing was that when he bowled alone, Alec was a good bowler, often outscoring Doc's average. But he could not perform well with the gang.

On one occasion, Doc staged a bowling competition among the gang members, offering prize money to the top scorers. Alec announced his intentions to win. When after the first few frames Alec was indeed ahead, the rest of the gang began to heckle him in a hostile fashion. He began to make mistakes and then began going out for drinks between turns. By the end, Alec's bowling score fell from first to last place. The gang members said it would not have been right if Alec had won.

After his defeat, Alec started challenging the number two man in the gang, "Long John," to bowl. He regularly defeated him. Hearing of this, Doc took Long John aside and told him that he must try harder, that he couldn't allow himself to be embarrassed by Alec. Long John's bowling began to improve and Alec no longer defeated him on a usual basis. Clearly, the Norton gang status hierarchy controlled its members' bowling performances almost independently of their actual skills. It appears to have done so through the positive and negative expectations the gang members held for one another and the social support (or discouragement) this provided for the individual member.

This early research record clearly shows that when people interact (particularly if the interaction is goal-oriented), a hierarchy of participation, evaluation, performance, and influence quickly develops, stabilizes and shapes future behavior. Members' goal-related behaviors and their evaluations of one another are particularly governed by the hierarchy. Such status structures develop whether group members are similar or different in social background or characteristics, although when such differences occur they shape the status structure. But the questions that remained were the theoretical ones before us here: Why and how do status structures emerge in interaction? Through what social processes do they operate?

Theoretical Approaches to Status Hierarchies

At least four theoretical perspectives have been used to explain the emergence of status structures: exchange theory, functionalism, symbolic interactionism, and conflict-dominance approaches. Exchange theory (e.g., Blau 1964; Homans 1961) views status as a reward that one actor grants to another by deferring to the other and accepting his/her influence. Status is granted in exchange for the recipient engaging in behaviors that produce rewards for other group members. In a goal-oriented group, for instance, status might be exchanged for a member's efforts to help the group attain its goal, since goal attainment provides rewards for all. If one member's contributions are thought to be more valuable to the group than another's, the first member will be granted greater deference and influence than the other, creating a hierarchy based on perceived value. In exchange theory, then, hierarchies develop from actors' rational interests in maximizing collective rewards by offering incentives for valuable contributions to collective activities.

The functionalist approach explains status hierarchies as a necessary mechanism that groups develop to adapt and survive in their environment (Bales 1953; Hare et al. 1955; Parsons and Bales 1955). It argues that to persist, groups must develop means of adapting to the outside environment, attaining collective goals, achieving internal cohesion, and maintaining organizational patterns. Status hierarchies address the first two functions. They provide a structure by which individual efforts are organized for effective decision-making and collective action in regard to group goals and the environment. When more competent members are given higher status, the group adapts and survives more successfully.

Bales (1953) further argued that while status hierarchies are functionally necessary, the invidious distinctions they create cause problems for internal cohesion that the group must also address, maintaining an equilibrium between the two contending concerns. Because there is a tension between status processes and internal cohesion, the implication is that the social or affective processes by which cohesion is maintained will be distinct from status processes and operate differently. While never clearly tested, this argument has been quite influential. Most contemporary approaches to status focus exclusively on the goal (task)-oriented behavior on which the hierarchy seems to turn, excluding affective behavior as a separate domain (but see Clark 1991 for an exception).

Symbolic interactionism, the third theoretical approach, views interaction as a process by which actors construct shared meanings (Blumer 1969: Mead 1934; Stryker and Statham 1985). Within this context, status is understood as the meaning and relative value attached to each actor's self as it is socially constructed in the situation (Alexander and Wiley 1981; Clark 1991). Each actor attempts to present and have accepted a valued social "face" (E. Goffman 1959, 1967), but each depends on the support of others to enact that face successfully in the group. As a result, the status order is negotiated through interaction as actors' face claims, reactions, and counterreactions mutually construct one another's selves in the situation (Alexander and Wiley 1981; E. Goffman 1956). According to this view, then, status hierarchies arise jointly out of the need to create shared definitions of the self for interaction and each actor's desire to be defined in the most valued way possible.

Exchange, functionalist, and symbolic interactionist perspectives all view status processes as essentially cooperative in nature. Each emphasizes the goal-oriented nature of interaction and the *positive interdependence* this creates among the actors. Because of their interdependence, they must cooperatively exchange deference for something they jointly want or need (rewards, functional task organization, a shared system of meaning). As a result, status is more *given* than *taken*.

This cooperative view contrasts with the more competitive perspective of the conflict-dominance approach (e.g., Archibald 1976; Keating 1985; Lee and Ofshe 1981; Mazur 1973; Wilson 1975). Traditionally, dominance analyses explain status hierarchies as a result of competition over scarce resources (e.g., food, mates, rewards, power), a type of *negative interdependence*. Individuals try to intimidate one another in a series of dominance contests to establish each other's rank in the hierarchy and, thus, access to resources. Once established, these hierarchies tend to stabilize because of individuals' shared interest in avoiding continual, destructive fighting. Thus, dominance approaches emphasize resource distribution rather than resource production (i.e., goal attainment) as the primary basis of status hierarchies.

Most dominance approaches seek similarities between animal and human hierarchies and some posit biological factors that contribute to an individual's standing in a
hierarchy (e.g., Mazur 1985).

Cooperative versus Competitive Hierarchy Formation

Evidence indicates that most status allocation is uncontested (Mazur 1973). Consequently, recent dominance analyses of humans and other primates have moderated
the traditional emphasis on agonistic competition and granted a role for cooperative
as well as competitive processes in the development of hierarchies (Mazur 1985;
Mitchell and Maple 1985). But why should cooperative status processes predomin-
ate? What happens to self-interest? The conflict-dominance approach raises basic
issues about hierarchy formation that must be considered, especially because the
traditional dominance perspective has been widely popularized and affects much
everyday thinking about status structures.

According to recent analyses, there may be structural reasons why status allocation in goal-oriented interaction is not purely competitive (Ridgeway and Diekema
1989). In a goal-oriented setting, actors have a cooperative interest in deferring to
one another on the basis of expected contributions to the goal to achieve maximum
collective rewards. On the other hand, they also have a competitive interest in
dominating others to increase their personal share of the rewards. Given these
conflicting possibilities, it is instructive to consider that the actors' dependence on
one another to accomplish the goal also creates a third set of interests. It makes it in
each actor's interest that all *other* actors grant status on the basis of expected
contributions to the goal, so that there will be some collective rewards to claim.
This suggests that actors are likely to pressure others to defer on the basis of expected
contributions, whatever they seek for themselves. As a result, even if each actor
pursues personal dominance above all, each is likely to face a coalition of others
unwilling to see status granted on any basis other than expected contributions.

As Emerson notes (1972), this implicit coalition effectively creates norms that
make deference on the basis of expected contributions the acceptable, legitimate
basis for status in goal-oriented settings. Claims to status on any other basis,
including pure dominance (i.e., threatening behavior), are subject to collective sanction. Tests of this argument, in fact, show that group members intervene to sanction
a member who claims status through threatening dominance behaviors (a raised
voice with a dismissive, commanding, interrogating manner and intrusive gestures,
such as pointing), and the domineering member fails to gain influence (Ridgeway
1987; Ridgeway and Diekema 1989). Because of this normative control process,
dominance alone is an ineffective means of gaining status in goal-oriented interaction.

It appears, then, that positive interdependence with respect to a goal creates
implicit norms that coerce actors from pursuing purely competitive claims to status
without regard to contributions to the collective. However, this doesn't eliminate
individuals' competitive interests from the status process. Rather, these norms redirect individual competition to the arena of the shared goal, so that actors compete to
appear competent in regard to the goal to "deserve" a more rewarding position in the
status order. It is through these processes that status hierarchies become collective

instruments of resource production as well as resource distribution. These processes highlight the importance of legitimating norms in the operation of status structures.

Systematic Theories of Status

The theoretical perspectives of exchange, functionalism, symbolic interaction, and conflict-dominance offer distinctive insights about status hierarchies. Yet none, by itself, has yielded a specific theory of status processes that can fully account for the existing empirical evidence on status structures. As Meeker (1981) notes, a strict exchange approach can explain much but has difficulty accounting for evidence that group members distort their perceptions of the quality of contributions by high- and low-status members. The functionalist explanation gives important attention to the role of the status order in accomplishing collective goals but seems to assume that merely because a behavior is "adaptive" it will occur. Symbolic interactionism points out the negotiated nature of status orders and the need for a shared definition of the situation for coordinated interaction to occur. But, perhaps because it focuses on selves rather than group structure, it has not yet produced a specific theory of status that can predict the structural form of hierarchies in differing situations. Finally, dominance theory reminds us of the role of competition and coercion in status process but must deal with the evidence that most status relations are cooperative and uncontested (Mazur 1973).

From such a diversity of insights and weaknesses, a variety of rather different systematic theories of status could be constructed. In fact, empirical studies of status have continued with a variety of approaches, such as symbolic interaction and conversational analysis (Kollock et al. 1985; West 1984; West and Garcia 1988) and dominance (Mazur and Cataldo 1989). However, *expectation states theory* has become the dominant systematic account. As the most conceptually developed and empirically verified theory of status-organizing processes available, it has been the focus of most recent research in the area. The intellectual roots of the theory are diverse, but it draws primarily on the concepts and insights of exchange theory, functionalism, and symbolic interactionism. As this suggests, it views the emergence of status orders as an essentially cooperative process arising from interactants' positive interdependence with respect to some collective goal.

Expectation States Theory

Expectation states theory developed in an explicit effort to explain the empirical findings of early status research (J. Berger, Wagner, and Zelditch 1985). Berger and colleagues (J. Berger, Conner, and Fisek 1974) proposed that the correlations demonstrated among speaking, being spoken to, evaluations of members and their contributions, and influence occurred because each of these behaviors is an observable indicator of a single, underlying phenomenon, a *power and prestige order*. The best way to understand how power and prestige (i.e., status) order emerges and operates, Berger et al. argue, is to separate the status process from other interactional processes analytically and study it on its own. Once status dynamics are understood they can then be placed back in context and analyzed in relation to other processes, such as conformity or affect, that occur simultaneously in face-to-face interaction.

Following this strategy, the theory limits its focus to the behavioral indicators of power and prestige, which in goal-oriented setting are goal- or task-related behaviors and evaluations. The theory's basic argument is that the dynamics of a power and prestige order arise out of group members' expectations about the value of their own and others' contributions to group activities and the way those expectations, called *performance expectations*, affect their task-related behavior toward one another.

Expectation states theory is distinctive in that it adopts a formal approach to theory construction, testing, and application. Explicit scope conditions specify the range of the phenomena the theory claims to explain, so that negative results can be clearly interpreted (Walker and Cohen 1985). The theory itself is stated in formal postulates that are usually linked with a mathematical calculus for expressing the stated relationships and deriving testable hypotheses. While theoretical postulates are often proposed to account for existing empirical evidence, they are subjected to independent tests in controlled experiments. Many of these experiments use a standardized experimental setting to allow clear comparisons of results across multiple experiments. While this theoretical and methodological strategy can make the theory seem forbidding to an outsider, it has been the secret of its success. It has enabled expectation states theory to generate a cumulative body of evidence with which to refine and expand its analysis. The resulting theory has been better able than its alternatives to predict and explain status processes both in controlled studies and applied settings, such as the classroom (E. Cohen 1982), and in corporate research and development teams (B. Cohen and Zhou 1991).

Expectation states theory takes the interactional *encounter*, rather than individuals, as its unit of analysis (J. Berger, Fisek, et al. 1985). It limits its scope to those encounters where actors are oriented toward the accomplishment of a shared goal or task for which they have a sense of success and failure and for which it is appropriate to take one another's opinions into account to achieve the best task outcome. An encounter can meet these conditions either because it is the meeting of an explicit task group, such as a committee, or because people interacting on another basis turn their attention to a collective task or decision.

The theory argues that when these conditions occur a *status organizing process* is activated by the actors' efforts to evaluate their own and others' task suggestions, to reach a successful collective decision about the task. To decide how to act, whether to speak up, who to listen to, and who to agree with when conflicts develop, actors look for a way to anticipate the likely usefulness of their own and each other's suggestions. In doing so, they form performance expectations for themselves compared to each other actor in the setting. Performance expectations are generally not conscious judgments, but rather implicit, unaware hunches about whose suggestions are more likely to be better. Because they are often implicit, the theory treats performance expectations as an unobserved theoretical construct that mediates changes in observable factors. The theory assumes that actors follow similar cognitive principles in forming performance expectations. Consequently, as long as interactants have roughly similar cultural beliefs and information about one another, the expectations they develop are shared, creating a roughly consensual *order of performance expectations* in the encounter.

Self–other performance expectations are important because they tend to guide behavior in a self-fulfilling manner. If an actor has a higher expectation for him- or herself than for another, the actor is more likely to speak up, offer opinions, and stick to them if challenged. If the same actor has lower expectations for him- or herself than for the other, the actor is more likely to hesitate in making suggestions, to ask for and respond positively to the other's opinions, and to assume that he or she is wrong when another disagrees. Thus, the theory proposes that the higher the expectations held for one actor compared to another: (1) the more opportunities the other will give the actor to participate; (2) the more task suggestions the actor will offer; (3) the more likely these suggestions are to be positively evaluated by the others; and (4) the more influential the actor will be over the others.

In this way, self–other performance expectations determine the inequalities in action opportunities, performance outputs, positive and negative evaluations, and influence that constitute the observable power and prestige order of the setting. Assuming a shared order of performance expectations, each actor's behaviors confirm the others' expectations. As a result, once formed, differentiated performance expectations tend to magnify and stabilize the behavioral differences between self and other in a manner consistent with expectations, stabilizing the power and prestige order. This argument is expressed in the theory's principal postulate (J. Berger et al. 1977: 130):

> Once actors have formed expectations for self and other(s), their power and prestige positions relative to the others will be a direct function of their expectation advantage over (or disadvantage compared to) those others.

For this postulate to be useful, however, we must ask: How and on what basis do actors form higher performance expectations for one person rather then another? Can the processes by which expectations are formed predict when there will be very large power and prestige differences among group members and when these differences will be relatively small? Much of expectation states theory is directed toward answering the first question in a manner that allows it to answer the second. Thus far, a variety of factors that create or change performance expectations and, consequently, positions in a power and prestige order have been analyzed. These include task-directed behaviors, nonverbal behaviors, status-valued characteristics of actors, evaluations from an outside source, and rewards. The theory's argument about each of these factors follows a similar form, expressed in its four additional postulates (J. Berger et al. 1977: 91–134; Fisek et al. 1991). It is this shared logical form that allows the theory to combine the effects of multiple factors on expectations to make predictions about the differing structures of power and prestige orders in different situation. A brief review of this logical form is useful before turning to the analysis of specific factors.

According to the second postulate, for any behavior, characteristic, reward, or other factor to affect expectations, it must first become *salient* in the situation. Factors become salient when they either provide a contrast among actors in the situation (e.g., gender in a mixed-sex setting) or are perceived to be relevant to the shared task. Because of this assumption, expectation states theory takes a *situational* approach to status orders. Although actors carry some of the same attributes from one situation to the next, whether they affect the status order in a given situation and, if so, how they affect it depends on other factors in the situation. Thus status orders are always socially constructed in the situation itself and never merely imported unchanged from outside the setting.

The third postulate states that when a factor is salient, unless it is specifically disassociated from the task, actors will use cultural beliefs about its status value in forming their expectations, even if the factor is logically irrelevant to the task. This is called the *burden-of-proof process*, because actors act as if the burden of proof lies in showing that a salient factor is not relevant to task competence rather than that it is relevant. Because of this postulate, the theory predicts that socially evaluated characteristics, such as race or gender, or behaviors that may be entirely unrelated to objective competence, such as talking more, still affect expectations for performance and, thus, power and prestige, when the members differ on them. Thus the theory predicts that power and prestige orders may be quite unmeritocratic sometimes, despite being based on expectations for performance, because of the way status-valued but logically irrelevant factors can bias perceptions of competence.

The fourth postulate states that whenever a new factor becomes salient in a situation, it becomes connected to all the other factors already salient, either strengthening or counteracting their implications for expectations. This is called the *structure completion* postulate, in reference to the formal graph structures by which the theory represents the impact all salient factors have on expectations in the setting (J. Berger et al. 1977). These graphs represent the actors' definition of the situation with respect to the task, themselves, and each other. The theory analyzes them by means of graph theory to produce precise metric predictions for a given setting of each actor's expectation advantage or disadvantage compared to the others.

The fifth postulate, *aggregation*, states that the impacts of all salient factors are combined to produce aggregated expectations for each actor compared to the others. Specifically, the negative implications of all factors are weighted by their perceived relevance to task performance, combined, and then subtracted from the weighted and combined positive implications of all factors to produce aggregated expectation states for each actor. The principal postulate, stated earlier, then takes over to state that power and prestige positions will be a direct function of these aggregated expectations. For the exact formulas and procedures for analyzing graphs, calculating aggregated expectations, and making metric predictions of observable power and prestige positions, see J. Berger et al. (1977: 91–134), Fisek et al. (1991), and Balkwell (1991a).

One implication of aggregation is that the theory can make predictions about the situations in which power and prestige differences between actors are likely to be large and those in which they will be slight (Humphreys and Berger 1981). When salient factors have inconsistent implications for task competence, power and prestige differences will be less than if the same number of factors have consistent implications for competence. Status orders where status characteristics, behavior, and rewards cross-cut are more likely to be egalitarian, then, than status orders where these factors are all aligned.

The five postulates of expectation states theory paint a picture of status processes as an outcome of the ongoing process of constructing a social definition of reality in a task-oriented setting to accomplish the shared goal. To figure out how to act, actors look for information with to create differential expectations for self and other, using whatever becomes salient. They notice differences in appearance or manner that indicate the social categories (e.g., gender or social class) each belongs to. They respond to the confidence or assertiveness of each other's eye gaze, speech, and overall demeanor. They notice distinctions in the socially valued possessions or rewards each controls. Aggregating all such information, actors form implicit expectations that self will have more (or less) to contribute to the situation than given others. Each then acts on these expectations by speaking up or hesitating, acting confident or nervous, arguing or deferring. In doing so, self and others jointly create a behavioral power and prestige order that implicitly fulfills their expectations. Although this power and prestige order tends to stabilize, new information and discordant events can modify expectations and alter the order.

With this framework in mind, let us turn to specific factors that affect expectations and power and prestige. Owing to space limitations we focus on verbal and non-verbal behavior, status characteristics, and rewards, although other factors, such as sources of evaluation, have also been shown to affect expectations (Webster and Sobieszek 1974). We begin with the role of behavior enacted in the setting to illustrate the theory's analysis of how a power and prestige order is negotiated through interaction.

Behavior and Performance Expectations

We know that status hierarchies form quickly even in homogeneous groups, where participants are initially status equals. In such groups, actions and demeanor are the only bases participants have to form differential judgments about one another. The theory proposes that such behavior itself creates differentiated performance expectations, even though, once formed, expectations then drive behavior (J. Berger and Conner 1974; Fisek et al. 1991).

At the core of goal-oriented interaction are the behavioral cycles in which participants offer task suggestions and have them accepted or rejected by others. In the simplest such *behavioral sequence*, an actor is given or takes an opportunity to speak (an action opportunity) and makes a task suggestion (a performance output), and others react positively or negatively to it. However structured, the sequence concludes when the actors jointly accept (positively evaluate) or reject (negatively evaluate) the task suggestion. If joint acceptance or rejection comes about because one actor changes his or her evaluation of the task suggestion to agree with the evaluation of another actor, then influence has occurred.

In their early formulation, Berger and Conner (1974) and Berger, Conner, and McKeown (1974) postulated that every time a task suggestion is positively or negatively evaluated or influence occurs, there is some probability that self and other(s) will form expectation states for one another corresponding to the evaluation or influence. This means the more task suggestions an actor makes compared to another, or the more positive evaluations he/she receives for those suggestions, the more likely it is that both the actor and the other will form higher expectations for the actor than the other. This prediction of the theory is consistent with evidence that participation levels are associated with perceived competence and influence.

Subsequent research has shown that whether an actor's task suggestions are accepted by others is also affected by nonverbal demeanor during interaction. Taking a seat at the head of the table, having an upright, relaxed posture, speaking up without hesitation in a firm, confident tone, and maintaining direct eye contact all make a group member's suggestions "sound better" and increase the likelihood that he or she will be influential (see Dovidio and Ellyson 1985; Ridgeway 1987; Ridgeway et al. 1985). Joseph Berger et al. (1986) refer to these demeanor variables as *task cues* because actors appear to read them as cultural signs of confidence and competence at the task.

Recently, Fisek et al. (1991) incorporated task cues into an expanded account of behavior and performance expectations that recasts the argument in terms of the theory's basic postulates. They note that evaluative reactions tend to encourage or discourage future suggestions from an actor and affect the actor's confidence and demeanor. Also, having one suggestion positively or negatively evaluated by others increases the chance that the actor's next suggestion will be similarly evaluated. Consequently, behavior sequences in a group tend to develop into stable patterns of interchange, as others have shown (Burke 1974). Fisek et al. define these *behavior interchange patterns* as sets of behavioral sequences that are consistent in their power and prestige significance with respect to the actors.

Consistently making more task suggestions or speaking in a forceful manner attracts attention. Consequently, Fisek et al. argue that actors implicitly recognize interchange patterns when they develop. They notice at some level that one actor is consistently speaking up while another only agrees. When recognized, interchange patterns make salient *status typifications*, which are socially constructed beliefs about what high-status and low-status, "leader-follower," behaviors and demeanors are like (this is the salience postulate of the theory). These cultural beliefs associate people who enact high-status behavioral cues with higher levels of ability or competence than those who display low-status behavioral cues. This, in turn, leads actors to expect more useful contributions to the task at hand from people who act high-status than from people who act low-status (the burden-of-proof postulate). This is how the theory explains the impact of demeanor on perceptions of competence. Through this sequence, interchange patterns lead to differentiated performance expectations. Every time a new interchange pattern becomes salient, it either strengthens or replaces the implications of the former pattern, creating a dynamic process (the structure completion postulate). Dynamic changes in performance expectations, in turn, produce changes in observable indicators of power and prestige, such as participation rates and nonverbal task cues (the principle postulate).

This sequence is represented in graph-theoretic terms so the effects of interchange patterns can be combined with other factors salient in the setting to predict aggregated expectation advantages and consequent differences in participation and other behaviors. Fisek et al. evaluate the model's ability to account for participation rates in open interaction groups by fitting it to several existing data sets, including Bales's (1970) original data from 208 groups. The rates of participation predicted by the model accounted for 89 to 99 percent of the variance of the actual observed participation rates. Thus the model can indeed describe the inequalities in participation that develop among actors in an open interaction setting.

Status Characteristics

Strodtbeck et al.'s (1957) jury study clearly demonstrated that characteristics that carry status value in society, such as occupation and gender, have a powerful impact on a person's behavior and position in a power and prestige order. But as they noted, the means or mechanism by which the status of the social categories to which one belongs affects one's behavior and standing in interaction were unknown. Expectation states theory sought to answer this question in its *status characteristics theory* (see J. Berger et al. 1977 for a formal statement; Webster and Foschi 1988: 1–20, for a brief review). The theory proposes that status characteristics, when salient in the situation, create performance expectations in goal-oriented settings and these shape the actors' behavior and, thus, rank in the power and prestige order (J. Berger et al. 1972; J. Berger et al. 1977; Webster and Foschi 1988).

A status characteristic is defined as an attribute on which individuals vary that is associated in society with widely held beliefs according greater esteem and worthiness to some states of the attribute (e.g., being male or a proprietor) than other states of the attribute (e.g., being female or a laborer). Because it is based in consensual beliefs, the status value of an attribute can change over time and vary among populations. The theory's most important insight is that the cultural beliefs that attach status value to a characteristic also associate it with implicit expectations for competence. Worthiness becomes presumed competence. Occupation, educational attainment, race, gender, and age are some of the status characteristics that carry such beliefs in the United States.

Status characteristics range from specific to diffuse, depending on the specificity of the competence associations they carry. Specific status characteristics are socially valued skills, expertise, or social accomplishments that imply a specific and bounded range of competencies. Computer skills are an example. Most interesting are diffuse status characteristics such as gender or race. These, too, are culturally associated with some specific skills but also carry general expectations for competence that are diffuse and unbounded in range. Yes, men are presumed by cultural stereotypes to be better at mechanics and worse at sewing than women, but they are also expected to be diffusely more able than women at almost any new task. This gives diffuse status characteristics a wide-ranging power to affect status relations in interaction.

Like any other factor, to affect power and prestige status characteristics must become salient in the setting either by discriminating among actors or by being perceived as task-relevant. This suggests that whether or not a given status characteristic affects an individual's power and prestige in a setting depends on the goals of the setting and how the characteristic compares with those of the other participants. A characteristic (e.g., a BA degree) that gives an actor an edge in one setting (with college dropouts) can have no effect in another (where others have BAs also and it is not task-relevant) or be a disadvantage in a third setting (where others have Ph.Ds). So the impact of status characteristics is situationally specific. By this account, there are no "master statuses" that doom a person to low status or guarantee high status in all situations.

Once a status characteristic is salient, its competence associations generalize to affect actors' expectations about their own and other's abilities at the specific task at hand. If the status characteristic is actually relevant to the task, it will have a very strong impact on performance expectations. But even if it is completely irrelevant it will have a significant, if weaker, impact on expectations (the burden-of-proof process). This is what makes status characteristics prejudicial. It means, for instance, that in a mixed-sex setting, general beliefs about men's greater overall competence will generalize to affect reactions to an idea offered by a man rather than a woman even if the task is unrelated to gender. Both men and women are likely to assume the idea is better if it comes from a man. Such unfortunate effects persist despite official ideologies of equality because they usually operate as unaware judgments made "without thinking." Part of the power of expectation states theory is its ability to explain these effects.

Several studies have demonstrated this *status generalization* process (see J. Berger, Fisek, et al. 1985). Many use expectation states theory's standardized experimental setting, where participants are placed in separate rooms and given controlled feedback about one another's characteristics. Then they work together on an ambiguous task by pushing buttons on a console to exchange opinions and agree on a decision over a series of trials. Although they believe they are working together, each participant actually receives preprogrammed feedback that shows their partner disagreeing with them on many trials. They then must stick to their own choice or change to agree with their partner, in effect accepting influence from the partner. This controlled setting allows the investigator to test whether knowledge of self and other's status characteristics alone will affect the participants' willingness to accept or reject influence from the other. Using this setting, studies have shown that status characteristics as diverse as educational attainment (Moore 1968), gender (Pugh and Wahrman 1983; Wagner et al. 1986), military rank (J. Berger et al. 1972), race (Webster and Driskell 1978), age (Freese and Cohen 1973), and specific abilities (Webster 1977) affect rates of influence even when they are completely irrelevant to the task.

The theory has also accurately predicted status generalization effects in open interaction settings (E. Cohen and Roper 1972; Carli 1990, 1991; Fisek et al. 1991; Lockheed and Hall 1976; Ridgeway 1982). In one such study, Wood and Karten (1986) demonstrated that the reason gender affected participation rates and other task behaviors in mixed-sex interaction was that it affected expectations for competence at the task, just as the theory argues. When these expectations were controlled, gender effects on task behaviors disappeared. Driskell and Mullen's (1990) meta-analysis of status generalization studies similarly shows that status characteristics affect influence by affecting perceived competence.

Other open interaction studies have shown that status generalization shapes nonverbal task cues in the manner the theory predicts (Dovidio et al. 1988; Leffler et al. 1982; Ridgeway et al. 1985; Smith-Lovin and Brody 1989). When a status characteristic places a person at an advantage in a given interaction, he or she becomes nonverbally assertive, as indicated by speech initiations, direct eye contact, looking at the other while speaking rather than while listening, gesturing, and interrupting. But when the same characteristic puts the person at a disadvantage in another interaction, his or her task cues become less assertive than those of others present. In a particularly clear demonstration of the theory's predictions, Dovidio et al. (1988) showed that when mixed-sex dyads shifted from a gender-neutral task, where the man had a status advantage, to a stereotypically feminine task, where the woman had a status advantage, the observable power and prestige orders reflected in their participation and nonverbal task cues reversed from one favoring the man to one favoring the woman.

Status characteristics in enduring groups

Most studies of status generalization have focused on relatively short-lived groups, where members have limited opportunities to get to know one another and discover their actual abilities and interests in the group. Knowledge of actual abilities will have a stronger impact on performance expectations and power and prestige than diffuse status characteristics, since it is more directly relevant to task performance. Does this mean status generalization is likely to affect only the initial period of hierarchy formation? Do status characteristics play a significant role in enduring groups?

The most powerful impact of observable status characteristics, such as gender and race, is at the beginning of interaction, when actors know little else about one another. However, status characteristics usually have a long-lasting impact on a power and prestige structure because, by affecting initial expectations and opportunities to participate, they shape the subsequent information actors are able to introduce about themselves. Also, as Whyte's (1943) study of the Nortons showed, expectations, shaped by status characteristics, can powerfully constrain actors' ability actually to perform well at group activities, regardless of their real skills. Thus, it is difficult, although not impossible, for actors to break out of the power and prestige position into which they are cast initially by the status generalization process (see E. Cohen 1982; Ridgeway 1982 for discussions of how status generalization may be overcome). Consequently, as Bernard Cohen and Xueguang Zhou's (1991) study of corporate research and development teams demonstrates, the power and prestige structures of most enduring groups continue to reflect the impact of status characteristics.

Recently, Foschi (1989, 1991) showed that status characteristics may have such a pervasive impact on power and prestige because, in addition to shaping performance expectations, they also create double standards for judging success and failure. Performance expectations make it unlikely that the same contribution from a status-advantaged and a status-disadvantaged person will be perceived to be of the same quality. But double standards mean that even if they are, a contribution of that quality will be seen as stronger evidence of genuine task ability (or weaker evidence of incompetence) for the status-advantaged person than the status-disadvantaged person. Double standards are another way the effects of status characteristics in interaction can become self-fulfilling.

Multiple status characteristics

Our discussion thus far has dealt with single status characteristics, such as gender, skills, or race. But what about gender *and* skills *and* race? No individual is only a man or a woman, African American or white, and not also a variety of other status characteristics. In open interaction, participants often differ simultaneously on multiple status characteristics, and these characteristics can have inconsistent implications for power and prestige. There was a debate at one time about whether interactants would deal with inconsistent status characteristics by ignoring one or more of the characteristics, perhaps the least flattering or least task-relevant ones (Freese and Cohen 1973; I. Goffman 1957; Sampson 1969). The evidence suggests that this is not the case (Webster and Driskell 1978; Zelditch et al. 1980). As the theory predicts, people act as though they create aggregated expectations for themselves and others by weighting positive and negative characteristics by task relevance and combining them (Balkwell 1991b; Berger et al. 1977).

Such weighted combining indicates that the competence expectations and power and prestige of a woman doctor in a mixed-sex medical setting will be more strongly affected by her occupational status than her gender, but gender will still have an effect. She is likely to have slightly lower power and prestige than a similar male doctor (cf. Floge and Merrill 1986). However, it also implies that a woman might have equal or higher power and prestige than some men in the setting if she is higher than them on enough relevant skills or other status characteristics, as a number of studies have demonstrated (E. Cohen and Roper 1972; Dovidio et al. 1988; Pugh and Wahrman 1983). Because people are complex packages of skills and status characteristics, the status structures people construct through interaction reflect that complexity. They are not merely mirror images of the stratification of the larger society, despite being strongly affected by that stratification.

An interesting implication of this is that people may experience power and prestige structures that challenge their usual expectations for individuals with given diffuse status characteristics. When this happens, the experience can transfer to the way they treat the next person they encounter with that characteristic. Studies have shown that a man's experience working with a woman clearly more competent than he causes him to have somewhat higher performance expectations for the next woman he works with (Markovsky et al. 1984; Pugh and Wahrman 1983). While the effects diminish with each transfer, sufficient "reversal" experiences could moderate the cultural beliefs that associate competence with the characteristic and reduce its biasing effect on power and prestige structures.

Rewards and Performance Expectations

As noted earlier, status hierarchies are both a result of actors' efforts to organize the production of collective rewards and systems for reward distribution. Not surprisingly, in established hierarchies rewards tend to be distributed in accordance with rank and help maintain the relative power of those ranks (Homans 1961). But rewards have more subtle effects as well that show their integral role in status processes. Rewards can affect the creation of status hierarchies, modify positions in an existing hierarchy, and produce judgments about the justice or injustice of the status system. We leave the justice issue aside for now, focusing instead on the way rewards shape status positions.

It is a common observation that distributing rewards equally in a group reduces the apparent status differences among the members, while unequal distribution tends to increase status differences (e.g., Lerner 1974). This suggests that rewards are interdependent with other sources of power and prestige in a group. Expectation states theory captures this idea by arguing that actors' expectations for rewards in a task setting are interdependent with their performance expectations and, so, power and prestige positions (J. Berger, Fisek, et al. 1985; Cook 1975). In an experimental test of this argument, Cook (1975) showed that when a third party gave differential rewards to subjects who had no other basis for evaluating their performances on a shared task, the subjects used the reward differences to infer ability differences. Those who receive higher rewards are presumed to have greater task ability than those with lower rewards, even when there is no explicit connection between the distribution of rewards and level of ability (Harrod 1980; Stewart and Moore 1992).

This important point highlights how the power or good luck represented in the unequal possession of rewards becomes legitimate status. Through the creation of performance expectations, the unequal rewards appear to be "deserved," and thus legitimately and justly bring respect, deference, and influence. It also suggests an association between possession of rewards and membership in a given racial, ethnic, or other social category may be one means by which such membership becomes or remains a status characteristic in society (Ridgeway 1991).

Expectation states theory considers rewards, like status characteristics and behavior, to be an additional factor that interactants include in their formation of aggregated performance expectations. These performance expectations, in turn, affect expectations for future rewards, with the result that interactants generally distribute future awards in accord with their standing in the power and prestige order.

A Critical Assessment

It is clear that expectation states theory is a powerful, well-documented theory that can successfully account for many of the structural forms and interactional dynamics of status orders in goal-oriented settings. But there are important questions about status orders that it has not yet addressed. One of the most obvious is to account for status orders in interactional settings not characterized by explicit goals, which expectation states theorists have only begun to discuss (Johnston 1988). Unfortunately, this problem has not been systematically addressed by other theories either, although McWilliams and Blumstein (1991) have offered some interesting initial thoughts on it. As they note, status characteristics, assertive behavior, and rewards are likely to be important to power and prestige in such settings also. But exactly how do they work? More important, does a weaker goal orientation in interaction reduce the importance or extent of status dynamics? Certainly this is the implication of the exchange and functionalist approaches to status that have dominated sociological analyses of status structures, including the expectation states theory.

A second important question is the role of expressive, emotionally oriented behavior in status dynamics. The organization of affective relations may indeed be a separate process, as Bales (1950) suggested. However, recent analyses suggest that, at the very least, status dynamics shape emotional reactions during interaction in ways that control and direct positive and negative expressive behavior (Clark 1991; Ridgeway and Johnson 1990; Smith-Lovin and Heise 1988). Other analyses indicate that affective relations moderate or magnify power and prestige differences (Shelly 1988). Much more data are needed to assess these ideas properly and understand the relationship between affect and status.

Finally, there is the problem of the role of conflict in status hierarchies. Expectation states theory focuses on consensual allocation, which evidence indicates predominates (Mazur 1973). But conflict does occur, and it needs to be explicitly addressed. Since status conflicts usually elicit emotions (Bales 1953; Ridgeway and Johnson 1990), the problem of conflict is related to the need to understand affect and status.

References

Alexander, C. Norman Jr. and Wiley, Mary Glenn. 1981. "Situated activity and identity formation." In M. Rosenberg and R. H. Turner (eds.) *Social Psychology: Sociological Perspectives*. New York: Basic Books, pp. 269–89.

Archibald, W. Peter. 1976. "Face-to-face: The alienating effects of class, status, and power divisions." *American Sociological Review* 41: 819–37.

Bales, Robert F. 1950. *Interaction Process Analysis: A Method for the Study of Small Groups*. Cambridge, Mass.: Addison-Wesley.

—— 1953. "The equilibrium problem in small groups." In T. Parsons, R. F. Bales, and E. A. Shils (eds.) *Working Papers in the Theory of Action*. Glencoe, Ill.: Free Press.

—— 1970. *Personality and Interpersonal Behavior*. New York: Holt, Rinehart and Winston.

Bales, Robert F. and Slater, Philip E. 1955. "Role differentiation in small decision-making groups." In T. Parsons and R. F. Bales (eds.) *The Family, Socialization, and Interaction Processes*. Glencoe, Ill.: Free Press, pp. 259–306.

Balkwell, James W. 1991a. "From expectations to behavior: An improved postulate for expectation states theory." *American Sociological Reivew* 56: 355–69.

—— 1991b. "Status characteristics and social interaction: An assessment of theoretical variants." In E. Lawler, B. Markovsky, C. Ridgeway, and H. Walker (eds.) *Advances in Group Processes*, vol 8. Greenwich, Conn.: JAI Press, pp. 135–76.

Berger, Joseph and Conner, Thomas L. 1974. "Performance expectations and behavior in small groups: A revised formulation." In J. Berger, T. Conner, and M. H. Fisek (eds.) *Expectation States Theory: A Theoretical Research Program*. Cambridge, Mass.: Winthrop, pp. 85–110.

Berger, Joseph, Cohen, Bernard P. and Zelditch, Morris Jr. 1972. "Status characteristics and social interaction." *American Sociological Review* 37: 241–55.

Berger, Joseph, Conner, Thomas L. and Fisek, M. Hamit. 1974. *Expectation States Theory: A Theoretical Research Program*. Cambridge, Mass.: Winthrop.

Berger, Joseph, Conner, Thomas L. and McKeown, William L. 1974. "Evaluations and the formation and maintenance of performance expectations." In J. Berger, T. Conner, and M. H. Fisek (eds.) *Expectation States Theory: A Theoretical Research Program*. Cambridge, Mass.: Winthrop, pp. 27–51.

Berger, Joseph, Wagner, David G. and Zelditch, Morris Jr. 1985. "Expectation states theory: Review and assessment." In Joseph Berger and Morris Zelditch (eds.) *Status, Rewards, and Influence*. San Francisco: Jossey-Bass, pp. 1–72.

Berger, Joseph, Fisek, M., Hamit, Norman, Robert Z., and Wagner, David G. 1985. "The formation of reward expectations in status situations." In J. Berger and M. Zelditch (eds.) *Status, Rewards, and Influence*. San Francisco: Jossey-Bass, pp. 215–61.

Berger, Joseph, Fisek, M. Hamit, Norman, Robert Z., and Zelditch, Morris Jr. 1977. *Status Characteristics in Social Interaction: An Expectation States Approach*. New York: Elsevier.

Berger, Joseph, Webster, Murray Jr., Ridgeway, Cecilia and Rosenholtz, Susan J. 1986. "Status cues, expectations and behavior." In E. Lawler (ed.) *Advances in Group Processes*, vol. 3. Greenwich, Conn.: JAI Press, pp. 1–22.

Blau, Peter. 1964. *Exchange and Power in Social Life*. New York: Wiley.

Blumer, Herbert. 1969. *Symbolic Interactionism: Perspective and Method*. Englewood Cliffs, NJ: Prentice-Hall.

Bonacich, Philip and Lewis, Gordon H. 1973. "Function specialization and sociometric judgment." *Sociometry* 36: 31–41.

Burke, Peter J. 1967. "The development of task and social-emotional role differentiation." *Sociometry* 30: 379–92.

—— 1968. "Role differentiation and the legitimation of task activity." *Sociometry* 31: 404–11.

—— 1971. "Task and socioemotional leadership role performance." *Sociometry* 34: 22–40.

—— 1974. "Participation and leadership in small groups." *American Sociological Review* 39: 832–43.

Carli, Linda L. 1990. "Gender, language, and influence." *Journal of Personality and Social Psychology* 59: 941–51.

Clark, Candace. 1991. "Emotions and micropolitics in everyday life: Some patterns and paradoxes of 'place'." In T. D. Kemper (ed.) *Research Agendas in the Sociology of Emotions*. Albany: State University of New York Press, pp. 305–33.

Cohen, Bernard P. and Zhou, Xueguang. 1991. "Status processes in enduring work groups." *American Sociological Review* 56: 179–88.

Cohen, Elizabeth G. 1982. "Expectation states and interracial interaction in school settings." *Annual Review of Sociology* 8: 209–35.

Cohen, Elizabeth G. and Roper, Susan S. 1972. "Modification of interracial interaction disability: An application of status characteristics theory." *American Sociological Review* 37: 643–57.

Cook, Karen S. 1975. "Expectations, evaluations, and equity." *American Sociological Review* 40: 372–88.

Dovidio, John F. and Ellyson, Steven L. 1985. "Patterns of visual dominance behavior in humans." In S. Ellyson and J. Dovidio (eds.) *Power, Dominance, and Nonverbal Behavior*. New York: Springer-Verlag, pp. 129–50.

Dovidio, John F., Brown, Clifford E., Heltman, Karen, Ellyson, Steven L., and Keating, Caroline F. 1988. "Power displays betwen women and men in discussions of gender-linked tasks: A multichannel study." *Journal of Personality and Social Psychology* 55: 580–7.

Driskell, James E. and Mullen, Brian. 1990. "Status, expectations, and behavior: A meta-analytic review and test of the theory." *Personality and Social Psychology Bulletin* 16: 541 53.

Emerson, Richard M. 1972. "Exchange theory, II: Exchange relations and networks." In J. Berger, M. Zelditch, and B. Anderson (eds.) *Sociological Theories in Progress*, vol. 2. Boston: Houghton Mifflin.

Fisek, M. Hamit, Berger, Joseph, and Norman, Robert Z. 1991. "Participation in heterogenous and homogenous groups: A theoretical integration." *American Journal of Sociology* 97: 114–42.

Fisek, M. Hamit and Ofshe, Richard. 1970. "The process of status evolution." *Sociometry* 33: 327–46.

Floge, Liliane and Merrill, Deborah M. 1986. "Tokenism reconsidered: Male nurses and female physicians in a hospital setting." *Social Forces* 64: 925–47.

Foschi, Martha. 1989. "Status characteristics, standards and attributions." In J. Berger, M. Zelditch, and B. Anderson (eds.) *Sociological Theories in Progress: New Formulations*. Newbury Park, Calif.: Sage Publications.

—— 1991. "Gender and double standards for competence." In C. Ridgeway (ed.) *Gender, Interaction, and Inequality*. New York: Springer-Verlag, pp. 181–207.

Freese, Lee and Cohen, Bernard P. 1973. "Eliminating status generalization." *Sociometry* 36: 177–93.

Goffman, Erving. 1956. "The nature of deference and demeanor." *American Anthropologist* 58: 473–502.

—— 1959. *The Presentation of Self in Everyday Life*. New York: Doubleday.

—— 1967. *Interaction Ritual*. New York: Anchor.

Goffman, Irwin W. 1957. "Status consistency and preference for change in power distribution." *American Sociological Review* 22: 275–81.

Hare, A. Paul, Borgatta, Edgar F., and Bales, Robert F. (eds.) 1955. *Small Groups: Studies in Social Interaction*. New York: Knopf.

Harrod, Wendy J. 1980. "Expectations from unequal rewards." *Social Psychology Quarterly* 43: 126–30.

Harvey, O. J. 1953. "An experimental approach to the study of status reactions in small groups." *American Sociological Review* 18: 357–67.

Homans, George C. 1961. *Social Behavior: Its Elementary Forms*. New York: Harcourt Brace.

Humphreys, Paul and Berger, Joseph. 1981. "Theoretical consequences of the status characteristics formulation." *American Journal of Sociology* 86: 953–83.

Johnston, Janet R. 1988. "The structure of ex-spousal relations: An exercise in theoretical integration and application." In M. Webster, Jr. and M. Foschi (eds.) *Status Generalization: New Theory and Research*. Stanford, Calif.: Stanford University Press, pp. 309–26, 509–10.

Keating, Caroline F. 1985. "Human dominance signals: The primate in us." In S. L. Ellyson and J. F. Dovidio (eds.) *Power, Dominance, and Nonverbal Behavior*. New York: Springer-Verlag, pp. 89–108.

Kollock, Peter, Blumstein, Philip, and Schwartz, Pepper. 1985. "Sex and power in interaction." *American Sociological Review* 50: 34–47.

Lee, Margaret T. and Ofshe, Richard. 1981. "The impact of behavioral style and status characteristics on social influence: A test of two competing theories." *Social Psychology Quarterly* 44: 73–82.

Leffler, Ann, Gillespie, Dair L. and Conaty, Joseph C. 1982. "The effects of status differentiation on nonverbal behavior." *Social Psychology Quarterly* 45: 153–61.

Lerner, Melvin J. 1974. "The justice motive: 'Equity' and 'parity' among children." *Journal of Personality and Social Psychology* 29: 539–50.

Lewis, Gordon H. 1972. "Role differentiation." *American Sociological Review* 37: 424–34.

Lineweber, David, Barr-Bryan, Dorine, and Zelditch, Morris Jr., 1982. "Effects of a legitimate authority's justification of inequality on the mobilization of revolutionary coalitions." Technical Report #84, Laboratory for Social Research, Stanford University.

Linton, Ralph, 1936. *The Study of Man: An Introduction*. New York: Appleton.

Lockheed, Marlaine E. and Hall, Katherine P. 1976. "Comceptualizing sex as a status characteristic." *Journal of Social Issues* 32: 111–24.

Markovsky, Barry, Smith, LeRoy F., and Berger, Joseph. 1984. "Do status interventions persist?" *American Sociological Review* 49: 373–82.

Mazur, Allan. 1973. "Cross-species comparison of status in established small groups." *American Sociological Review* 38: 111–24.

—— 1985. "A biosocial model of status in face-to-face primate groups." *Social Forces* 64: 377–402.

Mazur, Allan and Cataldo, Mima. 1989. "Dominance and deference in conversation." *Journal of Social Biology and Structure* 12: 87–99.

McWilliams, Susan and Blumstein, Philip 1991. "Evaluative hierarchy in personal relationships." In E. Lawler, B. Markovsky, C. Ridgeway, and H. Walker (eds.) *Advances in Group Processes*, vol. 8. Greenwich, Conn.: JAI Press, pp. 67–88.

Mead, George H. 1934. *Mind, Self, and Society*, ed. Charles C. Morris. Chicago: University of Chicago Press.

Meeker, Barbara F. 1981. "Expectation states and interpersonal behavior." In M. Rosenberg and R. H. Turner (eds.) *Social Psychology: Sociological Perspectives*. New York: Basic Books, pp. 290–319.

Mitchell, G. and Maple, Terry L. 1985. "Dominance in nonhuman primates." In S. Ellyson and J. Dovidio (eds.) *Power, Dominance, and Nonverbal Behavior*. New York: Springer-Verlag, pp. 49–68.

Moore, James C. Jr. 1968. "Status and influence in small group interactions." *Sociometry* 31: 47–63.

Parsons, Talcott and Bales, Robert F. 1955. *Family, Socialization, and Interaction Process*. New York: Free Press.

Pugh, Meredith D. and Wahrman, Ralph. 1983. "Neutralizing sexism in mixed-sex groups: Do women have to be better than men?" *American Journal of Sociology* 88: 746–62.

Ridgeway, Cecilia L. 1982. "Status in groups: The importance of motivation." *American Sociological Review* 47: 76–88.

——1987. "Nonverbal behavior, dominance, and the basis of status in task groups." *American Sociological Review* 52: 683–94.

——1991. "The social construction of status value: Gender and other nominal characteristics." *Social Forces* 70: 367–86.

Ridgeway, Cecilia L., and David Diekema. 1989. "Dominance and collective hierarchy formation in male and female task groups." *American Sociological Review* 54: 79–93.

Ridgeway, Cecilia L. and Johnson, Cathryn. 1990. "What is the relationship between socio-emotional behavior and status in task groups?" *American Journal of Sociology* 95: 1189–1212.

Ridgeway, Cecilia L., Berger, Joseph, and Smith, LeRoy. 1985. "Nonverbal cues and status: An expectation states approach." *American Journal of Sociology* 90: 955–78.

Riecken, Henry W. 1958. "The effect of talkativeness on ability to influence group solutions of problems." *Sociometry* 21: 309–21.

Riedesel, Paul L. 1974. "Bales reconsidered: A critical analysis of popularity and leadership differentiation." *Sociometry* 37: 557–64.

Roethlisberger, Fritz and Dickson, William J. 1939. *Management and the Worker*. Cambridge, Mass.: Harvard University Press.

Sampson, Edward E. 1969. "Studies in status congruence." In Leonard Berkowitz (ed.) *Advances in Experimental Social Psychology*, vol. 4. New York: Academic, pp. 225–70.

Shelly, Robert K. 1988. "Social differentiation and social integration." In M. Webster, Jr. and M. Foschi (eds.) *Status Generalization: New Theory and Research*. Stanford, Calif.: Stanford University Press, pp. 366–76 and 512–15.

Sherif, Muzafer, White, B. Jack, and Harvey, O. J. 1955. "Status in experimentally produced groups." *American Journal of Sociology* 60: 370–9.

Slater, Philip E. 1955. "Role differentiation in small groups." *American Sociological Review* 20: 300–10.

Smith-Lovin, Lynn and Brody, Charles. 1989. "Interruptions in group discussions: The effects of gender and group composition." *American Sociological Review* 54: 424–35.

Smith-Lovin, Lynn and Heise, David R. 1988. *Analyzing Social Interaction: Advances in Affect Control Theory*. New York: Gordon and Breach.

Stewart, Penni A. and Moore, James C. Jr. 1992. "Wage disparities and performance expectations." *Social Psychology Quarterly* 55: 78–85.

Strodtbeck, Fred L. and Mann, Richard D. 1956. "Sex role differentiation in jury deliberations." *Sociometry* 19: 3–11.

Strodtbeck, Fred L., James, Rita M., and Hawkins, Charles. 1957. "Social status in jury deliberations." *American Sociological Review* 22: 713–19.

Stryker, Sheldon and Statham, Anne. 1985. "Symbolic interaction and role theory." In G. Lindzey and E. Aronson (eds.) *The Handbook of Social Psychology*, 3rd edn, vol. 1. New York: Random House, pp. 311–78.

Torrance, E. Paul. 1954. "Some consequences of power differences in decision making in permanent and temporary three-man groups." In A. P. Hare, E. F. Borgatta, and R. F. Bales (eds.) *Small Groups*. New York: Knopf, pp. 600–9.

Veblen, Thorstein [1899] 1953. *The Theory of the Leisure Class: An Economic Study of Institutions*, rev. edn. New York: New American Library.

Wagner, David G., Ford, Rebecca S., and Ford, Thomas W. 1986. "Can gender inequalities be reduced?" *American Sociological Review* 51: 47–61.

Walker, Henry A. and Cohen, Bernard P. 1985. "Scope statements: Imperatives for evaluating theory." *American Sociological Review* 50: 288–301.

Weber, Max [1921] 1946. "Class, status, and party." In *From Max Weber: Essays in Sociology*, translated and ed. H. Gerth and C. W. Mills. New York: Oxford University Press, pp. 180–95.

Webster, Murray Jr. 1977. "Equating characteristics and social interaction: Two experiments." *Sociometry* 40: 41–50.

Webster, Murray Jr. and Driskell, James E. 1978. "Status generalization: A review and some new data." *American Sociological Review* 43: 220–36.

Webster, Murray Jr. and Foschi, Martha. 1988. *Status Generalization: New Theory and Research*. Stanford, Calif.: Stanford University Press.

Webster, Murray Jr. and Sobieszek, Barbara I. 1974. *Sources of Self-Evaluation: A Formal Theory of Significant Others and Social Influence*. New York: Wiley.

West, Candace. 1984. "When the doctor is a 'lady': Power, status and gender in physician–patient exchanges." *Symbolic Interaction* 7: 87–106.

West, Candace and Garcia, Angela. 1988. "Conversational shift work: A study of topical transition between men and women." *Social Problems* 35: 551–75.

Whyte, William F. 1943. *Street Corner Society*. Chicago: University of Chicago Press.

Wilson, Edward O. 1975. *Sociobiology: The New Synthesis*. Cambridge, Mass.: Harvard University Press.

Wood, Wendy and Karten, Steven J. 1986. "Sex differences in interaction style as a product of perceived sex differences in competence." *Journal of Personality and Social Psychology* 50: 341–7.

Zelditch, Morris Jr., Lauderdale, Patrick, and Stublarec, Stephen. 1980. "How are inconsistencies between status and ability resolved?" *Social Forces* 58: 1025–43.

21 Attention for Sale: The Hidden Privileges of Class

Charles Derber, with Yale Magrass

Suddenly, a sharp, dry cough was heard, and they all looked around. It came from a tall supercilious looking Rocket, who was tied to the end of a long stick. He always coughed before he made any observation, so as to attract attention.

"Ahem, Ahem," he said, and everybody listened... As soon as there was perfect silence, the Rocket coughed a third time and began. He spoke with a very slow distinct voice, as if he was dictating his memoirs, and always looked over the shoulder of the person to whom he was talking. In fact, he had a most distinguished manner. "I am a very remarkable Rocket, and come of remarkable parents. My mother was the most celebrated Catherine Wheel of her day, and was renowned for her graceful dancing. When she made her public appearance she spun around nineteen times before she went out and each time that she did so she threw into the air seven pink stars... My father was a Rocket like myself and of French extraction. He flew so high people were afraid that he would never come down. He did though, for he was of a kindly disposition, and he made a most brilliant descent in a shower of golden rain..."

"I am made for public life" said the Rocket, "and so are all my relations... Whenever we appear we excite great attention..."

Oscar Wilde, from "The Remarkable Rocket"

A high-school girl who detectives say wanted to put some zest in her life was charged with second-degree forgery yesterday in the theft of about $32,000 from her parents' saving accounts. Detectives said Sandra Lee Smart, 19, of Boulder, bought a new Thunderbird, Jaguar and a $25,000 Lincoln Continental to become popular and change her humdrum life-style. "She told me she knew she would be caught sooner or later, but it was worth it," said detective Steve Dillman. "She got people to notice her..."

Boston Globe, November 30, 1978 (UPI)

What is at issue here, however, is the question: how far is commodity exchange together with its structural consequences able to influence the total outer and inner life of society?

George Lukács, from History and Class-Consciousness

We have seen a close relation between attention and power. In America, wealth, occupation, and education all significantly affect who gets attention in everyday interactions, with members of privileged groups receiving the most and those in subordinate groups experiencing a certain daily invisibility. Inequalities of attention grow out of the most fundamental forms of social inequality and must be understood partly as a feature of a society divided into classes.

Socially dominant classes have the power to define themselves as having greater personal and social worth than those in inferior positions and thus more deserving of attention. They are best able to exhibit the prevailing societal symbols of worth,

Reprinted from *The Pursuit of Attention: Power and Ego in Everyday Life*, New York: Oxford University Press, 2000, pp. 57–77.

symbols described by Richard Sennett as "badges of ability" that all members of society accept as tangible measures of merit. By displaying these symbols, people affirm themselves in the eyes of others as individuals of special distinction, whose abilities and achievements give them unqualified claim to attention (see Richard Sennett and Jonathan Cobb, *The Hidden Injuries of Class*, 1973). In stratified societies, dominant classes largely define these symbols and assign them to achievements and possessions reflecting their own class advantages.

In America, the dominant classes are those which come to control economic, political, and cultural life. They include the monied class that owns economic resources and the emerging class of managers and professionals that exercises economic and cultural authority over the rest of the population. The subordinate classes include a marginal underclass comprising the poor, unemployed, and peripherally employed, and the working class whose members are employed, but do not own capital or exercise authority. Members of dominant classes have advantages in gaining attention in what we have called "formal" interactions principally because of their power and official status. They monopolize the commanding attention-getting roles in cultural and political life and in workplaces. In addition, they are advantaged in informal interactions because wealth, occupation, and education create added claims to attention in ordinary conversations. We shall begin by considering the relation of attention to wealth – first in formal, then in informal interactions – and then consider how occupational roles and educational standing affect the attention any individual receives.

Attention as a Commodity: Wealth and the Purchase of Attention

In modern industrial societies, a growing percentage of the individual's social life occurs in "secondary" relationships mediated by money and commercial interests. People must seek to satisfy their basic needs – including attention – in interactions governed directly or indirectly by the market. Attention has become increasingly available as a commodity to be purchased from people who give attention in the course of their work and expect to be paid for their services. Members of the dominant classes are best able to afford attention of this kind and consume the greatest amount.

Consider, for example, the purchase of attention in psychotherapy. Therapy is a market-based formal interaction explicitly structured to assure the client-purchaser most of the attention. In exchange for a fee, the client is assured that the only legitimate focus or "subject" of the interaction is herself. (The therapist who repeatedly seeks to introduce himself as the focus of attention violates the most fundamental norm of therapy.) The therapist is the quintessential professional attention-giver, for the focus of his training is the development of attention-giving skills and it is these skills for which he is paid.

In the therapeutic setting, unlike many other market settings, there is no subtlety cloaking the exchange of attention for money, as the therapist publicly offers his attention and the client openly purchases it. In the therapeutic process itself, however, the therapist must convince his client that he is giving his attention out of genuine concern and sympathy rather than for purely pecuniary ends or the therapeutic endeavor is likely to fail. This reflects the fact that people are most gratified by attention they believe others spontaneously choose to give. Thus, even people purchasing attention want to believe that the other is giving his attention freely rather than because his purchase requires it.

Psychoanalysis and psychotherapy continue to be a luxury enjoyed by business and professional classes. Members of subordinate classes can rarely afford to enter psychotherapy and so must seek other, and less expensive, forms of attention. The options are limited, however, as access to most of the attention-getting roles (and formal interactions) in the marketplace requires considerable money, and those roles which they may be able to afford offer less attention than those available to the privileged.

The purchase of attention in restaurants, a very different kind of market setting, illustrates this point well. Getting attention is part of the pleasure of "eating out," even in a modest restaurant where the amount of attention the customer can normally expect is limited to the simple serving of a meal.

But the attention purchased in the expensive restaurant is distinct. The reputation of an exclusive restaurant rests not only in the quality of its food, but in its capacity to deliver in delicately-structured interactions the extra attention which its affluent clientele is presumably deserving and able to pay for. Consider the following observation:

> We were greeted by the owner himself, who was dressed in extremely formal attire, but welcomed us informally, as if he were personally pleased to see us. All through the meal, one waiter hovered over our table watching to see if we needed anything. He moved quickly to fill our glasses and to make sure that we had the right sauces and condiments. The head waiter had a distinguished manner, with the expected French accent, and was extremely deferential. In taking our orders, he spoke softly and unobtrusively, yielding the floor immediately whenever one of us began to speak. He was responsive to our inquiries, showing considerable knowledge of gastronomy, but careful not to draw too much attention to himself. He listened solicitously to each person's order, nodding supportively or appreciatively at the selections and never allowing his gaze to wander. All staff members were, in fact, extremely attentive. The wine stewards, busboys, and waiters also approached us respectfully and served the food with a sense of exquisitely concentrated care and concern. (From the Attention-Interaction Project supervised by the author. All examples cited henceforth in this chapter are drawn from this research, unless otherwise specified. This particular report is one of a small number based on participant-observation.)

Here, the role of customer is a source of exceptional attention. The patron purchases the services of a variety of attention-givers, as well as the rights to a carefully cultivated face-to-face deference. He can immediately engage those serving him and, in face-to-face interaction, can expect unhurried and uninterrupted attention. These waiters are trained to give undivided visual attention, to listen solicitously, and to refrain from making themselves the focus of the interaction. This can involve considerable finesse, as in the case of the headwaiter, who is expected to speak with a certain elegance befitting an attendant of a distinguished patron, but not in a style that calls undue notice to himself.

The waiter–patron interchange in the expensive restaurant reflects the way attention is typically allocated in formal interactions, with people in the dominant classes gaining the attention and members of the subordinate classes giving it. Since attention-giving is related to offering deference and respect, the transaction not only reflects the economic power of those in the giving and getting roles, but symbolically affirms their relative social worth.

The privileged classes purchase attention not only in restaurants, shops, and other public settings, but also in formal interactions in private life, by employing attention-givers in the home. As depicted in chronicles of upper-class life...members of the dominant classes have historically surrounded themselves with servants recruited from the subordinate classes who must routinely give attention to whomever pays for their services. Even in the contemporary affluent household, cooks, cleaning ladies, governesses, and other domestic help are employed in attention-giving roles and are judged partly by the quality of the attention they give. In many upper-class homes, liveried servants continue to serve dinner, while valets and chauffeurs attend to the adults. The privileged classes are also able to purchase "overseers" (nannies, governesses, etc.) for their children, thus relieving parents of many attention-giving responsibilities.

Wealth and Informal Interactions: Attention and Consumption Displays

Attention is "purchased" in a different way in the informal interactions of everyday life. By displaying symbols of material success, an individual can increase his sense of his own worth and his rights to attention, while at the same time predisposing others to give the attention expected. Ostentatious or subtle exhibits of property can be used both to attract attention in public places and to help a person maintain the focus of attention in everyday conversations.

Displays of clothing are the most important evidences of property in ordinary interaction. Dressing fashionably is an extremely common means by which people seek to gain attention. Here, members of the dominant classes are especially advantaged, as they define style and can best afford to dress glamorously. For example:

> Two women were sitting over lunch in the restaurant associated with the museum. A third woman, elegantly coiffured and stylishly dressed, sat down to join them. In greeting her, her friends immediately focused their attention on her, looking intently at her outfit and commenting on how lovely she looked. Both commented specifically about her dress and she began to talk at some length about the dress itself and her experiences in shopping for it. The other women, after a few minutes, began to try to broaden the conversation and bring in some of their own shopping experience. By returning to one or another feature of the very striking dress she was wearing, the woman who had been dominating the conversation continued to redirect the conversation to her own clothes and experiences in shopping. The others subsided into a permanent listening role, only letting their attention wander occasionally when they scrutinized the outfits of other elegantly dressed women who were walking by.

Here, a stylish woman focuses the conversation on herself by referring constantly to her clothes. Clothing has special importance for women, who are taught to seek attention through glamor and sexuality. Moreover, women in the dominant classes can use their economic resources to gain added advantages not available to less affluent women in daily interactions. While the latter also learn to rely heavily on clothing to gain attention, they cannot normally afford the expensive jewelry, elegant wardrobes and other glamorous or very stylish items that win privileged women extra attention.

The automobile is another possession that symbolizes social worth and is "displayed" to bring attention to the self. By driving such luxury cars as Cadillacs, Continentals, Mercedes, and Rolls Royces, wealthy individuals attract attention in the streets and in public places. One millionaire's "outsize white Cadillac with a gold plated dashboard" has been described by C. Wright Mills as a lavish example from an earlier era. Nowadays, the acquisition of expensive but less blatantly garish vehicles, including sports cars, antique automobiles, and chauffeured limousines, remains a means by which dominant groups indirectly "purchase" attention.

There are many other areas in which dominant groups set standards of taste and draw attention by displays of consumer sophistication. Tasteful displays of furniture, art work, glassware, china and cutlery, stereophonic equipment, and other household items are used by members of affluent groups as subtle ways of establishing their worth and rights to special attention in everyday interactions.

In consumer economies, through advertising, members of subordinate classes also learn to depend on clothes, cars, and other consumer goods as attention-getting commodities. Advertising successfully persuades consumers that without certain products they will appear either ugly, uncultivated, or offensive, leading others to withdraw attention. Listerine ads warn people of the consequences of bad breath, cosmetic ads condemn unsightly, pimpled, or wrinkled skin. Buying commodities thus helps reduce personal anxieties about getting attention; if most members of the society cannot afford to buy the clothes and other expensive goods to make them fashionable or "glamorous" like the upper classes, at least they can avoid the "blemishes" that might mar their appearance by making relatively inexpensive consumer purchases.

Subordinate groups also buy goods to attract desirable attention. A given toothpaste will buy a winning smile with sparkling white teeth; a given perfume will attract and hold the attention of that glamorous man in the office. People in the subordinate classes, without access to institutional attention-getting roles, may come to depend especially on the acquisition of goods to compensate. The worker in the factory or the clerk in the office who get little or no attention in their work roles may be able to afford the flashy car, clothes, and other goods that bring some attention in personal interaction. While for many consumption is one of the few avenues for gaining attention, it is part of a system that best serves the privileged classes, as they can purchase the commodities which most symbolize worth.

We have examined some of the ways in which monied groups purchase attention in formal interactions and in everyday social life. One further point about the relation between money and attention, particularly in regard to the poor, deserves discussion. We suggested earlier that the attention-getting role is normally the powerful one, but there are exceptions affecting mainly the poor. A number of institutions, including welfare agencies, social work offices, and employment services, offer poor people roles in which they receive face-to-face attention. However, power in these interactions rests in the hands of those giving attention. Welfare client, as an example, is a role of weakness and helplessness, bringing attention at the cost of respect and requiring that the individual acknowledge personal incapacity, failure, or dependency.

Under these conditions, the attention-getting role is one the individual would ordinarily avoid. Those receiving such attention are less likely to feel supported or nurtured as intruded upon, violated, or humiliated. They have little control over the nature of the interaction and the attention given, or over how the parts of their personalities and life histories are examined and revealed. While attention is always potentially controlling or victimizing, this is especially true when the attention-giver represents social control agencies. Giving attention becomes part of the exercise of power and the attention itself a threat or weapon.

Attention and Work

In addition to being a commodity that can be purchased, attention is a reward of authority and prestige in work. People in the dominant occupations gain special attention in the formal interactions in their work life and also in their informal interactions in personal life. This is related both to the structure of work roles and to the growing importance of work as the governing symbol of social worth.

The claim to expertise is a primary source of power for those in dominant occupations and a formidable way of gaining attention. People approach most professionals for what they believe is valuable information, and not only pay generously for it, but give in return an uncommonly close form of attention. The worried patient will hang on every word of his doctor, the legal client will listen keenly to the advice of his lawyer, the avid student will give undivided attention to the professor who knows what the student wants to know. Professionals frequently use "displays" of knowledge to capture attention:

> This professor had an air of expertise that was extremely effective in capturing and holding the attention of his students. During the lecture, he referred constantly to the books he had written, as well as the one he was currently writing. These references seemed to have an effect, as students whose attention had been wandering refocused their gaze on him at these points.

More subtle displays are also common:

> The teacher is unpretentious and one of those rare instructors who makes it clear that he is not an absolute expert in the field. He confesses this fact frequently during the class. Laughing it off, he gains power and attention by giving the tacit implication that he knows more than he would admit to. Students keep their eyes riveted on him and do not stare out the window, whisper to each other or show other signs of diverted attention.

A professional is normally granted attention automatically on the basis of assumed expertise and knowledge. A resort to conscious "displays," even of the subtle kind illustrated here, is thus likely to happen only under those circumstances – which occur frequently in the classroom – where the professional is uncertain that those required by their role to listen him are actually doing so.

The control of rewards and punishments also assures professionals and managers attention in formal interactions. In a courtroom, all parties extend respectful attention to the judge, not only because of the ritual formalities but because of the inordinate power he or she wields over the fate of the petitioners. Similarly, at the workplace, because the employer hires and fires, and controls conditions of work, employees focus on her. In face-to-face interactions with his boss, a subordinate must give respectful attention even if he feels resentment or bitterness. This is a part of deference in formal interactions: the role of the subordinate is not only to listen and respond to instructions or commands, but also to show respect by being especially attentive and taking care not to draw undue attention to himself.

Professional services have traditionally required attention-giving to clients in face-to-face interactions. More recently, however, changes in professional work roles have shifted attention-giving responsibility from professionals to less skilled subordinates; the professional spends less of his time in interactions with clients and, during the time he does so, often gains attention as the "expert" rather than giving it as a helper. These changes are well illustrated in the following observation in a private hospital room:

> The patient is resting in a single room two days after abdominal surgery. She is seen primarily by nurses and aides who enter the room every couple of hours to check vital signs and the IV. The major attending nurse is solicitous and personally attentive. In the early afternoon she enters and asks how the patient is feeling. The patient smiles and indicates she is feeling stronger. She then says she is feeling more pain around the incision. She describes the pain and the nurse listens attentively. The nurse sits on the bed and feels carefully around the abdominal area. She touches her gently and with some nurturance. She tells the patient there is no indication of infection or other problems, but she should let her know about any acute pain that develops. She is reassuring and supportive. She also indicates that the doctor, whom the patient has seen only once since the operation, will be coming to see her in the afternoon.
>
> The doctor arrives an hour later. He is friendly, but formal and personally remote. He asks how the patient is doing; as she answers, he does not look at her but at a chart he is holding. He asks her a few questions in quick succession, now looking at the patient, but indicating by his manner that he does not have much time. She then asks quickly about her abdominal condition. She is interested in the exact prognosis of the disorder. He then begins a rather lengthy, authoritative description of the disease. He seems to enjoy talking about it and expounds on it for about five minutes. The attention in the interaction remains clearly focused on him for the rest of the time, and he leaves right after his exposition.

The difference in the two interactions is striking. With the nurse, the focus of attention remains on the patient and the nurse exhibits a "bedside manner" traditionally associated with family doctors. The doctor, on the other hand, interacts with the patient less as a caretaker than as expert consultant. In the "expert" role he becomes the focus of attention himself and offers relatively little attention to the patient.

The same dynamics are evident in higher education. Professors are "experts" who meet with students in large classes to impart knowledge. To the extent that students receive any attention, they are less likely to receive it from their professors in the classroom than from teaching assistants or graduate students who lead discussion groups, read papers, and meet with students in individual consultations. Like nurses and medical paraprofessionals, teaching assistants are part of an emerging stratum of subordinates who buffer professionals from demands of clients and take over the routine burden of attention-giving.

In the business world executives and bosses also delegate much of the responsibility of attention-giving to subordinates. The secretary-receptionist, for example, not only gives attention to clients, but must do so in a way conducive to her boss's interests. Secretaries give attention to their bosses as well as to clients, nurses to doctors as well as patients, and teaching assistants to professors as well as to students. These attention-givers thus benefit those in dominant occupations doubly, not only by lightening their attention-giving responsibilities but reinforcing their attention-getting status.

Invisibility at Work: Subordinate Occupations

The work roles of those not in dominant occupations are rarely attention-getting ones. Most sales and service workers, clerical workers, and industrial workers do not have subordinates expected to give them attention. The only attention that these workers can typically expect in their formal interactions is from supervisors who regulate their behavior.

It is useful to distinguish subordinate workers who remain visible and others who become invisible. Invisibility, as R. D. Laing has pointed out, is the most drastic form of attention-deprivation, ultimately more painful and dehumanizing than hostile or other "negative" attention. Anyone can become temporarily invisible in meetings, groups, and other kinds of everyday situations. But for those whose job is regarded as dirty, unpleasant, or unsightly, and are therefore required to work in hidden places such as kitchens or basements, it is routine to their daily experience. Other workers of very low status, such as the cleaning lady or the busboy, while they may work in the purview of other people, remain invisible because others feel no need to acknowledge their presence.

Erving Goffman's distinction between "front" and "back" regions of the workplace provides a basis for looking more closely at the difference between visible and invisible work roles. Goffman points out that work space can be divided into that accessible to the public or other outsiders (the "front" space) and those accessible only to the employees themselves (the "back" region). In a restaurant, the kitchen and stockroom are the back regions, while the diningroom is the front region. There are normally physical barriers between front and back regions, designed to prevent those in the front regions from seeing what takes place in the back regions. Certain workers, such as waitresses, have access to both regions while others, such as dishwashers, are confined to the back region.

Goffman was primarily concerned with understanding work as a kind of performance, and considered the back region as a backstage where the actors prepare the props and mobilize themselves for the drama in the front region. For our purposes, the distinction between front and back regions is useful in understanding who gives and gets attention. Those restricted to the front region can never give or get attention from those restricted to the back region and vice versa.

Workers restricted to the back regions become invisible to the public. The kitchen help, for example, remain completely unseen by the clientele of the restaurant. Similarly, stockboys, packers, inventory clerks, and many clerical workers, who are normally restricted to back regions of department stores, grocery stores, and other service or retail establishments, also work unnoticed.

Being in an invisible work role does not imply that the worker gets no attention at all in his job. The dishwasher may seek and get attention in informal interactions with fellow workers in his back region. Moreover, he is freed from having to give attention to the clientele. Nonetheless, his invisibility to the public is symbolic of his low worth and disadvantages him in gaining attention. Symbolically, it suggests that he is not entitled to acknowledgment or recognition from the clientele.

Workers confined to the back regions are not the only ones in invisible work roles. A more extreme form of dehumanization is experienced by those who work in front regions, but whose presence commands no attention whatsoever. The sweeper in the restaurant, for example, carries out his work in full view without anyone else noticing him and remains unseen unless he commits an offense which violates his role. In the movie *Charlie*, for example, the hero, a busboy, is portrayed in his invisible role until he drops and breaks a stack of dishes, thus exploding out of his invisible position. Similarly, transportation workers, and the janitors and groundskeepers in many establishments carry out their work in view of others and yet receive minimal recognition. A cleaning lady or other domestic servant may glide through the house performing her duties almost as a ghost, without family members taking any note of her presence.

On the other hand, there are many work settings where the lower-status employees occupy the front regions while those with the greatest power are sheltered in exclusive back regions. In a bank, for example, the tellers are visible, while the executives are hidden within imposing offices. Similarly, in many bureaucracies, clerks and other low-status office workers can normally be seen within a large office space while the more powerful employees gradually disappear into asylums as they move up the ranks. In these circumstances, "invisibility" is actually a symbol of status. The executive suite is, however, a very different kind of back region from, say, the restaurant kitchen, and the "invisibility" of the high official radically distinct from that of the dishwasher. The executive office is designed to serve the interest of the one who occupies it, functioning in many ways as a sanctuary from the demands of others. Moreover, the executive is invisible only when he chooses, as he has a staff of subordinate attention-givers (secretaries, personal aides, etc.) on whom he can call at any time. He also has access to the front region and can demand, if he desires, a great deal of attention from subordinates when he enters there.

Workers available to the public, moreover, such as bank tellers and receptionists, are normally in attention-giving roles. They typically receive from the public only the minimal acknowledgment of their presence that is required to conduct business. Their visibility merely reflects the obligation of giving attention to customers – a duty delegated to those in the front region – and not the privilege of receiving it, which is reserved for those in the back region.

As indicated earlier, all lower-status workers are assured, however, of getting the one kind of attention that all work establishments direct toward their employees, even the least favored in formal interactions: supervisory attention. Employers extend the attention required to insure that they are doing their job, maintaining discipline, and working at the rhythm and efficiency expected of them. On the assembly line, the foreman focuses his attention on the workers to regulate their behavior and prevent interruptions of the production process. The gaze of the foreman is the immediate expression, face-to-face, of a larger system of social control that institutionalizes the power of the employer over the worker; it is the most important and least desired of the forms of attention that workers receive.

Work Identity and Informal Interaction

We have seen that the competition for attention in ordinary informal interaction involves a struggle by each individual to establish his or her relative worth. High occupational status has become one of the most important symbols defining personal worth in ordinary social relations. As a result, professionals, executives, and others in dominant occupations enjoy a significant advantage in seeking and winning attention in ordinary conversation.

The importance of occupational status derives from the primacy of "ability" as a contemporary measure of worth. Richard Sennett has shown that ability (and accomplishment) has become a universal value that significantly affects the appraisal of members of all classes of their own worth and that of others. Occupational status is considered in modern culture the most tangible and compelling measure of ability and now carries the symbolic significance that wealth had in an earlier period.

To exploit occupational status as a means of getting attention, the individual must successfully display or communicate it to others. Obviously, a doctor cannot expect special attention in conversation unless he has made his professional identity known. Unlike a property display, disclosures of occupational identity are not usually communicated visually (although a doctor, for example, can give visual cues by wearing a "beeper" or his white coat when off the job). Such information normally surfaces in conversation either by being openly discussed or by being subtly communicated through use of technical language or knowledge. A doctor's professional identity will normally become apparent to strangers or acquaintances when he talks directly about his work, uses some kind of medical vocabulary, or steers the discussion to health-related topics in which he has expertise. At the beginning of conversations between strangers or new acquaintances, people normally break the ice with the familiar question "What do you do?" Occupation is thus revealed at the outset and helps to establish the relative status of the parties talking and the allocation of attention.

In most social relations, those in dominant occupations need not disclose this information, as it is already known to family, friends, and others with whom they regularly interact. As such, their occupational status is a permanently recognized "badge of ability" that establishes their special worth in the eyes of others and, in most informal situations, enhances their perceived rights to attention. As indicated earlier, fathers in high status jobs often gain added attention in their families because of the prestige they carry from the outside world. Those who cannot exhibit the occupational "badge" or whose occupational status is clearly inferior will find their worth constantly in question. In order to win attention, they must struggle to establish it in other ways. This is reflected in subtle dynamics in conversations among people of different occupational statuses. People of low status may feel the pressure to talk constantly simply to prevent others from withdrawing their attention altogether. This is reflected in the stereotypical "talkativeness" of housewives, who cannot draw on occupational status to secure attention in ordinary situations. An analysis of the talk of working-class housewives indicates that their lack of occupational status forces them to seek alternative strategies (obsessive talking is one possibility) to mitigate the fear that they might be completely disregarded.

Attention and Education

An individual's education also has a major effect on the attention he receives in everyday interactions. Since access to higher education depends on one's class position and is instrumental in one's gaining entry to dominant occupations, it becomes an indirect basis for access to the attention-getting roles already considered. In addition, independently of one's occupation and income, one's education can be a powerful claim on attention. In everyday conversation, people with college or advanced education have a number of advantages in gaining attention, stemming from the importance of schooling as a unique symbol of worth that entitles the individual to special forms of recognition.

This is partly due to the widespread tendency to equate schooling with intelligence. Intelligence is regarded as a fundamental kind of ability which commands enormous respect in contemporary culture, and its appearance or apparent absence has a major effect on the kinds of attention any individual receives. While there is no compelling evidence that those given special access to higher education are more intelligent than others, they are normally regarded as such, in part because education provides resources (mainly verbal skills and specialized information) for appearing so. Those without advanced education are widely considered deficient both in ability and intelligence, and thus lacking a claim to the interest and attention of others.

Education is also a badge or symbol of "self-development," another contemporary measure of worth, related to ability, but more explicitly concerned with the extent to which talents, skills, and faculties have been cultivated and actualized (in a sense, the extent to which ability has been realized). The criterion of self-development means that those perceived as most "evolved" or "accomplished" are viewed as especially deserving of attention.

Revelations about educational status are enormously important in shaping others' assessments of one's worth and regulating the flow of attention. People in dominant classes rely on their education as a major sign both of their "self-development" and their special rights to attention. Whenever the rights are in doubt, educated individuals will normally act to reaffirm their worth, often by displaying some expression of self-development or schooling. This display can be compared to the property or consumer display described earlier, by which individuals exhibit evidence of wealth. One does not ordinarily make explicit reference to educational accomplishments, although an individual who offhandedly mentions his undergraduate experience at Princeton or the fact that he has a Ph.D. will enhance his status. Usually, the display is more subtle and indirect, involving either the use of sophisticated vocabulary and manner of speaking or the display of specialized knowledge.

Speech is enormously important as an education display and attention-getting cue. Sociolinguists have accumulated considerable evidence that people can be identified in terms of class, subculture, and education on the basis of how they talk. Such matters as vocabulary, grammar, intonation, and diction significantly affect how people respond to one another. Members of dominant classes use an expanded vocabulary (including more technical, literary, or simply "big" words) as well as the "proper" or "standard" grammar and diction that others recognize as evidence of advanced schooling. Members of subordinate classes are likely to find themselves at a disadvantage when seeking attention in any face-to-face setting in which people of different classes are brought together. On the basis of speech patterns and other cues of educational background and class position, their ideas are less likely to be taken seriously, and others less disposed to cede air time or listen attentively to them. Studies in such diverse contexts as jury rooms, parent–teacher meetings, and community gatherings indicate that those who talk the most frequently and whose ideas are given the greatest attention are invariably individuals with high educational status and class background, and that those less educated normally speak less often and receive less attention.

Members of subordinate classes who do not exhibit the "standard" vocabulary, grammar, and diction are handicapped as soon as they begin to speak. These handicaps begin early in life, since the working- or lower-class child is less likely to get attention from teachers in school because of the way he talks. This experience is reproduced in adult life in most organizations and institutions; bureaucrats, employers, and others in positions of authority, attuned to the class symbols of worth, are likely to direct attention preferentially on the basis of speech cues indicating education and class status. This is one of the most subtle forms of discrimination by class, reproduced in the everyday interactions within all our institutions.

22 Contending with Everyday Discrimination: Effects and Strategies

Joe R. Feagin and Melvin P. Sikes

A few months before he died of AIDS in 1993, the black tennis star Arthur Ashe was asked if that deadly disease had been the most difficult challenge he had faced in his life. Reflecting on his battle with AIDS, which he had contracted through a blood transfusion, Ashe replied that another challenge was greater: "Being black is. No question about it. Even now it continues to feel like an extra weight tied around me" (Shuster 1993: 1C). In previous chapters of *Living with Racism* we have discussed the extra weight that discrimination imposes on black lives. We have discussed the character and impact of specific instances of discrimination in public places, businesses, schools, and neighborhoods, and touched briefly on countering strategies middle-class African Americans have used in particular cases. In this chapter we focus in detail on the important lifesaving skills and coping strategies that African Americans rely on to survive the ordeals of modern racism.

To our knowledge the recent social science literature contains no systematic analysis of the survival skills African Americans have developed in confronting bigotry. A few psychological studies have recognized the stress caused by discrimination and identified some of the psychological strategies devised in response. Humphrey noted that "an ethnic group's perception of another ethnic group's effect on the distortion of the rules of distributive justice will predict a sense of *anomie* among its members and consequently disturb their emotional homeostasis" (1986: 63). He suggested that facilitating a sense of powerfulness in a group reduces psychological *anomie*. Similarly, Thomas and Sillen (1977) have noted that racial stress can stimulate important coping mechanisms. Individual reactions to this stress may range from constructive adaptation to a breakdown of normal functioning. Significantly, many victims of discrimination have marshalled resources that were not previously obvious or strengths of which they were not aware (see also Mirowsky and Ross 1989). Much more social science research, in our view, needs to be done on black approaches to bias and discrimination.

Among middle-class African Americans there is much discussion of survival strategies. The oral tradition is a major source of the wisdom that has helped our respondents in struggling against everyday racism. Some programs within black organizations teach defensive survival tactics. A sophisticated repertoire of methods and tactics that have helped overcome racism becomes critical in a black person's life approach and life perspective.

Reprinted from *Living with Racism: The Black Middle Class Experience*, Boston: Beacon Press, 1994, pp. 272–318.

With great persistence and patience, middle-class blacks pursue personal dreams of achievement and prosperity in the face of discriminatory encounters. Dreams must not, a hospital administrator argues, be given up in the face of discrimination. He explained forcefully what it is like to persevere despite meeting racism:

> Being aware that the opportunities are there for black Americans to achieve, and also realizing that though the opportunities are there for achievement, the types of blockage or the types of pitfalls that are there – and also recognizing that the opportunities may be there to excel, but you may not have all the working tools and all the necessary mentors to open the doors for you. . . . There's going to be discrimination and racism out there, and as long as you can accomplish what you have set forth to accomplish, recognize it for what it is, understand it for what it is, and don't let it deter you from your dreams, don't let it deter you from your goals. When that *does* happen, though, then you have to formulate a plan of action to still accomplish your goal and let that be your number one priority. Don't let attacking racism and attacking discrimination cause you to lose sight of your goal. You keep that aside, and understanding that this is something that you had to deal with as you continue to pursue your goal. Because that happens when you start putting all your energy in trying to deal with a racist act that is preventing you from trying to accomplish something, you won't accomplish it. You have to understand that this is an obstacle that you're going to have to deal with, but while I'm dealing with this, I'm going to keep moving straight ahead.

He continued emphatically: "And I'm saying that we can't afford to get caught up in just attacking racism without pursuing on a continued basis our goal to accomplish our goals and to accomplish our dreams. My thoughts and my feelings are, yes, recognize racism, recognize discrimination, try to deal with it as you are continuing to pursue your dreams and your goals."

The Array of Situational Strategies

Prior to the 1960s the legalized mistreatment of black Americans, especially in the South, often demanded that they subordinate themselves to whites and routinely respond to them with obsequiousness. Today, even when whites expect obsequiousness, most middle-class blacks do no oblige. Indeed, as many of our respondents have described, there has been a significant increase in the number of African Americans with the professional and financial resources to fight discrimination, often directly. In examining specific examples of discrimination, we have seen that responses to everyday prejudice or mistreatment range from careful assessment to withdrawal, resigned acceptance, verbal confrontation, physical confrontation, or legal action. We will now turn to the more general discussions in our interviews of the impact, character, and meaning of these anti-discrimination strategies.

One way to deal with discrimination is to try to avoid situations where it might occur, even at some personal cost. A physician in a southwestern city responded to a question about dealing with discrimination this way: "It just depends on what the situation is, whether or not it's personal, business; it just kind of depends on what, you know, exactly what it is. I usually don't go places where I'm not wanted, so I'm not the kind of person that trailblazes – where people tell you that they don't want you in a certain situation and you persist. It's kind of a hard question to answer." Seen here is the tragic legacy for black Americans of having to "know one's place." One senses fear of physical harm and psychological pain in his words.

Yet avoidance helps only in certain situations, since being middle class almost by definition means venturing daily into a white-dominated world. As we have seen in accounts of discrimination in previous chapters, in that white world a common initial response to discrimination is to carefully evaluate or read the situation. A teacher commented on this evaluation procedure:

> First of all, within myself I try to analyze it. I try to look at all the pros and cons, all the ways in which the situation could've happened. Did I do my part, not necessarily as a black person but just as a person? Did I do everything that I was supposed to do in the particular situation, whether or not it was a conversation, whether or not it was being hired for a job, or whatever.... Then what I do is, again, I just say what I think, in a very professional way. I try not to get into stereotyping myself by becoming very loud, and loud and aggressive, because I think that's the way white people feel as though we are going to handle ourselves. But if I'm faced with it, I try to be professional and assertive. Because I believe with whites you have to deal with them the way that they are accustomed to being dealt with. And that is, putting something on paper, and being professional, assertive but not aggressive. And that's the way I deal with it. I identify the problem. I say, "This is what I feel has happened here." And I give the steps or the reasons that I feel like it has happened, what has drawn me to this conclusion.

This woman captures well the preference of many black Americans to see, if possible, negative action against them as rooted in some factor besides color. Discrimination creates a psychological dilemma. A standard psychological recommendation for dealing with life problems is to face them head on (see, e.g., Mirowsky and Ross 1989). From this perspective it may be healthier for blacks to say internally about mistreatment, "Yes, this is racism," for once a problem is named, it is often easier to solve. As we have suggested previously, many whites feel that black people are paranoid about discrimination and rush quickly to charges of racism. But the reality is often the opposite, as most middle-class blacks seem to evaluate a situation carefully before judging it discriminatory. We judge from our interviews that much discrimination is overlooked if possible. There is white hostility that blacks must ignore just to reduce the pain and to survive. If one can name racial discrimination something else, it may not hurt as much. For example, if blacks can attribute discriminatory acts to economic causes, then they can envisage how conditions might be changed to eliminate the negative behavior. They cannot change the color of their skins, and it is most disheartening to be damned for something over which one has no control.

Accuracy in assessing whites is usually necessary, as an administrative clerk in a publishing firm stressed:

> I'd say don't open your mouth and say anything that you're not 100 percent sure of. Don't have doubt. If you know this is where you want to go, and you know that these things are accurate, you shouldn't have doubt about it, no matter who comes through.... I don't care what the next person tells you. I've had people on my job to

tell me, "well, it's your imagination." [Even] black people now, that say, "Maybe it's just your imagination that this is going on." No, it's not my imagination . . . . Take Susan, one of the supervisors. [They say] "This is just her nature to treat people this way." No. That didn't make me doubt for a moment. It didn't make me have a second thought and say, "Well, is this really the way she is and that she's really not discriminating?" No. She's discriminating.

Beneath the surface we sense the psychological toll taken on a person who must fight to have her view of what is going on in her workplace acknowledged. Having to assess potentially discriminatory situations carefully before responding can create a strain on the energy and psyche of African Americans. What is at stake is often more than whether one is right in a particular assessment. A less obvious aspect of modern racism is the great difficulty black victims often have in establishing their perceptions as legitimate. Full racial integration of historically white institutions requires a change in white views and practices, as well as an increase in power for blacks. Such a major change will result in the power of African Americans to establish their own situational readings and constructions as legitimate in interactions with the whites. In addition, some black Americans say, "The right I want most as an American of African descent is the right to be wrong." Blacks in white institutions feel constantly scrutinized and that they can never "let down" or make a mistake. True racial integration would include the right to make a mistake without abnormal or racial repercussions.

Several respondents discussed how they reassess maltreatment after it has occurred. A manager in an electronics firm described how he applies a self-evalua-tion technique he learned in a management program:

When something happens, I'll take it and toss around in my head, replay it like a recorder, and see if there's maybe something that I did that could have caused it, or something I could have done differently that would have made the outcome different. Then once I feel comfortable with what I've analyzed, the one thing I'll do is I'll present, if need be, my argument to whoever it is that I'm dealing with, be it my manager or someone else.

Not every situation requires the same reaction. Punctuating his comments with some laughter, the owner of a chemical company described how he sometimes chooses to ignore minor incidents:

It depends on the importance of the situation that I'm dealing with. If it's in the grocery store, hey, I don't get upset about somebody [who] gets in front of me, tries to pretend I'm not there. It depends on how I'm feeling that day, but, you know, life is too short to get upset about something like that. If it meant that they wanted to short-change me in the line, you know just because I'm black, then we've got some problems. And we will deal with it head on. So we have to put it in the proper perspective because, like I said, there's always going to be discrimination and you just have to learn to deal with it; you just don't jump up and down in every instance.

A theme throughout many discussions of coping in our interviews is the struggle to keep some kind of balance and to contain one's frustrations in searching for the best response. In one situation, resigned acceptance is preferred; in another, active confrontation.

After the initial assessment of a situation one possible response is to retreat. Some street incidents allow only for a quick exit. Some type of acquiescence is another response forced on black Americans. A computer specialist for an East Coast bank described one such response, a "blocking out" method:

> My first way of dealing with discrimination is usually... acting like it doesn't exist. Back in the sixties, in my parents' days, Martin Luther King's days, it was outward, it was blatant. Now, you can't holler discrimination, because they're going to think that you're trying to get a lawsuit, or trying to [get] a free meal or something, so you really can't come out and say, "I'm being discriminated against." You've got to handle it in a more mature, more adult way, a more, I guess you could say, a more timid way. You've got to just know it's there, do all you can to avoid it.

Such acquiescence may sometimes be necessary, yet, as we suggested earlier, it may not be a psychologically healthy technique. It is possible too that by "a more timid way" he refers to an indirect or subtle means of deflecting discrimination.

The heavy price paid psychologically for this adaptation strategy can be seen in the comments of a banking executive in an eastern city:

> You become a chameleon. You take on the characteristics of what's going on there. It goes everything from patterns of speech, your philosophies, your thinking. Because I don't think all the time you're openly, I mean, you're not totally honest. You know what [white] people want to hear more than anything else and you give them back your feedback; you regurgitate back to them what you think they need to hear. There are times when you go against it, bucking the system, and then you just tell them your gut feelings or how you really feel about something, but most people that I know will hold that back until it's at the point when it needs to be said. But they don't normally, as a routine basis, do it.

Some agree that the struggle with whites requires acquiescence, but only up to a point; that is, they take the "run to fight another day" approach. In an earlier chapter we discussed a black lawyer's measured response to a white attorney who used the word "nigger" in his presence. Although he appeared at first to ignore the remark, when the white attorney later came by to ask how he was, he with some humor pressured him by suggesting that many white people need "help" in dealing with their sickness called racism. In his interview the black lawyer added these words:

> I think many blacks have lost out because we have become frustrated. We see what we're dealing with. And then it appears so hopeless, and we just say, "Oh, I can't help it." And we just throw in the towel.... It's a world in which they may have the advantage, but there's nothing that says it has to continue to be that way. And so our job then becomes: How do we turn whatever disadvantages may be ours into advantages. And I think there're certain ways to do it. But the strategy must sometimes vary, and we must control our tempers and our emotions. And then there are some times when we must just hide to live another day, which means, "I see what you're doing, I don't particularly care for what you're doing, but nothing will be gained by me pointing it out to you today." So I'll take it, and there'll be another day.

Confronting White Racists

Withdrawal and acquiescence are by no means the only strategies our respondents described. Confrontation is a common strategy for dealing with the racist attitudes and actions of white Americans. Indeed, there has been a long history of active resistance to racism on the part of African Americans, from the time the first Africans were enslaved on ships bound for the new American colonies. Historian Herbert Aptheker found evidence of 250 American slave revolts or conspiracies to revolt, a count that did not include the numerous mutinies aboard slave ships (1943: 12–18, 162). Later, during legal segregation, some blacks took great risks by confronting whites openly. In Blauner's interviews with blacks and whites in California, several black respondents reported acquaintances reacting aggressively to racial discrimination prior to the 1970s (Blauner 1989). After saying that "you have to choose your battles," a professor at a New England university commented on how she deals with racist remarks: "I would say, 'I don't think that's very funny,' you know. 'Look at what it is that you're [saying].' And they would say, 'Oh, it's *only* a joke.' But it isn't *only* a joke, you know. And I think it's really not uncommon even if it's not jokes given about blacks, but given about Arabs, for example. And I think that black people need to say, 'I don't think that's funny.'" Some whites have told the authors that the "black jokes are harmless" and that blacks should "lighten up" and laugh at them, the suggestion being that said jokes are a sign of integration into the core culture. While some middle-class blacks find themselves in situations where they feel pressured to laugh at anti-black and other ethnic jokes told by whites, this professor does not agree with such assent to joking.

By regularly confronting whites verbally, black Americans run the risk of being ostracized or labeled. Emphasizing an aggressive approach, a professional who directs a social welfare program in the Midwest spoke of confronting discrimination:

> There was a job that I just went through and filed a grievance like a big dog. And I called up all of the people that I know that would help raise hell – hell raisers – and that's what, really, what I did. I have never taken the back seat intentionally if I knew that I was taking the back seat. And I tell them. You know, when I came out of high school we had – in the seventies – we had a lot of pride, and one of the things we were taught is that you fought for what you believed in, regardless of how people felt about you, you did that. So as far as discrimination, you know, in my city people know me as a hell-raiser.

Called a "troublemaker," a social worker in an eastern city described her approach to white denial:

> Generally, I get myself into difficulties because I deal with it head on. And generally, I'm considered a troublemaker, or someone who's constantly looking at race, and someone who's looking to argue.... And what disturbed me and continues to disturb me is that whites will try to tell you that they're not being racist, when they can't tell you what you perceive, or how you've experienced something. And what they try to do is to deny your experience, and then invalidate it. And then in other words, you walk around like, well, I know this is happening to me, but you're telling me this is not happening to me, so it's not? No, it means you don't want to acknowledge that it's happening, so what I tend to

do is say, "you are doing this to me," and whether you acknowledge it or not, that's the way I experience it. So, I try to deal with it head on.

Again and again in the interviews we see that living with modern racism is a matter of accumulating experience. And it is the extensive experience that most African Americans have that makes them outraged at the common white denials of the reality of everyday racism.

A bank manager characterized her direct, but careful approach: "Being very direct, I tend to put them on the defensive. I don't, I'm not argumentative, but I always try to ask questions. I'm very direct with my accusations. I just don't fly off the handle. I usually have facts. I go right to the people involved, and I let them explain to me why things are happening. And it seems to shake them up a little bit, that someone can be as direct about the black–white issue."

A lawyer quoted previously sometimes deliberately uses a matter-of-fact but casual retort to racist comments: "Instead of just throwing temper tantrums, say, 'Oh, that's just because you're a racist.' They don't like to be called racist. . . . That's the exciting part. It's not always bad being the underdog. It's not. It's good to see people go through the mental gymnastics, you know." This lawyer characterizes his white antagonists as racists with a smile, using humor as an equalizer, but from the white point of view such a direct yet unheated accusation is disarming and it can provoke vigorous denials.

It is remarkable how many middle-class African Americans see it as their task to educate white Americans about racism and to remind them of the implications of the "liberty and justice" creed whites supposedly honor. One theme in some interviews is calling whites on the carpet, as a southern newspaper publisher explained:

> I think most people don't know what racism is. They consider it just part of the way of doing things. I think the most horrifying thing to me has been that when people have been racist and I have turned around and said, "That was very racist," it's almost been shocking to them. "Racist! I'm not a racist!" And then you explain to them how that's racist, and it's like, "Oh, I never thought of it like that." That's always been mind-boggling. Their perception is that it's not racist – that's the way they think, that's the way they function. So, if I had a choice, more black people would educate white people about what is racist.

The experience of being a victim often seems to generate considerably more thought and reflection about the character of US racial relations than the experience of being white victimizers.

In an earlier chapter of *Living with Racism* we discussed a television anchorperson's account of being discriminated against while attempting to buy a luxury car. In his interview he also described the educational approach he sometimes uses:

> I have found that probably the most effective way – at least it makes me feel better – you realize that basically discrimination is based on ignorance, so you try to educate people. And the best way to educate people I have found is to point out in a very subtle way, and a very intellectual way, the stupidity – I don't know how better to put it – the ignorance basically of why they are prejudiced. For example, the incident that I cited to you about

my buying the car, and the people, based on the [casual] way I was dressed, based on the fact that I was black, assuming that I was not in a position, or was not interested in purchasing that car. That's based on ignorance, and that's based on stereotyping.

As we have seen, racially insensitive or hostile remarks are the scourge of middle-class African Americans moving into formerly all-white situations. With an air of disapprobation, a management assistant in an eastern county government office recounted her reaction to a colleague's remark:

Another incident in that same department – somebody had said that an ambulance company had picked up a person that was so dirty and had lice, and they were appalled. And the next comment was, "And the person wasn't even black." Well, again . . . they looked at me, because they knew that that would be offensive to me and they also knew that I would have a retort for this person. And I said to him, "Do you think black people have a monopoly on dirt?" And the comment was made by the others in the group, which was said in jest, but probably very true, that the person who made the comment had no idea what the word "monopoly" meant. But they knew that he had offended me, and it was interesting. The refreshing thing about that was that the other people in the group were white and had very little exposure to blacks but because of my presence had become more sensitive.

Her presence and her quick response to racially barbed remarks apparently sensitized other whites in her work circle who had no experience with blacks.

For some middle-class black Americans, this desire to educate whites about a range of issues informs their everyday professional activities, as in the case of this professor who has taught at universities in the North and the Southwest:

Most of my class isn't black, two-thirds of any class I teach is white. And so when I'm politicizing black students, I'm also politicizing white students. And I do that because I think that as folks who are going to be participants in the big middle class, they probably won't be as well-off as their parents were, they might be at some point people who are interested in breaking the stranglehold that ideology has on the way we see the world. I think for example that a white male, who is just going to be the equivalent of a middle manager in an insurance company, can see the fact that what is happening to him is not tied to black people, but tied to the way the economy works, that individual will then be someone who in his own life interrupts the process of scapegoating another group. It's the only way I can think of to intervene, short of becoming part of a revolutionary group. Do you know what I mean? I mean, if I wasn't teaching, I'd be standing on a street corner with a machine gun, because I can't imagine what else I would be doing.

Mixing her commentary with occasional laughter, a black professional in a northern state discussed how her approach to educating whites depends on the situation and who the white person is:

I have very little tolerance for white people who expect me to change my behavior to make them comfortable. They don't change their behavior to make me comfortable. I am who I am. Either they sit with me and work with me respecting that, or you can't sit and work together. But I don't – and I see them uncomfortable, and I think to myself,

"Well, that's unfortunate." But, no, I don't go to any great lengths to make them any more comfortable in dealing with me. I sometimes see them choking on words, trying to find ways to say things. And I let them choke! But I'm serious! Why should I help them phrase it. Sometimes I think they're trying to say something about, "Well, do you think the other black members..." "Excuse me?" And I wait for them to come forward with it, and often times they end up not saying it because they're afraid of what my response will be. So they work around it, and I say, "Well, I think that's inappropriate." Then there are other people, who are personal friends, who may make a racist statement, and it's really based on their ignorance and their lack of understanding, and I'll take the time to deal with it. There's a young white woman that I work with now, and she's really not worked with a lot of different people of color, and she uses the term, "you people," and I bring it to her attention, and she's like, "oh, oh," and so it's an education, we're working together.

Differentiating between whites whose statements reflect ignorance and those whose comments show hostility, this professional takes the time to educate the former. Such a response seems to us to be psychologically healthy, for it offers a real solution to a chronic problem and gives the individual black person a sense of accomplishment.

In their everyday rounds some middle-class African Americans have the moxie and opportunity to create situations in which whites must come face to face with their racist views and assumptions. A manager for a southwestern computer firm described a "victory march":

One thing that used to always happen to me – [white] customers don't see me a lot, and their assumption is that I'm white when I talk to them over the phone.... I would go to a customer site, with one of my engineers. And they would come, and they would always talk to the engineer as though I was working for him. And what I would always do is have a game: I would make sure that I would walk to the other side of the room. And then the conversation would soon come to a point where the engineer would say, "I'm not the one that's going to get your problems resolved, that's my boss over there." I would make them come to me, sort of like a victory march!

Although calculated, the manager's response is more one of teaching a lesson than of seeking revenge – and again is wrapped in the commonplace black humor rather than in overt hostility.

Judging from our interviews it is very rare for black Americans to set out to annoy whites just out of vindictiveness. However, we did find a somewhat humorous example of a "payback time" reaction. A student at a predominantly white university recounted, with some laughter, how she and her black friends set up situations and took chances in taunting whites:

It's, I don't know, it's a sense of control in a way, I guess. And it's an acceptable way for me to lash out at white people, you know "acceptable." Because my friends and I, we'll do that a lot. We'll go to a restaurant and we'll talk so loud about racial issues, and we will just trip people out! We did that last Sunday at a restaurant as a matter of fact, no joke. And they would just turn around, and look and drop food and stuff! We would make sure that we sat around the most white people that we possibly could; and we would just talk about them, and just talk about them. And have the best time! I mean, I know it's mean, I know it's evil, but hell. Ok, I have no justification for it, I don't. I admit it, but I can't help it. I can't help myself. It's payback!

Specific incidents of racial discrimination often provoke a personal and collective sense of powerlessness. This payback action gives this young woman and her friends some sense of power and the confidence that they often do not feel in the white university environment. The retaliation strategy works, it should be noted, only because some whites overreact to loud black comments on racial issues. Significantly, the young respondent shows concern over the meanness of her actions. Judging from our interviews – surprisingly, perhaps, given the scale of the racial hostility they face – even more aggressive revenge against whites is not an openly expressed goal of middle-class African Americans.

Many if not most whites grow up with few significant or intimate contacts with African Americans. Some may have had contact with a black domestic or yard worker; and some may have had fleeting contacts with black clerks in stores or one or two black employees in the workplace. Some have no contact at all. For that reason white preconceptions about black Americans stem mostly from parents, friends, teachers, and the mass media. Still, white prejudices can change with greater contact with black Americans, but the character of that contact is very important. Contact between those of unequal status, such as between servants and employers, will seldom have major positive effects. The racial "contact hypothesis" discussed in social science research proposes that contacts between blacks and whites must be between those of roughly equal social status for the contact to lessen white prejudices and stereotypes (Allport 1958: 251–3). A research administrator at a southern university talked about how he helped a white associate deal with his prejudices:

> I'll tell you something that happened to me when I was in banking. I worked in the commercial finance division and I was supposed to go out and interview with somebody. I was the trainee, and this guy who was going out was an old-timer and stuff like that. But he told me, he said, "Listen, I never worked for black people." And in fact, he didn't like black people because he told me that his grandfather told him black people were no good and to watch out for them, that they were cheats and liars. I said, "You know, my mother told me the same thing. Watch out for white people. They're cheats, liars and thieves, and I've got to be very careful around them!" And he realized over the course of our relationship that all the things that he had been taught was just rhetoric, but he says, "I can't change. I've been taught this all my life." And by the time my little tour of duty in that area was over, we became very good friends. And that happens over and over and over again. I've worked with people, I was almost the only friend of this particular white guy that worked in this company. But all he had seen, because he grew up in areas – people may not believe this – but there are areas where white people haven't actually seen a real black person.

Some of the whites described in this section belong to that segment of white America for whom equal status contact with middle-class blacks seems to have changed certain anti-black attitudes. Yet a striking characteristic of the black middle-class experience is that so many middle-class whites seem to be little affected, especially in deep and lasting ways, by an increase in contacts with these middle-class black Americans. The attainment by the black middle class of a status more equal to that of the white middle class has not brought the fully integrated society that equal-status theory, and equality of opportunity laws, would seem to have foretold.

Using Official Channels and Court Suits

A more formal or official response to discrimination can range from writing a letter of protest to complaining to the relevant government agencies or filing a lawsuit. An administrator at a western university told the story of his wife driving past a white police officer who had given her an unclear signal. The officer hit her car hard with his fist, held her up in the middle of traffic, and then told her to get "that junk out of here." Reviewing the story, the administrator commented on how he prefers to handle mistreatment by working through channels:

> When I was younger, I dealt with it confrontation-style. But when I got older and smarter I dealt with it nonconfrontational-style. I deal with it through calling the proper people, writing the proper authorities, going through the proper channels and so forth . . . Oh, for example, that same situation with that police officer who beat on the car and told her it was a piece of junk and told her to pull over. What she should have done was written down his badge number and then phoned it in. And enough people do things like that, a pattern clearly develops against policemen who do things like that.

This emphasis on using proper channels of institutional authority is remarkable given the problems that Africans Americans . . . have with white police officers. In the recent past this type of protest would probably have been futile, if not dangerous. Yet this man's style signals how many middle-class African Americans have come to feel that the police system should be there to serve them. His resources have given him the grounds to demand respect as a citizen and taxpayer.

A number of our respondents have had to resort to threatening lawsuits or actually going to court to rectify maltreatment. A strong sense of justice and legal rights is evident in many of their specific accounts of discrimination. One account was given by an unemployed corporate executive in a northern state, who explored the implications and consequences of the litigation approach:

> I got to a certain level, which is to say a middle-management level of the corporation. I was in line for a *major* increase in position, and that position was given to a white male who was brought from outside the area, outside the area of expertise of the project. . . . He had lesser education, he had lesser experience, so it would seem fit to use the old boy network to bring him into it and to see evidence that that probably happens to many people. And I believe the reaction on the part of a lot of the other blacks is to either resign themselves to putting up with it, and a large number of others end up simply quitting and going elsewhere, and all the effort that they've put into getting where they've gotten at that point in time goes down the drain. . . . Now in my particular case, I am currently unemployed; you know, I'm pursuing a lawsuit. And I'm unable to gain other employment since it's well known in the area where I live at that I am suing my previous employer. And since there is a protective order in place whereby I cannot discuss the specifics of the case, specifically what information we got from the various

interrogatories and discovery material laying out what was done to me. But I cannot properly defend myself in front of potential employers, and, as a consequence, I'm affected so far as not being able to get employment.... It just kind of pulls you in and further essentially isolates you ... It's affected the way former associates, in the town I live in, particularly white associates, perceive and deal with me. It's a very overt avoidance at this point in time. It's even made black friends somewhat hesitant – black friends prior to the time I had to sue my previous employer, black friends who were very friendly toward me – after I had to sue and go into the situation I'm in right now, has made them hesitant so far as their relationships with me.

Seeking redress from discriminators in court, even if one wins, can be devastating professionally and personally. Given the isolation and possibility of retaliation, it is surprising that some middle-class black employees muster the courage to seek legal redress and jeopardize their current situations. Yet the black tradition of civil rights drives many to seek fair play. Despite the few legal recourses available to them, middle-class African Americans have in recent decades provided great and reinforcing support for the old US tradition of protesting injustice.

Personal Coping Styles and Defenses

In addition to strategies for countering specific instances of white discrimination, middle-class black Americans have developed broader personal philosophies, coping styles, and protective defenses for dealing with the accumulating impact of racism on their psyches and lives. Broader life philosophies and perspectives are required because of the harshness, intensity, and prevalence of modern racism. Some costs of white racism are material; others are psychological. Psychiatrists William Grier and Price Cobbs have written that "people bear all they can and, if required, bear even more. But if they are black in present-day America they have been asked to shoulder too much. They have had all they can stand. They will be harried no more. Turning from their tormentors, they are filled with rage" (1968: 4).

Most white Americans do not have any inkling of the rage over racism that is repressed by African Americans. Asked how often she got angry about actions by white people, a professor at a western university replied:

Any time there's any injustice either done to me, or I see it or read about it, it makes me angry. I don't think any human being has the right to feel superior, or act superior, or do things that say they're better than someone else, just because of the color of their skin. And every time I hear [about] incidents I get angry, it upsets me greatly. [*So, would you say that's once a day, once a week, once a month?*] In my profession you can hear it fifteen times on some days, it just depends on who you're seeing on that day, and what's going on in their lives.

The level of intensity this anger can reach is revealed in this vigorous comment of a retired professor in reply to the question, "On a scale of one to ten, where do you think your level of anger is?"

Ten! I think that there are many blacks whose anger is at that level. Mine has had time to grow over the years more and more and more until now I feel that my grasp on handling myself is tenuous. I think that now I would strike out to the point of killing, and not think anything about it. I really wouldn't care. Like many blacks you get tired, and you don't know which straw would break the camel's back.... And I'm angry at what's happening to our young people. I call it impotent rage, because it's more than anger, it's a rage reaction, but something that you can't do something about and that makes it even more dangerous when you do strike out.

Repressed rage over maltreatment is common, this professor argues later in the interview, to *all* African Americans. The psychological costs to African Americans of widespread prejudice and discrimination include this rage, as well as humiliation, frustration, resignation, and depression. Such high costs require major defensive strategies.

One strategy African Americans in all income classes use to cope is to put on their defensive "shields," the term used in a conversation the first author had with a retired music teacher. Now in her seventies, this black informant contrasted her life with that of a white woman, who, like her, bathes, dresses, and puts on her cosmetics before leaving the house each morning. Unlike the white woman, this black woman suggested, she must put on her "shield" just before she leaves the house. When quizzed about this term, she said that for decades, before leaving home she has had to be prepared psychologically and to steel herself in advance for racist insults and acts, to be prepared even if nothing adverse happens on a particular day. One of our respondents, a physical education teacher, spoke to us of her "guarded position" in life: "I feel as though most of the time I find myself being in a guarded position or somewhat on the defense. I somewhat stay prepared to be discriminated against because I never know when it's going to happen to me." A teacher in the Midwest put it this way: Middle-class blacks "can't sit back and relax at all; you have to be vigilant at all times; if you don't you'll be back in chains." Psychologists Thomas and Sillen have argued that such a defensive approach is realistic; in order to survive, they suggest, a black person should assume that "every white man is a potential enemy unles he personally finds out differently" (1977: 54).

The high energy costs of this vigilance and of actually dealing with white racism over a lifetime were described by the retired professor quoted earlier:

> If you can think of the mind as having 100 ergs of energy, and the average man uses 50 percent of his energy dealing with the everyday problems of the world – just general kinds of things – then he has 50 percent more to do creative kinds things that he wants to do. Now that's a white person. Now a black person also has 100 ergs; he uses 50 percent the same way a white man does, dealing with what the white man has [to deal with], so he has 50 percent left. But he uses 25 percent fighting being black, [with] all the problems being black and what it means.

One way that African Americans consume personal energy is in determined efforts to succeed in the face of racism, including overachieving to prove their worth in the face of whites' questioning black ability and competence. A college graduate in a western city described how he felt about having to prove himself:

> It's being constantly reminded that you're different, that you're not good enough, that you have to prove yourself, that you have to be better than average, just to be considered

normal...I am to the point now where when someone has a problem with my race, or my color, or my ability to be a human, and they only see me as an object, a black guy, a "blackie," I deal with it. When they have a problem, I leave it as their problem. I make sure that they understand that this problem that they're having is only theirs. If they have a problem with how I look, who I am, then maybe they should stop looking at me, stop associating with me.

The distress that comes from having to prove oneself in most situations has led this young black man to develop a defensive repertoire that includes making whites aware of who is at fault.

The professor quoted above explained a general approach many employ in dealing with whites:

I think sometimes I use the same strategy I've seen others use. I'll say that doesn't bother me, knowing it does. It's a matter of not letting it destroy you. So it's a matter of psychological strength. And I think most blacks have a tremendous amount of psychological strength. We're able to say this is unfair, but I won't let it destroy me. And that bulldog determination that you will not be destroyed, you will not be torn up, helps you to get over what I call many of the humps.

He tells blacks to recognize that discrimination is unfair, but to work to prevent it from destroying them.

Several respondents felt that it was common for black employees trying to prove themselves in white settings to overachieve, doing more than white employees with similar resources and credentials would have to do. Sprinkling his comments with some laughter, a professor at an eastern law school expounded on this strategy:

There's a lot of pressure, but one thing that there is, there is a byproduct of that that's good, because once you succeed, you *know* that you have the ability. There's no question about it, because you've had to do a little bit more than the next guy to even get through. Whereas we used to say when we were growing up, "If you're white you don't have any excuse for not succeeding in America." And if you're black and get into a position to pursue a certain goal, yes, you might have to work much harder, but that makes it a little bit better in the end, and a little bit more assured of your own ability. The way that things are done now is that everything that a black person does – not everything, but most of the things that some black people do – they try to discount it, say it's not as good, which is not true. And if you fall for that you really have a problem, but it's all a little game.

There is a lot of clearly a psychic cost to such an approach, yet there is also the benefit of knowing one has substantial ability when forced to demonstrate it.

Our interviews repeatedly demonstrated the importance of the inner strength required when African Americans enter indifferent or hostile white worlds. A professor at a historically white university underscored the need for a healthy self-concept:

You must develop some skills, but you also must develop a love of yourself, a liking of yourself. It's very important for you to do that. Now, the skills, that's difficult, because that's a very broad subject. You've got to put yourself in a position where you can learn, and sometimes you may be in a painful position, but once you have that confidence and the skills, you can make it. The liking of yourself is broader than just skills.... When you go to a predominantly white situation where people don't care about you, or a lot of them, and it's maybe even hostile at times, you need to love yourself. You truly need it. You need to get up in the morning and feel very self-contained.

This respondent links avoiding self-blame to liking oneself. Several of those with whom we talked discussed working to overcome excessive self-blaming inclinations, including this executive officer at a predominantly white chamber of commerce:

> Well, I think the thing that works for me is I know it's not me. And you're right, a lot of times when these crazy things happen, I'll sit down and call a friend. And then not even discuss that issue, but talk about something else. But the first part of my coping is to realize that I'm not the problem. I don't internalize it. And realize that I'm the victim, and so I don't blame the victim. I'm gentle on myself.

Psychologists Thomas and Sillen have suggested that, among blacks, anger at whites may be replacing self-derogation as a response to oppression. They suggest that this shift is a healthy sign, for it is saying, "I am condemning you for doing wrong to me" (1977: 54). From this perspective a positive means of coping results from a realistically targeted anger.

Young or old, the need to buttress one's self-image is a constant problem for our respondents. One college student, who has had epithets hurled at her by white students, explained that Stokely Carmichael's book *Black Power* had helped her strengthen her sense of self worth:

> This is crazy because I'm twenty-four, and all along I was thinking, "OK, he called me 'nigger,' he was just one, there's not a whole lot of them here." ... But reading *Black Power*, I mean, we've always heard about the civil rights movement, and we've always heard about this, that, and the other, but *Black Power* to me was a little bit more in-depth than that. This man had a plan of what we needed to do in order to, I guess, consolidate or to establish some kind of solidarity. And he explained in a very just, rational, manner why it was needed. Because before, yes, we need to get together, you'd hear that all the time, "Unity, unity." But it seems like we've been doing OK without it – that was a lot of the older attitude. I can see that attitude. But reading that book I understand a little bit more about just how hard it [unity] is.

Exposure to the black power literature provided the student with a stronger sense of linkage to other black Americans and thus more confidence in dealing with the white campus culture.

Our respondents reported an array of creative approaches they find effective in keeping their sanity in the face of white racism. For some a candid dialogue with God is one approach, as in this statement of a state legislator:

> It's quite frustrating. I chew God out sometimes. I don't mean it in a blasphemous way, or cursing, but I mean like some of the minor prophets did, you know, "God what's your problem? You're not moving; you're not acting. What's the deal here? Why aren't you doing something about this?" You see what I'm saying? You know, that kind of thing, and it's very frustrating. It's very hurting, because you go through the [black] community and when people say, "Oh, there's legislator Jones," and you tell people about being a

good American, and doing this, and doing that, and you know really, you can't promise them much, not very much at all really.

Taking a Jeremiah-like stance, this legislator has addressed God to express her anger over how little she can do the help her constituents. Reflecting the deeply-felt religious heritage of African Americans, a probation officer in the South emphasized the importance of prayer and positive thinking:

> Oh, I get angry. Frustrated. And then again, I pray. I remember back, I don't know, someone said, "What the mind can conceive and believe it can achieve." I've been a student of positive thinking, and I know if anybody can, I can. And that's the type of attitude I have to reach deep within myself to deal with that. . . . If not, it will eat you away and you'll wind up doing what we're seeing more and more of. I can remember when I grew up and I was growing up as a little kid, we didn't hear of suicides among blacks. But the older I get, the more suicides among blacks have taken place. A little godchild of mine, three months ago, took his life. Prime of his life. All because of these outside pressures, and he wasn't able to deal with them, a twenty-one-year-old kid. That's what I'm saying. You have to have an innermost strength to reach down and draw [on].

Using religious insights and resources to face racism has been at the core of black survival since slavery. The slave spirituals and much other prized religious music often refer to such conditions as a "home in Heaven" or to "rest, peace, and no more pain." Religion remains very important for many because the present life is so difficult that African Americans hope that somewhere there is a better life. African-American religion, including spirituals and other religious music, has long spoken of comfort and hope, as well as of resistance to oppression. From the beginning African-American religion has been a foundation from which to critique white oppression and to work to try to transform a racist society. (See Stuckey 1987: 27, 42–6.)

One other resource is often critical for black survival – the ability to laugh at one's fate and one's tormentors. In *An American Dilemma* Myrdal discussed the ways in which black southerners in the 1930s and 1940s used humor to deal with the gaping discrepancy between the American creed and discriminatory white behavior (1964: 38). All along, we have seen middle-class black respondents using humor and laughter to deal with poor treatment by whites. With great amusement a political consultant described how she and her husband were a fighting team: "Matter of fact, our hobby is to fight discrimination and challenge discrimination; that's a hobby for us. We've been doing it all our lives. We like it!" In conversations reviewing their encounters with whites, blacks sometimes say things like "I cut him, and he didn't even know he had been cut", or "I cut him so sharp, he didn't even bleed." In a particular situation such humor can be a means of covert retaliation, sometimes not even recognized by the white party but totally understood by other blacks. Such humor can help defang the white enemy, thereby protecting against retaliation. In difficult conditions humor can function to take some of the sting out of a situation or to side-step an action so that it goes by relatively harmlessly.

Numerous respondents chuckled or laughed as they gave accounts of encounters with whites. A college counselor at a western university explained this coping strategy:

Well, you know, one of the things that we've been able to use as a survival method is laughter. And there have been times and situations where friends, feeling like I do now, we've been able to talk about something that was quite serious, but we've been able to make light of it. Well, not to make light of it, but to laugh at it, at how bad something really is, just turn it over. That's a survival method. . . . It's very important, in order not to be a statistic in terms of stroke or heart attack.

Chuckling at painful events helps lessen the stress and perhaps decreases the probability of greater anguish. Here laughing at tragedy is part of social inter-action; this circle of friends is trying to manage psychologically the effects of mis-treatment.

The ability to laugh at pain rather than being overwhelmed is at the heart of heroic advice a lawyer in a southern city had for younger blacks:

> Having said all that, enjoy life. That'll get worked out over all these problems. There's a time to be serious, and there's a time to build, and there's a time to enjoy your life. And when all is said and done, don't be overcome by what you see, and by all means, don't let anybody else steal your joy. . . . And my attitude is real basic and simple, and that is, I may not live to see the struggle, the battle won, but my joy is just being right at this day in the struggle. We know how to get to the Promised Land. I just want to live to be in the fight.

Sources of Social Support

As we have already briefly discussed, social and psychological support from family and friends is crucial in surviving daily struggles with whites. This may appear surprising to some white readers who have seen much discussion of black families as pathological, dysfunctional, and unable to provide their members sufficient sustenance (see, e.g., Auletta 1982; Moynihan 1965). However, the everyday reality is usually different, for most black families in all income classes have been strong enough to provide havens of refuge for generations. A law professor described this heroic heritage.

> Well, the love and the support and the understanding, they're important. It just happens that this past weekend, I went to a family reunion. And we traced our families' roots and we had a chance to all sit around and talk about the kinds of values that are important. My family comes from the South, and they were slaves. And we talk about the people who were slaves, but [with] a great sense of family, and a real understanding of the meaning of the concept of fear. Again, as I said, my people were slaves, they lived through Jim Crow, through the Depression, and found their way to the sustaining concepts, the sustaining philosophies, the sustaining wisdom, love, family, and support. Understanding the concept of emotional and psychological healing, then you are always making a move to make the wound heal. You also understand how to avoid wounds. You know there are situations where you may not go head on against racism, you may step aside, you may deflect it. And I think that my family has put a lot in me that has helped me to be able to at least lessen some of the effects.

Family support as a means of coping with oppression has a long history among African Americans. Harriette McAdoo has researched the family in many areas of Africa and compared it with the African-American family. Among the salient dimensions of African family life are (1) an emphasis on kinship groups and tribal survival and (2) a guiding principle of humanitarianism and interdependence of members. Historically, there was a xenophilic rather than a xenophobic dimension to many African societies. Strangers were not automatically considered enemies (McAdoo 1988). Long before the intrusion of European slave traders and the enslavement in the Americas, the family system in west Africa generally encompassed every person. This system proved its importance during slavery in North America. Despite the many and varied tribes, customs, and languages, and the inhuman destruction of many family bonds by white slaveholders, enslaved African Americans forged strong bonds in order to survive and escape. The importance of strong family bonds under slavery and segregation has been demonstrated by Herbert Gutman and other historians over the two decades (Gutman 1976).

A woman who worked as a clerical employee in the Midwest, then moved to the South where she holds a personal service job, discussed the role of family and friends:

> Oh, we discuss, you know, naturally blacks always get together and talk about it and what we're going to do. It's discussed, but most of my friends and even my family, my mother has always been afraid for me. Especially when, me moving here, because she knows that I'm not going to take anything, you know. So, she would always say, "Now, Jane, you know they're not like they are up here. You have to watch your mouth. You have to watch the way you say things to people because you know, you can be real cutting verbally." And I know I can. And she's just afraid that I might be one that they hang on a tree. Like my sons. I've always taught them to be proud and strong and they've had a couple incidents down here we had to discuss it, you know.

The half-joking reference to lynching is striking as a reminder of the psychological currentness of brutal practices that persisted into the 1980s.

Emotional support in the face of everyday racism is critical, as a corporate executive quoted earlier made clear: "[My family has given] me the, I guess, warm emotional support one needs that says, 'Keep pushing. Don't give up. Hang in there, and don't let things make you do things you'll regret later. Just do the positive thing and recognize that it's going to take a long time.'" In managing encounters with racism middle-class black Americans are beginning to go to psychologists and psychiatrists. Until recently the great majority of mental health professionals have been white. These professionals, tending to make judgments in the form of white-normed diagnoses, have sometimes been considered the "enemy" in black communities. For example, for many years the anger and suspicion seen in black patients was too often diagnosed as paranoid schizophrenia. In recent years, however, mental health workers have examined these diagnoses more carefully and have found that for many black patients the feelings of anger and suspicion are reality-based and do not signal a psychosis. Very often the emotions have been generated by experiences with whites (see Bell and Evans 1981).

The social support of black friends is grounded in shared experiences, a point accentuated by a social worker:

Well, I think I have some friends who validate my experience which keeps me sane. I think it's real important that you have blacks that you can go to, that you can say, this has happened to me, it is disturbing me. The [white] person will not acknowledge what they have done. Can you help me validate whether this is off or not? Having somebody that you trust, that's objective, that will tell you, "Hey, you were off there, you shouldn't have said that. They probably were being racist, but you should have dealt with it a different kind of way." But I think that my friends help me balance, because when you're in the midst of it, you get so hurt and so angry. It's like these two emotions running at the same time. It's like how dare they do this to me, that's the anger. Don't they realize that I'm a human being too? So, you have all these emotions happening at the same time inside of you, and you just need somebody to say, yea, this probably is happening to you, and this is how you can deal with it. And my family, I was raised in a Christian home, and raised that you treat people the way you want to be treated.

Discussions with friends help by validating a black person's experience, as well as confirming one's sense of what is right and just.

Black organizations can also be places of refuge and sources of support. For example, one important survival tactic for black students encountering poor treatment at predominantly white colleges is to link up with local black organizations. A hospital supervisor and civil rights activist who lectures to black college students offered the following advice to those newly arrived at white campuses: "They should look up the black student organization on campus. . . . It is very important that they do this. A lot of what happens to black students that come to this university – I'm sure it happens in all of the big universities – is that their parents have misled them. That's the reason the majority of them can't survive on that campus." She felt strongly that black students must join together on a white campus:

> It is important that they hook up and become a very strong black organization member, to be there for each other. You can't walk that alone. You cannot be a lone black in a group of whites, because eventually that's going to wear so thin. . . . you need to first and foremost develop a real close relationship with the black organization. Go into the community, that's important, whether it's to the church, church activity, or a black organization in the community, but be a part of the community as well as part of the school community. Those are things that parents should tell their children.

From this point of view survival as an individual alone is impossible; only collective efforts ensure success. Thinking in a similar vein, one engineering student we interviewed on a white campus said: "I would have sought out more support groups."

The Role of Helpful Whites

In discussions with middle-class black Americans one senses a recognition that the problems of color discrimination in the United States will not be solved by either white or black Americans acting separately. Cooperation is deemed essential by most. On occasion, white reporters and colleagues of the authors have asked how helpful whites have been to middle-class African Americans as they have sought their personal goals in this society. Our respondents' answer to this question vary but most seemed to fall into two general categories: either they said they had not been helped by whites, or they cited one or two whites who had been important to them, often at a specific point in their lives. Into the first category fall respondents like this sales-person for an electronics firm, who was asked if any whites had been helpful in achieving his goals: "I wish I could think of someone, but realistically I really can't. And God forgive [me] if there was, and I don't remember. Maybe the system's had that much effect on me that . . . I can't bring it up to a conscious level."

Other respondents had a mixed reaction to the question. A human services manager in a northern city initially replied, "I can't think of any," but then qualified her answer with this comment:

> I've had white colleagues who have been very helpful in skills development. I tend not to be a numbers person, and hate dealing with the financial part of my job. I'm getting better at it, but there's a white woman at work who's been very good at helping me to do that. And at my old job, there was a white woman who – it's very funny, from a very, very, wealthy family in the United States, worth millions, but acted very much in the manner in which it was comfortable for me, did not flaunt that station of position in life, and we got to be very close personal friends. In fact, she worked with me, and no longer lives in this city, but at that particular job, she was very helpful in helping me, in fact, to gain the skills, computer skills, and connection skills, that I needed to do that job well, and for that I'll always be grateful.

The whites mentioned here were helpful in particular areas of skill development, yet this woman made it clear in her interview that no white person had been broadly and fundamentally helpful to her achievements.

The response of a clerk in a vehicle parts department to a question about whether whites had been especially "helpful to you in achieving your goals?" was positive:

> Yes. I would think so. They encouraged me. In fact, when I was deciding that I would bring this lawsuit against the company that I work for, I talked to this young guy – he's about thirty – and I asked him, I said, "I've decided I'm going to sue the company, so who should I go to for support, since the company's so large and I can't possibly do this on my own. Should I go to the National Organization for Women or the NAACP?" He said, "Why not go to the National Organization for Women because they are very visible and vocal. The NAACP is an old organization and they haven't done anything in a long time." This is a young white guy. He's now supervisor down where I work, but he wasn't then. He's still my friend, though. . . . I have, oh, the French class that I have, I study, all of those ladies support me and what I do. . . . There's a lady who works with me, she's part-time on this job, and the regular women in there won't associate with her for some reason or another. She's a Mediterranean lady, a white lady, and we've become very good friends.

This woman found a white male supporter in a workplace where a number of whites had racially and sexually harassed her. Similarly, a banking executive in an eastern city mentioned some white friends as helpful, but not as central to her goal pursuits: "I've had some white friends who were there if I needed help, but no one who's pushed me and said, you can do it if you do this and do that, and you can achieve what you want. I think it's my own inner self who really wanted to do it, and went for it."

White friends are usually not knowledgeable enough about, or sensitive enough to, the US racial situation to relate in a truly intimate way to the problems that their black friends face. Thus black students have noted that it is difficult to make close white friends, since few whites are willing to listen to their detailed accounts of or frustrations about racism on campus. We suggested earlier that many white males, including some who see themselves as liberals, are defensive in the presence of black men, a point emphasized in an interview with a security supervisor in a western city: "I don't feel that I have too many close white male friends.... Just associates at work, but I really can't consider them close friends, because there's nothing that we share together. Most white males have a tendency to be defensive and not honest as to their relationship with a black male." He added that he had an easier time relating to white women at work. An airline customer service representative in the South spoke of the limitations of white friendships:

> As sympathetic as white friends are, they don't understand. They just don't. They think: well, because we're friends, then surely they're not racist, so what's the whole problem, why are you even bothered about it? So I can't discuss it with white friends, and I do have white friends.... in the industry, the neighborhood, the situations that I'm in, there just aren't that many black people. So my husband and my family become the stabilizing force for bouncing off situations. And I guess just knowing that I'm not the only one who's experiencing it, you know, that safety in numbers.

This woman spoke of the insensitivity of even sympathetic white co-workers and neighbors to racist speech and action. For black Americans the most trustworthy white people may be those who candidly see themselves as "recovering racists."

The effort on the part of middle-class black students and employees to find nonracist or anti-racist whites who are helpful and supportive can be vital to survival because most historically white organizations, including colleges, corporations, and governmental agencies, do not have enough black Americans for there to be a critical mass and supportive social networks. A professor at a northeastern university recommended seeking out sympathetic whites, in spite of the difficulties.

> And then I think the other thing that blacks have to learn to do is to find whites in the system who are supportive and helpful to them, and there are such whites. I think that you can.... Some, even if they may have some attitudes that aren't totally liberated, they can sometimes still be helpful to people. And I think blacks have to learn how to utilize those kinds of resources, because if we don't, we won't make it, because there just aren't enough blacks in the system to serve that purpose.

Some respondents suggested that their relationships with whites in the outside world were strategic, somewhat like a chess game. A professor at a southwestern university explained how in some cases she was able to outthink whites with whom she was dealing, then added:

> I'm also very good at figuring out who has the power to make decisions – of someone I might be talking to. I'm pretty good at getting the occasional white person to be interested enough in what I do to intervene on my behalf. And I think that's a skill, [finding out] who makes the decision, who because of a particular idiosyncrasy might be

sympathetic to your case. And then you learn how to go to those white people, and make your case before them, and get them to intervene.

Preparing Children to Face Discrimination

Black middle-class parents face the daunting task of preparing their children for racial slights and obstacles. Many know well what playwright August Wilson has written: "Blacks know more about whites in white culture and white life than whites know about blacks. We have to know because our survival depends on it. White people's survival does not depend on knowing blacks" (quoted in Flowers 1989: 173). In an important research study James Jackson and his associates found that black parents took several different approaches to teaching children about racial issues. Some avoided the issue and gave no information; some imparted messages stressing the equality of blacks and whites; and some taught their children to distrust whites and stand up for their own rights (Jackson et al. 1991: 246–53).

In our interviews we found a greater variety of messages. Thus a law school administrator discussed his parents' view of whites:

> I think they have subtly prepared me for different things. My father was always very conscious and said, "There're just a lot of things that you have to do to make sure that things are going to be okay for you. You've got to be careful of what people think and how people see you." And I think those are the basic things that they've passed on to me, not suggestions of how to deal with discrimination, but how to avoid it. It's just like preventive medicine. We waste a lot of money trying to cure people instead of spending more money trying to prevent illness.

The father's cautionary socialization was based upon the preventive medicine of avoiding difficult situations. His warning to be careful of what white people think suggests another dimension of the black double-consciousness. In their book on counselling black clients, Peter Bell and Jimmy Evans (1981) have argued that in normal social interaction whites need to think mainly of how they see themselves and how other whites see them. For middle-class blacks, however, social interaction is usually much more complicated. Seeing themselves in relation to how other blacks see them is compounded by the requirement to orient themselves to whites' (mis)understandings. African Americans must work through a psychological maze as they develop the necessary relationships with white Americans. Not only must they determine how they see the variety of whites (from blatant racists, to covert racists, to the culturally ignorant, to the truly color blind), they must ascertain how they see themselves *in relation to* whites (as inferior, equal, superior, powerless, or powerful). Such determinations start at an early age, and parents are a major source of advice on how to handle white hostility and discrimination. This means devoting considerable time and energy to a task with which white parents are not burdened.

Lessons are taught by example as well as by mouth. And avoidance is not the only lesson taught by parents. A television anchorperson in a southwestern city described his mother's strong personal example:

The [white] lady in front did not have to have her ID checked, and my mother had hers checked. Now the woman in front was not even from the town, but then they asked my mom. And my mom was like, "Wait a minute, I've been shopping here for X amount of years, been living here all my life." She didn't tell them who she was. And she said, "and you're going to ask for my ID? I don't even want the groceries." And she left. But then she thought about it and said, "No, I'm going back and get the manager." And [once there she] said, "hey, I supply some money to this store, and I've been shopping here for years. And my son's in town, and my people are from here." And the guy was like, "Mrs James, I know that name." Because he knew me. She said, "don't give me the green light because of what my son does. He's younger than me. I was here before he was, so [don't] think because he's an athlete that that's going to be the green light for me to write a check in this store and not get my ID checked." So, I saw her do that kind of stuff. So, it's rubbed off on me.

Notable here is the discretionary character of white power in moments of interaction with black customers. Assertive adults can create outspoken children; this man reported responding aggressively to the discrimination he encountered in his own daily rounds as an adult.

The theme of a legacy of collective wisdom about racism was touched on or discussed by numerous respondents. Alluding to this inherited wisdom, a hospital administrator in a northern city discussed the conflict she felt:

My goals, in terms of for myself and for my family, are in trying to teach them those inherited ways that others have learned and the wisdom that was passed on as to how to overcome racism, how to overcome discrimination, how to make yourself as good as anyone else to achieve and to accomplish. And I guess I can get hung up on the racism and discrimination, which is going to be there, but I think that I'd rather get hung up on *my* attributes, on *my* success, on *my* qualifications, on *my* skills, on *my* intellect, and being able to overcome with strengths within myself the racisms that might be, you know, some of the stumbling blocks.

In the socialization of children there is some tension between teaching an unclouded knowledge of racism's realities and communicating a sense of personal strength and capability. In this woman's view black children should be taught there are major barriers, but they also need to be taught that they can be overcome – a difficult balancing act for parents.

However, a newspaper publisher suggested a cautionary note about teaching children too much optimism about American promises of equal opportunity: "I think we owe an obligation to our children to teach them about racism and how to deal with it, instead of giving them the false impression that if you get a good education, if you go to the better schools, if you appease the white man, then you will not have to really deal with racism." In the United States there is much exhortation to work hard and strive to succeed as individuals. In this philosophy of life personal failure is to be accepted as one's own fault. But this philosophy only makes sense if the social game is fair. An executive officer at a white chamber of commerce spoke of teaching young blacks the hard lesson that the game is rigged against them:

I think that, again, our children have got to realize that things really aren't fair, that there are barriers out there, that there are additional barriers, there are barriers in this world, and that everything that we face isn't because we're black. But we're going to face a certain amount of things that are because we're black. And I think if we teach our children on the front end of that tunnel, that that doesn't have to stop anything. We may have to figure out a different strategy, we may have to decide that instead of running IBM, we're going to run our own multinational corporation.

In her view, teaching black children about racial hostility is important, but so is teaching them how to circumvent the barriers they will face.

Not surprisingly, a number of respondents urged young black people to fall back on friends and family to bolster their sense of self. A university professor had the following recommendations for black youth:

> [I recommend] that they talk to other people about it constantly, because I think you need every sense of reinforcement that you can get – that you can get from your friends, people that are going through the same things, from your family, from your teachers, from any well-intentioned human being, who seems to have some inkling that when you say that things are happening to you, you are telling nothing but the truth, that you are not imagining that things are going wrong, that you are not imagining that you're being oppressed. What you need is to have constantly reinforced your sense that the world is not fine, and you are ... fine, and doing the best that you can under circumstances that are fairly horrendous. That's what I tell my students all the time, because what they tend to do is blame themselves for what happens to them.

White denial that the discrimination individual black Americans face is serious adds the burden of reality testing and fighting self-doubt to the burden of the discrimination itself.

Emotional support is critical to the black struggle. One mother, a therapist at a hospital, was blunt about getting black children, and black males generally, to share their pain: "I encourage my boys to share feelings. Not none of that macho shit where you fall down, and your knee's hanging off and you say, 'Don't cry, be a man.' And that's where a lot of our black men have gotten totally messed up at. It hurts, you cry."

Sharing one's pain and frustrations about life's troubles, including white oppression, was also recommended for blacks of all ages. A drug program director in the Midwest made this point:

> There is a population of older blacks, though, that are – like, my grandmother died when she was ninety-one – that don't like to talk a lot about that emotional pain that's there. . . . But there's an older population of blacks, when you start asking some of those [discrimination] questions, and they will choose not to talk about it because it hurts too bad. So, I agree we need to talk. But we need to also be encouraged by, and encourage, those [black Americans] because a lot of times they don't want to talk about it.

A social welfare program director, also in the Midwest, commented on the cost to all African Americans of repressing anger and rage over racism:

> [We need] to teach them, our people, how to talk about it and how to identify what it is. Because quite a lot of what we keep inside of us prevents us from being comfortable about who we are and where we want to go. I really believe that. I feel that a lot of us hold back our frustration and emotional pain because either we have not been able to

have that permission or learn how to talk about those things.... We can get out of that negative environment of feelings in the mind.

Conclusion

Earlier, we cited the view of Brittan and Maynard that the terms of racial and gender oppression are "profoundly shaped at the site of the oppression, and by the way in which oppressors and oppressed continuously have to renegotiate, reconstruct, and re-establish their relative positions in respect to benefits and power" (Brittan and Maynard 1984: 7). Today the interaction of blacks and whites in discriminatory situations has some similarities with that of the era of rigid segregation, but there are significant differences. The arrival on the scene of significant numbers of middle-class African Americans with substantial resources and power has created many situations where white Americans are forced into more explicit racial negotiation and where whites' assumptions of low black power are challenged. In the examples we have examined we frequently observe middle-class blacks establishing "power credibility," as whites realize that the blacks are not bluffing. Whether this perception will last beyond the particular incident is not clear, but it is a major change from the old racism.

Consequential too in this period of modern racism are the changing legal structure, the institutionalization of civil rights laws, and black Americans' belief in legal rights and civil justice. These statutes are momentous not only in themselves but also in the effect they have had of reinforcing the robust sense of justice that is a part of the black middle-class approach to everyday racism. In numerous accounts we have noted this black sense of justice due, of the right to fair play. The irony is that these African Americans are simply demanding to be treated like the average white person in this ostensibly democratic society.

Changes in interpersonal negotiation have not meant that the costs of discrimination have been eliminated. Throughout, we have reported the individual and collective price paid in dealing with life crises created by the omnipresent white discriminators. The anger of many middle-class black Americans is intense, if often repressed, or channelled into overachieving and hypertension. We have also observed the remarkable and pervasive ability of African Americans to laugh at adversity. And we have seen the vital support of family and friends. The tremendous energy drain caused by discrimination has taken a toll on black achievement and performance. The exceptional achievements of these Americans have come in spite of, and in the face of, energy-sapping racism. A central dilemma in fighting the internal stress of racism is how to cultivate a strong self-image, not only in oneself but also in one's children. At the heart of this positive self-image must be an enduring appreciation of black achievement and group worth, an avoidance of self-blame, and a recognition of the persisting flaws in the US social system.

References

Allport, Gordon. 1958. *The Nature of Prejudice*, abridged edn. Garden City, NY: Anchor Books.

Aptheker, Herbert. 1943. *American Negro Slave Revolts*. New York: International Publishers.

Auletta, Ken. 1982. *The Underclass*. New York: Random House.

Bell, Peter and Evans, Jimmy. 1981. *Counseling with the Black Client: Alcohol Use and Abuse in Black America*. Center City, Minn.: Hazelden.

Blauner, Bob. 1989. *Black Lives, White Lives*. Berkeley: University of California Press.

Brittan, Arthur and Maynard, Mary. 1984. *Sexism, Racism and Oppression*. Oxford: Basil Blackwell.

Flowers, Betty Sue (ed.) 1989. *Bill Moyers: A World of Ideas*. New York: Doubleday.

Grier, William H. and Cobbs, Price M. 1968. *Black Rage*. New York: Basic Books.

Gutman, Herbert. 1976. *The Black Family in Slavery and Freedom, 1750–1925*. New York: Random House.

Humphrey, James H. 1986. *Human Stress*. New York: AMS Press.

Jackson, James S., McCullough, Wayne R., and Gurin, Gerald. 1991. "Race identity." In James S. Jackson (ed.) *Life in Black America*. Newbury Park, Calif.: Sage Publications.

McAdoo, Harriette P. 1988. *Black Families*, 2nd edn. Beverly Hills, Calif.: Sage Publications.

Mirowski, John and Ross, Catherine E. 1989. *Social Causes of Psychological Distress*. New York: Aldine and de Gruyter.

Moynihan, Daniel P. 1965. *The Negro Family: The Case for National Action*. Washington, DC: US Government Printing Office.

Myrdal, Gunnar. [1944] 1964. *An American Dilemma*, vol. 1. New York: McGraw-Hill.

Shuster, Rachel. 1993. "Arthur Ashe: 1943–1993; Ashe legacy goes beyond sports, race." *USA Today*, February 8.

Stuckey, Sterling. 1987. *Slave Culture*. New York: Oxford University Press.

Thomas, Alexander and Sillen, Samuel. 1977. *The Theory and Application of Symbolic Interactionism*. Boston: Houghton Mifflin.

23 Hidden Power in Marriage

Aafke Komter

Listen here, as a woman you are not in this world to say: "Well, I am going to enjoy myself and be myself, and everything will be fine." No, I don't think that is fair towards men.

From an interview with an upper-class husband

As men's formal and institutionalized power decreases in western societies, informal and not necessarily institutionalized ways of sustaining and reproducing power inequality between women and men are becoming more visible. Without patriarchal laws and legally permitted gender discrimination, it becomes clearer that a powerful drawback to gender equality springs from norms about gender identity, concepts of masculinity and femininity, and tacit rules of interaction between women and men.

This article discusses a way to conceptualize the structure of informal power in gender relationships, using research into marital power carried out in the Netherlands between 1981 and 1984.

The research focused on power mechanisms and processes rather than on their outcomes. Theoretically, the study was based on Lukes's concept of power (1974), supplemented by Gramsci's notion of ideological hegemony (1971). Power was operationalized in such a way that the less visible, informal effects of power could be uncovered.

Theoretical Background

In their well-known study, *Husbands and Wives*, Blood and Wolfe (1960) laid the basis for a tradition of research into marital power in which decision-making was the main indicator. The focus on observable, behavioral outcomes of power, operationalized as conflicts over decisions, diverted attention from the underlying power processes, and the structural character of the unequal division of power resources between women and men was overlooked. Women and men were generally seen as having equal chances of getting the most advantageous outcomes in their negotiations on important marital matters, and their resources were considered as equivalent (Scanzoni 1972, 1979b). Despite manifold criticisms (Eichler 1981; Gillespie 1971; C. Johnson 1975; Safilios-Rothschild 1970), the outcome of decision-making is still considered the primary indicator of martial power (McDonald 1980: 846), and underlying structural inequality remains underestimated.

Blumstein and Schwartz (1983) examined the dynamics of influence and the negotiation of control between partners in different kinds of intimate relationships, comparing married, cohabiting, gay, and lesbian couples. Adopting an approach similar to that of Blood and Wolfe, the study focused on observable power outcomes,

Reprinted from *Gender and Society* 3(2) (June 1989): 187–216.

measuring power by who has the right or authority to exert control and by who has more say about important decisions affecting the relationship.

In order to develop an approach to marital power that tapped its underlying structure, I used concepts from Lukes (1974) and Gramsci (1971).

Lukes's Three-Dimensional View of Power

Lukes (1974) distinguishes three perspectives on power. The one-dimensional view is historically rooted in Max Weber's concept of power. Weber defined power as the ability of enforcing one's will, even against resistance. Studies carried out from a one-dimensional perspective focus on the question of who ultimately makes decisions and controls participation in decision-making. The assumption is that power is exercised in a direct, observable conflict over issues recognized as relevant.

Power can also be used to prevent issues from being raised. Two-dimensional approaches to power investigate nondecisions as well as decisions. A nondecision neutralizes or eliminates any latent or overt threat to the vested interests of the powerful. Nondecisions do not necessarily manifest themselves in overt behavior and do not relate to recognized issues only. The two-dimensional view of power focuses on potential issues, which remain invisible as a result of nondecisions. In this view, the exercise of power is not necessarily based on observable conflict, but may also ensue from covert, although in principle observable, conflict.

Lukes's three-dimensional view of power involves a thorough-going critique of the two previous views which, he feels, are too behavioral. He conceptualizes the different ways in which issues are kept out of an arena of conflict, whether through individual decisions, or through the operation of dominant values and institutional procedures. Genuine consensus does not necessarily exist because no grievances can be detected. Lukes says:

> Is it not the supreme and most insidious exercise of power to prevent people, to whatever degree, from having grievances by shaping their perceptions, cognitions and preferences in such a way that they accept their role in the existing order of things, either because they can see or imagine no alternative to it, or because they see it as natural and unchangeable, or because they value it as divinely ordained and beneficial? (1974: 24)

The third dimension Lukes adds is latent conflict, that is, a hidden discrepancy of interests of those exercising power and those subject to this power. The conflict is latent in the sense that it *would* arise if subordinates would express their wants and desires. These unexpressed desires or preferences that would be expressed in a condition of relative autonomy for powerless groups or individuals are considered real interests by Lukes.

According to Lukes, the attribution of an exercise of power involves the claim that A acts (or fails to act) in such a way that B does (or fails to do) what he or she would not do otherwise (the term *do* includes *think, feel,* or *want*). Specifically, Lukes offers two guidelines to the empirical identification of power. First, the relevant *counter-factual* has to be identified, that is, what B would have done (or failed to do) in the absence of A's power. In order to trace this counterfactual, we must explore those alternatives that are not realized. How would B react to a hypothetical or real opportunity to act differently from the way A had wanted him or her to? In the case of overt conflict, the relevant counterfactual is easily identified: if A and B are in conflict, A wanting x and B wanting y, then, if A prevails over B, we can assume that B would otherwise have done y. Where there is no overt conflict, we must provide other grounds for asserting that if A had not acted in a certain way, B would have acted differently from the way he or she did in reality.

Second, Lukes advocates uncovering the *mechanism* that enabled A to exercise power. In looking for the power mechanism, it must be acknowledged, according to Lukes, that the exercise of power can be the result of inaction, that power may be exercised by collectives and institutions, and that A has to be aware neither of the actual reason or motive for his or her action nor of the way in which B interprets A's action. When A is unable to perceive the effects that his or her action has on B, it is not justified, Lukes argues, to speak of the exercise of power. There can be an exercise of power only when A is actually capable of not exercising power by acting differently. In Lukes's view, the assignment of power is at the same time the assignment of partial or full responsibility for certain consequences.[1]

Most criticisms of Lukes focus on the concept of real interests (Bloch et al. 1979; Bradshaw 1976; Wrong 1979), arguing that it is evaluative, as Lukes himself (1974) pointed out. In view of this criticism, I decided in my own research not to attempt to uncover any real interests of married women and men. I rejected the notion of real interests mainly because of its association with the concept of false consciousness. I did not try to determine empirically which part of the respondents' consciousness reflected their most genuine beliefs. Instead, I aimed at identifying subjective preferences under hypothetical conditions of autonomy, the conditions, according to Lukes, to detect relevant counterfactuals, that is, what someone would have done if no power had been exercised or did not do because power was exercised. I attempted to uncover the power mechanisms that determine subjective preferences by looking for the hidden ideological forces that constitute women's and men's wants concerning certain domains of their marriage.

One crucial problem, however, remained to be solved: how to find empirical grounds to determine whether, in a situation in which no grievances are expressed, power is involved. If people turn out to be incapable of imagining any desired alternatives to their present situation as a result of a general state of resignation and passivity, what evidence can be provided for the hypothesis that power is involved? Gramsci's work on ideological hegemony offered a solution to this problem.

Gramsci's Concept of Ideological Hegemony

Gramsci (1971) conceives of ideological hegemony as the result of a slow social process in which consensus is developed between dominant and subordinate groups. Consensus is expressed in the approval by subordinate groups of the dominant values, symbols, beliefs, and opinions. Social institutions, such as the educational system, religion, and mass media, which serve to produce culture, contribute in significant ways to the evolution of social consensus. Public opinion and the prevailing cultural climate make actions performed by subordinate groups appear to be springing from their free will, whereas in fact they reflect a necessity resulting from existing relationships of dominance.

In Gramsci's notion of ideological hegemony, common sense plays a crucial part. Hegemonic control is achieved by generating representations in common-sense thought in which social contradictions figure as a unitary whole. Control, however, is not total, and the common-sense conception of the world is fragmentary, incoherent, and often inconsistent. It is in the ambiguities and contradictions of common sense that the differentiation between the values of dominant and subordinate groups becomes visible.

An ideology is hegemonic when it demonstrates three characteristics (Van den Brink 1978). First, the ideology has become part of everyday thought. Second, the ideology promotes social cohesion by representing contradictions as unitary. Third, the ideology represents necessity as freedom; particular interests of dominant groups are experienced as general interests and therefore can be freely accepted by subordinate groups.

These three characteristics can serve as empirical criteria to detect inconsistencies within the general consensus with respect to gender relationships. If it would be possible to trace these characteristics in common-sense thought and beliefs about women and men, it could tell us a great deal about the ideological underpinnings of power in gender relationships.

Conceptualizing Power in Marital Relationships

The central concern of the research reported here was the quality of power, as reflected in power processes and mechanisms, rather than the quantity, the way the "power cake" is divided up between married women and men. Power was studied within the context of interpersonal relationships between married women and men and was defined as the ability to affect consciously or unconsciously the emotions, attitudes, cognitions, or behavior of someone else. This definition incorporates both the possibility of changing the other and the possibility of resisting change. Such an interpersonal definition of power, however, did not assume that power in marital relationships was exclusively interpersonal; sociostructural (e.g., economic and cultural) factors also influence power processes in marriage.

Power processes, then, were considered to be taking place when marriage partners desired certain changes that, in the course of time, were either effectuated or thwarted in some way. Desired changes, as the expression of subjective preferences, were regarded as Lukes's relevant counterfactuals – what one spouse would have done (or failed to do) in the absence of the other spouse's power. Five elements in the process of change were distinguished: *desires* for, or *attempts* at, change; structural or psychological *impediments*; the partner's *reaction* to change; *conflicts* that might arise in the process of change; and *strategies* to realize or prevent change.

My assumption was that the reasons and motivations for both the presence and absence of desires for, or attempts at, change, can shed light on marital power. So can the reasons for the absence of conflict or refraining from conflict. If inconsistencies, ambiguities, or contradictions were detected in a respondent's statements, the three characteristics of Gramsci's concept of ideological hegemony – prevailing, masking contradictions, and allowing no real choice – were assumed to be part of the mechanisms of marital power.

A theoretical distinction was made among *manifest power, latent power,* and *invisible power.* Manifest power surfaces in visible outcomes such as attempts at change, conflicts, and strategies. Latent power can be at stake when no changes or no conflicts are reported. It can be identified when the needs and wishes of the more powerful person are anticipated, or when the reasons for not desiring or attempting change or refraining from conflict produce resignation in anticipation of a negative reaction or fear of jeopardizing the marital relationship. Invisible power was defined as the result of social or psychological mechanisms that do not necessarily surface in overt behavior, or in latent grievances, but that may be manifest in systematic gender differences in mutual and self-esteem, differences in perceptions of, and legitimations concerning, everyday reality. The effects of invisible power generally escape awareness of the people involved.

Research Design

Research Questions

Two main variables affect marital power: social class and the working status of the wife (Edgell 1980; Heer 1963; Komarovsky 1967; Safilios-Rothschild 1967). Although the literature about the influence of class is somewhat contradictory, most findings suggest that power inequality is more evident in the lower than in the upper social strata, where more egalitarian norms and practices are supposed to prevail. In many studies the power of wives has been found to increase when they become employed outside the home. In other studies, however, no increase of power is found among couples when the wife is employed. It seemed useful to test the validity of these mostly American findings in the Netherlands.

The general research question was: What is the nature of power in marital relationships? What is the connection between marital power and class and the employment status of the wife? From the relevant literature (Edgell 1980, Komarovsky 1967; Scanzoni 1972, 1979a, 1979b; Scanzoni and Scanzoni 1976; Young and Willmott 1973), several areas were identified in which marital power can be at stake: domestic labor, child caring and rearing, sexuality, leisure activities, and finances.

The specific research questions concerned the following: first, the extent to which women and men have desires for change in these areas, attempt to realize any of these desires, and experience impediments in this process; second, the extent to which conflicts emerge in the different areas; third, the strategies women and men employ in their attempts at effecting or preventing change; and fourth, possible gender differences in mutual and self-esteem, in perceptions of and legitimations concerning everyday reality.

Sample

In selecting the respondents for this study, the social positions of both women and men were calculated by using employment and educational levels. If a woman was not employed outside the home, her previous job was used. If she had never been so employed, her educational level was used. For pragmatic reasons, only two class levels could be studied. Measures of *lower-class* status were little or no vocational training and unskilled or semi-skilled labor; measures of *upper-class* status were higher education and skilled or academically qualified work.

The respondents were selected in and around an average-sized university city (Nijmegen) in the eastern part of the Netherlands. Two lists with addresses of employed women were used. One consisted of female cleaning personnel employed at the university, the other was made available by the Association of Academically Trained Women (VVAO). A letter to both spouses invited participation in research described as "women's and men's experience of marriage." As this procedure did not yield enough respondents, particularly from the lower class, letters with the request to participate were distributed at several other places where lower-class women were employed, and a call for subjects was placed in local papers. Couples who had already agreed to participate suggested other couples who might be inclined to take part in the study. This last procedure produced by far the most repondents, so the sample was in effect a snowball sample.

Sixty couples, aged 20–55, with children living at home, participated in the study. One half had a low, the other half a high socioeconomic background. Half of the women in each socioeconomic group had a paid job. The final sample had eight clusters: lower-class women working at paid jobs, their husbands, lower-class non-employed women, their husbands, upper-class employed women, their husbands, upper-class nonemployed women, and their husbands. Each cluster had an N of 15.

The average ages were lower-class women, 36.4 years; their husbands, 39.5 years; upper-class women, 36.9 years; and their husbands, 38 years.

The mean number of children was 2.3 in the lower-class group, with a mean age of 11.3 years. Among upper-class couples, the mean number of children was 2.1, with a mean age of 9.4 years.

Twelve percent of the couples had been married 0–5 years; 28 percent, 6–10 years; 27 percent, 11–15 years; 18 percent, 16–20 years; and 15 percent more than 20 years. The mean duration of the marriages was 13.6 years. First and subsequent marriages were included in the sample.

On a six-level occupational scale most respondents categorized as lower-class were in the lowest two levels; most respondents categorized as upper-class were in the two highest categories. As is true of the Netherlands as a whole, the women's occupational and educational levels were lower than those of their husbands. Compared with national statistics, there was a slight overrepresentation of Roman Catholics in the lower-class group, and those saying they were not religious were overrepresented in the upper-class group.

The sample of couples selected for this research was not representative of Dutch married couples, as the research was not meant to yield general valid statements about power in "the" Dutch marriage. Its prime aim was to gain theoretical insight into marital power processes.

Data Collection and Analysis

The research data were collected by seventeen women interviewers, all advanced students, and the author. A semi-structured interview was conducted with women and men separately. The interview started with questions about past expectations of the marriage, self-esteem, and esteem for the partner. Corresponding to the theoretical framework and problem of the research, the questions focused on desires for change, reactions of the partner to change, impediments to change, conflicts, and strategies for effecting or preventing change. Despite pilot interviewing, it became apparent only after a substantial amount of fieldwork that some respondents found it difficult to answer this whole series of questions for each of the main topics: domestic labor, child care, sexuality, leisure activities, and finances. The interviews lasted almost three hours, on the average. Interviews with upper-class respondents were slightly longer than those with lower-class respondents, and the interviews with the women were somewhat longer than those with the men in both social classes.

All interviews were recorded and transcribed verbatim and coded twice, with an agreement of about 90 percent. Differences between spouses were tested with the Wilcoxon Matched-Pairs Signed-Ranks test. Differences between lower-class and upper-class respondents, and between nonemployed and employed women were tested with the Mann–Whitney test. Except for the overall gender differences, no statistical tests were used to analyze leisure activities and finances because the number of valid answers was too small. The responses were, however, used in qualitative analysis, as were the respondents' common-sense notions about gender, the motivations for having no desires for change, or no conflicts, the nature of impediments, and strategies for change. Where enough responses were available, they were compared on class, gender, and the employment status of the women.[2]

Desires for Change and Conflicts over Change

The first research question concerned the extent to which women and men have desires for change in the areas of domestic labor, children, sexuality, leisure activities, and finances; their attempts to realize these desires; and the nature of impediments they experience in the process of change. The second question referred to the extent to which conflicts occurred in the process of change. Table 23.1 shows the degree to which respondents desired changes and reported conflicts in the areas of domestic labor, child care, and sexuality.

In all the areas studied except sexuality, the wives were significantly more likely to desire change. Upper-class husbands and wives tended to want more change, but for most of the areas, differences between upper- and lower-class couples were not significant. No significant differences were found between employed and non-employed wives or between their husbands. When spouses say they do not have any desire for change, this may indicate latent power if resignation and anticipation of the other spouse's reaction can be demonstrated.

Conflicts arise when attempts at change are thwarted or when spouses disagree about the specific content or the rapidity of the change. As such, conflicts are outcomes of manifest power. However, when no conflicts are reported, it is not necessarily an indication of contentment with the existing situation, nor does it prove that no power is involved. For example, a spouse may decide, after a long series of fruitless disputes, that further quarreling is pointless because he or she will be losing anyhow. Or a spouse may anticipate sanctions that might ensue if he or she started a

Table 23.1   Spouses' desire for change and reported conflicts by gender, class, and wife's employment status

Social status:	Lower class				Upper class				Totals	
Wife employed:	Yes		No		Yes		No			
Gender:	W	M	W	M	W	M	W	M	W	M
	%	%	%	%	%	%	%	%	%	%
Desired change										
domestic labor	50	0	67	21	87	50	69	38	68 (N = 59)	28 (N = 59)
child care	43	20	53	27	53	40	67	27	54 (N = 59)	28 (N = 60)
sexuality	43	27	67	53	73	67	71	79	64 (N = 58)	56 (N = 59)
Conflicts										
domestic labor	57	57	75	50	83	73	62	70	72 (N = 59)	62 (N = 60)
child care	50	33	57	40	60	36	73	71	60 (N = 58)	45 (N = 58)
sexuality	28	22	20	18	40	42	46	48	33 (N = 57)	32 (N = 58)

dispute. In these instances, latent power is at stake – power that results in preventing overt conflict.

Domestic Labor

Despite the emancipatory tendencies of the last decade, the wives in this study, both employed and nonemployed, performed most of the domestic work. Husbands of employed women did not have a significantly greater share compared with husbands whose wives were not employed outside the home. Significantly more women than men wanted changes in the area of housework (p < 0.05). Upper-class employed women had a greater desire for change than their lower-class counterparts (p < 0.05), and the same was true for their husbands (p < 0.01).

   Their stories reveal the well-known pattern of women's discontent with the division of household tasks and responsibilities. The wives wanted their husbands to take a greater share in the housework, preferably out of free will. Insofar as men desired any change at all, their wishes were a reflection of their wives' desires: they felt they ought to carry out more housework. Women's attempts at change were, on the whole, not very effective, mainly because of the unwilling attitude of their husbands. As one upper-class employed woman explained:

> Yes, I would like him to do some more housework. But if anybody hates arrangements, it's him. He is appalled by the idea of fixed schemes.

Efforts made by the men were always met with enthusiasm on the part of their wives, but often the matter ended with their good intentions. One upper-class man said:

> That she has the greater responsibility doesn't imply that I think that nothing should be done about it. And if I am saying that I am not fanatical in trying to change, that doesn't

mean that I disagree with the idea of change. But I am not the kind of person to walk after her the whole day to try to change things.

Women encountered more relational impediments than did their husbands. Apart from interpersonal barriers, women also mentioned more guilt: they felt that they should not bother their husbands with their "small problems."

If women and men desired no change in the division of household tasks and responsibilities, the women's attitudes were more often ones of resignation, whereas their husbands were unequivocally satisfied with the status quo. Two examples from lower-class respondents may illustrate this. A nonemployed woman said in response to the question of whether she desired change in domestic tasks:

No ... things are as they are, aren't they? You can't have everything settled as you prefer it.

Her husband said:

No. As long as I know that everything runs smoothly, I don't have to worry about it. If things would run out of control, then I would have to interfere.

The pattern with child care was similar. Significantly more women than men wanted changes in child care and rearing ($p < 0.05$). The overall gender difference came mostly from the couples in which the wife was not employed, particularly those in the upper class, who were the most eager to change the existing pattern. In this area, too, men's negative responses formed a major obstacle to the women's attempts at change. A lower-class employed woman said:

Yes, I would like some changes. But I never settled it, so to speak. He says: "What others are doing does not affect me." Well, and then you are played out. Here it is always: "Mom, Mom, Mom," and that's what you hear. I sometimes say: "I am father and mother at the same time."

When no desires for change were mentioned, the women, especially those in the lower class, displayed more feelings of resignation. A lower-class employed woman said: "It's all up to me in the end, so what should I do?"

A lower-class man said:

No, not really wanting changes, no. Oh well, sometimes I must do something for this wife of mine, you know, but ... not that I really would like to ... no, that's not my cup of tea.

An upper-class man said.

No, I really take off my hat to the way she deals with the children. It is fantastic, the attention she pays to them. Really, I am glad that she did most of the rearing because I think that if I had done it, and if she had gone to work, the impact on the children would have been much less than the impact she has had on them. I am convinced that she has much more patience than I, to give the children the attention they just need.

As table 23.1 shows, the division of tasks and responsibilities in the domains of domestic labor and child care were the most disputed topics. More women than men reported conflicts on these issues, but there was no statistical significance. In all areas, upper-class couples seemed to disagree more frequently than their lower-class counterparts. However, the differences were not statistically significant by class either. Although egalitarian norms may be a more frequent topic of discussion among upper-class couples, which may cause more conflicts, more egalitarian practices did not occur. Upper-class employed women reported the greatest amount of conflict about domestic labor, whereas upper-class women who had no paid job had the highest number of conflicts about child-caring tasks and responsibilities. In general, conflicts were not very effective in producing desired changes.

Some women did succeed in bringing about changes in this area. In 8 of the 60 couples, 4 in each social class, a more equal division of domestic and caring tasks had been accomplished, often as a result of continued debates and arguments. When these 8 couples advocated no further changes, they were clearly expressing contentment with the achieved situation.

Sexuality

As opposed to the other areas, an almost equal number of women and men desired changes in sexuality. Upper-class couples were somewhat more interested in changing their sexual relationship than lower-class couples were, and upper-class husbands were significantly more dissatisfied with their sexual relationship than lower-class men were ($p < 0.05$). Upper-class husbands whose wives were not employed were least content in this respect.

The nature of the desires for change varied greatly between women and men. The women wanted a sexual relationship in which intercourse would take a less central role; they wanted more emotional involvement, warmth, and tenderness. They also wanted their own attitudes toward sex to be changed: they wanted to be less inhibited, to have a greater desire for intercourse, and to enjoy sex more. Their husbands also wanted more frequent relations, more variation, and more initiation from their wives. The women's statements about their sexual wishes were often highly ambivalent. An example from a lower-class woman:

> Yes, I would like a change, what should I say...once a week or once a month, uh...sexual...uh...things, that is what would be good for me, I guess. But you do these things together, so you don't have so much of a say yourself...I don't know. My ideal? Oh well, then I say to myself: I wouldn't miss it. If it possibly would not be necessary, then for me there would be no need.

Attempts at change in this area were not very successful for either the women or the men. The women saw their own inhibitions as the major obstacle, and they tended to subordinate their needs. They feared jeopardizing the relationship and anticipated a negative response from their husbands, who, they felt, might regard attempts at change as a criticism.

The men pointed to their wives' attitudes as the greatest impediment to change. An upper-class man said:

Yes, I really would appreciate it enormously if she showed a bit more spontaneity, if she demonstrated more that it really means something for her.

The general picture was that the women were inclined to satisfy their husband's wishes more than their husbands did theirs. The women said they expressed their wishes only very hesitantly and were often not met by a response. Many women, especially in the lower class, expressed a sense of duty about meeting their husbands' needs. They felt guilty if they failed to do this and tended to describe bringing up their own needs as egotistic.

Resignation and passivity were expressed in the statements of women who said they did not want any change, particularly in lower-class women. An example of a lower-class woman's anticipation of her husband's reaction was the following:

No, for me it's okay. I don't need sex so much. And if I would talk about it, I am afraid that I have to do many more things...so I don't say anything about it. I believe that he only would...be going to try some other things, uh, which he did not experience yet, but for me there's no need.

For lower-class men, the situation was often different:

No, I am content as things go now. If I feel some need, I am always admitted, that's no problem. But my opinion is [that] you should not use your wife as a pig.

Sexuality gave rise to many desires for change but to a relatively small number of conflicts. However, the limited number of conflicts should not be interpreted as a lack of strain felt in this area. Sexuality was not an easily discussable subject. Ideologies about what is "normal" and "abnormal" are strongly interwoven with women's and men's psychosexual identities, and wives often had great difficulty in saying what they liked and disliked about their sexual relationship. Many potential conflicts, for example, those about differences in sexual needs, were "solved" in advance because women gave in to their husbands' desires, particularly among lower-class couples.

One reason for this rather traditional picture of sexual relationships might be that many lower-class couples were Roman Catholics or were brought up in a Catholic family. Roman Catholicism, with its strong emphasis on female duties and male prerogatives in sexual matters, is the leading religion in the region where the research was carried out.

Finances and Leisure Activities

The wives (36 percent of 52) were more dissatisfied with the way finances were managed or spent than their husbands (10 percent of 51) and had a significantly greater desire for change ($p < 0.05$). Lower-class women in particular expressed great dissatisfaction with finances. They wanted their husbands to take a greater share in financial matters and to become more aware of women's efforts to made ends meet. However, most lower-class husbands saw it as the wives' task to handle finances, and they showed little interest in it. Upper-class women's wishes concerned a greater financial independence, for example, having their own income and being free to spend it as they wished. Their husbands sometimes felt threatened by this need and insisted that the family live exclusively on their income. Some men in both social classes were proud when there was "no need" for their wives to work.

Significantly more women (75 percent of 53) than men (50 percent of 48) wanted changes in leisure activities ($p < 0.1$). Upper-class couples were particularly interested in changes here. Mostly, spouses wanted to spend more time together by visiting friends or going out. Time was the main barrier to leisure in the upper class; money shortage played an important role in the lower class.

Here, too, the women who were seeking change in their leisure pursuits met with greater opposition from their husbands than men did from their wives. The women, particularly in the lower class, more often gave up their hobbies or their own friends because "he does not like it" than vice versa.

Conflicts about leisure pursuits and finances seemed to be the least important ones in terms of the strain involved and the frequency with which they were repeated. Only a minority (about a quarter) of the spouses reported having conflicts about these issues. In all areas, women and men gave partly different reasons when they said they had *no* conflicts. Women who reported no conflict explained that they were inclined to avoid conflicts because they were afraid to disturb their relationship. This type of motivation is lacking in the men's statements about "no conflict"; they reflect a state of satisfaction more unequivocally. Also, the women's statements displayed more resignation: they expect to lose anyhow, and they therefore refrained from having any further arguments. An example is the statement of a lower-class woman without a paid job:

> No, we don't have conflicts often. When you really have something, you don't say anything to prevent having an argument. If, for example, I am depressed about something which relates to my husband, I usually keep it to myself as long as possible, and would only say it when it really can last no longer. The most important thing is that you get on well together and have no arguments. For if a cup is crazed, it will soon burst.

A lower-class man said:

> No, we rarely have conflicts. If I have a bad temper, you know, then I am sometimes messing about, but otherwise I don't mix up with things. Otherwise I don't mind.

To summarize, manifest and latent power, as expressed in the process of change, and conflicts over change, were found to operate in both social classes in a similar way, although latent power was more pronounced among lower-class couples and manifest power was more characteristic of upper-class husbands and wives. The effect of both forms of power was that the existing pattern of gender roles – with its implied inequality – was confirmed. Change toward more gender equality in marital relationships not only was slow because of all the husbands' clinging to the traditional pattern but it also was hampered by the women's tendency to anticipate their husbands' possible negative reactions or to resign themselves to the existing state of affairs.

Strategies for Change

The third research question was concerned with strategies for change. By "strategy" is meant a conscious or unconscious way of self-expression (verbal or nonverbal) in order to achieve what one wants or to prevent what one does not want. Strategies that are used in the process of change are elusive and often not conscious phenomena. Complicated and subtle psychological and interactional processes are involved that cannot easily be tapped empirically. It is, for example, pointless to ask for strategies in any direct way, for example: "What kind of strategies do you use to change the division of domestic labor?" The implied suggestion is that people are conscious of the fact that they are using strategies and of their exact nature. Instead, in the research reported here, respondents were to tell how they proceeded when they desired anything to be changed in their relationship and if they could give any examples. Because not all respondents had desires for change, and because not all women and men were able to provide some insight into how they proceeded, data about strategies pertained to a limited number of respondents and could not, therefore, be analyzed quantitatively. The following presentation is based on a qualitative analysis of the respondents' statements concerning strategies.

Strategies emerged most clearly in the areas of domestic labor, child care, and sexuality. Strategies that could be distilled from the respondents' statements were cautiousness, sanctioning, waiting, reasonableness, and ignoring. Cautiousness was typically used by women. Its effect was limited because of its indirectness (cf. P. Johnson 1976). Sanctioning and waiting were used by both women and men, but these strategies seemed to be more effective when used by men. Reasonableness and ignoring were reported only by men and turned out to be rather effective, at least in the short run. No clear differences between couples in which the wife did or did not work outside the home were found. Class differences were limited to the strategy of reasonableness, which was found only among upper-class husbands.

Women's Strategies

Only a few women tried to change their relationship in a very clear and direct manner. Much more common among women was the indirect strategy of cautiousness. Although in the long run, a direct approach seemed to be the most profitable, many women reported that direct efforts to realize changes, particularly in the field of household tasks and responsibilities, boomeranged. So they tried to get things changed in a cautious way, for example, by hinting, grumbling, and giving sly digs.

Step-by-step strategies were another instance of cautiousness. By this means, the women attempted to effect change in a gradual way, without having any conflicts. An upper-class employed woman said:

> I really proceed very slowly. I want to change things in a gradual way. You have to be very careful not to fall back in the old pattern. . . . But I reckon a lot with his feelings and I don't want to jeopardize my marriage because of my own things and wishes. I believe, if you are too radical, you risk destroying a lot.

This strategy often produced much internal frustration, because change proceeded so slowly. The effectiveness of cautiousness was also often limited, because the appeal made to the partner was too indirect to be perceived as such. Cautiousness was effective for some women who had been worried about their husband's possible negative reactions to their being employed outside the home. As one woman said:

> He was more sensitive about my working than he had thought in advance. So I thought: I have to do it in such a way that he is not bothered in any way by the fact I work, because otherwise we will get such an enormous trouble that I will feel obliged to stop working. So I managed to not let him notice anything. Afterwards we talked about it, and he never noticed anything.

Women's and Men's Strategies

Some behavior of the partner, which is experienced as undesirable, can be sanctioned or threatened with sanctions. For example, a husband who repeatedly did not keep his promise to be at home for dinner in time was offered a cold meal. Some women refused to take care of certain essential domestic supplies their husbands had promised to provide. Or, they left the kitchen in a mess for days, hoping that their husbands would, in the end, clear away the rubbish, as they promised. As the husbands did not seem to be bothered very much, the strategy was scarcely effective. Some lower-class men sanctioned their wives for their lack of sexual interest by threatening to "go to another woman." Or they criticized their wives for not having done the laundry by scattering the dirty laundry around the room. Or, again in the lower class, when women told their husbands that they wanted to look for a job, their husbands threatened to become café-habitués. An upper-class husband's reaction was the proposition to resign from his own job, so that his wife would have to support the whole family.

On the whole, sanctioning was used more often by men than by women. When women used this strategy, it seemed to be less effective than it was in the hands of men, perhaps because the sanctions the men had at their disposal carried more weight.

Waiting was also used by women and men. However, they had different aims in waiting rather than trying to make changes. The women waited to see a change in some respect and hoped it would come about in time, whereas the men were inclined to be passive, in the expectation that their wives would handle the matter. For example, women waited silently for their husbands to take an initiative in housekeeping or child care, and their husbands did the same. On the whole, waiting seemed to be more profitable for husbands than for wives because of women's inclination to jump in and do the necessary domestic tasks. An upper-class man said:

> I do nothing. I sit down and, well, it's up to you to look after the children, and I make clear by simply remaining seated here: it's up to you. This runs smoothly, in general she accepts it.

Men's Strategies

Ignoring was more often a men's than a women's strategy. Most frequently, it was a reaction to the wife's discontent or anger. By turning a deaf ear to what she is saying, her complaints could be denied. As one upper-class husband said:

> If she is angry I sometimes find it such a ridiculous reason why she is angry. Then, uh, I laugh a bit, which makes her still more angry of course. When my mother was so angry, I did not say anything either, I just went my own way, and I do this with my wife in a similar way. I simply do not react sometimes: I don't want to hear it, and then I don't hear it.

The strategy seemed to be effective only in the short run because most women eventually came back to the matter at issue.

Probably because of their greater verbal skills, reasonableness was a strategy that appeared to be used mostly by upper-class husbands. They tried to convince their wives of the irrationality of their demands or of the rationality of their own viewpoint. They made an appeal to their wives' good sense and reasonableness. Husbands often used a lot of arguments to convince their wives that they should be satisfied in being housewives: they had plenty of time, lots of freedom, and plenty of praise for their work in the home, so there was nothing to complain about. However, the wives' underlying feelings were ignored, and the central issue for the wife was bypassed. An upper-class nonemployed woman said:

> Or he finds that I don't see it the right way. Then he says: "That's not true because yesterday...," this and that. And then I think: Oh yes, I forgot about that. It happens often that I have some feeling, and that he sets me right on a factual basis. But probably, then, something else is wrong because I keep having the feeling that... even if it doesn't correspond to the facts. But then I think that it is my own fault, or... I don't know what.

In the sexual domain, this strategy was used to ensure that wives recognized the importance of meeting their husbands' sexual needs. Appeals were made to "love," "a good sexual relationship as a precondition for a good marriage," or "being forced to have extramarital relationships."

The effectiveness of reasonableness was often great because the women felt disconcerted by the force of the arguments and had difficulty in expressing their own feelings in such a way that their husbands would feel obliged to reckon with them.

The findings on strategies corroborated those on change and conflicts in the relative ineffectiveness of women's attempts to alter their relationship. Manifest power as expressed in strategies tends to reinforce the status quo, because women's strategies are too indirect, and men's sanctions carry more weight. In the long run, only unambiguous and direct efforts to change the relationship seem to be effective.

In terms of Lukes's conceptualization of power, the search for counterfactuals – by asking for desired alternatives – is a method supposed to uncover three-dimensional power. However, this study's findings about change, conflicts, and strategies uncovered only the first two dimensions of power: power surfacing in overt behavior or resulting in nonbehavior. In order to tap the third dimension of power – invisible power – the ideological underpinnings of marital power have to be examined.

Invisible Power

Invisible power refers to the implicit values, beliefs, or preconceptions that precede behavior. The focus of the fourth research question was on gender differences in mutual and self-esteem, perceptions of, and legitimations about everyday reality in married life. These may be regarded as invisible power mechanisms because they confirm and justify power inequality ideologically, unintentionally, and often unconsciously. Three invisible power mechanisms were distilled: inequality in esteem for women and men, perceptual bias, and apparent consensus. These mechanisms were found in all categories of respondents, but they appeared to be most pronounced among upper-class couples in which the wife was not employed outside the home.

Inequality of Esteem

In the beginning of the interview, respondents were asked to tell what they liked most about themselves and about their partners. Although the question focused on positive characteristics, negative qualities were mentioned spontaneously. The number of positive and negative characteristics a respondent generated was used as an indicator of the degree of esteem. Women expressed less self-esteem than men ($p < 0.01$). The gender difference in self-esteem was greatest among the couples in which the wife was not employed, particularly in the upper-class ($p < 0.05$). Wives described themselves as significantly less cognitively competent than their husbands ($p < 0.001$). The gender difference was greater between spouses when the wife was not employed than among couples when she had a paid job ($p < 0.01$ and $p < 0.05$, respectively). Husbands tended to esteem their own personal competence more highly than their wives did ($p < 0.1$), particularly husbands of nonemployed wives ($p < 0.05$).

Women also mentioned significantly more negative personal qualities than men did ($p < 0.001$). Again, nonemployed wives were the most negative about themselves, particularly those in the upper class, but the gender difference was also significant comparing employed women and their husbands ($p < 0.05$).

Wives had more esteem for their husbands than their husbands had for them ($p < 0.1$). Wives esteemed their husbands for their cognitive competence more than their husbands esteemed them. Gender differences were relatively greater between nonemployed wives and their husbands' ($p < 0.05$) and were greatest in the upper class. Wives esteemed their husbands' personal competence more than husbands esteemed that of their wives ($p < 0.05$). Again, the greatest difference was found between nonemployed women and their husbands, particularly in the upper class.

Both wives and husbands described themselves and each other in terms of classical gender-role stereotypes. Husbands possessed a higher degree of self-esteem, and they were also valued by themselves and their wives for highly valued characteristics. The husbands' greater self-esteem gave them greater marital bargaining power. In addition, the effect of the implicit hierarchy in worth, whereby every individual man benefits from the cultural valuation of men over women, and men's characteristics over women's characteristics, attached to women and men, which increased men's power in the marriage. The power effect is invisible because the apparent naturalness of the assumed differences in personality traits prevents wives and husbands from acknowledging it.

Perceptual Bias

Another invisible power mechanism was found in the perception of daily life. Self-reports on "Who has the greatest responsibility for domestic labor" and "Who does in fact perform most of the domestic labor" were compared with lists where respondents had filled in the concrete amount of time spent on different activities in one week. Husbands underestimated their wives' share in household tasks ($p < 0.05$). This was particularly the case with husbands of nonemployed wives ($p < 0.01$). Husbands also underestimated their wives' responsibilities ($p < 0.05$) and concrete share in child care ($p < 0.01$). Their own contribution was correspondingly overestimated. These gender differences were greatest in the upper class, particularly when the wife had no paid job, and were statistically significant. This perceptual bias offers husbands the obvious psychological benefit that they do not have to feel obliged to meet their wives' request to take a greater share; their perception of the existing division of labor makes such a request seem unjustified.

Husbands overestimated the sexual (here coital) needs of their wives ($p < 0.05$), thereby demonstrating wishful thinking. By attributing greater sexual appetite to their wives than their wives said they had, husbands could assume that they were more welcome sexually than was really the case.

Apparent Consensus

Just like strategies, legitimations about everyday life are difficult to operationalize empirically. For example, it would make no sense to pose direct questions about legitimations because most people do not realize that they are using justifications and legitimations. However, one can ask for the reasons and explanations of the existing state of affairs in marriage.

In this study, husbands and wives seemed to agree on the reasons for the present situation in their marriage. Examples of legitimations concerning the division of domestic and child-caring tasks included the following: "she has more time available," "he has no feeling for it," "he is not born to it," "it does not fit his character," "she has more talent for it," "it is a woman's natural duty," "she has chosen to be a housewife and mother," and "she enjoys it more than he does."

The implied consensus in these legitimations, however, was only apparent. For example, both wives and husbands claimed that "women enjoy parenting more than men." However, when asked directly about their experience of parenthood, the women enjoyed it somewhat less than the men. Husbands emphasized how they enjoyed parenting in the evenings and weekends. Wives frequently said they felt that they failed in some way in their parenting and reported feelings of guilt, which made their experience of parenthood less unproblematically joyful, compared with their husbands'. Men's attitude toward domestic labor was more positive than women's feelings about it, presumably because they did it less. Men's positive feelings about household chores were not reflected in legitimations of the division of household labor. On the contrary, "he dislikes it," or "she has more pleasure in doing it" *were* frequently mentioned.

Several other inconsistencies emerged, all pointing to a contradiction between common-sense truths about reality and the way reality was experienced. Common-sense thought contains a strong element of justification: reality *has* to be the way it is. Acceptance therefore needs suppression of one's own actual experience, especially for women (Smith 1987). Wives were less contented than husbands in all of the areas studied, as their greater desire for change on almost all domains demonstrated. Husbands legitimized the existing situation more frequently and were more inclined to emphasize the inevitability of the present situation by perceiving it as natural, necessary, and unchangeable. Upper-class husbands of nonemployed wives seemed to report more legitimations than did other categories of respondents, but otherwise no clear-cut class differences were found. An upper-class husband said about his lack of domestic talent:

> The finishing touch, I never succeed in managing that. I contrive to let it look acceptable up to a certain degree, but to clean up the slab completely is beyond my reach.

A lower-class husband said:

> My wife just has to do it, that is what she's a wife for. Isn't she? That's the wife's task, although one doesn't seem to agree with that anymore, these times.

An upper-class husband said:

> But I have the idea that she just has more fun doing it, more than I have. That's fine with me.

In the area of sexuality, typical legitimations were "Men have a greater appetite than women," "Men are the active party in sexual matters," and "Men are conquerors." Ample reference was made to such inevitabilities as nature, creation, genes, and instinct.

These legitimations are not causal explanations. Rather, they express normative views on everyday married life. The truths contained in them serve primarily to justify the situation as it has evolved. Because they are largely taken for granted, legitimations contribute forcefully to the perception of daily reality as unchangeable and inevitable and so become part of invisible power.

Class, Wife's Employment Status and Marital Power

The general problem addressed by this research was the nature of marital power and its connection with class and the employment status of the wife. Manifest power was slightly more apparent among upper-class couples than among lower-class husbands and wives, but the wife's employment status did not make a difference. Latent power seemed to play a more prominent role in the lower than in the upper class, particularly in the area of sexuality. Here, wives were inclined to anticipate their husbands' needs and meet them, rather than to make changes or impose their own wishes. For latent power, too, class differences were slight, and there were no differences among couples in which the wife had or did not have a paid job.

The most clear-cut differences regarding class and the employment status of wives was found with the manifestation of invisible power, which was particularly prominent among upper-class couples in which the wife was not employed. Women in this category had the lowest self-esteem compared with women in the other categories of respondents, whereas their husbands esteemed themselves more than any other category of husbands. Moreover, these husbands had comparatively low esteem for their wives, who, on the contrary, were inclined more than other categories of wives to place their husbands on a pedestal. Upper-class couples in which the wife was not employed had the most perceptual bias regarding each partner's activities and wishes, and husbands in this category were most inclined to legitimate the status quo.

Two possible explanations might be suggested for these findings. First, a comparatively large discrepancy existed between husbands and wives in this category with respect to social position (in terms of education, family status, and prestige of husband's occupation). Second, egalitarianism was more keenly desired in upper than in lower social classes (cf. Weeda 1983), but by means of invisible power, wives and husbands both contributed to the perpetuation of marital inequality. Invisible power, then, might be considered as a subterranean answer to the threat to existing inequality that is implied in the egalitarian strivings of upper-class women. This interpretation is in line with the ambivalence about their own position expressed by upper-class wives who were not employed. Respondents were asked, "Would you want to exchange roles and positions with your partner?" "Who has the easier life, you or your partner?" and "If you could start a new life, would you plan it in a different way?" Although gender differences were small, women seemed to have a slight preference for their husbands' lives, whereas men rejected their wives' lives in a much more unambiguous way. One woman said in answer to the question whether she would like to exchange roles and status with her husband:

> Oh no . . . well, to the extent that . . . I would want to be in his place because he . . . has a reasonable dose of ambition and he has so much pleasure in his work. Really, he never says: "Oh well, today I am going to be ill," you know. I find this so admirable. That's what I would want to exchange with him, yes.

Summary and Conclusions

Lukes's concept of three-dimensional power was operationalized in this research to detect relevant counterfactuals, or alternatives, as well as power mechanisms. On this basis, it was possible to analyze manifest and latent power – Lukes's first two dimensions of power – in marital relationships. These two forms of power usually consisted of the husbands' negative responses or negative attitudes to changes proposed by their wives, or the anticipation of husbands' perceived needs and preferences by their wives and their not causing conflict as a result. Both manifest and latent power tend to work to the advantage of husbands because the status quo of traditional gender roles, beliefs, and practices is confirmed as a result. The married women we interviewed did not seem to be powerful enough on their own to bring about the substantial changes in their marriages that they desired. They needed the support of their husbands, who still showed considerable reluctance concerning a greater gender equality in marriage, whether or not the wife had a paid job, in both social classes. Blumstein and Schwartz (1983), however, found that in the United States, in marriages in which the wife was employed power was more often equally shared than in marriages in which the wife was a full-time homemaker.

Lukes's concept of three-dimensional power has enriched theorizing about power by including those forms of power that prevent people from having grievances at all by ideologically shaping their beliefs and preferences. In this research, this type of power was called invisible power. To explore invisible power, Gramsci's notion of ideological hegemony was used.

All three characteristics of Gramsci's ideological hegemony were encountered in the research findings. Culturally prevailing notions of femininity and masculinity were reflected in the everyday thinking of the married women and men we interviewed. For example, in legitimations of everyday married life, reference was made to (presumed) differences between women and men that were accepted as normal and inevitable. In these legitimations, the contradictory and ambiguous character of everyday experience was represented as a unitary whole. Particularly among upper-class couples, frequent reference was made to the freedom for married women to choose motherhood and domestic responsibility, work outside the home, or some combination of these. However, alternatives to domestic responsibility are far more numerous for men than for women. Social "necessity" then, while called "freedom," is experienced as such mostly by husbands, and rarely by wives.

Subtly, and probably at a largely unconscious level, invisible power reflects the already existing power inequality between husbands and wives, at the same time justifying and confirming it. By means of the unequal esteem expressed by the women and men interviewed, the stereotyped way in which husbands and wives perceived themselves and each other, their selective perception of their contribution to the marriage, and legitimations of everyday married life, these husbands and wives – unintentionally and unconsciously – reinforced the power inequality that character-ized their marriages. The ideological underpinnings of inequality in marital power that are confirmed by means of invisible power do not reflect accidental beliefs and opinions, but express cultural and societal hegemonic values about women, men, and what is appropriate and natural. The findings on esteem, perceptions, and legitima-tions pointed to the subtle ways in which the acceptance of gender roles and gendered identities as natural and unchangeable are reinforced ideologically. The focus on spouses' mutual esteem and self-esteem, their perceptions and legitimations, then, made it possible to study Lukes's third dimension of power empirically.

When the idea of normalcy and rightness of prevailing patterns in gender relations characterizes both husbands' and wives' perceptions and experience in marriage, inequality in marital power is confirmed in an unobtrusive and invisible way, automatically as it were, without brute power. Although among many couples, particularly in the upper class, the new values of equal partnership and equal chances for women and men were endorsed, both manifest and latent power operated in favor of men. Invisible power particularly contributed to the continuation of inequality in marriage in two ways. First, ideological justifications of presumed gender differences were used to confirm the status quo. Second, selective perception averted differences that could imply a threat to the status quo from consciousness.

These ideological processes might be considered more general characteristics of power in gender relations: reality is perceived in such a way that it confirms and justifies gendered identities and averts from consciousness information that threatens the stability of these identities. The concept of gender itself, with its implied hierarchy in values, symbols, beliefs, and statuses, is a cornerstone of the edifice of gendered inequality. Any conscious or unconscious effort to undermine this cornerstone tends to be experienced as deeply threatening because it is so fundamentally tied to the psychosexual and social identities of women and men. And since marriages are created from gendered identities, activities, and statuses, one might ask if the partners can ever be equal.

Measurements of power that are based on decision-making indicators as in the work of Blood and Wolfe (1960), or on self-reports about who has the right to control – the approach of Blumstein and Schwartz – do not pay justice to the underlying structure of marital power. The husbands and wives we interviewed were strongly inclined to state that most important decisions were made together. Egalitarian results, however, were exceptional. Tapping into the invisible power that sustains inequality can tell us if real shifts are taking place – shifts in power that could be reflected in everyday understandings and legitimations of the status quo. Real changes in marital power can occur only if husbands and wives recognize their stereotyped self-concepts and ways of seeing each other, as well as the discrepancies between their respective perceptions of marital life, and the effect of these stereotypes and discrepancies in maintaining the status quo. A revived and strengthened women's movement could help by continued efforts to lay bare the sociocultural and psychic roots of gender inequality. Important sources of power inequality in marriage are still taken for granted. As Dorothy Dinnerstein notes:

> The most potent sources of sexual conservatism are buried in the dark, silent layers of our mental life: it is this burial that keeps them potent. (1976: 3)

Notes

1 From the introduction to a more recent publication (Lukes 1986, pp. 1–19), it appears that Lukes has revised some of his earlier views on power. Power is, in his 1986 view, not necessarily linked to interests. Also, Lukes now recognizes the possibility of power in which no conflict is involved. Finally, Lukes does not link power to responsibility in the same direct way that he did in 1974. The research reported here, however, was based on Lukes's (1974) theoretical analysis.

2 Only those results that are relevant to the theoretical background and the research problem are presented here. For a more complete and detailed discussion, see Komter (1985, 1987).

References

Bloch, M. et al. 1979. "Power in social theory: A non-relative view." In S. C. Brown (ed.) *Philosophical Disputes in the Social Sciences*. Sussex: Harvester Press, pp. 243–59.

Blood, R. O. and Wolfe, D. M. 1960. *Husbands and Wives*. New York: Free Press.

Blumstein, P. and Schwartz, P. 1983. *American Couples: Money, Work, Sex*. New York: Morrow.

Bradshaw, A. 1976. "A critique of Steven Lukes' *Power: A Radical View.*" *Sociology* 10: 121–7.

Dinnerstein, D. 1976. *The Mermaid and the Minotaur: Sexual Arrangements and Human Malaise*. New York: Harper and Row.

Edgell, S. R. 1980. *Middle-class Couples: A Study of Segregation, Domination and Inequality in Marriage*, London: Allen and Unwin.

Eichler, M, 1981. "Power, dependency, love and the sexual division of labour." *Women's Studies International Quarterly* 4: 201–19.

Gillespie, D. 1971. "Who has the power: The marital struggle." *Journal of Marriage and the Family* 33: 445–58.

Gramsci, A. 1971. *Selections from the Prison Notebooks*, edited and translated by Q. Hoare and G. Nowell-Smith. London: Lawrence and Wishart.

Heer, D. M. 1963. "The measurement and bases of family power: An overview." *Marriage and Family Living* 25: 133–9.

Johnson, C. 1975. "Authority and power in Japanese-American marriage." In R. E. Cromwell and D. H. Olson (eds.) *Power in Families*. New York: Wiley.

Johnson, P. 1976. "Women and power: Toward a theory of effectiveness." *Journal of Social Issues* 3: 99–110.

Komarovsky, M. 1967. *Blue-collar Marriage*. New York: Vintage.

Komter, A. 1985. *De Macht van de Vanzelfsprekendheid: Relaties tussen Vrouwen en Mannen*. Den Haag: VUGA (in Dutch).

—— 1987. "Why bad mothers are worse than bad fathers: Power mechanisms in the family." In T. Knijn and A. C. Mulder (eds.) *Unraveling Fatherhood*. Dordrecht: Foris, pp. 27–37.

Lukes, S. 1974. *Power: A Radical View*. London: Macmillan.

—— 1986. *Power*. Oxford: Basil Blackwell.

McDonald, G. W. 1980. "Family power: A decade of theory and research, 1970–1979." *Journal of Marriage and the Family* 32: 841–55.

Safilios-Rothschild, C. 1967. "A comparison of power structure and marital satisfaction in urban Greek and French families." *Journal of Marriage and the Family* 29: 345–52.

—— 1970. "The study of family power structure: A review, 1960–1969." *Journal of Marriage and the Family* 32: 539–52.

Scanzoni, J. 1972. *Sexual Bargaining: Power Politics in the American Marriage*. Englewood Cliffs, NJ: Prentice-Hall.

—— 1979a. *Sex Roles, Women's Work, and Marital Conflict*. Lexington, Mass.: Heath.

—— 1979b. "Social processes and power in families." In F. I. Nye and I. Reiss (eds.) *Contemporary Theories About the Family*, vol. 1. New York: Free Press.

Scanzoni, L. and Scanzoni, J. 1976. *Men, Women and Change: A Sociology of Marriage and the Family*. New York: McGraw-Hill.

Smith, D. 1987. *The Everyday World as Problematic: A Feminist Sociology*. Toronto: University of Toronto Press.

Van den Brink, G. 1978. "Ideologie en hegemonie bij Gramsci." Te Elfder ure 24, *Ideologietheorie* 1: 10–58. Nijmegen: SUN (in Dutch).

Weeda, C. J. 1983. *Van Huwelijk tot Echtscheiding: En Regenboog van Ervaringen*. Wageningen: Mededelingen Vakgroep Sociologie (in Dutch).

Wrong, D. 1979. *Power: Its Forms, Bases and Uses*. Oxford: Basil Blackwell.

Young, M. and Willmott, P. 1973. *The Symmetrical Family: A Study of Work and Leisure in the London Region*. London: Routledge and Kegan Paul.

24 The Velvet Glove

Mary Jackman

The Sweetest Persuasion: Paternalism

Dominant groups resort to alternative modes of persuasion as circumstances change, but the enduring beacon to which they are drawn and from which they depart only reluctantly and by degrees is an ideology of paternalism. Webster's definition of paternalism is "the principle or system of governing or controlling a country, group of employees, etc. in a manner suggesting a father's relationship with his children" (Webster 1975). An earlier edition of Webster's defined paternalism in more detail:

> Paternalism: the care or control of subordinates (as by a government or employer) in a fatherly manner; *esp.*: the principles or practices of a government that undertakes to supply needs or regulate conduct of the governed in matters affecting them as individuals as well as in their relations to the state and to each other. (Webster's 1965)

The traditional father–child relationship on which the term is based was one in which the father authoritatively dictated all the behaviors and significant life-decisions of his children within a moral framework that credited the father with an unassailable understanding of the needs and best interests of his children. They, in turn, accepted implicitly and absolutely the authority of their father; occasional bouts of independence were not unexpected, but never tolerated. Good children learned to comply with and defer to the wishes of their fathers.

No arrangement could be more desirable for a group that dominates another. Yet fathers love their children, and thus the traditional father–child relationship might seem an inappropriate analogy for the ideology that accompanies and bolsters a relationship of inequality between social groups. Because of our ensnarement in the "conflict versus consensus" debate, we have implicitly regarded discrimination as the inalienable expression of hostility: within that framework, affection and exploitation are incompatible. Here, however, I separate hostility from discrimination. I argue that it is only in the limiting case that they become linked. Affection, far from being alien to exploitative relations, is precisely the emotion that dominant groups wish to feel toward those whom they exploit. The everyday practice of discrimination does not require feelings of hostility, and, indeed, it is not at all difficult to have fond regard for those whom we subordinate, especially when the subject of our domination accedes to the relationship compliantly. To denote this phenomenon of discrimination without the expression of hostility, I use the term paternalism.

Paternalism is a time-worn term that has had indefinite meaning in common usage. Among analysts of intergroup relations, it has occupied an uncertain and

Reprinted from "Prologue," in *The Velvet Glove: Paternalism and Conflict in Gender, Class, and Race Relations*, Berkeley: University of California Press, 1994, pp. 9–16.

marginal role because of the overriding concern with conflict and hostility. In one of the few explicit analyses of paternalistic relations, van den Berghe (1967) relegated it to preindustrial societies in which a numerically small minority dominates over more numerous subordinates. Myrdal (1944), in his classic treatment of black–white relations in the United States, regarded paternalism as a cultural anachronism, out of place in an industrial, democratic society. Paternalism found its most penetrating exposition in Genovese's work on master–slave relations in the antebellum American South (1974), and more recently, some scholars have applied the concept to an analysis of management–labor relations in anachronistic pockets of the developing industrial enterprise (Burawoy 1984; Lockwood 1966; Newby 1977a, 1977b; Staples 1987). More commonly, paternalism indefinitely connotes the colonial days and the "white man's burden" of the nineteenth century. The prevailing effect has been to associate paternalism with a bygone era. Most research on contemporary intergroup relations has brushed the phenomenon aside, like a relic, to be regarded occasionally with quiet dismay.

My argument, however, is that paternalism has a significance that is both general and contemporary. It is a powerful ideological mold that offers the most efficient and gratifying means for the social control of relationships between unequal groups. The attitude structure that it comprises – the combination of positive feelings for a group with discriminatory intentions toward the group – has been underestimated by students of intergroup relations and unheeded in research on intergroup attitudes. And yet the ideology of dominant groups departs from the comforting mold of paternalism only reluctantly and under duress. The abiding quest is to preserve an amicable relationship with subordinates and thus to preempt or subvert conflict. The expression of hostility invites the exercise of force, and that remains the option of last resort.

Paternalism versus Benevolence

An awkward ambiguity has pervaded both popular and scholarly uses of the term "paternalism" over the extent to which paternalism connotes benevolence. Fathers, after all, were presumed to have benevolent intentions toward their children, even as they exercised absolute authority over them. And in the analysis of intergroup relations, the tendency to link malevolence with hostility has been so habitual that analysts have inferred that the development of bonds of affection between the members of dominant groups and their subordinates must erode the ability of dominant-group members to control their relations with subordinates.

Thus, the observation of affection toward subordinates in paternalistic systems has promoted the inference that paternalism involves at least some degree of benevolence. For example, in a discussion in "Paternalism in industry," Blumer wrote:

> [A] sense of responsibility and of obligation for the welfare of the worker is the most outstanding mark of paternalism. It is a tempering influence on the mere proprietary and control relationship and imparts to that relationship a personal and benevolent character. (Blumer 1951: 26)

A similar confounding of affection and benevolence is found in a more recent treatment of paternalism by Weiner (1985/1986). In assessing the effect of slave-owners' wives on the institution of slavery, Weiner comments:

> Allston was not the only plantation mistress who found pleasure in plantation life or developed strong bonds of affection for slaves. The teachings of the ideology of domesticity and southern paternalism together defined caring for slaves as central to southern womanhood.... While men created paternalism as a mechanism of social control, women inadvertently assumed a significant portion of the responsibility for putting it into practice on a daily basis.... In their efforts to ameliorate the physical and emotional hardships experienced by slaves, women quite unwittingly became the agents of paternalism.... Ironically then, one result ... was to enable slavery to continue to exist by making life more tolerable for slaves and thus helping to defuse discontent. (Weiner 1985/1986: 382)

Even the most critical exponents of paternalism have seen it as an ideological system fraught with contradictions, stemming from a tensive intermixture of domination with benevolence (see, for example, Genovese 1974; Newby 1977b). Dominant-group members are seen as being trapped by their affectionate inclinations and by paternalism's moral shroud of mutual obligation into giving more than they might otherwise to subordinates.

The appearance of benevolence in paternalistic intergroup relations is indeed pervasive, but it is important to recognize that it is nothing more than an appearance. It is helpful here to consider a neutral definition of paternalism that portrays the phenomenon as benevolently motivated. In VanDeVeer's exhaustive and probing book, *Paternalistic Intervention: The Moral Bounds of Benevolence*, paternalistic acts are defined as those "in which one person, A, interferes with another person, S, in order to promote S's own good" (1986: 12). VanDeVeer specifically rules out callousness or maliciousness as a motive for paternalistic acts. He cites many diverse examples of paternalistic acts: his long list includes legal requirements that motorcyclists wear helmets, compulsory education of the young, legal prohibitions on voluntary euthanasia, required courses at universities, required waiting periods for divorce, distribution of welfare in kind (e.g., food stamps) rather than in cash, involuntary sterilization, and compulsory participation in systems providing for adequate income on retirement (e.g., Social Security) (1986: 13–15). What all these acts have in common is the intervening party's presumptive claim to a superior understanding of the subject's best interests than the subject may possess him- or herself. In essence, then, VanDeVeer's paternalistic actor is distinguished by the coupling of two characteristics: an un-self-interested, benevolent intent, and a presumption of greater moral competence than the subject of his or her intervention.

We now return to the inferred benevolence of the father's authority over his children. The father's benevolent exercise of authority is, of course, based on the notion that children are not the maturational or moral equals of their parents. An argument can be made that the exercise of authority over those who lack the maturity or moral competence to make the "wisest" decisions for themselves may be construed as being in the best interests of those who are thus treated, as "taking care" of them. Individuals who are encompassed by this criterion might (arguably) include children, students, the seriously retarded, the mentally ill, and people who are physically unconscious.

However, even here, legitimate disputes can arise about both the definition of the morally incompetent population (at what point does someone cease to be a child or a student? is someone who is depressed and wishes to commit suicide to be considered mentally ill?), and about the extent of intervention that is justified (should parental consent be required for teenagers to have abortions? should involuntary hospitalization be required for the mentally ill?). These moral ambiguities hover over even the most neutral examples of paternalism (VanDeVeer 1986), and they are compounded by yet another tier of difficulties.

When an actor presumes to have superior moral competence, he or she becomes the final arbiter of what is considered to be the best interests of the subject of the intervention. What protection does such a system offer for a truly disinterested assessment of the subject's best interests? Indeed, is the paternalist capable of assessing the best interests of others, separate from his or her own interests and free from the limitations of his or her own moral perspective? Bear in mind that when fathers exercised paternalistic authority over their children, they did not selflessly evaluate the best interests of their children. Children owed an allegiance to their families: their personal interests were defined, at best, as inseparable from those of their families, and in the event of a conflict, personal interests were subjugated to the financial, status, or political interests of the family. To what extent do similar constraints operate when faculty decide what is "in the best interests" of students, or when civil authorities decide what is "in the best interests" of the mentally ill or the seriously retarded? Do faculty consider what knowledge students should learn without consideration to what would be easiest for the faculty to teach and uninfluenced by their own prior investment in a particular body of knowledge? Do social institutions consider what is best for social dependents without concern for the costs to the rest of society of alternative options?

And, finally, how is the observer to distinguish acts that are altruistically or benevolently motivated from malevolent acts that merely purport to be benevolent? VanDeVeer acknowledges the existence of "illegitimate constraints placed on persons 'for their own good' – with the invitation to comfortable self-righteousness implicit in such an expression." He adds: "Given our strong desire to believe that we are 'reasonable persons of good will' we . . . are less likely to avoid the self-deceptions associated with acts which are seemingly innocent instances of 'doing good'" (1986: 426).

These layers of doubts and ambiguities plague even a generous interpretation of paternalism, as when an agent intervenes with good will on behalf of a subject who is maturationally younger or morally incompetent. But these issues are heightened dramatically when an agent presumes superior moral competence over a subject who is the equal of the agent either maturationally or in the physical ability to think and reason. Indeed, VanDeVeer argues that even acts of benevolently motivated paternalism are unjustified in such cases: when we "view and treat other competents as our moral inferiors," we indulge our own moral sensibilities at the expense of others' liberties (1986: 423–4).

These issues are heightened still further when a social group presumes moral superiority over another group from whom it is expropriating valued societal resources. To begin, the lack of reciprocity implicit in such a presumption of moral superiority (that is, the dominant group does not grant that subordinates may at times have a superior understanding of the interests of dominant-group members) carries with it a tacit status-ranking of the two groups. Insidiously, that status-ranking coincides with the expropriative pattern in the intergroup relationship. The preexisting relationship between the two groups hardly positions dominant group members for disinterested, benevolent intervention on behalf of subordinates. In such circumstances, it is implausible that the members of the dominant group might dissociate their own best interests from those of the group that is providing their privileges. The presumption of moral superiority over a group with whom one has an expropriative relationship is thus flatly incompatible with the spirit of altruistic benevolence, no matter how much affection and breast-beating accompanies it. In the analysis of unequal relations between social groups, paternalism must be distinguished from benevolence.

Mastering the Illusion of Benevolence

But the agenda for dominant groups is to create an ideological cocoon whereby they can define their discriminatory actions as benevolent. In this way, the beneficiaries of the inequality assuage their own sensibilities at the same time as they avoid the awkwardness of having to withhold something from the demanding grasp of subordinates. Subordinates do not demand something unless they define it as a need. Dominant groups thus mimic the traditional father–child relationship by claiming superior moral competence and attempting to define the needs of subordinates. They can then provide – with pleasant sentimentality and with a satisfying *feeling* of benevolence – for the fulfillment of those needs.

To that end, their unequal relationship is swathed in a morality that identifies subordinates' worth and value within the terms of that relationship. Such an orientation must rest on persuasion rather than on force and can only be really effective in the circumstance of mutual affection between the groups. With affection comes the ability of those in command to shape the needs and aspirations of subordinates and to portray discriminatory arrangements as being in the best interests of all concerned. Conflict is obviated because those who must initiate it – the have-nots – are bound emotionally and cognitively in a framework that is of the dominant group's definition. Far from undermining their domination over subordinates, the expression of affection for subordinates thus strengthens the dominant group's control.

The Wages of Love

A great deal has been written, spoken, and above all, sung, about the virtues of love. Love in all its forms is extolled. Whether it is in reference to the relations between parents and children, sexual partners, siblings, friends, social groups, or nations, we are daily exhorted to strive for love. Before its radiant power, problems melt. We all know that "love is blind," that to love is to give of oneself, to embrace the other to oneself, to lay oneself open, and to dissolve barriers. We revere love as the highest human emotion.

But something is missing. Many husbands who profess to love their wives beat them, and after humble contrition and apologies, they beat them again. Many fathers who profess love for their children beat them or sexually abuse them. Slave-owners in the Old South who professed affection for their slaves subjected their slaves to harsh physical punishments. I submit that love is overrated. It seems to offer little protection in human relations.

Is love given freely, or is it offered on terms? Does love instill feelings of protectiveness, or feelings of possession? Is love blind, or carefully circumscribed? Does love make people do anything for someone, or does it give them a license to do anything *to* someone? Do we give more to those whom we love, or do we demand more from our loved ones? Is love a feeling of dependence ("I can't live without her"), or a feeling of being indispensable ("He needs me")? The problem is that almost anything can be done, and has been done, in the name of love. Idealized love and the practice of love appear to have little connection.

The single achievement of love is to entangle the affected parties with an intricate and complex emotional bond. That bond does not dissolve other elements present in the relationship. It neither alters the personalities of the participants nor changes the way resources are distributed between them. If one participant has more resources, love does not move him to give those advantages up. The distinction between the pleasures afforded by love and by privilege is brought out sharply in the words of an upper-middle-class white Virginian, interviewed in the 1940s:

> As a boy I played with colored children. I loved my Negro mammy and kissed her as I would my white mother. The social side has nothing to do with the human side. I wouldn't have gone to school with the colored boys, but I was in sports with them, camped out with them, ate and slept with them. I remember one old friend, Jim, who had been a body guard to an old general. I saw him in back of the house when I was home last – he almost opened his arms to me. I shook his hand, just as familiarly. That's the human side of your old type Negro. If he came to my house he'd go around to the back door; he wouldn't think of going to the front. (Quoted in Johnson 1943: 210; for similar reports showing the acute distinction between affection and status differentiation in whites' relations with African Americans in the South in the early twentieth century, see Powdermaker 1968: 31–2)

What love does accomplish is to infuse the inequalities in a relationship with an intricate bond that lubricates the contact points between the participants. By these sweet means, the actor with more resources is granted an ease of access to the other party of which he might otherwise only dream.

Longstanding relationships of social inequality are not driven by feelings of hostility; nor do such feelings provide a sound bolster for the inequality. In such relations, the intent to discriminate springs directly from the privileged interests of the dominant group, and the emotional accompaniment of choice is not hostility, but affection. Groups who dominate social relationships strive to keep hostility out of those relationships, not in order to foster equality, but rather to deepen and secure the inequality. They have learned that persuasion is better than force.

References

Blumer, Herbert. 1951. "Paternalism in industry." *Social Process in Hawaii* 15: 26–31.

Burawoy, Michael. 1984. "Karl Marx and the Satanic mills: Factory politics under early capitalism in England, the United States, and Russia." *American Journal of Sociology* 90(2): 247–82.

Genovese, Eugene, D. 1974. *Roll, Jordan, Roll: The World the Slaves Made*. New York: Random House.

Johnson, Charles S. 1943. *Patterns of Negro Segregation*. New York: Harper and Brothers.

Lockwood, David. 1966. "Sources of variation in working class images of society." *Sociological Review* 14 (November): 249–67.

Myrdal, Gunnar. 1944. *An American Dilemma: The Negro Problem and Modern Democracy*. New York: Harper and Brothers.

Newby, Howard. 1977a. *The Deferential Worker: A Study of Farm Workers in East Anglia*. London: Allen Lane.

——, —— 1977b. "Paternalism and capitalism." In Richard Scase (ed.) *Industrial Society: Class, Cleavage and Control*. London: Allen and Unwin, pp. 59–73.

Powdermaker, Hortense. [1939] 1968. *After Freedom: A Cultural Study in the Deep South*. New York: Russell and Russell.

Staples, William G. 1987. "Technology, control, and the social organization of work at a British hardware firm, 1791–1891." *American Journal of Sociology* 93(1): 62–88.

van den Berghe, Pierre L. 1967. *Race and Racism: A Comparative Perspective*. New York: John Wiley and Sons.

VanDeVeer, Donald, 1986. *Paternalistic Intervention: The Moral Bounds of Benevolence*. Princeton, NJ: Princeton University Press.

Webster's Third New International Dictionary of English Language. 1965, 1975. Ed. Philip Babcock Gove. Springfield, Mass.: G. and C. Merriam Company.

Weiner, Marli F. 1985/6. "The intersection of race and gender: The antebellum plantation mistress and her slaves." *Humboldt Journal of Social Relations* 13(1, 2): 374–86.

Index